Dewey Decimal Classification

Devised by Melvil Dewey

2021

Volume 3

Edited by

Alex Kyrios, Editor

OCLC
OCLC, Inc.
Dublin, Ohio
2021

OCLC, Inc.
6565 Kilgour Place
Dublin, OH 43017-3395 USA
www.oclc.org/dewey

ISBN: (vol. 3) 978-1-55653-181-1

600

600   Technology (Applied sciences)

Class here inventions

See also 303.483 for technology as a cause of cultural change; also 306.46 for sociology of technology; also 338.1–338.4 for economic aspects of industries based on specific technologies; also 338.926 for technology transfer; also 338.927 for appropriate technology

See Manual at 300 vs. 600; also at 363 vs. 302–307, 333.7, 570–590, 600; also at 363.1 vs. 600; also at 583–585 vs. 600

SUMMARY

630	**Agriculture and related technologies**
.1–.9	Standard subdivisions
631	**Specific techniques; apparatus, equipment, materials**
632	**Plant injuries, diseases, pests**
633	**Field and plantation crops**
634	**Orchards, fruits, forestry**
635	**Garden crops (Horticulture)**
636	**Animal husbandry**
637	**Processing dairy and related products**
638	**Insect culture**
639	**Hunting, fishing, conservation, related technologies**

640	**Home and family management**
.1–.9	Standard subdivisions; specific aspects of household management; evaluation and purchasing guides
641	**Food and drink**
642	**Meals and table service**
643	**Housing and household equipment**
644	**Household utilities**
645	**Household furnishings**
646	**Sewing, clothing, management of personal and family life**
647	**Management of public households (Institutional housekeeping)**
648	**Housekeeping**
649	**Child rearing; home care of people with disabilities and illnesses**

650	**Management and auxiliary services**
.01–.09	Standard subdivisions
.1	Personal success in business
651	**Office services**
652	**Processes of written communication**
653	**Shorthand**
657	**Accounting**
658	**General management**
659	**Advertising and public relations**

660	**Chemical engineering and related technologies**
.01–.09	Standard subdivisions and chemical technologies of specific states of matter
.2–.7	[General topics in chemical engineering, biotechnology, industrial stoichiometry]
661	**Technology of industrial chemicals**
662	**Technology of explosives, fuels, related products**
663	**Beverage technology**
664	**Food technology**
665	**Technology of industrial oils, fats, waxes, gases**
666	**Ceramic and allied technologies**
667	**Cleaning, color, coating, related technologies**
668	**Technology of other organic products**
669	**Metallurgy**

670	**Manufacturing**
.1–.9	Standard subdivisions and special topics of manufacturing
671	**Metalworking processes and primary metal products**
672	**Iron, steel, other iron alloys**
673	**Nonferrous metals**
674	**Lumber processing, wood products, cork**
675	**Leather and fur processing**
676	**Pulp and paper technology**
677	**Textiles**
678	**Elastomers and elastomer products**
679	**Other products of specific kinds of materials**

680	Manufacture of products for specific uses
681	Precision instruments and other devices
682	Small forge work (Blacksmithing)
683	Hardware and household appliances
684	Furnishings and home workshops
685	Leather and fur goods, and related products
686	Printing and related activities
687	Clothing and accessories
688	Other final products, and packaging technology

690	Construction of buildings
.01–.09	Standard subdivisions
.1–.8	Special topics of construction of buildings
691	Building materials
692	Auxiliary construction practices
693	Construction in specific types of materials and for specific purposes
694	Wood construction
695	Roof covering
696	Utilities
697	Heating, ventilating, air-conditioning engineering
698	Detail finishing

601 Philosophy and theory

602 Miscellany

.18 Standards

Class interdisciplinary collections of standards in 389.6

[.72] Patents

Do not use; class in 608

.75 Trademarks and service marks

Class here comprehensive works on trademarks generally used for products rather than services

Class interdisciplinary works on trademarks and service marks in 929.95

.9 Commercial miscellany

Class commercial miscellany of products and services used in individual and family living in 640.29; class commercial miscellany of manufactured products in 670.29; class interdisciplinary commercial miscellany in 381.029

603 Dictionaries, encyclopedias, concordances

604 Technical drawing, hazardous materials technology; groups of people

.2 Technical drawing

Class here engineering graphics, mechanical drawing

For architectural drawing, see 720.284. For technical drawing in a specific subject, see the subject, e.g., map drawing 526, electronic drafting 621.381

See also 006.6 for computer graphics

3

.22	Arrangement and organization of drafting rooms, preservation and storage of drawings
.24	Specific drafting procedures and conventions
.242	Production illustration

Nontechnical graphic representations

.243	Dimensioning; lettering, titling; shades, shadows
.245	Projections

Including isometric, orthographic, spherical projections; perspectives

.25	Preparation and reading of copies

Standard subdivisions are added for either or both topics in heading

Including blueprints, photostats

See also 686.42 for printing blueprints

.7 **Hazardous materials technology**

Methods of extracting, manufacturing, processing, utilizing, handling, transporting, storing solids, liquids, gases of corrosive, explosive, flammable, infectious, radioactive, toxic nature

Class interdisciplinary works on hazardous materials in 363.17. Class technology of a specific hazardous material with the technology, e.g., explosives 662.2; class safety techniques for a specific application of hazardous materials with the application outside 300, plus notation 0289 from Table 1, e.g., safety techniques in working with hazardous paving materials 625.80289 (*not* 363.179)

See Manual at 604.7 vs. 660.2804

.8 **Groups of people**

Add to base number 604.8 the numbers following —08 in notation 081–089 from Table 1, e.g., women 604.82

605 Serial publications

606 Organizations

[.8] **Management**

Do not use; class in 658

607 Education, research, related topics

Notation 07 from Table 1 as modified below

.01–.03	Education, research, related topics in areas, regions, places in general; in ancient world

Add to base number 607.0 notation 1–3 from Table 2, e.g., technical training in ancient Rome 607.0376

[.04–.09]   Education, research, related topics in specific continents, countries, localities in modern world

>   Do not use; class in 607.4–607.9

.1   Education

.2   Research

>   Class here industrial, products research

>   Class product planning in management in 658.5038; class management of research for new and improved products in 658.57

[.201–.209]   Geographic treatment of research

>   Do not use; class in 607.21–607.29

.21   Research in areas, regions, places in general

>   Do not use for research methods; class in 607.2

>   Add to base number 607.21 the numbers following —1 in notation 11–19 from Table 2, e.g., industrial research in Western Hemisphere 607.21812

[.22]   Historical research

>   Do not use; class in 607.2

.23   Research in the ancient world

>   Do not use for descriptive research; class in 607.2

>   Add to base number 607.23 the numbers following —3 in notation 31–39 from Table 2, e.g., research in ancient Egypt 607.232

.24   Research in Europe

>   Do not use for experimental research; class in 607.2

>   Add to base number 607.24 the numbers following —4 in notation 41–49 from Table 2, e.g., industrial research in Norway 607.2481

.25   Research in Asia

>   Add to base number 607.25 the numbers following —5 in notation 51–59 from Table 2, e.g., industrial research in Japan 607.252

.26   Research in Africa

>   Add to base number 607.26 the numbers following —6 in notation 61–69 from Table 2, e.g., industrial research in South Africa 607.268

.27   Research in North America

>   Do not use for statistical methods; class in 607.2

>   Add to base number 607.27 the numbers following —7 in notation 71–79 from Table 2, e.g., industrial research in Canada 607.271

.28   Research in South America

           Do not use for presentation of statistical data; class in 607.2

           Add to base number 607.28 the numbers following —8 in notation 81–89 from Table 2, e.g., industrial research in Argentina 607.282

.29   Research in other parts of the world

           Add to base number 607.29 the numbers following —9 in notation 91–99 from Table 2, e.g., industrial research in New Zealand 607.2993

.3   Other aspects of education, research, related topics

           Add to base number 607.3 the numbers following —07 in notation 074–079 from Table 1, e.g., fairs and exhibitions 607.34

           Class commercial aspects of fairs and exhibitions in 381.1; class interdisciplinary works on fairs and exhibitions in 907.4

.4–.9   Education, research, related topics in specific continents, countries, localities in modern world

           Do not use for museums, collections, exhibits and their activities and services; review and exercise; use of apparatus and equipment in study and teaching; competitions, festivals, awards, financial support; class in 607.3

           Add to base number 607 notation 4–9 from Table 2, e.g., education and research in Japan 607.52

608   Patents

           Do not use for history and description of technology with respect to groups of people; class in 604.8

           Class here interdisciplinary collections of patents

           Class interdisciplinary works on patents in 346.0486

           For patents in a specific subject, see the subject, plus notation 0272 from Table 1, e.g., patents in chemical engineering 660.0272

[.09]   History, geographic treatment, biography

           Do not use for history and geographic treatment; class in 608.7

[.092]   Biography

           Do not use; class in 609.2

.7   History and geographic treatment

[.700 1–.700 8]   Standard subdivisions

           Do not use; class in 608.01–608.08

[.700 9]   History, geographic treatment, biography

           Do not use for history and geographic treatment; class in 608.7

[.700 92]   Biography

           Do not use; class in 609.2

.701–.705   Historical periods

> Add to base number 608.70 the numbers following —090 in notation 0901–0905 from Table 1, e.g., 20th century patents 608.704

.71   Areas, regions, places in general; oceans and seas

> Add to base number 608.71 the numbers following —1 in notation 11–18 from Table 2, e.g., patents from developing regions 608.71724

.73–.79   Specific continents, countries, localities

> Add to base number 608.7 notation 3–9 from Table 2, e.g., patents from Brazil 608.781

609   History, geographic treatment, biography

> *See Manual at 300 vs. 600: Interdisciplinary works*

.009   Archaeology

> Class here interdisciplinary works on industrial archaeology

> *For economic aspects of industrial archaeology, see 338.09009*

.2   **Biography**

> Class here biography of inventors, of patentees

610   Medicine and health

> Standard subdivisions are added for medicine and health together, for medicine alone

> Class here technology of medical services

> Class social welfare problems of and services to people with physical illness, interdisciplinary works on social provision of medical services and technology of medical services in 362.1; class home care by nonprofessionals of people with illnesses and disabilities in 649.8

> *For veterinary medicine, see 636.089*

> *See Manual at 362.1–362.4 vs. 610; also at 571–573 vs. 610; also at 610 vs. 616*

[.23]   Medicine and health as a profession, occupation, hobby

> Do not use; class in 610.69

.28   Auxiliary techniques and procedures; apparatus, equipment, materials

> Class here comprehensive works on biomedical engineering

> *For biological aspects of biomedical engineering, see 570.28*

.6   **Organizations, management; group practice; medical personnel and relationships**

> Notation 06 from Table 1 as modified below

.65   Group practice

> Class economics of group practice in 338.7–338.8; class social aspects in 362.1042

.69   Medical personnel and relationships

> Standard subdivisions are added for medical personnel and relationships together, for medical personnel alone

> Nature of duties, characteristics of the professions of medical personnel

> Class here medical missionaries

> Class medical secretaries in 651.3741; class medical records librarians in 651.504261. Class nature of duties, characteristics of profession, relationships of medical personnel of a specific specialty with the specialty, plus notation 023 from table under 616.1–616.9, notation 023 from table under 617, or notation 023 from table under 618.1–618.8, e.g., obstetricians 618.20232, obstetrical nurses 618.20231; class critical appraisal and description of work, individual and collected biographies with the specialty, plus notation 092 from Table 1, e.g., biography of coroners 614.1092, of psychiatrists 616.890092

> *For nursing personnel, see 610.73069; for allied health personnel, see 610.737069*

.695   Physicians

.696   Medical relationships

> Including relationships between medical personnel and patients, between medical personnel and the public, within medical professions

.7   Education, research, nursing, services of allied health personnel

> Notation 07 from Table 1 as modified below

.724   Experimental research

> Class here comprehensive works on experimental biomedical research

> *For experimental biology, see 570.724; for clinical trials, see 615.50724; for experimental medicine, see 616.027*

.73   Nursing and services of allied health personnel

Standard subdivisions are added for nursing and services of allied health personnel together, for nursing alone

Class here comprehensive works on the nursing process; comprehensive works on nursing care plans, on nursing interventions so long as the works cover both diagnosis and therapy

> *For school nursing, see 371.712; for forensic nursing, see 614.1; for patient education by nurses, see 615.5071. For a specific part of the nursing process, a specific part of a nursing care plan, a specific type of nursing intervention, see the part or type in 614–618, e.g., vaccinations provided by nurses 614.47, exercise therapy provided by nurses 615.82, nursing assessment and nursing diagnosis 616.075; for nursing for a specific disease or group of diseases or a specific medical specialty, see the disease or group of diseases or medical specialty in 616–618, plus notation 0231 from table under 616.1–616.9, notation 0231 from table under 617, or notation 0231 from table under 618.1–618.8 if role or work of nursing personnel is emphasized, e.g., a work about cancer nursing that gives much general medical information about cancer 616.994, a work about cancer nursing that focuses on instructions for nurses 616.9940231, a work about geriatric nursing that gives much general information about geriatrics 618.97, a work about geriatric nursing that emphasizes the role and techniques of the geriatric nurse 618.970231*

[.730 23]   Nursing and work of allied health personnel as a profession, occupation, hobby

Do not use; class in 610.73069

.730 6   Organizations and personnel

Notation 06 from Table 1 as modified below

.730 68   Management

Do not use for management of services of nurses; class in 362.173068

.730 69   Nursing personnel

Nature of duties, characteristics of the profession, relationships

Class here comprehensive works on nursing personnel and allied health personnel

Class comprehensive works on techniques of nursing operations in 610.73

> *For allied health personnel, see 610.737069*

.730 692   Professional nurses

Including associate-degree nurses

Class here nurse practitioners

Class physician assistants in 610.7372069

.730 693   Practical nurses

Including registered nursing assistants

.730 698   Auxiliary nursing personnel

> Class here nurses' aides, nursing assistants other than registered nursing assistants
>
> Class registered nursing assistants in 610.730693

.730 699   Relationships of nurses

> Including relationships between nurses and patients, between nurses and the public, within nursing profession

---

\>   **610.732–610.736 Nursing**

Class comprehensive works in 610.73

.732   **Private duty nursing**

.733   **Institutional nursing and ward management**

> Standard subdivisions are added for either or both topics in heading
>
> Class nonmedical aspects of ward management in 362.173068

.734   **Public health nursing**

> Class here Red Cross nursing

.734 3   Community and district nursing

> Standard subdivisions are added for either or both topics in heading
>
> Including work of health visitors, visiting nurses; home nursing by professionals
>
> Class home nursing by nonprofessionals in 649.8

.734 6   Occupational health nursing (Industrial nursing)

.734 9   Disaster nursing

.736   **Long-term care nursing**

.737   **Services of allied health personnel**

> Class here services of medical assistants, medical technicians
>
> *For a specific part of the work of allied health personnel, see the part in 614–618, e.g., exercise therapy provided by medical technicians 615.82; for services of allied health personnel for a specific disease or group of diseases or a specific medical specialty, see the disease or group of diseases or medical specialty in 616–618, plus notation 0233 from table under 616.1–616.9, notation 0233 from table under 617, or notation 0233 from table under 618.1–618.8 if role or work of allied health personnel is emphasized, e.g., a work about services of medical technicians with respect to geriatric patients that gives much general information about geriatrics 618.97, a work that emphasizes the role and techniques of the medical technician with respect to geriatric patients 618.970233*

[.737 023]   Work of allied health personnel as a profession, occupation, hobby

> Do not use; class in 610.737069

.737 06	Organizations and personnel

Notation 06 from Table 1 as modified below

.737 069	Allied health personnel

Nature of duties, characteristics of the profession, relationships

Class here medical assistants, medical technicians

Class comprehensive works on techniques of allied health personnel, medical assistants, medical technicians in 610.737

For physician assistants, see 610.7372069

.737 2	Services of physician assistants
[.737 202 3]	Work of physician assistants as a profession, occupation, hobby

Do not use; class in 610.7372069

.737 206	Organizations and personnel

Notation 06 from Table 1 as modified below

.737 206 9	Physician assistants

People educated in the medical model and licensed to perform diagnostic and therapeutic procedures under the supervision of a physician

Nature of duties, characteristics of the profession, relationships

Class nurse practitioners in 610.730692

.92	Biography

See Manual at 610.92 vs. 615.534092

611   Human anatomy, cytology, histology

Standard subdivisions are added for human anatomy, cytology, histology together; for human anatomy alone

For pathological anatomy, see 616.07

See Manual at 599.94 vs. 611; also at 612 vs. 611

.001–.009	Standard subdivisions
.01	Anatomic embryology, cytology, histology

Class here specific systems, organs, regions

.013	Anatomic embryology
.018	Histology and cytology

Standard subdivisions are added for histology and cytology together, for histology alone

.018 1	Cytology (Cell biology)

Class cytology and cells of specific systems and organs in 612.1–612.8; class cytology and cells of specific regions in 612.9

For connective tissue cells, see 611.01826; for adipocytes (fat cells), see 611.018276; for epithelial cells, see 611.01876

.018 15	Pathology (Cytopathology)
.018 16	Physiological genetics

Class here nucleic acids

.018 166	DNA (Deoxyribonucleic acid)
.018 166 3	Molecular structure

Class here DNA topology, genetic code; chromosome, gene, genome mapping; base, gene, nucleotide sequences

.018 167	Chromosomes

Class mapping chromosomes in 611.0181663

>   611.018 2–611.018 7 Histology (Tissue biology)

Class here histogenesis, histophysiology, histopathology, tissue regeneration

Class comprehensive works in 611.018

.018 2	Connective tissues and connective tissue cells

Standard subdivisions are added for connective tissues and connective tissue cells together, for connective tissues alone

Including collagen, elastic tissues, extracellular matrix

Class connective tissues of specific systems and organs in 612.1–612.8; class connective tissues of specific regions in 612.9

.018 26	Connective tissue cells

Including mast cells

.018 27	Adipose tissues and adipocytes

Standard subdivisions are added for adipose tissues and adipocytes together, for adipose tissues alone

.018 276	Adipocytes (Fat cells)
.018 7	Epithelial tissues and cells

Standard subdivisions are added for epithelial tissues and cells together, for epithelial tissues alone

Including endothelium; serous and mucous membranes

Class epithelial tissues of specific systems and organs in 612.1–612.8; class epithelial tissues of specific regions in 612.9

.018 76	Epithelial cells

> **611.1–611.9 Gross anatomy**

Class comprehensive works in 611

> **611.1–611.8 Gross anatomy of specific systems and organs**

Class comprehensive works in 611; class comprehensive works on gross anatomy and tissue structure of specific systems and organs in 612.1–612.8

See Manual at 612.1–612.8

.1 Cardiovascular organs

Class hematopoietic system in 611.41

.11 Pericardium

.12 Heart

Including ventricles, auricles, endocardium, myocardium

For pericardium, see 611.11

.13 Arteries

Class here comprehensive works on blood vessels

For veins, see 611.14; for capillaries, see 611.15. For blood vessels of a specific system or organ, see the system or organ, e.g., cerebral blood vessels 611.81

.14 Veins

.15 Capillaries

.2 Respiratory organs

.21 Nose and paranasal sinuses

Standard subdivisions are added for nose and paranasal sinuses together, for nose alone

.22 Larynx

Including epiglottis, glottis, laryngeal muscles

.23 Trachea and bronchi

.24 Lungs

.25 Pleura

.26 Diaphragm

.27 Mediastinum

.3 Digestive tract organs

.31 Mouth

.313 Tongue

.314	Teeth
.315	Palate
.316	Salivary glands
.317	Lips
.318	Cheeks
.32	Pharynx, tonsils, esophagus
.33	Stomach

Including pylorus

Class here comprehensive works on gastrointestinal organs

For intestine, see 611.34

.34	Intestine
.341	Small intestine

Including duodenum, jejunum, ileum

.345	Cecum, vermiform appendix
.347	Large intestine

Including sigmoid colon

Class here colon

For cecum, vermiform appendix, see 611.345; for rectum, see 611.35

.35	Rectum and anus

See also 611.96 for perineum

.36	Biliary tract and liver

Standard subdivisions are added for biliary tract and liver together, for biliary tract alone

Including gallbladder, bile ducts

.37	Pancreas and islands of Langerhans

Standard subdivisions are added for pancreas and islands of Langerhans together, for pancreas alone

.38	Peritoneum

Including mesentery, omentum

.4	**Hematopoietic, lymphatic, glandular systems**

Class here endocrine system

For glandular organs of a specific system, see the system, e.g., salivary glands 611.316

.41 Bone marrow and spleen

> Class here comprehensive works on anatomy of hematopoietic (blood-forming, hemopoietic) system

> *For liver, see 611.36; for lymphatic system, see 611.42*

.42 Lymphatic system

> *For spleen, see 611.41; for lymphatic glands, see 611.46*

.43 Thymus gland

.44 Thyroid and parathyroid glands

.45 Adrenal glands

.46 Lymphatic glands

.47 Carotid body; pituitary and pineal glands

.49 Breasts

.6 Urogenital system

.61 Kidneys and ureters

> Standard subdivisions are added for kidneys and ureters together, for kidneys alone

> Class here comprehensive works on anatomy of urinary organs

> *For bladder and urethra, see 611.62*

.62 Bladder and urethra

.63 Testes, prostate, scrotum

> Class here comprehensive works on male genital organs

> *For penis, see 611.64*

.64 Penis

.65 Ovaries and fallopian tubes

> Class here comprehensive works on female genital organs

> *For uterus, see 611.66; for vagina, hymen, vulva, see 611.67*

.66 Uterus

> Including uterine cervix

.67 Vagina, hymen, vulva

.7 Musculoskeletal system, integument

> Standard subdivisions are added for musculoskeletal system, integument together; for musculoskeletal system alone

.71 Bones

> *For ossicles, see 611.85*

.711 Bones of spinal column

.712	Bones of chest

> Including ribs
>
> *For sternum, see 611.713*

.713	Sternum
.715	Bones of skull

> *For bones of face, see 611.716; for mastoid processes, see 611.85*

.716	Bones of face
.717	Bones of upper extremities

> Including scapulas, clavicles, humeri, radii, ulnas, carpal and metacarpal bones, phalanges and sesamoid bones of hands
>
> Class comprehensive works on bones of extremities in 611.718

.718	Bones of lower extremities

> Including hip bones, femurs, patellas, tibias, fibulas, tarsal and metatarsal bones, phalanges and sesamoid bones of feet
>
> Class here comprehensive works on bones of extremities
>
> *For bones of upper extremities, see 611.717*

.72	Joints and ligaments

> Standard subdivisions are added for joints and ligaments together, for joints alone

.73	Muscles

> *For muscles of a specific system or organ, see the system or organ, e.g., heart muscles 611.12*

.731	Muscles of back
.732	Muscles of head
.733	Muscles of neck
.735	Muscles of chest
.736	Muscles of abdomen and pelvis
.737	Muscles of upper extremities

> Including muscles of shoulders, arms, hands
>
> Class comprehensive works on muscles of extremities in 611.738

.738	Muscles of lower extremities

> Including muscles of hips, buttocks, thighs
>
> Class here leg muscles, comprehensive works on muscles of extremities
>
> *For muscles of upper extremities, see 611.737*

.74	Connective tissues

Including tendons, fasciae

For ligaments, see 611.72; for bursae, sheaths of tendons, see 611.75

.75	Bursae, sheaths of tendons
.77	Integument

For hair and nails, see 611.78

.78	Hair and nails

Including hair follicles

.8   Nervous system

Class here neuroanatomy, sense organs

.81	Brain

Class here central nervous system

For spinal cord, see 611.82

.82	Spinal cord
.83	Nerves and ganglia

Class nerves of a specific system or organ with the system or organ, e.g., optic nerves 611.84

.84	Eyes

Class here orbits

.85	Ears

Including mastoid processes, ossicles

.86	Olfactory organs
.87	Gustatory organs
.88	Tactile organs

.9   Regional and topographical anatomy

Standard subdivisions are added for either or both topics in heading

Including back

Class specific systems or organs in a region in 611.1–611.8; class comprehensive works on gross anatomy and tissue structure of specific regions in 612.9

.91	Head

For face, see 611.92

.92	Face

See also 611.317 for lips; also 611.318 for cheeks

.93	Neck

.94   Thorax

.95   Abdomen

                Epigastric through lumbar regions

.96   Perineum and pelvic region

.97   Upper extremities

                Class comprehensive works on extremities in 611.98

.98   Lower extremities

                Class here legs, comprehensive works on extremities

                  For upper extremities, see 611.97

612   Human physiology

        Class here comprehensive works on human anatomy and physiology

        Class physiological psychology in 152

          For human anatomy, cytology, histology, see 611; for pathological physiology, see 616.07

          See Manual at 612 vs. 611; also at 613 vs. 612, 615.8; also at 616 vs. 612

.001   Philosophy and theory

[.001 571 4]   Biophysics

                Do not use; class in 612.014

[.001 572]   Biochemistry

                Do not use; class in 612.015

.001 579   Microorganisms, fungi, algae

                Class here comprehensive works on human microbiome, on human microbiota, on microbiology of human body; on beneficial and harmful microorganisms in human body; on beneficial microorganisms in human body

                  For comprehensive works on harmful microorganisms in human body, see 616.9041. For microorganisms in relation to specific aspects of human body, see the aspect in 611–618, e.g., gastrointestinal microbiome 612.3601579, probiotics as therapy for human diseases 615.329, works that emphasize poisons produced by microorganisms 615.9529

.002–.009   Standard subdivisions

.01   Biophysics and biochemistry

.014   Biophysics

.014 2   Physical phenomena in humans

                Including human aura when scientifically considered

                  See also 133.892 for the aura as a manifestation of psychic power

.014 21	Bioenergetics
	For body heat, see 612.01426; for bioelectricity, see 612.01427; for energy metabolism, see 612.39
.014 26	Body heat
	Including regulation
	Class here production, maintenance
.014 27	Bioelectricity
	Including electrophysiology
.014 4	Effects of terrestrial agents
	Including aerospace physiology
	Class space physiology in 612.0145
.014 41	Mechanical forces
.014 412	Gravitational forces
.014 414	Acceleration and deceleration
	Standard subdivisions are added for either or both topics in heading
.014 415	Pressure
	Including submarine physiology
.014 42	Electricity and magnetism
.014 44	Visible light
.014 45	Mechanical vibrations, sound, related vibrations
.014 453	Sound
.014 455	Ultrasonic vibrations
.014 46	Thermal forces
.014 462	Heat and high temperatures
	Standard subdivisions are added for either or both topics in heading
.014 465	Cold and low temperatures
	Standard subdivisions are added for either or both topics in heading
	For cryogenic temperatures, see 612.014467
.014 467	Cryogenic temperatures
.014 48	Radiation (Radiobiology)
	Class radiation sickness and radiation injuries in 616.9897
	For visible light, see 612.01444

.014 480 287	Testing and measurement

Class here radiometry (radiation dosimetry)

> *For a specific application of radiometry, see the application, e.g., use of radiometry in radiotherapy 615.842, use for prevention of diseases due to radiation 616.989705*

.014 481	Radio waves and microwaves

Standard subdivisions are added for either or both topics in heading

.014 482	Infrared radiation
.014 484	Ultraviolet radiation
.014 485	X rays
.014 486	Particle radiation

Including cosmic rays; beta, gamma, neutron radiation

For X rays, see 612.014485

.014 5	Extraterrestrial biophysics

Class here bioastronautics, space physiology

Class aerospace physiology in 612.0144; class space medicine in 616.980214

.014 53	Effects of mechanical forces
.014 532	Gravitational forces
.014 534	Acceleration and deceleration

Standard subdivisions are added for either or both topics in heading

.014 535	Pressure
.015	Biochemistry

Class metabolism in 612.39

For physiological genetics, see 611.01816

.015 01	Philosophy and theory

Class theoretical biochemistry in 612.01582

.015 02	Miscellany
.015 028	Auxiliary techniques and procedures; apparatus, equipment, materials

Class analytical biochemistry in 612.01585

.015 1	Enzymes

Add to base number 612.0151 the numbers following 572.7 in 572.75–572.79, e.g., saccharolytic enzymes 612.015156, lipolytic enzymes 612.015157

.015 2	Fluids, inorganic constituents, pigments
.015 22	Fluids

Including fluid balance, water, water-electrolyte balance

Class here fluid metabolism

.015 24	Inorganic constituents

Including minerals

Class inorganic fluids in 612.01522; class inorganic pigments in 612.01528

.015 28	Pigments

Class biochemistry of skin pigmentation in 612.7927

.015 4	Biosynthesis
.015 7	Organic compounds

For nucleic acids, see 611.01816; for enzymes, see 612.0151; for organic fluids, see 612.01522; for organic pigments, see 612.01528; for vitamins, see 612.399; for hormones, see 612.405

.015 75	Proteins
.015 756	Components of proteins

Class here amino acids, peptides, polypeptides

.015 77	Lipids

Including steroids

Class here fats, fatty acids

.015 78	Carbohydrates

Including sugars

.015 8	Theoretical, physical, analytical biochemistry

Class physical, theoretical, analytical biochemistry of a specific constituent with the constituent, e.g., physical chemistry of carbohydrates 612.01578

.015 82	Theoretical biochemistry
.015 83	Physical biochemistry
.015 85	Analytical biochemistry
.02	Control processes and tissue and organ culture
.022	Control processes

Including biological rhythms, homeostasis

For control processes in biophysics, see the process in 612.014, e.g., body heat regulation 612.01426; for control processes in biochemistry, see the process in 612.015, e.g., water-electrolyte balance 612.01522

.028	Tissue and organ culture
.04	Physiology of specific activities

Class here comprehensive works on the physiology of physical movements in relation to multiple physiological systems

For physiology of physical movements in relation to a specific system, see the system, e.g., musculoskeletal system 612.76

.042	Work
.044	Exercise and sports

Standard subdivisions are added for either or both topics in heading

Including walking

Class here recreation

For physiology of exercise on the job, see 612.042

> ### 612.1–612.8 Specific functions, systems, organs

Class here cytology and cells of specific systems and organs, histology and tissues of specific systems and organs, comprehensive works on gross anatomy and tissue structure of specific systems and organs

Except for modifications shown under specific entries, add to each subdivision identified by * as follows:
```
04       Tissues and cells
045         Tissues
               Class here histology (tissue biology); histogenesis,
               histophysiology, histopathology, tissue regeneration
046         Cells
               Including cytopathology
               Class here cytology (cell biology)
```

Class comprehensive works in 612

See Manual at 612.1–612.8

.1	***Circulatory system**

Class here cardiovascular system, circulation

For lymphatic system, see 612.42. For circulation in a specific system or organ, see the system or organ, e.g., brain 612.824

.11	Blood

Class hematopoietic system in 612.41; class blood transfusion in 615.39

For blood chemistry, see 612.12

.111	Erythrocytes (Red corpuscles)
.111 1	Biochemistry

Including hemoglobins

---

*Add as instructed under 612.1–612.8

.111 2		Counts and counting
.112	Leukocytes (White corpuscles)	
.112 1		Biochemistry
.112 7		Counts and counting
.115	Coagulation (Clotting)	

> Including role of fibrin, fibrinoplastin, plasma, thrombin in clotting

.116	Plasma

> Class blood plasma transfusion in 615.39

> *For role of plasma in clotting, see 612.115*

.117	Platelets
.118	Biophysics and biological properties
.118 1	Biophysics

> Physical properties and phenomena, effect of physical agents

> Including hemorheology (study of blood flow)

> *For biophysics of a specific component or function, see the compound or function in 612.111–612.117, e.g., biophysics of platelets 612.117*

.118 2	Biological properties
.118 25	Blood types and typing (Blood groups and grouping)

> Standard subdivisions are added for any or all topics in heading

.12	Blood chemistry

> Including cholesterol, lipids, sugar

> Class biological properties in 612.1182

> *For chemistry of a specific component or function, see the component or function in 612.111–612.117, e.g., chemistry of coagulation 612.115*

>   612.13–612.18 Circulation

> Class comprehensive works in 612.1

.13	*Blood vessels

> Class here vascular circulation

> *For vasomotors, see 612.18*

.133	*Arteries

> Class here arterial circulation

---

*Add as instructed under 612.1–612.8

.134	*Veins
	Class here venous circulation
.135	*Capillaries
	Class here capillary circulation
.14	Blood pressure
.17	*Heart
.171	Biophysics

Including contraction and dilation of heart cavities, valvular activity

For blood pressure, see 612.14

.173   Biochemistry

Including metabolism

.178   *Innervation

.18   *Vasomotors

Nerves causing dilation (vasodilators) and constriction (vasoconstrictors) of blood vessels

.2   *Respiratory system

Class here respiration

.21   Biophysics

Including respiratory sounds

Class here respiratory mechanics

.22   Biochemistry

Including oxygen supply, gas exchange, carbon dioxide removal

.23   Nose, paranasal sinuses, larynx, trachea, bronchi

.232   *Nose and paranasal sinuses

Class here comprehensive works on physiology of the nose

Subdivisions are added for nose and paranasal sinuses together, for nose alone

For physiology of the nose as an olfactory organ, see 612.86

.233   *Larynx

Including epiglottis, glottis

For physiology of glottis as an organ of speech, see 612.78

.234   *Trachea and bronchi

Subdivisions are added for either or both topics in heading

*Add as instructed under 612.1–612.8

.24	*Lungs
.25	Pleura, diaphragm, mediastinum
.26	Tissue respiration
.28	*Innervation of respiratory system

.3   ***Digestive system**

Class here digestion, nutrition

For dietetics and applied nutrition, see 613.2

.31   *Mouth and esophagus

Including ingestion and start of digestion

Subdivisions are added for mouth and esophagus together, for mouth alone

.311   *Teeth

Including mastication

.312   Tongue and tonsils

Class here comprehensive works on physiology of tongue

For physiology of tongue as a gustatory organ, see 612.87

.313   *Salivary glands

Including saliva

.315   *Esophagus

.32   *Stomach

Including gastric secretions

Class here comprehensive works on gastrointestinal organs and secretions

For intestine and intestinal secretions, see 612.33

.320 157 9   Microorganisms, fungi, algae

Do not use for comprehensive works on gastrointestinal microbiome, gastrointestinal microbiota; class in 612.3601579

.33   *Intestine

Including intestinal secretions

For large intestine, see 612.36

.330 157 9   Microorganisms, fungi, algae

Do not use for comprehensive works on intestinal microbiome, intestinal microbiota; class in 612.3601579

.34   *Pancreas

Including pancreatic secretions

*Add as instructed under 612.1–612.8

.35	*Biliary tract and liver

Including gallbladder, bile and bile ducts

Subdivisions are added for biliary tract and liver together, for biliary tract alone

.352	*Liver
.36	*Large intestine

Including defecation

.360 157 9	Microorganisms, fungi, algae

Class here comprehensive works on gastrointestinal microbiome, on gastrointestinal microbiota

Class comprehensive works on human microbiome, on human microbiota in 612.001579

For microbiome, microbiota of a specific part of gastrointestinal tract, see the part, plus notation 01579 from Table 1, e.g., microbiome, microbiota of small intestine 612.3301579

.38	Absorption

Transfer of digested food from alimentary canal into blood stream

Class absorption in a specific part of the alimentary canal with the part, e.g., intestine 612.33

.39	Metabolism

Including energy metabolism

Class bioenergetics in 612.01421

For biosynthesis, see 612.0154; for metabolism of drugs, see 615.7; for metabolism of toxic substances, see 615.9. For metabolism within a specific function, system, or organ, see the function, system, or organ, e.g., metabolism of plasma 612.116

.391	Hunger and thirst mechanisms
.392	Metabolism of inorganic substances

Class here minerals

.392 3	Water

Class electrolytic, fluid balance; comprehensive works on fluid metabolism in 612.01522

.392 4	Elements

Including iron, phosphorus, sulfur

.392 6	Compounds other than water

Including salts

*Add as instructed under 612.1–612.8

.396	Carbohydrate metabolism

> Class glycemic index as dietetic guide in 613.283

.397	Lipid metabolism

> Including fats

.398	Protein metabolism
.399	Vitamins
.4	***Hematopoietic, lymphatic, glandular, urinary systems**

> Class here endocrine system, exocrine glands, secretion

For glands and glandular activity in a specific system or organ, see the system or organ, e.g., salivary glands 612.313, mammary glands and lactation 612.664

.400 1–.400 9	Standard subdivisions
.405	Hormones
.41	*Spleen and bone marrow

> Class here hematopoiesis, comprehensive works on hematopoietic (blood-forming, hemopoietic) system

For liver, see 612.352; for lymphatic system, see 612.42

.415	*Spleen
.416	*Bone marrow
.42	*Lymphatic system

> Class here lymph

For spleen, see 612.415

.43	*Thymus gland
.44	*Thyroid and parathyroid glands

> Subdivisions are added for thyroid and parathyroid glands together, for thyroid gland alone

.448	*Parathyroid glands
.45	*Adrenal glands
.46	*Urinary system

> Class here comprehensive works on excretion, excretory system

For defecation, see 612.36

.461	Urine
.463	*Kidneys
.467	Ureters, bladder, urethra

*Add as instructed under 612.1–612.8

.467 3	*Bladder
.49	Carotid body; pituitary and pineal glands
.492	*Pituitary and pineal glands

> Subdivisions are added for pituitary and pineal glands together, for pituitary gland alone

| .6 | ***Reproduction, development, maturation** |

> Class here genital system, comprehensive medical works on sex

> Class interdisciplinary works on sex in 306.7

> *For a specific aspect of sex, see the aspect, e.g., sexual disorders 616.69*

| .61 | *Male reproductive system |

> Including function in sexual activity

> *For climacteric, see 612.665*

| .614 | *Testes and scrotum |

> Subdivisions are added for testes and scrotum together, for testes alone

.616	*Penis
.618	*Prostate
.62	*Female reproductive system

> Including function in sexual activity

> *For pregnancy and childbirth, see 612.63; for menstruation, see 612.662; for climacteric, see 612.665*

| .625 | *Ovaries and fallopian tubes |

> Subdivisions are added for ovaries and fallopian tubes together, for ovaries alone

| .627 | *Uterus |

> Including uterine cervix

| .628 | Vagina, hymen, vulva |
| .63 | Pregnancy and childbirth |

> Including placenta

> Class comprehensive works on pregnancy and childbirth in 618.2

> *For physiology of embryo and fetus, see 612.64*

| .64 | Physiology of embryo and fetus |

> Class here comprehensive works on embryology

> *For anatomic embryology, see 611.013*

| .640 01–.640 09 | Standard subdivisions |

*Add as instructed under 612.1–612.8

.640 1	Development of specific systems, organs, regions

Add to base number 612.6401 the numbers following 611 in 611.1–611.9, e.g., development of the eye 612.640184

.646	Development of embryo
.647	Development of fetus

>   612.65–612.67 Postnatal development

Class comprehensive works in 612.6

For postnatal development of a specific system, organ, region, see the system, organ, region, e.g., postnatal development of teeth 612.311

.65	Child development
.652	Development of newborn (neonate)

First month of postnatal development

.654	Development from infancy to beginning of puberty

From second month of postnatal development

.66	Adult development and maturity

For aging, see 612.67

.661	Puberty and development prior to attainment of full maturity
.662	Menstruation

Including menarche

.663	Full maturity
.664	*Mammary glands

Class here lactation

.665	Climacteric

Including menopause

.67	Aging

Class here physical gerontology

See also 616.078 for death

.68	Longevity factors
.7	***Musculoskeletal system, integument**

Subdivisions are added for musculoskeletal system, integument together; for musculoskeletal system alone

---

*Add as instructed under 612.1–612.8

.74   *Muscles

> Class locomotion, exercise, rest in 612.76. Class muscles of a specific system or organ with the system or organ, e.g., cardiac muscles 612.17, eye muscles 612.846

.740 45   Muscle tissues

> Number built according to instructions under 612.1–612.8

> Including skeletal muscle tissue, smooth muscle tissue

.741   Biophysics

> Including contractions, elasticity, irritability, tonus

.743   *Innervation

.744   Biochemistry

> Including fatigue products

.75   Bones, joints, connective tissues

> Class locomotion, exercise, rest in 612.76

.751   *Bones and cartilage

> Subdivisions are added for bones and cartilage together, for bones alone

> Class bone marrow in 612.416

> *For mastoid processes, ossicles, see 612.854*

.751 045   Bone tissues

> Number built according to instructions under 612.1–612.8

> Including periosteum

.751 7   Cartilage

> Including elastic cartilage, hyaline cartilage; fibrocartilage

.751 76   Cartilage cells (Chondrocytes)

.752   Joints and ligaments

> Standard subdivisions are added for joints and ligaments together, for joints alone

.757   Connective tissues

> Class comprehensive works on histology of connective tissues in 611.0182

> *For bone tissues, see 612.751045; for cartilage tissues, see 612.7517; for ligament tissues, see 612.752*

*Add as instructed under 612.1–612.8

.76	Locomotion, exercise, rest

Including body mechanics

Class total physiology of physical movements (including muscle contractions, breathing, blood flow, digestion during exercise) in 612.04

.78	Voice and speech

Standard subdivisions are added for either or both topics in heading

Class here organs of speech

Class neurolinguistics in 612.82336

.79	*Integument

Class here integumentary system, skin

.791	Biophysics of skin

Including absorbency, contractions, irritability, resistivity, tonus

.792	Biochemistry of skin
.792 7	Pigmentation
.793	Glands of skin

Including perspiration

Class here glandular secretions

.798	*Innervation of skin
.799	Hair and nails

Including hair follicles

.8	**Nervous system**

Class here neurophysiology, psychophysiology, sensory functions

See Manual at 612.8 vs. 152

.804	Special topics of nervous functions
.804 2	Neurochemistry

Including cerebrospinal fluid

.804 3	Biophysics of nervous system

---

*Add as instructed under 612.1–612.8

.81	*Nerves and nerve fibers

Class here peripheral nervous system

Subdivisions are added for nerves and nerve fibers together, for nerves alone

Class comprehensive works on nerves, nerve fibers, central nervous system in 612.8

> *For nerves and nerve fibers in central nervous system, see 612.82; for autonomic nervous system, see 612.89. For innervation and neural activity in a specific system or organ, see the system or organ, e.g., heart innervation 612.178*

.810 46	Nerve cells

Number built according to instructions under 612.1–612.8

Including neuroglia

Class here neurons

.811	Motor and sensory nerves
.813	Biophysics

Including electrophysiology

> *For irritability, see 612.816. For biophysics of a specific kind of nerve, see the nerve, e.g., biophysics of cranial nerves 612.819*

.814	Biochemistry

> *For biochemistry of a specific kind of nerve, see the nerve, e.g., biochemistry of motor nerves 612.811*

.816	Irritability
.819	Cranial and spinal nerves
.82	*Central nervous system

Class here brain

> *For spinal cord, see 612.83*

.821	Sleep phenomena

Physiology of brain during sleep and dreams

Class effect of sleep on other psychological activity, interdisciplinary works on sleep in 154.6; class dreams as phenomena that have meaning in themselves or in the life of the dreamer, interdisciplinary works on dreams in 154.63

.822	Biochemistry and biophysics

> *For biochemistry and biophysics of a specific part of brain, see the part, e.g., biophysics of cerebrum 612.825*

.823	Emotions, conscious mental processes, intelligence

*Add as instructed under 612.1–612.8

| .823 2 | Emotions |
| | Class here feelings |

.823 3 Conscious mental processes and intelligence

Standard subdivisions are added for conscious mental processes and intelligence together, for conscious mental processes alone

Class here cognitive neuroscience

Add to base number 612.8233 the numbers following 153 in 153.1–153.9, e.g., neurolinguistics 612.82336, physiology of brain with respect to memory 612.823312, with respect to intelligence 612.82339; however, for kinesthesis, see 612.88

.824 Circulation

For circulation in a specific part of brain, see the part, e.g., circulation in cerebellum 612.827

.825 *Cerebrum

Including cerebral hemispheres, convolutions, corpus striatum, cortex, rhinencephalon

Class here prosencephalon (forebrain)

For cerebral commissures and peduncles, see 612.826; for diencephalon, see 612.8262

.825 2 Localization of motor functions

.825 5 Localization of sensory functions

.826 Diencephalon and brain stem

Including cerebral commissures and peduncles

For medulla oblongata, see 612.828

.826 2 *Diencephalon

Including geniculate bodies, hypothalamus, thalamus

.826 4 *Mesencephalon (Midbrain)

Including corpora quadrigemina

.826 7 *Pons Variolii

.827 *Cerebellum

.828 *Medulla oblongata

.83 *Spinal cord

> 612.84–612.88 Sensory functions

Class here sense organs

Class comprehensive works in 612.8

*Add as instructed under 612.1–612.8

.84	*Eyes
	Class here eyeballs; physiological optics; vision
.841	Fibrous tunics, conjunctivas, anterior chambers
	Including corneas, scleras
.842	*Uveas
	Including choroids, ciliary bodies, irises
.843	Optic nerves and retinas
.844	Aqueous humors, crystalline lenses, vitreous bodies
.846	Movements
	Class here ocular neuromuscular mechanism
.847	Eyelids and tear ducts
	Class conjunctivas in 612.841
.85	*Ears
	Class here hearing
.851	*External ears
.854	*Middle ears
	Including eustachian tubes, mastoid processes, ossicles, tympanic membranes
.858	*Internal ears
	Including cochleas, labyrinths, semicircular canals, vestibules
.86	*Nose
	Class here chemical senses, smelling
	Class comprehensive works on physiology of nose in 612.232
	For tasting, see 612.87
.87	*Tongue
	Class here tasting
	Class comprehensive works on physiology of the tongue in 612.312
.88	Other sensory organs
	Including kinesthesis, proprioceptive senses; tactile senses; pain sensations and reactions
.89	*Autonomic nervous system
	Including sympathetic and parasympathetic nervous systems

*Add as instructed under 612.1–612.8

.9   **Regional physiology**

Including back

Class here cytology and cells of specific regions, histology and tissues of specific regions, comprehensive works on gross anatomy and tissue structure of specific regions

Add to base number 612.9 the numbers following 611.9 in 611.91–611.98, e.g., physiology of face 612.92

Class physiology, cytology, histology of specific systems and organs in specific regions in 612.1–612.8

613   Personal health and safety

Standard subdivisions are added for personal health and safety together, for personal health alone

Class here measures to promote health and prevent disease taken by individuals and their medical advisers, comprehensive medical works on personal and public measures to promote health and prevent disease

For public measures to promote health and prevent disease, see 614; for personal measures to prevent poisoning, see 615.905. For personal measures to prevent a specific disease or group of diseases, see the disease or group of diseases in 616–618, plus notation 05 from table under 616.1–616.9, notation 052 from table under 617, or notation 052 from table under 618.1–618.8, e.g., personal measures to prevent cardiovascular diseases 616.105

See Manual at 613 vs. 612, 615.8

.04   Personal health of people by gender, sex, or age group

Class here comprehensive works on personal health and safety of specific gender, sex, and age groups

For personal safety of specific gender, sex, and age groups, see 613.6081–613.6084

.042   Personal health of specific sex groups

.042 3   Males

.042 32   Males under twelve

Class here comprehensive works on boys

For boys twelve and older, see 613.04233

.042 33   Males twelve to twenty

.042 34   Adult men

.042 4   Females

.042 42   Females under twelve

Class here comprehensive works on girls

For girls twelve and older, see 613.04243

.042 43   Females twelve to twenty

.042 44	Adult women
.043	**Personal health of specific age groups**
	Class personal health of specific age groups of specific sexes in 613.042
.043 2	Infants and children
	Through age eleven
	Class here pediatric preventive measures
.043 3	Young people twelve to twenty
.043 4	Mature adults
	Including young adults, middle-aged people
	For people in late adulthood, see 613.0438
.043 8	People in late adulthood
	Class here geriatric preventive measures
[.081–.084]	**People by gender, sex, or age group**
	Do not use; class in 613.04
.1	**Environmental factors**
	Class here acclimatization, comprehensive works on personal environmental health
	For artificial environments, see 613.5; for industrial and occupational health, see 613.62; for travel health, see 613.68; for survival, see 613.69; for environmental toxicology, see 615.902; for environmental diseases, see 616.98
.101 579	Microorganisms, fungi, algae
	Class here microorganisms, fungi, algae in the environment around humans
	Class microorganisms, fungi, algae that live on and in humans in 612.001579
.11	**Weather and climate**
	Standard subdivisions are added for either or both topics in heading
	Including humidity, seasonal changes
[.110 911]	Weather and climate in frigid zones
	Do not use; class in 613.111
[.110 913]	Weather and climate in torrid zone (tropics)
	Do not use; class in 613.113
.111	**Cold weather and climate**
	Standard subdivisions are added for either or both topics in heading
	Including arctic climate

.113	Hot weather and climate

       Standard subdivisions are added for either or both topics in heading

       Including tropical climate

.12	Physiographic and other regions

       Including mountains, seashore

.122	Health resorts
.19	Air and light
.192	Breathing

       Class here breathing exercises

       Class breathing exercises in respiratory therapy in 615.836; class comprehensive works on exercises in 613.71

.193	Sun bathing
.194	Nudism
.2	**Dietetics**

Class here applied nutrition; guides to nutritional aspects of food, of beverages; comprehensive works on personal health aspects of food, of beverages

Class human nutritional requirements considered in relation to physiological processes and the role of nutrients in the body in 612.3; class personal aspects of preventing alcohol abuse in 613.81; class diet therapy in 615.854; class nutritive values of specific beverages in 641.2; class nutritive values of specific foods in 641.33–641.39; class comprehensive works on diet and physical fitness in 613.7; class interdisciplinary works on food safety in 363.192. Class diets to prevent or treat a specific disease with the disease, plus notation 0654 from table under 616.1–616.9, notation 0654 from table under 617, or notation 0654 from table under 618.1–618.8, e.g., diets to prevent or treat hypertension 616.1320654; however, class diets that exclude a specific food or group of foods with the diet in 613.268, e.g., diets that exclude wheat to prevent or treat an allergy 613.268311 (*not* 616.9750654)

See also 616.39 for conditions resulting from nutritional deficiencies; also 641.563 for cooking for preventive and therapeutic diets

See Manual at 363.8 vs. 613.2, 641.3

.201 579   Microorganisms, fungi, algae

> Do not use for personal health aspects of mushrooms and truffles as food; class in 613.2758. Do not use for personal health aspects of marine algae, seaweeds as food; class in 613.2798

> Class here comprehensive works on probiotic foods (foods with probiotics)

> Class interdisciplinary works on probiotics in 615.329; class interdisciplinary works on food microbiology, on probiotic foods in 641.3001579

> *For specific probiotic foods, see the foods, e.g., probiotic dairy products 613.277*

> *See also 641.563 for cooking probiotic foods*

.208 2   Women

> Class dietetics for nursing women in 613.269; class dietetics for pregnant women in 618.242

.208 3   Young people

> Class home economics and child-rearing aspects of feeding children, interdisciplinary works on feeding children in 649.3

.208 32   Infants

> Class breast feeding in 613.269

.208 5   Relatives

.208 52   Mothers

> Class dietetics for nursing mothers in 613.269

.23   Calories

> Class here calorie counters

> Class high-calorie diet in 613.24; class low-calorie diet in 613.25

.24   Weight-gaining diet

> Class weight-gaining diet focused on a specific nutritive element in 613.28

.25   Weight-losing diet (Reducing diet)

> Class here caloric restriction, low-calorie diet

> Class weight-losing diet focused on a specific nutritive element in 613.28; class diet therapy for obesity in 616.3980654; class comprehensive works on exercise and diet for weight loss in 613.712

.26   Specific diets

> Class human breast milk diet in 613.269

> *For weight-gaining diet, see 613.24; for weight-losing diet, see 613.25; for diets that promote specific foods, see 613.27; for diets involving specific nutritive elements, see 613.28*

[.260 1–.260 9]	Standard subdivisions

Do not use; class in 613.201–613.209

.262   Vegetarian diet

Plant-based diet that excludes meat from land animals but may include milk products, eggs, seafood

Class here lacto-ovo vegetarian diet, pescatarian diet; interdisciplinary works on vegetarianism

For ethics of vegetarianism, see 179.3; for religious ethics of vegetarianism, see 205.693; for macrobiotic diet, see 613.264; for vegetarian foods, see 641.303; for vegetarian cooking, see 641.5636

.262 2   Vegan diet

.263   High-fiber and low-fiber diets

Standard subdivisions are added for either or both topics in heading

Class vegetarian diet in 613.262; class raw food diet in 613.265

.264   Macrobiotic diet

.265   Raw food diet

Class vegetarian diet in 613.262

.268   Diets that exclude specific foods

Including diets that exclude specific meats or seafood, e.g., pork-free diet

Class here diet therapy that excludes a specific food or group of foods, diets to prevent a specific disease if the diets exclude a specific food or group of foods

Class vegetarian diet in 613.262; class sugar-free diet in 613.28332; class salt-free diet in 613.285223; class comprehensive works on diets that exclude specific foods and diets that promote specific foods in 613.27; class comprehensive works on diet therapy in 615.854

.268 3–.268 5   Diets that exclude specific foods from plant crops

Add to base number 613.268 the numbers following 63 in 633–635 for the food to be excluded, e.g., wheat-free diet 613.268311

.268 311   Wheat-free diet

Number built according to instructions under 613.2683–613.2685

Class here comprehensive works on gluten-free diet

For rye-free diet, see 613.268314; for barley-free diet, see 613.268316

.268 7   Diets that exclude dairy and related products

Class here dairy-free diet; casein-free diet, lactose-free diet

Add to base number 613.2687 the numbers following 637 in 637.1–637.5 for the food to be excluded, e.g., milk-free diet 613.26871, egg-free diet 613.26875

.269   **Human breast milk diet**

> Class here nutritional and general health aspects of breast feeding for both mother and infant, comprehensive medical works on breast feeding
>
> Class interdisciplinary works on breast feeding in 649.33
>
> > *For a specific medical aspect of breast feeding not provided for here, see the aspect, e.g., prolactin and physiology of human lactation 612.664*

.27   **Specific foods**

> Class here personal health aspects of specific foods; diets that promote specific foods; comprehensive works on diets that promote specific foods and diets that exclude specific foods
>
> Add to base number 613.27 the numbers following 641.3 in 641.33–641.39, e.g., honey 613.278
>
> Class vegetarian diet in 613.262; class high-fiber diet in 613.263; class interdisciplinary works on nutritional value of specific foods in 641.3
>
> > *For diets that exclude specific foods, see 613.268; for human breast milk diet, see 613.269*

.28   **Specific nutritive elements**

> Class here weight-gaining diet focused on a specific nutritive element, weight-losing diet focused on a specific nutritive element
>
> Class probiotic foods in 613.201579; class calories in 613.23; class high-fiber and low-fiber diets in 613.263; class diets that exclude specific foods in 613.268; class diets that promote specific foods in 613.27

[.280 1–.280 9]   Standard subdivisions

> Do not use; class in 613.201–613.209

.282   Proteins

> > *For gluten-free diet, see 613.268311; for casein-free diet, see 613.2687*

.283   Carbohydrates

> Class here glycemic index as dietetic guide
>
> Class physiology of carbohydrate metabolism in 612.396

.283 3   Low-carbohydrate diet (Carbohydrate-restricted diet)

.283 32   Sugar-free diet

> Diet that avoids added and refined sugars but may use substitute sweeteners (e.g., honey)
>
> > *For lactose-free diet, see 613.2687*

.284   Fats and oils

> Standard subdivisions are added for either or both topics in heading

.284 3   Low-fat diet (Fat-restricted diet)

.284 32	Low-cholesterol diet
.285	Minerals
.285 1	Calcium, iron, copper

Class here metals

For metals other than calcium, iron, copper, see 613.2852

.285 16	Calcium
.285 2	Metals other than calcium, iron, copper
.285 22	Sodium
.285 223	Sodium-restricted diet

Class here low-salt diet, salt-free diet

.286	Vitamins

Including antioxidants

.287	Water
.4	**Personal cleanliness and related topics**

Standard subdivisions are added for personal cleanliness and related topics together, for personal cleanliness alone

.41	Bathing

Including saunas, Turkish baths; showering

.48	Clothing and cosmetics
.482	Clothing

Only health aspects

Class clothing selection and dressing with style in 646.3

.488	Cosmetics

Only health aspects

Class cosmetics in grooming in 646.72

.5	**Artificial environments**

In enclosed spaces

Including homes, offices; indoor air quality; indoor temperatures and air conditioning

Class toxicology in 615.9

.6 **Personal safety and special topics of health**

> Standard subdivisions are added for personal safety and special topics of health together, for personal safety alone
>
> Class here accident prevention for individuals, crime prevention for individuals
>
> Class social services to victims of crimes in 362.88; class public safety programs, interdisciplinary works on safety in 363.1; class works on why individuals become victims of specific crimes in 364.1; class crime prevention for society as a whole in 364.4
>
> > *For prevention of identity theft, see 332.024; for household security, see 643.16. For personal safety in a specific field, see the field, plus notation 0289 from Table 1, e.g., personal safety in recreational boating 797.10289*

.62 Industrial and occupational health

> Standard subdivisions are added for either or both topics in heading

.66 Self-defense

> Class here prevention of violent crimes for individuals
>
> Class works on why people become victims of specific violent crimes in 364.15; class martial arts for self-defense, interdisciplinary works on martial arts in 796.8
>
> > *See also 362.88 for general works on why people become victims of crimes; also 613.7148 for exercises from martial arts traditions for fitness*

.660 82 Women

> Class here self-defense for women
>
> Class rape prevention in 613.663

.663 Rape prevention for individuals

.68 Travel health

.69 Survival

> After accidents and disasters, in other unfavorable circumstances
>
> Class here survival housekeeping
>
> Class survival as a safety aspect of a specific sport with the sport in 796, plus notation 0289 from Table 1, e.g., survival as a safety aspect of mountaineering 796.5220289
>
> > *For self-defense, see 613.66*

.7 **Physical fitness**

> Class here comprehensive works on diet and physical fitness
>
> > *For diet, see 613.2*

.704 Special topics of physical fitness

> 613.704 2–613.704 5 Specific age and sex groups

Class physical yoga of specific age and sex groups in 613.7046; class comprehensive works in 613.704

.704 2   Physical fitness of children

.704 3   Physical fitness of young people twelve to twenty

.704 4   Physical fitness of adults

For physical fitness of adult women, see 613.7045

.704 46   Physical fitness of people in late adulthood

Class physical fitness of men in late adulthood in 613.70449

.704 49   Physical fitness of adult men

Class here physical fitness of males

For physical fitness of boys under twelve, see 613.7042; for physical fitness of young men twelve to twenty, see 613.7043

.704 5   Physical fitness of adult women

Class here physical fitness of females

For physical fitness of girls under twelve, see 613.7042; for physical fitness of young women twelve to twenty, see 613.7043

.704 6   Physical yoga

Class here hatha yoga

Class exercises from the martial arts and related traditions in 613.7148

[.708 1–.708 4]   People by gender, sex, or age group

Do not use; class in 613.7042–613.7045

.71   Exercise and sports activities

Standard subdivisions are added for exercise and sports activities together, for exercise alone

Class here aerobic exercise, comprehensive works on care of physique and form

Class physical yoga in 613.7046; class exercises to aid childbirth in 618.244; class parental supervision of children's exercise and sports activities in 649.57; class exercise and sports activities as recreation in 796; class comprehensive works on physiological processes of exercise and sports in 612.044

For breathing exercises, see 613.192

[.710 247 96]   The subject for people occupied with athletics and sports

Do not use; class in 613.711

.710 82	Women

> Class exercise for pregnant women in 618.244

.710 88	Occupational and religious groups
[.710 887 96]	People occupied with athletics and sports

> Do not use; class in 613.711

.711 Fitness training for sports

Including fitness training for specific sports not provided for in 613.713–613.717, e.g., soccer

Class here personal health of athletes

Class a specific kind of fitness training with the kind, e.g., weight lifting 613.713; class fitness training for a specific sport listed in 613.713–613.717 with the sport, e.g., swimming 613.716

.712 Exercise for weight loss

Class here reducing, reducing exercises, comprehensive works on exercise and diet for weight loss

Class exercise therapy for obesity in 616.398062

For diet for weight loss, see 613.25

.713 Weight lifting

Class here interdisciplinary works on bodybuilding

For weight lifting as a sport, bodybuilding contests, see 796.41

.714 Calisthenics and isometric exercises

Standard subdivisions are added for calisthenics and isometric exercises together, for calisthenics alone

Class here gymnastic exercises

See also 613.713 for weight lifting; also 613.715 for aerobic dancing; also 613.716 for aquatic exercises

.714 8 Exercises from the martial arts traditions and related traditions

Standard subdivisions are added for exercises from the martial arts traditions and related traditions together, for exercises from the martial arts traditions alone

Class here fitness training for the martial arts

Class interdisciplinary works on martial arts in 796.8

.714 81–.714 86 Exercises from specific combat sports

Add to base number 613.7148 the numbers following 796.8 in 796.81–796.86, e.g., exercises from karate 613.7148153, exercises from boxing 613.71483

.714 815 5	Exercises from Chinese forms of martial arts

Number built according to instructions under 613.71481–613.71486

Class here interdisciplinary works on tai chi

For tai chi as a sport, see 796.8155

.714 89	Qi gong
.714 9	Isometric exercises
.715	Aerobic dancing
.716	Aquatic exercises and swimming
.717	Running and walking

See also 796.42 for running and walking as sports

.717 2	Running

Class here jogging

.717 6	Walking
.718	Stretching exercises, and exercises for muscles of specific parts of body
.718 2	Stretching exercises

See also 613.72 for massage

.718 8	Exercises for muscles of specific parts of body

Add to base number 613.7188 the numbers following 611.73 in 611.731–611.738, e.g., abdominal exercises 613.71886

.719	Specific systems of exercises for health

Class physical yoga in 613.7046; class exercises from the martial arts traditions and related traditions in 613.7148

.719 2	Pilates method
.72	Massage

Class here massage for health, fitness, relaxation

Class therapeutic massage, interdisciplinary works on massage in 615.822

.78	Correct posture
.79	Relaxation, rest, sleep
.792	Relaxation

Class breathing for relaxation in 613.192; class massage for relaxation in 613.72

.794	Sleep

.8   **Substance abuse (Drug abuse)**

> Only personal preventive aspects
>
> Including abuse of analgesics, depressants, inhalants, sedatives, tranquilizers
>
> Class here appeals to the individual to avoid substance abuse for health reasons
>
> Class comprehensive medical works on addictive drugs in 615.78; class stopping substance abuse, comprehensive medical works on substance abuse as a disease in 616.86; class interdisciplinary works on substance abuse in 362.29

.81   Alcohol

.83   Narcotics, hallucinogens, psychedelics, cannabis

.835   Cannabis

> Class here specific kinds of cannabis, e.g., hashish, marijuana

.84   Stimulants and related substances

> Standard subdivisions are added for stimulants and related substances together, for stimulants alone
>
> Including amphetamine, ephedrine; cocaine
>
> Class nicotine in 613.85

.85   Tobacco

> Class smoking cessation in 616.86506

.9   **Birth control, reproductive technology, sex hygiene, sexual techniques**

> Including sexual abstinence as a method of birth control and disease prevention
>
> Class sexual abstinence for birth control in 613.94; class sexual abstinence for disease prevention in 613.95

.907 1   Education

> Class sex education of children in the home in 649.65

.94   Birth control and reproductive technology

> Standard subdivisions are added for birth control and reproductive technology together, for birth control alone
>
> Only personal health aspects
>
> Including artificial insemination, measures to increase the likelihood of having a child of the desired sex
>
> Class here family planning
>
> Class comprehensive medical works on human reproductive technology in 616.69206; class comprehensive medical works on birth control and family planning in 618.18; class interdisciplinary works on birth control and family planning in 363.96

.942 Surgical methods of birth control

Including tubal sterilization, vasectomy

Class comprehensive works on surgical methods of birth control for males in 617.463; class comprehensive works on surgical methods of birth control for females in 618.1

.943 Chemical, natural, mechanical methods of birth control

.943 2 Chemical methods of birth control

Including contraceptive drug implants, postcoital contraceptives (morning after pills)

.943 22 Oral contraceptives

Class postcoital contraceptives in 613.9432

.943 4 Natural family planning

Class here ovulation detection method, rhythm method

.943 5 Mechanical methods of birth control

Including intrauterine devices, comprehensive works on condoms

For use of condoms for disease prevention, see 613.95

.95 Sex hygiene

Including use of condoms for disease prevention

Class here techniques for disease prevention

See also 613.96 for sexual techniques

[.950 81–.950 84] People by gender, sex, or age group

Do not use; class in 613.951–613.955

.951 Sex hygiene of young people

To age twenty

For sex hygiene of males to age twenty, see 613.953; for sex hygiene of females to age twenty, see 613.955

.952 Sex hygiene of adult men

Class here sex hygiene of males

For sex hygiene of males to age twenty, see 613.953

.953 Sex hygiene of males to age twenty

.954 Sex hygiene of adult women

Class here sex hygiene of females

For sex hygiene of females to age twenty, see 613.955

.955 Sex hygiene of females to age twenty

.96   Sexual techniques

Class here techniques for enhancing sexual enjoyment

See also 613.95 for techniques for disease prevention

614   Forensic medicine; incidence of injuries, wounds, disease; public preventive medicine

Class social provision for public health services other than those concerned with incidence and prevention of disease in 362.1; class environmental problems and services in 363.7; class incidence of poisoning in 615.904

.1   Forensic medicine

Including forensic nursing

Class here forensic pathology, medical jurisprudence

.12   Forensic chemistry

Class forensic toxicology in 614.13

.13   Forensic toxicology

.15   Forensic psychology and psychiatry

Standard subdivisions are added for either or both topics in heading

.17   Forensic anthropology

Class here forensic osteology

.18   Forensic dentistry

.3   Incidence of injuries and wounds

Standard subdivisions are added for either or both topics in heading

Including athletic injuries, crash injuries

Add to base number 614.3 the numbers following 617.1 in 617.11–617.19, e.g., gunshot wounds 614.345

Class public safety programs and social provision for prevention of injuries in 363.1

For incidence of injuries and wounds of a specific system, region, organ, see the system, region, organ in 614.59, e.g., eye injuries 614.5997

.4   Incidence of and public measures to prevent disease

Class here epidemiology

For incidence of and public measures to prevent specific diseases and kinds of diseases, see 614.5

See also 353.59 for registration and certification of births and deaths

See Manual at 614.4; also at 362.1–362.4 and 614.4–614.5

.409	History, geographic treatment, biography

For geographic treatment of incidence of diseases, see 614.42; for history of epidemics, see 614.49

.42	Incidence

Range, rate, or amount of occurrence

Class here prevalence; health surveys, medical geography

[.420 91]	Areas, regions, places in general

Do not use; class in 614.422

[.420 93–.420 99]	Specific continents, countries, localities

Do not use; class in 614.423–614.429

.422	Areas, regions, places in general

Add to base number 614.422 the numbers following —1 in notation 11–19 from Table 2, e.g., diseases in the tropics 614.4223

.423–.429	Specific continents, countries, localities

Add to base number 614.42 notation 3–9 from Table 2, e.g., diseases in the United States 614.4273

.43	Disease vectors and disease transmission by water

Standard subdivisions are added for disease vectors and disease transmission by water together, for disease vectors alone

Class here control of disease-carrying pests

Class comprehensive works on water supply in 363.61; class medical microbiology of waterborne pathogens in 616.9041

See also 614.5 for specific diseases transmitted by vectors or by water

.432	Insects
.432 2	Flies
.432 3	Mosquitoes
.432 4	Fleas and lice

Standard subdivisions are added for either or both topics in heading

.433	Arachnids

Including mites, ticks

.434	Birds
.438	Rodents
.44	Public preventive medicine

For specific preventive measures, see 614.45–614.48

>   **614.45–614.48 Specific preventive measures**

        Class comprehensive works in 614.44

.45   Patient isolation

        Class quarantine in 614.46

.46   Quarantine

        Class patient isolation in 614.45

.47   Immunization

        Class here vaccination

.48   Disinfection, fumigation, sterilization

        Standard subdivisions are added for any or all topics in heading

.49   History of epidemics

        Add to base number 614.49 notation 1–9 from Table 2, e.g., history of epidemics in the United Kingdom 614.4941

.5   **Incidence of and public measures to prevent specific diseases and kinds of diseases**

        Class incidence of and public measures to prevent mental and emotional illnesses and disturbances in 362.2; class incidence of injuries and wounds in 614.3

         See Manual at 362.1–362.4 and 614.4–614.5

.51   Salmonella infections, bacillary diseases, clostridium infections, diphtheria, cholera, dysenteries, influenza

.511   Salmonella infections

.511 2   Typhoid fever

.511 4   Paratyphoid fever

.512   Clostridium infections, diphtheria

        Standard subdivisions are added for clostridium infections and diphtheria together, for clostridium infections alone

        Class here bacillaceae infections, bacillary infections

         For bacillary dysentery, see 614.516; for anthrax, see 614.561

.512 3   Diphtheria

.512 5   Botulism

.512 8   Tetanus

.514   Cholera

.516   Dysenteries

        Including amebic dysentery, bacillary dysentery (shigellosis)

.518	Influenza

.52   Smallpox, scarlet fever, measles, rubella, chickenpox, rickettsial diseases

.521   Smallpox and attenuated forms

Standard subdivisions are added for smallpox and attenuated forms together, for smallpox alone

Including cowpox

.522   Scarlet fever

.523   Measles

.524   Rubella

.525   Chickenpox

.526   Rickettsial diseases

Add to base number 614.526 the numbers following 616.922 in 616.9222–616.9225, e.g., North Queensland tick typhus 614.5263, Q fever 614.5265

.53   Protozoan infections

Add to base number 614.53 the numbers following 616.936 in 616.9362–616.9364, e.g., malaria 614.532

For amebic dysentery, see 614.516

.54   Miscellaneous diseases

Limited to the diseases provided for below

.541   Yellow fever

.542   Tuberculosis

.543   Whooping cough (Pertussis)

.544   Mumps

.545   Puerperal septicemia and pyemia

Standard subdivisions are added for puerperal septicemia and pyemia together, for puerperal septicemia alone

Class comprehensive works on incidence of and public measures to prevent septicemia and pyemia in 614.577

.546   Hansen's disease (Leprosy)

.547   Sexually transmitted diseases

Including chancroid, condylomata acuminata (genital warts), herpes genitalis, lymphogranuloma venereum

For acquired immune deficiency syndrome (AIDS), see 614.599392

.547 2   Syphilis

For neurosyphilis, see 614.5983

.547 8	Gonorrhea
.549	Poliomyelitis

Including postpoliomyelitis syndrome

.55	Parasitic diseases and diseases due to fungi (mycoses)

Add to base number 614.55 the numbers following 616.96 in 616.962–616.969, e.g., schistosomiasis 614.553; however, for trichinosis, see 614.562

For protozoan infections, see 614.53; for parasitic skin diseases, see 614.5957; for fungal skin diseases, see 614.59579

.56	Zoonoses

For incidence of and public measures to prevent a specific zoonotic disease not provided for here, see the disease, e.g., Q fever 614.5265

.561	Anthrax
.562	Trichinosis
.563	Rabies
.564	Glanders
.565	Brucellosis
.566	Psittacosis
.57	Bacterial diseases

Including escherichia coli infections, pseudomonas infections, mycoplasma infections

Class here comprehensive works on gram-negative bacterial infections

For specific bacterial disease or group of bacterial diseases not provided for here, see the diseases, e.g., rickettsial diseases 614.526, brucellosis 614.565

.573	Pasteurella infections, yersinia infections, chlamydia infections, tularemia

Standard subdivisions are added for pasteurella infections, yersinia infections, chlamydia infections, tularemia together; for pasteurella infections alone

.573 2	Plague
.573 5	Chlamydia infections
.573 9	Tularemia
.574	Borrelia infections
.574 4	Relapsing fevers
.574 6	Lyme disease

.577   Bacterial blood diseases

                     Including pyemia, septicemia

                     Class puerperal septicemia and pyemia in 614.545

.579   Gram-positive bacterial infections

                     Including mycobacterium infections

                          For a specific gram-positive bacterial infection or group of gram-positive bacterial infections not provided for here, see the infection or group of infections, e.g., clostridium infections 614.512, anthrax 614.561

.579 7   Staphylococcal infections

                     Including toxic shock syndrome

.579 8   Streptococcal infections

                     Including necrotizing fasciitis

                          For scarlet fever, see 614.522; for erysipelas, see 614.59523

.58   Virus diseases

                          For a specific virus disease or group of virus diseases not provided for here, see the disease or group of diseases, e.g., chickenpox 614.525

.581   DNA virus infections

                     Including human papillomavirus infections

                          For a specific DNA virus infection not provided for here, see the infection, e.g., smallpox 614.521

.581 2   Herpesvirus diseases

                     Including infectious mononucleosis

                          For a specific herpesvirus disease or group of herpesvirus diseases not provided for here, see the disease or group of diseases, e.g., herpes genitalis 614.547

.588   RNA virus infections

                     Including Colorado tick fever, hantavirus infections, retroviridae infections, Rift Valley fever

                          For a specific RNA virus infection or retroviridae infection not provided for here, see the infection, e.g., measles 614.523, HIV infections 614.599392

.588 5   Flavivirus infections

                          For yellow fever, see 614.541

.588 52   Dengue

                     Including dengue hemorrhagic fever

.588 56   West Nile fever

.59   **Diseases of regions, systems, organs; other diseases**

> Class here incidence of injuries and wounds of specific regions, systems, organs
>
> Class comprehensive works on incidence of injuries and wounds in 614.3

.591–.598   **Diseases of regions, systems, organs**

> Add to base number 614.59 the numbers following 616 in 616.1–616.8, e.g., epidemic diarrhea 614.593427, erysipelas 614.59523, heart disease 614.5912, nutritional diseases 614.5939, neurosyphilis 614.5983; however, for mental and emotional illnesses, see 362.2; for allergies affecting specific regions, systems, organs, see 614.5993; for tumors (neoplasms) of regions, systems, organs, see 614.5999

.593 9   Nutritional and metabolic diseases

> Number built according to instructions under 614.591–614.598
>
> Class here nutrition surveys that emphasize malnutrition
>
> Subdivisions are added for either or both topics in heading
>
> Class comprehensive works on nutrition surveys in 363.82

.599   **Other diseases**

.599 2   Gynecologic, obstetrical, pediatric, geriatric disorders

> Add to base number 614.5992 the numbers following 618 in 618.1–618.9, e.g., pediatric disorders 614.599292; however, for puerperal septicemia and pyemia, see 614.545

.599 3   Diseases of immune system

> Class here allergies, failures of immunity
>
> Add to base number 614.5993 the numbers following 616.97 in 616.973–616.979, e.g., acquired immune deficiency syndrome (AIDS) 614.599392

.599 6   Dental diseases

> Including fluoridation of water supply

.599 7   Eye diseases

.599 8   Ear diseases

.599 9   Cancers

> Including benign neoplasms, benign tumors
>
> Class here carcinoma, malignant neoplasms, malignant tumors, neoplastic diseases; comprehensive works on benign and malignant neoplasms, on benign and malignant tumors
>
> Class public programs to control cancer-causing agents in 363.179; class public programs to control carcinogens in food in 363.192

.599 94   Specific cancers

[.599 940 1–.599 940 9]	Standard subdivisions

Do not use; class in 614.599901–614.599909

.599 941–.599 949   Subdivisions for specific cancers

Add to base number 614.59994 the numbers following 616.994 in 616.9941–616.9949, e.g., breast cancer 614.5999449

.6   Disposal of the dead

Class social aspects and services in 363.75

615   Pharmacology and therapeutics

Class comprehensive works on pharmacology in 615.1; class comprehensive works on therapeutics in 615.5

.1   Drugs (Materia medica)

Substances used for diagnosis, cure, mitigation, treatment, or prevention of disease

Class here patent medicines, pharmacology, pharmacy

Class drug therapy in 615.58

For specific drugs and groups of drugs, see 615.2–615.3; for practical pharmacy, see 615.4; for physiological and therapeutic action of drugs, see 615.7

See Manual at 615.1 vs. 615.2–615.3; also at 615.1 vs. 615.7

[.101 513]   Arithmetic

Do not use; class in 615.1401513

[.101 54]   Chemistry

Do not use; class in 615.19

.107 24   Experimental research

Class here experimental research on new drugs before they are ready for clinical trials, e.g., testing on cells in vitro or on animals; comprehensive works on drug testing

For experimental research in development and manufacture of drugs, see 615.1900724; for clinical drug trials, see 615.580724

.11   Pharmacopoeias

[.110 93–.110 99]   Specific continents, countries, localities

Do not use; class in 615.113–615.119

.113–.119   Specific continents, countries, localities

Add to base number 615.11 notation 3–9 from Table 2, e.g., pharmacopoeias of Japan 615.1152

.13   Formularies

Class here dispensatories

[.130 93–.130 99]		Specific continents, countries, localities
		Do not use; class in 615.133–615.139
.133–.139		Specific continents, countries, localities

> Add to base number 615.13 notation 3–9 from Table 2, e.g., formularies of United States 615.1373

.14   Prescription writing

> Including measures to avoid incompatibilities in prescriptions

> Class here dosage determination, posology

.140 151 3   Arithmetic

> Class here pharmaceutical arithmetic

.18   Drug preservation techniques

> Class here packaging designed to preserve drug quality and potency

.19   Pharmaceutical chemistry

> Including specific pharmaceutical dosage forms (forms of medication), e.g., ointments and emulsions; pills, capsules, tablets, troches, powders; solutions and extracts

> Class here drug design, drug development, pharmaceutical technology, comprehensive works on drug compounding

> *For drug compounding closely associated with dispensing, see 615.4*

.190 01		Philosophy and theory
.190 02		Miscellany
[.190 028 7]		Testing and measurement
		Do not use; class in 615.1901
.190 03–.190 09		Standard subdivisions
.190 1		Chemical analysis

> Class clinical drug trials in 615.580724; class toxicity testing of drugs in 615.7040724

> **615.2–615.3 Specific drugs and groups of drugs**

> Class here pharmaceutical chemistry, preservation, general therapeutics

> Class a specific drug or group of drugs affecting a specific system in 615.7; class comprehensive works in 615.1

> *See Manual at 615.1 vs. 615.2–615.3; also at 615.2–615.3 vs. 615.7*

.2   Inorganic drugs

> Add to base number 615.2 the numbers following 546 in 546.2–546.7, e.g., calomel (mercurous chloride) 615.2663

> Class use of radioactive elements, of radioisotopes in 615.842

.3   **Organic drugs**

.31   Synthetic drugs

> Add to base number 615.31 the numbers following 547.0 in 547.01–547.08, e.g., sulfonamides 615.3167

> *For a specific synthetic drug not provided for here, see the drug, e.g., synthetic vitamins 615.328*

.32   Drugs derived from plants and microorganisms

.321   Drugs derived from plants

> Class here herbal medicine, herbals, medicinal plants, minimally processed alkaloids, pharmacognosy; comprehensive works on crude drugs and simples (products that serve as drugs with minimal processing, e.g., medicinal teas)

> Class enzymes of plant origin in 615.35

> *For drugs derived from specific plants, see 615.322–615.327*

.321 9   Aromatherapy

.322   Drugs derived from bryophytes

> Add to base number 615.322 the numbers following 588 in 588.2–588.3, e.g., drugs derived from Musci 615.3222

.323–.327   Drugs derived from specific plants

> Add to base number 615.32 the numbers following 58 in 583–587, e.g., belladonna 615.3239593

> *For drugs derived from bryophytes, see 615.322; for drugs derived from fungi and algae, see 615.329*

.328   Vitamins

> Including synthetic vitamins, vitamins of animal origin

> Class here vitamin therapy

.329   Drugs derived from microorganisms, fungi, algae

> Class here comprehensive works on antibiotics, interdisciplinary works on probiotics

> Add to base number 615.329 the numbers following 579 in 579.2–579.8, e.g., streptomycin 615.329378

> Class comprehensive works on beneficial microorganisms in human body in 612.001579

> *For pharmacokinetics of antibiotics, see 615.7922; for probiotic foods, see 641.3001579*

.34   Fish-liver oils

.35   Enzymes

> Including enzymes of plant origin

.36   **Drugs of animal origin**

Class here drugs of animal origin prepared by recombinant DNA technology, hormones

For a drug of animal origin not provided for here, see the drug, e.g., fish-liver oils 615.34

.363   Pituitary hormones

Including ACTH (adrenocorticotrophic hormone)

.364   Adrenal hormones

Including aldosterone, cortisone

For sex hormones, see 615.366

.365   Insulin

.366   Sex hormones

.37   Immunologic drugs and immune serums

Standard subdivisions are added for either or both topics in heading

Class here antitoxins, immune gamma globulins, immunoglobulins

.372   Vaccines

Including toxoids

Class here development and manufacture of vaccines

Class use of vaccines in 614.47. Class use of specific vaccines with the disease in 614.5, e.g., use of influenza vaccines 614.518

.39   Human blood products and their substitutes

Standard subdivisions are added for human blood products and their substitutes together, for human blood products alone

Including blood and blood plasma transfusion

For immune gamma globulins, immunoglobulins, immune serums, see 615.37

See also 362.1784 for blood and blood plasma banks

.399   Blood substitutes

Including blood plasma substitutes

.4   **Prescription filling**

Class here drug compounding closely associated with filling prescriptions

Class comprehensive works on pharmacy in 615.1; class drug compounding by drug manufacturers, comprehensive works on drug compounding in 615.19

See also 615.14 for prescription writing

.401 513   Arithmetic

Class pharmaceutical arithmetic in 615.1401513

.5   **Therapeutics**

Class here comprehensive works on alternative therapies, on iatrogenic diseases, on patient compliance, on placebo effect

Class works on alternative medicine that include pathology and etiology in addition to therapeutics in 610 (or, if arranged by kind of disease, in 616). Class therapies applied to a specific disease or group of diseases with the disease or group of diseases in 616–618, plus notation 06 from table under 616.1–616.9, notation 06 from table under 617, or notation 06 from table under 618.1–618.8, e.g., therapies for cardiovascular diseases 616.106

> *For specific therapies and kinds of therapies other than drug therapy, chemotherapy, see 615.8; for emergency care, see 616.025; for intensive care, see 616.028; for palliative and terminal care, see 616.029. For a specific occurrence of iatrogenic diseases, patient compliance, placebo effect, see the occurrence, e.g., drug interactions not anticipated by a doctor 615.7045, surgical infections 617.9195*

.501 9   Psychological principles

Do not use for psychological therapies; class in 615.851

.507 1   Education

Class here comprehensive works on patient education

> *For patient education on a specific topic, see the topic, plus notation 071 from Table 1, e.g., patient education about diabetes mellitus 616.4620071*

.507 2   Research

.507 24   Experimental research

Class here comprehensive works on clinical trials

> *For clinical trials of diagnostic procedures, see 616.0750724. For clinical trials of a specific therapy, see the therapy, plus notation 0724 from Table 1, e.g., clinical drug trials 615.580724; for clinical trials of therapies for a specific disease or group of diseases, see the disease or group of diseases in 616–618, plus notation 060724 or other subdivision of 06 from table under 616.1–616.9, notation 060724 or other subdivision of 06 from table under 617, or notation 060724 or other subdivision of 06 from table under 618.1–618.8, e.g., clinical trials of therapies for cancer 616.994060724, clinical trials of drugs for cancer 616.9940610724*

.508 3   Young people

Do not use for therapeutics for infants and children up to puberty, comprehensive works on child and adolescent therapeutics; class in 615.542

.508 35   Young people twelve to twenty

Do not use for therapeutics for young people twelve to twenty who have not reached puberty; class in 615.542

Class here therapeutics for adolescents

.508 4   People in specific stages of adulthood

[.508 46]	People in late adulthood
	Do not use; class in 615.547
.53	General therapeutic systems

Including anthroposophical therapy, eclectic medicine

Class drug therapy regardless of system in 615.58

See also 615.321 for botanic remedies, herbal medicine; also 615.88 for folk remedies, traditional remedies

See Manual at 615.53

.532	Homeopathy
.533	Osteopathy

As a therapeutic system

Class comprehensive works on osteopathy as a medical science in 610. Class a specific application of osteopathy with the application, e.g., osteopathic discussion of thyroid diseases 616.44

.534	Chiropractic
.534 092	Biography

See Manual at 610.92 vs. 615.534092

.535	Naturopathy
.538	Ayurvedic medicine
.54	Pediatric and geriatric therapeutics
.542	Pediatric therapeutics

Class here comprehensive works on child and adolescent therapeutics

For adolescent therapeutics, see 615.50835. For a specific aspect of pediatric therapeutics, see the aspect, plus notation 083 from Table 1, e.g., exercise therapy for children 615.82083

.547	Geriatric therapeutics

For a specific aspect of geriatric therapeutics, see the aspect, plus notation 0846 from Table 1, e.g., acupuncture as therapy for people in late adulthood 615.8920846

.58	Drug therapy

Class here chemotherapy

Class general therapeutics of a specific drug or group of drugs in 615.2–615.3

For methods of administering drugs, see 615.6

.580 724	Experimental research

Class here clinical drug trials

Class chemical analysis of drugs in 615.1901; class toxicity testing of drugs in 615.7040724. Class clinical trials for drugs for specific diseases or groups of diseases with the disease or group of diseases in 616–618, plus notation 0610724 from table under 616.1–616.9, notation 0610724 from table under 617, or notation 0610724 from table under 618.1–618.8, e.g., clinical trials of drugs for cancer 616.9940610724

.6   Methods of administering drugs

Only works that focus narrowly on methods of administering drugs

Including inhalation, oral, topical administration; injections; parenteral infusions

Class here drug administration routes

Class general works on a specific type of therapy with the therapy, e.g., drug therapy 615.58, inhalation therapy 615.836

> *For methods of administering a specific drug or group of drugs, see 615.2–615.3*

.7   Pharmacokinetics

Class here biopharmaceutics, pharmacodynamics

Class use of a drug to treat a specific disease or group of diseases with the disease or group of diseases in 616–618, plus notation 061 from table under 616.1–616.9, notation 061 from table under 617, or notation 061 from table under 618.1–618.8, e.g., drug treatment for diseases of liver 616.362061

> *For toxicology, see 615.9*

> *See Manual at 612.1–612.8; also at 615.1 vs. 615.7; also at 615.2–615.3 vs. 615.7; also at 615.7 vs. 615.9*

.704	Special effects and actions of drugs

Class here adverse reactions, toxic reactions

Class toxicity testing of drugs in 615.7040724; class drug allergies in 616.9758

.704 028 7	Testing and measurement

Do not use for toxicity testing of drugs; class in 615.7040724

.704 2	Side effects
.704 5	Interactions

Including drug-herb interactions, drug incompatibilities

.704 52	Drug-nutrient interactions

.71   **Drugs affecting cardiovascular and hematopoietic systems**

> Standard subdivisions are added for drugs affecting cardiovascular and hematopoietic systems together, for drugs affecting cardiovascular system alone

.711   Cardiotonic agents

> Class here heart stimulants

.716   Anti-arrhythmia agents

> Class here heart depressants, myocardial depressants

.718   **Drugs affecting blood and hematopoietic system**

.72   **Drugs affecting respiratory system**

> Including bronchodilator agents, cough remedies, expectorants

.73   **Drugs affecting digestive system and metabolism**

> Standard subdivisions are added for drugs affecting digestive system and metabolism together, for drugs affecting digestive system alone
>
> Class drug-nutrient interactions in 615.70452

.732   Cathartics

> Class here laxatives

.739   Drugs affecting metabolism

> Including antilipemic agents

.74   **Drugs affecting lymphatic and glandular systems**

.76   **Drugs affecting urogenital system**

.761   Drugs affecting urinary system

> Including diuretics, antidiuretics

.766   Drugs affecting reproductive system

> Including abortifacient, contraceptive, fertility drugs

.766 9   Aphrodisiacs

.77   **Drugs affecting musculoskeletal system, integument**

> Standard subdivisions are added for drugs affecting musculoskeletal system, integument together; for drugs affecting musculoskeletal system alone

.771   Drugs affecting bones

.773   Drugs affecting muscles

.778   Drugs affecting integument

> *For drugs affecting nails and hair, see 615.779*

.779   Drugs affecting nails and hair

.78   Drugs affecting nervous system

Class here addictive drugs, psychopharmacology

Class personal aspects of preventing drug addiction in 613.8; class drug therapy for mental disorders in 616.8918; class comprehensive medical works on addictions as diseases in 616.86; class interdisciplinary works on drug addiction in 362.29

See also 178 for the ethics of using addictive drugs

.781   Anesthetics

.782   Central nervous system depressants

Class here hypnotics, sedatives

For anesthetics, see 615.781; for analgesics, see 615.783; for tranquilizers, see 615.7882

.782 1   Barbiturates

.782 2   Narcotics

Including narcotic antagonists

.782 7   Cannabis

Including marijuana

.782 8   Alcohol

.783   Analgesics

Including antipyretics

.784   Anticonvulsants and antispasmodics

Standard subdivisions are added for anticonvulsants and antispasmodics together, for anticonvulsants alone

Including parasympatholytics

.785   Central nervous system stimulants

For aphrodisiacs, see 615.7669

.788   Psychotropic drugs

.788 2   Tranquilizers

Including anti-anxiety, antipsychotic drugs; chlorpromazine, diazepam, meprobamate

.788 3   Hallucinogens

Class here psychedelic drugs

For cannabis, see 615.7827

.79   Miscellaneous classes of drugs

Limited to those provided for below

.792   **Anti-infective agents**

> Including antifungal agents, antiparasitic agents

.792 2   **Anti-bacterial agents**

> Class here antibiotics
>
> Class interdisciplinary works on antibiotics in 615.329

.792 4   **Antiviral agents**

> Including anti-retroviral agents, anti-HIV agents

.794   **Anti-inflammatory agents**

.796   **Anti-allergic agents**

.798   **Antineoplastic agents**

.8   **Specific therapies and kinds of therapies**

> Class comprehensive works in 615.5
>
> *For drug therapy, see 615.58; for surgery, see 617*
>
> *See Manual at 615.8; also at 613 vs. 612, 615.8*

[.801–.809]   **Standard subdivisions**

> Do not use; class in 615.501–615.509

.82   **Physical therapies**

> Including Alexander technique
>
> Class here physiotherapy, therapeutic manipulations and exercises
>
> > *For phototherapy, thermotherapy, climatotherapy, respiratory therapy; therapeutic use of sound, see 615.83; for radiotherapy, electric stimulation therapy, magnetotherapy, see 615.84; for hydrotherapy and balneotherapy, see 615.853*

.822   **Therapeutic massage**

> Including Rolfing
>
> Class here interdisciplinary works on massage
>
> Class aromatherapy in 615.3219
>
> > *For massage for health and fitness, see 613.72*

.822 2   **Acupressure**

> Class here shiatsu
>
> Class comprehensive works on acupuncture and acupressure in 615.892

.822 4   **Reflexology**

.83   **Phototherapy, thermotherapy, climatotherapy, respiratory therapy; therapeutic use of sound**

> Class music therapy in 615.85154

.831	Phototherapy
.831 2	Color therapy
.831 4	Heliotherapy
.831 5	Ultraviolet therapy

Class here actinotherapy

.832	Thermotherapy
.832 3	Diathermy

Class here ultrasonic therapy

.832 9	Cryotherapy

For cryosurgery, see 617.05

.834	Climatotherapy
.836	Respiratory therapy

Including breathing exercises, hyperbaric oxygenation, oxygen inhalation therapy

Class here aerotherapy, inhalation therapy

Class aromatherapy in 615.3219

.836 2	Artificial respiration
.84	Radiotherapy, electric stimulation therapy, magnetotherapy
.842	Radiotherapy

Class phototherapy in 615.831

.842 2	X-ray therapy
.842 3	Radium therapy
.842 4	Radioisotope therapy

Class radium therapy in 615.8423

.845	Electric stimulation therapy and magnetotherapy

Standard subdivisions are added for electric stimulation therapy and magnetotherapy together, for electric stimulation therapy alone

Class here electrotherapeutics, therapeutic use of electricity

Class diathermy in 615.8323; class electroacupuncture in 615.892

.845 4	Magnetotherapy

Class here therapeutic use of magnetism

.85	Miscellaneous therapies

Limited to the therapies provided for below

.851	Psychological and activity therapies

Class mental healing (psychic healing) in 615.8528; class comprehensive works on psychotherapy in 616.8914

.851 2	Hypnotherapy
.851 22	Self-hypnosis

Class here autogenic training

Class therapeutic use of biofeedback in 615.8514

.851 4	Biofeedback therapy

Class here therapeutic use of biofeedback training

.851 5	Activity therapy

Including therapeutic use of gardening

Class here occupational therapy

For bibliotherapy, writing therapy, educational therapies, see 615.8516

.851 53	Recreational therapy

Class here play therapy

Class therapeutic use of horsemanship in 615.851581

.851 54	Music therapy
.851 55	Dance therapy
.851 56	Art therapy
.851 58	Therapeutic use of animals

Class here therapeutic use of pets

Class works that focus on the therapy animal and training it for therapeutic use with the animal in 636, e.g., training therapy dogs 636.7088

.851 581	Therapeutic use of horses

Class here therapeutic use of horsemanship

.851 6	Bibliotherapy, writing therapy, educational therapies
.851 62	Bibliotherapy (Therapeutic use of reading)

Standard subdivisions are added for therapeutic use of reading in general and for therapeutic use of reading specific literary or nonliterary forms

Class here comprehensive works on therapeutic use of reading and writing

For therapeutic use of writing, see 615.85163

.851 63	Writing therapy

Standard subdivisions are added for therapeutic use of writing in general and for therapeutic use of writing in specific literary or nonliterary forms

Class comprehensive works on therapeutic use of reading and writing in 615.85162

.852	Religious and psychic therapies

Standard subdivisions are added for religious and psychic therapies together, for religious therapies alone

Including healing touch (therapeutic touch), Reiki

Class here faith healing, spiritual therapies

See Manual at 615.852 vs. 203.1, 234.131, 292–299

.852 8	Psychic therapies

Including psychic surgery

Class here healing facilitated by spiritualism; mental healing (psychic healing)

.853	Hydrotherapy and balneotherapy

Standard subdivisions are added for either or both topics in heading

.854	Nutrition therapy

Class here diet therapy

For diet therapy that excludes a specific food or group of foods, see the diet in 613.268, e.g., gluten-free diet 613.268311; for diet therapy emphasizing a single food, see the food as a type of drug in 615.3, e.g., a diet emphasizing soy 615.32363, a diet emphasizing garlic 615.32478

.854 8	Nutrition support

Class here artificial feeding

.854 82	Enteral nutrition

Class here tube feeding

.854 84	Parenteral nutrition

Class here intravenous feeding

.855	Parenteral therapy

For a specific kind of parenteral therapy, see the kind, e.g., parenteral drug therapy 615.58, parenteral feeding 615.85484

.856	Controversial and spurious therapies

Standard subdivisions are added for either or both topics in heading

Class here quackery

For a specific controversial or spurious therapy, see the therapy, e.g., controversial diet therapy 615.854

.88   Traditional remedies

Only therapeutics

Class here folk remedies, home remedies

Class theoretical works on traditional general therapeutic systems in 615.53; class works on traditional medicine that include pathological or etiological beliefs in 610 (or, if arranged by class of disease, in 616). Class a specific kind of traditional remedy with the kind, e.g., medicinal herbs 615.321, acupuncture 615.892

.880 9   History, geographic treatment, biography

.880 901   To 499 A.D.

Class here ancient remedies

.880 902   6th-15th centuries, 500–1499

Class here medieval remedies

.89   Other therapies

.892   Acupuncture

Including moxibustion, electroacupuncture

Class here comprehensive works on acupuncture and acupressure

For acupressure, see 615.8222

.895   Gene therapy

.9   **Toxicology**

Class here poisons and poisoning

Class forensic toxicology in 614.13. Class effects of poisons on a specific system or organ with the system or organ, plus notation 071 from table under 616.1–616.9, notation 071 from table under 617, or notation 071 from table under 618.1–618.8, e.g., effect of poisons on the liver 616.362071

See Manual at 615.7 vs. 615.9

.900 1   Philosophy and theory

.900 2   Miscellany

[.900 287]   Testing and measurement

Do not use; class in 615.907

.900 3–.900 9   Standard subdivisions

.902   Industrial toxicology

Including toxicology of pollution

Class here environmental toxicology

Class environmental diseases, environmental medicine in 616.98

For toxic reactions and interactions of drugs, see 615.704; for toxicology of food additives, see 615.954

.904	Incidence of poisoning
.905	Prevention of poisoning

Class public safety programs and social provision for prevention of poisoning in 363.1791

.907	Tests, analysis, detection of poisons and poisoning

Class here diagnoses and prognoses of poisoning

Topics listed under 616.075 Diagnoses and prognoses are all included here

.908	Treatment of poisoning

Class here antidotes

.91	Gaseous poisons

Including asphyxiating gases

Class here lethal gases

.92	Inorganic poisons

For gaseous inorganic poisons, see 615.91; for radiation poisoning, see 616.9897

.921	Acids

For specific acids, see 615.925

.922	Alkalis

For specific alkalis, see 615.925

.925	Specific inorganic poisons

Add to base number 615.925 the numbers following 546 in 546.2–546.7, e.g., mercurial poisons 615.925663

.94	Animal poisons
.942	Venoms

Including bee, scorpion, snake, spider venoms

.945	Poisonous food animals

Only works that emphasize poisons

Including poisonous fishes; food animals made poisonous by plants or microorganisms, e.g., shellfish made poisonous by red tides

Class comprehensive medical works on a specific type of communicable disease that involves poisons with the type of disease in 616.9, e.g., salmonella infections 616.927

.95	Organic poisons

For gaseous organic poisons, see 615.91; for animal poisons, see 615.94

.951   Synthetic and manufactured poisons

       Add to base number 615.951 the numbers following 547.0 in
       547.01–547.08, e.g., ethers 615.95135
        Subdivisions are added for either or both topics in heading

.952   Plant and microorganism poisons, poisons derived from plants and microorganisms

       Standard subdivisions are added for all topics in heading together, for plant poisons alone, for poisons derived from plants alone

       Class food animals made poisonous by plants and microorganisms in 615.945

.952 3–.952 8 Specific plant poisons, poisons derived from specific plants

       Add to base number 615.952 the numbers following 58 in 583–588, e.g., opium 615.952335

        For fungi and algae poisons, poisons derived from fungi and algae, see 615.9529

.952 9   Microorganism, fungi, algae poisons; poisons derived from microorganisms, fungi, algae

       Only works that emphasize poisons

       Add to base number 615.9529 the numbers following 579 in 579.2–579.8, e.g., bacterial food poisons 615.95293

       Class comprehensive medical works on a specific type of communicable disease that involves poisons with the type of disease in 616.9, e.g., salmonella infections 616.927, botulism 616.9315

.954   Food poisons

       Only works that emphasize poisons

       Including toxicology of food additives

       Class poisonous food animals in 615.945. Class a specific plant poison and poisons derived from specific plants and microorganisms with the poison in 615.952, e.g., bacterial food poisons 615.95293

616 Diseases

     Class here clinical medicine, evidence-based medicine, internal medicine

     For incidence of and public measures to prevent disease, see 614.4; for therapeutics, see 615.5; for injuries and wounds, surgical treatment of diseases, diseases by body region, diseases of teeth, eyes, ears, see 617; for gynecologic, obstetrical, fetal, pediatric, geriatric diseases, see 618

     See Manual at 610 vs. 616; also at 616 vs. 612; also at 616 vs. 616.075; also at 616 vs. 617.4; also at 616 vs. 618.92

>   616.001–616.009 Standard subdivisions

     Class comprehensive works in 616

     See Manual at 610 vs. 616: Standard subdivisions

.001	Philosophy and theory

.001 9   Psychological principles

> Do not use for psychosomatic medicine; class in 616.08

.002   Miscellany

[.002 3]   Work with diseases as a profession, occupation, hobby

> Do not use; class in 610.69

.002 8   Auxiliary techniques and procedures; apparatus, equipment, materials

[.002 87]   Testing and measurement

> Do not use; class in 616.075

.003–.006   Standard subdivisions

.007   Education, research, related topics

[.007 24]   Experimental research

> Do not use; class in 616.027

.008   Groups of people

> Do not use for incidence of disease in groups of people; class in 614.4208

.008 3   Young people

> Do not use for diseases of infants and children up to puberty, comprehensive works on child and adolescent medicine; class in 618.92

.008 35   Young people twelve to twenty

> Do not use for diseases of young people twelve to twenty who have not reached puberty; class in 618.92

> Class here adolescent medicine

.008 4   People in specific stages of adulthood

[.008 46]   People in late adulthood

> Do not use; class in 618.97

.009   History, geographic treatment, biography

> Do not use for history and geographic treatment of incidence of disease; class in 614.42. Do not use for history of epidemics; class in 614.49

[.009 11–.009 13]   Frigid, temperate, tropical zones

> Do not use; class in 616.9881–616.9883

.009 2   Biography

> Class life with a physical disease in 362.19. Class life with a mental disorder with the disorder in 616.85–616.89, plus notation 0092 from table under 616.1–616.9, e.g., life with manic-depressive illness 616.8950092

.02	**Special topics of diseases**	

Class special topics applied to special medical conditions in 616.04

.024	**Domestic medicine**

Diagnosis and treatment of ailments without direction of physician

Including advice on when to go to a doctor

> *For first aid, see 616.0252. For a specific kind of therapy, see the therapy in 615, e.g., drug therapy 615.58*

.025	**Medical emergencies**

Class here emergency care nursing, resuscitation, comprehensive works on emergency medicine

> *For intensive care, see 616.028. For a specific kind of emergency therapy, see the therapy in 615, e.g., oxygen therapy 615.836; for a specific kind of resuscitation, see the kind, e.g., cardiopulmonary resuscitation 616.1025*

.025 2	First aid
.027	**Experimental medicine**

Including use of cultured or genetically engineered tissue, use of human fetal tissue

Class ethics of animal experimentation in 179.4; class ethics of experimentation on human subjects and comprehensive works on ethics of medical experimentation in 174.28; class comprehensive works on clinical trials in 615.50724; class comprehensive works on clinical trials of diagnostic procedures in 616.0750724; class fetal tissue transplantation in 617.954; class breeding, genetic engineering, care, maintenance of laboratory animals in 636.0885

.027 3	Mammals other than humans

As models for experimental research on human diseases

Including rabbits, swine

Class here transgenic mammals as experimental animals

Class experimental research using mammalian cells in 616.0277

.027 33	Rodents

Including guinea pigs, hamsters, rats

.027 333	Mice (Mus)
.027 38	Primates

Including apes, monkeys

.027 7	Cells

Use for experimental research on human diseases

Class here cell lines

.027 74	Stem cells

.028   Intensive care

Class here critical care, intensive care nursing

For a specific kind of intensive care therapy, see the therapy in 615, e.g., oxygen therapy 615.836

.029   Palliative and terminal care

Standard subdivisions are added for either or both topics in heading

Class here terminal care nursing

For a specific kind of palliative and terminal care therapy, see the therapy in 615, e.g., drug therapy 615.58; for palliative treatment of a specific symptom, see the symptom, e.g., pain 616.0472

.04   Special medical conditions

.042   Genetic diseases (Hereditary diseases)

Class here genetic aspects of diseases with complex causation, comprehensive works on medical genetics

For gene therapy, see 615.895; for immunogenetics, see 616.0796; for prenatal procedures to diagnose genetic diseases (e.g., amniocentesis and chorionic villus biopsy), see 618.3204275

.043   Congenital diseases

Including teratology

Class congenital diseases of genetic origin in 616.042

.044   Chronic diseases

For chronic fatigue syndrome, see 616.0478

.047   Symptoms and general pathological processes as problems in their own right

Including edema, fever, gangrene

Class here pathology, diagnosis, treatment of symptoms of various etiologies; symptomatology

Class comprehensive works on palliative care in 616.029; class interpretation of symptoms for diagnosis and prognosis in 616.075; class infections in 616.9; class results of injuries and wounds in 617.2; class surgical complications and sequelae in 617.919. Class symptoms and pathological processes of a specific disease or class of diseases with the disease or class of diseases, e.g., symptoms of heart diseases 616.12

.047 2   Pain

Class headaches in 616.8491

.047 3   Inflammation

.047 5   Shock and multiple organ failure

Standard subdivisions are added for either or both topics in heading

For shock associated with injury or surgery, see 617.21

.047 8   **Chronic fatigue syndrome**

Class here chronic fatigue syndrome discussed as a specific kind of disease, myalgic encephalomyelitis

See also 616.044 for chronic diseases

>   **616.07–616.09 Pathology, psychosomatic medicine, case histories**

Class pathology, psychosomatic medicine, case histories applied to special medical conditions in 616.04; class comprehensive works in 616

.07   **Pathology**

For cytopathology, see 611.01815; for histopathology, see 611.0182–611.0187; for forensic pathology, see 614.1; for medical microbiology, see 616.9041; for symptoms and general pathological processes as problems in their own right, see 616.047

.071   **Etiology**

Class here pathogenesis, risk factors

Class social factors contributing to spread of a disease in 362.1042; class genetic diseases, genetic aspects of diseases with complex causation in 616.042

For pathogenic microorganisms as causes of communicable diseases, see 616.9041

.075   **Diagnosis and prognosis**

Standard subdivisions are added for diagnosis and prognosis together, for diagnosis alone

Class here differential diagnosis; disability evaluation; nursing assessment, nursing diagnosis

Class nonprofessional diagnosis in 616.024

See Manual at 616 vs. 616.075

.075 072 4   **Experimental research**

Class here clinical trials of diagnostic procedures

Class comprehensive works on clinical trials of diagnostic procedures and therapy in 615.50724

.075 1   **Medical history taking**

.075 4   **Physical diagnosis**

Including thermography

Class here comprehensive works on diagnostic imaging

For radiological diagnosis, see 616.0757

.075 43	Diagnostic ultrasound
	Class here comprehensive works on ultrasonography (sonography, echography)
	Class comprehensive works on tomography in 616.0757
	For ultrasonic therapy, see 615.8323
.075 44	Diagnosis by sound
	Class here auscultation
.075 45	Optical diagnosis
	Class here comprehensive works on endoscopy
	Class microscopy in 616.0758
	For endoscopic surgery, see 617.057
.075 47	Electrodiagnosis
.075 48	Magnetic diagnosis
	Class here magnetic resonance imaging, nuclear magnetic resonance imaging, proton spin tomography
	Class comprehensive works on tomography in 616.0757
.075 6	Chemical diagnosis
	Including diagnostic serology, immunodiagnosis
	Class here clinical chemistry, laboratory diagnosis
	For radioimmunoassay, see 616.0757; for microscopy in diagnosis, see 616.0758
.075 61	Blood analysis
	Including phlebotomy
	See also 616.15075 for diagnosis of diseases of blood
.075 63	Analysis of gastroenteric contents
	See also 616.3075 for diagnosis of diseases of digestive system
.075 66	Urinalysis
	Class radioscopic urinalysis in 616.0757; class urinary manifestations of diseases of urogenital system in 616.63
	See also 616.6075 for diagnosis of diseases of urogenital system

.075 7	Radiological diagnosis

Including radioimmunoassay, radioscopic urinalysis

Class here diagnostic radiology; comprehensive works on medical radiology, on tomography

Class diagnostic radiology limited to use of X-rays in 616.07572; class comprehensive works on diagnostic imaging in 616.0754

For radiotherapy, see 615.842; for magnetic resonance imaging, see 616.07548

.075 72	Radiography (X-ray examination)

Including fluoroscopy

Class diagnostic radiology covering use of X-rays, radioactive materials, other ionizing radiation in 616.0757

.075 722	X-ray computed tomography

Class here computerized axial tomography (CAT scan, CT)

.075 75	Radioisotope scanning

Variant names: nuclear medicine, radionuclide imaging

Including positron emission tomography (PET), radioimmunoimaging, single-photon emission-computed tomography (SPECT)

See also 616.07548 for nuclear magnetic resonance imaging

.075 8	Microscopy in diagnosis

Class here biopsy

.075 81	Bacteriological examination
.075 82	Cytological examination
.075 83	Histological and histochemical examination
.075 9	Autopsy (Postmortem examination)

Class forensic autopsy in 614.1

.078	Death

Class interdisciplinary works on human death in 306.9

.079	Immunity

Class here disease resistance, immune system, immunochemistry, immunology, leukocytes, lymphocytes

Class immune serums and immunologic drugs in 615.37; class diagnostic immunochemistry, immunodiagnosis in 616.0756; class diseases of hematopoietic system in 616.41; class diseases of immune system in 616.97

> 616.079 1–616.079 6 Immunochemistry

Class comprehensive works in 616.079. Class applications of immunochemistry to a specific type of cell or to reactions associated with a specific type of cell with the cell or reaction in 616.0797–616.0799, e.g., immunochemistry of antigen-antibody reactions 616.07987

.079 1   Interferons

.079 2   Antigens

.079 5   Immune response

Including clonal selection

Class here antigen recognition, comprehensive works on serology

Class immune reactions associated with specific types of cells in 616.0797–616.0799

For diagnostic serology, see 616.0756

.079 6   Immunogenetics

.079 7   T cells (T lymphocytes)

Class here cell-mediated (cellular) immunity, cytotoxic T cells

See also 616.0799 for killer cells

.079 8   B cells (B lymphocytes)

Class here antibodies (immunoglobulins)

For antibody-dependent immune mechanisms, see 616.0799

.079 87   Antigen-antibody reactions

.079 9   Phagocytes and complement

Standard subdivisions are added for phagocytes and complement together, for phagocytes alone

Including granulocytes, killer cells

Class here antibody-dependent immune mechanisms, reticuloendothelial system

See also 616.0797 for cytotoxic T cells

.079 95   Macrophages

.079 97   Complement

Class activation of macrophages by complement in 616.07995

.08   Psychosomatic medicine

Use only for psychosomatic aspects of diseases defined in 616.1–616.7, 616.9

Class somatoform disorders in 616.8524; class diseases caused by stress in 616.98; class comprehensive works on psychological and psychosomatic aspects of disease in 616.0019

.09   Case histories

>

616.1–616.9 Specific diseases

All notes under 616.02–616.08 are applicable here

Except for modifications shown under specific entries, add to each subdivision identified by * as follows:

001	Philosophy and theory
002	Miscellany
[0023]	The subject as a profession, occupation, hobby
	Do not use; class in notation 023 from this table
0028	Auxiliary techniques and procedures; apparatus, equipment, materials
00284	Apparatus, equipment, materials
	Do not use for self-help devices for people with disabilities; class in notation 03 from this table
[00287]	Testing and measurement
	Do not use; class in notation 075 from this table
003–006	Standard subdivisions
007	Education, research, related topics
[00724]	Experimental research
	Do not use; class in notation 027 from this table
008	Groups of people
	Do not use for incidence of specific diseases or kinds of diseases in groups of people; class in 614.5
0083	Young people
	Do not use for diseases of infants and children up to puberty, comprehensive works on diseases of children and adolescents; class in 618.92
00835	Young people twelve to twenty
	Do not use for diseases of young people twelve to twenty who have not reached puberty; class in 618.92
	Class here diseases of adolescents
0084	People in specific stages of adulthood
[00846]	People in late adulthood
	Do not use; class in 618.97
009	History, geographic treatment, biography
	Do not use for history and geographic treatment of incidence of specific diseases or kinds of diseases; class in 614.5
0092	Biography
	Class life with a physical disease in 362.19. Class life with a mental disease with the disease in 616.85–616.89, plus notation 0092 from this table, e.g., life with depression 616.85270092
>01–03	Medical microbiology, special topics, rehabilitation
	Class microbiology, special topics, rehabilitation applied to special classes of diseases in notation 04 from this table; class comprehensive works in 616 without adding from this table
01	Medical microbiology
	When the cause of a disease or class of diseases is known to be a single type of microorganism, use 01 without further subdivision for works about the type of microorganism
	Class works on a whole disease and its course, cure, and prevention with the disease without adding from this table, e.g., comprehensive works on tuberculosis 616.995
	See Manual at 616.1–.9: Add table: 071 vs. 01

> **616.1–616.9 Specific diseases**

014	Medical bacteriology
	Including medical microbiology of rickettsiae
015	Medical mycology
016	Medical protozoology
019	Medical virology
02	Special topics
023	Personnel
0231	Nurses

Class here nature of duties, characteristics of profession, relationships; nursing with respect to specific diseases; works that emphasize technology of operations performed by nurses, e.g., works that emphasize techniques used by a cardiovascular nurse 616.10231, by an orthopedic nurse 616.70231

Class works that emphasize a specific technique used by nurses with the technique, e.g., nursing diagnosis 075, nursing diagnosis of cardiovascular diseases 616.1075

0232	Physicians

Class here nature of duties, characteristics of profession, relationships

Do not use for works that emphasize technology of operations performed by physicians; class with the subject without 0232, e.g., works that emphasize techniques used by a physician with respect to cardiovascular diseases 616.1

Class works that emphasize a specific technique used by physicians with the technique, e.g., diagnosis by a physician 075, diagnosis by a physician of cardiovascular diseases 616.1075

0233	Allied health personnel

Class here nature of duties, characteristics of profession, relationships; works that emphasize technology of operations performed by allied health personnel, e.g., works that emphasize techniques used by allied health personnel with respect to cardiovascular diseases 616.10233

Class works that emphasize a specific technique used by allied health personnel with the technique, e.g., diagnosis by allied health personnel 075, diagnosis of cardiovascular diseases by allied health personnel 616.1075

02332	Physician assistants
024	Domestic medicine

Class a specific kind of therapy with the therapy in notation 06 from this table, e.g., drug therapy 061

For first aid, see notation 0252 from this table

025	Medical emergencies

Class here comprehensive works on emergency therapy for specific diseases or kinds of diseases

For intensive care, see notation 028 from this table. For a specific kind of emergency therapy, see the therapy in notation 06 from this table, e.g., emergency drug therapy 061

0252	First aid
027	Experimental medicine

>

616.1–616.9 Specific diseases

 028   Intensive care

       Class here critical care

        For a specific kind of intensive care therapy, see the therapy in notation 06 from this table, e.g., drug therapy 061

 029   Palliative and terminal care

        For a specific kind of palliative or terminal care therapy, see the therapy in notation 06 from this table, e.g., drug therapy 061

 03   Rehabilitation

       Including self-help devices for people with disabilities

       Class rehabilitative therapy in notation 06 from this table; class comprehensive works on rehabilitation in 617.03

 04   Special classes of diseases

       Limited to the classes named below

 042   Genetic diseases (Hereditary diseases)

       Class here genetic aspects of diseases with complex causation, medical genetics

 0421–0423 Microbiology, special topics, rehabilitation

       Add to 042 the numbers following 0 in notation 01–03 from table under 616.1–616.9, e.g., experimental medicine for genetic diseases 04227

 0425–0429 Preventive measures, therapy, pathology, psychosomatic medicine, case histories

       Add to 042 the numbers following 0 in notation 05–09 from table under 616.1–616.9, e.g., therapy for genetic diseases 0426, gene therapy 042695

 043   Congenital diseases

       Class congenital diseases of genetic origin in notation 042 from this table

 0431–0433 Microbiology, special topics, rehabilitation

       Add to 043 the numbers following 0 in notation 01–03 from table under 616.1–616.9, e.g., experimental medicine for congenital diseases 04327

 0435–0439 Preventive measures, therapy, pathology, psychosomatic medicine, case histories

       Add to 043 the numbers following 0 in notation 05–09 from table under 616.1–616.9, e.g., therapy for congenital diseases 0436

>05–09 Preventive measures, therapy, pathology, psychosomatic medicine, case histories

       Class preventive measures, therapy, pathology, psychosomatic medicine, case histories applied to specific classes of diseases in notation 04 from this table; class comprehensive works in 616 without adding from this table

 05   Preventive measures

       By individuals and by medical personnel

       Class comprehensive works on public and private measures for preventing diseases in 613. Class public measures for preventing a specific disease, use of specific vaccines with the disease in 614.5, e.g., mosquito control for prevention of malaria 614.532, use of influenza vaccines 614.518; class a specific kind of therapy used for prevention with the kind of therapy in notation 061–069 from this table, e.g., drug therapy 061

> **616.1–616.9 Specific diseases**

     06   Therapy

Class here alternative therapy; rehabilitative therapy; specific kinds of therapy used in domestic medicine, medical emergencies, intensive care, palliative and terminal care

Class comprehensive works on therapy in 615.5; class comprehensive works on therapy for specific diseases or kinds of diseases in domestic medicine in notation 024 from this table; class comprehensive works on therapy for specific diseases or kinds of diseases in medical emergencies in notation 025 from this table; class comprehensive works on therapy for specific diseases or kinds of diseases in intensive care in notation 028 from this table; class comprehensive works on therapy for specific diseases or kinds of diseases in palliative or terminal care in notation 029 from this table; class comprehensive works on rehabilitative therapy and training for people with a specific disease or kind of disease in notation 03 from this table; class comprehensive works on prevention, therapy, etiology of a specific disease or kind of disease if all related to a specific kind of therapy in notation 061–069 from this table, e.g., diet therapy 0654. Class comprehensive works on therapy and pathology of a specific disease or kind of disease if not all related to a specific kind of therapy with the disease or kind of disease, without adding from this table, e.g., cause, course, and cure of heart disease 616.12 (*not* 616.1206)

     060724   Experimental research

Class here clinical trials

Class clinical trials of a specific kind of therapy with the kind of therapy, plus notation 0724 from Table 1, e.g., clinical drug trials 0610724

     >061–069   Specific therapies

Class here specific kinds of therapy used for prevention; comprehensive works on prevention, therapy, etiology if these all relate to a specific kind of therapy, e.g., nutritional aspects of a disease and diet therapy 0654

     061   Drug therapy

     0610724   Experimental research

Class here clinical drug trials

     062–069   Other therapies

Add to 06 the numbers following 615.8 in 615.82–615.89, e.g., X-ray therapy 06422, psychotherapies 0651

     07   Pathology

     071   Etiology

Including effects of poisons on specific systems and organs as cause of disease

Class social factors contributing to spread of a disease in 362.19; class comprehensive works on medical toxicology in 615.9

See Manual at 616.1–.9: Add table: 071 vs. 01

     075–079   Diagnosis, prognosis, death, immunity

Add to 07 the numbers following 616.07 in 616.075–616.079, e.g., diagnosis 075, clinical trials of diagnostic procedures 0750724

     08   Psychosomatic medicine

     09   Case histories

> ### 616.1–616.9 Specific diseases

Class comprehensive works in 616. Class a work treating all the complications of a disease with the disease, e.g., all the complications of diabetes mellitus 616.462; class a work that focuses on one specific complication with the complication, e.g., peripheral nerve disorders associated with diabetes mellitus 616.856

See Manual at 612.1–612.8

> ### 616.1–616.8 Diseases of specific systems and organs

Class comprehensive works in 616

For diseases of immune system, see 616.97; for tumors and cancers of specific systems and organs, see 616.994; for tuberculosis of specific systems and organs, see 616.995

.1   ***Diseases of cardiovascular system**

Class here cardiopulmonary diseases

Class cardiopulmonary resuscitation (CPR) in 616.1025; class diseases of blood-forming system in 616.41

For pulmonary diseases, see 616.24

.11   *Diseases of endocardium and pericardium

.12   *Diseases of heart

Including cor pulmonale

Class here cardiology

For diseases of endocardium and pericardium, see 616.11

.122   *Angina pectoris

.123   *Coronary diseases (Ischemic heart diseases)

Class works on heart attacks limited to myocardial infarction in 616.1237; class comprehensive works on cardiac arrest, on heart attacks in 616.123025. Class cardiac arrest and heart attacks not caused by narrowing or blocking of coronary arteries with the cause, e.g., heart attacks caused by congestive heart failure 616.129025

For angina pectoris, see 616.122

.123 028 ·   Intensive care

Number built according to instructions under 616.1–616.9

Class coronary care covering intensive care for any serious heart disease in 616.12028

.123 2   *Coronary arteriosclerosis

---

*Add as instructed under 616.1–616.9

.123 7   *Myocardial infarction

.124   *Myocarditis

        Class here comprehensive works on diseases of myocardium

        For myocardial infarction, see 616.1237

.125   *Valvular diseases

.127   *Rheumatic heart diseases

        For rheumatic valvular diseases, see 616.125

.128   *Arrhythmia

        Class here atrial fibrillation, ventricular fibrillation

        Class electric countershock (electric defibrillation) in 616.1280645; class implantation of heart pacers and defibrillators in 617.4120592; class functioning of heart pacers and implanted defibrillators in 617.4120645

.129   *Heart failure

        Class here congestive heart failure

        Class comprehensive works on cardiac arrest in 616.123025

.13   *Diseases of blood vessels

        Including arterial occlusive diseases

        Class here angiology; diseases of arteries; diseases of blood vessels in a specific region, e.g., abdominal and pelvic cavities

        Class a specific arterial occlusive disease with the disease, e.g., arteriosclerosis 616.136; class diseases of blood vessels in a specific system or organ with the system or organ, e.g., cerebrovascular diseases 616.81

        For diseases of veins and capillaries, see 616.14

.131   *Peripheral vascular diseases

>   616.132–616.136 Hypertension, aneurysms, arterial embolisms and thromboses, arteriosclerosis

        Class hypertension, aneurysms, embolisms, thromboses, arteriosclerosis of aorta in 616.138; class comprehensive works in 616.13

.132   *Hypertension

        Including renal hypertension

        For pulmonary hypertension, see 616.24; for portal hypertension, see 616.362

.133   *Aneurysms

*Add as instructed under 616.1–616.9

.135	*Arterial embolisms and thromboses

Class here comprehensive works on embolisms, on thromboses

For venous embolisms and thromboses, see 616.145; for pulmonary embolisms and thromboses, see 616.249

.136	*Arteriosclerosis

Class here atherosclerosis

.138	*Diseases of aorta
.14	*Diseases of veins and capillaries

Subdivisions are added for diseases of veins and capillaries together, for diseases of veins alone

.142	*Phlebitis

Including thrombophlebitis

.143	*Varicose veins (Varix)
.145	*Venous embolisms and thromboses

Class thrombophlebitis in 616.142; class comprehensive works on embolisms, on thromboses in 616.135

.148	*Diseases of capillaries

Including telangiectasis, telangitis

.15	*Diseases of blood

Class here hematology, comprehensive works on hemic and lymphatic diseases

For lymphatic diseases, see 616.42; for bacterial blood diseases, see 616.94

See also 616.07561 for use of blood analysis in diagnosis of diseases in general

.151	*Diseases of erythrocytes

Class here hemoglobin disorders

For anemia, see 616.152; for polycythemia, see 616.153

.152	*Anemia

Including iron-deficiency anemia, thalassemia

.152 7	*Sickle cell anemia
.153	*Polycythemia
.154	*Diseases of leukocytes

Including agranulocytosis

*Add as instructed under 616.1–616.9

.157   *Hemorrhagic diseases

> Including von Willebrand disease
>
> Class here comprehensive works on disorders of blood coagulation, on blood platelet disorders
>
>> *For arterial embolisms and thromboses, see 616.135; for venous embolisms and thromboses, see 616.145*

.157 2   *Hemophilia

.2   **Diseases of respiratory system**

> Class here dyspnea

.200 1–.200 3   Standard subdivisions

> As modified in notation 001–003 from table under 616.1–616.9

.200 4   Special topics of diseases of respiratory system

> Add to base number 616.2004 the numbers following 0 in notation 01–09 from table under 616.1–616.9, e.g., diagnosis of respiratory diseases 616.200475

.200 5–.200 9   Standard subdivisions

> As modified in notation 005–009 from table under 616.1–616.9

.201   *Croup

.202   *Respiratory allergies

> Class here hay fever
>
> Class asthma in 616.238

.203   *Influenza

.204   *Whooping cough (Pertussis)

.205   *Common cold

.208   *Hyperventilation

.209   *Sleep apnea syndromes

> Class here snoring

.21   *Diseases of nose, nasopharynx, paranasal sinuses, larynx

> Class here rhinology
>
> Subdivisions are added for diseases of nose, nasopharynx, paranasal sinuses, larynx together; for diseases of nose alone
>
> Class allergic rhinitis in 616.202; class common cold in 616.205; class otolaryngology, comprehensive works on diseases of ears, nose, throat in 617.51
>
>> *For diseases of larynx, see 616.22*

*Add as instructed under 616.1–616.9

| .212 | *Diseases of paranasal sinuses |
| .22 | *Diseases of larynx, epiglottis, glottis, vocal cords |

> Class here laryngology
>
> Subdivisions are added for diseases of larynx, epiglottis, glottis, vocal cords; for diseases of larynx alone

| .23 | *Diseases of trachea and bronchi |

> Including bronchiectasis, tracheitis
>
> Subdivisions are added for either or both topics in heading
>
> Class bronchopneumonia in 616.241

| .234 | *Bronchitis |
| .238 | *Asthma |

> Class here bronchial asthma
>
> *For cardiac asthma, see 616.12*

| .24 | *Diseases of lungs |

> Including chronic obstructive pulmonary disease, pulmonary hypertension
>
> Class here comprehensive works on diseases of lungs and bronchi
>
> Class cystic fibrosis in 616.372; class pulmonary sarcoidosis in 616.429; class pulmonary tuberculosis in 616.995; class comprehensive works on cardiopulmonary diseases in 616.1
>
> *For diseases of bronchi, see 616.23*

| .241 | *Pneumonia |

> *See also 616.245 for necropneumonia*

| .241 2 | *Bacterial pneumonia |

> Including Legionnaires' disease

.241 4	*Viral pneumonia
.241 6	*Fungal pneumonia
.244	*Pneumoconiosis

> Including asbestosis, black lung disease, byssinosis (brown lung disease), pulmonary abscesses, silicosis

.245	*Necropneumonia
.248	*Emphysema
.249	*Pulmonary embolisms and thromboses

> Class comprehensive works on embolisms, on thromboses in 616.135

*Add as instructed under 616.1–616.9

.25   *Diseases of pleura

         Class pleural pneumonia in 616.241

.27   *Diseases of mediastinum

.3   *Diseases of digestive system

         Class allergies of digestive system in 616.975

         See also 616.07563 for use of analysis of gastroenteric contents in diagnosis of diseases in general

.31   *Diseases of mouth and throat

         Subdivisions are added for diseases of mouth and throat together, for diseases of mouth alone

         Class oral region (a broader concept than mouth as a digestive organ) in 617.522; class diseases of teeth and gums in 617.63

         For diseases of larynx, see 616.22; for diseases of pharynx, see 616.32

.312   *Necrotizing ulcerative gingivitis (Trench mouth)

.313   *Mumps

.314   *Diseases of tonsils

.316   *Diseases of salivary glands

         For mumps, see 616.313; for Sjogren's syndrome, see 616.775

.32   *Diseases of pharynx and esophagus

         Subdivisions are added for either or both topics in heading

         Class diseases of tonsils in 616.314

.323   *Deglutition disorders

         Class here dysphagia

.324   *Gastroesophageal reflux

         Class here heartburn

.33   *Diseases of stomach

         Class here gastroenteritis, comprehensive works on gastroenterology (gastrointestinal diseases)

         For diseases of intestine, see 616.34; for typhoid fever, see 616.9272; for cholera, see 616.932; for dysentery, see 616.935; for hiatal hernia, see 617.559

.332   *Functional disorders

         Including disorders of secretion; dyspepsia

         Class gastroesophageal reflux, heartburn in 616.324

.333   *Gastritis

*Add as instructed under 616.1–616.9

.334	*Stomach ulcers

Class comprehensive works on ulcers in 616.343

.34	*Diseases of intestine

Including appendicitis, giardiasis

For hernias, see 617.559

.342	*Functional disorders

Including irritable bowel syndrome (irritable colon), obstructions

.342 7	*Diarrhea
.342 8	*Constipation
.343	*Peptic ulcers

Class here comprehensive works on stomach and peptic ulcers

For stomach ulcers, see 616.334

.343 3	*Duodenal ulcers
.344	*Enteritis

Including duodenitis, jejunitis

Class here Crohn disease, inflammatory bowel diseases

See also 616.342 for irritable bowel syndrome

.344 5	*Ileitis
.344 7	*Colitis
.344 73	*Ulcerative colitis
.35	*Diseases of rectum and anus

Including fecal incontinence

Class here proctology

Subdivisions are added for diseases of rectum and anus together, for diseases of rectum alone

.352	*Hemorrhoids
.36	*Diseases of biliary tract and liver

Subdivisions are added for diseases of biliary tract and liver together, for diseases of biliary tract alone

.362	*Diseases of liver

Including portal hypertension

For hepatic encephalopathy, Reye syndrome, see 616.83

*Add as instructed under 616.1–616.9

.362 3	*Hepatitis
	Class here viral hepatitis
.362 4	*Cirrhosis
.362 5	*Jaundice
.365	*Diseases of gallbladder and bile duct

Subdivisions are added for diseases of gallbladder and bile duct together, for diseases of gallbladder alone

Class comprehensive works on diseases of biliary tract in 616.36

.37	*Diseases of pancreas

Class diseases of pancreatic internal secretion in 616.46

.372	*Cystic fibrosis
.38	*Diseases of peritoneum
.39	*Nutritional and metabolic diseases

Class here food intolerance

Subdivisions are added for either or both topics in heading

Class inborn (inherited) errors of metabolism in 616.39042; class comprehensive works on food intolerance and food allergies in 616.975. Class nutritional and metabolic diseases of a specific system or organ outside the digestive system with the system or organ, e.g., iron-deficiency anemia 616.152

For endocrinology, see 616.4

.390 654	Diet therapy

Number built according to instructions under 616.1–616.9

For diet therapy that excludes a specific food or group of foods, see the diet in 613.268, e.g., wheat-free diet 613.268311

>   616.392–616.396   Deficiency diseases

Class comprehensive works in 616.39

.392	*Beriberi
.393	*Pellagra
.394	*Scurvy
.395	*Rickets

*Add as instructed under 616.1–616.9

.396   Other deficiency diseases and states

Including emaciation, kwashiorkor

Class anorexia nervosa in 616.85262

For multiple deficiency states, see 616.399

.398   *Obesity

.398 08   Psychosomatic medicine

Number built according to instructions under 616.1–616.9

For eating disorders, see 616.8526

.399   Other nutritional and metabolic diseases

Including multiple deficiency states, porphyria

Class here malabsorption syndromes

.399 1   Miscellaneous nutritional and metabolic diseases

Limited to the diseases provided below

.399 12   *Celiac disease and other non-allergic gluten-related disorders

Including non-celiac gluten sensitivity

Subdivisions are added for celiac disease and other non-allergic gluten-related disorders together, for celiac disease alone

Class gluten-free diet in 613.268311; class wheat allergy in 616.975

[.399 120 654]   Diet therapy

Do not use; class in 613.268311

.399 2   *Body fluid disorders

Including acid-base imbalances

Class here water-electrolyte imbalances

.399 5   *Diseases of protein metabolism

Including amyloidosis, phenylketonuria

.399 7   *Diseases of lipid metabolism

Including hypercholesterolemia, hyperlipidemia

.399 8   *Diseases of carbohydrate metabolism

.399 82   *Lactose intolerance

Class lactose-free diet in 613.2687

[.399 820 654]   Diet therapy

Do not use; class in 613.2687

*Add as instructed under 616.1–616.9

.399 9   *Gout

.4   ***Diseases of endocrine, hematopoietic, lymphatic, glandular systems; diseases of male breast**

> Class here endocrinology, comprehensive works on diseases of glands
>
> Subdivisions are added for diseases of endocrine, hematopoietic, lymphatic systems, of male breast together; for diseases of endocrine system alone
>
> Class endocrinal obesity in 616.398. Class diseases of glands in a specific system or organ with the system or organ, e.g., diseases of female sex glands 618.1

.41   *Diseases of spleen and bone marrow

> Class here diseases of hematopoietic (blood-forming) system
>
> *For anemia, see 616.152*

.42   *Diseases of lymphatic system

> Class filiarial elephantiasis in 616.9652; class Hodgkin disease in 616.99446
>
> *For diseases of spleen, see 616.41*

.429   *Sarcoidosis

> Class here pulmonary sarcoidosis

> 616.43–616.48   Diseases of endocrine system
>
> Class comprehensive works in 616.4

.43   *Diseases of thymus gland

.44   *Diseases of thyroid and parathyroid glands

> Subdivisions are added for diseases of thyroid and parathyroid glands together, for diseases of thyroid alone

.442   *Goiter

.443   *Hyperthyroidism

> Including Graves' disease

.444   *Hypothyroidism

> *For myxedema, see 616.858848*

.445   *Diseases of parathyroid glands

> Including hyperparathyroidism, hypoparathyroidism

.45   *Diseases of adrenal glands

> Including Addison's disease, Cushing syndrome, hyperadrenalism, hypoadrenalism

.46   *Diseases of islands of Langerhans

*Add as instructed under 616.1–616.9

.462	*Diabetes mellitus

Class here comprehensive works on diabetes

Class diabetic nephropathies in 616.61

For diabetes insipidus, see 616.47

.462 2	*Diabetes mellitus, type 1 (Insulin-dependent diabetes)
.462 4	*Diabetes mellitus, type 2 (Non-insulin-dependent diabetes)
.466	*Hypoglycemia
.47	*Diseases of pituitary gland

Including acromegaly, diabetes insipidus, pituitary dwarfism, pituitary gigantism, hypopituitarism

.48	*Diseases of other glands of endocrine system

Including hyperpinealism, polyglandular disorders

.49	*Diseases of male breast

Class comprehensive works on diseases of breast in 618.19

.5	***Diseases of integument**

Class here dermatology, skin diseases

Class porphyria in 616.399; class mastocytosis in 616.77

For allergies of skin, see 616.973; for dermatological manifestations of food and drug allergies, see 616.975

.51	*Dermatitis, photosensitivity disorders, urticaria

Including contact dermatitis

Class here eczema

Subdivisions are added for dermatitis, photosensitivity disorders, urticaria together; for dermatitis alone

Class bacterial and viral skin diseases in 616.52

For allergic contact dermatitis, see 616.973

.515	*Photosensitivity disorders

Including sunburn

.517	*Urticaria (Hives)

Class urticaria pigmentosa in 616.77

.52	Viral and bacterial skin diseases; psoriasis

*Add as instructed under 616.1–616.9

.522	*Viral skin diseases
	Including herpes labialis (cold sores, fever blisters), shingles (herpes zoster)
	Class herpes genitalis in 616.9518; class comprehensive works on herpesvirus diseases in 616.9112
.523	*Bacterial skin diseases
	Including boils, carbuncles, erysipelas, impetigo, pinta, yaws
.526	*Psoriasis
.53	*Diseases of sebaceous glands
	Including acne, blackheads, seborrhea, wens
.54	*Skin hypertrophies and ulcerations; diseases of scalp, hair, nails
	For pigmentary changes, see 616.55
.544	*Skin hypertrophies
	Including callosities, corns, ichthyosis, keratosis, scleroderma, warts
.545	*Skin ulcerations
	Class here decubitus ulcers (bedsores)
.546	*Diseases of scalp, hair, hair follicles
	Including baldness (alopecia), dandruff, excessive hairiness (hypertrichosis)
.547	*Diseases of nails
.55	*Pigmentary changes
	Including albinism, birthmarks, moles, pigmentary nevi, vitiligo
	Class urticaria pigmentosa in 616.77
	For birthmarks that are capillary hemangiomas, see 616.99315
.56	*Diseases of sweat glands
.57	*Parasitic and fungal skin diseases
	Subdivisions are added for parasitic and fungal skin diseases together, for parasitic skin diseases alone
	Class leishmaniasis in 616.9364
.572	*Lice infestations
	Class here pediculosis
.573	*Mite infestations
	Class here scabies

*Add as instructed under 616.1–616.9

.579   *Fungal skin diseases (Dermatomycoses)

  Including athlete's foot (tinea pedis), ringworm (tinea)

.58   *Chapping, chilblains, frostbite

  Subdivisions are added for any or all topics in heading

.6   *Diseases of urogenital system

  Class here diseases of urinary system; urology

─────────────

>   616.61–616.64 Diseases of urinary system

  Class comprehensive works in 616.6

.61   *Diseases of kidneys and ureters

  Class here diabetic nephropathies, nephrology

  Subdivisions are added for kidneys and ureters together, for kidneys alone

  Class renal hypertension in 616.132; class kidney dialysis in 617.461059

  For kidney stones, see 616.622

.612   *Nephritis

  Class here glomerulonephritis

  For pyelonephritis, see 616.613

.613   *Pyelonephritis and pyelocystitis

  Subdivisions are added for pyelonephritis and pyelocystitis together, for pyelonephritis alone

.614   *Renal failure

  Class here chronic renal failure

  Class hemodialysis, peritoneal dialysis in 617.461059

.62   *Diseases of bladder and urethra

  Including urinary incontinence

  Class here urination disorders

  Subdivisions are added for either or both topics in heading

  For diseases of male urethra, see 616.64; for enuresis, see 616.849

.622   *Urinary calculi

  Class here bladder stones, kidney stones

.623   *Cystitis

.624   *Urethritis

*Add as instructed under 616.1–616.9

.63   *Urinary manifestations of diseases of urogenital system

         Including albuminuria, hematuria, proteinuria

         Class interpretation of symptoms for diagnosis and prognosis of diseases of urogenital system in 616.6075. Class urinary manifestations of a specific disease or of disease in a specific organ with the disease or organ, e.g., urinary manifestations of renal failure 616.614

         See also 616.07566 for use of urinalysis to diagnose diseases in general

.635   *Uremia

.64   *Diseases of male urethra

.65   *Diseases of genital system

         Class here diseases of male genital system, diseases of prostate gland

         Class comprehensive works on reproductive toxicology in 616.65071

         For sexual disorders, see 616.69; for diseases of female genital system, see 618.1. For diseases of a specific male genital organ not provided for here, see the organ, e.g., diseases of male urethra 616.64

.66   *Diseases of penis

.67   *Diseases of scrotum

.68   *Diseases of testes and accessory organs

         Subdivisions are added for diseases of testes and accessory organs together, for diseases of testes alone

.69   *Sexual disorders

         Class here male sexual disorders

         For psychiatric sexual disorders, see 616.8583; for female sexual disorders, see 618.17

.692   *Infertility and impotence

         Class here comprehensive works on male and female infertility

         Subdivisions are added for infertility and impotence together, for infertility alone

         For female infertility, artificial insemination, see 618.178

.692 06   Therapy

         Number built according to instructions under 616.1–616.9

         Class here comprehensive medical works on human reproductive technology

         For human reproductive technology applied to female infertility, see 618.17806

.692 1   *Male infertility

         Class impotence in 616.6922

*Add as instructed under 616.1–616.9

| .692 2 | *Impotence |

For impotence as a psychological disorder, see 616.85832

| .693 | *Male climacteric disorders |

Class comprehensive works on climacteric disorders in 618.175

| .694 | *Intersexuality |

Class here hermaphroditism, comprehensive medical works on sex differentiation disorders

Class interdisciplinary works on intersexuality in 306.7685. Class a specific sex differentiation disorder with the disorder, e.g., congenital adrenal hyperplasia 616.45, congenital adrenal hyperplasia in children 618.9245

See also 616.8583 for gender-identity disorders

| **.7** | ***Diseases of musculoskeletal system** |

Class here comprehensive works on orthopedics

For orthopedic surgery of musculoskeletal system, see 617.47; for orthopedic regional medicine, orthopedic regional surgery, see 617.5

| .71 | *Diseases of bones |

Class here chronic diseases of skeletal system

Class pituitary gigantism, pituitary dwarfism in 616.47; class Marfan syndrome in 616.773

For diseases of spine, see 616.73; for fractures, see 617.15

| .712 | *Osteitis |

Including osteochondritis, periostitis

Class here osteitis deformans

| .715 | *Osteomyelitis |

| .716 | *Disorders of metabolic origin |

Class here osteoporosis

For rickets, see 616.395

| .72 | *Diseases of joints |

For gout, see 616.3999

| .722 | *Arthritis |

| .722 3 | *Osteoarthritis |

| .722 7 | *Rheumatoid arthritis |

For ankylosing spondylitis, see 616.73; for Sjogren's syndrome, see 616.775

*Add as instructed under 616.1–616.9

.723   *Rheumatism

> Class here rheumatology, rheumatic diseases

>> *For a specific rheumatic disease, see the disease, e.g., rheumatoid arthritis 616.7227, rheumatic fever 616.991*

.73   *Diseases of spine

> Including ankylosing spondylitis

> Class backache in 617.564

.74   *Diseases of muscles

> Class diseases of muscles in a specific system or organ with the system or organ, e.g., diseases of heart muscle (myocardium) 616.124

.742   *Myalgia

> Class here fibromyalgia (muscular rheumatism)

>> *See also 616.0478 for chronic fatigue syndrome*

.743   *Myositis

.744   *Neuromuscular diseases

> Class myalgic encephalomyelitis in 616.0478; class neuromuscular diseases resulting from disorders of central nervous system in 616.83

.744 2   *Myasthenia gravis

.748   *Muscular dystrophy

.75   *Diseases of tendons and fasciae

>> *See also 616.76 for diseases of sheaths of tendons*

.76   *Diseases of bursae and sheaths of tendons

.77   *Diseases of connective tissues

> Including Ehlers-Danlos syndrome, mastocytosis

> Class here collagen diseases

> Class carpal tunnel syndrome in 616.856

>> *For rheumatoid arthritis, see 616.7227; for diseases of tendons and fasciae, see 616.75*

.772   *Systemic lupus erythematosus

.773   *Marfan syndrome

.775   *Sjogren's syndrome

---

*Add as instructed under 616.1–616.9

.8 **Diseases of nervous system and mental disorders**

Class here diseases of brain; neurology; neuropsychiatry

Class diseases of cranial, spinal, peripheral nerves in 616.856; class diseases of autonomic nervous system in 616.8569. Class diseases of nerves needed to make a specific system or organ function properly with the system or organ, e.g., neuromuscular diseases 616.744, diseases of optic nerves 617.732

Diseases of nerves needed to make a region function properly are classed with diseases of nerves, e.g., disease of peripheral nerves needed to make the hand function properly are classed with diseases of peripheral nerves in 616.856

.800 1–.800 9   Standard subdivisions

.801–.803   Standard subdivisions of neurology, of diseases of nervous system, of diseases of brain

As modified in notation 001–003 from table under 616.1–616.9

.804   Special topics of diseases of nervous system, of diseases of brain

Add to base number 616.804 the numbers following 0 in notation 01–09 from table under 616.1–616.9, e.g., diagnosis of brain diseases 616.80475
Subdivisions are added for any or all topics in heading

Class manifestations of neurological diseases as problems in their own right in 616.84

.805–.809   Standard subdivisions of neurology, of diseases of nervous system, of diseases of brain

As modified in notation 005–009 from table under 616.1–616.9

.81   *Cerebrovascular diseases

Class here stroke

.812   *Vascular dementia

Class comprehensive works on dementia in 616.831

.82   *Meningeal diseases

Including meningitis

Class meningoencephalitis in 616.832

*Add as instructed under 616.1–616.9

.83   **Other organic diseases of central nervous system**

> Including ataxia telangiectasia, chorea and choreatic disorders other than Huntington disease, Creutzfeldt-Jakob syndrome (both familial form and variant associated with bovine spongiform encephalopathy), Friedreich ataxia, hepatic encephalopathy, neuronal ceroid-lipofuscinosis, neurosyphilis, prion diseases, Reye syndrome, spina bifida, tardive dyskinesia, Tourette syndrome

> Class here diseases of basal ganglia, of spinal cord; comprehensive works on memory disorders, on movement disorders

> Class phenylketonuria in 616.3995; class comprehensive works on syphilis in 616.9513

> > *For orthopedic aspects of spina bifida, see 616.73; for Huntington disease, see 616.851; for epilepsy, see 616.853*

.831   **Dementia

> Including frontotemporal dementia

> Class here senile dementia, comprehensive works on dementia

> Class senile dementia of the Alzheimer type in 616.8311

> > *For a specific kind of dementia or dementia-causing disease not provided for here, see the dementia or disease, e.g., vascular dementia 616.812, dementia caused by AIDS 616.9792*

.831 1   **Alzheimer disease

.832   **Encephalitis

> Class here meningoencephalitis

> Class postencephalitic Parkinson disease in 616.833

> > *See also 616.0478 for myalgic encephalomyelitis*

.833   **Parkinson disease and Lewy body dementia

> Including postencephalitic Parkinson disease

> Subdivisions are added for Parkinson disease and Lewy body dementia together, for Parkinson disease alone

.833 6   **Lewy body dementia

> Class here Lewy body dementia discussed as a separate disease, Lewy body dementia discussed as an aspect of Parkinson disease, dementia in Parkinson disease

.834   **Multiple sclerosis

.835   **Poliomyelitis

> Including postpoliomyelitis syndrome

.836   **Cerebral palsy

.839   **Amyotrophic lateral sclerosis

*Add as instructed under 616.1–616.9

.84	Manifestations of nervous system diseases

Symptoms as problems in their own right

Class here pathology, diagnosis, treatment of symptoms

Class interpretation of symptoms for diagnosis and prognosis of neurological diseases in 616.80475; class manifestations of mental disorders in 616.89. Class diagnostic and prognostic interpretation of symptoms of a specific disease or class of diseases with the disease or class of diseases, e.g., interpretation of symptoms of cerebrovascular diseases 616.81075

.841	Dizziness and vertigo

Standard subdivisions are added for either or both topics in heading

.842	Paralysis

Including neurological aspects of paraplegia

Class comprehensive works on neurological and surgical aspects of paraplegia in 617.58

.845	Convulsions
.849	Miscellaneous symptoms

Only those named below

Including coma, enuresis, pain

Class comprehensive works on urinary incontinence in 616.62

.849 1	*Headaches

Class here vascular headaches

.849 12	*Migraine
.849 13	*Cluster headache
.849 14	*Tension headache
.849 8	*Sleep disorders

Including narcolepsy, somnambulism

For sleep apnea and snoring, see 616.209

.849 82	*Insomnia
.85	Miscellaneous diseases of nervous system and mental disorders

Only those named below

.851	*Huntington disease
.852	*Neuroses

Including adjustment disorders

Class neurotic aspects of a specific disease with the disease, e.g., neurotic aspects of asthma 616.238

*Add as instructed under 616.1–616.9

.852 1	*Traumatic neuroses
	Class here post-traumatic stress disorders
.852 12	*War neuroses (Combat disorders)
.852 2	*Anxiety disorders
	For traumatic neuroses, see 616.8521
.852 23	*Panic disorder
.852 25	*Phobic disorders
	Including agoraphobia
.852 27	*Obsessive-compulsive disorder
	Class comprehensive works on compulsive behavior in 616.8584
.852 3	*Dissociative disorders and amnesia
	Subdivisions are added for dissociative disorders and amnesia together, for dissociative disorders alone
.852 32	*Amnesia
	Class here amnestic disorders
.852 36	*Multiple personality disorder
.852 4	*Somatoform disorders
	Class here conversion disorder, hysteria, somatization disorder
	For hypochondria, see 616.8525
	See also 616.8581 for histrionic personality disorder
.852 5	*Hypochondria
.852 6	*Eating disorders
	Class here appetite disorders, food addiction
.852 62	*Anorexia nervosa
.852 63	*Bulimia
.852 7	*Depressive disorder
	Including seasonal affective disorder
	Class here comprehensive works on depression, on mood disorders
	For manic-depressive illness, see 616.895; for postpartum depression, see 618.76
.852 8	*Neurasthenia
	See also 616.0478 for chronic fatigue syndrome
.853	*Epilepsy

*Add as instructed under 616.1–616.9

.855	*Speech and language disorders

Class here articulation disorders, communication disorders

Subdivisions are added for either or both topics in heading

Class comprehensive works on learning and communication disorders in 616.85889

.855 2	*Neurological language disorders

Including dysarthria

Class here aphasias

For written language disorders, see 616.8553

.855 3	*Written language disorders

Including agraphia

Class here dyslexia

.855 4	*Stuttering

Class here stammering

.855 6	*Voice disorders
.856	*Diseases of cranial, spinal, peripheral nerves; diseases of autonomic nervous system

Including carpal tunnel syndrome, neuralgias, neuritis, polyradiculoneuritis, sciatica; cutaneous sensory disorders, disorders of smell and taste

Subdivisions are added for diseases of cranial, spinal, peripheral nerves and for diseases of autonomic nervous system together; for diseases of cranial, spinal, peripheral nerves alone

Class neurofibromatosis in 616.99383; class comprehensive works on overuse injuries in 617.172

For shingles, see 616.522; for diseases of optic nerves, see 617.732; for diseases of aural nervous system, see 617.886

.856 9	*Diseases of autonomic nervous system

Including parasympathetic nervous system, sympathetic nervous system

.858	Personality, sexual, gender-identity, impulse-control, factitious, developmental, learning disorders; violent behavior; intellectual disabilities

*Add as instructed under 616.1–616.9

.858 1   *Personality disorders

Including compulsive, dependent, histrionic, paranoid, passive-aggressive, schizoid, schizotypal personality disorders

Class impulsive personality, comprehensive works on compulsive behavior in 616.8584

For a specific type of personality disorder not provided for here, see the disorder, e.g., borderline personality disorder 616.85852

See also 616.85227 for obsessive-compulsive disorder; also 616.8524 for hysteria; also 616.897 for paranoid disorders; also 616.898 for schizophrenia

.858 2   *Antisocial personality disorders, family violence and abuse

Class here self-destructive behavior, violent behavior

Subdivisions are added for antisocial personality disorders, family violence and abuse together; for antisocial personality disorders alone

Class sexual disorders in 616.8583

For a specific type of self-destructive or violent behavior, see the behavior, e.g., suicide 616.858445

.858 22   *Family violence and abuse

Class here intimate partner abuse, spouse abuse

Subdivisions are added for either or both topics in heading

.858 223   *Child abuse

Including Munchausen syndrome by proxy

Class incest involving children, sexual abuse of children in 616.85836; class abused children in 618.92858223

.858 223 9   *Adult victims of child abuse

Class a specific problem of adult victims of child abuse with the problem, e.g., depression 616.8527

.858 3   *Sexual disorders and gender-identity disorders

Including homosexuality treated as a medical disorder

Subdivisions are added for sexual and gender-identity disorders together, for sexual disorders alone

Class interdisciplinary works on gender identity in 305.3; class interdisciplinary works on LGBT identity in 306.76; class interdisciplinary works on homosexuality in 306.766; class interdisciplinary works on transgender identity in 306.768

See also 616.694 for intersexuality

See Manual at 616.8583

*Add as instructed under 616.1–616.9

.858 32	*Frigidity and impotence
	Subdivisions are added for either or both topics in heading
	Class comprehensive works on impotence in 616.6922
.858 33	*Sex addiction
	Class here nymphomania, satyromania
.858 35	*Sadism and masochism
	Subdivisions are added for either or both topics in heading
.858 36	*Sexual abuse of children and adolescents
	Class here incest
	Subdivisions are added for either or both topics in heading
	Class sexually abused children in 618.9285836
.858 369	*Adult victims of childhood and adolescent sexual abuse
	Subdivisions are added for either or both topics in heading
	Class a specific problem of adult victims of childhood and adolescent sexual abuse with the problem, e.g., multiple personality disorder 616.85236
.858 4	*Disorders of impulse control; homicidal and suicidal behavior
	Including compulsive shopping
	Class here impulsive personality, comprehensive works on compulsive behavior
	For obsessive-compulsive disorder, see 616.85227; for compulsive eating disorders, see 616.8526; for compulsive personality disorder, see 616.8581; for compulsive sexual disorders, see 616.8583; for substance abuse, see 616.86
.858 41	*Pathological gambling
.858 42	*Kleptomania
.858 43	*Pyromania
.858 44	Homicidal and suicidal behavior
.858 445	*Suicidal behavior
.858 5	Borderline and narcissistic personality disorders
.858 52	*Borderline personality disorder
.858 54	*Narcissistic personality disorder
.858 6	*Factitious disorders
	Including Munchausen syndrome
	Class Munchausen syndrome by proxy in 616.858223

*Add as instructed under 616.1–616.9

.858 8	*Intellectual disabilities; developmental and learning disorders

Class here mental disorders usually first diagnosed in infancy, childhood, adolescence

Subdivisions are added for intellectual disabilities, developmental and learning disorders together; for intellectual disabilities alone; for developmental disorders alone

For attention deficit disorder with hyperactivity, see 616.8589

.858 82	*Autism

Class here comprehensive works on pervasive development disorders

For pervasive development disorders other than autism, see 616.85883

.858 83	Other pervasive development disorders

Including childhood disintegrative disorder

For Rett syndrome, see 616.85884

.858 832	*Asperger syndrome
.858 84	Intellectual disabilities due to genetic disorders, other congenital abnormalities

Class phenylketonuria in 616.3995; class learning disorders due to genetic disorders, other congenital abnormalities, and not associated with intellectual disabilities in 616.85889

.858 841	*Fragile X syndrome
.858 842	*Down syndrome
.858 843	*Hydrocephalus
.858 844	*Microcephaly
.858 845	*Cerebral sphingolipidosis

Class here Tay-Sachs disease

.858 848	*Myxedema

Class congenital myxedema in 616.858848043

*Add as instructed under 616.1–616.9

.858 89   *Learning disorders

Regardless of level of intelligence

Class here learning disorders due to genetic disorders, other congenital abnormalities, and not associated with intellectual disabilities; comprehensive works on learning and communication disorders

Class learning disorders associated with a specific disorder with the disorder, e.g., minimal brain dysfunction 616.8589

For communication disorders, see 616.855

.858 9   *Attention deficit disorder with hyperactivity

Class here hyperkinesia, minimal brain dysfunction

.86   †Substance abuse (Drug abuse)

Including abuse of analgesics, depressants, inhalants, sedatives, tranquilizers

Class here addiction, dependence, habituation, intoxication

Class personal measures to prevent substance abuse in 613.8; class food addiction in 616.8526; class comprehensive medical works on addictive drugs in 615.78; class comprehensive works on compulsive behavior in 616.8584; class interdisciplinary works on substance abuse in 362.29

See Manual at 616.86 vs. 158.1, 204.42, 248.8629, 292–299, 362.29

.861   †Alcohol

Class here alcoholism

.861 9   *Effect of alcoholism on people close to alcoholics

Class here adult children of alcoholics, codependent spouses of alcoholics

Class minor children of alcoholics in 618.928619. Class a specific problem of people close to alcoholics with the problem, e.g., depression 616.8527

\>   616.863–616.865 Substances other than alcohol

Including effects on people close to substance abusers

Class minor children of substance abusers in 618.92863–618.92865; class comprehensive works in 616.86. Class a specific problem of people close to substance abusers with the problem, e.g., depression 616.8527

.863   †Narcotics, hallucinogens, psychedelics, cannabis

---

*Add as instructed under 616.1–616.9

†Add as instructed under 616.1–616.9, except do not use 05; class prevention in 613.8 or its subdivisions

.863 2   †Narcotics

                Opium and its derivatives and synthetic equivalents

                Class here specific narcotics, e.g., heroin, morphine

.863 4   †Hallucinogens and psychedelics

                Class here specific hallucinogens and psychedelics, e.g., LSD, mescaline, PCP

                Subdivisions are added for either or both topics in heading

                Class cannabis in 616.8635

.863 5   †Cannabis

                Class here specific kinds of cannabis, e.g., hashish, marijuana

.864   †Stimulants and related substances

                Class here specific kinds of stimulants, e.g., amphetamine, ephedrine

                Subdivisions are added for stimulants and related substances together, for stimulants alone

                Class nicotine in 616.865

.864 7   †Cocaine

                Class here specific forms of cocaine, e.g., crack

.865   †Tobacco

.869   *Effect of substance abuse on people close to substance abusers

                Class here adult children of substance abusers, codependent spouses of substance abusers

                Class minor children of substance abusers in 618.92869. Class effect of abuse of a specific substance on people close to abusers with the abuse of the specific substance, e.g., effect of alcoholism on people close to alcoholics 616.8619, effect of cocaine abuse on people close to cocaine abusers 616.8647; class a specific problem of people close to substance abusers with the problem, e.g., depression 616.8527

---

*Add as instructed under 616.1–616.9
†Add as instructed under 616.1–616.9, except do not use 05; class prevention in 613.8 or its subdivisions

.89   *Mental disorders

Including manifestations of mental disorders

Class here abnormal and clinical psychologies, comparative abnormal behavior of animals, psychiatry, psychoses

Class a specific organic psychosis not provided for here with the psychosis, e.g., psychosis due to brain tumors 616.99481

For neuroses, see 616.852; for personality, sexual, gender-identity, impulse-control, factitious, developmental, learning disorders; violent behavior, see 616.858; for puerperal mental disorders, see 618.76

See Manual at 616.89 vs. 150.195

[.890 6]   Therapy

Do not use; class in 616.891

.891   Therapy

.891 2   Convulsive therapy

Variant name: shock therapy

Including insulin and other drug shock therapies

.891 22   Electroconvulsive therapy

.891 3   Physical therapies

For electroconvulsive therapy, see 616.89122; for psychosurgery, see 617.481

.891 4   Psychotherapy

Class psychotherapy applied to a specific disorder with the disorder, plus notation 0651 from table under 616.1–616.9, e.g., psychotherapy applied to borderline personality disorder 616.858520651

For group and family psychotherapy, see 616.8915; for psychological and activity therapies, see 616.8916; for psychoanalysis, see 616.8917

.891 42   Behavior therapy (Behavior modification therapy)

.891 425   Cognitive therapy

.891 43   Gestalt therapy

.891 44   Milieu therapy

.891 45   Transactional analysis

.891 47   Brief psychotherapy

Class a brief form of a specific kind of psychotherapy with the kind, e.g., brief cognitive therapy 616.891425

.891 5   Group and family psychotherapy

Class specific psychological and activity therapies in 616.8916

*Add as instructed under 616.1–616.9

.891 52	Group psychotherapy
.891 523	Psychodrama
	Including role playing
.891 56	Family psychotherapy
.891 562	Marital psychotherapy
	Class here couples therapy
.891 6	Psychological and activity therapies

Add to base number 616.8916 the numbers following 615.851 in 615.8512–615.8516, e.g., hypnotherapy 616.89162

Class psychotherapy in 616.8914; class group and family psychotherapy in 616.8915; class psychoanalysis in 616.8917

.891 7	Psychoanalysis
[.891 701 9]	Psychological principles

Do not use for comprehensive works; class in 150.195. Do not use for applications to therapy; class in 616.8917

.891 8	Drug therapy

Class drug shock therapy in 616.8912

.895	*Bipolar disorder

Variant name: Manic-depressive illness

Including depressive reactions, involutional psychoses

Class here circular and alternating manic-depressive psychoses

Class comprehensive works on depression, on mood disorders in 616.8527

.897	*Paranoid disorders

See also 616.8581 for paranoid personality disorder

.898	*Schizophrenia

See also 616.8581 for schizoid personality disorder, schizotypal personality disorder

.9	**Other diseases**

Class here communicable diseases, infections

[.900 1–.900 9]	Standard subdivisions of other diseases

Do not use; class in 616.001–616.009

.901–.903	Standard subdivisions of communicable diseases

As modified in notation 001–003 from table under 616.1–616.9

*Add as instructed under 616.1–616.9

.904   Special topics of communicable diseases

Add to base number 616.904 the numbers following 0 in notation 01–09 from table under 616.1–616.9, e.g., diagnosis of communicable diseases 616.90475

.904 1   Medical microbiology

Number built according to instructions under 616.904

Class here drug resistance in microorganisms, comprehensive works on harmful microorganisms in human body

Class resistance to specific drugs in 615; class comprehensive works on human microbiome, on human microbiota, on microbiology of human body, on beneficial and harmful microorganisms in human body, on beneficial microorganisms in human body in 612.001579; class comprehensive works on etiology of diseases in 616.071; class comprehensive works on communicable diseases and their course, cure, and prevention in 616.9; class comprehensive works on etiology of communicable diseases in 616.90471. Class medical microbiology of a specific disease or group of diseases with the disease or group of diseases, plus notation 01 from table under 616.1–616.9, e.g., medical microbiology of cancer 616.99401, medical microbiology of tuberculosis 616.99501

> *For works that emphasize poisons produced by microorganisms, see 615.9529*
>
> *See also 615.329 for probiotics*
>
> *See Manual at 579.165 vs. 616.9041*

.904 71   Etiology

Number built according to instructions under 616.904

Class here comprehensive works on etiology of communicable diseases, e.g., environmental and genetic risk factors plus pathogenic microorganisms

> *For pathogenic microorganisms as causes of communicable diseases, see 616.9041*

.905–.908   Standard subdivisions of communicable diseases

As modified in notation 005–008 from table under 616.1–616.9

.909   History, geographic treatment, biography of communicable diseases

[.909 11–.909 13]   Frigid, temperate, tropical zones

Do not use; class in 616.9881–616.9883

>   616.91–616.96   Specific communicable diseases

Class here diseases caused by microorganisms or parasites even if the diseases are not communicable

Class comprehensive works in 616.9

For a specific communicable disease not provided for here, see the disease, e.g., mumps 616.313

.91   *Virus diseases

For a specific virus disease or group of virus diseases not provided for here, see the disease or group of diseases, e.g., viral hepatitis 616.3623

See also 616.0478 for chronic fatigue syndrome

.910 1   Medical virology

Number built according to instructions under 616.1–616.9

Class here medical microbiology of ultramicrobes

.911   *DNA virus infections

Including human papillomavirus infections

For a specific DNA virus infection not provided for here, see the infection, e.g., smallpox 616.912, condylomata acuminata 616.9518

.911 2   *Herpesvirus diseases

For a specific herpesvirus disease or group of herpesvirus diseases not provided for here, see the disease or group of diseases, e.g., shingles 616.522, herpes genitalis 616.9518

.911 22   *Infectious mononucleosis

.912   *Smallpox

For mild forms of smallpox, see 616.913

.913   *Mild forms of smallpox; cowpox

Including alastrim (amaas, Cuban itch, variola minor)

.914   *Chickenpox

.915   *Measles

.916   *Rubella

.918   *RNA virus infections

Including Colorado tick fever, hantavirus infections, Rift Valley fever

For a specific RNA virus infection not provided for here, see the infection, e.g., measles 616.915

.918 5   *Flavivirus infections

*Add as instructed under 616.1–616.9

.918 52	*Dengue

Including dengue hemorrhagic fever

.918 54	*Yellow fever

.918 56	*West Nile fever

.918 8	*Retroviridae infections

For a specific retroviridae infection not provided for here, see the infection, e.g., HIV infections 616.9792

.918 801	Medical microbiology of retroviridae

Number built according to instructions under 616.1–616.9

For retroviridae as oncogenic viruses, see 616.994019

.92	*Bacterial diseases

Including pseudomonas infections, mycoplasma infections

Class here comprehensive works on gram-negative bacterial infections

For a specific bacterial disease or group of bacterial diseases not provided for here, see the disease or group of diseases, e.g., bacterial skin diseases 616.523, brucellosis 616.957

.922	*Rickettsial diseases

.922 2	*Epidemic louse-borne typhus and endemic flea-borne typhus

.922 3	*Tick-borne rickettsia infections

Including boutonneuse fever

Class here North Queensland tick typhus, Rocky Mountain spotted fever

.922 4	*Tsutsugamushi disease (Scrub typhus)

.922 5	*Q fever

.923	*Pasteurella infections, yersinia infections, chlamydia infections, tularemia

Subdivisions are added for pasteurella infections, yersinia infections, chlamydia infections, tularemia together; for pasteurella infections alone

.923 2	*Plague

.923 5	*Chlamydia infections

.923 9	*Tularemia

.924	*Borrelia infections

.924 4	*Relapsing fevers

.924 6	*Lyme disease

.926	*Escherichia coli infections

*Add as instructed under 616.1–616.9

.927	*Salmonella infections
.927 2	*Typhoid fever
.927 4	*Paratyphoid fever
.929	*Gram-positive bacterial infections

> *For a specific gram-positive bacterial infection or group of gram-positive bacterial infections not provided for here, see the infection or group of infections, e.g., clostridium infections 616.931, anthrax 616.956*

.929 4	*Mycobacterium infections

> *For tuberculosis, see 616.995; for Hansen's disease, see 616.998*

.929 7	*Staphylococcal infections

Including toxic shock syndrome

.929 8	*Streptococcal infections

Including necrotizing fasciitis

.929 87	*Scarlet fever
.93	Clostridium infections, diphtheria, cholera, dysenteries, protozoan infections
.931	*Clostridium infections, diphtheria

Class here bacillaceae infections, bacillary infections

Subdivisions are added for clostridium infections and diphtheria together, for clostridium infections alone

> *For anthrax, see 616.956*

> *See also 616.9355 for bacillary dysentery*

.931 3	*Diphtheria
.931 5	*Botulism
.931 8	*Tetanus
.932	*Cholera
.935	*Dysenteries
.935 3	*Amebic dysentery
.935 5	*Bacillary dysentery (Shigellosis)
.936	*Protozoan infections

Class giardiasis in 616.34

> *For amebic dysentery, see 616.9353*

.936 2	*Malaria

*Add as instructed under 616.1–616.9

.936 3	*Trypanosomiasis

Class here African sleeping sickness (African trypanosomiasis), Chagas disease (South American trypanosomiasis)

.936 4	*Leishmaniasis

Including cutaneous leishmaniasis (oriental sores), visceral leishmaniasis (kala-azar)

.94	*Bacterial blood diseases
.944	*Septicemia

Including pyemia

For puerperal septicemia, see 618.74

.95	Sexually transmitted diseases, zoonoses
.951	*Sexually transmitted diseases

For acquired immune deficiency syndrome (AIDS), see 616.9792

.951 3	*Syphilis

For neurosyphilis, see 616.83

.951 5	*Gonorrhea
.951 8	Other sexually transmitted diseases

Including chancroid, condylomata acuminata (genital warts), herpes genitalis, lymphogranuloma venereum

Class comprehensive works on chlamydia infections in 616.9235; class comprehensive works on human papillomavirus infections in 616.911; class comprehensive works on herpesvirus diseases in 616.9112

See also 616.522 for herpes labialis

.953	*Rabies
.954	*Glanders
.956	*Anthrax
.957	*Brucellosis
.958	*Psittacosis
.959	*Zoonoses

For a specific zoonotic disease, see the disease, e.g., tularemia 616.9239, rabies 616.953

*Add as instructed under 616.1–616.9

.96   *Parasitic diseases and diseases due to fungi (mycoses)

Class here medical parasitology

Subdivisions are added for parasitic diseases and diseases due to fungi together, for parasitic diseases alone

For parasitic skin diseases, see 616.57; for protozoan infections, see 616.936

> 616.962–616.968 Parasitic diseases

Class comprehensive works in 616.96

.962   *Diseases due to endoparasites

Class here comprehensive works on diseases due to worms

For a specific disease due to worms, see 616.963–616.965

> 616.963–616.965 Diseases due to worms

Class here medical helminthology

Class comprehensive works in 616.962

.963   *Diseases due to flukes (Trematode infections)

Including schistosomiasis (bilharziasis)

.964   *Diseases due to tapeworms (Cestode infections)

Including echinococcosis

.965   *Diseases due to roundworms (Nematode infections)

.965 2   *Diseases due to filariae

Including elephantiasis, onchocerciasis

Class here filariasis

.965 4   Diseases due to other nematodes

Including ascariasis, enterobiasis, hookworm infections, trichinosis

.968   *Diseases due to ectoparasites

Class here medical entomology

For a specific entomological disease, see the disease, e.g., lice infestations 616.572

.969   *Diseases due to fungi (Mycoses)

For fungal skin diseases, see 616.579

.969 3   *Candidiasis

*Add as instructed under 616.1–616.9

.97   *Diseases of immune system

Class here comprehensive works on allergies

Class sarcoidosis in 616.429

For a specific allergy not provided for here, see the allergy, e.g., hay fever 616.202

.973   *Contact allergies

Class here allergic contact dermatitis, allergies of skin

Class comprehensive works on contact dermatitis in 616.51; class dermatological manifestations of food and drug allergies in 616.975

.975   *Food and drug allergies

Class here allergies of digestive system; comprehensive works on food allergies and food intolerance

Subdivisions are added for food and drug allergies together, for food allergies alone

For food intolerance, see 616.39

See also 616.39912 for celiac disease and other non-allergic gluten-related disorders

.975 065 4   Diet therapy

Number built according to instructions under 616.1–616.9

For diet therapy that excludes a specific food or group of foods, see the diet in 613.268, e.g., egg-free diet 613.26875

.975 8   *Drug allergies

.978   *Autoimmune diseases

Class here autoimmunity

For a specific autoimmune disease, see the disease, e.g., celiac disease 616.39912, systemic lupus erythematosus 616.772

.979   *Immune deficiency diseases

.979 2   *Acquired immune deficiency syndrome (AIDS)

Class here HIV infections

*Add as instructed under 616.1–616.9

.98   Noncommunicable diseases and environmental medicine

> Standard subdivisions are added for either or both topics in heading

> Including Persian Gulf syndrome

> Class here communicable diseases as part of environmental medicine, diseases due to stress

>> *For poisoning, see 615.9. For a specific noncommunicable or environmentally linked disease or type of disease provided for elsewhere, see the disease or type of disease, e.g., mental disorders 616.89, malaria 616.9362, cancer 616.994*

.980 01–.980 08   Standard subdivisions

.980 09   History, geographic treatment, biography

[.980 091 1–.980 091 3]   Frigid, temperate, tropical zones

>> Do not use; class in 616.9881–616.9883

.980 2   Specialized medical fields

> Including travel medicine

>> *For industrial and occupational medicine, see 616.9803; for sports medicine, see 617.1027*

.980 21   Aerospace medicine

.980 213   Aviation medicine

.980 214   Space medicine

.980 22   Submarine medicine

> Class here diving medicine

> Class diseases due to compression and decompression in 616.9894

.980 23   Military medicine

>> *For naval medicine, see 616.98024*

.980 24   Naval medicine

> Class submarine medicine in 616.98022

.980 3   Industrial and occupational medicine

> Standard subdivisions are added for either or both topics in heading

>> *See also 613.62 for industrial and occupational health; also 615.902 for industrial toxicology*

.988   *Diseases due to climate and weather

> Class here medical climatology, medical meteorology

> Subdivisions are added for either or both topics in heading

---

*Add as instructed under 616.1–616.9

.988 1–.988 3	Diseases of frigid, temperate, tropical zones

Class here communicable diseases of frigid, temperate, tropical zones

Add to base number 616.988 the numbers following —1 in notation 11–13 from Table 2, e.g., diseases due to tropical climate 616.9883

.989   *Diseases due to heat, cold, motion, altitude, compression, decompression, sound, other vibrations, radiation

Including heat exhaustion, hypothermia

Class here comprehensive works on diseases due to physical forces

For diseases due to light, see 616.5; for chapping, chilblains, frostbite, see 616.58

.989 2   *Diseases due to motion

.989 3   *Diseases due to altitude

Class here mountain sickness

.989 4   *Diseases due to compression and decompression

Subdivisions are added for either or both topics in heading

.989 6   *Diseases due to sound and diseases due to other vibrations

Subdivisions are added for diseases due to sound and diseases due to other vibrations together, for diseases due to sound alone

.989 7   *Diseases due to radiation

Class here radiation injuries

Class comprehensive works on radiation dosimetry in 612.01448

.99   Tumors and miscellaneous communicable diseases

Only those named below

[.990 1–.990 9]   Standard subdivisions

Do not use; class in 616.99

.991   *Rheumatic fever

.993   †Benign tumors

Variant name: benign neoplasms

Medical and surgical treatment

Including adenomas

.993 1–.993 9   Benign tumors of specific systems and organs

Add to base number 616.993 the numbers following 611 in 611.1–611.9, e.g., benign skin tumors 616.99377, neurofibromatosis 616.99383; then add further as instructed under 618.1–618.8, e.g., therapy for neurofibromatosis 616.9938306

*Add as instructed under 616.1–616.9
†Add as instructed under 618.1–618.8

.994	†Cancers

Variant names: malignant neoplasms, malignant tumors, neoplastic diseases

Medical and surgical treatment

Class here carcinoma, oncology, tumors

For benign tumors, see 616.993

.994 1	†Cancers of cardiovascular organs and blood
.994 11–.994 15	Cancers of cardiovascular organs

Add to base number 616.9941 the numbers following 611.1 in 611.11–611.15, e.g., cancer of heart 616.99412; then add further as instructed under 618.1–618.8, e.g., therapy for cancer of heart 616.9941206

.994 18	†Cancer of blood

Including multiple myeloma

For cancer of leukocytes, see 616.99419

.994 19	†Leukemia

Cancer of leukocytes

.994 2–.994 9	Cancers of other organs and of regions

Add to base number 616.994 the numbers following 611 in 611.2–611.9, e.g., breast cancer 616.99449; then for organs, systems, regions having their own number add further as instructed under 618.1–618.8, e.g., surgery for breast cancer 616.99449059
Subdivisions are added for a specific type of cancer if subdivisions are added for comprehensive works on cancer of the organ or region, e.g., surgery for Hodgkin disease (a cancer of lymphatic glands) 616.99446059

.995	*Tuberculosis

Class here pulmonary tuberculosis

.995 1	Tuberculosis of cardiovascular system

Add to base number 616.9951 the numbers following 611.1 in 611.11–611.15, e.g., tuberculosis of heart 616.99512; then add further as instructed under 616.1–616.9, e.g., therapy for tuberculosis of heart 616.9951206

.995 2	Tuberculosis of respiratory system

*Add as instructed under 616.1–616.9
†Add as instructed under 618.1–618.8

.995 21–.995 23   Tuberculosis of nose and nasal accessory sinuses, of larynx, of trachea and bronchi

Add to base number 616.9952 the numbers following 611.2 in 611.21–611.23, e.g., laryngeal tuberculosis 616.99522; then add further as instructed under 616.1–616.9, e.g., therapy for laryngeal tuberculosis 616.9952206

.995 25–.995 27   Tuberculosis of pleura, diaphragm, mediastinum

Add to base number 616.9952 the numbers following 611.2 in 611.25–611.27, e.g., pleural tuberculosis 616.99525; then add further as instructed under 616.1–616.9, e.g., therapy for pleural tuberculosis 616.9952506

.995 3–.995 9   Tuberculosis of other specific systems and organs

Add to base number 616.995 the numbers following 611 in 611.3–611.9, e.g., tuberculosis of teeth and surrounding tissues 616.995314, of bones 616.99571, of eyes 616.99584, of ears 616.99585; then add further as instructed under 616.1–616.9, e.g., therapy for tuberculosis of bones 616.9957106

.998   *Hansen's disease (Leprosy)

*Add as instructed under 616.1–616.9

617   **Surgery, regional medicine, dentistry, ophthalmology, otology, audiology**

> Standard subdivisions are added for surgery alone; however, do not add for surgery, regional medicine, dentistry, ophthalmology, otology, audiology together; class in 616.001–616.009

> Except where contrary instructions are given, all notes under 616.02–616.08 and in table under 616.1–616.9 are applicable here

> Except for modifications shown under specific entries, add to each subdivision identified by * as follows:

001–007	Standard subdivisions
	As modified in notation 001–007 from table under 616.1–616.9
008	Groups of people
0083	Young people
	Notation 0083 is used for pediatric aspects of specific kinds of wounds and injuries, e.g., burns and scalds in children 617.110083; for surgery of a specific organ, system, disorder, e.g., brain surgery in children 617.4810083; for specific aspects of pediatric dentistry, e.g., caries in children 617.670083
	Class comprehensive works on pediatric dentistry in 617.645; class comprehensive works on surgery for infants and children up to puberty in 617.98; class comprehensive works on pediatrics in 618.92; class regional medicine, ophthalmology, otology, audiology for infants and children up to puberty in 618.92097
00835	Young people twelve to twenty
	Notation 00835 is used for adolescent medicine aspects of all topics in 617, e.g., brain surgery in adolescents 617.48100835, comprehensive works on surgery for adolescents 617.00835
0084	People in specific stages of adulthood
00846	People in late adulthood
	Notation 00846 is used for geriatric aspects of specific kinds of wounds and injuries, e.g., burns and scalds in late adulthood 617.1100846; for surgery of a specific organ, system, disorder, e.g., heart surgery in late adulthood 617.41200846
	Class comprehensive works on geriatric surgery in 617.97; class comprehensive works on geriatrics in 618.97; class regional medicine, dentistry, ophthalmology, otology, audiology for people in late adulthood in 618.9775–618.9778
0088	Occupational and religious groups
0088355	Military personnel
	Class military surgery in 617.99
[009]	History, geographic treatment, biography
	Do not use; class in notation 09 from this table
>01–03	Surgical complications, preoperative, intraoperative, postoperative care, special topics, rehabilitation
	Class surgical complications, preoperative, intraoperative, postoperative care, special topics, rehabilitation applied to special classes of diseases in notation 04 from this table; class comprehensive works in 617, without adding from this table

617   Surgery, regional medicine, dentistry, ophthalmology, otology, audiology

01   Surgical complications; preoperative, intraoperative, postoperative care

> Standard subdivisions are added for any or all topics in heading
> Including surgical shock; complicating preconditions, e.g., heart problems
> Class intensive care in notation 028 from this table

02   Special topics

023   Personnel

0231   Nurses

> Class here specific surgical nursing specialties; nature of duties, characteristics of profession, relationships; works that emphasize technology of operations performed by nurses, e.g., works that emphasize techniques used by a heart surgery nurse 617.4120231
> Class works that emphasize a specific technique used by nurses with the technique, e.g., nursing diagnosis 075, nursing diagnosis with respect to gunshot wounds 617.145075

0232   Physicians

> Class here nature of duties, characteristics of profession, relationships
> Do not use for works that emphasize technology of operations performed by physicians; class with the subject without 0232, e.g., works that emphasize techniques used by a physician with respect to gunshot wounds 617.145
> Class works that emphasize a specific technique used by physicians with the technique, e.g., diagnosis by a physician 075, diagnosis by a physician with respect to gunshot wounds 617.145075

0233   Allied health personnel

> Class here nature of duties, characteristics of profession, relationships; works that emphasize technology of operations performed by allied health personnel, e.g., works that emphasize techniques used by allied health personnel with respect to gunshot wounds 617.1450233
> Class works that emphasize a specific technique used by allied health personnel with the technique, e.g., diagnosis by allied health personnel 075, diagnosis by allied health personnel with respect to gunshot wounds 617.145075

02332   Physician assistants

024   Domestic medicine

> *For first aid, see notation 0262 from this table*

026   Emergencies

0262   First aid

027   Experimental medicine

028   Intensive care

03   Rehabilitation

> Including self-help devices for people with disabilities
> Class rehabilitative therapy in notation 06 from this table

04   Special classes of diseases

> Limited to the classes named below

042   Genetic diseases (Hereditary diseases)

617   Surgery, regional medicine, dentistry, ophthalmology, otology, audiology

0421–0423	Surgical complications, preoperative, intraoperative, postoperative care, special topics, rehabilitation
	Add to 042 the numbers following 0 in notation 01–03 from table under 617, e.g., experimental medicine for genetic diseases 04227
0425–0428	Preventive measures, surgery, therapy, pathology, psychosomatic medicine
	Add to 042 the numbers following 0 in notation 05–08 from table under 617, e.g., diagnosis of genetic diseases 04275
043	Congenital diseases
	Add to 043 the numbers following 042 in notation 0421–0428 from table under 617, e.g., experimental medicine for congenital diseases 04327
	Class congenital diseases of genetic origin in notation 042 from this table
044	Injuries and wounds
	Including results of injuries and wounds
	Class here trauma
	Add to 044 the numbers following 042 in notation 0421–0428 from table under 617, e.g., experimental medicine for injuries 04427
	Subdivisions are added for either or both topics in heading
	See also 01 for surgical shock
>05–08	Preventive measures, surgery, therapy, pathology, psychosomatic medicine
	Class preventive measures, surgery, pathology, psychosomatic medicine applied to special classes of diseases in notation 04 from this table; class comprehensive works on prevention, therapy, etiology of a specific disease or kind of disease if all related to a specific kind of therapy in notation 061–069 from this table, e.g., diet therapy 0654; class comprehensive works in 617, without adding from this table
05	Preventive measures and surgery
052	Preventive measures
	By individuals and by medical personnel
	Class public measures for preventing specific diseases in 614.5; class comprehensive works on prevention in 613. Class a specific kind of therapy used for prevention with the kind of therapy in notation 061–069 from this table, e.g., drug therapy 061
059	Surgery
	Limited to operative surgery
	Including surgery utilizing specific instruments or techniques, e.g., catheterization, cryosurgery, microsurgery, radiosurgery
	Class laser microsurgery in notation 0598 from this table; class nonoperative physical procedures in notation 06 from this table
	For surgical complications; preoperative, intraoperative, postoperative care, see notation 01 from this table
0592	Cosmetic and restorative plastic surgery, transplantation of tissue and organs, implantation of artificial organs
	Including implantation and removal of prostheses, other medical devices
0597	Endoscopic surgery

617   Surgery, regional medicine, dentistry, ophthalmology, otology, audiology

0598		Laser surgery

               Including laser coagulation
               Class here laser microsurgery

06   Therapy

      Class here rehabilitative therapy

      Class comprehensive works on rehabilitative therapy and training for people with a specific disease or kind of disease in notation 03 from this table; class comprehensive works on prevention, therapy, etiology of a specific disease or kind of disease if all related to a specific kind of therapy in notation 061–069 from this table, e.g., diet therapy 0654

      For surgery, see notation 059 from this table

      See Manual at 617: Add table: 06

060724   Experimental research

         Class here clinical trials

         Class clinical trials of a specific kind of therapy with the kind of therapy, plus notation 0724 from Table 1, e.g., clinical drug trials 0610724

>061–069   Specific therapies

      Class here specific kinds of therapy used for prevention; comprehensive works on prevention, therapy, etiology if these all relate to a specific kind of therapy, e.g., nutritional aspects of a disease and diet therapy 0654

061   Drug therapy

0610724   Experimental research

         Class here clinical drug trials

062–069   Other therapies

      Add to 06 the numbers following 615.8 in 615.82–615.89, e.g., X-ray therapy 06422, rehabilitative activity therapies 06515

07   Pathology

071   Etiology

      Including effects of poisons on specific systems and organs as cause of disease

      Class social factors contributing to spread of a disease in 362.19; class comprehensive works on medical toxicology in 615.9

075–079   Diagnosis, prognosis, death, immunity

      Add to 07 the numbers following 616.07 in 616.075–616.079, e.g., physical diagnosis 0754

08   Psychosomatic medicine

09   History, geographic treatment, biography

0901–0905   Historical periods

      Add to 09 the numbers following —090 in notation 0901–0905 from Table 1, e.g., the subject in late 20th century 09045

091–099   Geographic treatment and biography

      Add to 09 notation 1–9 from Table 2, e.g., the subject in India 0954

Class comprehensive works on minor surgery in 617.024; class comprehensive works on emergency surgery in 617.026; class comprehensive works on surgery by instrument and technique in 617.05; class comprehensive works on surgical pathology in 617.07; class comprehensive works on operative surgery and special fields of surgery in 617.9

For surgical treatment of tumors, see 616.993–616.994

617   Surgery, regional medicine, dentistry, ophthalmology, otology, audiology

See Manual at 618.92097 vs. 617; also at 618.977 vs. 617

>   617.001–617.008   Standard subdivisions of surgery

       Class comprehensive works in 617

.001   Philosophy and theory of surgery

.002   Miscellany of surgery

[.002 3]   Surgery as a profession, occupation, hobby

       Do not use; class in 617.023

[.002 8]   Auxiliary techniques and procedures; apparatus, equipment, materials

       Do not use; class in 617.9

[.002 87]   Testing and measurement

       Do not use; class in 617.075

.003–.007   Standard subdivisions of surgery

.008   Surgery for groups of people

.008 3   Young people

       Do not use for surgery for infants and children up to puberty; class in 617.98

.008 35   Young people twelve to twenty

       Do not use for comprehensive works on surgery for young people twelve to twenty who have not reached puberty; class in 617.98

       Class here adolescent surgery

.008 4   People in specific stages of adulthood

[.008 46]   People in late adulthood

       Do not use; class in 617.97

.008 8   Occupational and religious groups

[.008 835 5]   Military personnel

       Do not use; class in 617.99

[.009]   History, geographic treatment, biography of surgery

       Do not use; class in 617.09

>   617.02–617.09   General topics of surgery; history, geographic treatment, biography of surgery

       Class comprehensive works in 617

.02	Special topics of surgery
.023	Personnel

.023 1   Surgical nurses

> Class here general surgical nursing, general works that emphasize technology of operations performed by surgical nurses; nature of duties, characteristics of profession, relationships

> Class works that emphasize a specific technique used by surgical nurses with the technique, e.g., physical diagnosis by surgical nurses 617.0754

.023 2   Surgeons

> Class here nature of duties, characteristics of profession, relationships

> Do not use for general works on technology of operations that surgeons perform; class in 617

> Class works that emphasize a specific technique used by surgeons with the technique, e.g., physical diagnosis by surgeons 617.0754

.023 3   Surgical allied health personnel

> Class here nature of duties, characteristics of profession, relationships of surgical technicians and assistants; general works that emphasize technology of operations performed by surgical technicians and assistants

> Class works that emphasize a specific technique used by surgical technicians and assistants with the technique, e.g., techniques of sterilization for surgery by surgical assistants 617.9101

.023 32   Surgical physician assistants

> Class here nature of duties, characteristics of profession, relationships; general works that emphasize technology of operations performed by surgical physician assistants

> Class works that emphasize a specific technique used by surgical physician assistants with the technique, e.g., physical diagnosis by surgical physician assistants 617.0754

.024	Minor surgery

> Class here outpatient surgery

.026	Emergency surgery
.03	Rehabilitation

> Class here comprehensive works on rehabilitation

> Class rehabilitative therapy in 617.06. Class rehabilitation from a specific disease or injury with the disease or injury in 616–618, plus notation 03 from table under 616.1–616.9, notation 03 from table under 617, or notation 03 from table under 618.1–618.8, e.g., rehabilitation for patients with heart disease 616.1203

.033   **Self-help devices for people with disabilities**

> Including wheelchairs

> *For orthopedic self-help devices for people with disabilities, see 617.9*

.05   **Surgery utilizing specific instruments and techniques or specific groups of instruments and techniques**

> Including catheterization, cryosurgery, microsurgery; geriatric surgery, pediatric surgery, or military surgery utilizing a specific instrument or technique not provided in 617.91–617.96

> Class radiosurgery in 617.481059

.057   **Endoscopic surgery**

> Class comprehensive works on endoscopy in 616.07545

.058   **Laser surgery**

> Including laser coagulation

> Class here laser microsurgery

.06   **Nonsurgical therapy**

> Class here rehabilitative therapy

> Add to base number 617.06 the numbers following 615.8 in 615.82–615.89, e.g., X-ray therapy 617.06422, rehabilitative activity therapies in 617.06515

> Class comprehensive works on rehabilitative therapy and training in 617.03

.07   **Pathology**

> Add to base number 617.07 the numbers following 616.07 in 616.071–616.079, e.g., physical diagnosis 617.0754

.075   **Diagnosis and prognosis**

> Number built according to instructions under 617.07

> Class comprehensive works on a diagnostic technique used in general medicine, including techniques that involve minor surgery, with the technique in 616.075, e.g., biopsy 616.0758

.09   **History, geographic treatment, biography of surgery**

.090 1–.090 5   Historical periods

> Add to base number 617.090 the numbers following —090 in notation 0901–0905 from Table 1, e.g., history of surgery in late 20th century 617.09045

.091–.099   Geographic treatment and biography

> Add to base number 617.09 notation 1–9 from Table 2, e.g., collected biographies of surgeons 617.0922

.1   **Injuries and wounds**

Standard subdivisions are added for either or both topics in heading

Class here traumatology

Class frostbite in 616.58; class heat stress disorders in 616.989; class motion sickness in 616.9892; class results of injuries and wounds in 617.2

> *For injuries and wounds of a specific system, region, or organ, see the system, region, or organ in 617.4–617.5, plus notation 044 from table under 617, e.g., thoracic injuries 617.54044*

.100 1–.100 9   Standard subdivisions

.102   Special topics of injuries and wounds

.102 6   Emergencies

.102 62   First aid

> *For first aid for a specific type of injury or wound, see the type, plus notation 0262 from table under 617, e.g., first aid for athletic injuries 617.1027, first aid for gunshot wounds 617.1450262*

.102 7   Athletic and dance injuries

Standard subdivisions are added for athletic and dance injuries together, for athletic injuries alone

Class here sports medicine

Class a specific branch of sports medicine with the branch, e.g., promotion of health of athletes 613.711

.102 75   Dance injuries

.102 76–.102 79   Injuries associated with specific kinds of sports

Add to base number 617.1027 the numbers following 79 in 796–799, e.g., skiing injuries 617.1027693

.102 8   Crash injuries

Injuries resulting from transportation accidents

.103   Rehabilitation

Including self-help devices for people with disabilities

Class rehabilitative therapy in 617.106

.106   Nonsurgical therapy

Class here rehabilitative therapy

Add to base number 617.106 the numbers following 615.8 in 615.82–615.89, e.g., therapeutic massage 617.10622, rehabilitative activity therapies 617.106515

Class comprehensive works on rehabilitative therapy and training in 617.103

.107   Pathology

> Add to base number 617.107 the numbers following 616.07 in 616.071–616.079, e.g., physical diagnosis 617.10754

.11   *Burns and scalds

> Subdivisions are added for either or both topics in heading

> Class burns and scalds resulting from injuries from electricity in 617.12

.12   *Injuries from electricity

.13   *Abrasions, contusions, lacerations

> Subdivisions are added for any or all topics in heading

.14   *Penetrating wounds

.143   *Incisions and punctures

> Class here needlestick injuries, stab wounds

> Subdivisions are added for either or both topics in heading

.145   *Gunshot wounds

.15   Fractures

> Add to base number 617.15 the numbers following 611.71 in 611.711–611.718, e.g., fracture of femur 617.158

.16   *Dislocations

.17   *Sprains and strains

> Subdivisions are added for either or both topics in heading

.172   *Cumulative trauma disorders

> Variant names: overuse injuries, repetitive strain injuries

> > *For a specific cumulative trauma disorder, see the disorder, e.g., carpal tunnel syndrome 616.856*

.18   *Asphyxia

> Including drowning, near drowning

.19   *Blast injuries

> > *For a specific kind of blast injuries, see the kind of injury, e.g., fractures 617.15*

.2   Results of injuries and wounds

> Standard subdivisions are added for either or both topics in heading

> > *For results of injuries and wounds of a specific system, region, or organ, see the system, region, or organ in 617.4–617.5, plus notation 044 from table under 617, e.g., results of thoracic injuries 617.54044*

> > *See also 617.103 for rehabilitation; also 617.106 for rehabilitative therapy*

---

*Add as instructed under 617

.21   Traumatic and surgical shock

> Standard subdivisions are added for either or both topics in heading

> Class comprehensive medical works on shock in 616.0475

.22   Fever, infections, inflammation

> *See also 617.9195 for fever, infections, inflammation as surgical complications*

> **617.4–617.5 Surgery by systems and regions**

> Class here injuries and wounds of specific systems, regions, organs; surgery of specific organs

> Class comprehensive works in 617

.4   **Surgery by systems**

> *For respiratory system, see 617.54*

> *See Manual at 612.1–612.8; also at 616 vs. 617.4*

.41   †Cardiovascular system

.412   †Heart

> Class implantation of heart pacers in 617.4120592; class functioning of heart pacers in 617.4120645

.413   †Arteries

> Class here comprehensive works on surgery of blood vessels (vascular surgery)

> Class surgery of blood vessels in a specific system or organ with the system or organ, e.g., cerebrovascular surgery 617.481

> *For veins, see 617.414; for capillaries, see 617.415*

.414   †Veins

.415   †Capillaries

.43   †Digestive system

> Including surgical treatment of morbid obesity

> *For surgery of specific organs of digestive system, see 617.5*

> *See also 617.952 for lipectomy*

.44   †Blood-forming, lymphatic, glandular systems

> Class here endocrine system

> *For surgery of a specific gland, see the gland, e.g., thyroid gland 617.539*

---

†Add as instructed under 617, except use 059 by itself only for surgery utilizing specific instruments or techniques and do not use 06 by itself

.441	†Bone marrow
.46	†Urogenital system

           For gynecologic and obstetrical surgery, see 618

.461	†Kidneys, adrenal glands, ureters

Class here comprehensive works on surgery of urinary organs

Subdivisions are added for kidneys, adrenal glands, ureters together; for kidneys alone

Class hemodialysis, peritoneal dialysis in 617.461059

For bladder and urethra, see 617.462

.462	†Bladder and urethra
.463	†Male genital organs

Including circumcision; surgical methods of birth control in males, vasectomy

.47	†Musculoskeletal system, integument

Class here orthopedic surgery

Subdivisions are added for musculoskeletal system, integument together; for musculoskeletal system alone

Class orthopedic regional surgery in 617.5

For amputations, see 617.58059

.471	†Bones

Class chronic diseases of skeletal system in 616.71; class spine surgery involving both spinal column and spinal cord in 617.56059

For skull, see 617.514; for jaws, see 617.522

See also 617.441 for bone marrow

.471 044	Injuries and wounds

Number built according to instructions under 617

For fractures, see 617.15

.472	†Joints

For jaws, see 617.522; for joints of extremities, see 617.58

.472 044	Injuries and wounds

Number built according to instructions under 617

For dislocations, see 617.16

.473	†Muscles

---

†Add as instructed under 617, except use 059 by itself only for surgery utilizing specific instruments or techniques and do not use 06 by itself

.473 044	Injuries and wounds
	Number built according to instructions under 617
	For sprains and strains, see 617.17
.474	†Tendons
.475	†Bursae
.477	†Integument
	Including surgery of nails
	Class here surgery of skin
.477 044	Injuries and wounds
	Number built according to instructions under 617
	For abrasions, see 617.13
.477 9	†Hair
	Including removal
.48	†Nervous system
	Class here neurosurgery
	For ophthalmologic surgery, see 617.71; for otologic surgery, see 617.8059
.481	†Brain
	Including psychosurgery
.481 03	Rehabilitation
	Number built according to instructions under 617
	Class rehabilitation of brain-injured patients in 617.4810443
.482	†Spinal cord
	Including surgical treatment of spina bifida
	Class surgery involving both spinal column and spinal cord in 617.56059
.483	†Nerves
	Class surgery of nerves of a specific system or organ with the system or organ, e.g., neuromuscular surgery 617.473

---

†Add as instructed under 617, except use 059 by itself only for surgery utilizing specific instruments or techniques and do not use 06 by itself

.5	**Regional medicine**

Class here regional surgery; orthopedic regional medicine, orthopedic regional surgery

Class nonsurgical medicine of specific systems or organs in specific regions in 616; except as provided for below, class surgery of a specific system in a specific region in 617.4

See also 617.15 for fractures

See Manual at 617.5

.508 3	Young people

Do not use for nonsurgical regional medicine of infants and children up to puberty, comprehensive works on child and adolescent medicine; class in 618.920975

.508 35	Young people twelve to twenty

Do not use for nonsurgical regional medicine of young people twelve to twenty who have not reached puberty; class in 618.920975

Class here comprehensive works on nonsurgical regional medicine of adolescents

.508 4	People in specific stages of adulthood
.508 46	People in late adulthood

Do not use for nonsurgical regional medicine; class in 618.9775

.51	*Head

Class here otolaryngology, otorhinolaryngology, comprehensive works on diseases of ears, nose, throat

For face, see 617.52; for throat, see 617.531; for eyes, see 617.7; for ears, see 617.8

.514	†Skull

Limited to surgery

Class here skull base

.52	*Face

Class eyes in 617.7

.522	*Oral region

Including lips, tongue, jaws, parotid gland

Class nonsurgical works on mouth as a digestive organ in 616.31

For teeth, see 617.6

---

*Add as instructed under 617
†Add as instructed under 617, except use 059 by itself only for surgery utilizing specific instruments or techniques and do not use 06 by itself

.522 059		Surgery

Number built according to instructions under 617

Class comprehensive works on kinds of oral surgery commonly performed by dentists in 617.605. Class a specific kind of oral surgery performed by dentists with the kind in 617.6, e.g., periodontal surgery 617.632059, tooth extraction 617.66

.522 5	*Palate
.523	*Nose

Class here comprehensive works on nose and throat

Class comprehensive works on diseases of ears, nose, throat in 617.51

For throat, see 617.531

.53	*Neck
.531	*Throat

For pharynx, see 617.532; for larynx and trachea, see 617.533

.532	†Pharynx

Limited to surgery

Including tonsils

.533	†Larynx and trachea

Limited to surgery

Including epiglottis, vocal cords

.539	†Thyroid and parathyroid glands

Limited to surgery

.54	*Thorax (Chest) and respiratory system

Regional medicine and surgery of thorax; surgery of respiratory system

Subdivisions are added for thorax and respiratory system together, for thorax alone

For surgery of heart, see 617.412; for surgery of nose, see 617.523; for surgery of larynx and trachea, see 617.533

.542	†Lungs

Limited to surgery

.543	†Pleura

Limited to surgery

---

*Add as instructed under 617

†Add as instructed under 617, except use 059 by itself only for surgery utilizing specific instruments or techniques and do not use 06 by itself

.544	†Bronchi
	Limited to surgery
.545	†Mediastinum
	Limited to surgery
.546	†Thymus gland
	Limited to surgery
.547	†Diaphragm
	Limited to surgery
.548	†Esophagus
	Limited to surgery
.549	†Male breast
	Limited to surgery
	Class comprehensive works on surgery of breast in 618.19059
.55	*Abdominal and pelvic cavities
	For urogenital system, see 617.46
.551	†Spleen
	Limited to surgery
.553	†Stomach
	Limited to surgery
	Including pylorus
.554	†Intestine
	Limited to surgery
.554 1	†Small intestine
	Limited to surgery
	Including duodenum, jejunum, ileum
.554 5	†Cecum, vermiform appendix
	Limited to surgery
	Subdivisions are added for either or both topics in heading

*Add as instructed under 617
†Add as instructed under 617, except use 059 by itself only for surgery utilizing specific instruments
 or techniques and do not use 06 by itself

.554 7   †Large intestine

         Limited to surgery

         Including sigmoid colon

         Class here colon

         For cecum and vermiform appendix, see 617.5545; for rectum, see 617.555

.555   †Rectum, anus, perineum

         Limited to surgery

         Subdivisions are added for rectum, anus, perineum together; for rectum alone

.556   †Biliary tract and liver

         Limited to surgery

         Subdivisions are added for biliary tract and liver together, for biliary tract alone

.556 2   †Liver

         Limited to surgery

.556 5   †Gallbladder

         Limited to surgery

.556 7   †Bile ducts

         Limited to surgery

.557   †Pancreas and islands of Langerhans

         Limited to surgery

         Subdivisions are added for pancreas and islands of Langerhans together, for pancreas alone

.558   †Peritoneum

         Limited to surgery

         Including mesentery, omentum

.559   *Hernias in abdominal region

         Including hiatal hernia

         Class here inguinal hernia

.56   *Back

         Class shoulders in 617.572; class hips in 617.581

.564   *Backache

---

*Add as instructed under 617

†Add as instructed under 617, except use 059 by itself only for surgery utilizing specific instruments or techniques and do not use 06 by itself

.57	***Upper extremities**

Class here surgery of joints of upper extremities

Class comprehensive works on extremities in 617.58; class comprehensive works on amputations, on surgery of joints of extremities in 617.58059

.572	***Shoulders**
.574	***Arms, elbows, wrists**

Subdivisions are added for arms, elbows, wrists together; for arms alone

Class carpal tunnel syndrome in 616.856

.575	***Hands**

Class carpal tunnel syndrome in 616.856

.58	***Lower extremities**

Class here legs; comprehensive works on extremities, on paraplegia

Class works about "legs" when used to mean segment of lower limb between knee and ankle in 617.584

For neurological aspects of paraplegia, see 616.842; for upper extremities, see 617.57

See also 616.72 for nonsurgical medical aspects of joints

.580 59	Surgery

Number built according to instructions under 617

Class here comprehensive works on amputations, on surgery of joints of extremities

For amputations of upper extremities, surgery of joints of upper extremities, see 617.57059. For surgery of a specific joint, see the joint, e.g., surgery of knees 617.582059

.581	***Hips**
.582	***Knees and thighs**

Subdivisions are added for knees and thighs together, for knees alone

.584	***Legs between knee and ankle, ankles**
.585	***Feet**

Class here podiatry

.6	***Dentistry**
.600 83	Young people

Do not use for dentistry for infants and children up to puberty; class in 617.645

---

*Add as instructed under 617

.600 835   Young people twelve to twenty

> Do not use for dentistry for young people twelve to twenty who have not reached puberty; class in 617.645

> Class here adolescent dentistry

.601   Oral hygiene and preventive dentistry

> Do not use for surgical complications, preoperative, intraoperative, postoperative care; class in 617.605

> Standard subdivisions are added for either or both topics in heading

> Class here dental hygiene

.605   Surgery

> Number built according to instructions under 617

> Do not use for preventive measures; class in 617.601

> Including surgical complications; preoperative, intraoperative, postoperative care

>> *For a specific kind of dental surgery, see the kind, e.g., extractions 617.66, dental implantation 617.693*

[.605 9]   Surgery

> Do not use; class in 617.605

.63   *Dental diseases

> Class here diseases of teeth

>> *For tumors of teeth and surrounding tissues, see 616.994314; for tuberculosis of teeth and surrounding tissues, see 616.995314*

.632   *Diseases of gums and tooth sockets

> Including gingivitis, periapical abscesses, periodontitis

> Class here periodontics

> Subdivisions are added for either or both topics in heading

.634   *Diseases of tooth tissues

> Including diseases of cementum, dentin, enamel

>> *For caries, see 617.67*

.634 2   *Diseases of dental pulp

> Class here endodontics

.64   Orthodontics and pediatric dentistry

.643   *Orthodontics

*Add as instructed under 617

.645   *Pediatric dentistry

Class here comprehensive works on pediatric and adolescent dentistry

For adolescent dentistry, see 617.600835. For a specific aspect of pediatric dentistry, see the aspect, plus notation 0083 from table under 617, e.g., periodontics for children 617.6320083

.66   *Extraction

Class here exodontics

.67   *Caries (Cavities)

.672   Preparation and treatment

Standard subdivisions are added for either or both topics in heading

.675   Fillings and inlays

Standard subdivisions are added for either or both topics in heading

Including metallic and ceramic fillings and inlays

.69   Prosthodontics

Class here dental restoration

For fillings and inlays, see 617.675

.690 284   Apparatus and equipment

Do not use for materials; class in 617.695

.692   Dentures, bridges, crowns

Standard subdivisions are added for dentures, bridges, crowns; for dentures alone

For implant-supported dentures, see 617.693

.692 2   Crowns

.693   Dental implantation

Class here dental implants, implant-supported dentures

.695   Materials

Class here dental materials used for dental restoration

For materials used as fillings and inlays, see 617.675

.7   ***Ophthalmology**

Class here eye diseases

For tumors of eyes, see 616.99484; for tuberculosis of eyes, see 616.99584

[.704 4]   Injuries and wounds

Do not use; class in 617.713

---

*Add as instructed under 617

[.705 9]	Surgery

Do not use; class in 617.71

[.707]	Pathology

Do not use; class in 617.71

.71	Pathology and surgery of eyes

Class surgical complications; preoperative, intraoperative, postoperative care in 617.701. Class pathology and surgery of a specific disease or part of eyes with the disease or part, e.g., diagnosis of glaucoma 617.741075

.712	*Blindness and partial blindness

Subdivisions are added for either or both topics in heading

See also 617.75 for disorders of refraction and accommodation, color vision defects

.713	*Injuries and wounds

Class here trauma

Subdivisions are added for either or both topics in heading

.715	Diagnosis and prognosis

Add to base number 617.715 the numbers following 616.075 in 616.0751–616.0759, e.g., physical diagnosis 617.7154
Subdivisions are added for diagnosis and prognosis together, for diagnosis alone

.719	*Diseases of corneas and scleras

Subdivisions are added for corneas and scleras together, for corneas alone

See also 362.1783 for eye banks

.72	*Diseases of uveas

Including diseases of choroids, ciliary bodies, irises

.73	*Diseases of optic nerves, of retinas
.732	*Diseases of optic nerves

Class diseases of ocular neuromuscular mechanism in 617.762

.735	*Diseases of retinas
.74	*Diseases of eyeballs

For diseases of corneas and scleras, see 617.719; for diseases of uveas, see 617.72; for diseases of retinas, see 617.735

.741	*Glaucoma
.742	*Diseases of crystalline lenses

Class here cataracts

*Add as instructed under 617

.742 059 2	Cosmetic and restorative plastic surgery, transplantation of tissue and organs, implantation of artificial organs
	Number built according to instructions under 617
	Do not use for implantation of intraocular lenses; class in 617.7524
.746	*Diseases of vitreous bodies
.75	Disorders of refraction and accommodation, color vision defects
	Class here optometry
	See also 617.712 for blindness and partial blindness
.750 3	Rehabilitation
	Number built according to instructions under 617
	Do not use for eyeglasses, contact lenses; class in 617.752
.752	Eyeglasses, contact lenses, intraocular lenses
	Class here opticianry
.752 2	Eyeglasses
.752 3	Contact lenses
.752 4	Intraocular lenses
	Including implantation of intraocular lenses
.755	Disorders of refraction and accommodation
	Including astigmatism, hyperopia, myopia, presbyopia
	For correction of disorders of refraction or accommodation by eyeglasses, contact lenses, intraocular lenses, see 617.752; for aniseikonia, see 617.758. For surgical correction of disorders of refraction or accommodation, see the specific part of the eye upon which surgery is done, e.g., surgery on corneas to correct myopia 617.719059
.758	Aniseikonia
.759	Color vision defects
.76	Diseases of ocular neuromuscular mechanism and lacrimal apparatus
.762	*Diseases of ocular neuromuscular mechanism
	Including diplopia, strabismus
	Class here ocular motility disorders, orthoptics
.764	*Diseases of lacrimal apparatus
	For Sjogren's syndrome, see 616.775
.77	Diseases of eyelids and conjunctivas

*Add as instructed under 617

.771	*Diseases of eyelids
.772	*Trachoma
.773	*Conjunctivitis

> For trachoma, see 617.772

| .78 | *Diseases of orbits |
| .79 | Artificial eyes |

> Class intraocular lenses in 617.7524; class orbital implants in 617.780592

.8   *Otology and audiology

Class here deafness, partial hearing loss

Subdivisions are added for either or both topics in heading

> For tumors of ears, see 616.99485; for tuberculosis of ears, see 616.99585

| .803 | Rehabilitation |

Number built according to instructions under 617

Do not use for hearing aids; class in 617.89

| .81 | *Diseases of external ears |

> For diseases of auricles, see 617.82; for diseases of auditory canals, see 617.83

.82	*Diseases of auricles
.83	*Diseases of auditory canals
.84	*Diseases of middle ears

> For diseases of tympanic membranes, see 617.85; for diseases of eustachian tubes, see 617.86; for diseases of mastoid processes, see 617.87

.842	*Diseases of ossicles
.85	*Diseases of tympanic membranes
.86	*Diseases of eustachian tubes
.87	*Diseases of mastoid processes
.88	*Diseases of internal ears and of aural nervous system
.882	*Diseases of internal ears

Including Meniere's disease; semicircular canals, vestibules

Class here diseases of labyrinths

Class vertigo as a symptom of neurological disease in 616.841; class motion sickness in 616.9892

| .882 2 | *Diseases of cochleas |

*Add as instructed under 617

.886   *Diseases of aural nervous system

            Including sensorineural hearing loss

.89   Correction of impaired hearing

            Including hearing aids

> *For surgical methods of correction that are limited to a specific part of the hearing apparatus, see the part in 617.81–617.88, plus notation 059 from table under 617, e.g., cochlear implants 617.88220592; for nonsurgical methods of correction that are limited to a specific part of the hearing apparatus, see the part in 617.81–617.88, plus notation 06 from table under 617, e.g., drug therapy for diseases of middle ears 617.84061*

.9   **Operative surgery and special fields of surgery**

> Class here orthopedic equipment; auxiliary techniques and procedures; apparatus, equipment, materials; comprehensive works on surgical equipment, on prostheses

> Class comprehensive works on orthopedic and nonorthopedic self-help devices for people with disabilities in 617.033

> *For a specific piece of equipment or prosthesis, see the use of the equipment or prosthesis, e.g., dentures 617.692*

> 617.91–617.96   Surgical techniques, procedures, apparatus, equipment, materials

> Class comprehensive works in 617.9. Except for anesthesiology, class techniques, procedures, apparatus, equipment, materials of surgery of a specific system, organ, or region with the surgical therapy of the system, organ, or region, e.g., preoperative care in neck surgery 617.53059

.91   Operative surgery

> *For anesthesiology, see 617.96*

.910 01   Philosophy and theory

.910 02   Miscellany

[.910 028]   Auxiliary techniques and procedures; apparatus, equipment, materials

            Do not use; class in 617.9178

.910 03–.910 09   Standard subdivisions

.910 1   Asepsis and antisepsis

            Standard subdivisions are added for either or both topics in heading

            Class here sterilization

.917   Operating rooms

*Add as instructed under 617

.917 8   Surgical instruments, apparatus, equipment, materials

For surgical dressings, see 617.93

.919   Surgical complications; preoperative, intraoperative, postoperative care

Including complicating preconditions, e.g., heart problems

For surgical complications associated with anesthesia, see 617.96041

.919 2   Preoperative care

.919 5   Postoperative care and complications

Standard subdivisions are added for either or both topics in heading

Including surgical infections

For surgical shock, see 617.21

.93   Surgical dressings

.95   Cosmetic and restorative plastic surgery, transplantation of tissue and organs, implantation of artificial organs

.952   Cosmetic and restorative plastic surgery

Standard subdivisions are added for either or both topics in heading

Class transplantation of tissue for cosmetic and restorative purposes in 617.954; class implantation of artificial tissue for cosmetic and restorative purposes in 617.956

For cosmetic and restorative plastic surgery of a specific system, region, or organ, see the system, region, or organ in 617.4–617.5, plus notation 0592 from table under 617, e.g., plastic surgery of face 617.520592; for cosmetic and restorative plastic surgery in gynecologic and obstetrical surgery, see the tissue or organ in 618, plus notation 0592 from table under 618.1–618.8, e.g., mammaplasty 618.190592

.954   Transplantation of tissue and organs

Including transplantation of fetal tissue

Class blood and blood plasma transfusion in 615.39; class transplantation of fetal tissue in experimental medicine in 616.027

For transplantation of tissue of a specific system, region, or organ; or transplantation of a specific organ, see the system, region, or organ in 617.4–617.5, plus notation 0592 from table under 617, e.g., skin transplantation 617.4770592, heart transplantation 617.4120592; for transplantation of tissue of a specific system, region, or organ; or transplantation of a specific organ in gynecological or obstetrical surgery, see the system, region, or organ in 618, plus notation 0592 from table under 618.1–618.8, e.g., transplantation of ovarian tissue 618.110592

See also 362.1783 for tissue and organ banks; also 618.1780599 for gamete, zygote, embryo transfer for purpose of human reproduction

.956   **Implantation of artificial tissue and organs**

         Including implantation and removal of prostheses, other medical devices

> *For implantation of artificial tissue of a specific system, region, or organ; or implantation of an artificial substitute, artificial part, or assistive device for a specific organ, see the system, region, or organ in 617.4–617.5, plus notation 0592 from table under 617, e.g., implantation of bone substitutes 617.4710592, implantation of heart-assist devices 617.4120592; for implantation of artificial tissue, artificial organs, or medical devices in gynecologic and obstetrical surgery, see the tissue or organ in 618, plus notation 0592 from table under 618.1–618.8, e.g., breast implants 618.190592*

.96   **Anesthesiology**

         Class acupuncture anesthesia in 615.892

.960 4   Special topics of anesthesiology

.960 41   Complications

.960 42   Emergencies

         Class resuscitation in 616.025

>   **617.962–617.966   Types of anesthesia**

         Class anesthesiology regardless of type for specific kinds of surgery in 617.967; class comprehensive works in 617.96

.962   **General anesthesia**

         Including inhalation, intravenous, rectal anesthesias

.964   **Regional anesthesia**

         Including epidural, spinal anesthesias

         Class here conduction anesthesia

> *For local anesthesia, see 617.966*

.966   **Local anesthesia**

.967   **Anesthesiology for specific kinds of surgery**

         General, regional, local anesthesia

         Add to base number 617.967 the numbers following 617 in 617.1–617.9, e.g., dental anesthesia 617.9676

> *For anesthesiology for gynecology and obstetrics, see 617.968*

.968   **Anesthesiology for gynecology and obstetrics**

.968 1   Gynecology

.968 2   Obstetrics

> 617.97–617.99 Special fields of surgery

Class comprehensive works in 617.9

For surgery of tumors and cancers, see 616.993–616.994; for gynecologic surgery, see 618.1059. For surgery of a specific organ, system, region, or disorder, see the organ, system, region, or disorder in 617, e.g., brain surgery in children 617.4810083, abdominal surgery in children 617.55059083

.97 *Geriatric surgery

[.970 59] Operative surgery

Do not use for comprehensive works; class in 617.97; do not use for comprehensive works on geriatric surgery utilizing a specific instrument or technique not provided in 617.91–617.96; class in 617.05, e.g., cryosurgery on people in late adulthood 617.05, laser surgery on people in late adulthood 617.0580846; do not use for a specific surgical technique provided in 617.91–617.96; class in 617.91–617.96, e.g., anesthesiology of people in late adulthood 617.960846

[.970 592] Cosmetic and restorative plastic surgery, transplantation of tissue and organs, implantation of artificial organs

Do not use; class in 617.950846

.98 *Pediatric surgery

Class here comprehensive works on pediatric and adolescent surgery

For adolescent surgery, see 617.00835

[.980 59] Operative surgery

Do not use for comprehensive works; class in 617.98; do not use for comprehensive works on pediatric surgery utilizing a specific instrument or technique not provided in 617.91–617.96; class in 617.05, e.g., cryosurgery on children 617.05, laser surgery on children 617.058083; do not use for a specific surgical technique provided in 617.91–617.96; class in 617.91–617.96, e.g., anesthesiology of children 617.96083

[.980 592] Cosmetic and restorative plastic surgery, transplantation of tissue and organs, implantation of artificial organs

Do not use; class in 617.95083

.99 *Military surgery

*Add as instructed under 617

[.990 59]	Operative surgery

Do not use for comprehensive works; class in 617.99; do not use for comprehensive works on military surgery utilizing a specific instrument or technique not provided in 617.91–617.96; class in 617.05, e.g., cryosurgery on military personnel 617.05, laser surgery on military personnel 617.058088355; do not use for a specific surgical technique provided in 617.91–617.96; class in 617.91–617.96, e.g., military anesthesiology 617.96088355

[.990 592]	Cosmetic and restorative plastic surgery, transplantation of tissue and organs, implantation of artificial organs

Do not use; class in 617.95088355

618   Gynecology, obstetrics, pediatrics, geriatrics

Standard subdivisions are added for gynecology, obstetrics, pediatrics, geriatrics together; for gynecology and obstetrics together

.01	Philosophy and theory
.02	Miscellany
[.028 7]	Testing and measurement

Do not use; class in 618.0475

.03	Dictionaries, encyclopedias, concordances
.04	Special topics of gynecology, obstetrics, pediatrics, geriatrics

Add to base number 618.04 the numbers following 0 in notation 01–09 from table under 618.1–618.8, e.g., drug therapy 618.0461; however, for gynecology, obstetrics, pediatrics, geriatrics as a profession, occupation, hobby, see 618.023

.05–.07	Standard subdivisions
.08	Groups of people
.083	Young people

Do not use for infants and children up to puberty; class in 618.92098

.083 5	Young people twelve to twenty

Do not use for young people twelve to twenty who have not reached puberty; class in 618.92098

Class here adolescent gynecology and obstetrics

.084	People in specific stages of adulthood
.084 6	People in late adulthood

Do not use for patients; class in 618.978

.09	History, geographic treatment, biography

Class life with a disease in 362.198

> ### 618.1–618.8 Gynecology and obstetrics

Medical and surgical

Except where contrary instructions are given, all notes under 616.02–616.08 and in table under 616.1–616.9 are applicable here

Except for modifications shown under specific entries, add to each subdivision identified by * as follows:

001–007	Standard subdivisions
	As modified in notation 001–007 from table under 616.1–616.9
008	Groups of people
0083	Young people
	Do not use for infants and children up to puberty; class in 618.92098
00835	Young people twelve to twenty
	Do not use for young people twelve to twenty who have not reached puberty; class in 618.92098
	Class here adolescent gynecology and obstetrics
0084	People in specific stages of adulthood
00846	People in late adulthood
	Do not use for patients; class in 618.978
009	History, geographic treatment, biography
0092	Biography
	Class life with a disease in 362.198
01–03	Microbiology, special topics, rehabilitation
	Add to 0 the numbers following 0 in notation 01–03 from table under 616.1–616.9, e.g., experimental medicine 027
	Class microbiology, special topics, rehabilitation applied to special classes of diseases in notation 04 from this table
04	Special classes of diseases
	Limited to the classes named below
042	Genetic diseases (Hereditary diseases)
0421–0423	Microbiology, special topics, rehabilitation
	Add to 042 the numbers following 0 in notation 01–03 from table under 616.1–616.9, e.g., experimental medicine for genetic diseases 04227
0425–0429	Preventive measures, surgery, therapy, pathology, psychosomatic medicine, case histories
	Add to 042 the numbers following 0 in notation 05–09 from table under 618.1–618.8, e.g., therapy for genetic diseases 0426
043	Congenital diseases
	Add to 043 the numbers following 042 in notation 0421–0429 from table under 618.1–618.8, e.g., experimental medicine for congenital diseases 04327
	Class congenital diseases of genetic origin in notation 042 from this table

> **618.1–618.8 Gynecology and obstetrics**

>05–09   Preventive measures, surgery, therapy, pathology, psychosomatic medicine, case histories

> Class preventive measures, surgery, therapy, pathology, psychosomatic medicine applied to special classes of diseases in notation 04 from this table; class comprehensive works on prevention, therapy, etiology of a specific disease or kind of disease if all related to a specific kind of therapy in notation 061–069 from this table, e.g., diet therapy 0654; class comprehensive works in 618.1–618.8, without adding from this table

05   Preventive measures and surgery

052   Preventive measures

> By individuals and by medical personnel
> Class public measures preventing specific diseases in 614.5992; class comprehensive works on prevention in 613. Class a specific kind of therapy used for prevention with the kind of therapy in notation 061–069 from this table, e.g., drug therapy 061

059   Surgery

> Limited to operative surgery
> Including preoperative, intraoperative, postoperative care; surgery utilizing specific instruments or techniques, e.g., catheterization, cryosurgery, microsurgery, radiosurgery; surgical complications
> Class laser microsurgery in notation 0598 from this table; class nonoperative physical procedures in notation 06 from this table

0592   Cosmetic and restorative plastic surgery, transplantation of tissue and organs, implantation of artificial organs

> Including implantation and removal of prostheses, other medical devices

0597   Endoscopic surgery

0598   Laser surgery

> Including laser coagulation
> Class here laser microsurgery

06   Therapy

> Class here rehabilitative therapy
> Class comprehensive works on rehabilitative therapy and education for living with handicaps and disabilities in notation 03 from this table; class comprehensive works on prevention, therapy, etiology of a specific disease or kind of disease if all related to a specific kind of therapy in notation 061–069 from this table, e.g., diet therapy 0654
> *For surgery, see notation 059 from this table*

060724   Experimental research

> Class here clinical trials
> Class clinical trials of a specific kind of therapy with the kind of therapy, plus notation 0724 from Table 1, e.g., clinical drug trials 0610724

>061–069   Specific therapies

> Class here specific kinds of therapy used for prevention; comprehensive works on prevention, therapy, etiology if these all relate to a specific kind of therapy, e.g., nutritional aspects of a disease and diet therapy 0654

061   Drug therapy

>   **618.1–618.8 Gynecology and obstetrics**

     0610724   Experimental research
                                 Class here clinical drug trials

     062–069   Other therapies
                      Add to 06 the numbers following 615.8 in 615.82–615.89,
                      e.g., X-ray therapy 06422

     07   Pathology

     071   Etiology
                      Including effects of poisons on specific systems and organs
                      as cause of disease
                      Class social factors contributing to spread of a disease in
                      362.19; class comprehensive works on medical toxicology in
                      615.9

     075–079   Diagnosis, prognosis, death, immunity
                      Add to 07 the numbers following 616.07 in 616.075–616.079,
                      e.g., physical diagnosis 0754

     08   Psychosomatic medicine

     09   Case histories

        Class comprehensive works in 618

.1   ***Gynecology**

        Including endocrine gynecology, endometriosis

        Class tumors of genital system in 616.99465

        For puerperal diseases, see 618.7

        See also 616.9297 for toxic shock syndrome

.100 83   Young people

        Do not use for gynecology for infants and children up to puberty;
        class in 618.92098

.100 835   Young people twelve to twenty

        Do not use for gynecology for young people twelve to twenty
        who have not reached puberty; class in 618.92098

        Class here adolescent gynecology

.11   *Diseases of ovaries

.12   *Diseases of fallopian tubes

.14   *Diseases of uterus

        Class here diseases of uterine cervix

        See also 618.1 for endometriosis

[.140 59]   Surgery

        Do not use; class in 618.145

---

*Add as instructed under 618.1–618.8

.142	*Infections
	Including cervicitis, endometritis
	For leukorrhea, see 618.15
	See also 618.1 for endometriosis
.144	*Malformations
	Including prolapse of uterus
.145	Surgery
.145 3	Hysterectomies
.145 8	Dilatation and curettage
	See also 618.88 for surgical abortion
.15	*Diseases of vagina
	Including leukorrhea
.16	*Diseases of vulva
.17	*Functional and systemic disorders
	Class here female sexual disorders
	Class comprehensive medical works on sexual disorders in 616.69
.172	*Menstruation disturbances
	Including amenorrhea, dysmenorrhea, menorrhagia, oligomenorrhea, premenstrual syndrome (PMS)
.175	*Menopause disorders
	Class here disorders of perimenopause, of postmenopause; comprehensive works on climacteric disorders
	For male climacteric disorders, see 616.693
.178	*Infertility
	Including artificial insemination
	Class comprehensive works on male and female infertility in 616.692
.178 059	Surgery
	Number built according to instructions under 618.1–618.8
.178 059 9	Gamete, zygote, embryo transfer; fertilization in vitro
	Standard subdivisions are added for any or all topics in heading

*Add as instructed under 618.1–618.8

.178 06	Therapy

Number built according to instructions under 618.1–618.8

Class here human reproductive technology applied to female infertility

Class comprehensive works on human reproductive technology in 616.69206

For surgery, see 618.178059

.18	Birth control

Class here contraception, family planning

Class personal health aspects of birth control in 613.94; class interdisciplinary works on birth control in 363.96. Class surgical methods of birth control in females with the kind of surgery in 618.1, e.g., tubal sterilization 618.12059

For nonsurgical methods of birth control in males, see 616.65; for surgical methods of birth control in males, see 617.463

.182	Chemical methods of birth control

Including contraceptive drug implants, spermatocidal agents

Class pharmacokinetics of chemical contraceptives in 615.766

.182 2	Oral contraceptives

Class postcoital contraceptives in 618.1825

.182 5	Postcoital contraceptives

Class here morning after pills

.184	Natural family planning

Class here ovulation detection method, rhythm method

.185	Mechanical methods of birth control

Including female condoms, vaginal diaphragms

.185 2	Intrauterine devices
.19	*Diseases of breast

Class here comprehensive works on diseases of male and female breast

For diseases of male breast, see 616.49; for tumors of breast, see 616.99449; for diseases of lactation, see 618.71

.190 59	Surgery

Number built according to instructions under 618.1–618.8

Class here comprehensive works on surgery of male and female breast

For surgery of male breast, see 617.549

*Add as instructed under 618.1–618.8

.2   ***Obstetrics**

> Class here midwifery, comprehensive works on pregnancy and childbirth

> *For physiology of pregnancy and childbirth, see 612.63; for diseases, disorders, management of pregnancy, childbirth, puerperium, see 618.3–618.8*

.200 835   Young people twelve to twenty

> Class here adolescent obstetrics

[.205 2]   Preventive measures

> Do not use; class in 618.24

[.205 9]   Surgery

> Do not use; class in 618.8

.207 5   Diagnosis

> Number built according to instructions under 618.1–618.8

> Class here comprehensive works on diagnosis of diseases and complications of pregnancy, diagnosis of labor complications, diagnosis of puerperal diseases

> To be classed here a work should be broader than diagnosis of diseases and complications of pregnancy; it should include also diagnosis of labor complications (618.5) or diagnosis of puerperal diseases (618.7075)

> *For diagnosis of diseases and complications of pregnancy, see 618.3075; for diagnosis of labor complications, see 618.5; for diagnosis of puerperal diseases, see 618.7075*

.24   Prenatal care and preparation for childbirth

> Standard subdivisions are added for either or both topics in heading

.242   Dietetics and nutrition for pregnant women

> Standard subdivisions are added for either or both topics in heading

> *See also 641.56319 for cooking for pregnant women*

.244   Exercise for pregnant women

.25   *Multiple pregnancy and childbirth

> Subdivisions are added for either or both topics in heading

.29   Nonsurgical methods of abortion

> Class here use of abortifacient agents

> Class surgical abortion, comprehensive works on induced abortion in 618.88

---

*Add as instructed under 618.1–618.8

> **618.3–618.8 Diseases, disorders, management of pregnancy, childbirth, puerperium**

Class comprehensive works in 618.2

See also 618.25 for multiple pregnancy and childbirth

.3   *Diseases and complications of pregnancy

.31   *Ectopic pregnancy

Including abdominal, tubal pregnancies

.32   *Fetal disorders

Class here perinatal medicine (perinatology)

Class neonatal medicine in 618.9201; class comprehensive works on congenital diseases in 616.043

For childbirth, see 618.4

.320 75   Diagnosis

Number built according to instructions under 618.1–618.8

Class procedures to diagnose genetic diseases, e.g., amniocentesis and chorionic villi sampling, in 618.3204275

.326   Diseases of specific systems and organs

.326 1   *Diseases of cardiovascular system

.326 8   *Diseases of nervous system

.326 86   *Substance-related disorders

Effects on fetus of use of substances by mother

Including effect of tobacco use

Class here drug dependence; comprehensive works on fetal disorders and pregnancy complications associated with substance use and abuse

For pregnancy complications associated with substance use and abuse, see 618.3686

.326 861   *Alcohol-related disorders

Class here fetal alcohol syndrome

.34   *Diseases of placenta and amniotic fluid

Subdivisions are added for diseases of placenta and amniotic fluid together, for diseases of placenta alone

*Add as instructed under 618.1–618.8

.36	Pregnancy complications due to co-occurrence of pregnancy and disease in the mother

Pre-existing diseases and diseases induced by pregnancy

Including communicable diseases

.361	*Diseases of cardiovascular system
.361 3	*Diseases of blood vessels
.361 32	*Hypertension

Including eclampsia

Class here pregnancy toxemias

For puerperal eclampsia, see 618.7

.364	*Diseases of endocrine, hematopoietic, lymphatic systems

Class here diseases of glands

Subdivisions are added for diseases of endocrine, hematopoietic, lymphatic systems together; for diseases of endocrine system alone

.364 6	*Diabetes

Class here diabetes mellitus, gestational diabetes

.368	*Diseases of nervous system and mental disorders
.368 6	*Substance abuse (Drug abuse)

Including alcohol, tobacco

Class here substance use that would not be considered a problem except during pregnancy

Class comprehensive works on fetal disorders and pregnancy complications associated with maternal substance use and abuse in 618.32686

.39	Miscarriage, stillbirth, premature labor
.392	*Miscarriage and stillbirth

Subdivisions are added for either or both topics in heading

Class here perinatal death, spontaneous abortion

See also 155.937085 for psychology of bereavement

.397	*Premature labor

Class here premature birth

.4	**Childbirth**

Class here labor

Class a specific aspect not provided for here with the aspect, e.g., Cesarean section 618.86

---

*Add as instructed under 618.1–618.8

.42	Presentation
.45	Natural childbirth

.5 **Labor complications**

> Class here dystocia

.54	Uterine hemorrhage

.6 **Normal puerperium**

> Class here postnatal care

.7 ***Puerperal diseases**

> Including postpartum hemorrhage, Sheehan's syndrome

[.707 8]	Death

> Do not use; class in 618.79

.71	*Diseases of lactation
.74	*Puerperal infections

> Including infectious puerperal peritonitis, puerperal metritis, puerperal pyemia

> Class here childbed fever, puerperal septicemia

.76	*Puerperal mental disorders

> Class here postpartum depression

> Class comprehensive works on depression in 616.8527

.79	Maternal death

.8 **Obstetrical surgery**

> Class embryo transfer in 618.1780599

.82	Version and extraction
.85	Minor surgery

> Including episiotomy

.86	Cesarean section
.88	Surgical abortion

> Including embryotomy

> Class here comprehensive medical works on abortion

> Class interdisciplinary works on abortion in 362.19888

> *For nonsurgical methods of abortion, see 618.29*

> *See also 615.766 for abortifacient drugs*

*Add as instructed under 618.1–618.8

.9   **Pediatrics and geriatrics**

.92   Pediatrics

               Medicine for infants and children up to puberty

               Class here comprehensive works on child and adolescent medicine

                  For medicine for young people who have reached puberty (adolescent medicine), see 616.00835; for pediatric aspects of injuries and wounds, see 617.10083; for pediatric aspects of results of injuries and wounds, see 617.2083; for pediatric dentistry, see 617.645; for pediatric surgery, see 617.98

                  See Manual at 616 vs. 618.92

.920 001–.920 007   Standard subdivisions

                  As modified in notation 001–007 from table under 616.1–616.9

.920 008   Groups of people

.920 009   History, geographic treatment, biography

.920 009 2   Biography

                  Class life with a physical disease in 362.19892.
                  Class life with a mental disorder with the disorder
                  in 618.9285–618.9289, e.g., life with depression
                  618.9285270092

.920 01–.920 09   General topics of pediatrics

                  Add to base number 618.920 notation 01–09 from table under
                  616.1–616.9, e.g., congenital diseases 618.920043; however,
                  for pediatric preventive measures, see 613.0432; for pediatric
                  therapeutics, see 615.542

                  Class chronic diseases; symptoms and general pathological
                  processes as problems in their own right in 618.9204

.920 1   Newborn infants (Neonates)

               In first month after birth

               Class here neonatal medicine (neonatology)

               Class perinatal medicine in 618.32; class comprehensive works on
               congenital diseases in 616.043

.920 11   Premature infants

                  Class here low birth weight infants

.920 2   Infants

               Through age two

               Class a specific medical condition or disease not provided for here
               with the condition or disease, e.g., pain in infants 618.9204720832,
               diarrhea in infants 618.92342700832

                 For infants in first month after birth, see 618.9201

.920 26	†Sudden infant death
	Variant names: cot death, crib death, sudden infant death syndrome (SIDS)
.920 4	Chronic diseases; symptoms and general pathological processes as problems in their own right
	Add to base number 618.9204 the numbers following 616.04 in 616.044–616.047, e.g., pain in childen 618.920472
.920 9	Special branches of medicine
	Class pediatric sports medicine in 617.1027083; class pediatric dentistry in 617.645; class pediatric surgery in 617.98
.920 97	Regional medicine, ophthalmology, otology, audiology
	See Manual at 618.92097 vs. 617
.920 975	Regional medicine
	Add to base number 618.920975 the numbers following 617.5 in 617.51–617.58, e.g., disorders of face 618.92097522; however, for pediatric regional surgery, see 617.5083
.920 977–.920 978	Ophthalmology, otology, audiology
	Add to base number 618.92097 the numbers following 617 in 617.7–617.8, e.g., trachoma in children 618.92097772; however, for pediatric surgery of eyes, see 617.71; for pediatric surgery of ears, see 617.8059083
.920 98	†Gynecology
	For pediatric gynecologic surgery, see 618.1059083
.920 981	Specific diseases
	Add to base number 618.920981 the numbers following 618.1 in 618.11–618.19, e.g., diseases of uterus 618.9209814; however, for surgery for pediatric gynecologic diseases, see 618.11–618.19
.921–.929	Specific diseases
	Add to base number 618.92 the numbers following 616 in 616.1–616.9, e.g., heart diseases in children 618.9212
	Class sudden infant death in 618.92026
	For pediatric dental diseases, see 617.645; for pediatric regional medicine diseases, pediatric diseases of eyes and ears, pediatric gynecologic diseases, see 618.9209
.97	†Geriatrics
	For geriatric aspects of injuries and wounds, see 617.100846; for geriatric aspects of results of injuries and wounds, see 617.20846; for geriatric surgery, see 617.97

†Add as instructed under 616.1–616.9

[.970 42]	Genetic diseases (Hereditary diseases)
	Do not use; class in 618.976042
[.970 43]	Congenital diseases
	Do not use; class in 618.976043
[.970 52]	Preventive measures
	Do not use; class in 613.0438
[.970 6]	Therapy
	Do not use; class in 615.547

.976   **Special medical conditions, specific diseases**

[.976 01–.976 03]	Standard subdivisions
	Do not use; class in 618.97001–618.97003
.976 04	Special medical conditions

Add to base number 618.97604 the numbers following 616.04 in 616.042–616.047, e.g., pain in geriatric patients 618.9760472

[.976 05–.976 09]	Standard subdivisions
	Do not use; class in 618.97005–618.97009
.976 1–.976 9	Specific diseases

Add to base number 618.976 the numbers following 616 in 616.1–616.9, e.g., geriatric mental disorders 618.97689

.977   **Miscellaneous branches of medicine other than surgery**

Only those branches named below

See Manual at 618.977 vs. 617

[.977 01–.977 02]	Standard subdivisions
	Do not use; class in 618.977
.977 03	Rehabilitation

Do not use for dictionaries, encyclopedias, concordances; class in 618.977

Class rehabilitation from a specific disease with the disease in 618.976–618.978, plus notation 03 from table under 616.1–616.9, notation 03 from table under 617, or notation 03 from table under 618.1–618.8, e.g., rehabilitation for geriatric patients with heart disease 618.9761203

[.977 04–.977 09]	Standard subdivisions
	Do not use; class in 618.977

.977 5–.977 8	Regional medicine, dentistry, ophthalmology, otology, audiology

Add to base number 618.977 the numbers following 617 in 617.5–617.8, e.g., geriatric dentistry 618.9776; however, for geriatric regional surgery, see 617.50846; for geriatric dental surgery, see 617.6050846; for geriatric surgery of eyes, see 617.71; for geriatric surgery of ears, see 617.80590846

.978	†Gynecology

For geriatric gynecologic surgery, see 618.10590846

.978 1	Specific diseases

Add to base number 618.9781 the numbers following 618.1 in 618.11–618.19, e.g., diseases of uterus 618.97814; however, for surgery for geriatric gynecologic diseases, see 618.11–618.19

[619]   [Unassigned]

Most recently used in Edition 21

620   Engineering and allied operations

Standard subdivisions are added for engineering and allied operations together, for engineering alone

Class here manufacturing of products of various branches of engineering

Class comprehensive works on manufacturing in 670

For chemical engineering, see 660

.001	Philosophy and theory
.001 1	Systems

Class design of engineering systems in 620.0042; class manufacturing systems in 670.11; class interdisciplinary works covering systems of agriculture, home economics, or management in addition to engineering in 601.1; class interdisciplinary works on systems in 003

.001 13	Computer modeling and simulation

Class computer-aided design in 620.00420285

.001 17	Kinds of systems
.001 171	Large-scale systems

Class here systems engineering

.001 5	Scientific principles
[.001 53]	Physical principles in engineering

Do not use; class in 621

[.001 531]	Mechanical principles in engineering

Do not use; class in 620.1

†Add as instructed under 616.1–616.9

[.001 534]	Principles of sound and related vibrations in engineering
	Do not use; class in 620.2
.002	Miscellany
[.002 87]	Testing and measurement
	Do not use; class in 620.0044
[.002 88]	Maintenance and repair
	Do not use; class in 620.0046
[.002 89]	Safety measures
	Do not use; class in 620.86
.003	Dictionaries, encyclopedias, concordances
.004	Design, testing, measurement, quality, maintenance, repair
.004 2	Engineering design
	See also 621.988 for three-dimensional printing
.004 202 85	Computer applications
	Class here computer-aided design (CAD)
	Class comprehensive works on computer-aided design and computer-aided manufacturing (CAD/CAM) in 670.285
.004 4	Testing and measurement
	Including inspection, simulation
	Class interdisciplinary works on measurement in 530.8
.004 5	Quality
	Including interchangeability, maintainability, precision
	Class testing and measurement for quality in 620.0044; class maintenance in 620.0046
.004 52	Reliability
.004 54	Durability
.004 6	Maintenance and repair
	Class here interdisciplinary works on maintenance and repair
	For maintenance and repair in a specific subject, see the subject, plus notation 0288 from Table 1, e.g., clock and watch repair 681.110288
.005–.008	Standard subdivisions
.009	History, geographic treatment, biography

.009 1	Areas, regions, places in general

Class engineering to overcome problems of specific kinds of geographic environments in 620.41

.009 2	Biography

Class biography of engineers known primarily as entrepreneurs in 338.76

.009 9	Other parts of the world
[.009 99]	Extraterrestrial worlds

Do not use; class in 620.419

.1 Engineering mechanics and materials

Standard subdivisions are added for engineering mechanics and materials together, for engineering mechanics alone

Class here applied mechanics

.100 1–.100 9	Standard subdivisions

> 620.103–620.107 Engineering mechanics (Applied mechanics)

Class comprehensive works in 620.1

For fine particle technology, see 620.43

See also 531 for mechanics as a subject in physics

.103	Applied statics

For applied solid statics, see 620.1053; for applied fluid statics, see 620.1063; for applied gas statics, see 620.1073

.104	Applied dynamics

For applied solid dynamics, see 620.1054; for applied fluid dynamics, see 620.1064; for applied gas dynamics, see 620.1074

.105	Applied solid mechanics

Class structural theory in 624.17

For mechanical vibration, see 620.3

See also 621.811 for physical principles of machinery

.105 3	Statics
.105 4	Dynamics
.106	Applied fluid mechanics

Class here applied hydromechanics, comprehensive works on fluid-power technology

For applied gas mechanics, see 620.107; for steam engineering, see 621.1; for hydraulic-power technology, see 621.2; for hydraulic engineering, see 627

.106 3	Statics
.106 4	Dynamics

         Including cavitation, pressure surge, water hammer

         Class here flow

           See also 621.4022 for convective transport, heat convection

.107   **Applied gas mechanics**

         Class here applied aeromechanics

           For steam engineering, see 621.1; for pneumatic and vacuum technology, see 621.5; for aeromechanics of flight, see 629.1323; for air-conditioning engineering, see 697.93

.107 3	Statics
.107 4	Dynamics
.11	**Engineering materials**

         Class comprehensive works on materials, manufacture of materials in 670

         For specific kinds of materials, see 620.12–620.19

.110 287	Testing and measurement

           Do not use for nondestructive testing; class in 620.1127

.112   **Properties of materials and nondestructive testing**

         Standard subdivisions are added for properties of materials and nondestructive testing together, for properties of materials alone

         Class here failure, resistance, strength of materials

         Class properties and nondestructive testing of porous, organic, composite materials in 620.116–620.118

\>   620.112 1–620.112 6   Resistance to specific forces

     Class comprehensive works in 620.112

.112 1	Resistance to thermal forces

         Class resistance to thermal radiation in 620.11228

           See also 620.11296 for thermal properties

.112 15	Changes in temperature
.112 16	Low temperatures

         Including cryogenic temperatures

.112 17	High temperatures

.112 2	Resistance to decay, decomposition, deterioration
	Standard subdivisions are added for any or all topics in heading
	Physicochemical actions not basically thermal or mechanical
	Including action of pests
.112 23	Biodegradation, corrosion, weathering
	Including rot, rust
.112 28	Resistance to radiation
.112 3	Resistance to mechanical deformation (Mechanics of materials)
	For resistance to specific mechanical stresses, see 620.1124; for resistance to fracture, see 620.1126
.112 302 87	Testing and measurement
	Including strain gauges
.112 32	Temporary deformation (Elasticity)
	Including elastic limit
.112 33	Permanent deformation (Plasticity)
	Including creep, plastic flow
	For properties affecting permanent deformation, see 620.1125
.112 4	Resistance to specific mechanical stresses
	Class resistance to change of form, regardless of stress, in 620.1125; class resistance to fracture, regardless of stress, in 620.1126
.112 41	Tension
.112 42	Compression
.112 43	Torsion
.112 44	Flexure
.112 45	Shearing
.112 48	Vibrations
.112 5	Properties affecting permanent deformation
	Including impact strength, rigidity, shock resistance; ductility, malleability
.112 6	Resistance to fracture (Fracture mechanics)
	Including brittleness, hardness
	Class here crack resistance, resistance to penetration and breaking; fatigue; fatigue, fracture, rupture strength
.112 7	Nondestructive testing
.112 72	Radiographic testing
	Class here X-ray testing

.112 73	Tracer testing
.112 74	Ultrasonic testing
.112 78	Magnetic testing
.112 9	Other properties
.112 92	Mechanical properties

> Including adhesiveness, roughness, texture; friction and wear resistance
>
> Class comprehensive works on friction in 621.89
>
> *See also 620.44 for surface technology*

.112 94	Acoustical properties
.112 95	Optical properties

> Including luminescence, photoelasticity, refractivity

.112 96	Thermal properties

> Including heat conductivity
>
> *See also 620.1121 for resistance to thermal forces*

.112 97	Electrical, electronic, magnetic properties
.112 972	Semiconductivity
.112 973	Superconductivity
.112 99	Microphysical properties

> Including crystallographic and molecular properties; microstructure
>
> *For electronic properties, see 620.11297*

> 620.115–620.118 Nanostructured, porous, organic, composite materials

Class comprehensive works in 620.11

> *For a specific kind of nanostructured, porous, organic, composite material, see 620.12–620.19*

.115	*Nanostructured materials

> Class nanoporous materials in 620.116; class nanostructured organic materials in 620.117; class nanostructured composite materials in 620.118

.116	*Porous materials

> Including nanoporous materials
>
> Class porous organic materials in 620.117; class porous composite materials in 620.118

*Add as instructed under 620.12–620.19

.117   *Organic materials

Class organic composite materials in 620.118

.118   *Composite materials

For a specific composite material, see the predominant component in 620.12–620.19, e.g., reinforced concrete 620.137

>   620.12–620.19 Specific kinds of materials

Add to each subdivision identified by * as follows:
    0287   Testing and measurement
           Do not use for nondestructive testing; class in notation 7 from this table
    1–9   Specific properties and nondestructive testing
           Add the numbers following 620.112 in 620.1121–620.1129, e.g., nondestructive testing 7

Class comprehensive works in 620.11. Class manufacturing and chemical properties of a specific kind of material with the material, e.g., wood 674

For porous, organic, composite materials, see 620.116–620.118

.12   *Wood

Including laminated wood

.13   Masonry materials

For brick, terra-cotta, tile, see 620.142

.130 287   Testing and measurement

Do not use for nondestructive testing; class in 620.130427

.130 4   Special topics of masonry materials

.130 42   *Specific properties and nondestructive testing

.132   *Natural stones

.135   *Cement

Class here masonry adhesives

.136   *Concrete

For reinforced and prestressed concrete, see 620.137; for concrete blocks, see 620.139

.137   *Reinforced and prestressed concrete

Subdivisions are added for either or both topics in heading

.139   Artificial stones

Including cinder and concrete blocks

---

*Add as instructed under 620.12–620.19

.139 028 7	Testing and measurement
	Do not use for nondestructive testing; class in 620.1390427
.139 04	Special topics of artificial stones
.139 042	*Specific properties and nondestructive testing
.14	**Ceramic and allied materials**

Standard subdivisions are added for ceramic and allied materials together, for ceramic materials alone

Class masonry materials in 620.13

.140 287	Testing and measurement
	Do not use for nondestructive testing; class in 620.140427
.140 4	Special topics of ceramic and allied materials
.140 42	*Specific properties and nondestructive testing
.142	**Brick, terra-cotta, tile**
.143	***Refractory materials**

Including fireclays

Class refractory metals in 620.16

For asbestos, see 620.195

.144	***Glass**

Including fiber glass

.146	**Enamel and porcelain**
.16	***Metals**

Class here alloys

For ferrous metals, see 620.17; for nonferrous metals, see 620.18

.17	***Ferrous metals**

Class here iron, steel

.18	**Nonferrous metals**

Class here nonferrous alloys

.180 287	Testing and measurement
	Do not use for nondestructive testing; class in 620.180427
.180 4	Special topics of nonferrous metals
.180 42	*Specific properties and nondestructive testing

*Add as instructed under 620.12–620.19

.182	*Copper

Class here brass, Muntz metal; bronze, gunmetal; copper-aluminum alloys; copper-beryllium alloys

.183	*Lead
.184	Zinc and cadmium
.184 2	*Zinc

For brass, Muntz metal, see 620.182

.184 6	*Cadmium
.185	*Tin

For bronze, gunmetal, see 620.182

.186	*Aluminum

For copper-aluminum alloys, see 620.182

.187	*Magnesium
.188	*Nickel
.189	Other metals
.189 1	*Mercury
.189 2	Precious, rare-earth, actinide-series metals

Add to base number 620.1892 the numbers following 669.2 in 669.22–669.29, e.g., uranium 620.1892931

.189 3	Metals used in ferroalloys

For nickel, see 620.188

.189 302 87	Testing and measurement

Do not use for nondestructive testing; class in 620.18930427

.189 304	Special topics of metals used in ferroalloys
.189 304 2	*Specific properties and nondestructive testing
.189 32	Titanium, manganese, vanadium
.189 322	*Titanium
.189 33	*Cobalt
.189 34	Chromium, molybdenum, tungsten
.189 35	Zirconium and tantalum
.189 352	*Zirconium
.189 4	*Beryllium

For copper-beryllium alloys, see 620.182

*Add as instructed under 620.12–620.19

.189 5	Antimony, arsenic, bismuth
.189 6	Alkali and alkaline-earth metals
.189 602 87	Testing and measurement

> Do not use for nondestructive testing; class in 620.18960427

.189 604	Special topics of alkali and alkaline-earth metals
.189 604 2	*Specific properties and nondestructive testing
.19	Other engineering materials
.191	Soils and related materials

> Standard subdivisions are added for soils and related materials together, for soils alone

> Including aggregates, clay, gravel, sand

> Class foundation soils in 624.151; class interdisciplinary works on soils in 631.4

.191 028 7	Testing and measurement

> Do not use for nondestructive testing; class in 620.1910427

.191 04	Special topics of soils and related materials
.191 042	*Specific properties and nondestructive testing
.192	Polymers

> *For elastomers, see 620.194*

.192 028 7	Testing and measurement

> Do not use for nondestructive testing; class in 620.1920427

.192 04	Special topics of polymers
.192 042	*Specific properties and nondestructive testing
.192 3	*Plastics

> Class here plastic laminating materials

.192 4	*Gums and resins

> Subdivisions are added for either or both topics in heading

.193	Nonmetallic elements

> Including carbon, silicon

.193 028 7	Testing and measurement

> Do not use for nondestructive testing; class in 620.1930427

.193 04	Special topics of nonmetallic elements
.193 042	*Specific properties and nondestructive testing

*Add as instructed under 620.12–620.19

.194   *Elastomers

                Class here rubber

.195   Insulating materials

                Including asbestos, corkboard, kapok, rock wool; dielectric materials

.195 028 7   Testing and measurement

                        Do not use for nondestructive testing; class in 620.1950427

.195 04   Special topics of insulating materials

.195 042   *Specific properties and nondestructive testing

.196   Bituminous materials

                Including asphalt, tar

.196 028 7   Testing and measurement

                        Do not use for nondestructive testing; class in 620.1960427

.196 04   Special topics of bituminous materials

.196 042   *Specific properties and nondestructive testing

.197   Organic fibrous materials

                Including paper, paperboard, rope, textiles

.197 028 7   Testing and measurement

                        Do not use for nondestructive testing; class in 620.1970427

.197 04   Special topics of organic fibrous materials

.197 042   *Specific properties and nondestructive testing

.198   Other natural and synthetic minerals

                Including corundum, feldspar, gems, graphite, oil, quartz, water

.199   Adhesives and sealants

                Class here comprehensive works on laminating materials

                For masonry adhesives, see 620.135; for plastic laminating materials, see 620.1923

.199 028 7   Testing and measurement

                        Do not use for nondestructive testing; class in 620.1990427

.199 04   Special topics of adhesives and sealants

.199 042   *Specific properties and nondestructive testing

*Add as instructed under 620.12–620.19

.2   **Sound and related vibrations**

> Standard subdivisions are added for sound and related vibrations together, for sound alone
>
> Class here applied acoustics (acoustical engineering)
>
> *See also 534 for physics of sound*

> 620.21–620.25   Applied acoustics (Acoustical engineering)

> Class electroacoustical communications in 621.3828; class engineering works on architectural acoustics in 690.2; class comprehensive works in 620.2; class interdisciplinary works on architectural acoustics in 729.29

.21   General topics of applied acoustics

> Including reflection and refraction of sound

.23   Noise and countermeasures

> Standard subdivisions are added for either or both topics in heading

.25   Acoustics in specific physical environments

> Including underwater acoustics

.28   Applied subsonics and ultrasonics

> *For ultrasonic testing of materials, see 620.11274*

.3   **Mechanical vibration**

> Class effects of vibrations on materials in 620.11248
>
> *For sound and related vibrations, see 620.2*

.31   Generation and transmission

.37   Effects and countermeasures

> Standard subdivisions are added for either or both topics in heading

.4   **Engineering for specific kinds of geographic environments, fine particle and remote control technology, surface engineering**

.41   Engineering for specific kinds of geographic environments

> Class a specific technology with the technology, plus notation 091 from Table 1 when the environment is not inherent in the subject, e.g., ergonomics for deserts 620.8209154, nautical engineering 623.8

.411–.417   Specific kinds of terrestrial environments

> Add to base number 620.41 the numbers following —1 in notation 11–17 from Table 2, e.g., ocean engineering 620.4162; however, for engineering of estuaries, see 627.124
>
> Class hydraulic engineering in 627

.419   Extraterrestrial environments

.43	Fine particle technology

> Including dust, liquid particle technology
>
> Class here powder technology

.44	Surface engineering
.46	Remote control and telecontrol

> Standard subdivisions are added for either or both topics in heading

.5   Nanotechnology

> Technology that manipulates matter on the atomic or molecular scale
>
> Class a specific application of nanotechnology with the technology, e.g., nanostructured materials 620.115, nanotechnology used in manufacturing thin-film circuits 621.3815

.8   Human factors and safety engineering

> Class here work environment engineering
>
> Class a specific application of human factors engineering with the application, e.g., engineering of the home kitchen work environment 643.3
>
> *See also 628 for environmental protection engineering*

.82	Human factors engineering

> Variant names: biotechnology, design anthropometry, ergonomics

.86	Safety engineering

> Class interdisciplinary works on safety in 363.1
>
> *For safety engineering of a specific technology, see the technology, plus notation 0289 from Table 1, e.g., safety in machine engineering 621.80289*

621   Applied physics

> Class here mechanical engineering
>
> Class a specific application of applied physics with the application, e.g., military engineering 623
>
> *For engineering mechanics, see 620.1; for applied acoustics, see 620.2*

.04	Special topics of applied physics
.042	Energy engineering

> Class here engineering of alternative and renewable energy sources
>
> Class interdisciplinary works on energy in 333.79

.044	Plasma engineering

> Class interdisciplinary works on plasma in 530.44

> **621.1–621.2 Fluid-power technologies**

Class comprehensive works in 620.106

.1   **Steam engineering**

> 621.15–621.16 Specific kinds of steam engines

Class comprehensive works in 621.1

For marine steam engines, see 623.8722; for steam locomotives, see 625.261; for steam tractors and rollers, see 629.2292

.15   Portable engines

Class comprehensive works on specific structural types of steam engines in 621.16

.16   Stationary engines

Class here comprehensive works on specific structural types of steam engines

For portable engines of specific structural types, see 621.15

.164   Reciprocating engines

.165   Turbines

.18   Generating and transmitting steam

Standard subdivisions are added for generating and transmitting steam together, for generating steam alone

Class generating steam in specific kinds of steam engines in 621.15–621.16; class generating steam in central stations in 621.19

> 621.182–621.183 Generating steam

Class comprehensive works in 621.18

.182   Fuels

.183   Boilers and boiler furnaces

Standard subdivisions are added for either or both topics in heading

Including chimneys, mechanical stokers

.185   Transmitting steam

Including insulation, pressure regulators, safety valves, steam pipes

.19   Central stations

.194   Boiler operations (Boiler-house practices)

.197   Accessories

Including condensers, cooling towers, superheaters

.199	Cogeneration of electric power and heat

Class interdisciplinary works on cogeneration of electricity and heat in 333.793

.2	**Hydraulic-power technology**

Class hydraulic control in 629.8042

.204	Special topics of hydraulic-power technology
.204 2	Specific liquids
[.204 201–.204 209]	Standard subdivisions

Do not use; class in 621.201–621.209

.204 22	Water
.204 24	Hydraulic fluids

Other than water

.21	Water mills

Class here comprehensive works on waterwheels

For waterwheels used as water-lifting devices, see 621.69

.24	Turbines
.25	Pumps and accumulators
.252	Pumps

Class comprehensive works on pumps in 621.69

.254	Accumulators
.26	Hydraulic transmission

Class specific liquids in hydraulic transmission in 621.2042

For rams, see 621.27

.27	Rams
.3	**Electrical, magnetic, optical, communications, computer engineering; electronics, lighting**

Standard subdivisions are added for electromagnetic engineering, for combined electrical and electronic engineering, for electrical engineering alone

See also 537 for physics of electricity and electromagnetism

.302 84	Apparatus, equipment, materials

Do not use for electrical equipment; class in 621.31042

.302 87	Testing and measurement

Do not use for electrical testing and measurement; class in 621.37

.31	Generation, modification, storage, transmission of electric power

Class here alternating current

.310 4   Special topics of generation, modification, storage, transmission of electric power

.310 42   Electrical machinery and equipment

Standard subdivisions are added for either or both topics in heading

Including eddy currents, shaft currents

Class a specific application with the application, e.g., refrigerators 621.57

For electric motors, see 621.46

.312   Generation, modification, storage

For equipment for generation, modification, control, see 621.313–621.317

.312 1   Generation

Class here central and auxiliary power plants, mechanical generation

For direct energy conversion, see 621.3124

.312 13   Specific kinds of mechanical generation

[.312 130 1–.312 130 9]   Standard subdivisions

Do not use; class in 621.312101–621.312109

.312 132   Steam-powered generation

Class here comprehensive works on generation from fossil fuels

For generation by internal-combustion engines, see 621.312133; for nuclear steam-powered generation of electricity, see 621.483

.312 133   Generation by internal-combustion engines

.312 134   Hydroelectric generation

Including tidal generation

Class engineering of dams for hydroelectric power in 627.8

.312 136   Wind-powered generation

.312 4   Direct energy conversion

.312 42   Electrochemical energy conversion

Class here batteries

Class comprehensive works on electrochemical engineering in 660.297

For solar batteries, see 621.31244

.312 423   Primary batteries

.312 424   Secondary batteries (Storage batteries)

.312 429	Fuel cells	

.312 43   Thermoelectric generation

> Including radioisotope thermoelectric generation; thermionic converters

> Class generation of electricity from solar radiation in 621.31244

.312 44   Generation of electricity from solar radiation

> Class here photovoltaic generation, use of solar batteries and cells

.312 45   Magnetohydrodynamic generation

.312 6   Modification and storage

> Including operation of transformer, converter substations

> *For storage of electrical energy by chemical methods, see 621.312424*

> **621.313–621.317 Machinery and equipment for generation, modification, control**

> Class comprehensive works in 621.31042

.313   Generating machinery and converters

> Standard subdivisions are added for either or both topics in heading

> Class here comprehensive works on generators and motors

> *For details and parts of generators, see 621.316; for electric motors, see 621.46*

.313 2   Direct-current machinery

> Including converters to alternating current, dynamos

.313 3   Alternating-current machinery

> Class here synchronous machinery

> *For synchronous generators, see 621.3134; for synchronous converters to direct current, see 621.3135; for asynchronous machinery, see 621.3136*

.313 4   Synchronous generators

.313 5   Synchronous converters to direct current

> *For rectifiers, see 621.3137*

.313 6   Asynchronous machinery

> *For rectifiers, see 621.3137*

.313 7   Rectifiers

.314   Transformers

.315   Capacitors (Condensers)

.316   **Details and parts of generators**

> Including armatures, brushes, commutators, contactors, electromagnets
>
> *For a specific part not provided for here, see the part, e.g., transformers 621.314*

.317   **Control devices**

> Including circuit breakers, fuses, grounding devices, lightning arresters, relays, rheostats
>
> Class here power electronics, switching equipment
>
> Class switches at service end of line in 621.31924

.319   **Transmission**

> Including power failure
>
> Class here electrification
>
> Class interdisciplinary works on electrification, on power failure in 333.7932
>
> *For electric power transmission for railroads, see 621.33*

[.319 011]   Systems

> Do not use; class in 621.3191

.319 1   Systems

> Class circuitry and lines in 621.3192

.319 12   Direct-current systems

.319 13   Alternating-current systems

> Including high-tension systems

.319 15   Composite current systems

> Direct and alternating currents combined

.319 2   Networks (Circuitry and lines)

.319 21   Physical phenomena in circuits

> Including heat losses in lines, transients

.319 22   Overhead lines

.319 23   Underground lines

.319 24   Apparatus at service end of line

> Including extension cords, outlets, sockets, switches
>
> Class here interior wiring
>
> *For exterior wiring, see 621.31925*

.319 25   Exterior wiring

.319 3	Equipment and components

Class equipment for generation, modification, control in 621.313–621.317; class use of equipment and components in lines and circuitry in 621.3192

.319 33	Wires
.319 34	Cables
.319 37	Insulators

Class here insulation

.32	Lighting

Class here electric lighting

.321	Principles of lighting

Class principles of specific kinds of lighting with the kind, e.g., principles of residential lighting 621.3228

.321 1	Layouts, calculations, photometry
.321 4	Floodlighting

Class here directed lighting

Class exterior floodlighting in 621.3229

.322	Lighting in specific situations

Class here interior lighting

Class specific forms of lighting in 621.323–621.327

For public lighting, see 628.95; for lighting of airports, see 629.1365

.322 01–.322 09	Standard subdivisions for interior lighting

Do not use for comprehensive works on lighting in specific situations; class in 621.3201–621.3209

.322 5–.322 8	Interior lighting for specific kinds of buildings

Add to base number 621.322 the numbers following 72 in 725–728, e.g., lighting for office buildings 621.322523

.322 9	Exterior lighting

Including advertising and display lighting, garden and patio lighting

---

>   **621.323–621.328 Specific forms of lighting**

Class comprehensive works in 621.32

.323	Nonelectrical lighting

Including candles, oil-burning devices, torches

For gas lighting, see 621.324

.324	Gas lighting

>   **621.325–621.328 Electric lighting**

           Class comprehensive works in 621.32

.325   **Arc lighting**

           Electric-discharge lighting in which light is produced by consumable electrodes or by vapors emanating from consumable electrodes

.326   **Incandescent lighting**

.327   **Vapor lighting (Luminous-tube lighting)**

.327 3   Fluorescent lighting

.327 4   Mercury-vapor lighting

.327 5   Neon lighting

.327 6   Sodium-vapor lighting

.328   **LED lighting (Light-emitting diode lighting)**

.33   **Electric power transmission for railroads**

.34   **Magnetic engineering**

           Class here artificial magnets, electromagnets

           Class electromagnets as parts of generators in 621.316; class electromagnets as parts of electric motors in 621.46; class comprehensive works on electromagnetic technology in 621.3

           See also 538 for physics of magnetism; also 538.4 for natural magnets

.35   **Superconductivity**

           Class here superconductors

           Class superconductor circuits in 621.3815

.36   **Optical engineering**

           Class here applied optics; works on infrared and ultraviolet technology together

           Class manufacture of optical instruments in 681.4; class interdisciplinary works on photography in 770

           For lighting, see 621.32

           See also 535 for optics and light as subjects in physics; also 620.11295 for optical properties of engineering materials

.361   **Spectroscopy**

>   **621.362–621.364 Infrared and ultraviolet technology**

           Class infrared and ultraviolet spectroscopy in 621.361; class infrared and ultraviolet photography in 621.3672; class comprehensive works in 621.36

.362   **Infrared technology**

.364	Ultraviolet technology
.365	Photonics
.366	Lasers

> For laser communications, see 621.3827

.366 1	Solid-state lasers
.366 2	Fluid-state lasers

> For gaseous-state lasers, see 621.3663

.366 3	Gaseous-state lasers
.366 4	Chemical and dye lasers
.367	Technological photography and photo-optics

Standard subdivisions are added for either or both topics in heading

Including spectrography, stroboscopic photography

Class here image processing, optical data processing

> For photoelectric and photoelectronic devices, see 621.381542; for optical communications, see 621.3827

> See Manual at 006.37 vs. 006.42, 621.367, 621.391, 621.399

.367 2	Infrared and ultraviolet photography
.367 3	Radiography (Gamma-ray and X-ray photography)
.367 5	Holography
.367 8	Remote sensing technology

> For photogrammetry, see 526.982

.369	Other branches of applied optics
.369 2	Fiber optics

> See also 621.381045 for optoelectronics

.369 3	Integrated optics
.369 4	Nonlinear optics
.37	Testing and measurement of electrical quantities

Instruments and their use

> For testing and measurement of a specific apparatus, part, or function, see the apparatus, part, or function, plus notation 0287 from Table 1, e.g., testing overhead lines 621.319220287

.372	Units and standards of measurement

Including calibration of electrical instruments

.373	Recording meters

Class meters recording specific electrical quantities in 621.374

.374	Instruments for measuring specific electrical quantities
[.374 01–.374 09]	Standard subdivisions

         Do not use; class in 621.3701–621.3709

.374 2	Instruments for measuring capacitance, inductance, resistance

         Including bridges, ohmmeters, resistance boxes, shunts; comprehensive works on electrical bridges (bridge circuits)

         For frequency bridges, see 621.3747

.374 3	Instruments for measuring potential

         Including electrometers, potentiometers, voltage detectors, voltmeters

.374 4	Instruments for measuring current

         Including ammeters, ampere-hour meters, coulometers, galvanometers, milliammeters, voltameters

.374 5	Instruments for measuring energy

         Including electric meters, watt-hour meters

.374 6	Instruments for measuring power

         Including electrodynamometers, volt-ammeters, wattmeters

.374 7	Instruments for measuring frequency

         Including frequency bridges, oscillographs

         Class electric phasemeters in 621.3749

.374 9	Instruments for measuring phase

         Including power-factor meters, synchroscopes

.38	Electronics, communications engineering

         Unless other instructions are given, class a subject with aspects in two or more subdivisions of 621.38 in the number coming last, e.g., antennas for amateur radio 621.38416 (*not* 621.384135)

.381	Electronics

         Class here microelectronics, molecular electronics

         Class signal processing in 621.3822; class electronic interference and noise in 621.38224. Class a specific application of electronics with the application, e.g., laser technology 621.366

         See also 537.5 for physics of electronics

.381 04	Special topics of electronics
.381 044	Power and energy in electronic systems
.381 045	Optoelectronics

         See also 621.3678 for remote sensing technology; also 621.3692 for fiber optics

.381 046	Packaging

.381 3	Microwave electronics
.381 31	Wave propagation and transmission
	Including interference
.381 32	Circuits

Add to base number 621.38132 the numbers following 621.38153 in 621.381532–621.381537, e.g., amplifiers 621.381325

.381 33	Components and devices

Standard subdivisions are added for either or both topics in heading

Class use of components in specific circuits in 621.38132

.381 331	Wave guides
.381 332	Cavity resonators
.381 333	Klystrons
.381 334	Magnetrons
.381 335	Traveling-wave tubes
.381 336	Masers
.381 5	Components and circuits

Standard subdivisions are added for either or both topics in heading

Class here analog, digital, integrated, microelectronic, semiconductor, superconductor, thin-film circuits; circuits and components common to electronics and communications engineering

Class components and circuits of a specific branch of communications engineering in 621.383–621.389; class very large scale integration in 621.395

For microwave components and circuits, see 621.3813

[.381 502 87]	Testing and measurement

Do not use; class in 621.381548

>   621.381 51–621.381 52   Components

Class use of components in specific circuits in 621.38153; class devices not intrinsic to circuits in 621.38154; class analog-to-digital and digital-to-analog converters in 621.38159; class comprehensive works in 621.3815

.381 51	Electronic tubes
.381 512	Vacuum tubes
.381 513	Gas tubes
.381 52	Semiconductors

Class here crystal devices, miniaturization, optoelectronic devices, thin-film technology

.381 522	Diodes
	Including junction diodes, light-emitting diodes (LEDs), tunnel diodes (Esaki diodes), Zener diodes; varactors
	Class LED lighting (light-emitting diode lighting) in 621.328
.381 528	Transistors and thyristors
	Standard subdivisions are added for transistors and thyristors together, for transistors alone
	Including phototransistors
	Class here bipolar transistors
.381 528 2	Junction transistors
.381 528 4	Field-effect transistors
.381 528 7	Thyristors
.381 53	Printed circuits and circuits for specific functions
.381 531	Printed circuits
	Including microlithography
	Class printed circuits for specific functions in 621.381532–621.381537

>   **621.381 532–621.381 537 Circuits for specific functions**

Class comprehensive works in 621.3815

.381 532	Converters, filters, interference eliminators
.381 532 2	Converters (Rectifiers and inverters)
.381 532 4	Filters
.381 533	Oscillators
	Class use of oscillators in pulse circuits in 621.381534
.381 534	Pulse circuits
	Including counting circuits, pulse generators and processes
	Class modulation and demodulation (detection) of pulses in 621.3815365
.381 535	Amplifiers and feedback circuits
	Standard subdivisions are added for amplifiers and feedback circuits together, for amplifiers alone
	Class operational amplifiers in 621.395
.381 536	Modulators and demodulators (detectors)
	Class here modulation, demodulation (detection)

.381 536 2	Amplitude
	Including attenuators
.381 536 3	Frequency
	See also 621.3815486 for frequency synthesizers
.381 536 4	Phase
	Including phase-locked loops
.381 536 5	Pulse
.381 537	Switching, control, trigger circuits, relays
.381 537 2	Switching theory
	Class switching theory in logic circuit design in 621.395
.381 54	Supplementary components
	Devices not intrinsic to circuits
	Class here electronic instrumentation (applications of electronics)
	Class instrumentation in a specific field with the field, e.g., electronic control 629.89
.381 542	Photoelectric and photoelectronic components
	Including electric eyes; photoconductive, photoemissive, photovoltaic cells; photomultipliers; phototubes
	See also 621.367 for image processing; also 621.381045 for optoelectronics
.381 542 2	Video display components
	Including liquid crystal displays
.381 548	Testing and measuring components
	Including bridges (bridge circuits); signal, square-wave, sweep generators; thermistors
	Class here testing and measuring electronic circuits and components, instruments for testing and measuring electronic signals
	Class testing and measuring a specific circuit or component with the circuit or component, plus notation 0287 from Table 1, e.g., testing amplifiers 621.3815350287
.381 548 3	Oscilloscopes
	Including oscillographs
.381 548 6	Frequency synthesizers

.381 59	Analog-to-digital and digital-to-analog converters

Standard subdivisions are added for either or both topics in heading

Class analog-to-digital and digital-to-analog converters in data communications engineering in 621.39814

.382	Communications engineering

Including Internet telephony

Class here analog, digital, electronic communications; telecommunications; comprehensive works on digital data and telecommunications engineering

Unless other instructions are given, class a subject with aspects in two or more subdivisions of 621.382 in the number coming last, e.g., signal processing in acoustical communications 621.3828 (*not* 621.3822)

Class comprehensive works on wireless communication in 621.384. Class a component or circuit common to electronics and communications engineering with the component or circuit in 621.3815, e.g., amplifiers 621.381535, switching circuits 621.381537

For specific communications systems, see 621.383–621.389; for data communications engineering, see 621.3981

See Manual at 004.6 vs. 621.382, 621.3981

[.382 028 546 2]	Interfacing and communications protocols (standards)

Do not use; class in 621.38212

[.382 028 546 5]	Communications network architecture

Do not use; class in 621.38215

[.382 028 546 6]	Data transmission modes and data switching methods

Do not use; class in 621.38216

.382 1	Communications networks

For communications networks based on a specific technology, see the technology, e.g., telephone networks 621.385

.382 12	Communications protocols (Communications standards)
[.382 120 218]	Standards

Do not use; class in 621.38212

.382 15	Communications network architecture

Class here systems analysis, design, topology (configuration) of communications networks

.382 16	Data transmission modes and data switching methods

Including circuit and packet switching, multiplexing, asynchronous and synchronous transfer modes

.382 2	Signal processing
	Class here information theory
	Class interdisciplinary works on information theory in 003.54
.382 23	Signal analysis and theory
	Standard subdivisions are added for either or both topics in heading
.382 24	Interference and noise
	Standard subdivisions are added for either or both topics in heading
	Class here electronic interference and noise
.382 3	Miscellaneous topics
	Limited to studios, transmission facilities, and the topics provided for below
.382 32	Power supply in communications systems
.382 34	Recording devices
	Including discs, tapes
	For a recording device of a specific communication system, see the device in 621.383–621.389, e.g., video recorders 621.38833, sound recorders 621.38932
.382 35	Facsimile transmission
	By wire or radio wave
	Class here telefacsimile
.382 38	Space communications
	See also 621.3825 for satellite communication
.382 4	Antennas and propagation
.382 5	Relay communication
	Class here satellite communication
.382 54	Antennas and propagation
.382 7	Optical communications
	Transmission of sound, visual images, other information by light
	Including optical disc technology
	Class here laser communications
	Class optoacoustic communications in 621.3828
.382 75	Optical-fiber communication
	Class here guided-light communication

.382 8   Acoustical communications

                   Audio systems covering broadcasting and transmission as well as recording and reproduction of sound

                   Including acousto-optical communications

                   Class here electroacoustical communications

                   Class audio systems limited to recording and reproduction of sound in 621.3893

.382 84   Specific devices

                   Including microphones, speakers

                   Class antennas in 621.3824

>   621.383–621.389   Specific communications systems

               Class comprehensive works in 621.382

.383   Telegraphy

                   For radiotelegraphy, see 621.3842

.384   Radio and radar

                   Standard subdivisions are added for radio and radar together, for radio alone

                   Class here broadcasting stations, digital audio broadcasting; comprehensive engineering works on radio and television, on wireless communication

                   Class interdisciplinary works on radio and television in 384.5; class interdisciplinary works on broadcasting stations in 384.5453

                   For satellite communication, see 621.3825; for television, see 621.388

.384 028 8   Maintenance and repair

                     Class maintenance and repair of radio receiving sets in 621.384187

>   621.384 1–621.384 5   Radio

               Class comprehensive works in 621.384

.384 1   Specific topics in general radio

[.384 101–.384 109]   Standard subdivision

                   Do not use; class in 621.38401–621.38409

.384 11   Wave propagation and transmission

                   Including interference

                   See also 384.54524 for allocation of frequencies

.384 12	Circuits

> Including amplifiers, filters, interference eliminators, modulation circuits, oscillators, rectifiers
>
> Class a specific application of circuits with the application, e.g., receiving set circuits 621.38418

.384 13	Components and devices

> Standard subdivisions are added for either or both topics in heading

.384 131	Transmitters
.384 132	Tubes

> Class use of tubes in specific circuits in 621.38412

.384 133	Miscellaneous supplementary devices

> Limited to condensers (capacitors), grounding devices, inductors, microphones, resistors, testing equipment

.384 134	Semiconductor devices

> Class use of semiconductor devices in specific circuits in 621.38412

.384 135	Antennas
.384 15	Systems by wave type, satellite and relay systems

> Standard subdivisions are added for systems by wave type, satellite and relay systems together; for systems by wave type alone

>

621.384 151–621.384 153 Systems by wave type

Class relay and satellite systems of a specific wave type in 621.384156; class comprehensive works in 621.38415

.384 151	Shortwave systems

> Including ultrahigh frequency (UHF), very-high-frequency (VHF) systems
>
> *For frequency-modulation systems, see 621.384152*

.384 152	Frequency-modulation (FM) systems
.384 153	Long-wave systems

> Including amplitude modulation (AM), single-sideband, very-low-frequency (VLF) systems

.384 156	Relay and satellite systems

> Class here satellite radio

.384 16   Amateur radio (Ham radio)

> Limited to long distance communication
>
> Class here comprehensive works on amateur and citizens band radio
>
> *For citizens band radio, see 621.38454*

.384 18   Radio receiving sets

[.384 180 288]   Maintenance and repair

> Do not use; class in 621.384187

.384 187   Maintenance and repair

.384 19   Special developments

.384 191   Direction and position finding

> Standard subdivisions are added for either or both topics in heading
>
> Including loran, radio beacons, radio compasses
>
> Class here GPS receivers

.384 192   Identification and locating

> Standard subdivisions are added for either or both topics in heading
>
> Including radio frequency identification (RFID) systems
>
> Class here automatic identification and data capture (AIDC); real-time locating systems (RTLS)

.384 196   Radio control

> Variant names: remote control, telecontrol

.384 197   Space communication

.384 2   Radiotelegraphy

.384 5   Radiotelephony

> Including portable radios, walkie-talkies
>
> Class here mobile radio stations, comprehensive works on radio transmission in telephony
>
> *For radio relays, see 621.38782*

.384 54   Citizens band radio

> Limited to local communication (ca. 10 miles or 15 kilometers)
>
> Class comprehensive works on amateur and citizens band radio in 621.38416

.384 56   Mobile telephone systems

> Variant names: cellular radio, cellular telephone systems, portable telephone systems

.384 8	Radar
.384 83	Specific instruments and devices
	Including antennas
.384 85	Systems
	Including continuous, monopulse, pulse-modulated systems
.385	Telephony

Class here telephone systems based on wires, cables, lasers, optical fibers

Class mobile telephone systems in 621.38456; class data communications engineering in 621.3981; class interdisciplinary works on telephony in 384.6

For Internet telephony, see 621.382; for radiotelephony, see 621.3845; for telephone terminal equipment, see 621.386; for telephone transmission and nonterminal equipment, see 621.387

.385 1	Network analysis
.385 7	Automatic and semiautomatic switching systems
	Including direct distance dialing
.386	Telephone terminal equipment
	Dialing, transmitting, receiving equipment
.386 7	Telephone answering and message recording devices
.386 9	Pay telephones
.387	Telephone transmission and nonterminal equipment
	Including switching systems
.387 8	Transmission

Class comprehensive works on radio transmission in telephony in 621.3845

.387 82	Long-distance systems
	Including radio relays
.387 83	Local systems
.387 84	Transmission lines and cables
.388	Television

Class here interactive television (TV programming with interactive content and/or enhancements, e.g., interactive program guides, personalized multi-camera angles, real-time voting, video-on-demand)

.388 001	Philosophy and theory
.388 002	Miscellany

.388 002 88	Maintenance and repair
	Class here maintenance and repair of broadcast and transmission equipment, of comprehensive works on television repair
	For maintenance and repair of receiving sets, see 621.38887
.388 003–.388 009	Standard subdivisions
.388 02	Black-and-white television
.388 04	Color television
.388 06	High-definition television (HDTV)
.388 07	Digital television
	Including mobile television
.388 1	Wave propagation and transmission
	Including interference
.388 3	Components and devices
	Standard subdivisions are added for either or both topics in heading
.388 31	Transmitters
.388 32	Semiconductors, transistors, tubes
.388 33	Video recorders and video recordings
	Standard subdivisions are added for video recorders and video recordings together, for video recorders alone
[.388 330 288]	Maintenance and repair
	Do not use; class in 621.388337
.388 332	Video recordings
	Including cassettes, discs
[.388 332 028 8]	Maintenance and repair
	Do not use; class in 621.388337
.388 337	Maintenance and repair of video recorders and video recordings
.388 34	Cameras and components
.388 35	Antennas
.388 5	Communication systems
.388 53	Satellite television
.388 57	Cable television
.388 6	Stations
.388 8	Television sets

[.388 802 88]	Maintenance and repair	

Do not use; class in 621.38887

.388 87	Maintenance and repair
.389	Security, sound recording, related systems
.389 2	Public address, security, related systems

Including paging systems, sirens

.389 28   Security electronics

Including surveillance systems, e.g., electronic eavesdropping devices

Class here alarm systems

For fire alarms, see 628.9225

.389 3   Sound recording and reproducing systems

Audio systems limited to recording and reproduction of sound

Class here digital audio engineering

Class telephone message recording in 621.3867; class comprehensive works on acoustical communications, on audio systems covering transmission as well as recording and reproduction in 621.3828

.389 32   Recorders and recordings

Including compact discs

.389 324   Tape recorders and recordings

Including cassettes

.389 33   Reproducers

Including compact disc players, jukeboxes, phonographs

Class combination recorders-reproducers in 621.38932

.389 332   High-fidelity systems (Hi-fi)

For stereophonic systems, see 621.389334

.389 334   Stereophonic systems

Including quadraphonic systems

.389 5	Sonar
.389 7	Audiovisual engineering

.39	**Computer engineering**

Class here electronic digital computers, central processing units, computer reliability, general computer performance evaluation

Unless other instructions are given, class a subject with aspects in two or more subdivisions of 621.39 in the number coming last, e.g., circuitry of computer internal storage 621.3973 (*not* 621.395)

Class selection and use of computer hardware, works treating both hardware and either software development or software in 004. Class a specific application of computers with the application, e.g., use of computers to regulate processes automatically 629.895

See Manual at 004–006 vs. 621.39

[.390 287]	Testing and measurement

Do not use; class in 621.392

.391	**General works on specific types of computers**

Including optical computers

Class here specific types of processors, e.g., multiprocessors

Class programmable calculators in 681.14

See Manual at 006.37 vs. 006.42, 621.367, 621.391, 621.399

>   621.391 1–621.391 6 Digital computers

Class comprehensive works in 621.39

See Manual at 004.11–004.16

.391 1	Supercomputers
.391 2	Mainframe computers

For supercomputers, see 621.3911

.391 4	Midrange computers

Class here minicomputers, server class computers

Class comprehensive works on midrange and personal computers in 621.3916

.391 6	Personal computers

Class here specific types of personal computers; comprehensive works on midrange and personal computers

For midrange computers, see 621.3914

.391 67	Mobile computing devices

Class here specific mobile computing devices

.391 9	Analog and hybrid computers

Standard subdivisions are added for either or both topics in heading

.392	Systems analysis and design, computer architecture

Including hardware description languages

See Manual at 004.21 vs. 004.22, 621.392

.395	Circuitry

Class here logic circuits, logic design of circuits, very large scale integration (VLSI)

.397	Storage
.397 3	Internal storage (Main memory)

Class here random-access memory (RAM), read-only memory (ROM)

Class CD-ROM (compact disc read-only memory) in 621.3976

.397 32	Semiconductor memory

Class here bipolar, metal-oxide-semiconductor (MOS), thin-film memory

.397 6	External storage (Auxiliary storage)

Including punched cards

.397 63	Magnetic storage

Including floppy disks, floppy disk drives; magnetic tapes, e.g., cartridges, cassettes, reel-to-reel tapes; tape drives

Class here hard disks, hard disk drives; magnetic bubble memory

.397 67	Optical storage

Including CD-ROM (compact disc read-only memory), DVD, WORM (write once read many) discs and drives

Class storage of pictorial data in optical storage devices in 621.367

.397 68	Semiconductor storage

Class here solid-state storage; flash drives, memory cards

.398	Interfacing and communications devices, peripherals
.398 1	Interfacing and communications devices

Class here data communications engineering

Class Internet telephony in 621.385

See Manual at 004.6 vs. 621.382, 621.3981

.398 14	Analog-to-digital and digital-to-analog converters

Standard subdivisions are added for either or both topics in heading

Including modems

.398 4	Peripherals
	Class peripheral storage in 621.3976
	For peripherals combining input and output functions, see 621.3985; for input peripherals, see 621.3986; for output peripherals, see 621.3987
.398 5	Peripherals combining input and output functions
	Class here computer terminals
	Class tape and disk devices in 621.3976
.398 6	Input peripherals
	Including keyboards
.398 7	Output peripherals
	Including monitors (video display screens), printers
	See also 621.3996 for computer graphics
.399	Devices for special computer methods
	Including computer sound synthesis
	See Manual at 006.37 vs. 006.42, 621.367, 621.391, 621.399
.399 3	Computer vision
.399 4	Computer pattern recognition
.399 6	Computer graphics
.4	**Prime movers and heat engineering**
	Standard subdivisions are added for prime movers and heat engineering together, for prime movers alone
	Class here engines, power plants, propulsion systems
	For steam engineering, see 621.1; for hydraulic-power technology, see 621.2
.400 1–.400 9	Standard subdivisions
.402	Heat engineering
	For low-temperature technology, see 621.56. For a kind of heat engineering, see the kind, e.g., geothermal engineering 621.44, heating buildings 697
	See also 536 for physics of heat
.402 1	Thermodynamics
.402 2	Heat transfer
	Including heat exchange
.402 23	Conduction
.402 25	Convection

.402 27	Radiation
.402 3	Fuels and combustion

Class pollution by-products of combustion in 628.532

.402 4	Insulation
.402 5	Equipment

Including furnaces, heat engines, heat exchangers, heat pumps

Class solar furnaces in 621.477

.402 8   Specific heat systems

Not provided for elsewhere

Including distribution and storage systems; electric heating

Class a specific aspect of a specific heat system with the aspect, e.g., heat transfer in electric heating 621.4022

.406   Turbines

Class here turbomachines

.42   Stirling engines and air motors

For wind engines, see 621.45

.43   Internal-combustion engines

Class generation of electricity by internal-combustion engines in 621.312133

For internal-combustion engines for a specific type of transportation, see the type, e.g., internal-combustion engines of ships 623.8723

\>   621.433–621.436 Specific internal-combustion engines

Class parts and accessories of specific engines in 621.437; class comprehensive works in 621.43

.433   Gas turbines and free-piston engines

Standard subdivisions are added for gas turbines and free-piston engines, for gas turbines alone

For turbojet engines, see 621.4352

.433 5   Free-piston engines

.434   Spark-ignition engines

Nondiesel piston engines

Including rotary spark-ignition engines

Class here reciprocating spark-ignition engines

.435   Jet and rocket engines

.435 2   Jet engines

Including turbojet engines

.435 6	Rocket engines
	Class here interdisciplinary works on rocketry
	For a specific aspect of rocketry, see the aspect, e.g., rocket weapons 623.4519, booster rockets 629.475
.436	Diesel and semidiesel engines
	Standard subdivisions are added for either or both topics in heading
	Class here compression-ignition engines
[.436 028 8]	Maintenance and repair
	Do not use; class in 621.4368
.436 1	General topics of diesel and semidiesel engines
	Including combustion
.436 2	Design and construction
.436 8	Operation, maintenance, repair
.437	Parts and accessories of internal-combustion engines
	Including carburetors, connecting rods, cylinders, governors, ignition devices, pistons, valves
.44	Geothermal engineering
.45	Wind engines
	Class wind-powered generation of electricity in 621.312136
.453	Windmills
.46	Electric and related motors
	Standard subdivisions are added for electric and related motors together, electric motors alone
.47	Solar-energy engineering
	Class engineering of secondary sources of solar energy with the secondary source, e.g., generation of electricity from solar radiation 621.31244, wind energy 621.45
.471	General topics of solar-energy engineering
.471 2	Heat storage
.472	Solar collectors
.473	Solar engines
.477	Solar furnaces
.48	Nuclear engineering
	Fission and fusion technology
	See also 539.7 for nuclear physics

.483	Nuclear reactors, power plants, by-products

Standard subdivisions are added for nuclear reactors, power plants, by-products together; for nuclear reactors alone; for nuclear power plants alone

Class here fission reactors, nuclear steam-powered generation of electricity; comprehensive works on fission and fusion reactors, power plants, by-products

For fusion reactors, power plants, by-products, see 621.484

.483 015 3	Physical principles

Do not use for reactor physics; class in 621.4831

.483 028 6	Green technology (Environmental technology)

Do not use for waste technology; class in 621.4838

[.483 028 9]	Safety measures

Do not use; class in 621.4835

.483 1	Reactor physics

Including critical size

Class here physics of reactor cores

Class physics of a specific component, material, or process with the component, material, or process, plus notation 0153 from Table 1, e.g., nuclear reactions in fuel elements 621.483350153976

.483 2	Design, construction, shielding, siting
.483 23	Shielding
.483 3	Materials
.483 32	Structural materials
.483 35	Fuel element materials

Fuels and cladding

.483 36	Coolants
.483 37	Moderators
.483 4	Specific types of reactors

Classified by neutron energy, moderator, fuel and fuel conversion, coolant

Including breeder reactors

Class a specific aspect of a specific type with the aspect, e.g., shielding of fast reactors 621.48323

.483 5	Operation, control, safety measures

.483 7	Radioactive isotopes

Class here comprehensive technological works on radioisotopes

For a specific application of radioisotopes, see the application, e.g., radioactive isotope therapy 615.8424, radioisotope thermoelectric generation 621.31243

.483 8	Waste technology
.484	Fusion reactors, fusion power plants, by-products

Standard subdivisions are added for fusion reactors, fusion power plants, by-products together; for fusion reactors alone; for fusion power plants alone

Variant name for fusion reactors: thermonuclear reactors

Including tokamaks

Class comprehensive works on fission and fusion reactor, power plants, by-products in 621.483

.485	Nuclear propulsion
.5	**Pneumatic, vacuum, low-temperature technologies**
.51	Pneumatic technology

Class here air compression technology, air compressors

For a specific kind of pneumatic technology, see the kind, e.g., compressed-air transmission 621.53, pneumatic control 629.8045

.53	Compressed-air transmission
.54	Pneumatic conveying and cleaning

Including carriers, cleaners, sandblasters

.55	Vacuum technology

Including vacuum pumps

See also 533.5 for vacuum physics

.56	Low-temperature technology

Class here refrigeration

For freezers and refrigerators, see 621.57; for ice manufacture, see 621.58; for cryogenic technology, see 621.59

See also 536.56 for physics of low temperatures

.563	Heat pumps
.564	Refrigerants
.57	Freezers and refrigerators
.58	Ice manufacture
.59	Cryogenic technology

Including liquefaction and solidification of gases having low boiling points

.6	**Blowers, fans, pumps**
.61	Blowers and fans

Standard subdivisions are added for either or both topics in heading

For rotary blowers and fans, see 621.62; for centrifugal blowers and fans, see 621.63

.62	Rotary blowers and fans

Standard subdivisions are added for either or both topics in heading

.63	Centrifugal blowers and fans

Standard subdivisions are added for either or both topics in heading

---

> 621.64–621.69 Pumps

Class hydraulic pumps in 621.252; class comprehensive works in 621.69

.64	Hand pumps
.65	Reciprocating pumps
.66	Rotary pumps
.67	Centrifugal pumps
.69	Pneumatic pumps

Class here water-lifting devices, comprehensive works on pumps

For a specific kind of pump, see the kind, e.g., hydraulic pumps 621.252

.691	Jet pumps
.699	Density and direct-fluid-pressure displacement pumps
.8	**Machine engineering**

Class a specific kind of machinery not provided for here with the kind, e.g., hydraulic machinery 621.2; class a specific use of machinery with the use, e.g., gears in clocks 681.112

[.801 53]	Physical principles

Do not use; class in 621.811

.802 87	Testing and measuring

Class here strength tests of mechanisms

[.802 88]	Maintenance and repair

Do not use; class in 621.816

.81	General topics of machine engineering
.811	Physical principles

Including vibration

.812	Power and speed control devices

.815	Machine design	
.816	Maintenance and repair	

> Including balancing

.82	Machine parts

> Including rotors
>
> *For gears, ratchets, cams, see 621.83; for valves, pistons, see 621.84*

.821	Journals
.822	Bearings

> Including ball, roller, sliding bearings
>
> Class journals in 621.821

.823	Shafts

> Including axles
>
> Class bearings in 621.822
>
> *For journals, see 621.821*

.824	Springs
.825	Clutches, couplings, universal joints
.827	Connecting rods, cranks, eccentrics
.83	Gears and cams

> Including pawls, ratchets

.833	Gears

> Class here gearing

.833 1	Spur gears
.833 2	Bevel and skew bevel gears
.833 3	Spiral and worm gears
.838	Cams
.84	Valves and pistons

> Standard subdivisions are added for valves and pistons, for valves alone
>
> Variant names for valves: cocks, faucets, taps

.85	Power transmission systems

> Class power transmission systems for materials-handling equipment in 621.86. Class a specific machine part of a transmission system with the part, e.g., shafts 621.823

.852	Power transmission by belt
.853	Power transmission by rope
.854	Power transmission by wire

.859   Power transmission by chain

.86   Materials-handling equipment

> *For cranes, elevators, see 621.87*

.862   Hoisting equipment

> *For chain hoists, fork lifts, tackles, see 621.863; for capstans, winches, windlasses, see 621.864*

.863   Chain hoists, fork lifts, tackles

.864   Capstans, winches, windlasses

.865   Excavating machinery

> Class here earthmoving machinery, power shovels

.867   Conveying equipment

> *For telpherage, see 621.868*

.867 2   Pipes

> Including pipe laying

> Class here pipelines

> Class coal pipelines in 662.624; class petroleum pipelines in 665.544; class industrial gases pipelines in 665.744. Class manufacturing pipes of a specific material with the material, e.g., metal pipes 671.832

.867 5   Belt conveyors

.867 6   Escalators

.868   Telpherage

> Including chair lifts, ski tows

> Class here comprehensive works on people movers

> *For escalators, see 621.8676; for elevators, see 621.877*

.87   Cranes and elevators

.873   Cranes

> Including cherry pickers, derricks

.877   Elevators

> Including jacks

.88   Fasteners

> *See also 621.97 for fastening equipment*

.882   Bolts, nuts, screws

.883   Cotters

.884   Nails and rivets

.885   Sealing devices

.89   Tribology

Including lubrication, lubricants, wear

Class here friction

For bearings, see 621.822

.9   Tools

Class here fabricating equipment

Class a specific use with the use, e.g., lathes in woodworking 684.08

.900 1–.900 9   Standard subdivisions

.902   Machine tools

.902 3   Numerical control

.904   Pneumatic tools

.908   Hand tools

.91   Planing and milling tools

See also 671.35 for machining metal

.912   Planers, shapers, slotters

.914   Crushing tools

.92   Abrading and grinding tools

Standard subdivisions are added for either or both topics in heading

.922   Lapping tools

Including buffing, polishing tools

.923   Emery wheels and grindstones

.924   Filing tools

.93   Cutting, disassembling, sawing tools

Including axes, crowbars, scissors, shears, slicers, trimmers

.932   Knives

.934   Saws

.94   Turning tools

Class turning tools used for perforating in 621.95

.942   Lathes

.944   Gear-cutting, pipe-threading, screw-cutting tools

For tapping tools, see 621.955

.95 Perforating and tapping tools

> Standard subdivisions are added for perforating and tapping tools together, for perforating tools alone

> *For punching tools, see 621.96*

.952 Drilling tools

> Class here boring tools

.954 Broaching and reaming tools

.955 Tapping tools

> *See also 621.84 for taps (valves)*

.96 Punching tools

> Class die punches in 621.984

.97 Fastening and joining equipment

> Standard subdivisions are added for either or both topics in heading

> Class fasteners in 621.88

.972 Screwdrivers and wrenches

> Variant name for wrenches: spanners

.973 Hand hammers

.974 Power hammers

.977 Soldering and welding equipment

.978 Riveting equipment

.98 Pressing equipment, impressing equipment, molding equipment, additive manufacturing equipment

> Standard subdivisions are added for pressing, impressing, molding, additive manufacturing equipment together; for pressing equipment alone

.982 Bending tools

.984 Impressing and molding equipment

> Including dies, molds, stamps

.988 Additive manufacturing equipment

> Class here three-dimensional printers

> Class additive manufacturing applications in a subject with the subject, plus notation 028 from Table 1, e.g., three-dimensional printing applied to creation of costume jewelry as artistic work 745.5942028

.99 Other tools and equipment

.992 Guiding, holding, safety equipment

> Including chucks, clamps, guards, jigs, vises

622   Mining and related operations

Standard subdivisions are added for mining and related operations together, for mining alone

[.028 9]   Safety measures

Do not use; class in 622.8

.1   Prospecting

Class here exploratory operations

> 622.12–622.17 General topics of prospecting

Class general topics of prospecting applied to specific materials in 622.18; class general topics of prospecting applied to treasure in 622.19; class comprehensive works in 622.1

.12   Surface exploration

Including biogeochemical, geobotanical, geological prospecting

.13   Geochemical prospecting

Including mineral surveys (qualitative and quantitative measurement of mineral content)

Class biogeochemical prospecting in 622.12

.14   Mine surveys

Determination of size, depth, shape of mines

.15   Geophysical prospecting

.152   Gravitational prospecting

.153   Magnetic prospecting

.154   Electrical prospecting

.159   Other methods of prospecting

Including gas-detection, geothermal, radioactivity prospecting

.159 2   Seismic prospecting

Variant names: acoustical, vibration prospecting

.17   Underwater prospecting

.18   Prospecting for specific materials

Add to base number 622.18 the numbers following 553 in 553.2–553.9, e.g., prospecting for petroleum 622.1828; however, for prospecting for water, see 628.11

Standard subdivisions are added for specific materials even if only one type of prospecting is used, e.g., seismic exploration for petroleum in Texas 622.182809764

.19   Prospecting for treasure

         Underground and underwater

         Class here treasure hunting

         Class archaeological methods and equipment in 930.1028

.2   **Excavation techniques**

         Class here underground (subsurface) mining

         Class extraction techniques for specific materials in 622.3

         See also 622.4–622.8 for nonextractive mining technologies

---

>   622.22–622.28   Underground mining

         Class comprehensive works in 622.2

.22   In-situ processing

         Class here leach mining wells, solution mining

         See Manual at 622.22, 622.7 vs. 662.6, 669

.23   Underground blasting and drilling

.24   Underground boring

.25   Shaft sinking

         Class here shafts

.26   Tunneling

         Class here tunnels

.28   Supporting structures

         Class here control of roof and wall failure (rock failure)

.29   Surface and underwater mining

.292   Surface mining

         Class here open-pit and strip mining

         Class reclamation after surface mining in 631.64

         For quarrying, see 622.35

.292 7   Alluvial mining

         Including hydraulic and placer mining

.295   Underwater mining

         Class here offshore mining, mineral extraction from ocean floor

.3   ***Mining for specific materials**

> Class here extraction techniques of specific materials
>
> Class prospecting for specific materials in 622.18. Class a nonextractive mining technology relating to specific materials with the technology in 622.4–622.8, e.g., ore dressing 622.7
>
> *For surface mining of specific materials, see 622.292*

.33   ***Carbonaceous materials**

.331–.337   Coal, graphite, solid and semisolid bitumens

> Add to base number 622.33 the numbers following 553.2 in 553.21–553.27, e.g., coal 622.334; however, for safety measures, see 622.8

.338   ***Oil, oil shales, tar sands, natural gas**

> Use 622.338 for extraction of petroleum covering oil and gas, use 622.3382 for petroleum limited to oil
>
> Class comprehensive technical works on petroleum in 665.5; class interdisciplinary works on petroleum in 553.28

.338 1   *Drilling techniques

> Including use of drilling muds (drilling fluids)

.338 19   *Offshore drilling

> Class here comprehensive works on offshore petroleum extraction
>
> *For a specific aspect of offshore petroleum extraction, see the aspect, e.g., offshore enhanced oil recovery 622.3382*

.338 2   *Oil

> Including well blowouts
>
> Class here reservoir engineering; enhanced, secondary, tertiary recovery; well flooding
>
> Class techniques of drilling for oil in 622.3381

.338 27   *Specific enhanced oil recovery methods

> Including enhanced recovery by use of bacteria

.338 3   *Oil shale and tar sands

> Variant names for oil shale: bituminous, black shale; for tar sands: bituminous, oil sands
>
> Class extraction of oils from oil shale and tar sands in 665.4

.338 5   *Natural gas

> Class techniques of drilling for natural gas in 622.3381

---

*Do not use notation 0289 from Table 1 for safety measures; class in 622.8

.339	*Fossil resins and gums

> Standard subdivisions are added for fossil resins and gums together, for fossil resins alone

.34	*Metals

> Class here the ore of the metal

.341	*Iron

> 622.342–622.349 Nonferrous metals

Class comprehensive works in 622.34

.342	*Precious metals
.342 2	*Gold
.342 3	*Silver
.342 4	*Platinum
.343–.349	Other nonferrous metals

> Add to base number 622.34 the numbers following 553.4 in 553.43–553.49, e.g., uranium ores 622.34932; however, for safety measures, see 622.8

.35–.39	Other materials

> Add to base number 622.3 the numbers following 553 in 553.5–553.9, e.g., gem diamonds 622.382; however, for safety measures, see 622.8; for water, see 628.114

.35	Structural and sculptural stone

> Number built according to instructions under 622.35–622.39

> Class here quarrying

> *For quarrying of other economic materials, see 622.36*

> **622.4–622.8 Nonextractive mining technologies**

Class here nonextractive mining technologies relating to specific materials

Class comprehensive works in 622

.4	**Mine environment**

> *For mine drainage, see 622.5; for mine health and safety, see 622.8*

.42	Ventilation and air conditioning

> *For temperature control, see 622.43*

.43	Temperature control
.47	Illumination

*Do not use notation 0289 from Table 1 for safety measures; class in 622.8

.473   Portable lamps

.474   Electric lighting systems

.48   Electricity

> Class electricity applied to a specific operation with the operation, e.g., temperature control 622.43

.49   Sanitation

.5   Mine drainage

.6   Mine transport systems

> Haulage and hoisting

.65   Hand and animal haulage

.66   Mechanical haulage

> Including mine railroads
>
> Class vertical haulage in 622.68

.67   Direct-driven and gear-driven hoists

.68   Elevators

> Including skips

.69   Surface transportation

> Including loading, unloading, transshipment

.7   Ore dressing

> Class here dressing of specific mineral ores
>
> *See Manual at 622.22, 622.7 vs. 662.6, 669*

.73   Crushing and grinding

.74   Sizing

> Including screening

> 622.75–622.77   Ore concentration

> Variant names: beneficiation, ore separation
>
> Class comprehensive works in 622.7

.75   Mechanical separation

.751   Gravity concentration

.752   Flotation

.77   Electrostatic and magnetic separation

.79   Milling plants

> Class specific milling-plant operations in 622.73–622.77

.8 **Mine health and safety**

Standard subdivisions are added for either or both topics in heading

Class control of roof and wall failure (rock failure) in 622.28; class interdisciplinary works on mine safety in 363.119622

For comprehensive works on safety measures for excavation techniques, see 622.20289; for sanitation, see 622.49. For safety measures for a specific excavation technique, see the technique in 622.22–622.29, plus notation 0289 from Table 1, e.g., safety measures in tunneling 622.260289

.82 Control of gas and explosions

Class here comprehensive works on fire control, on respiratory safety

For dust control, see 622.83

.83 Dust control

.89 Rescue operations

623 Military and nautical engineering

Standard subdivisions are added for military and nautical engineering together, for military engineering alone

See Manual at 355–359 vs. 623

.04 Special topics of military engineering

.042 Optical engineering

Class here infrared and ultraviolet technology

.043 Electronic engineering

.044 Nuclear engineering

.045 Mechanical engineering

.047 Construction engineering

> **623.1–623.7 Military engineering**

Class special topics of military engineering in 623.04; class naval engineering in 623.8; class comprehensive works in 623

.1 **Fortifications**

Class here forts and fortresses

Class architectural aspects in 725.18

.109 History and biography

Do not use for geographic treatment; class in 623.19

.15 Temporary fortifications

.19		Geographic treatment

         Add to base number 623.19 notation 1–9 from Table 2, e.g., forts in France 623.1944

.2		**Mine laying and clearance, demolition**
.26		Mine laying and clearing

         Standard subdivisions are added for either or both topics in heading

         See also 623.45115 for manufacture of mines

.27		Demolition
.3		**Engineering of defense**

         Class warning systems in 623.737

         See also 623.4 for ordnance

.31		Defense against invasion

         Including countermining, flooding, mechanical barriers, moats, traps

         Class architectural aspects of moats in 725.98

         For fortifications, see 623.1; for mine laying, demolition, see 623.2

.38		Protective construction

         Including air raid shelters

.4		**Ordnance**

         Class here weapons, nonlethal weapons

         Class combat ships in 623.82; class comprehensive works on engineering and manufacturing of weapons in 683.4

         For combat vehicles, see 623.74

.41		Artillery

         For specific pieces of artillery, see 623.42; for artillery projectiles, see 623.4513

.412		Field artillery
.417		Coast artillery
.418		Naval artillery
.419		Space artillery
.42		Specific pieces of artillery

         Including crew-served rocket launchers

.422		Catapults

         Class here trebuchets

.424		Cannons
.425		Mortars

.427	Howitzers
.43	Gun mounts
.44	Small arms and miscellaneous weapons

Standard subdivisions are added for small arms and miscellaneous weapons together, for small arms alone

Only those named below

Class here side arms

Class artistic aspects of arms and armor in 739.7. Class vehicle-mounted small arms with the vehicle, e.g., armored cars 623.7475

See also 623.455 for small arms ammunition

.441	Small arms of pre-firearm origin

Including bayonets, maces

Class here comprehensive works on engineering and manufacturing of small arms of pre-firearm origin

For engineering and manufacturing of small arms of pre-firearm origin for civilian use, see 683.4

.441 2	Knives

Class here daggers

.441 3	Swords
.441 4	Axes

Including tomahawks

.441 5	Spears
.441 6	Bows and arrows
.441 8	Armor

Including shields

.442	Portable firearms

For handguns, see 623.443

.442 4	Automatic firearms

Including automatic rifles, machine and submachine guns

Class automatic pistols and revolvers in 623.443

.442 5	Carbines, muskets, rifles
.442 6	Portable rocket launchers (Bazookas)
.443	Handguns
.443 2	Pistols
.443 6	Revolvers

.445   **Chemical weapons**

> Including flame throwers; rifle attachments for launching smoke and gas canisters
>
> Class artillery for launching chemical projectiles in 623.41; class chemical delivery devices in 623.4516
>
> *For chemical agents, see 623.4592*

.446   **Destructive radiation weapons**

> Including laser weapons, thermal weapons

.447   **Destructive vibration weapons**

> Including ultrasonic weapons

.45   **Ammunition and other destructive agents**

> Standard subdivisions are added for ammunition and other destructive agents together, for ammunition alone

.451   **Charge-containing devices**

> Class here bombs, missiles, projectiles
>
> Class interdisciplinary works on bombs in 355.8251; class interdisciplinary works on missiles in 358.17182
>
> *For tactical rockets, see 623.4543*
>
> *See also 623.455 for small arms ammunition*

.451 1   Grenades, mines, nuclear weapons

> Class grenades and mines with special types of charges in 623.4516–623.4518

.451 14   Grenades

> Class here hand and rifle grenades

.451 15   Mines

> Class mine laying and clearance in 623.26

.451 19   Nuclear weapons

> Including artillery projectiles, bombs
>
> *For nuclear missiles, see 623.4519*

.451 3   Artillery projectiles

> Class artillery projectiles with special types of charges in 623.4516–623.4518; class nuclear artillery projectiles in 623.45119

.451 4   Antipersonnel devices

Including booby traps

Class here shrapnel devices

For a specific antipersonnel device other than booby traps and shrapnel devices, see the device, e.g., antipersonnel hand grenades 623.45114

>   623.451 6–623.451 8   Devices with special types of charges

Class comprehensive works in 623.451

For nuclear weapons, see 623.45119

.451 6   Chemical and biological devices

Projectiles and related devices containing incendiary materials, microbes, poison gas, smoke

Standard subdivisions are added for chemical and biological devices together, for chemical devices alone

Class here weapons of mass destruction

Class chemical agents in 623.4592; class biological agents in 623.4594

For nuclear weapons, see 623.45119

.451 7   High-explosive devices

Including blockbusters, high-explosive-antitank (HEAT) projectiles, torpedoes

For bangalore torpedoes, see 623.4545

.451 8   Armor-piercing devices

.451 9   Guided missiles

Nuclear and nonnuclear missiles

Class here storage and launching equipment, launch vehicles; strategic missiles, comprehensive works on rocket weapons

Class comprehensive works on rocketry in 621.4356

For tactical rockets, see 623.4543

.451 91   Air-to-air guided missiles

.451 92   Air-to-surface guided missiles

.451 93   Air-to-underwater guided missiles

.451 94   Surface-to-air guided missiles

Class here antimissile missiles, interceptor missiles

.451 95   Ballistic missiles

Class here surface-to-surface guided missiles

.451 952	Short-range ballistic missiles
.451 953	Intermediate-range ballistic missiles
.451 954	Long-range ballistic missiles

> Class here intercontinental ballistic missiles

.451 96	Surface-to-underwater guided missiles
.451 97	Underwater guided missiles

> Including underwater-to-air, underwater-to-surface, underwater-to-underwater missiles

.451 98	Space guided missiles
.452	Explosives
.452 6	Burning and deflagrating explosives

> Including cordite, guncotton, gunpowder, smokeless powder

> Class here propellant explosives

.452 7	High explosives

> Including dynamite, nitroglycerin, TNT

.454	Detonators, tactical rockets, demolition charges
.454 2	Detonators

> Including fuses, percussion caps, primers

.454 3	Tactical rockets

> Unguided nuclear and nonnuclear rockets

> Class comprehensive works on rocket weapons, on rocket-propelled guided missiles in 623.4519

.454 5	Demolition charges

> Including bangalore torpedoes, destructors, shaped charges

> Class shaped charges in bombs, missiles, projectiles in 623.451

.455	Small arms ammunition

> Including bazooka rockets, bullets, cartridges

.459	Nonexplosive agents

> Class here detection of nonexplosive agents

.459 2	Chemical agents

> Including tear gas

> Class here poisons and gases

.459 4	Biological agents
.46	Accessories

> Including range finders, sighting apparatus

.5		**Ballistics and gunnery**
.51		Ballistics
.513		Interior ballistics

Motion of projectiles within the bore

.514		Exterior ballistics

Motion of projectiles after leaving gun tube

.516		Terminal ballistics

Effect of projectiles on targets

.55 Gunnery

For recoil, see 623.57

.551 Land gunnery

.553 Naval gunnery

.555 Aircraft gunnery

.556 Spacecraft gunnery

.557 Target selection and detection

Class range and sighting apparatus in 623.46; class application to specific types of gunnery in 623.551–623.556

.558 Firing and fire control

Standard subdivisions are added for either or both topics in heading

Class application to specific types of gunnery in 623.551–623.556

For target selection and detection, see 623.557

.57 Recoil

.6 **Military transportation technology**

For vehicles, see 623.74

.61 Land transportation

For roads, see 623.62; for railroads, see 623.63; for bridges, see 623.67; for tunnels, see 623.68

.62 Roads

.63 Railroads

.631 The way

Earthwork and track

.633 Rolling stock

.64		Naval facilities

> Including artificial harbors, docks
>
> Class here naval bases
>
> Class architectural aspects of naval facilities in 725.34

.66		Air facilities

> Class here air bases, airports, comprehensive works on military aerospace engineering
>
> Add to base number 623.66 the numbers following 629.136 in 629.1361–629.1368, e.g., airstrips 623.6612
>
> Class architectural aspects of air facilities in 725.39
>
> *For military astronautics, see 623.69; for aircraft, see 623.746*

.67		Bridges
.68		Tunnels
.69		Space facilities

> Class here comprehensive works on military astronautics
>
> *For spacecraft, see 623.749*

.7		**Communications, vehicles, sanitation, related topics**
.71		Intelligence and reconnaissance topography

> Standard subdivisions are added for intelligence and reconnaissance topography together, for intelligence alone
>
> Including sketching and map making
>
> *For photography and photogrammetry, see 623.72*

.72		Photography and photogrammetry
.73		Communications technology

> Class comprehensive works on military electronics in 623.043

.731		Visual signals
.731 2		Flag signals, heliographs, semaphores
.731 3		Pyrotechnical devices
.731 4		Electrooptical devices
.732		Telegraphy

> *For radiotelegraphy, see 623.7342*

.733		Telephony

> *For radiotelephony, see 623.7345*

.734	Radio and radar

Standard subdivisions are added for radio and radar together, for radio alone

.734 1	Shortwave radio
.734 2	Radiotelegraphy

Class shortwave radiotelegraphy in 623.7341

.734 5	Radiotelephony

Class shortwave radiotelephony in 623.7341

.734 8	Radar
.735	Television
.737	Warning systems

Class here air raid warning systems

.74	Vehicles

Support vehicles, combat vehicles and their ordnance

For ammunition and other destructive agents, see 623.45; for railroad rolling stock, see 623.633; for nautical craft, see 623.82

See Manual at 629.046 vs. 388

.741	Lighter-than-air aircraft

For specific types of lighter-than-air aircraft, see 623.742–623.744

> 623.742–623.744 Specific types of lighter-than-air aircraft

Class comprehensive works in 623.741

.742	Free balloons

Class here comprehensive works on military balloons

For barrage balloons, see 623.744

.743	Airships (Dirigibles)
.743 5	Rigid airships
.743 6	Semirigid airships
.743 7	Nonrigid airships
.744	Barrage balloons
.746	Heavier-than-air aircraft

Class here comprehensive works on aircraft

For lighter-than-air aircraft, see 623.741

.746 04	Special topics of aircraft

>   623.746 042–623.746 047   General types of heavier-than-air aircraft

Class here piloting general types of heavier-than-air aircraft

Class comprehensive works in 623.746; class comprehensive works on piloting in 623.746048

.746 042   Propeller-driven airplanes

.746 044   Jet planes

            Class jet powered-lift aircraft in 623.7460476

.746 047   Vertical-lift aircraft (VTOL aircraft)

.746 047 2   Rotorcraft

            Class here helicopters

.746 047 6   Powered-lift aircraft

            Class here convertiplanes

.746 048   Piloting

            Class piloting of a specific type of heavier-than-air aircraft with the aircraft, e.g., piloting jet planes 623.746044, piloting fighters 623.7464

.746 049   Components

            Including engines, escape equipment, instrumentation (avionics)

            Class components of a specific type of aircraft with the aircraft, e.g., components of jet planes 623.746044, of fighters 623.7464

            For aircraft ordnance, see 623.7461

.746 1   Aircraft ordnance

            For charge-containing devices, see 623.451

>   623.746 2–623.746 7   Heavier-than-air aircraft for specific uses

Class here piloting heavier-than-air aircraft for specific uses

Add to each subdivision identified by * the numbers following 623.74604 in 623.746042–623.746047, e.g., jet fighters 623.74644

Class aircraft ordnance regardless of type of aircraft in 623.7461; class drones regardless of type in 623.7469; class comprehensive works in 623.746; class comprehensive works on piloting in 623.746048

.746 2   *Trainers

---

*Add as instructed under 623.7462–623.7467

.746 3	*Bombers and fighter-bombers
	Class here attack airplanes, close support aircraft
	Subdivisions are added for either or both topics in heading
.746 4	*Fighters
.746 5	*Transport aircraft
	Cargo and personnel
.746 6	*Rescue aircraft
.746 7	*Reconnaissance aircraft
.746 9	Drones
	Variant names: guided aircraft, pilotless aircraft
	Add to base number 623.7469 the numbers following 623.746 in 623.7462–623.7467, e.g., reconnaissance drones 623.74697
.747	Motor land vehicles
.747 2	Motor land vehicles for transporting personnel
	Class armored personnel carriers in 623.7475
.747 22	Jeeps and similar vehicles
	Standard subdivisions are added for jeeps and similar vehicles together, for jeeps alone
.747 23	Buses
.747 24	Ambulances
.747 4	Motor land vehicles for transporting supplies
.747 5	Motor land vehicles for combat
	Including armored personnel carriers
.747 52	Tanks
.748	Air-cushion vehicles
.748 2	Overland air-cushion vehicles
.748 4	Overwater air-cushion vehicles
.748 5	Amphibious air-cushion vehicles
.749	Spacecraft
.75	Sanitation and safety engineering
	Class here health engineering
.751	Water supply
.753	Sewage treatment and disposal

*Add as instructed under 623.7462–623.7467

.754	Garbage and refuse treatment and disposal
.76	Electrical engineering
.77	Camouflage and concealment

.8   **Nautical engineering and seamanship**

> Nautical engineering: engineering of ships and boats and their component parts
>
> Standard subdivisions are added for nautical engineering and seamanship together, for nautical engineering alone
>
> Class here naval engineering, comprehensive works on military water transportation
>
> Class harbors, ports, roadsteads in 627.2
>
> *For naval facilities, see 623.64*

.802 84   Apparatus, equipment, materials

> Do not use for equipment and outfit of nautical craft; class in 623.86

.81   Naval architecture

> Variant names: marine architecture, naval design

.812   Design of craft

.812 04   Design of general types of craft

> Add to base number 623.81204 the numbers following 623.820 in 623.8202–623.8205, e.g., design of submersible craft 623.812045

.812 1–.812 9   Design of specific kinds of craft

> Add to base number 623.812 the numbers following 623.82 in 623.821–623.829, e.g., design of sailboats 623.81223

.817   Structural analysis and design

> Add to base number 623.817 the numbers following 624.17 in 624.171–624.177, e.g., structural analysis 623.8171, wreckage studies 623.8176
>
> Class structural analysis and design of general and specific kinds of craft in 623.812; class structural analysis and design of specific metals in 623.818

.818   Design in specific materials

> Add to base number 623.818 the numbers following 624.18 in 624.182–624.189, e.g., design in steel 623.81821
>
> Class design of general and specific kinds of craft in a specific material in 623.812

.82   Nautical craft

> Class shipyards in 623.83; class overwater hovercraft in 629.324

> *For naval architecture, see 623.81; for parts and details of nautical craft, see 623.84–623.87*

> *See Manual at 629.046 vs. 388*

.820 01   Philosophy and theory

.820 02   Miscellany

[.820 022 8]   Models and miniatures

> Do not use; class in 623.8201

.820 03–.820 09   Standard subdivisions

.820 1   Models and miniatures

> Class ships in bottles in 745.5928

.820 104   Models and miniatures of general types of craft

> Add to base number 623.820104 the numbers following 623.820 in 623.8202–623.8205, e.g., models of sailing craft 623.8201043

.820 11–.820 19   Models and miniatures of specific types of craft

> Add to base number 623.8201 the numbers following 623.82 in 623.821–623.829, e.g., models of battleships 623.820152

>   623.820 2–623.820 5   General types of craft

> Class general types of craft in specific materials in 623.8207; class specific types of craft in 623.821–623.829; class comprehensive works in 623.82

.820 2   *Small craft

> Class small sailing craft in 623.8203; class small submersible craft in 623.8205; class small power-driven craft in 623.823

.820 23   *Pleasure craft

> Including yachts

.820 26   *Working craft

.820 3   *Sailing ships

.820 4   *Power-driven ships

> Including hydrofoils, steamships

> Class power-driven submersible craft in 623.8205; class small power-driven craft in 623.823

.820 5   *Submersible craft

---

*Do not use notation 0228 from Table 1 for models and miniatures; class in 623.8201

.820 7	*Craft of specific materials
	Class works limited to hulls of specific materials in 623.84
.821	*Ancient and medieval craft
	Including biremes, caravels, galleys, triremes

> ### 623.822–623.829 Modern craft

Class comprehensive works in 623.82

.822	*Modern wind-driven ships
	Including rotor ships
	Class comprehensive works on ancient, medieval, and modern wind-driven ships in 623.8203
.822 3	*Pleasure craft
	Including sailing yachts
.822 4	*Merchant ships
	Including clipper ships
.822 5	*Warships
.822 6	*Work ships
	Including research ships
	For merchant ships, see 623.8224

> ### 623.823–623.828 Power-driven craft

Class comprehensive works in 623.8204

.823	*Small and medium power-driven ships
	For small and medium power-driven craft not provided for here, see 623.824–623.828
.823 1	*Motorboats
	Class here speedboats
.823 13	*Outboard motorboats
.823 14	*Inboard motorboats
	Including hydroplanes, motor yachts
.823 15	*Inboard-outboard motorboats
.823 2	*Tugboats and towboats
.823 4	*Ferryboats

*Do not use notation 0228 from Table 1 for models and miniatures; class in 623.8201

.824   *Power-driven merchant and factory ships

Standard subdivisions are added for power-driven merchant and factory ships together, for power-driven merchant ships alone

Class trawlers in 623.828

.824 3   *Passenger ships

Class ferryboats in 623.8234

.824 32   *Ocean liners

.824 36   *Inland-waterway ships

Including river steamers

.824 5   *Cargo ships

Including bulk carriers, freighters, tankers

.824 8   *Factory ships

Including ship canneries, whaleboats

.825   *Power-driven warships

For support warships, see 623.826

.825 1   Naval ordnance

Class here armor, weapons

For naval artillery, see 623.418; for charge-containing devices, see 623.451

> 623.825 2–623.825 8 Specific types of combat warships

Class naval ordnance in 623.8251; class comprehensive works in 623.825

.825 2   *Battleships

.825 3   *Cruisers

.825 4   *Destroyers and destroyer escorts

Standard subdivisions are added for destroyers and destroyer escorts together, for destroyers alone

.825 5   *Aircraft carriers

.825 6   *Landing craft

.825 7   *Submarines

Class comprehensive works on submersible craft in 623.8205

.825 72   *Diesel-engine and electric-motor powered submarines

.825 74   *Nuclear-powered submarines

*Do not use notation 0228 from Table 1 for models and miniatures; class in 623.8201

.825 8		*Light combat craft
		Including torpedo boats
.826		*Support warships and other government ships
.826 2		*Minelayers and minesweepers
.826 3		*Coast guard ships, police boats, revenue cutters
.826 4		*Hospital ships and military transports
.826 5		*Military supply ships
.827		*Nonmilitary submersible craft
		Including bathyscaphes, bathyspheres
		Class comprehensive works on submersible craft in 623.8205
.828		*Other power-driven ships
		Including dredgers, drilling ships, icebreakers
.828 2		*Fishing boats
		Including trawlers
		For whaling ships, see 623.8248
.829		*Hand-propelled and towed craft
		Including barges, canoes, coracles, lifeboats, rafts, rowboats, scows, towed canalboats
.83		Shipyards
		Including dry docks, floating dry docks

> 623.84–623.87 Parts and details of nautical craft

Class here design

Class comprehensive works in 623.82

.84	Hulls of nautical craft
	Class hydrodynamics of hulls in 623.812
.842	Lofting
.843	Metalwork
.843 2	Riveting and welding
.843 3	Ship fitting
.844	Carpentry

*Do not use notation 0228 from Table 1 for models and miniatures; class in 623.8201

.845	Construction with ceramics, masonry, allied materials

Add to base number 623.845 the numbers following 624.183 in 624.1832–624.1838, e.g., concrete hulls 623.8454

.848	Resistant construction

Including corrosion-resistant, fire-resistant construction

.85	Engineering systems of nautical craft

For power plants, see 623.87

.850 01–.850 09	Standard subdivisions
.850 1	Mechanical systems
.850 3	Electrical systems
.850 4	Electronic systems
.852	Electric lighting
.853	Temperature controls and air conditioning

Standard subdivisions are added for temperature controls and air conditioning together, for temperature controls alone

.853 5	Cooling

Including refrigeration

.853 7	Heating and air conditioning
.854	Water supply and sanitation
.854 2	Potable water
.854 3	Seawater

Used for fire fighting and sanitation

.854 6	Sanitation

Class seawater for sanitation in 623.8543

.856	Communication systems

Add to base number 623.856 the numbers following 623.73 in 623.731–623.737, e.g., flag systems 623.85612

.86	Equipment and outfit of nautical craft

Including flares, other portable lights

Class use of equipment and outfit in 623.88

.862	Gear and rigging

Including anchors, cordage, masts, rope, rudders, sails, spars

.863	Nautical instruments

.865   Safety equipment

      Including fire fighting, lifesaving equipment

      Class comprehensive works on marine safety technology in 623.888

.866   Furniture

.867   Cargo-handling equipment

      Class cargo handling in 623.8881

      For onshore cargo-handling equipment, see 627.34

.87   Power plants of nautical craft

      Class here marine engineering

.872   Specific kinds of engines

[.872 01–.872 09]   Standard subdivisions

      Do not use; class in 623.8701–623.8709

.872 2   Steam engines

.872 3   Internal-combustion engines

      Class here inboard motors

      Add to base number 623.8723 the numbers following 621.43 in 621.433–621.437, e.g., outboard motors 623.87234, diesel engines 623.87236

.872 6   Electric engines

.872 7   Solar engines

.872 8   Nuclear engines

.873   Engine auxiliaries

      Including boilers, pipes, propellers, pumps, shafts

.874   Fuels

.88   Seamanship

      For navigation, see 623.89

[.880 289]   Safety measures

      Do not use; class in 623.888

.881   Ship handling

      Class safety and related topics in handling craft in 623.888

      For handling specific types of craft, see 623.882

.881 2–.881 5   Handling general types of craft

      Add to base number 623.881 the numbers following 623.820 in 623.8202–623.8205, e.g., handling small craft 623.8812

.882   Handling various specific types of craft

Class safety and related topics in handling specific types of craft in 623.888

[.882 01–.882 09]   Standard subdivisions

Do not use; class in 623.88101–623.88109

.882 1–.882 9   Specific types of craft

Add to base number 623.882 the numbers following 623.82 in 623.821–623.829, e.g., handling power-driven merchant ships 623.8824

.888   Specific topics of seamanship

Class here marine safety technology

For safety equipment, see 623.865

[.888 01–.888 09]   Standard subdivisions

Do not use; class in 623.8801–623.8809

.888 1   Loading and unloading of nautical craft

Standard subdivisions are added for either or both topics in heading

Class here cargo handling

.888 2   Knotting and splicing ropes and cables

Class here interdisciplinary works on knotting and splicing

For a specific application of knotting and splicing, see the application, e.g., knotting in camping 796.545

.888 4   Prevention of collision and grounding

Including rules of the road

.888 5   Wreckage studies

Class wreckage studies in marine architecture in 623.8176

.888 6   Fire fighting technology

See also 623.865 for manufacture of fire fighting equipment

.888 7   Rescue operations

.89   Navigation

Selection and determination of course

Class navigation procedures to prevent collision and grounding in 623.8884

.892   Geonavigation

For electronic aids to geonavigation, see 623.893

.892 021   Tabulated and related materials

Do not use for tide and current tables; class in 623.8949

.892 2   Piloting and pilot guides

                          Positioning craft by visual observation of objects of known position

                          Standard subdivisions are added for either or both topics in heading

                          Class here nautical charts

                          For piloting in and pilot guides to specific marine harbors and shores, see 623.8929

[.892 209 163–.892 209 167]   Treatment by specific oceans and seas

                          Do not use; class in 623.89223–623.89227

.892 209 168   Treatment by specific oceanographic forms

                          Do not use for inland seas; class in 623.89229

.892 209 169   Treatment by fresh and brackish waters

                          Do not use for specific inland waters; class in 623.89229

.892 23–.892 27   Piloting in and pilot guides to specific oceans and intercontinental seas

                          Add to base number 623.8922 the numbers following —16 in notation 163–167 from Table 2, e.g., pilot guides to North Sea 623.8922336; however, for piloting in and pilot guides to specific marine harbors and shores, see 623.8929

.892 29   Piloting in and pilot guides to specific inland waters

                          Add to base number 623.89229 notation 4–9 from Table 2, e.g., pilot guides to Great Lakes 623.8922977; however, for piloting in and pilot guides to specific marine harbors and shores, see 623.8929

.892 3   Dead reckoning

.892 9   Piloting in and pilot guides to specific marine harbors and shores

                          Standard subdivisions are added for either or both topics in heading

                          Class here approach and harbor piloting and pilot guides

[.892 909 1]   Areas, regions, places in general

                          Do not use; class in 623.89291

[.892 909 3–.892 909 9]   Specific continents, countries, localities

                          Do not use; class in 623.89293–623.89299

.892 91   Piloting in and pilot guides to specific areas, regions, places in general

                          Add to base number 623.89291 the numbers following —1 in notation 11–19 from Table 2, e.g., pilot guides of developing countries 623.89291724; however, for approach and harbor piloting and pilot guides dealing comprehensively with specific oceans and intercontinental seas, see 623.89223–623.89227
                          Subdivisions are added for either or both topics in heading

.892 93–.892 99   Piloting in and pilot guides to specific continents, countries, localities

> Add to base number 623.8929 notation 3–9 from Table 2, e.g., pilot guides of India 623.892954
> Subdivisions are added for either or both topics in heading

.893   Geonavigation aids

> Class here electronic aids to geonavigation, navigation aids

> *For nonelectronic aids to geonavigation, see 623.894*

>   623.893 2–623.893 3   Direction-finding and position-finding devices

> Class comprehensive works in 623.893

.893 2   Radio aids

> Including compasses, loran, radio

.893 3   Microwave aids

> Including racon, radar, shoran

> Class here GPS receivers

.893 8   Sounding devices

> Including echo-ranging and sound-ranging devices, e.g., sonar

.894   Nonelectronic aids to geonavigation

.894 2   Lighthouses

> Class interdisciplinary works on lighthouses in 387.155

.894 3   Lightships

.894 4   Light beacons, buoys, daymarks

.894 5   Light lists

.894 9   Tide and current tables

> Standard subdivisions are added for either or both topics in heading

624   Civil engineering

Including engineering of landscape architecture

Class here construction engineering

> *For military construction engineering, see 623.047. For a specific branch of civil engineering not provided for here, see the branch, e.g., construction of buildings 690*

> *See Manual at 624 vs. 624.1; also at 624 vs. 690*

.029   Commercial miscellany

> Class interdisciplinary works on quantity surveying in 692.5

.1   **Structural engineering and underground construction**

> Standard subdivisions are added for structural engineering and underground construction together, for structural engineering alone
>
> Class a specific application of structural engineering with the application, e.g., structural engineering of dams 627.8
>
> *See Manual at 624 vs. 624.1*

.101   Philosophy and theory

> Class structural theory, theory of structure in 624.17

.15   Foundation engineering and engineering geology

> Standard subdivisions are added for foundation engineering and engineering geology together, for foundation engineering alone

.151   Engineering geology

> Class here geotechnical engineering, properties of foundation soils

.151 09   History, geographic treatment, biography

> Class soil surveys in 624.1517

.151 3   Rock and soil mechanics

.151 32   Rock mechanics

.151 36   Soil mechanics

> Including drainage properties, permeability; permafrost

.151 362   Soil consolidation

.151 363   Soil stabilization

> Class here soil compaction

.151 4   Soil content analysis

.151 7   Soil surveys

> Class interdisciplinary works on soil surveys in 631.47

[.151 709 1]   Areas, regions, places in general

> Do not use; class in 624.15171

[.151 709 3–.151 709 9]   Specific continents, countries, localities

> Do not use; class in 624.15173–624.15179

.151 71   Areas, regions, places in general

> Add to base number 624.15171 the numbers following —1 in notation 11–19 from Table 2, e.g., soil survey of tropical regions 624.151713

.151 73–.151 79   Specific continents, countries, localities

> Add to base number 624.1517 notation 3–9 from Table 2, e.g., soil survey of Japan 624.151752

>   624.152–624.158   Foundation engineering

       Class engineering geology of foundations in 624.151; class comprehensive works in 624.15

.152   Excavation

         Including grading, shoring

         Class here earthwork

         Class embankments in 624.162

.152 6   Blasting

.153   Foundation materials

         Add to base number 624.153 the numbers following 620.1 in 620.12–620.19, e.g., iron 624.1537

         Class foundation materials for specific types of foundations in 624.154–624.158

>   624.154–624.158   Specific types of foundations

       Class comprehensive works in 624.15

.154   Pile foundations

.156   Floating foundations

         Including cantilever and platform foundations

.157   Underwater foundations

         Including caissons, cofferdams

         Class underwater pier foundations in 624.158; class comprehensive works on underwater constuction in 627.702

.158   Pier foundations

.16   Supporting structures other than foundations

         Class temporary supporting structures during excavation in 624.152

.162   Embankments

.164   Retaining walls

.17   Structural analysis and design

Standard subdivisions are added for structural analysis and design together, for structural analysis alone

Class here mechanics of structures, structural elements, structural theory, interdisciplinary works on structural analysis and design

Unless other instructions are given, class a subject with aspects in two or more subdivisions of 624.17 in the number coming last, e.g., wind loads on shells 624.17762 (*not* 624.175)

For a specific application of structural analysis and design, see the application, e.g., structural analysis of aircraft 629.1341

.171   Specific elements of structural analysis

Including structural control, failures, stability

For loads, see 624.172; for stresses and strains, see 624.176

.171 2   Graphic statics

.171 3   Statically indeterminate structures

Including static determinacy and indeterminacy

.171 4   Deflections

.171 5   Moment distribution method

.172   Loads

For wind loads, see 624.175

.175   Wind loads

.176   Stresses and strains (Deformation)

Standard subdivisions are added for either or both topics in heading

Including blast-resistant construction

Class here wreckage studies

.176 2   Earthquake engineering

.177   Structural design and specific structural elements

[.177 01–.177 09]   Standard subdivisions

Do not use; class in 624.1701–624.1709

.177 1   Structural design

For design with specific materials, see 624.18

.177 13   Structural optimization

> 624.177 2–624.177 9 Specific structural elements

Class here specific structural elements in metal, design and construction of specific elements

Class specific structural elements in materials other than metal in 624.18; class comprehensive works in 624.17

.177 2   Beams, girders, cylinders, columns, slabs

.177 23   Beams and girders

Standard subdivisions are added for either or both topics in heading

.177 25   Columns

.177 3   Trusses and frames

Standard subdivisions are added for either or both topics in heading

.177 3   Trusses and frames

Standard subdivisions are added for either or both topics in heading

.177 4   Cables, wires, bars, rods

.177 5   Arches and domes

.177 6   Shells and plates

.177 62   Shells

.177 65   Plates

.177 9   Sandwich and honeycomb constructions

Standard subdivisions are added for either or both topics in heading

Class specific sandwich and honeycomb constructions in 624.1772–624.1776

.18   Materials

Class here design and construction

.182   Metals

Class specific structural elements in metal in 624.1772–624.1779

.182 1   Iron and steel (Ferrous metals)

Standard subdivisions are added for either or both topics in heading

.182 2–.182 9   Nonferrous metals

Add to base number 624.182 the numbers following 620.18 in 620.182–620.189, e.g., construction in aluminum 624.1826

.183   Masonry, ceramic, allied materials

.183 2   Stone

Including artificial stone, e.g., concrete blocks

.183 3	Cement
.183 4	Concrete

Class concrete and cinder blocks in 624.1832

See also 721.0445 for visual concrete

.183 41	Reinforced concrete (Ferroconcrete)

Class a specific concrete structural element of reinforced concrete in 624.18342–624.18349

.183 412	Prestressed concrete
.183 414	Precast concrete
.183 42–.183 49	Specific concrete structural elements

Add to base number 624.1834 the numbers following 624.177 in 624.1772–624.1779, e.g., concrete shells 624.183462

.183 6	Brick and tile
.183 8	Glass
.184	Wood and laminated wood

Standard subdivisions are added for wood and laminated wood together, for wood alone

.189	Other materials

Add to base number 624.189 the numbers following 620.19 in 620.191–620.199, e.g., design in plastics 624.18923

.19	Underground construction

Class here ventilation

Class subsurface mining in 622.2

For construction of underground waste disposal facilities, see 628.44566

.192	Mountain tunnels
.193	Tunnels

Class architectural aspects in 725.98

For military tunnel engineering, see 623.68; for mountain tunnels, see 624.192; for underwater tunnels, see 624.194

.194	Underwater tunnels
.2	**Bridges**

Class here compound bridges, long-span bridges

Unless other instructions are given, class a subject with aspects in two or more subdivisions of 624.2 in the number coming last, e.g., movable truss bridges 624.24 (*not* 624.217)

Class architecture of bridges in 725.98

For military bridge engineering, see 623.67

.209 3–.209 9   Specific continents, countries, localities

> Class specific bridges of a specific kind in 624.21–624.24

>   624.21–624.24   Specific kinds of bridges

Class comprehensive works in 624.2

.21   Girder and related kinds of bridges

Standard subdivisions are added for girder and related kinds of bridges together, for girder bridges alone

Including beam bridges, tubular bridges

Class here continuous bridges

.215   Box-girder bridges

.217   Iron and steel truss bridges

Standard subdivisions are added for either or both topics in heading

.218   Timber truss bridges

Class here covered bridges

.219   Cantilever bridges

.22   Arch bridges

.225   Masonry arch bridges

.23   Suspension and cable-stayed bridges

Standard subdivisions are added for suspension and cable-stayed bridges together, for suspension bridges alone

.238   Cable-stayed bridges

.24   Movable bridges

.25   Structural analysis and design

Standard subdivisions are added for either or both topics in heading

Class structural analysis and design of specific kinds of bridges in 624.21–624.24

.252   Loads, stresses, strains

.257   Specific structural elements

For floors and foundations, see 624.28

[.257 01–.257 09]   Standard subdivisions

Do not use; class in 624.201–624.209

.28   Floors and foundations

.283   Floors

Class here structural analysis and design of floors

.284   Foundations

Class here structural analysis and design of foundations

625   Engineering of railroads and roads

Class tunnel engineering in 624.193; class bridge engineering in 624.2; class land transportation engineering in 629.049

.1   Railroads

Including comprehensive works on special-purpose railroads

Class here comprehensive works on broad-gage, narrow-gage, standard-gage railroads

Class electrification of railroads in 621.33; class interdisciplinary works on railroads in 385

For military railroad engineering, see 623.63; for railroad rolling stock, see 625.2; for special-purpose railroads, see 625.3–625.6

.100 1   Philosophy and theory

.100 2   Miscellany

[.100 228]   Models and miniatures

Do not use; class in 625.19

.100 288   Maintenance and repair

Including snow removal operations

.100 3–.100 9   Standard subdivisions

.11   Surveying and design

Including final location surveys; determination of grades, switchbacks, right-of-way

---

>   625.12–625.16   Permanent way

Class comprehensive works in 625.1

For permanent way of special-purpose railroads, see 625.3–625.6

.12   Earthwork

.122   Engineering geology

Including rock and soil mechanics

Class here properties of soils that support structures (foundation soils)

.123   Roadbed preparation

Including excavation

.13   Protective structures

Including retaining walls, snow fences, snowsheds

.14   Track

> *For rails and rail fastenings, see 625.15; for track accessories, see 625.16*

.141   Ballast

.143   Ties (Sleepers)

> Including tie plates

.144   Track laying

> *For laying of tracks over ice, see 625.147*

.147   Tracks over ice

.15   Rails

> Including rail fastenings

.16   Track accessories

.163   Turnouts and crossings

> Including frogs, switches, sidings

.165   Control devices

> Including signals, signs

.18   Railroad yards

.19   Model and miniature railroads and trains

> Standard subdivisions are added for either or both topics in heading

> Add to base number 625.19 the numbers following 625.2 in 625.21–625.26, e.g., models of steam locomotives 625.1961

> Class play with model railroads and trains in 790.133

> > *For models and miniatures of a specific kind of special-purpose railroad, see the kind in 625.3–625.6, e.g., models of subways 625.420228, models of monorail rolling stock 625.44*

.2   **Railroad rolling stock**

> Class here comprehensive works on specific types of cars, on rolling stock for roads with two running rails

> *For rolling stock for special-purpose railroads, see 625.3–625.6*

> *See Manual at 629.046 vs. 388*

[.202 28]   Models and miniatures

> Do not use; class in 625.19

.21   *Running gear

         Including axles, bearings, springs, wheels

         Class here running gear for specific types of cars

>   625.22–625.24   Specific types of cars

         Class running gear for specific types of cars in 625.21; class accessory equipment for specific types of cars in 625.25; class comprehensive works in 625.2

.22   *Work cars (Nonrevenue rolling stock)

         Including cabooses, handcars, railroad snowplows

.23   *Passenger-train cars

         Including coaches; baggage, dining, sleeping cars

.24   *Freight cars

         Including boxcars, gondola cars, refrigerator cars, tank cars

.25   *Accessory equipment

         Including brakes, buffers, couplings

         Class here accessory equipment for specific types of cars

.26   *Locomotives

         Class running gear in 625.21; class accessory equipment in 625.25

.261   *Steam locomotives

.262   *Gas-turbine locomotives

.263   *Electric locomotives

         For diesel-electric locomotives, see 625.2662

.265   *Air-compression-powered locomotives

.266   *Diesel and semidiesel locomotives

         Standard subdivisions are added for either or both topics in heading

.266 2   *Diesel-electric locomotives

.266 4   *Diesel-hydraulic locomotives

.27   Mechanical operation

*Do not use notation 0228 from Table 1; class in 625.19

> **625.3–625.6   Special-purpose railroads**

    Class here roadbeds, tracks and accessories, rolling stock

    Class comprehensive works in 625.1

    For mine railroads, see 622.66

.3   **Inclined, mountain, ship railroads**

.32   Funicular railroads

.33   Rack railroads

.39   Ship railroads

.4   **Local rail transit systems**

    Including guided-way systems

    Class here local surface rail systems using conventional (heavy) rail technology; commuter rail systems, rapid transit rail systems, urban and suburban rail systems; comprehensive works on local rail transit systems with multiple transit modes

    For light rail transit systems, see 625.6

.42   Underground systems (Subways)

.44   Elevated systems

    Including monorail systems

.5   **Cable and aerial railways**

    For funicular railroads, see 625.32

.6   **Light rail transit systems**

    Class here interurban railroads (streetcar lines running between urban areas or from urban to rural areas); streetcar systems, tramways, trolley-car systems

.65   Roadbeds, tracks, accessories

.66   Rolling stock

    Class here streetcars, trams, trolley cars

.7   **Roads**

    Class here highways, streets

    Class grade crossings (road crossings of railroads) in 625.163; class interdisciplinary works on roads and highways in 388.1; class interdisciplinary works on urban roads and streets in 388.411

    For military road engineering, see 623.62; for artificial road surfaces, see 625.8; for forestry roads, see 634.93

[.702 88]   Maintenance and repair

    Do not use; class in 625.76

.72   **Surveying and design**

.723   Surveying

            Class soil surveys in 625.732

.725   Design

            Including determination of bankings, grades

.73   **Earthwork**

.732   Engineering geology

            Including rock and soil mechanics

            Class here properties of soils that support structures (foundation soils)

.733   Foundation preparation

            Including excavation

.734   Drainage

            Including conduits, dikes, ditches, gutters, pipes

.734 2   Culverts

.735   Subsurface highway materials

.74   **Dirt roads**

            Stabilized and unstabilized

            Including soil stabilization processes

            For surfacing dirt roads, see 625.75

.75   **Surfacing dirt roads**

.76   **Maintenance and repair**

            Class maintenance and repair of a specific kind of road or associated feature with the road or feature, plus notation 0288 from Table 1, e.g., maintenance of dirt roads 625.740288, of roadside areas 625.770288

.761   Damages and their repairs

            Standard subdivisions are added for either or both topics in heading

            Including resurfacing, shoulder maintenance

.763   Snow and ice control measures

            Including use of snowplows, snow fences

.77   **Roadside areas**

            Including parking turnouts, picnic areas, rest areas; planting and cultivation of roadside vegetation

.79   **Ice crossings, traffic control equipment, protective roadside barriers**

            For public lighting for roads, see 628.95

.792   Ice crossings

       Class here ice and snow-compacted roads

.794   Traffic control equipment

       Including markings, signals, signs

.795   Protective roadside barriers

       Including dividers, fences

       Class snow fences in 625.763; class curbs in 625.888

.8   **Artificial road surfaces**

       Class here comprehensive works on paving

       For a paving surface not provided for here, see the surface, e.g., airport runways 629.13634

[.802 88]   Maintenance and repair

       Do not use; class in 625.76

>   625.81–625.86 Pavements in specific materials

       Class sidewalks in specific materials in 625.881–625.886; class comprehensive works in 625.8

.81   Flagstones

.82   Brick and stone

       Including gravel and crushed stone pavements

       For flagstones, see 625.81

.83   Wood

.84   Concretes

       For asphalt concrete, see 625.85

.85   Bituminous materials

       Including tar

       Class here asphalt, asphalt concrete

       For macadam, see 625.86

.86   Macadam and telford surfaces

.88   Sidewalks and auxiliary pavements

       Standard subdivisions are added for sidewalks and auxiliary pavements together, for sidewalks alone

.881–.886   Sidewalks in specific materials

       Add to base number 625.88 the numbers following 625.8 in 625.81–625.86, e.g., brick sidewalks 625.882

.888   Curbs

.889   Auxiliary pavements

      Including driveways, parking aprons

      For curbs, see 625.888

[626]   [Unassigned]

      Most recently used in Edition 14

627   Hydraulic engineering

      The branch of engineering dealing with utilization and control of natural waters of the earth

      Class here hydraulic structures, water resource engineering

      Class comprehensive works on ocean engineering in 620.4162

      For water supply engineering, see 628.1

[.015 325]   Hydrodynamics

      Do not use; class in 627.042

.04   Special topics of hydraulic engineering

.042   Hydrodynamics of waterways and water bodies

      Standard subdivisions are added for either or both topics in heading

.046   Recreational waters

.1   **Inland waterways**

      For underwater operations, see 627.7

.12   Rivers and streams

      Standard subdivisions are added for either or both topics in heading

      Class interdisciplinary works on rivers and streams in 551.483

      For canalized rivers, see 627.13

[.120 153 25]   Hydrodynamics

      Do not use; class in 627.125

.122   Sediment and silt

      Standard subdivisions are added for either or both topics in heading

.123   Water diversion

      Including construction of barrages

.124   Estuaries and river mouths

      Standard subdivisions are added for either or both topics in heading

.125   Applied hydrodynamics

.13 Canals

Class here canalized rivers, comprehensive engineering works on canals

Class tunnels carrying canals in 624.193; class bridges carrying canals in 624.2; class interdisciplinary works on canals in 386.4

For irrigation canals, see 627.52

.131 Surveying and design

.133 Bank protection and reinforcement

Standard subdivisions are added for either or both topics in heading

.135 Auxiliary devices

.135 2 Gates, locks, sluices

.135 3 Inclines, lifts, ramps

> 627.137–627.138 Specific types of navigation canals

Class engineering and construction details of specific types of canals in 627.131–627.135; class comprehensive works in 627.13

.137 Ship canals

.138 Barge canals

.14 Lakes

.2 Harbors, ports, roadsteads

Standard subdivisions are added for harbors, ports, roadsteads together; for harbors alone; for ports alone

Class interdisciplinary works on harbors, ports, roadsteads in 387.1

For port facilities, see 627.3; for underwater operations, see 627.7

.22 Roadsteads, anchorages, mooring grounds

Standard subdivisions are added for any or all topics in heading

Including supertanker berthing areas

Class freestanding mooring and berthing structures in 627.32

.23 Channels

Class here fairways

.24 Protective structures

Including breakwaters, jetties, seawalls

Class comprehensive works on seawalls in 627.58

.3 Port facilities

Class architectural aspects in 725.34

For navigation aids, see 623.893

>   **627.31–627.34 Specific types of structures and equipment**

> Class specific types of structures in marinas in 627.38; class comprehensive works in 627.3

.31   Docks

> Class here piers, quays, wharves

.32   Freestanding mooring and berthing structures

.34   Cargo-handling equipment

> Class comprehensive works on cargo-handling equipment in 623.867

.38   Marinas

.4   **Flood control**

> Including flood wreckage studies

> Class here use of dams and reservoirs for flood control

> Class construction of dams and reservoirs for flood control in 627.8. Class flood control for and wreckage studies of a specific type of structure with the structure, e.g., flood wreckage studies of bridges 624.2

.42   Flood barriers

> Including seawalls

> Class here embankments, levees; comprehensive works on dikes

> Class comprehensive works on seawalls in 627.58

> *For dikes and seawalls in reclamation from sea, see 627.549*

.44   Water impoundment

.45   Water diversion

.5   **Reclamation, irrigation, related topics**

> Class here comprehensive technological works on erosion and its control

> Class interdisciplinary works on land reclamation in 333.73153; class interdisciplinary works on erosion in 551.302

> *For erosion of agricultural soils and its control, see 631.45; for reclamation of agricultural soils, see 631.6; for revegetation and surface mine reclamation, see 631.64*

.52   Irrigation

> Class here construction and use of irrigation canals

> Class construction of dams and reservoirs for irrigation in 627.8

> *For on-farm irrigation, see 631.587*

.54   Drainage and reclamation from sea

> Standard subdivisions are added for drainage and reclamation from sea together, for drainage alone

.549   Reclamation from sea

           Including dikes

           Class here polders

.56   Artificial recharge of groundwater

           Class comprehensive works on engineering of groundwater in 628.114

.58   Shore protection

           Including stabilization of coastal dunes by engineering means, comprehensive works on seawalls

           Class here beach erosion and its control, shore reclamation, comprehensive works on coastal engineering

           Class dune stabilization by revegetation, comprehensive works on dune stabilization in 631.64

           For harbor seawalls, see 627.24; for seawalls as flood barriers, see 627.42. For a specific aspect of coastal engineering, see the aspect, e.g., reclamation from sea 627.549

.7   **Underwater operations**

.700 1–.700 9   Standard subdivisions

       627.702–627.704   General topics of underwater operations

           Class comprehensive works in 627.7

.702   Underwater construction

.703   Salvage operations

.704   Research operations

.72   Diving

           Class here interdisciplinary works on diving

           For diving sports, see 797.2

.73   Dredging

.74   Blasting

.75   Drilling

.8   **Dams and reservoirs**

           Standard subdivisions are added for dams and reservoirs together, for dams alone

           Class here construction of dams and reservoirs for specific purposes

           Class a specific use of dams and reservoirs with the use, e.g., water storage and conservation 628.132

.81   Earthwork, planning, surveying

> Class earthwork, planning, surveying for specific kinds of dams in 627.82–627.84; class earthwork, planning, surveying for reservoirs in 627.86; class earthwork, planning, surveying for ancillary structures in 627.88

\>   **627.82–627.84 Specific kinds of dams**

> Class ancillary structures of specific kinds of dams in 627.88; class comprehensive works in 627.8

.82   Masonry dams

.83   Earth-fill and rock-fill dams

> Standard subdivisions are added for either or both topics in heading

.84   Movable dams

.86   Reservoirs

> Including silting control

> Class ancillary structures of reservoirs in 627.88

.88   Ancillary structures

.882   Gates, penstocks, sluices

.883   Spillways and weirs

.9   Other hydraulic structures

.98   Offshore structures

> Class here artificial islands, drilling platforms

> Class a specific use of offshore structures with the use, e.g., use of drilling platforms in petroleum extraction 622.33819

> *For freestanding mooring and berthing structures, see 627.32*

628 Sanitary engineering

Class here environmental engineering (environmental health engineering, environmental protection engineering), green technology (environmental technology), municipal engineering, public sanitation technology, sustainable engineering (sustainable technology)

Class interdisciplinary works on sustainability in 304.2; class interdisciplinary works on environmental protection in 363.7

> *For military sanitary engineering, see 623.75; for plumbing, see 696.1. For a specific aspect of municipal engineering not provided for here, see the aspect, e.g., road and street engineering 625.7, laying gas pipelines 665.744; for a specific social aspect of environmental engineering, green technology, sustainable engineering, see the aspect in 300, without use of notation 0286 from Table 1, e.g., economics of sustainable development through use of green technology 338.927; for a specific technology aspect of environmental engineering, green technology, sustainable engineering not provided for here, see the aspect, plus notation 0286 from Table 1, e.g., green technology in electronic circuits 621.38150286, green technology in fashion design 746.920286*

> *See Manual at 300 vs. 600; also at 363 vs. 302–307, 333.7, 570–590, 600*

.1 Water supply

Class here comprehensive works on engineering of water supply, sewers, sewage treatment and disposal

Class interdisciplinary works on water supply in 363.61

> *For sewers, see 628.2; for sewage treatment and disposal, see 628.3*

.102 87   Measurement

Do not use for testing; class in 628.161

.11 Sources

Class here protection and engineering evaluation of sources

Class economic and social evaluation of adequacy, development requirements, conservation of sources in 333.91; class hydraulic engineering in 627; class interdisciplinary works on sources, on evaluation of sources in 553.7

> *See also 628.132 for reservoirs*

.112 Lakes, rivers, springs

Class artesian wells in 628.114

.114 Groundwater

Including artesian wells, prevention of seawater intrusion, prospecting for water

Class here wells

.116 Seawater

Class desalinization in 628.167

.13   **Storage and conservation**

> Standard subdivisions are added for either or both topics in heading

> Including storage tanks, water towers

> Class construction of dams for water storage and conservation in 627.8

.132   **Reservoirs**

> Including evaporation control

> Class engineering of reservoirs for water supply, comprehensive works on protection of reservoirs in 627.86

.14   **Collection and distribution systems**

> *For construction of dams and reservoirs, see 627.8; for storage and conservation, see 628.13; for water mains and service pipes, see 628.15*

.142   **Collection systems**

.144   **Distribution systems**

.15   **Water mains and service pipes**

> Class here aqueducts

.16   **Testing, analysis, treatment, pollution countermeasures**

> *See Manual at 363.61*

.161   **Testing and analysis**

> Class here testing and measurement of pollution

.162   **Treatment**

> Class here treatment of sewage effluent for reuse; comprehensive engineering works on treatment of water supply and sewage

> *For mechanical treatment, see 628.164; for chemical treatment, see 628.166; for desalinization, see 628.167; for sewage treatment, see 628.3*

.162 2   **Coagulation (Flocculation), screening, sedimentation (settling)**

.164   **Mechanical treatment**

> Including filtration, membrane (osmotic) processes

> Class membrane processes for desalinization in 628.1674

> *For screening, sedimentation, see 628.1622*

.165   **Aeration**

> Including deaeration

> *See also 628.1662 for ozone treatment*

.166   **Chemical treatment**

> *For coagulation, see 628.1622; for aeration, see 628.165*

.166 2	Disinfection

Including chlorination, copper sulfate treatment, ozone treatment, ultraviolet radiation

.166 3	Fluoridation

Class interdisciplinary works on fluoridation in 614.5996

.166 6	Demineralization

Including softening

For desalinization, see 628.167

.167	Desalinization
.167 2	Distillation
.167 23	Distillation using nuclear energy
.167 25	Solar desalinization
.167 3	Electrolysis
.167 4	Membrane processes
.167 44	Reverse osmosis
.168	Pollution countermeasures

Class prevention of natural pollution of water sources in 628.11; class interdisciplinary works on water pollution countermeasures in 363.7394

For countermeasures that consist of routine water treatment, see 628.162; for countermeasures that consist of sewage treatment, see 628.3

[.168 028 7]	Testing and measurement

Do not use; class in 628.161

.168 2	Countermeasures for domestic wastes and sewage
.168 25	Wastes in sanitary landfills
.168 3	Countermeasures for industrial wastes

For countermeasures for radioactive wastes, see 628.1685. For countermeasures in a specific technology other than sanitary engineering, see the technology, plus notation 0286 from Table 1, e.g., pollution control in metallurgy plants 669.0286

.168 31	Thermal pollution
.168 32	Acid mine drainage
.168 33	Oil spills
.168 36	Wastes from chemical and related industries

Standard subdivisions are added for wastes from chemical and related industries together, for wastes from chemical industries alone

.168 37	Manufacturing wastes
	Class thermal pollution from manufacturing processes in 628.16831
	For wastes from chemical and related technologies, see 628.16836
.168 4	Countermeasures for agricultural wastes
.168 41	Soil improvement wastes
	Including fertilizers, irrigation return flow
.168 42	Pesticides
.168 46	Animal wastes
	Class here feedlot runoff
.168 5	Countermeasures for radioactive wastes
.2	**Sewers**
	Class road drainage in 625.734
.21	Sewer systems for handling precipitation
	Including overflows
	Class here urban runoff
.212	Storm sewers
.214	Combined sewers
.23	Deodorization and ventilation of sewers
	Including ventilators
.24	Design and construction
.25	Appurtenances of sewers
	Including catch basins, house connections, manholes
.29	Pumping stations
.3	**Sewage treatment and disposal**
	Standard subdivisions are added for sewage treatment and disposal together, for sewage treatment alone
	For treatment and disposal of sewage in a specific technology, see the technology, plus notation 0286 from Table 1, e.g., treatment of sewage from beverage plants by beverage makers 663.0286
	See Manual at 363.61

>	628.32–628.35 Treatment
	Class comprehensive works in 628.3
.32	Disinfection

.34   **Primary treatment**

Including primary sedimentation, screening

Class comprehensive works on a specific process used in both primary and secondary treatment in 628.351–628.354

.35   **Secondary and tertiary treatment**

Standard subdivisions are added for secondary and tertiary treatment together, for secondary treatment alone

Class here aeration, biological treatment

>   **628.351–628.354 Secondary treatment**

Class comprehensive works in 628.35

.351   **Oxidation ponds**

Variant names: sewage lagoons, stabilization ponds

Including oxidation ditches

.352   **Filtration**

.353   **Secondary sedimentation**

.354   **Activated sludge process**

.357   **Tertiary treatment**

Including nitrogen removal

Class comprehensive works on a specific process used in both secondary and tertiary treatment in 628.351–628.354

For demineralization, see 628.358

.358   **Demineralization**

.36   **Disposal**

For disposal into water, see 628.39

.362   **Sewage effluent disposal**

For disposal by artificial recharge of groundwater, see 627.56; for treatment for reuse as water supply, see 628.162

.362 3   Sewage irrigation

.364   **Sewage sludge disposal**

Including sanitary landfills

For underground disposal of sludge other than in sanitary landfills, see 628.366; for incineration of sludge, see 628.37; for utilization of sludge, see 628.38

.366   Underground disposal of sludge

         Other than in sanitary landfills

         Including construction of facilities, storage

.368   Unsewered sewage disposal

         Including composting toilets, portable toilets, septic tanks

.37   Incineration of sludge

.38   Utilization of sludge

         Class here biosolids

           For a specific use of sludge, see the use, e.g., use as fertilizer 631.869

.39   Disposal of sewage, sewage effluent, sewage sludge into water

.4   **Waste technology, public toilets, street cleaning**

         Standard subdivisions are added for waste technology, public toilets, street cleaning together; for waste technology alone

         Class here industrial waste treatment and disposal

         Class pollution from wastes in 628.5; class interdisciplinary works on wastes in 363.728

           For gaseous wastes, see 628.53; for agricultural waste technology and animal wastes, see 628.7. For control and utilization of wastes in a specific technology, see the technology, plus notation 0286 from Table 1, e.g., waste technology in fuel processing 662.60286

.42   Hazardous and toxic wastes

         Standard subdivisions are added for either or both topics in heading

         Waste technology only

         Class social services for hazardous and toxic wastes in 363.7287

           For hazardous and toxic liquid wastes, see 628.43; for hazardous and toxic solid wastes, see 628.44; for hazardous and toxic gaseous wastes, see 628.53

.43   Liquid wastes

           For liquid wastes released into bodies of water, see 628.168; for sewage treatment and disposal, see 628.3

.44   Solid wastes (Refuse)

         Class agricultural solid waste technology in 628.74

.442   Collection

.445   Treatment and disposal

         Standard subdivisions are added for either or both topics in heading

>   628.445 6–628.445 9   Disposal

          Class comprehensive works in 628.445

.445 6	Disposal on land and underground
.445 62	Open dumps
.445 64	Sanitary landfills
.445 66	Underground disposal

               Other than in sanitary landfills

               Including construction of facilities, storage

.445 7	Incineration
.445 8	Conversion into useful products

               Class here recycling technology

               For a specific conversion technology, see the technology, e.g., converting garbage into fertilizer 668.6375

.445 9	Disposal into water
.45	Public toilets
.46	Street cleaning
.5	**Pollution control technology and industrial sanitation engineering**

          Standard subdivisions are added for pollution control technology and industrial sanitation engineering together, for pollution control technology alone

          Class here industrial pollution technology

          Class interdisciplinary works on pollution in 363.73

          For noise control, see 620.23; for water pollution control, see 628.168. For pollution control technology in a specific technology, see the technology, plus notation 0286 from Table 1, e.g., engineering to control pollution in fuel processing plants 662.60286

.51	Industrial sanitation engineering

          Class here plant sanitation

.52	Specific kinds of pollutants

          Class here movement through environment

          Class specific kinds of pollutants in water in 628.168; class specific kinds of pollutants in air in 628.53; class specific kinds of pollutants in soil in 628.55

.529	Pesticides
.53	Air pollution

          Class here gaseous wastes, dispersal of pollutants from source

          Class air quality surveys in 363.73922

.532   Products of combustion

        Class here smog

.535   Radioactive substances

        Including radon

.536   Microorganisms

.55   Soil pollution

.7   Agricultural waste technology and animal wastes

.74   Agricultural waste technology

        Class animal wastes in 628.76

.76   Animal wastes

        For use of animal wastes as fertilizer, see 631.86

.9   Other branches of sanitary and municipal engineering

.92   Fire safety and fire fighting technology

        Including general disaster and rescue technology

        Class interdisciplinary works on fire hazards and their control in 363.37

        For a specific disaster and rescue technology, see the technology, e.g., first aid 616.0252

.922   Fire safety technology

        Including fire escapes, rescue operations

        Class here fire prevention

.922 2   Flammability studies and testing

        Standard subdivisions are added for either or both topics in heading

        Class development of fire resistance in products in 628.9223

.922 3   Fireproofing and fire retardation

        Including fire doors, fire retardants

        For fireproofing a specific product, see the product, e.g., textiles 677.689, buildings 693.82

.922 5   Fire detection and alarms

.925   Fire fighting technology

        Class here use of equipment and supplies, comprehensive works on their manufacture

        For shipboard fire fighting technology, see 623.8886; for fire fighting technology in airports, see 629.1368; for forest fire technology, see 634.9618. For manufacture of a specific kind of equipment and supplies, see the kind, e.g., nautical fire fighting equipment 623.865, fire resistant clothing 687.16, fire stations 690.519

.925 2	Extinction with water

Including hydraulic systems, sprinkler systems

.925 4	Extinction with chemicals

.925 9	Fire fighting vehicles

Class here fire engines

For construction of fire engines, see 629.225

.95	Public lighting

Class lighting of airports in 629.1365

.96	Pest control

Class here household pests, comprehensive works on pest control technology

Class interdisciplinary works on pest control in 363.78

For control of disease-carrying pests, see 614.43; for control of plant pests, see 628.97; for control of agricultural pests, see 632.6

.964	Mollusks

Class here slugs, snails

.965	Terrestrial invertebrates

.965 7	Insects

Including ants, cockroaches, house flies, mosquitoes, termites

.968	Birds

.969	Mammals

.969 3	Rodents

Class here rat control

.97	Control of plant pests

629   Other branches of engineering

.04	Transportation engineering

Unless other instructions are given, class a subject with aspects in two or more subdivisions of 629.04 in the number coming last, e.g., land vehicles 629.049 (*not* 629.046)

Class military transportation technology in 623.6; class operation of transportation equipment for recreational purposes in 796–797; class interdisciplinary works on transportation in 388. Class technical problems peculiar to transportation of a specific commodity with the commodity, e.g., slurry transportation of coal 662.624

.040 289	Safety measures

Including comfort equipment, e.g., air conditioning; control devices, e.g., markings, signals, signs

.045	Navigation

> *For celestial navigation, see 527*

.046	Transportation equipment

Including remote-control vehicles

Class here vehicles, autonomous vehicles

> *See also 629.8932 for mobile robots*

> *See Manual at 629.046 vs. 388*

.046 022 8	Models and miniatures

Class interdisciplinary works on remote-control models in 796.15

> *See Manual at 796.15 vs. 629.0460228*

.047	Stationary transportation facilities

Class here trafficways

> *For transportation buildings, see 690.53*

>   629.048–629.049   Engineering of transportation in specific mediums

Class comprehensive works in 629.04

> *For aerospace engineering, see 629.1*

.048	Water transportation engineering

> *For nautical engineering and seamanship, see 623.8; for inland waterways, see 627.1; for harbors, ports, roadsteads, see 627.2; for overwater air-cushion vehicles, see 629.324*

.049	Land transportation engineering

> *For pipes and pipelines, see 621.8672; for railroads, roads, highways, see 625; for motor land vehicles, cycles, see 629.2; for overland air-cushion vehicles, see 629.322; for nonmotor land vehicles, see 688.6*

.1	**Aerospace engineering**

Class military aerospace engineering in 623.66

> *For astronautics, see 629.4*

.11	Mechanics and operation of aerospace flight

Class mechanics and operation of a specific type of aerospace flight with the type, e.g., astromechanics 629.411

| .12 | Aerospace vehicles and stationary facilities |

Aerospace vehicles: vehicles that function equally well in the atmosphere and space

Class a specific facility with the facility, e.g., air-cushion vehicles 629.3

For vehicles that function primarily in the atmosphere, see 629.133; for vehicles that function primarily in space, see 629.47

| .13 | Aeronautics |

See Manual at 629.046 vs. 388

.130 01–.130 09	Standard subdivisions
.130 1	Philosophy and theory of flight
[.130 153 36]	Aeromechanics of flight

Do not use; class in 629.1323

| [.130 155 15] | Aviation meteorology |

Do not use; class in 629.1324

| .130 2–.130 8 | Standard subdivisions of flight |
| .130 9 | History, geographic treatment, biography of flight |

Do not use for flight guides; class in 629.13254

Record of flying activities in all types of aircraft

| .130 92 | Biography of flight |

Class here fliers, pilots

| .132 | Mechanics of flight; flying and related topics |

| [.132 01–.132 09] | Standard subdivisions |

Do not use; class in 629.1301–629.1309

| .132 2 | Aerostatics |
| .132 3 | Aerodynamics |

Including aircraft noise

Class here comprehensive works on aeromechanics

For aerostatics, see 629.1322; for weather aerodynamics, see 629.1324

.132 300 1–.132 300 9	Standard subdivisions
.132 303	Subsonic aerodynamics
.132 304	Transonic aerodynamics

Including sonic booms

| .132 305 | Supersonic aerodynamics |
| .132 306 | Hypersonic aerodynamics |

.132 31	Gliding and soaring
	Standard subdivisions are added for either or both topics in heading
.132 32	Airflow
	Including turbulence
	For boundary layers, see 629.13237
.132 322	Incompressible airflow
.132 323	Compressible airflow
.132 327	Air pockets (Air holes)
.132 33	Lift and thrust
.132 34	Drag (Air resistance)
.132 35	Pressure distribution and aerodynamic load
	Standard subdivisions are added for either or both topics in heading
.132 36	Stability and control
.132 362	Aeroelasticity, flutter, vibration
.132 364	Moments of inertia
	Including pitch, roll, yaw; restoring torques and damping
.132 37	Boundary layers
.132 38	Propulsion principles
.132 4	Aviation meteorology
	Weather conditions and aerodynamics
	Class piloting in bad weather in 629.1325214
.132 5	Flying and related topics
	Standard subdivisions are added for flying and related topics together, for flying alone
	Class flying model airplanes in 796.154; class flying kites in 796.158; class air sports in 797.5
	For aviation meteorology, see 629.1324; for automatic control, see 629.1326
	See Manual at 796.15 vs. 629.0460228
[.132 509]	History, geographic treatment, biography of flight
	Do not use; class in 629.1309
.132 51	Navigation

.132 52   Piloting

Class here comprehensive works on piloting and navigation, on piloting airplanes

For navigation, see 629.13251

[.132 520 92]   Biography

Do not use; class in 629.13092

.132 521   General topics of piloting

Unless other instructions are given, class a subject with aspects in two or more subdivisions of 629.132521 in the number coming first, e.g., landing during bad weather 629.1325213 (*not* 629.1325214)

Class general topics of specific types of aircraft in 629.132522–629.132528

.132 521 2   Takeoff

.132 521 3   Landing

.132 521 4   Piloting under adverse conditions

Including bad weather, disablement of craft, nighttime

Class here instrument flying

.132 521 6   Piloting commercial craft

.132 521 7   Piloting private craft

.132 522   Piloting lighter-than-air aircraft

.132 523–.132 529   Piloting specific types of heavier-than-air aircraft

Add to base number 629.13252 the numbers following 629.1333 in 629.13333–629.13339, e.g., piloting helicopters 629.1325252; however, for comprehensive works on piloting airplanes, see 629.13252; for piloting commercial craft, see 629.1325216; for piloting private craft, see 629.1325217

Class hang gliding in 629.14

.132 54   Flight guides (Pilot guides)

Class here charts, logbooks, maps

[.132 540 91–.132 540 99]   Geographic treatment

Do not use; class in 629.132541–629.132549

.132 541–.132 549   Specific geographic areas

Add to base number 629.13254 notation 1–9 from Table 2, e.g., pilot guides to Spain 629.1325446

.132 55   Wreckage studies

.132 6	Automatic control	

Manned and guided aircraft

See also 629.1352 for automatic pilots

.133   Aircraft types

Class components of specific aircraft types in 629.134

[.133 022 8]   Models and miniatures

Do not use; class in 629.1331

[.133 028 7]   Testing and measurement

Do not use; class in 629.1345

[.133 028 8]   Maintenance and repair

Do not use; class in 629.1346

.133 028 9   Safety measures

Class safety equipment in 629.13443

.133 1   Models and miniatures

Add to base number 629.1331 the numbers following 629.133 in 629.1332–629.1333, e.g., models of helicopters 629.1331352

Class comprehensive works on models and miniatures of military aircraft in 623.7460228; class flying model aircraft, interdisciplinary works on building and flying model aircraft in 796.154. Class models and miniatures of a specific type of military aircraft with the type in 623.741–623.746, plus notation 0228 from Table 1, e.g., models of fighters 623.74640228; class models and miniatures of a specific aircraft component with the component in 629.134–629.135, plus notation 0228 from Table 1, e.g., models of turboprop engines 629.13435320228

See Manual at 796.15 vs. 629.0460228

.133 2   *Lighter-than-air aircraft

.133 22   *Free and captive balloons

Including hot air balloons

Class dirigible balloons in 629.13324

.133 24   *Airships (Dirigibles)

For specific types of airships, see 629.13325–629.13327

>   629.133 25–629.133 27   Specific types of airships

Class comprehensive works in 629.13324

.133 25   *Rigid airships

---

*Do not use notation 0228 from Table 1; class in 629.1331

.133 26	*Semirigid airships
.133 27	*Nonrigid airships (Blimps)
.133 3	*Heavier-than-air aircraft
.133 32	*Kites

     Class flying kites in 796.158

.133 33	*Gliders

     Class hang gliders in 629.14

.133 34	Airplanes

     For rocket planes, see 629.13338

[.133 340 228]	Models and miniatures

     Do not use; class in 629.133134

[.133 340 287]	Testing and measurement

     Do not use; class in 629.1345

[.133 340 288]	Maintenance and repair

     Do not use; class in 629.1346

.133 340 4	Special topics of airplanes
.133 340 42	General topics of airplanes
.133 340 422	*Private airplanes

     Class private short takeoff and landing airplanes in 629.133340426

.133 340 423	*Commercial airplanes

     Class commercial short takeoff and landing airplanes in 629.133340426

.133 340 426	*Short takeoff and landing airplanes (STOL airplanes)
.133 343	*Propeller-driven airplanes

     Piston and turboprop

     Including ultralight airplanes

     Class propeller-driven seaplanes in 629.133347; class propeller-driven amphibious planes in 629.133348

.133 347	*Seaplanes
.133 348	*Amphibious planes
.133 349	*Jet airplanes

     Class jet seaplanes in 629.133347; class jet amphibious planes in 629.133348

---

*Do not use notation 0228 from Table 1; class in 629.1331

.133 35	*Vertical-lift aircraft (VTOL aircraft)
	Including autogiros, convertiplanes, flying automobiles
.133 352	*Rotorcraft
	Class here helicopters
.133 36	*Orthopters (Ornithopters)
.133 38	*Rocket planes
.133 39	*Drones
	Variant names: guided aircraft, pilotless aircraft

.134   Aircraft components and general techniques

For aircraft instrumentation, see 629.135

[.134 028 7]   Testing and measurement

Do not use; class in 629.1345

[.134 028 8]   Maintenance and repair

Do not use; class in 629.1346

.134 1   Analysis and design

Class analysis and design of parts in 629.1343; class analysis and design of interiors and special equipment in 629.1344

.134 2   Manufacturing and assembling

Class manufacturing and assembling of parts in 629.1343; class manufacturing and assembling of interiors and special equipment in 629.1344

.134 3   Parts

Class here components

For interiors and special equipment, see 629.1344

.134 31   Airframes

Class a specific component part with the component, e.g., fuselages 629.13434

.134 32   Airfoils

Including wing accessories

Class here wings

For control surfaces, see 629.13433; for propellers, vertical lift rotors, see 629.13436

.134 33   Control surfaces

Including ailerons, flaps, rudders

.134 34   Fuselages

*Do not use notation 0228 from Table 1; class in 629.1331

264

.134 35	Engines and fuels

Standard subdivisions are added for engines and fuels together, for engines alone

Including pollution control

.134 351	Fuels

Class here propellants

Class fuels and propellants for specific engines in 629.134352–629.134355

.134 352	Reciprocating and compound engines

Piston and compound piston-turbine engines

Class comprehensive works on reciprocating, compound, gas-turbine, jet engines in 629.13435

.134 353	Gas-turbine and jet engines

Standard subdivisions are added for either or both topics in heading

.134 353 2	Turboprop engines
.134 353 3	Turbojet engines
.134 353 4	Turboramjet engines
.134 353 5	Ramjet engines
.134 353 6	Pulse-jet engines
.134 353 7	Fan-jet engines
.134 354	Rocket engines
.134 355	Nuclear power plants
.134 36	Propellers and vertical lift rotors
.134 37	Rigging and bracing equipment

Standard subdivisions are added for either or both topics in heading

.134 38	Other equipment
.134 381	Landing gear

See also 678.32 for manufacture of tires

.134 386	Escape equipment

Including capsule cockpits, parachutes, pilot ejection seats

.134 4	Interiors and special equipment
.134 42	Comfort equipment

Including air conditioning, heating, pressurization, soundproofing, ventilating equipment

.134 43	Safety equipment
	Including fire prevention equipment, life rafts, safety belts
.134 45	Interiors
	Including cabins
.134 5	Tests and measurements
	Standard subdivisions are added for either or both topics in heading
	Aircraft and airplanes in general
	Class wreckage studies in 629.13255

For test and measurements of a specific type of aircraft other than airplanes in general or a specific part, see the type of aircraft or part, plus notation 0287 from Table 1, e.g., tests and measurements of seaplanes 629.1333470287, of interiors 629.134450287

.134 52	Ground tests and inspection
	Standard subdivisions are added for either or both topics in heading
	Including wind and shock tunnels
.134 53	Flight tests
.134 6	Maintenance and repair
	Standard subdivisions are added for either or both topics in heading
	Aircraft and airplanes in general

For maintenance and repair of specific types of aircraft other than airplanes in general or of a specific part, see the type of aircraft or part, e.g., maintenance and repair of seaplanes 629.1333470288, of interiors 629.134450288

.135	Aircraft instrumentation (Avionics)
.135 1	Navigation instrumentation
	Including landing and navigation lights
.135 2	Flight instrumentation
	Including accelerometers, altimeters, Machmeters; automatic pilots; air-speed, vertical-speed, turn and bank indicators; directional gyros, gyrohorizons
.135 3	Power-plant monitoring instrumentation
.135 4	Electrical systems
	Class electrical systems of a specific kind of instrumentation in 629.1351–629.1353
.135 5	Electronic systems
	Class electronic systems of a specific kind of instrumentation in 629.1351–629.1353

.136	Airports
	Class here commercial land airports
.136 1	Types other than commercial land airports
	Including floating airports (seadromes)
	Class details of airports in 629.1363–629.1368
.136 12	Airstrips
.136 16	Heliports

> 629.136 3–629.136 8 Details of airports

Class comprehensive works in 629.136

.136 3	Runways
.136 34	Pavements
.136 35	Drainage systems
.136 37	Snow removal and compaction
.136 5	Lighting systems
.136 6	Air traffic control systems
	See Manual at 629.1366 vs. 387.740426
.136 8	Fire fighting equipment
.14	Portable flight vehicles
	Units intended to be carried by a single person
	Including hang gliders and gliding
	Class hang gliding as a sport in 797.55
.2	**Motor land vehicles, cycles**
	Standard subdivisions are added for motor land vehicles, cycles together; for motor land vehicles alone
	Class here automotive engineering
	Class military motor land vehicles in 623.747
	See Manual at 629.046 vs. 388
[.202 28]	Models and miniatures
	Do not use; class in 629.221
.202 84	Apparatus and equipment
	Do not use for materials; class in 629.232
[.202 87]	Testing and measurement
	Do not use; class in 629.282

[.202 88]   Maintenance and repair

                     Do not use; class in 629.287

.202 89   Safety measures

                     Class safety engineering of motor land vehicles in 629.2042

.204   **Special topics of motor land vehicles**

.204 2   Safety engineering of motor land vehicles

                     Class here comprehensive works on motor land vehicle and highway safety engineering

                     For highway safety engineering, see 625.70289

.204 6   Autonomous motor land vehicles

                     Class a specific type of autonomous motor land vehicle with the type, e.g., self-driving cars 629.222

.22   **Types of vehicles**

                     Unless otherwise indicated, class hybrid vehicles and bi-fuel (dual-mode) vehicles with the type of vehicle coming later in the schedules, e.g., vehicles powered by both a gasoline-fueled internal combustion engine and an electric motor 629.2293, vehicles powered by both gasoline and compressed natural gas, stored in separate tanks 629.22973

                     Class design, materials, construction of a specific type of vehicle in 629.23; class parts of a specific type of vehicle in 629.24–629.27; class driving a specific type of vehicle in 629.283; class nonsurface motor land vehicles, vehicles for extraterrestrial surfaces in 629.29. Class flexible fuel vehicles with the fuel that predominates, e.g., automobiles powered by fossil fuels with biofuel additives 629.222. Class comprehensive works on autonomous motor land vehicles in 629.2046

[.220 228]   Models and miniatures

                     Do not use; class in 629.221

[.220 287]   Testing and measurement

                     Do not use; class in 629.282

[.220 288]   Maintenance and repair

                     Do not use; class in 629.287

.220 289   Safety measures

                     Class safety accessories in 629.276

.221   Models and miniatures

Including models and miniatures of off-road vehicles

Add to base number 629.221 the numbers following 629.22 in 629.222–629.229, e.g., models of racing cars 629.2218

Class comprehensive works on models and miniatures of military motor land vehicles in 623.7470228; class operating remote-control models in 796.156. Class models and miniatures of a specific type of military motor land vehicles with the type in 623.7472–623.7475, plus notation 0228 from Table 1, e.g., models of tanks 623.747520228

See Manual at 796.15 vs. 629.0460228

>   629.222–629.228 Vehicles powered by fossil fuels and human-powered vehicles

Class here comprehensive works on a specific type of vehicle regardless of source of power, e.g., comprehensive works on trucks 629.224

Class three-wheeled motor vehicles in 629.222; class two-wheeled motor vehicles in 629.2275; class comprehensive works in 629.22

For natural gas vehicles, see 629.22973

.222   *Passenger automobiles

Including cyclecars, microcars, minivans, station wagons

Class here three-wheeled automobiles; comprehensive works on three-wheeled motor vehicles

Class passenger automobiles rebuilt or modified for high speed in 629.2286

For a specific type of three-wheeled motor vehicle, see the type, e.g., three-wheeled motorcycles 629.2275

See also 629.2234 for vans

.222 1   *Sports cars

Class racing cars in 629.228

For specific named sports cars, see 629.2222

.222 2   Specific named passenger automobiles

(Option: Arrange alphabetically by name or make of car)

[.222 201–.222 209]   Standard subdivisions

Do not use; class in 629.22201–629.22209

.222 3   *Passenger automobiles for public transportation

.222 32   *Taxicabs and limousines

---

*Do not use notation 0228 from Table 1 for models and miniatures; class in 629.221. Do not use notation 0287 from Table 1 for testing and measurement; class in 629.282. Do not use notation 0288 from Table 1 for maintenance and repair; class in 629.287

.222 33	*Buses

For guided-way systems, see 625.4; for trolleybuses, see 629.2293

.222 34	*Ambulances
.223	*Light trucks
.223 2	*Pickup trucks
.223 4	*Vans

See also 629.222 for minivans

.224	*Trucks (Lorries)

Class here tractor trailers (articulated lorries, semi-trailers)

For light trucks, see 629.223

.225	*Work vehicles

Including bulldozers, fire engines

For automotive materials-handling equipment, see 621.86; for trucks, see 629.224

.225 2	*Tractors

For steam tractors, see 629.2292

.226	*Campers, motor homes, trailers (caravans)

Standard subdivisions are added for any or all topics in heading

Class here comprehensive works on recreational vehicles (RVs)

Class construction of towed mobile homes in 690.879

For a specific kind of recreational vehicle not provided for here, see the vehicle, e.g., dune buggies 629.222

See also 629.224 for tractor trailers

See Manual at 643.29, 690.879, 728.79 vs. 629.226

.227	*Cycles
.227 1	*Monocycles

One-wheeled vehicles with pedals, regardless of motorized assistance

.227 2	*Bicycles

Two-wheeled vehicles with pedals, regardless of motorized assistance

Class two-wheeled motor vehicles in 629.2275

For mopeds and motor bicycles, see 629.2275; for tandem bicycles, see 629.2276

---

*Do not use notation 0228 from Table 1 for models and miniatures; class in 629.221. Do not use notation 0287 from Table 1 for testing and measurement; class in 629.282. Do not use notation 0288 from Table 1 for maintenance and repair; class in 629.287

.227 3	*Tricycles
	Three-wheeled vehicles with pedals, regardless of motorized assistance
	Class three-wheeled motor vehicles in 629.222
.227 4	*Quadracycles
	Four-wheeled vehicles with pedals, regardless of motorized assistance
	Including pedal cars
	Class four-wheeled motor vehicles in 629.222–629.226
.227 5	*Motorcycles
	Including minibikes, mopeds, motor bicycles; three-wheeled motorcycles
	Class here motorscooters, two-wheeled motor vehicles
	Class cycles with pedals in 629.2271–629.2274; class comprehensive works on three-wheeled motor vehicles in 629.222
.227 6	*Tandem bicycles
	Regardless of motorized assistance
.228	**Racing cars and off-road vehicles**
.228 5	*Racing cars
	Conventional and converted
	Including karts
	For hot rods, see 629.2286
.228 6	*Hot rods
.228 8	*Off-road vehicles
	Including all-terrain vehicles, dune buggies, snowmobiles
.229	*Vehicles powered by other sources and vehicles powered by natural gas
	Class here alternative fuel vehicles
	Class comprehensive works on a specific type of vehicle regardless of source of power in 629.222–629.228, e.g., comprehensive works on trucks 629.224
.229 2	*Steam-powered vehicles
	Including steam tractors and steamrollers
	Class comprehensive works on tractors in 629.2252

---

*Do not use notation 0228 from Table 1 for models and miniatures; class in 629.221. Do not use notation 0287 from Table 1 for testing and measurement; class in 629.282. Do not use notation 0288 from Table 1 for maintenance and repair; class in 629.287

.229 3	*Electric-powered vehicles

Including trolleybus systems, trolleybuses

For solar energy-powered vehicles, see 629.2295; for fuel cell vehicles, see 629.22974

.229 4	*Air-compression-powered vehicles
.229 5	*Solar energy-powered vehicles
.229 6	*Nuclear-powered vehicles
.229 7	Natural gas vehicles and hydrogen-powered vehicles
.229 73	*Natural gas vehicles

Class comprehensive works on vehicles powered by fossil fuels in 629.22

.229 74	*Hydrogen-powered vehicles

Class here fuel cell vehicles

.23	Design, materials, construction

Class materials for, design and construction of parts in 629.24–629.27

.231	Analysis and design

Standard subdivisions are added for either or both topics in heading

Including ergonomic and safety design

Class safety accessories in 629.276

.232	Materials
.234	Manufacturing techniques

Including factory inspection

>	629.24–629.27 Parts

Class comprehensive works in 629.2

.24	Chassis
.242	Supporting frames
.243	Suspension systems

Class here springs and shock absorbers

.244	Transmission devices
.244 6	Automatic transmission devices
.245	Rear axles, differentials, drive shafts

*Do not use notation 0228 from Table 1 for models and miniatures; class in 629.221. Do not use notation 0287 from Table 1 for testing and measurement; class in 629.282. Do not use notation 0288 from Table 1 for maintenance and repair; class in 629.287

.246   Brakes

            Including brake fluids

.247   Front axles and steering gear

.248   Wheels

.248 2   Tires

            See also 678.32 for manufacture of tires

.25   Engines

            Class here pollution control

            Most works covering automobile engines as a whole focus on spark-ignition engines and are classed in 629.2504

.250 01–.250 09   Standard subdivisions

>   629.250 1–629.250 9   Specific types of engines

            Engines, parts, auxiliary systems

            Class comprehensive works in 629.25

.250 1   Steam engines

.250 2   Electric engines

.250 24   Power systems of electric engines

            Including batteries, fuel cells

.250 3–.250 6   Internal-combustion engines

            Add to base number 629.250 the numbers following 621.43 in 621.433–621.436, e.g., spark-ignition engines 629.2504

.250 7   Air-compression engines

.250 8   Solar engines

.250 9   Nuclear engines

>   629.252–629.258   Parts and auxiliary systems of internal-combustion engines

            Class here comprehensive works on specific kinds of parts and auxiliary systems of automotive engines

            Class comprehensive works in 629.25

            For a specific part or auxiliary system of noninternal-combustion engines, see the type of engine in 629.2501–629.2509, e.g., power systems of electric engines 629.25024

.252   Motor parts of internal-combustion engines

            Including mufflers (silencers)

.252 8   Emission control devices

.253	Fuel systems and fuels of internal-combustion engines

Standard subdivisions are added for fuel systems and fuels together, for fuel systems alone

Class here electronic fuel injection systems

.253 3	Carburetors
.253 8	Fuels
.254	Ignition, electrical, electronic systems of internal-combustion engines

Standard subdivisions are added for ignition, electrical, electronic systems together; for ignition systems alone; for electrical systems alone

Class a specific use of electrical and electronic systems with the use, e.g., electronic fuel injection 629.253, electric starters 629.257

.254 2	Batteries
.254 8	Auxiliary electrical systems

For lighting equipment, see 629.271

.254 9	Electronic systems
.255	Lubricating systems of internal-combustion engines

Class here lubricants

.256	Cooling systems of internal-combustion engines

Including antifreeze solutions

.257	Starting devices of internal-combustion engines
.258	Throttles and spark control devices of internal-combustion engines
.26	Bodies

Including convertible tops, doors, fenders, running boards, seats

.260 288	Maintenance and repair

Class here bodywork

Class comprehensive works on customizing and detailing in 629.287

.262	Decorations
.266	Windows and windshields

Standard subdivisions are added for either or both topics in heading

.27	Other equipment
.271	Lighting equipment

.272	Electronic systems

Class here computer systems

For an electronic system of a specific part of a motor land vehicle, see the part, e.g., electronic fuel injection systems 629.253

.273	Panel instrumentation
.275	Hardware

Including handles, hinges, locks

.276	Safety accessories

Including air bags, bumpers, mirrors, seat belts, windshield wipers and washers

Class comprehensive works on safety design in 629.231

.277	Comfort, convenience, entertainment equipment

Including glove compartments, telephones, two-way radios

.277 2	Heaters, ventilators, air-conditioners
.277 4	Entertainment equipment

Including audio systems, televisions

Class here in-car entertainment (in-vehicle infotainment)

.28	Tests, driving, maintenance, repair
.282	Tests and related topics

Class testing and measurement of a specific part with the part, plus notation 0287 from Table 1, e.g., testing brakes 629.2460287

For factory inspection, see 629.234

.282 4	Road tests (Performance tests)
.282 5	Periodic inspection and roadability tests
.282 6	Wreckage studies

Determination of mechanical failure through examination of remains

.283	Driving (Operation)

Class here driving private passenger automobiles

Class self-driving vehicles in 629.2046

For driving vehicles other than internal-combustion passenger vehicles, see 629.284

.283 04	Special topics of driving

Including factors in safe driving

.283 042	Driving off-road vehicles

Including all-terrain vehicles, snowmobiles

.283 3	Driving public transportation vehicles

.283 32	Taxicabs and limousines
.283 33	Buses
.283 34	Ambulances
.284	Driving vehicles other than internal-combustion passenger vehicles

> Add to base number 629.284 the numbers following 629.22 in 629.223–629.229, e.g., driving trucks 629.2844

.286	Services provided by garages and service stations

> *For maintenance and repair, see 629.287*

> *See also 690.538 for construction of garage and service stations*

.287	Maintenance and repair

> Standard subdivisions are added for either or both topics in heading

> Class here customizing, detailing

> Class works on car tune-ups limited to maintenance and repair of the engine in 629.2500288. Class maintenance and repair of a specific part with the part, plus notation 0288 from Table 1, e.g., maintenance of bodies 629.260288

.287 04	Special topics of maintenance and repair of types of vehicles

> Including three-wheel vehicles

.287 042	Maintenance and repair of off-road vehicles

> Including all-terrain vehicles, snowmobiles

> *For dune buggies, see 629.2872*

.287 043	Maintenance and repair of natural gas vehicles
.287 1–.287 9	Maintenance and repair of specific kinds of vehicles and of models and miniatures

> Add to base number 629.287 the numbers following 629.22 in 629.222–629.229, e.g., repair of motorcycles 629.28775

> (Option: Arrange alphabetically by trade name under each type of vehicle)
> (Option: Arrange all vehicles regardless of type alphabetically by trade name)

.29	Specialized land vehicles

> *For autonomous motor land vehicles, see 629.2046; for overland air-cushion vehicles, see 629.322*

.292	Nonsurface motor land vehicles

> Including subterranean, ocean floor vehicles

.295	Vehicles for extraterrestrial surfaces

> Including moon cars

.3   **Air-cushion vehicles (Ground-effect machines, Hovercraft)**

Class military air-cushion vehicles in 623.748

.31   General topics of air-cushion vehicles

Class general topics applied to specific types of vehicles in 629.32

.313   Lift systems

.314   Propulsion systems

.317   Structural analysis and design

.32   Types of vehicles

.322   Overland air-cushion vehicles

Class amphibious air-cushion vehicles in 629.325

.324   Overwater air-cushion vehicles

Class amphibious air-cushion vehicles in 629.325

.325   Amphibious air-cushion vehicles

.4   **Astronautics**

Class military astronautics in 623.69; class interdisciplinary works on space policy in 333.94

See also 500.5 for space sciences

See Manual at 629.046 vs. 388

[.401 521]   Astromechanics

Do not use; class in 629.411

.409 2   Astronautical engineers

Class astronauts in 629.450092

.41   Space flight

Class preparation for flight to a specific celestial body with the flight, e.g., preparation for manned lunar flight 629.454

For unmanned space flight, see 629.43; for manned space flight, see 629.45

.411   Astromechanics

.411 1   Gravitation

.411 3   Orbits

.415   Planetary atmospheres

Including reentry problems

.415 1   Aerodynamics

.415 2   Atmospheric thermodynamics

.416	Space phenomena and environments affecting flight
	Standard subdivisions are added for either or both topics in heading
	Including meteoroids, radiation
.418	Weightlessness
.43	Unmanned space flight
	See Manual at 629.43, 629.45 vs. 559.9, 919.904, 910.919
.432	Launching
.433	Guidance and homing
	Class here mission control
	For communication and tracking, see 629.437
.434	Flight of artificial satellites
	Class satellite flight for a specific purpose with the purpose, e.g., weather satellites 551.6354
.435	Astronautical exploratory and data-gathering flights
.435 2	Ionospheric and near-space flights
	Standard subdivisions are added for either or both topics in heading
.435 3	Lunar flights
.435 4	Planetary flights
	Add to base number 629.4354 the numbers following 523.4 in 523.41–523.49, e.g., Venusian probes 629.43542
.437	Communications and tracking
.44	Auxiliary spacecraft
.441	Space shuttles
.442	Space stations
	Class here space colonies, laboratories
.45	Manned space flight
	Class auxiliary spacecraft in 629.44
	See Manual at 629.43, 629.45 vs. 559.9, 919.904, 910.919
.450 01–.450 09	Standard subdivisions
.450 7	Selection and training of astronauts
	Standard subdivisions are added for either or both topics in heading
.452	Launching and takeoff
	Standard subdivisions are added for either or both topics in heading

.453	Guidance, homing, navigation
	Class here mission control
	For communication and tracking, see 629.437
.454	Circumterrestrial and lunar flights
.455	Planetary flights
	Class here flights to planetary satellites
	Add to base number 629.455 the numbers following 523.4 in 523.41–523.49, e.g., flights to Mars 629.4553
.457	Communications and tracking
.458	Piloting and related activities
.458 2	Piloting
.458 3	Rendezvous with other spacecraft
.458 4	Extravehicular activities
	Including space walks
.458 5	Rescue operations
.458 8	Atmospheric entry and landing
.46	Engineering of unmanned spacecraft
	Class here artificial satellites
	Add to base number 629.46 the numbers following 629.47 in 629.471–629.478, e.g., environmental control 629.467
.47	Astronautical engineering
	Class here comprehensive works on spacecraft
	For auxiliary spacecraft, see 629.44; for engineering of unmanned spacecraft, see 629.46
.471	Structural analysis and design of spacecraft
	Standard subdivisions are added for either or both topics in heading
.472	Spacecraft materials and components
.473	Spacecraft construction
.474	Spacecraft engineering systems
	For propulsion systems, see 629.475; for life-support systems, see 629.477
.474 2	Flight operations systems
	Including guidance, homing, landing, navigation, piloting systems
.474 3	Communication and tracking systems
.474 4	Auxiliary power systems

.474 43	Nuclear power systems
.474 45	Electric and magnetohydrodynamic power systems
.475	Propulsion systems

> Including fuels, auxiliary equipment and instrumentation
>
> Class here booster rockets, engines
>
> Class fuels, auxiliary equipment and instrumentation of a specific type of propulsion in 629.4752–629.4755; class comprehensive works on rocketry in 621.4356

.475 2	Chemical propulsion
.475 22	Liquid propellant
.475 24	Solid propellant
.475 3	Nuclear propulsion
.475 4	Photon propulsion
.475 5	Electric and magnetohydrodynamic propulsion

> Including plasma and ion propulsion

.477	Environmental control and life-support systems

> Standard subdivisions are added for either or both topics in heading

.477 2	Space suits
.477 3	Food and water supply
.477 4	Sanitation and sterilization

> Including control of wastes

.477 5	Control of temperature, humidity, air supply and pressure
.478	Terrestrial facilities

> Including launch complexes, space ports; spacecraft maintenance, ground testing, repair facilities

.8	**Automatic control engineering**

> Class here automatons that are not computer controlled
>
> Class a specific application with the application, e.g., numerical control of machine tools 621.9023

.801	Philosophy and theory

> *For control theory, see 629.8312*

.804	Special topics of automatic control engineering
.804 2	Hydraulic control

> Class here fluidics

.804 3   Electric control

Class computer control in 629.89

.804 5   Pneumatic control

.82   Open-loop systems

Mechanisms in which outputs have no effect on input signals

Including vending machines

Class computer control of open-loop systems in 629.89

.83   Closed-loop systems (Feedback systems)

Mechanisms which maintain prescribed relationships between the controlled outputs and the inputs

Class computer control of closed-loop systems in 629.89

.830 1   Philosophy and theory

For control theory, see 629.8312

.831   General principles

Class general principles of specific mechanisms and systems in 629.832–629.836

.831 2   Control theory

Mathematical design, analysis, synthesis

Including optimal control

Class here comprehensive works on control theory

Class interdisciplinary works on control theory in 003.5

For control theory for open-loop systems, see 629.82; for computer control theory, see 629.89

.831 3   Circuitry

.831 4   Feedback characteristics

.831 5   System components

Including error correctors, error detectors

.831 7   Construction and assembly

\>   629.832–629.836 Specific systems

Including components, circuitry

Class here mechanisms

Class comprehensive works in 629.83

.832   Linear systems

.832 3   Servomechanisms

.833	Multiple-loop systems
.836	Nonlinear systems

> Including adaptive control systems

.89	Computer control

> Class here electronic control, comprehensive works on computer control

> *For computer factory operations in manufacturing, see 670.427*

.892	Robots

> Unless it is redundant, add to base number 629.892 the numbers following 00 in 004–006, e.g., use of digital personal computers 629.892416, but use of digital computers as a whole 629.892 (*not* 629.8924)

> *For specific kinds of robots, see 629.893*

.893	Specific kinds of robots
.893 2	Mobile robots

> *For autonomous vehicles, see 629.046*

.893 3	Manipulators

> Class here robot hands

.895	Computerized process control

> Use of computers to keep conditions of continuous processes as close as possible to desired values or within a desired range by controlling continuous variables such as temperature or pressure

> Unless it is redundant, add to base number 629.895 the numbers following 00 in 004–006, e.g., use of digital personal computers 629.895416, but use of digital computers as a whole 629.895 (*not* 629.8954)

630   Agriculture and related technologies

> Standard subdivisions are added for agriculture and related technologies together, for agriculture alone

> Class here farming, farms, plant crops; interdisciplinary works on plants of agricultural importance

> Class agricultural sociology in 306.349; class agricultural economics in 338.1

> *For a specific nonagricultural aspect of domestic plants, see the aspect, e.g., biology of domestic plants 580*

> *See also 307.72 for rural sociology; also 333.76 for agricultural land economics; also 909.09734 for general works on rural conditions and civilization; also 930–990, plus notation 009734 from table under 930–990, for rural conditions and civilization in specific areas*

> *See Manual at 571–575 vs. 630; also at 630 vs. 579–590, 641.3*

[.15]   Scientific principles

                 Do not use; class in 630.21–630.29

.2   **Miscellany and scientific principles**

                 Notation 02 from Table 1 as modified below

.201   Tabulated, illustrative, related materials; humorous treatment; audiovisual treatment

.201 1–.201 2   Tabulated, illustrative, related materials

                     Add to base number 630.201 the numbers following —02 in notation 021–022 from Table 1, e.g., agricultural pictures 630.20122

.201 7   Humorous treatment

.201 8   Audiovisual treatment

.202   Synopses and outlines

.203–.209   Other miscellany

                     Add to base number 630.20 the numbers following —02 in notation 023–029 from Table 1, e.g., directories 630.205; however, for apparatus, equipment, materials, see 631

.21–.29   Scientific principles

                 Do not use for miscellany; class in 630.201–630.209

                 Add to base number 630.2 the numbers following 5 in 510–590, e.g., agricultural meteorology 630.2515; however, for agricultural genetics, see 631.5233

.7   **Education, research, related topics**

.71   Education

                 Notation 071 from Table 1 as modified below

.715   Adult education and on-the-job training

                 Class here extension departments and services

                 For extension work for young people, see 630.717

.717   Extension work for young people

631   **Specific techniques; apparatus, equipment, materials**

                 Topics common to plant and animal husbandry or limited to plant culture

                 Class comprehensive works on apparatus, equipment, materials used in a specific auxiliary technique or procedure in 630.208, e.g., computers 630.2085

                 For plant injuries, diseases, pests, see 632; for specific techniques, apparatus, equipment, materials for specific plant crops, see 633–635; for specific techniques, apparatus, equipment, materials for animal husbandry, see 636.08

[.01–.09]   Standard subdivisions

                 Do not use; class in 630.1–630.9

.2   **Agricultural structures**

Class construction of farm buildings and structures other than farmhouses in 690.537

.21   Farmhouses

Class construction of farmhouses in 690.86

.22   General-purpose buildings

Class here barns

For housing for domestic animals, see 636.0831

.25   Machine and equipment sheds

.27   Fences, hedges, walls

Construction and use

.28   Roads, bridges, dams

Class construction of bridges in 624.2; class construction of farm roads in 625.74; class construction of dams in 627.8

.3   **Tools, machinery, apparatus, equipment**

Class manufacture of tools, machinery, apparatus, equipment in 681.763. Class manufacture of a specific article with the article, e.g., tractors 629.2252

See also 631.2 for agricultural structures

.304   Workshops

.34   Equipment for care and shelter of plants

For equipment for a specific purpose, see the purpose, e.g., greenhouses 631.583

.37   Power and power machinery

For a specific use of power and power machinery, see the use, e.g., use of combines 633.1045

.371   Kinds of power

Including human, animal, mechanical, electric power

.372   Tractors

.373   Transport equipment

Including trucks, wagons

.4   **Soil science**

Class here interdisciplinary works on soils

For a specific aspect of soils, see the aspect, e.g., soil formation 551.305, engineering use of soils 624.151

[.401 2]   Classification of soils

Do not use; class in 631.44

[.401 5]	Scientific principles
	Do not use; class in 631.4
[.409]	History, geographic treatment, biography
	Do not use; class in 631.49
.41	Soil chemistry

For soil fertility, acidity, alkalinity, see 631.42

.416	Inorganic chemistry

Including salinity

Class use of soil conditioners in 631.82

.417	Organic chemistry

Including humus

Class here soil biochemistry

.42	Soil fertility, acidity, alkalinity
.422	Soil fertility

For use of fertilizers, see 631.8

.43	Soil physics
.432	Moisture and hydromechanics

Standard subdivisions are added for either or both topics in heading

.433	Soil mechanics

Including effect of gas content, micropedology

Class here soil texture

Class interdisciplinary works on soil mechanics in 624.15136

For hydromechanics, see 631.432

.436	Soil temperature
.44	Soil classification
.45	Soil erosion

Class here control of soil erosion, soil conservation, comprehensive agricultural works on soil and water conservation

Class comprehensive technological works on soil erosion in 627.5; class interdisciplinary works on soil conservation in 333.7316; class interdisciplinary works on soil erosion in 551.302

For revegetation, see 631.64; for water conservation, see 631.7

.451	Conservation tillage

Including mulch tillage

For tillage for water conservation, see 631.586

.452   Crop rotation and cover crops

> Class comprehensive works on crop rotation in 631.582

.455   Contouring and terracing

.456   Strip cropping

.46   Soil biology

> *For soil biochemistry, see 631.417*

.47   Soil and land-use surveys

> Standard subdivisions are added for either or both topics in heading
>
> Soil surveys are detailed studies covering small areas (the size of a county or smaller)
>
> Class geographic studies of soils (less detailed than soil surveys and usually covering larger areas) in 631.49

.470 01–.470 08   Standard subdivisions

[.470 09]   History, geographic treatment, biography

> Do not use for history without subdivision; class in 631.47

[.470 090 1–.470 090 5]   Historical periods

> Do not use; class in 631.4701–631.4705

[.470 091–.470 099]   Geographic treatment

> Do not use; class in 631.471–631.479

.470 1–.470 5   Historical periods

> Add to base number 631.470 the numbers following —090 in notation 0901–0905 from Table 1, e.g., 20th century soil surveys 631.4704
> Subdivisions are added for either soil or land-use surveys or both together

.471–.479   Geographic treatment

> Class here soil types in specific areas
>
> Add to base number 631.47 notation 1–9 from Table 2, e.g., soil survey of Gonzales County, Texas 631.47764257
> Subdivisions are added for either soil or land-use surveys or both together

.49   History, geographic treatment, biography of soil science

> Class here geographic studies of soils (less detailed than soil surveys and usually covering areas larger than jurisdictions like counties)
>
> *For soil and land-use surveys, see 631.47*

.490 1–.490 5   Historical periods

> Add to base number 631.490 the numbers following —090 in notation 0901–0905 from Table 1, e.g., 20th century soil studies 631.4904

.491–.499   Geographic treatment, biography

> Add to base number 631.49 notation 1–9 from Table 2, e.g., soil science in China 631.4951

.5   Cultivation and harvesting

> Standard subdivisions are added for cultivation and harvesting together, for cultivation alone

.51   Soil working (Tillage)

> Before and after planting
>
> Class here cultivation limited to tillage
>
> Class soil working in special methods of cultivation in 631.58
>
> *For conservation tillage, see 631.451*

.52   Production of seeds, bulbs, tubers, new varieties

> Standard subdivisions are added for production of seeds, bulbs, tubers, new varieties together; for production of seeds, bulbs, tubers alone
>
> Including domestication, plant selection, seedlings
>
> Class here nursery practice, plant breeding

.521   Seeds

.523   Development of new varieties

> Including plant introduction
>
> Class here germ plasm, hybrids
>
> Class interdisciplinary works on germ plasm in 333.9534

.523 3   Agricultural genetics

> Class here genetic engineering

.526   Bulbs and tubers

> Standard subdivisions are added for either or both topics in heading

.53   Plant propagation

> Class here comprehensive works on plant propagation and nursery practice
>
> *For nursery practice, see 631.52; for grafting, pruning, training, see 631.54*

.531   Propagation from seeds (Sowing)

.532   Propagation from bulbs and tubers

> Standard subdivisions are added for either or both topics in heading

.533   Propagation from suckers, runners, buds

> Class propagation from tubers in 631.532; class propagation from cuttings in 631.535

.534   Propagation by layering

.535	Propagation from cuttings and slips
.536	Transplanting
	Class here planting seedlings
.54	Grafting, pruning, training
	Most works on grafting and pruning will be classed in 634.044 and cognate numbers in 634.1–634.8 or in 635.9
.541	Grafting
.542	Pruning
.546	Training
.55	Harvesting
	Including mowing, reaping
	Class operations subsequent to harvesting in 631.56
.558	Yields
	See Manual at 338.1 vs. 631.558
.56	Operations subsequent to harvesting
	Including cleaning, husking, packing
.567	Grading
.568	Storage
.57	Varieties and kinds of organisms used in agriculture
	Class here description of cultivated varieties that contain little or no information on how to grow them
	Class biology of varieties of agricultural plants in 580
	For development of new varieties, see 631.523
.58	Special methods of cultivation
	Including double cropping, multiple cropping, permaculture
	Class special methods of cultivation as topics in land economics in 333.76; class special methods of cultivation as topics in agricultural economics in 338.162
.581	Reduced cultivation methods
	Class here minimum tillage, surface tillage
.581 2	Fallowing
.581 4	No-tillage
.581 8	Shifting cultivation (Slash-and-burn agriculture)
.582	Crop rotation
	For crop rotation to control erosion, see 631.452

.583 Controlled-environment agriculture

> Including forcing, retarding, hotbeds, use of artificial light

> Class here greenhouse agriculture

> Most works on use of artificial light in agriculture will be classed in 635.0483 and 635.9826

> *For greenhouse gardening, see 635.0483*

.584 Organic farming

> *For organic gardening, see 635.0484. For a specific aspect of organic farming, see the aspect, e.g., compost 631.875*

.585 Soilless culture (Hydroponics)

> Most works on soilless culture will be classed in 635.0485 and cognate numbers in 635.1–635.9

.586 Dry farming

> Class here tillage for water conservation

.587 Irrigation

> Use only for works describing what is done on the farm, e.g., installation and use of center-pivot sprinkler systems

> Class digging wells in 628.114; class interdisciplinary works on technological aspects of irrigation, works on obtaining irrigation water from off-farm sources in 627.52; class interdisciplinary works on irrigation in 333.913

> *For sewage irrigation, see 628.3623*

.6 **Clearing, drainage, revegetation**

> Class here reclamation

> Class interdisciplinary works on technological aspects of reclamation in 627.5

.61 Clearing

.62 Drainage

> Class off-farm drainage projects, interdisciplinary works on technological aspects of drainage in 627.54

.64 Revegetation

> Including inland dune stabilization, surface mine reclamation

> Class reforestation in 634.956

.7 **Water conservation**

> *For tillage for water conservation, see 631.586*

.8   **Fertilizers, soil conditioners, growth regulators**

Standard subdivisions are added for fertilizers, soil conditioners, growth regulators together; for fertilizers alone

Class here interdisciplinary works on agricultural chemicals

Class comprehensive works on soil fertility in 631.422

> *For pesticides, see 632.95; for manufacture of agricultural chemicals, see 668.6*

.81   Nutritive principles, complete fertilizers, methods of application

> *For nutritive principles and methods of application of specific fertilizers, see 631.83–631.87*

.811   Nutritive principles

.813   Complete fertilizers

.816   Methods of application

.82   Soil conditioners

Including conditioners for control of salinity

.821   Acid-soil conditioners

Including lime

.825   Alkaline-soil conditioners

.826   Conditioners for soil texture

Including peat

\>   631.83–631.87 Specific kinds of fertilizers

Class comprehensive works in 631.8

.83   Potassium fertilizers

.84   Nitrogen fertilizers

.841   Ammonium, cyanamide, urea fertilizers

> *For ammonium nitrate, see 631.842*

.842   Nitrate fertilizers

Including ammonium nitrate

.843   Slaughterhouse residues

> *For bone meal, see 631.85*

.847   Biological methods of soil nitrification

Use of nitrifying bacteria, nitrifying crops

.85   Phosphorus fertilizers

Including bone meal

.86	Organic fertilizers

Class here use of animal wastes as fertilizer

Class interdisciplinary works on animal wastes in 363.7288

> *For slaughterhouse residues, see 631.843; for vegetable manures and converted household garbage, see 631.87*

.861	Farm manure
.866	Guano
.869	Biosolids

Class here human manure (humanure), sewage sludge

.87	Vegetable manures and converted household garbage

Standard subdivisions are added for vegetable manures and converted household garbage together, for vegetable manure alone

.874	Green manures
.875	Compost

Including converted household garbage

> *See also 628.368 for composting toilets; also 631.869 for human waste as fertilizer*

.89	Growth regulators

632   Plant injuries, diseases, pests

Standard subdivisions are added for plant injuries, diseases, pests together; for plant injuries alone

Class here pathology of agricultural plants; comprehensive works on plant and animal injuries, diseases, pests

Class works on both physiology and pathology of agricultural plants in 571.2; class use of agricultural plants in studies of basic pathological processes in 571.92

> *For injuries, diseases, pests of specific plant crops, see 633–635; for veterinary medicine, see 636.089*

.1	**Damages caused by environmental factors**

Class here damages caused by climatic change, by weather

.11	Frost injury

Including other low-temperature injuries

.12	Drought and heat damage
.14	Hail damage
.15	Lightning damage
.16	Wind and rain damage
.17	Flood damage

.18   Fire damage

.19   Pollution damages

> Class here air pollution damages, diseases caused by pollution

---

> **632.2–632.8 Specific diseases and pests**

> Class here control of specific diseases

> Class comprehensive works on diseases and pests together in 632; class comprehensive works on diseases in 632.3; class comprehensive works on pests in 632.6; class comprehensive works on disease and pest control in 632.9

> *For pesticides regardless of disease or pest, see 632.95*

> *See Manual at 632.95 vs. 632.2–632.8*

.2   **Galls**

> Class here gall-producing organisms

.3   **Diseases**

> Including protozoan diseases, radiation injury

> Class here disease control

> *For diseases caused by pollution, see 632.19; for galls, see 632.2; for fungus diseases, see 632.4; for viral diseases, see 632.8; for pesticides used in disease control, see 632.95*

.32   Bacterial diseases

> Including rickettsial diseases

.4   **Fungus diseases**

> Add to base number 632.4 the numbers following 579.5 in 579.52–579.59, e.g., rusts 632.492, smuts 632.493

.5   **Weeds**

> Including poisonous plants

> Class here plant pests, weed control

> *For herbicides, see 632.954*

.52   Parasitic weeds

> Class parasitic microorganisms in 632.3

.6 **Animal pests**

Class here pests, control of specific animal pests

Add to base number 632.6 the numbers following 59 in 592–599, e.g., nematodes 632.6257, common rats 632.69352; however, for gall-producing animal pests, see 632.2; for protozoan diseases, see 632.3; for insect pests, see 632.7

Class comprehensive works on agricultural pest control, on specific topics of pest control other than pesticides in 632.9; class interdisciplinary works on pest control technology in 628.96; class interdisciplinary works on pests, works on pest control services in 363.78

> *For weeds, see 632.5; for pesticides, see 632.95; for predator control in animal husbandry, see 636.0839*

.7 **Insect pests**

Add to base number 632.7 the numbers following 595.7 in 595.72–595.79, e.g., locusts 632.726, beetles 632.76

.8 **Virus diseases**

.9 **General topics of pest and disease control**

Standard subdivisions are added for pest and disease control together, for pest control alone

Including genetic engineering for pest resistance

Class here control of animal pests, integrated pest management

> *For disease control, see 632.3; for weed control, see 632.5; for control of specific animal pests, see 632.6*

.902 84   Apparatus and equipment

Do not use for materials; class in 632.95

.93   Plant quarantine

.94   Crop-dusting, fumigation, spraying

.940 284   Apparatus and equipment

Do not use for materials; class in 632.95

.95   Pesticides

Including algicides

Class here pesticides used to control animal pests, interdisciplinary works on pesticides

Class chemicals used in biological control in 632.960284

> *For manufacture of pesticides, see 668.65*

> *See Manual at 632.95 vs. 632.2–632.8*

.950 4   Special topics of pesticides

Including fumigants

.950 42   Undesired effects and their control

                       Including pesticide resistance

                       Class interdisciplinary works on environmental effects of pesticides in 363.7384

.951   Pesticides used to control specific kinds of animal pests

                       Including rodenticides, vermicides

                       Class comprehensive works on pesticides used to control animal pests in 632.95

[.951 01–.951 09]   Standard subdivisions

                       Do not use; class in 632.9501–632.9509

.951 7   Insecticides

                       Including DDT

                       Class here pesticides used to control arthropods

.952   Fungicides

.953   Bactericides

.954   Herbicides

.96   Biological control

>   ## 633–635 Specific plant crops

         Add to each subdivision identified by * as follows:
            1–6   Cultivation and harvesting
                     Add the numbers following 631.5 in 631.51–631.56, e.g., harvesting 5
                     For special cultivation methods, see notation 8 from this table
            7   Varieties and kinds
                     Class specific techniques of cultivation and harvesting specific varieties in notation 1–6 from this table; class fertilizers, soil conditioners, growth regulators for specific varieties in notation 89 from this table; class injuries, pests, diseases of specific varieties in notation 9 from this table
            8   Special cultivation methods; fertilizers, soil conditioners, growth regulators
            81–87   Special cultivation methods
                     Add to 8 the numbers following 631.58 in 631.581–631.587, e.g., organic farming 84
            89   Fertilizers, soil conditioners, growth regulators
                     Add to 89 the numbers following 631.8 in 631.81–631.89, e.g., compost 8975
            9   Injuries, diseases, pests
                     Add to 9 the numbers following 632 in 632.1–632.9, e.g., insect pests 97
         Class comprehensive works in 630

         See Manual at 633–635

633   Field and plantation crops

Large-scale production of crops intended for agricultural purposes or industrial processing other than preservation

Standard subdivisions are added for either or both topics in heading

Class truck farming in 635

For a specific field or plantation crop not provided for here, see the crop, e.g., bananas 634.772

[.028]   Auxiliary techniques and procedures; apparatus, equipment, materials

Do not use for auxiliary techniques and procedures; class in 630.208

[.028 4]   Apparatus, equipment, materials

Do not use; class in 631

.1   **Cereals**

Including grain amaranths

For cereal crops grown for forage, see 633.25

.104   *Cultivation, harvesting, related topics

.11   *Wheat

.12   *Buckwheat

.13   *Oats

.14   *Rye

.15   *Corn

Variant names: Indian corn, maize

Class sweet corn in 635.672

For popcorn, see 635.677

.16   *Barley

.17   Millets, grain sorghums, upland and wild rice

.171   *Millets (Panicum and related genera)

.174   *Grain sorghums

Class sweet sorghums in 633.62

.178   *Wild rice

.179   *Upland rice

*Add as instructed under 633–635

.18   *Rice

Class here paddy rice

For upland rice, see 633.179

See also 633.178 for wild rice

.2   **Forage crops**

Class here forage grasses, Pooideae grasses

For forage crops other than grasses, see 633.3

.200 1–.200 9   Standard subdivisions

.202   Pastures and their grasses

Class here range management

Class pasture use of forests in 634.99; class comprehensive works on ranches and farms devoted to livestock in 636.01

For specific pasture grasses, see 633.21–633.28

.208   *Cultivation, harvesting, related topics of forage crops

.21   *Bluegrasses (Poa)

.22   *Orchard grass

Variant name: cocksfoot

.23   *Bent grasses (Agrostis)

.24   *Timothy

.25   Cereal grasses

Add to base number 633.25 the numbers following 633.1 in 633.11–633.18, e.g., rye grasses 633.254

.26   Sedges

.27   Panicoideae grasses

For corn, see 633.255; for millets, see 633.2571; for sorghums, see 633.2574

.28   Other Pooideae grasses

Including fescues (Festuca)

.3   **Legumes, forage crops other than grasses and legumes**

Standard subdivisions are added for legumes and forage crops other than grasses and legumes together, for legumes alone

Class here forage legumes, grain legumes

Class interdisciplinary works on legumes as food in 641.3565

For leguminous fruits, see 634.46; for garden legumes, see 635.65

*Add as instructed under 633–635

.304	*Cultivation, harvesting, related topics
.31	*Alfalfa

Variant name: lucerne

.32	*Trifolium clovers

Class here trefoils

Class sweet clovers in 633.366

.33	*Cowpeas

Variant name: black-eyed peas

.34	*Soybeans

Variant names: sojas, soyas

.35	*Vetches
.36	Lespedeza, sweet clovers, lupines, peanuts, field peas
.364	*Lespedeza

Variant name: bush clover

.366	*Sweet clovers (Melilotus)
.367	*Lupines
.368	*Peanuts

Variant name: groundnuts

.369	*Field peas

Variant names: Austrian winter peas, Pisum arvense

.37	Other legumes

Including chick-peas, fava beans (broad beans), lentils, lima beans, Pisum sativum

.372	*Common beans (Phaseolus vulgaris)
.39	Forage crops other than grasses and legumes
.5	**Fiber crops**

Class here soft-fiber crops

Class fiber plants grown for paper pulp in 633.89

>	633.51–633.56 Soft fibers

Class comprehensive works in 633.5

.51	*Cotton
.52	*Flax

*Add as instructed under 633–635

.53	*Hemp (Cannabis sativa)

               See also 633.79 for marijuana

.54	*Jute
.55	*Ramie
.56	Other soft fibers

               Including kenaf

.57	Hard fibers

               For hard fibers not provided for below, see 633.58

.571	*Manila hemp

               Variant name: abaca

.576	*Pineapple fibers
.577	*Sisal (Agave fibers)
.58	Other hard fibers

               Including bamboo, rattan, other basketwork and wickerwork plants

.6	**Sugar, syrup, starch crops**

               Standard subdivisions are added for sugar, syrup, starch crops together; for sugar crops alone; for syrup crops alone

.61	*Sugarcane
.62	*Sorgo

               Variant name: sweet sorghums

.63	*Sugar beets
.64	*Sugar maples
.68	Starch crops

               Including arrowroot, sago, taro

               Class a crop raised for starch and another product with the other product, e.g., potatoes 635.21

.682	*Cassava (Manioc)
.7	**Alkaloidal crops**
.71	*Tobacco
.72	*Tea
.73	*Coffee
.74	*Cacao
.75	*Poppies (Papaver somniferum)

*Add as instructed under 633–635

| .76 | *Kola nuts (Cola nuts) |
| .77 | *Maté |

>> Variant name: Paraguay tea

| .78 | *Chicory |
| .79 | *Marijuana |

>> Class here hashish

>> *See also 633.53 for hemp*

.8   Other crops grown for industrial processing

.81   Perfume-producing plants

.82   Flavoring-producing plants

>> Including hops, mints, sassafras, vanilla, wintergreen

>>> *For spices, see 633.83; for alliaceous plants, see 635.26; for aromatic and sweet herbs, see 635.7*

.83   Spices

>> Including allspice, clove, horseradish, nutmeg, saffron

>>> *For peppers, see 633.84. For non-spice uses of spice crops, see the use, e.g., ginger as candy 641.853*

.832   Ginger, cardamom, turmeric

>> Standard subdivisions are added for ginger, cardamom, turmeric together; for ginger alone

.834   Cinnamon and cassia

>> Standard subdivisions are added for either or both topics in heading

.837   Mustard

.84   Peppers

>> Peppers as spices regardless of taxonomic classification

>> Including paprika

>> Class allspice in 633.83

>>> *For sweet peppers, see 641.35643*

.85   Plants producing nonvolatile oils

>> Class here oilseed plants

>>> *For a specific plant producing a nonvolatile oil not provided for here, see the plant, e.g., corn 633.15; coconuts 634.61; olives 634.63*

.851   *Oil palms

.853   *Rapeseed

---

*Add as instructed under 633–635

.86	Dye-producing plants
.87	Tannin-producing plants

Including canaigre

.88	Medicine-producing plants

Add to base number 633.88 the numbers following 58 in 583–588, e.g., ginsengs 633.883988; however, for a crop producing medicine as a secondary product, see the primary product, e.g., poppy 633.75

.89	Crops grown for other industrial purposes
.895	Rubber-producing and resin-producing plants
.895 2	*Rubber tree (Hevea brasiliensis)
.895 9	*Turpentine-producing plants
.898	Insecticide-producing plants

634   Orchards, fruits, forestry

Fruits: reproductive bodies of seed plants having an edible more or less sweet pulp associated with the seed

Standard subdivisions are added for orchards, fruits, forestry together; for orchards alone; for fruits alone

Class here comprehensive works on tree crops

For trees grown for plantation crops, see 633; for pepos, see 635.61; for ornamental trees, see 635.977

.04	*Cultivation, harvesting, related topics of orchards, of fruits, of trees

---

>   **634.1–634.6   Orchards and their fruits**

Class comprehensive works in 634

.1	**Pomaceous fruits**
.11	*Apples
.13	*Pears

See also 634.653 for alligator pears

.14	*Quinces
.15	*Medlars (Mespilus germanica)

See also 634.16 for Japanese medlars

.16	*Loquats

Variant name: Japanese medlars

*Add as instructed under 633–635

.2 **Stone fruits**

> Variant name: Drupaceous fruits

.21 *Apricots

.22 *Plums

.23 *Cherries

.25 *Peaches

.257 Varieties and kinds

> Number built according to instructions under 633–635
>
> Including nectarines

.3 **Citrus and moraceous fruits**

.304 *Citrus fruits

> *For specific citrus fruits, see 634.31–634.34*

.31 *Oranges

.32 *Grapefruit

.33 Citron group

.331 *Citrons

.334 *Lemons

.337 *Limes

.34 *Kumquats

.36 *Moraceous fruits

> *For figs, see 634.37; for mulberries, see 634.38; for breadfruit, see 634.39*

.37 *Figs

.38 *Mulberries

.39 *Breadfruit

.4 **Other fruits**

> Class tropical and subtropical fruits not provided for here in 634.6

.41 Annonaceous fruits

> Including papaws

.42 Myrtaceous and passifloraceous fruits

.421 *Guavas

.425 *Passion fruit

.43 Sapotaceous fruits

*Add as instructed under 633–635

.44   Anacardiaceous fruits

      Including mangoes

      Class cashews in 634.573

.45   *Persimmons

.46   Leguminous fruits

      Including carob

      Class comprehensive works on legumes in 633.3

.5   Nuts

.51   *Walnuts

.52   *Pecans

.53   *Chestnuts

.54   *Filberts

.55   *Almonds

.57   Cashews, pistachios, Brazil nuts

.573   *Cashews

.574   *Pistachios

.575   *Brazil nuts

.6   Tropical and subtropical fruits

      Not provided for elsewhere

      For herbaceous tropical and subtropical fruits, see 634.77

.61   *Coconuts

.62   *Dates

.63   *Olives

.64   *Pomegranates

.65   Papayas, avocados, mangosteens

.651   *Papayas

.653   *Avocados

      Variant name: alligator pears

.655   *Mangosteens

*Add as instructed under 633–635

.7   **Berries and herbaceous tropical and subtropical fruits**

Standard subdivisions are added for berries and herbaceous tropical and subtropical fruits together, for berries alone

Class here comprehensive works on small fruits

For a specific small fruit not provided for here, see the fruit, e.g., mulberries 634.38, grapes 634.8

.71   Cane fruits (Rubus)

.711   *Raspberries

.713   *Blackberries

.714   *Loganberries

.717   *Dewberries

.718   *Boysenberries

.72   Ribes

.721   *Currants

.725   *Gooseberries

.73   Huckleberries and blueberries

.732   *Huckleberries (Gaylussacia)

.737   *Blueberries (Vaccinium)

.74   Other bush fruits

Including barberries, juneberries

.75   *Strawberries

.76   *Cranberries

.77   Herbaceous tropical and subtropical fruits

Class comprehensive works on tropical and subtropical fruits in 634.6

.772   *Bananas

.773   *Plantains

.774   *Pineapples

.775   Cactus fruits

.8   **Grapes**

Class here viticulture

.82   Injuries, diseases, pests

Add to base number 634.82 the numbers following 632 in 632.1–632.9, e.g., fungus diseases 634.824

---

*Add as instructed under 633–635

.83   Varieties and kinds

Class a specific aspect of varieties and kinds with the aspect, e.g., fungus diseases of muscadines 634.824

.88   Cultivation and harvesting

Add to base number 634.88 the numbers following 631.5 in 631.51–631.58, e.g., pruning 634.8842; however, for varieties, see 634.83

.9   Forestry

[.906 85]   Management of production

Do not use; class in 634.92

>   634.92–634.96   General topics of forestry

Class general topics applied to a specific kind of tree in 634.97; class comprehensive works in 634.9

For exploitation and products, see 634.98

.92   Forest management

Class here production management in forestry

Class comprehensive works on management in forestry in 634.9068. Class production management of a specific aspect of forestry with the aspect, e.g., production management of logging 634.980685

.928   Production planning and mensuration

.928 3   Production planning

.928 5   Mensuration

Including estimation

.93   Access and safety features

Including lookout towers, roads

.95   Silviculture

.953   Forest thinning

.955   Brush disposal

Including prescribed burning

.956   Forestation

Class here afforestation, reforestation, plant breeding

Class interdisciplinary works on afforestation in 333.75152; class interdisciplinary works on reforestation in 333.75153

.956 2   Producing seeds and seedlings

See also 634.9565 for propagation with seeds and seedlings

.956 4	Nursery practice

For producing seeds and seedlings, see 634.9562

.956 5	Propagation at permanent site

Including seeding at permanent site

.96	Injuries, diseases, pests

Add to base number 634.96 the numbers following 632 in 632.1–632.9, e.g., forest fire technology 634.9618

.97	Kinds of trees

Class here general topics of forestry applied to specific kinds of trees

Add to each subdivision identified by † as follows:
2–6   General topics
      Add the numbers following 634.9 in 634.92–634.96, e.g., reforestation 56
        For exploitation and products, see notation 8 from this table
7   Varieties and kinds
      Class a specific general topic with respect to a specific variety or kind with the topic, e.g., reforestation of a variety 56
8   Exploitation and products
      Standard subdivisions are added for either or both topics in heading
      Class here logging, logs, lumbering
        For minor products, see 634.985–634.987; for sawmill operations, see 674.2
83   Pulpwood

.972	Dicotyledons

Class here hardwoods

For other dicotyledons, see 634.973

.972 1	†Oaks
.972 2	†Maples
.972 3	†Poplars

Class aspens, cottonwoods in 634.97369

See also 634.974 for yellow poplar (tulip tree)

.972 4	†Chestnuts
.972 5	†Beeches
.972 6	†Birches
.972 7	†Lindens
.972 77	Varieties and kinds

Number built according to instructions under 634.97

Including basswood (American linden), lime (European linden)

†Add as instructed under 634.97

.972 8   †Elms

.973   Other dicotyledons

> Add to base number 634.973 the numbers following 583 in 583.2–583.9, e.g., eucalyptus 634.973733

.974   Magnoliids, basal angiosperms, monocots

> Class here palm forestry

> *See also 633.58 for rattan palms; also 633.851 for oil palms; also 634.61 for coconut palm; also 635.977484 for ornamental palms*

.975   Gymnosperms

> 634.975 1–634.975 8   Coniferous trees

> Class comprehensive works in 634.975

> *For coniferous trees not provided for here, see 634.9759*

.975 1   †Pines

> Class dammar, huon pines in 634.97593

.975 2   †Spruces

.975 3   †Hemlocks

.975 4   †Firs

.975 5   †Cypresses

.975 6   †Cedars

.975 7   †Larches

.975 8   †Sequoias

.975 9   Other gymnosperms

> Add to base number 634.9759 the numbers following 585 in 585.2–585.9, e.g., kauris (dammar pines) 634.97593

.98   Forest exploitation and products

> Standard subdivisions are added for either or both topics in heading

> Class here logging, logs, comprehensive works on lumbering

> Class exploitation and products of specific kinds of trees in 634.97; class lumber in 674. Class trees cultivated for a specific product other than lumber or pulp with the product, e.g., turpentine trees 633.8959, pecan trees 634.52

> *For sawmill operations, see 674.2*

.983   Pulpwood

> Class nonwoody plants grown for paper pulp in 633.89

†Add as instructed under 634.97

>   **634.985–634.987 Exploitation of minor forest products**

Use only for products that have not been cultivated

Class here minor products of specific kinds of trees

Class comprehensive works in 634.987

.985   Bark

.986   Sap

.987   Minor forest products

Including fruits, seeds, nuts

For bark, see 634.985; for sap, see 634.986

.99   Agroforestry

Forestry in combination with other farming

Including farm forestry, woodlots; pasture use of forestry

Class a specific forestry aspect of agroforestry with the aspect, e.g., logging 634.98

635   Garden crops (Horticulture)

Class here vegetables (crops grown primarily for human consumption without intermediate processing other than cooking and preservation); home gardening, truck farming

Class orchards in 634

.04   *Cultivation, harvesting, related topics

>   **635.1–635.8 Edible garden crops**

Class comprehensive works in 635

.1   **Edible roots**

For cassava, see 633.682

.11   *Beets

.12   Turnips, rutabagas, celeriac

.125   *Turnips

Class rutabagas in 635.126

.126   *Rutabagas

Variant names: Russian turnips, swedes, Swedish turnips

.128   *Celeriac

.13   *Carrots

*Add as instructed under 633–635

.14	*Parsnips
.15	*Radishes
.16	*Salsify
.2	**Edible tubers and bulbs**

> Standard subdivisions are added for edible tubers and bulbs together, for edible tubers alone

> *For taro, see 633.68*

.21	*Potatoes
.22	*Sweet potatoes
.23	*Yams (Dioscorea)
.24	*Jerusalem artichokes
.25	*Onions
.26	Alliaceous plants

> Including chives, garlic, leeks, shallots

> *For onions, see 635.25*

.3   **Edible leaves, flowers, stems**

> *For cooking greens and rhubarb, see 635.4; for salad greens, see 635.5*

.31	*Asparagus
.32	*Artichokes

> *See also 635.24 for Jerusalem artichokes*

.34	*Cabbage

> Class here comprehensive works on cultivation of Brassica oleracea

> *For cauliflower and broccoli, see 635.35; for Brussels sprouts, see 635.36*

.347	Varieties and kinds

> Number built according to instructions under 633–635

> Including kale (collards)

.35	*Cauliflower and broccoli

> Subdivisions are added for either or both topics in heading

.36	*Brussels sprouts
.4	**Cooking greens and rhubarb**

> Standard subdivisions are added for cooking greens and rhubarb together, for cooking greens alone

*Add as instructed under 633–635

.41	*Spinach
.42	*Chard
.48	*Rhubarb
.5	**Salad greens**
.51	*Dandelions
.52	*Lettuce
.53	*Celery

> *See also 635.128 for celeriac*

.54	*Chicory
.55	*Endive
.56	Sorrel and cresses
.6	**Edible garden fruits and seeds**
.61	Pepos

> Class here melons
>
> *For squashes and pumpkins, see 635.62; for cucumbers, see 635.63*

.611	*Muskmelons
.615	*Watermelons
.62	*Squashes and pumpkins

> Subdivisions are added for either or both topics in heading

.63	*Cucumbers
.64	Other garden fruits
.642	*Tomatoes
.643	*Sweet peppers

> Variant names: bell, green peppers

.646	*Eggplants
.648	*Okra
.65	Garden legumes

> Class comprehensive works on legumes in 633.3

.651	*Broad beans
.652	*Common beans (Phaseolus vulgaris)
.653	*Lima beans

*Add as instructed under 633–635

.655   *Soybeans

          Variant names: sojas, soyas

.656   *Peas

          Variant names: English peas, garden peas, Pisum sativum

.657   *Chick-peas

.658   *Lentils

.659   Other garden legumes

.659 2   *Black-eyed peas

          Variant name: cowpeas

.659 6   *Peanuts

          Variant name: groundnuts

.67   Corn

          Variant names: Indian corn, maize

.672   *Sweet corn

.677   *Popcorn

.7   **Aromatic and sweet herbs**

          Standard subdivisions are added for either or both topics in heading

          Class here herb gardens

.8   **Mushrooms and truffles**

          Standard subdivisions are added for mushrooms and truffles together, for mushrooms alone

.9   **Flowers and ornamental plants**

          Standard subdivisions are added for either or both topics in heading

          Class here floriculture

          Class landscape architecture of flower gardens in 712

          For planting and cultivation of roadside vegetation, see 625.77

          See Manual at 635.9 vs. 582.1

[.902 84]   Apparatus, equipment, materials

          Do not use; class in 635.91

*Add as instructed under 633–635

.91   Specific techniques; apparatus, equipment, materials

Add to base number 635.91 the numbers following 631 in 631.2–631.8, e.g., propagating ornamental plants 635.9153; however, for propagation from bulbs and tubers, see 635.94; for special methods of cultivation, see 635.98

Class specific techniques, apparatus, equipment, materials of specific groupings of ornamental plants in 635.93–635.97

.92   Injuries, diseases, pests

Add to base number 635.92 the numbers following 632 in 632.1–632.9, e.g., fungus diseases 635.924

For injuries, diseases, pests of specific groupings of plants, see 635.93–635.97

>   635.93–635.97   Groupings of plants

Unless other instructions are given, class a subject with aspects in two or more subdivisions of 635.93–635.97 in the number coming first in the schedule, e.g., succulent house plants 635.9525 (*not* 635.965)

Class comprehensive works in 635.9

.93   Groupings by life duration; taxonomic groupings

.931   Groupings by life duration

Class specific taxonomic kinds regardless of life duration in 635.933–635.938

For perennials, see 635.932

.931 2   *Annuals

.931 4   *Biennials

.932   *Perennials

.933–.938   Taxonomic groupings

Add to base number 635.93 the numbers following 58 in 583–588, e.g., cacti 635.933885, roses 635.933644, orchids 635.93472; however, for everlastings, see 635.973; for comprehensive works on dicotyledons, see 635.9; for taxonomic groupings of trees, see 635.9773–635.9775

.94   Plants propagated from bulbs and tubers

Standard subdivisions are added for either or both topics in heading

Class here propagating ornamental plants from bulbs, from tubers

.95   Groupings by environmental factors

.951   Native habitats

Add to base number 635.951 notation 4–9 from Table 2, e.g., ornamentals native to Scotland 635.951411

---

*Add as instructed under 633–635

.952	Groupings by climatic factors

           Including arctic plants

           Class comprehensive works on temperate-zone plants in 635.9

.952 3   *Tropical plants

.952 5   *Desert plants

           Including drought-resistant plants

           Class here succulent plants

           Class works on succulent plants emphasizing cactus in 635.93356

.952 8   *Alpine plants

           Including alpine gardens, high-altitude plants

           Class"alpine gardens" in the sense synonymous with rock gardens (that is, as rock gardens with nonalpine as well as alpine plants) in 635.9672

.953   Groupings by seasonal and diurnal factors

           Including winter-flowering plants, morning-blooming and night-blooming plants

.954   Groupings by natural light factors

           Including plants favoring sunlight

              See also 635.9826 for artificial-light gardening

.954 3   *Shade-tolerant plants

.955   Groupings by soil factors

           Including plants favoring difficult, problem, sandy soils

           Class plants suitable for rock gardens in 635.9672

.96   Groupings by special areas and purposes

           Class comprehensive works on plants for all purposes in 635.9

              For foliage plants, see 635.975; for butterfly gardening, see 638.5789

.962   *Flower beds

.963   *Borders and edgings

           Subdivisions are added for either or both topics in heading

.964   Ground cover

           Class here grass

.964 2   *Turf

           Class lawns in 635.9647

.964 7   *Lawns

*Add as instructed under 633–635

.965   *House plants

>   Class here indoor gardening in the home
>
>   Class window-box gardening in 635.9678; class comprehensive works on container gardening in 635.986
>
>   *For bonsai, see 635.9772*

.966   *Flowers for cutting

>   Class flower arrangement in 745.92

.967   Special kinds of gardens

.967 1   Roof, balcony, patio gardens

>   Class comprehensive works on container gardening in 635.986

.967 2   *Rock gardens

>   *See also 635.9528 for alpine gardening*

.967 4   *Water gardens

.967 6   *Wild-flower gardens

>   Class wild flowers of a specific native habitat in 635.951

.967 8   *Window-box gardens

.968   Plants grown for fragrance and color

.97   Other groupings of ornamental plants

.973   *Everlastings

.974   *Vines

>   Class here climbing plants

.975   *Foliage plants

.976   *Shrubs and hedges

>   Subdivisions are added for either or both topics in heading
>
>   Class hedges used as fences in 631.27

.977   Trees

>   Class here urban forestry; potted, shade, street trees
>
>   Including tree planting
>
>   Class comprehensive works on container gardening in 635.986

.977 1   General kinds of ornamental trees

>   Class general kinds of trees of a specific taxa in 635.9773–635.9775; class comprehensive works in 635.977
>
>   *For bonsai, see 635.9772*

*Add as instructed under 633–635

.977 13	*Flowering trees
.977 15	*Evergreen trees

> Class Christmas trees, evergreen trees in the sense of conifers in 635.9775

.977 2	*Bonsai

> Class here dwarf potted trees, miniature trees, penjing

> Class specific taxonomic kinds of bonsai in 635.9773–635.9775

.977 3–.977 5	Taxonomic groupings

> Add to base number 635.977 the numbers following 58 in 583–585, e.g., elms 635.9773648; however, for comprehensive works on dicotyledonous trees, see 635.977

.98	Special methods of cultivation in floriculture

> Class special methods of cultivation of specific groupings of plants in 635.93–635.97; class comprehensive works on special methods of cultivating vegetables and ornamental plants in 635.048

.982	Controlled-environment gardening

> *For bell-jar gardening, see 635.985*

.982 3	*Greenhouse gardening
.982 4	*Terrariums
.982 6	*Artificial-light gardening
.985	*Bell-jar gardening
.986	*Container gardening

> Class here pot gardening

.987	Organic gardening

> Class a specific aspect of organic gardening in floriculture with the aspect in 635.91–635.98, e.g., compost 635.91875

636   Animal husbandry

> Class here interdisciplinary works on species of domestic mammals

> *For culture of nondomesticated animals, see 639. For a specific nonagricultural aspect of domestic mammals, see the aspect, e.g., biology 599*

> *See Manual at 800, T3C—362 vs. 398.245, 590, 636*

.001	Philosophy and theory
[.001 576 5]	Genetics

> Do not use; class in 636.0821

.002	Miscellany

*Add as instructed under 633–635

[.002 77]	Ownership marks
	Do not use; class in 636.0812
.003–.006	Standard subdivisions
.007	Education, research, related topics
.007 9	Competitions, awards, financial support
	Do not use for animal shows and related awards; class in 636.0811
.008–.009	Standard subdivisions
.01	Ranches and farms
	Class feeding livestock in 636.084
	See also 636.0845 for range management
.07	Young of animals
	Class production and maintenance, rearing for specific purposes, veterinary medicine of young animals in 636.08
.08	Specific topics in animal husbandry
	Unless other instructions are given, class a subject with aspects in two or more subdivisions of this schedule in the number coming last, e.g., care and maintenance of pets 636.0887 (*not* 636.083)
	For ranches and farms, see 636.01; for young of animals, see 636.07
[.080 1–.080 9]	Standard subdivisions
	Do not use; class in 636.001–636.009
.081	Selection, showing, ownership marks
	For selection in breeding, see 636.082
.081 1	Showing
	Class here judging; show animals
.081 2	Ownership marks
	Class here branding
.082	Breeding
	Including breeding stock
.082 1	Genetics
	Including germ plasm
	Class here genetic engineering
	Class interdisciplinary works on livestock genetic resources in 333.954
.082 2	Breeding records
	Class here herdbooks, pedigrees, studbooks
.082 4	Breeding and reproduction methods

.082 45	Artificial insemination
.083	**Care, maintenance, training**

> Including transportation
>
> Class here stable management
>
> *For feeding, see 636.084*

.083 1	Housing

> Including barns, cages, stockyards
>
> Class waste management in 636.0838; class construction of housing for domestic animals in 690.892
>
> *See also 636.0843 for feedlot management*

.083 2	Animal welfare

> Class here animal rescue, animal shelters, condition of livestock
>
> Class veterinary care of animals in 636.089
>
> *See also 179.3 for ethical aspects of animal care*

.083 21	Animal hospitals

> Variant name: veterinary hospitals

.083 3	Individual tending

> Including dipping, shearing
>
> Class here grooming

.083 5	Training

> Class training for a specific purpose in 636.088

.083 7	Harnesses and accessories

> Most works on harnesses and accessories will be classed under horses in 636.10837

.083 8	Animal waste management
.083 9	Predator control

> *For predator control in wildlife conservation, see 639.966*

.084	**Feeding**

> *For feeds and applied nutrition, see 636.085*

.084 3	Feedlot management

> *For feedlot waste management, see 636.0838*

.084 5	Grazing

> Class here browsing, herding, range management
>
> *For development of pasturage, see 633.202; for pasture use of forests, see 634.99*

.085	Feeds and applied nutrition
.085 2	Applied nutrition

Class here composition and food value

For composition and food value of a specific feed, see the feed, e.g., food value of silage 636.0862

.085 21	Nitrogen
.085 22	Proteins
.085 27	Minerals

Class here trace elements

.085 28	Vitamins
.085 5	Feeds

Class growing forage crops in 633.2; class grazing in 636.0845

For field-crop feeds, see 636.086

.085 56	Feed from wastes

Class here feed from agricultural wastes

.085 57	Feed additives and formula feeds
.086	Field-crop feeds

Including dry fodder, green fodder

.086 2	Silage
.088	Animals for specific purposes

See Manual at 636.1–636.8 vs. 636.088

.088 2	Beasts of burden

Class here draft animals, pack animals

Class comprehensive works on work animals in 636.0886

.088 3	Animals raised for food

For animals raised for eggs and milk, see 636.08842

.088 4	Animals raised for special products

For animals raised for food, see 636.0883

.088 42	Animals raised for eggs and milk

Class milk processing in 637.1; class egg processing in 637.5

See Manual at 636.1–636.8 vs. 636.088

.088 44	Animals raised for hide

Class fur farming in 636.97

For hair, see 636.08845

.088 45	Animals raised for hair and feathers
	Including bristles, wool
.088 5	Laboratory animals
.088 6	Work animals

Including animals used to guard and herd

Class use of work animals with the use, e.g., use of work animals on police patrols 363.232

For beasts of burden, see 636.0882; for sport and stunt animals, see 636.0888

.088 7	Pets

Class here obedience training

Class reminiscences about and true accounts of pets in 808.883. Class reminiscences about and true accounts of pets in a specific literature with the literature in 800, plus notation 803 from Table 3B under the appropriate language, e.g., reminiscences in English about pets 828.03; class literary treatment of pets other than reminiscences with the appropriate literary form in 800, e.g., a late 20th century English novel about pets 823.914

See Manual at 800, T3C—362 vs. 398.245, 590, 636

.088 8	Sport and stunt animals

Including circus animals, fighting animals, hunting animals, game animals, racing animals

Class show animals in 636.0811; class comprehensive works on work animals in 636.0886. Class use of sport and stunt animals with the use in 700, e.g., use of animals in circuses 791.32

.088 9	Zoo animals
.089	Veterinary medicine

Class here veterinary sciences

Add to base number 636.089 the numbers following 61 in 610–618, e.g., veterinary viral diseases 636.089691

Class animal welfare in 636.0832; class animal hospitals in 636.08321

>   **636.1–636.8 Specific kinds of domestic animals**

Except for modifications shown under specific entries, add to each subdivision identified by * as follows:

01	Philosophy and theory
[015765]	Genetics
	Do not use; class in notation 2 from this table
02–06	Standard subdivisions
07	Education, research, related topics
079	Competitions, awards, financial support
	Do not use for animal shows and related awards; class in notation 1 from this table
08–09	Standard subdivisions
1	Showing
	Class here judging
2	Breeding
22	Breeding records
	Class here origin of the breed or breeds; herdbooks, pedigrees, studbooks
3	Care, feeding, training, veterinary medicine
35	Training
39	Veterinary medicine

Class comprehensive works in 636

See Manual at 636.1–636.8 vs. 636.088

.1   Horses

Class here equines

.100 1–.100 9   Standard subdivisions

Notation from Table 1 as modified under 636.001–636.009

.101–.108   **Specific topics in husbandry of horses**

Add to base number 636.10 the numbers following 636.0 in 636.01–636.08, e.g., housing horses 636.10831; however, for racehorses, see 636.12; for riding horses, see 636.13; for draft horses, see 636.15

Class training of riders and drivers, comprehensive works on training horses and their riders and drivers in 798

.109   **Miniature horses**

Regardless of breed

>   **636.11–636.17 Specific breeds and kinds of horses**

Class miniature horses regardless of breed in 636.109; class comprehensive works in 636.1

.11   **Oriental horses**

.112   *Arabian horse

*Add as instructed under 636.1–636.8

.12	*Racehorses

> *For a specific breed of racehorse, see the breed, e.g., Thoroughbred horse 636.132*

.13	Saddle horses (Riding horses)

Including American saddlebred, Tennessee walking horses; American paint, Appaloosa, Morab, mustang, pinto

> *For wild mustang, see 599.6655; for Oriental horses, see 636.11; for comprehensive works on racehorses, see 636.12*

.132	*Thoroughbred horse
.133	*Quarter horse
.138	*Lippizaner horse
.14	*Carriage horses

Including Cleveland bay and Hackney horses

Class here coach horses, comprehensive works on harness horses (carriage horses and light harness horses)

Class comprehensive works on harness and draft horses in 636.15

> *For light harness horses, see 636.17*

.15	*Draft horses

Including Belgian draft, Clydesdale, Shire horses

Class here comprehensive works on harness and draft horses

> *For harness horses, see 636.14*

.16	*Ponies

Including Chincoteague, Iceland, Shetland, Welsh ponies

.17	*Light harness horses
.175	*Standardbred horse

Class here trotters

.177	*Morgan horse
.18	Other equines

Including zebras

.182	*Donkeys (Burros)
.183	*Mules

*Add as instructed under 636.1–636.8

.2   **Cattle and related animals**

> Class here bovidae, bovines, ruminants
>
> Subdivisions are added for cattle and related animals together, for cattle alone
>
> *For sheep and goats, see 636.3; for Tragulidae, see 636.963*

.200 1–.200 9   Standard subdivisions

> Notation from Table 1 as modified under 636.001–636.009

.201–.208   Specific topics on husbandry of cattle and related animals together, of cattle alone

> Add to base number 636.20 the numbers following 636.0 in 636.01–636.08, e.g., heifers 636.207; however, for cattle for specific purposes, see 636.21

.21   Cattle for specific purposes

> Class here production, maintenance, training
>
> Add to base number 636.21 the numbers following 636.088 in 636.0882–636.0889, e.g., raising cattle for beef 636.213, for milk 636.2142
>
> Class veterinary science in 636.2089; class specific breeds of cattle for specific purposes in 636.22–636.28; class milking and milk processing in 637.1

>   636.22–636.28   Specific breeds of cattle
>
> Class comprehensive works in 636.2

.22   British breeds of cattle

.222   English beef breeds

> Including Hereford and Shorthorn cattle

.223   Scottish, Welsh, Irish beef breeds

> Including Aberdeen Angus, Galloway, Highland cattle

.224   Channel Island dairy breeds

> Including Guernsey and Jersey cattle

.225   Scottish and Irish dairy breeds

> Including Ayrshire and Dexter cattle

.226   Dual-purpose breeds

> Including Devon, English Longhorn, Polled Shorthorn cattle

.23   German, Dutch, Danish, Swiss breeds of cattle

.232   Beef breeds

.234   Dairy breeds

> Including Brown Swiss and Holstein-Friesian cattle

.236		Dual-purpose breeds
.24		French and Belgian breeds of cattle
.242		Beef breeds
.244		Dairy breeds
.246		Dual-purpose breeds
.27		Other European breeds of cattle
.28		Non-European breeds of cattle
.29		Other larger ruminants and Camelidae

Including Giraffidae

.291	Zebus (Brahmans)
.292	Bison

Variant names: American buffalo, buffalo

See also 636.293 for water buffalo

.293	Other Bovoidea

Including water buffalo

.294	Cervidae (Deer)
.294 4	Cervus
.294 42	*Cervus elephas

Variant names: American elk, red deer, wapiti

.294 5	*Dama (Fallow deer)
.294 8	*Rangifer

Variant names: caribou, reindeer

.295	*Camels

Subdivisions are added for specific breeds

.296	Camelidae

Including vicuña

For camels, see 636.295

.296 6	*Llamas (Guanaco, Alpacas)

Subdivisions are added for specific breeds

.3   Sheep and goats

Subdivisions are added for sheep and goats together, for sheep alone

---

* Add as instructed under 636.1–636.8

.300 1–.300 9   Standard subdivisions

                  Notation from Table 1 as modified under 636.001–636.009

.301–.308   Specific topics in husbandry of sheep and goats together, of sheep alone

                  Add to base number 636.30 the numbers following 636.0 in 636.01–636.08, e.g., sheep ranches 636.301; however, for sheep for specific purposes, see 636.31

.31   Sheep for specific purposes

                  Class here production, maintenance, training

                  Add to base number 636.31 the numbers following 636.088 in 636.0882–636.0889, e.g., raising sheep for mutton 636.313, for wool 636.3145

                  Class veterinary science in 636.3089; class specific breeds of sheep for specific purposes in 636.32–636.38

\>   636.32–636.38 Specific breeds of sheep

                  Class comprehensive works in 636.3

.32   British breeds of sheep

.33   German, Dutch, Swiss breeds of sheep

.34   French and Belgian breeds of sheep

.35   Italian breeds of sheep

.36   Merino breeds

                  Class here Spanish breeds of sheep

.366   Spanish Merino breeds

.367   Other European Merino breeds

.368   Non-European Merino breeds

.37   Other European breeds of sheep

.38   Non-European breeds of sheep

                  For non-European Merino breeds, see 636.368

.381   American breeds

.385   Asian breeds

.386   African breeds

.39   Goats

.390 01–.390 09   Standard subdivisions

                  Notation from Table 1 as modified under 636.001–636.009

.390 1–.390 8	Specific topics in husbandry of goats

Add to base number 636.390 the numbers following 636.0 in 636.01–636.08, e.g., goat farms 636.301; however, for goats for specific purposes, see 636.391

.391	Goats for specific purposes

Class here production, maintenance, training

Add to base number 636.391 the numbers following 636.088 in 636.0882–636.0889, e.g., raising goats for hair 636.39145

Class veterinary science in 636.39089; class specific breeds of goats for specific purposes in 636.392–636.398

.392–.398	Specific breeds of goats

Add to base number 636.39 the numbers following 636.3 in 636.32–636.38, e.g., Angora goat 636.3985

.4   Swine

.400 1–.400 9	Standard subdivisions

Notation from Table 1 as modified under 636.001–636.009

.401–.408	Specific topics in husbandry of swine

Add to base number 636.40 the numbers following 636.0 in 636.01–636.08, e.g., swine for specific purposes other than food 636.4088

Class swine for food in 636.4

>   636.42–636.48 Specific breeds of swine

Class comprehensive works in 636.4

.42–.47	European breeds of swine

Add to base number 636.4 the numbers following 636.3 in 636.32–636.37, e.g., British breeds 636.42

.48	Non-European breeds of swine
.482	Poland China swine
.483	Duroc-Jersey swine
.484	American breeds

Including Cheshire, Chester White, Hampshire, Victoria swine

For Poland China swine, see 636.482; for Duroc-Jersey swine, see 636.483

.485	Asian breeds
.486	African breeds
.489	Pacific Ocean island breeds

.5   **Chickens and other kinds of domestic birds**

Class here poultry, comprehensive works on raising birds, interdisciplinary works on species of domestic birds

Subdivisions are added for chickens and other kinds of domestic birds together, for chickens alone

> *For birds other than poultry, see 636.6. For a specific nonagricultural aspect of domestic birds, see the aspect, e.g., biology of domestic birds 598*

.500 1–.500 9   Standard subdivisions

Notation from Table 1 as modified under 636.001–636.009

.501–.508   Specific topics of husbandry of chickens and other kinds of domestic birds together, of chickens alone

Add to base number 636.50 the numbers following 636.0 in 636.01–636.08, e.g., chicken breeding 636.5082; however, for poultry for specific purposes, see 636.51

.51   Poultry for specific purposes

Class here production, maintenance, training

Add to base number 636.51 the numbers following 636.088 in 636.0882–636.0889, e.g., raising chickens for meat 636.513, for eggs 636.5142

Class veterinary science in 636.5089; class specific breeds of chickens for specific purposes in 636.52–636.58; class poultry other than chickens for specific purposes in 636.59

>   636.52–636.58 Specific breeds of chickens

Class comprehensive works in 636.5

.52–.57   European breeds of chickens

Add to base number 636.5 the numbers following 636.3 in 636.32–636.37, e.g., Leghorn 636.55

> *For diminutive varieties of European breeds of chickens, see 636.587*

.58   Non-European and diminutive breeds of chickens

.581   American breeds

> *For Plymouth Rock chicken, see 636.582; for Wyandotte chicken, see 636.583; for Rhode Island Red chicken, see 636.584; for diminutive varieties of American breeds, see 636.587*

.582   Plymouth Rock chicken

.583   Wyandotte chicken

.584   Rhode Island Red chicken

.585   Asian breeds

> *For diminutive varieties of Asian breeds, see 636.587*

.587	Diminutive varieties	
.587 1	*Bantams	
.587 2	Cornish fowl	
.59	Other poultry	
.592	Turkeys	

.592 001–.592 009   Standard subdivisions

           Notation from Table 1 as modified under 636.001–636.009

.592 01–.592 08   Specific topics in husbandry of turkeys

           Add to base number 636.5920 the numbers following 636.0 in 636.01–636.08, e.g., raising turkeys for meat 636.5920883

.593	Guinea fowl	
.594	Pheasants	
.595	Peafowl	
.596	*Pigeons	

         Subdivisions are added for specific breeds

.597   *Ducks

         Subdivisions are added for specific breeds

.598   Geese

.6   **Birds other than poultry**

         Class comprehensive works on birds in 636.5

.61   Birds raised for feathers

         Class a specific kind of bird raised for feathers with the kind, e.g., ostriches 636.694

.63   Game birds

.68   Ornamental birds, songbirds, hawks

         Standard subdivisions are added for ornamental birds, songbirds, hawks together; for ornamental birds alone; for songbirds alone

         Including mynas, toucans

         Class here aviary birds, cage birds

           For peafowl, see 636.595

.681   Swans

.686   Finches, parrots, hawks

.686 2   *Finches

---

*Add as instructed under 636.1–636.8

.686 25	*Canaries

Subdivisions are added for specific varieties

.686 4	*Budgerigars

Variant names: lovebirds; grass, shell parakeets

Subdivisions are added for specific varieties

Class comprehensive works on parakeets in 636.6865

See also 636.6865 for lovebirds (Agapornis)

.686 5	*Parrots

Including cockatoos, conures, lories, lovebirds (Agapornis), macaws, comprehensive works on parakeets

For budgerigars (lovebirds), see 636.6864

.686 56	*Cockatiels

Subdivisions are added for specific varieties

.686 9	*Hawks

Class here falcons

Subdivisions are added for specific varieties

.69	Ratites
.694	*Ostriches

.7 Dogs

.700 1–.700 9	Standard subdivisions

Notation from Table 1 as modified under 636.001–636.009

.701–.708	Specific topics in husbandry of dogs

Add to base number 636.70 the numbers following 636.0 in 636.01–636.08, e.g., breeding 636.7082; however, for sled dogs, watchdogs, see 636.73; for hunting dogs, see 636.75

See also 636.73 for working dogs as a recognized group of dog breeds; also 636.752 for sporting dogs as a recognized group of dog breeds

See Manual at 636.70886, 636.70888 vs. 636.73, 636.752

.71	Breeds of dogs

For specific breeds, see 636.72–636.76

*Add as instructed under 636.1–636.8

>   636.72–636.75   Specific breeds and groups of dogs

       Class comprehensive works in 636.71

       For toy dogs of any breed, see 636.76

       See Manual at 636.72–636.75

.72   Nonsporting dogs

       Including bichon frise, Boston terrier, bulldog, Chinese Shar-Pei, chow chow, Dalmatian, Finnish spitz, French bulldog, Keeshond, Lhasa apso, Schipperke, Tibetan spaniel, Tibetan terrier

       Class here utility breeds (United Kingdom)

       Class comprehensive works on terriers in 636.755

.728   *Poodles

       Class here miniature poodle

       Subdivisions are added for specific breeds

.73   Working and herding dogs

       Standard subdivisions are added for working and herding dogs together, for working dogs alone

       Including sled dogs, watchdogs (guard dogs)

       Including akita, Alaskan Malamute, Bernese mountain dog, boxer, bullmastiff, Eskimo dogs, Great Dane, Great Pyrenee, Komondor, Kuvasz, mastiffs, Newfoundland, Portuguese water dog, Rottweiler, Saint Bernard, Samoyed, Schnauzers (standard and giant), Siberian husky

       Class Finnish spitz in 636.72; class Norwegian elkhound in 636.753; class miniature Schnauzer in 636.755

       See also 636.70886 for dogs as working animals

       See Manual at 636.70886, 636.70888 vs. 636.73, 636.752

.736   *Doberman pinscher

       Class miniature pinscher in 636.76

.737   Herding dogs

       Including Australian cattle dog, Belgian Malinois, Belgian Tervuren, Bouvier des Flandres, Briard, Puli, Welsh corgis; sheep dogs other than collies and German shepherd dog

.737 4   *Collies

       Subdivisions are added for specific breeds

.737 6   *German shepherd dog (German police dog)

---

*Add as instructed under 636.1–636.8

.75	Sporting dogs, hounds, terriers

Class here hunting dogs, sporting dogs (United Kingdom)

.752	Sporting dogs

Including Brittany, Vizsla, Weimaraner, wirehaired pointing griffon

Class here bird dogs, gundogs (United Kingdom)

See also 636.70888 for dogs as sport animals

See Manual at 636.70886, 636.70888 vs. 636.73, 636.752

.752 4	*Spaniels

Subdivisions are added for specific breed

See also 636.72 for Tibetian spaniel; also 636.76 for Japanese spaniel (chin)

.752 5	*Pointers

Subdivisions are added for specific breeds

.752 6	*Setters

Subdivisions are added for specific breeds

.752 7	*Retrievers

Subdivisions are added for specific breeds

.753	Hounds

Including Norwegian elkhound

See Manual at 636.72–636.75: Hounds

.753 2	Gazehounds (Sighthounds)

Including Ibizan hound, Saluki, Scottish deerhound, whippet

For Afghan hound, see 636.7533; for greyhound, see 636.7534; for Borzoi, Irish wolfhound, see 636.7535

.753 3	*Afghan hound
.753 4	*Greyhound

Class Italian greyhound in 636.76; class greyhound racing in 798.8

.753 5	*Wolfhounds

Including Borzoi, Irish wolfhound

.753 6	Scent hounds (Tracking hounds)

Including Basenji, basset hound, black and tan coonhound, bloodhound, foxhounds, harrier, otterhound, petit basset griffon vendéen, pharaoh hound, Rhodesian ridgeback

For beagle, see 636.7537; for dachshund, see 636.7538

*Add as instructed under 636.1–636.8

.753 7		*Beagle
.753 8		*Dachshund

                 Class miniature dachshund in 636.76

.755   Terriers

                 Including miniature Schnauzer

                 For Boston and Tibetan terriers, see 636.72; for toy terriers, see 636.76

.755 9   *Bull terriers

                 Class here pit bull terriers

                 Subdivisions are added for specific breeds

.76   Toy dogs

                 Including affenpinscher, Brussels griffon, Chihuahua, Chinese crested, English toy spaniel, Italian greyhound, Japanese chin, Maltese, Mexican hairless (Xoloitzcuintli), miniature dachshund, miniature pinscher, Papillon, Pekingese, Pomeranian, pug, shih tzu, silky terrier, toy Manchester terrier, toy poodle, Yorkshire terrier

                 Class miniature poodle in 636.728; class miniature Schnauzer in 636.755

.8   **Cats**

.800 1–.800 9   Standard subdivisions

                 Notation from Table 1 as modified under 636.001–636.009

.801–.808   Specific topics in husbandry of cats

                 Add to base number 636.80 the numbers following 636.0 in 636.01–636.08, e.g., breeding cats 636.8082, cats for specific purposes other than pets 636.8088

                 Class cats as pets in 636.8

>   636.82–636.83   Specific breeds and kinds of domestic cats

                 Class comprehensive works in 636.8

                 See Manual at 636.82–636.83

.82   Shorthair cats

                 Including Chartreaux, Russian blue cats

                 Class here foreign (Oriental) shorthair cats

.822   Common shorthair cats

                 Breeds of British Isles, Canada, United States

                 Including Bengal, Manx, rex cats

*Add as instructed under 636.1–636.8

636   *Agriculture and related technologies*   636

.824	*Burmese cat	

Subdivisions are added for specific varieties

.825	*Siamese cat

Subdivisions are added for specific varieties

.826	*Abyssinian cat

Subdivisions are added for specific varieties

.83	Longhair cats

Including Himalayan, Maine coon, Turkish Angora, Turkish Van cats

.832	*Persian cat

Subdivisions are added for specific varieties

.89	Nondomestic cats

Including cheetah, ocelot

.9   **Other mammals**

Class here other mammals as pets

Add to base number 636.9 the numbers following 599 in 599.2–599.8, e.g., hamsters 636.9356, fur-bearing animals 636.97; however, for Equidae, see 636.1; for ruminants other than Tragulidae, see 636.2; for Camelidae, see 636.296; for Felidae, see 636.8

637   Processing dairy and related products

Class comprehensive works on dairy farming in 636.2142

.1   **Milk processing**

>   637.12–637.14 Cow's milk

Class comprehensive works in 637.1

.12	Milking and inspection of cow's milk
.124	Milking
.127	Inspection and testing

Standard subdivisions are added for either or both topics in heading

.127 6	Butterfat tests
.127 7	Bacterial counts
.14	Processing specific forms of cow's milk

>   637.141–637.146   Whole milk

Class comprehensive works in 637.1

*Add as instructed under 636.1–636.8

.141   Fresh whole milk

           Including comprehensive works on pasteurization, homogenization, vitamin D treatment

           For pasteurization, homogenization, vitamin D treatment of products other than fresh whole milk, see the product, e.g., cream 637.148

.141 028 7   Measurement

           Do not use for testing; class in 637.127

.142   Concentrated liquid forms of whole milk

.142 2   Evaporated milk

.142 4   Sweetened condensed milk

.143   Dried whole milk

.146   Cultured whole milk

           For yogurt from whole milk, see 637.1476

.147   Skim milk

.147 3   Dried skim milk

.147 6   Cultured skim milk

           Class here yogurt

.148   Cream

.17   Milk other than cow's milk

.2   **Butter processing**

.24   By-products

           Class here buttermilk

.3   **Cheese processing**

           Including by-products

.35   Varieties

.352   Cream cheese

.353   Ripened soft cheeses

           Including Brie

.354   Hard cheeses

           Including cheddar and Swiss cheeses

.356   Fresh cheeses

           Including cottage cheese

           For cream cheese, see 637.352

.358   Cheese foods

.4   **Manufacture of frozen desserts**

> Class here ice cream

.5   **Egg processing**

> Class raising hens for eggs in 636.5142; class raising poultry other than chickens for eggs in 636.59

.54   Dried eggs

> Including dried egg whites and yolks

638   Insect culture

.1   **Bee keeping (Apiculture)**

.12   Varieties of bees

> Class a specific aspect of a specific variety of bee with the aspect, e.g., pasturage 638.13

.13   Pasturage for bees

.14   Hive management

.144   Supplementary feeding of bees

.145   Queen rearing

.146   Swarming control

.15   Injuries, diseases, pests

.151–.158   Specific injuries, diseases, pests

> Add to base number 638.15 the numbers following 632 in 632.1–632.8, e.g., diseases 638.153
>
> *For adverse effects of pesticides, see 638.159*

.159   Adverse effects of pesticides

.16   Honey processing

> Class here comprehensive works on bee products
>
> *For wax, see 638.17*

.17   Wax

.2   **Silkworms**

.5   **Other insects**

.57   Specific insects

> Add to base number 638.57 the numbers following 595.7 in 595.72–595.79, e.g., butterfly gardening 638.5789

639   **Hunting, fishing, conservation, related technologies**

> Class here culture of nondomesticated animals
>
> *For sports hunting and fishing, see 799*

.091 6   Treatment in air and water

> Class aquaculture in 639.8

.1   **Hunting**

> Class here trapping, subsistence hunting
>
> Class comprehensive works on commercial and sports hunting in 799.2

.11   Hunting mammals

> Add to base number 639.11 the numbers following 599 in 599.2–599.8, e.g., bison (buffalo) hunting 639.11643, hunting fur-bearing animals 639.117; however, for whaling, see 639.28; for sealing, see 639.29
>
> Most works on trapping mammals are on fur trapping, and will be classed in 639.117
>
> > *See also 333.9549 for resource economics of game mammals in general; also 333.959 for resource economics of specific mammals; also 636.97 for fur farming; also 799.2 for sports hunting*

.12   Hunting birds

> Most works on hunting game birds will be classed in 333.958 (resource economics) or 799.24 (sports hunting)

.128   Specific kinds of birds

> Add to base number 639.128 the numbers following 598 in 598.3–598.9, e.g., waterfowl 639.12841

.13   Hunting amphibians

> > *See also 639.378 for amphibian farming*

.14   Reptile hunting

> Add to base number 639.14 the numbers following 597.9 in 597.92–597.98, e.g., hunting alligators 639.1484
>
> > *See also 639.39 for reptile farming*

.2   **Commercial fishing, whaling, sealing**

> Standard subdivisions are added for commercial fishing, whaling, sealing together; for commercial fishing alone
>
> Class here works on fisheries encompassing culture as well as capture, on fisheries encompassing invertebrates as well as fishes
>
> Class comprehensive works on aquaculture in 639.8
>
> > *For culture of fishes, see 639.3; for fisheries for invertebrates, see 639.4*

> 639.21–639.22 Fishing in specific types of water

Class fishing for specific kinds of fishes regardless of kind of water in 639.27; class comprehensive works in 639.2

.21   Fishing in fresh water

.22   Fishing in salt waters

Including fishing in brackish waters

Class here deep-sea fishing

.27   Fishing for specific kinds of fishes

Add to base number 639.27 the numbers following 597 in 597.2–597.7, e.g., salmon fishing 639.2756

.28   Whaling

.29   Sealing

.3   Culture of cold-blooded vertebrates

Class here cold-blooded vertebrates as pets; culture of fishes

> 639.31–639.34 Fish culture

Class comprehensive works in 639.3

For culture of specific kinds of fishes, see 639.372–639.377

.31   Fish culture in fresh water

Class here fishponds, freshwater fish farming

For fish culture in freshwater aquariums, see 639.34

.311   Fish hatcheries

.312   Fish culture in lakes

.313   Fish culture in streams

Class here fish culture in rivers

.32   Fish culture in salt waters

Including fish culture in brackish waters

For fish culture in marine aquariums, see 639.342

.34   Fish culture in aquariums

Class here freshwater aquariums, home aquariums

Class interdisciplinary works on aquariums in 597.073

.342   Marine aquariums

.344   Institutional aquariums

> Class interdisciplinary works on educational and scientific aquariums in 597.073

> *For marine aquariums, see 639.342*

.37   Culture of amphibians and specific kinds of fishes

[.370 1–.370 9]   Standard subdivisions

> Do not use; class in 639.301–639.309

.372–.377   Culture of specific kinds of fishes

> Add to base number 639.37 the numbers following 597 in 597.2–597.7, e.g., carp, koi 639.37483; goldfish 639.37484

.378   Amphibian culture

> Add to base number 639.378 the numbers following 597.8 in 597.82–597.89, e.g., frog culture 639.3789

.39   Reptile culture

> Add to base number 639.39 the numbers following 597.9 in 597.92–597.98, e.g., turtle culture 639.392

.4   **Mollusk fisheries and culture**

> Standard subdivisions are added for either or both topics in heading

> Class here Bivalvia; comprehensive works on harvest and culture of invertebrates, on shellfish fisheries and culture

> *For crustacean fisheries, see 639.5; for crustacean culture, see 639.6; for harvest and culture of invertebrates other than mollusks and crustaceans, see 639.7*

>   639.41–639.46   Bivalvia

> Class comprehensive works in 639.4

.41   Oysters

> Class here edible oysters

.412   Pearl oysters

.42   Mussels

.44   Clams

.46   Scallops

.48   Mollusks other than Bivalvia

.482   Minor classes of Mollusca

> Add to base number 639.482 the numbers following 594.2 in 594.27–594.29, e.g., chitons 639.4827

.483   Gastropoda

> Add to base number 639.483 the numbers following 594.3 in 594.32–594.38, e.g., land snails 639.4838

.485   Cephalopoda

> Add to base number 639.485 the numbers following 594.5 in 594.52–594.58, e.g., octopuses 639.4856

.5   **Crustacean fisheries**

> Class here comprehensive works on crustacean fisheries and culture

> Add to base number 639.5 the numbers following 595.38 in 595.384–595.388, e.g., shrimps 639.58

> *For crustacean culture, see 639.6*

.6   **Crustacean culture**

> Add to base number 639.6 the numbers following 595.38 in 595.384–595.388, e.g., crayfish culture 639.64

.7   **Harvest and culture of invertebrates other than mollusks and crustaceans**

> Standard subdivisions are added for either or both topics in heading

> *For insect culture, see 638*

.75   Worms

> Class here bait worm culture, earthworms (night crawlers), fishworms, worm farming

.8   **Aquaculture**

> Class here mariculture

> Class aquaculture of a specific kind of animal with the kind, e.g., aquaculture of fishes 639.3

.89   Aquaculture of plants

> Class hydroponics in 631.585

.9   **Conservation of biological resources**

> Class here conservation of animals, game animals, mammals, vertebrates, wildlife; game protection

> Class interdisciplinary works on conservation of biological resources in 333.9516; class interdisciplinary works on conservation of animals, vertebrates, mammals in 333.95416

> *See also 636.0888 for raising warm-blooded game animals*

>   639.92–639.96   Specific topics in conservation

         Class specific topics in conservation of specific kinds of animals in 639.97; class specific topics in conservation of plants in 639.99; class comprehensive works in 639.9

.92   Habitat improvement

.93   Population control

.95   Maintenance of reserves and refuges

         Standard subdivisions are added for either or both topics in heading

.96   Control of injuries, diseases, pests

.964   Diseases

.966   Pests

         Class here predator control

         Class comprehensive works on pest control in agriculture in 632.6; class comprehensive works on predator control in agriculture in 636.0839

.969   Adverse effects of pesticides

.97   Specific kinds of animals

         Other than vertebrates taken as a whole, mammals taken as a whole

         See Manual at 333.955–333.959 vs. 639.97

[.970 1–.970 9]   Standard subdivisions

         Do not use; class in 639.901–639.909

.971–.978   Specific kinds of animals other than mammals

         Add to base number 639.97 the numbers following 59 in 591–598, e.g., protecting marine animals 639.97177, attracting birds 639.978

         See also 598.07234 for bird watching; also 638.5789 for butterfly gardening; also 639.3 for raising game fishes; also 690.8927 for building bird houses

.979   Specific kinds of mammals

         Class comprehensive works on mammals in 639.9

[.979 01–.979 09]   Standard subdivisions

         Do not use; class in 639.901–639.909

.979 1–.979 8   Subdivisions for specific kinds of mammals

         Add to base number 639.979 the numbers following 599 in 599.1–599.8, e.g., habitat improvement for deer 639.97965

.99   Plant conservation

640   Home and family management

Standard subdivisions are added for home and family management together, for home management alone

Class here home economics, household management

Use 640 for housekeeping covering activities related to running the home, e.g., preparing meals and doing routine repairs as well as cleaning. Use 648 for housekeeping limited to cleaning

Class personal health in 613; class management of public households in 647

[.288]   Maintenance and repair

         Do not use; class in 643.7

.29   Commercial miscellany

         Do not use for evaluation and purchasing manuals; class in 640.73

.4   Specific aspects of home management

         Class comprehensive works on home management in 640

.41   Helpful hints and miscellaneous recipes

.43   Time management

         Class interdisciplinary works on time management in 650.11

.46   Management of household employees

         Duties, hours, selection, training

         Class management of institutional household employees in 647.2

.6   Organizations

[.68]   Management

         Do not use for comprehensive works; class in 640. Do not use for specific aspects; class in 640.4

.7   Education, research, related topics; evaluation and purchasing guides

         Notation 07 from Table 1 as modified below

.73   Evaluation and purchasing guides

         Class here consumer education for home and personal needs

         Class comprehensive works on managing household money in 332.024; class interdisciplinary evaluation and purchasing guides and works on consumer education in 381.33. Class evaluation and purchasing guides for a specific product or service with the product or service, plus notation 029 from Table 1, e.g., manual on evaluating automobiles 629.222029

641   Food and drink

Class applied nutrition in 613.2

For meals and table service, see 642

.01   Philosophy and theory, gastronomy

             Notation 01 from Table 1 as modified below

.013   Gastronomy

             Class here pleasures of food and drink, comprehensive works on the slow
             food movement

             *For a specific aspect of the slow food movement, see the aspect,
             e.g., purchasing food at farmers markets 381.4, growing heirloom
             tomatoes 635.642, slow food cooking in restaurants 641.572*

.2   **Beverages (Drinks)**

             Class here interdisciplinary works on beverages

             Class comprehensive works on nutritive values of beverages in 613.2. Class
             nutritive values of a specific beverage with the beverage, e.g., nutritive value of
             wine 641.22

             *For a specific aspect of beverages, see the aspect, e.g., manufacture
             (commercial preparation) 663*

.21   Alcoholic beverages

             Class home preparation of alcoholic beverages, bartending in 641.874

             *For wine, see 641.22; for brewed and malted beverages, see 641.23; for
             distilled liquor, see 641.25*

.22   Wine

             Class here grape wine, comprehensive works on white and red wine,
             comprehensive works on specific white and red wines (specific brands,
             estate wines)

             Class home preparation of wine in 641.872

             See also 641.23 for mead, rice wine

.222   Kinds of grape wine

             Including ice wine

[.222 01–.222 09]   Standard subdivisions

             Do not use; class in 641.2201–641.2209

.222 2   White wine

             Class here specific white wines (specific brands, estate wines,
             varietals)

             Class comprehensive works on white and red wine in 641.22; class
             white ice wine in 641.222

             *For sparkling white wine, see 641.2224; for fortified white wine,
             see 641.2226*

.222 3	Red wine

> Class here specific red wines (specific brands, estate wines, varietals)
>
> Class red ice wine in 641.222
>
> *For sparkling red wine, see 641.2224; for fortified red wine, see 641.2226*

.222 32	Rosé wine

> Class here specific rosé wines (specific brands, estate wines, varietals)

.222 4	Sparkling wine

> Class here specific sparkling wines (specific brands, estate wines, varietals)
>
> Class comprehensive works on white wine in 641.2222; class comprehensive works on red wine in 641.2223

.222 6	Fortified wine

> Class here specific fortified wines (specific brands, estate wines, varietals)
>
> Class comprehensive works on white wine in 641.2222; class comprehensive works on red wine in 641.2223

.229	Nongrape wine

> Including fermented cider

.23	Brewed and malted beverages

> Including mead (honey wine), pulque, rice wine
>
> Class here beer, ale
>
> Class malt whiskey in 641.252; class home brewing in 641.873

.25	Distilled liquor

> Including mescal, potato whiskey, tequila, vodka

.252	Whiskey

> Class potato whiskey in 641.25

.253	Brandy
.255	Compound liquors

> Including absinthe, gin
>
> Class here cordials, liqueurs

.259	Rum

.26   **Nonalcoholic beverages**

Including carbonated, malted, mineralized beverages

> *For specific nonalcoholic beverages made from a single principal ingredient, see 641.3, e.g., orange juice 641.3431; for nonalcoholic beverages made from multiple ingredients, see 641.875*

.3   **Food**

Class here interdisciplinary works on food

> *For interdisciplinary works on specific dishes, see 641.8. For a specific aspect of food, see the aspect, e.g., manufacture (commercial preparation) 664*

> *See Manual at 363.8 vs. 613.2, 641.3; also at 630 vs. 579–590, 641.3*

.300 1   Philosophy and theory

.300 157 9   Microorganisms, fungi, algae

Do not use for mushrooms and truffles; class in 641.358. Do not use for marine algae, seaweeds as food; class in 641.398

Class here interdisciplinary works on food microbiology, on probiotic foods (foods with probiotics)

Class interdisciplinary works on probiotics in 615.329

> *For microbiology in commercial food technology, see 664.001579. For specific probiotic foods, see the foods, e.g., probiotic dairy products 641.37*

> *See also 641.563 for cooking probiotic foods*

.300 2   Miscellany

.300 29   Commercial miscellany

Do not use for evaluation and purchasing manuals; class in 641.31

.300 3–.300 9   Standard subdivisions

.302   Health foods

Class here natural foods, organically grown foods

Class dietetics in 613.2; class probiotic foods in 641.3001579

> *See also 641.563 for health cooking*

.303   Food from plants

Class here vegetarian foods

Class interdisciplinary works on vegetarianism in 613.262

> *For specific food from plant crops, see 641.33–641.35*

> *See also 641.5636 for vegetarian cooking*

.306   Food from animals

> *For specific food from animals, see 641.36–641.39*

.308   Food additives

Class substitutes for specific foods excluded from specific diets in 641.309

.309   Alternative foods for diets that exclude specific foods

Including alternative foods for diets that exclude specific meats or seafood, e.g., pork-free foods

Class here food substitutes

Class comprehensive works on vegetarian foods in 641.303. Class alternative foods or food substitutes made with a specific food with the food, e.g., alternative foods made with soybeans 641.35655

.309 3–.309 5   Alternative foods for diets that exclude specific foods from plant crops

Add to base number 641.309 the numbers following 63 in 633–635 for the food to be excluded, e.g., wheat-free foods 641.309311

.309 311   Wheat-free foods

Number built according to instructions under 641.3093–641.3095

Class here comprehensive works on gluten-free foods

For rye-free foods, see 641.309314; for barley-free foods, see 641.309316

.309 7   Alternative foods for diets that exclude dairy and related products

Class here dairy-free foods, casein-free foods, lactose-free foods

Add to base number 641.3097 the numbers following 637 in 637.1–637.5 for the food to be excluded, e.g., milk-free foods 641.30971, egg-free foods 641.30975

.31   Evaluation and purchasing manuals

Class comprehensive works on applied nutrition in 613.2; class evaluation and purchasing manuals of specific food in 641.33–641.39

.33–.35   Specific food from plant crops

Class here nutritive values

Add to base number 641.3 the numbers following 63 in 633–635, e.g., field legumes 641.3565

Class comprehensive works on food from plants in 641.303

>   **641.36–641.39 Specific food from animals; miscellaneous foods**

Class here nutritive values

Class comprehensive works on food from animals in 641.306

.36	Meat

Add to base number 641.36 the numbers following 636 in 636.1–636.8, e.g., ham 641.364

For game and seafood, see 641.39

.37   Dairy and related products

Add to base number 641.37 the numbers following 637 in 637.1–637.5, e.g., skim milk 641.37147

.38   Honey

.39   Game, seafood, miscellaneous foods

Add to base number 641.39 the numbers following 641.69 in 641.691–641.698, e.g., oysters 641.394

.4   Food preservation and storage

Standard subdivisions are added for food preservation and storage together, for food preservation alone

Class interdisciplinary works on food preservation in 664.028

> 641.41–641.46 Preservation techniques for fruit and vegetables, for food as a whole

Class comprehensive works in 641.4

For preservation techniques for meat and allied food, see 641.49

.41   Preliminary treatment

.42   Canning

.44   Drying and dehydrating

Including freeze-drying

.45   Low-temperature techniques

.452   Cold storage

.453   Deep freezing

For freeze-drying, see 641.44

.46   Pickling, smoking, other forms of chemical preservation

Class here chemical preservation

.462   Pickling and brining

Standard subdivisions are added for either or both topics in heading

Class here pickles

.463   Fermenting

.465   Smoking

.48   Storage

.49	Meat

Class storage of meat in 641.48

.492	Red meat

Add to base number 641.492 the numbers following 641.4 in 641.41–641.46, e.g., canning red meat 641.4922

.493	Poultry

Add to base number 641.493 the numbers following 641.4 in 641.41–641.46, e.g., freezing poultry 641.49353

.494	Seafood

Add to base number 641.494 the numbers following 641.4 in 641.41–641.46, e.g., brining seafood 641.4946

.495	Other animal flesh

.5	**Cooking**

Preparation of food with and without use of heat

Unless other instructions are given, observe the following table of preference, e.g., outdoor cooking for children 641.5622 (*not* 641.578):

Cooking for special situations, reasons, ages	641.56
Quantity, institutional, travel, outdoor cooking	641.57
Money-saving and timesaving cooking	641.55
Cooking with specific fuels, appliances, utensils	641.58
Cooking specific meals	641.52–641.54
Beginner and gourmet cooking	641.51
Cooking characteristic of specific geographic environments, ethnic cooking	641.59

Class menus and meal planning in 642

For cooking specific materials, see 641.6; for specific cooking processes and techniques, see 641.7; for cooking specific kinds of dishes, preparing beverages, see 641.8

.502	Miscellany

.502 8	Auxiliary techniques and procedures

[.502 84]	Apparatus, equipment, materials

Do not use; class in 643.3

.508	Cooking with respect to groups of people

.508 3	Cooking with respect to young people

Do not use for cooking by children; class in 641.5123. Do not use for cooking for young people; class in 641.5622

.508 4	Cooking with respect to people in specific stages of adulthood

Do not use for cooking for people in specific stages of adulthood; class in 641.562

.508 7   Cooking with respect to people with disabilities, gifted people

Do not use for cooking for people with illnesses; class in 641.5631

.508 8   Cooking with respect to occupational groups

[.508 82]   Cooking with respect to religious groups

Do not use; class in 641.567

[.508 9]   Cooking with respect to ethnic and national groups

Do not use for cooking with respect to Jews as an ethnic group; class in 641.5676. Do not use for cooking with respect to other ethnic and national groups; class in 641.592

.509   History, geographic treatment, biography

Do not use for cooking characteristic of specific geographic environments; collections of recipes from specific restaurants associated with cooking characteristic of specific geographic environments, with ethnic cooking; class in 641.59

Class here collections of recipes from specific restaurants associated with general cooking

.51   Beginner and gourmet cooking

.512   Beginner cooking

Class here easy dishes

.512 3   Children's cooking

Class cooking of food for consumption by children in 641.5622

.514   Gourmet cooking

Class gourmet ethnic cooking in 641.59

For gourmet cooking characteristic of specific geographic environments, see 641.59

>   641.52–641.54 Cooking specific meals

Class comprehensive works in 641.5

.52   First meal of the day

Class here breakfasts, brunches

.53   Light meals

Class here snacks; dinners, lunches, suppers, teas as light meals

Class breakfasts and brunches in 641.52; class dinners, lunches, suppers, teas as main meals in 641.54

.54   Main meal of the day

Class here dinners, lunches, suppers, teas as main meals

Class breakfasts and brunches in 641.52; class dinners, lunches, suppers, teas as light meals in 641.53

.55	Money-saving and timesaving cooking
.552	Money-saving cooking
	Including leftovers
.555	Timesaving cooking
	Class here make-ahead meals
.56	Cooking for special situations, reasons, ages
.561	Cooking for one or two people
.561 1	Cooking for one
.561 2	Cooking for two
.562	Cooking for people of specific ages
.562 2	Young people
	Class here cooking for children
	Class cooking by children in 641.5123
.562 22	Cooking for infants
	Class here baby food
	Class comprehensive works on baby food in 641.300832
.562 7	People in late adulthood
.563	Cooking for health, appearance, personal reasons
	Standard subdivisions are added for cooking for health, appearance, personal reasons together; for cooking for health alone
	Class here cooking to prevent illness; comprehensive works on cooking probiotic foods (foods with probiotics)
	For cooking specific kinds of probiotic foods, see the foods, e.g., cooking probiotic dairy products 641.67
.563 1	Cooking for people with medical conditions
	Class cooking for specific diets for specific medical conditions in 641.5632–641.5639
.563 11	People with heart disease
.563 14	People with diabetes
.563 18	People with food allergies
	Class here cooking for diets that exclude multiple different foods to which people are commonly allergic, comprehensive works on cooking for people with food allergies
	For cooking for diets that exclude specific foods, see 641.5639
.563 19	Pregnant women
.563 2	Cooking with specified vitamin and mineral content

.563 23   Low-salt cooking

             Class here low-sodium cooking, salt-free cooking

.563 5   Low-calorie cooking

             Class here cooking for overweight people

             Class cooking with respect to low carbohydrate, fat, protein content in 641.5638

.563 6   Vegetarian cooking

             Cooking for plant-based diet that excludes meat from land animals but may include milk products, eggs, seafood

             Class here cooking for lacto-ovo vegetarian diet, cooking for pescatarian diet

             Class comprehensive works on vegetarian foods in 641.303; class interdisciplinary works on vegetarianism in 613.262

             See also 641.65 for cooking vegetables

.563 62   Vegan cooking

.563 7   Health-food cooking

             Class cooking for diets that exclude specific foods in 641.5639; class comprehensive works on health cooking in 641.563

.563 8   Cooking with respect to carbohydrate, fat, protein content

             Class cooking for diets that exclude specific foods in 641.5639

             For gluten-free cooking, see 641.5639311; for casein-free cooking, see 641.56397

.563 83   Low-carbohydrate cooking

.563 837   Sugar-free cooking

                Cooking for diet that avoids added and refined sugars but may use substitute sweeteners (e.g., honey)

                For lactose-free cooking, see 641.56397

.563 84   Low-fat cooking

                Class here fat-free cooking

.563 847   Low-cholesterol cooking

.563 9   Cooking for diets that exclude specific foods

             Including cooking for diets that exclude specific meats or seafood, e.g., cooking for pork-free diet

             Class cooking for diets that exclude multiple different foods to which people are commonly allergic, comprehensive works on cooking for people with food allergies in 641.56318; class vegetarian cooking in 641.5636; class sugar-free cooking in 641.563837; class salt-free cooking in 641.56323

.563 93–.563 95	Cooking for diets that exclude specific foods from plant crops

Add to base number 641.5639 the numbers following 63 in 633–635 for the food to be excluded, e.g., wheat-free cooking 641.5639311

.563 931 1	Wheat-free cooking

Number built according to instructions under 641.56393–641.56395

Class here comprehensive works on gluten-free cooking

For rye-free cooking, see 641.5639314; for barley-free cooking, see 641.5639316

.563 97	Cooking for diets that exclude dairy and related products

Class here dairy-free cooking; casein-free cooking, lactose-free cooking

Add to base number 641.56397 the numbers following 637 in 637.1–637.5 for the food to be excluded, e.g., milk-free cooking 641.563971, egg-free cooking 641.563975

.564	Seasonal cooking

Class cooking for special occasions in 641.568

.566	Cooking for Christian church limitations and observances

Including Lent

Class here cooking for specific Christian groups

For cooking for Christmas, see 641.5686

.567	Cooking for religious limitations and observances

Class here cooking for days of feast and fast, cooking with respect to religious groups

Add to base number 641.567 the numbers following 29 in 292–299, e.g., Jewish cooking 641.5676

For cooking for Christian church limitations and observances, see 641.566

.568	Cooking for special occasions

Class here cooking for holidays, for parties

Class cooking that emphasizes religious aspects of holidays in 641.567; class comprehensive works on food service and cooking for parties in 642.4

.568 6	Christmas cooking
.57	Quantity, institutional, travel, outdoor cooking

Including cooking for armed services

Class here short-order cooking

Class naval cooking in 641.5753

.571	School cooking	
.572	Hotel and restaurant cooking	
	Standard subdivisions are added for either or both topics in heading	
.575	Travel cooking	
	Including airline, bus, camper (caravan), dining car cooking	
.575 3	Marine cooking (Shipboard cooking)	
	Class here naval cooking	
.577	Canteen cooking	
	Temporary or mobile facilities for serving food	
.578	Outdoor cooking	
	Class here cookouts	
	Class cooking in campers (caravans) in 641.575	
.578 2	Camp cooking	
.578 4	Cooking at an outdoor grill	
	Class here cooking at outdoor barbecues	
	Class comprehensive works on techniques of barbecuing in 641.76	
.579	Cooking for health care facilities	
	Class here cooking for hospitals	
.58	Cooking with specific fuels, appliances, utensils	
	Including convection-oven cooking, wood-stove cooking	
	Class outdoor cooking in 641.578. Class a specific use of a specific appliance or utensil with the use, e.g., frying with frying pans 641.77	
.584	Gas	
.585	Alcohol-based fuels	
	Class here cooking with chafing dishes	
.586	Electricity	
	Cooking with electric ranges and appliances	
	Class convection-oven cooking in 641.58; class microwave cooking in 641.5882; class electric slow cooking in 641.5884	
.587	Steam and pressure cooking	
	Standard subdivisions are added for either or both topics in heading	
.588	Slow and fireless cooking	
.588 2	Microwave cooking	
.588 4	Electric slow cooking	

.589	Specific utensils

Including clay pots, Dutch ovens, foils, specially coated utensils

Class cooking with specific utensils using specific fuels in 641.584–641.588

.589 2	Food processors
.589 3	Blenders
.59	Cooking characteristic of specific geographic environments, ethnic cooking

Class here gourmet cooking characteristic of specific geographic environments, ethnic cooking; collections of recipes from specific restaurants associated with cooking characteristic of specific geographic environments, with ethnic cooking; international cooking

Class history and geographic treatment of general cooking, collections of recipes from specific restaurants associated with general cooking, in 641.509

.591	Cooking characteristic of areas, regions, places in general

Add to base number 641.591 the numbers following —1 in notation 11–19 from Table 2, e.g., arctic and cold-weather cooking 641.5911, tropical and hot-weather cooking 641.5913

.592	Ethnic cooking
.592 001–.592 009	Standard subdivisions
.592 05–.592 09	Specific ethnic and national groups with ethnic origins from more than one continent, of European descent

Add to base number 641.592 notation 05–09 from Table 5, e.g., cooking of ethnic groups of European descent 641.59209

.592 1–.592 9	Specific ethnic and national groups

Add to base number 641.592 notation 1–9 from Table 5, e.g., African American cooking 641.59296073; however, for Jewish cooking, see 641.5676; for cooking of ethnic groups dominant in their areas, see 641.593–641.599

.593–.599	Cooking characteristic of specific continents, countries, localities

Add to base number 641.59 notation 3–9 from Table 2, e.g., Southern cooking (United States) 641.5975

Class ethnic cooking of nondominant groups in 641.592

.6	**Cooking specific materials**

Class specific kinds of dishes featuring specific materials in 641.8

For leftovers, see 641.552

.61   Cooking preserved foods

> Add to base number 641.61 the numbers following 641.4 in 641.42–641.46, e.g., cooking using frozen foods 641.6153

> Class home preservation in 641.4; class cooking using specific preserved foods in 641.63–641.69

.62   Cooking with beverages and their derivatives

> Including vinegar

> Class home preparation of beverages in 641.87. Class cooking with a specific nonalcoholic beverage with the product from which it is derived, e.g., cooking with chocolate 641.6374, with apple juice 641.6411

.622   Wine

.623   Beer and ale

> Standard subdivisions are added for either or both topics in heading

.625   Distilled liquor

>   **641.63–641.69 Specific foods**

> Class comprehensive works in 641.6

.63–.67   Cooking food derived from plant crops and domesticated animals

> Add to base number 641.6 the numbers following 63 in 633–637, e.g., legumes 641.6565 (*not* 641.633), garden legumes 641.6565, meat 641.66, chicken meat 641.665; however, for ices, sherbet, sorbet, see 641.863

> Class vegetarian cooking in 641.5636; class comprehensive works on cooking with beverages in 641.62

> *For cooking with honey, see 641.68*

.68   Cooking with honey

.69   Cooking game, seafood, miscellaneous foods

> Only foods named below

> Class here cooking food derived from nondomesticated animals

.691   Game

> Mammals and birds

.692   Fish

> Class here seafood

> *For mollusks, see 641.694; for crustaceans, see 641.695*

.694   Mollusks

> Including clams, mussels, octopuses, oysters, snails, squid

> Class here shellfish

> *For crustaceans, see 641.695*

.695   Crustaceans

> Including crabs, lobsters, shrimp

.696   Amphibians, insects, reptiles

.698   Seaweeds

> Class here marine algae

.7   Specific cooking processes and techniques

> Class specific processes applied to specific materials in 641.6; class specific processes applied to specific kinds of dishes, preparing beverages in 641.8

[.701–.709]   Standard subdivisions

> Do not use; class in 641.501–641.509

.71   Baking and roasting

> Standard subdivisions are added for baking and roasting together, for baking alone

.73   Boiling, braising, simmering, steaming, stewing

.76   Barbecuing, broiling, grilling

> Standard subdivisions are added for barbecuing, broiling, grilling together; for barbecuing alone

> Including skewer cooking

> *For barbecuing, broiling, grilling at outdoor grills, see 641.5784*

.77   Frying and sautéing

> Standard subdivisions are added for either or both topics in heading

> Class braising in 641.73

.774   Stir frying

> Class here wok cooking

.79   Preparation of cold dishes

> Class here chilled dishes

.8   Cooking specific kinds of dishes and preparing beverages

> Class here interdisciplinary works on specific dishes

> *For manufacture (commercial preparation) of complete dishes, see 664.65*

[.801–.809]   Standard subdivisions

> Do not use; class in 641.501–641.509

.81   **Side dishes, sauces, garnishes**

> Standard subdivisions are added for side dishes, sauces, garnishes together; for side dishes alone
>
> Side dishes other than salads, sandwiches, desserts
>
> Including stuffing
>
> Class here specific side dishes treated as main dishes

.811   **Side dishes made with specific foods**

> *For appetizers, see 641.812; for soups, see 641.813; for sauces and salad dressings, see 641.814; for bread and bread-like foods, see 641.815; for garnishes, see 641.819*

>   641.811 3–641.811 7 Side dishes made with a specific food derived from plant crops and domesticated animals
>
> Add to base number 641.811 the numbers following 63 in 633–637, e.g., sauerkraut 641.811534

.811 9   Side dishes made with game, seafood, miscellaneous foods

> Add to base number 641.8119 the numbers following 641.69 in 641.691–641.698, e.g., crab dip 641.81195

.812   **Appetizers**

> Including dips, pâtés, relishes
>
> Class here finger foods, hors d'oeuvres, savories, starters, tapas

.813   **Soups**

.814   **Sauces and salad dressings**

> Standard subdivisions are added for sauces and salad dressings together, for sauces alone

.815   **Bread and bread-like foods**

> Standard subdivisions are added for bread and bread-like foods together, for bread alone
>
> Including crackers, unleavened breads
>
> Class here yeast breads, comprehensive works on baked goods
>
> Class main dishes based on bread and bread-like foods in 641.82; class sandwiches and related dishes in 641.84
>
> *For pastries, see 641.865*

.815 3   Crepes, pancakes, waffles

> Standard subdivisions are added for any or all topics in heading

.815 7   Quick breads

> Class here biscuits, muffins, scones
>
> *See also 641.8654 for biscuits (cookies)*

.819	Garnishes
.82	Main dishes

Including quiches, soufflés, sushi

Class here entrées, one-dish cooking

Class a side dish, salad, sandwich or stuffed food regarded as a main dish with the topic elsewhere in 641.8, e.g., soup 641.813, hamburger on a roll 641.84

.821	Casserole dishes
.822	Noodle and pasta dishes

Standard subdivisions are added for either or both topics in heading

.823	Stews
.823 6	Chili
.824	Meat and cheese pies

Including meat loaf

.824 8	Pizza
.83	Salads
.84	Sandwiches and related dishes

Standard subdivisions are added for either or both topics in heading

Class here sandwiches and related dishes of any type, e.g., open-faced sandwiches, grilled sandwiches, wraps

.85	Preserves and candy
.852	Jams, jellies, marmalades, preserves

Standard subdivisions are added for any or all topics in heading

See also 641.8642 for jellies (gelatin desserts)

.853	Candy

Variant name: sweets

.86	Desserts

Class here comprehensive works on candies and desserts

For preserves and candy, see 641.85

.862	Frozen desserts

Including frozen yogurt, ice milk

Class here ice cream

For ices, sherbet, sorbet, see 641.863

.863	Ices, sherbet, sorbet

Standard subdivisions are added for any or all topics in heading

.864		Gelatin desserts; puddings
.864 2		Gelatin desserts

Variant name: jellies

See also 641.852 for jellies (preserves)

.864 4		Puddings
.865		Pastries

Class comprehensive works on baked goods in 641.815

.865 2	Pies and tarts

Standard subdivisions are added for either or both topics in heading

.865 3	Cakes

See also 641.8659 for coffee cakes

.865 39	Cake decoration

Class here cake icing, sugar art

.865 4	Cookies

Variant name: biscuits

See also 641.815 for crackers; also 641.8157 for biscuits (quick breads)

.865 9	Danish, French, related pastries

Including coffee cakes, cream puffs, eclairs

.87	Preparing beverages

Class interdisciplinary works on beverages in 641.2

See also 641.62 for cooking with beverages

.872	Wine
.873	Alcoholic brewed beverages

Class here beer, ale

.874	Alcoholic beverages

Class here bartending, comprehensive works on cocktails (mixed drinks)

For wine, see 641.872; for alcoholic brewed beverages, see 641.873; for bottled and canned cocktails, see 663.1

.875	Nonalcoholic beverages

Including carbonated drinks, fruit drinks, juices, malted drinks

For nonalcoholic brewed beverages, see 641.877

.877	Nonalcoholic brewed beverages

Including cocoa, coffee, teas; their concentrates and substitutes

Class cooking with cocoa, coffee, tea in 641.637

642 Meals and table service

Class here menus, menu cookbooks, specific meals

Class banquets, catered meals in 642.4; class comprehensive works on cookbooks in 641.5

> ## 642.1–642.5 Meals in specific situations

Class here comprehensive works on meals and table service in specific situations

Class comprehensive works in 642

For table service in specific situations, see 642.6

.1 Meals for home, family, individuals

Standard subdivisions are added for meals for home, family, individuals together; meals for home alone, for family alone

Class family and individual meals for camp, picnic, travel in 642.3

.3 Meals for camp, picnic, travel

.4 Meals for social and public occasions

Including banquets, catered meals

Class here entertaining and catering for social and public occasions

Class party cooking in 641.568; class picnics in 642.3; class catering that includes restaurant operations in 647.95; class interdisciplinary works on entertaining in 793.2

.5 Meals in public and institutional eating places

Standard subdivisions are added for either or both topics in heading

Class here meals in cafeterias and restaurants

Class meals for social and public occasions in 642.4; class operation of public eating places in 647.95

.56 Health care facilities

Class here hospitals

.57 Schools

Regardless of level

.6 Table service

Including carving, place setting, seating guests

Class here table service at specific meals, waiting on tables

Class comprehensive works on meals and table service in specific situations in 642.1–642.5

For table furnishings, see 642.7; for table decorations, see 642.8

.7   **Table furnishings**

Including dinnerware, glassware, silverware, table linens

For table decorations other than folded napkins, see 642.8

.79   Napkin folding

.8   **Table decorations**

For folded napkins, see 642.79

643   Housing and household equipment

Works for owner-occupants or renters covering activities of members of household

[.028 4]   Apparatus, equipment, materials

Do not use; class in 643

[.028 8]   Maintenance and repair

Do not use; class in 643.7

.1   **Housing**

For special-purpose housing and special kinds of housing, see 643.2

See also 690.8 for construction of houses; also 728 for comprehensive works on design and construction of houses

See Manual at 363.5 vs. 643.1

[.102 88]   Maintenance and repair

Do not use; class in 643.7

.102 9   Commercial miscellany

Do not use for evaluation and purchasing guides; class in 643.12

.12   Selecting, buying, selling homes

Standard subdivisions are added for any or all topics in heading

Including site selection, supervision of construction

Class here evaluation and purchasing guides; home buying, home inspection

Class moving in 648.9

See also 333.338 for economics of home acquisition; also 346.043 for law of real property

.16   Household security

Class here burglarproofing

Class burglary in 364.1622

.2   **Special-purpose housing and special kinds of housing**

Including houseboats, modular and prefabricated houses

Class comprehensive works on single-family houses in 643.1. Class a specific aspect of special-purpose housing or a special kind of housing with the aspect, e.g., renovating vacation homes 643.7

.25   Vacation homes

.27   Apartments

Including condominium and cooperative apartments

Class management of condominiums and cooperative apartment houses in 647.92

.29   Mobile homes

See also 388.346 for motorized homes

See Manual at 643.29, 690.879, 728.79 vs. 629.226

>   **643.3–643.5 Specific areas of the home**

Class household utilities in 644; class household furnishings in 645; class comprehensive works in 643.1

See also 684.08 for home workshops

.3   ***Kitchens**

Including cooking apparatus, equipment, materials

Class cooking with specific appliances and utensils not limited to a specific kind of cooking in 641.58. Class a specific appliance or utensil used for a specific kind of cooking with the kind of cooking, e.g., frying with frying pans 641.77

.4   ***Eating and drinking areas**

Standard subdivisions are added for either or both topics in heading

Class here dining areas

.5   ***Other areas of the home**

Including attics, basements, storage areas

.52   *Bathrooms

Class plumbing, plumbing fixtures in 644.6

.53   *Bedrooms

.54   *Living rooms, drawing rooms, parlors

Standard subdivisions are added for any or all topics in heading

---

*Do not use notation 0284 from Table 1; class in base number

.55	*Recreation areas

Indoor and outdoor

Including family and recreation rooms, patios, porches

.556	*Swimming pools
.58	*Study and work areas

Including dens

See also 658.0412 for management of home-based enterprises

.6   Appliances and laborsaving installations

Standard subdivisions are added for either or both topics in heading

Class appliances and installations for specific areas in 643.3–643.5; class appliances and installations for specific household utilities in 644; class appliances and installations for specific kinds of household furnishings in 645. Class appliances and installations for a specific purpose with the purpose, e.g., sewing machines 646.2044

See also 683.8 for manufacture of household appliances

.602 88	Maintenance and repair

Class here maintenance and repair by members of household, maintenance and repair of electrical appliances

.7   Renovation, improvement, remodeling

Standard subdivisions are added for any or all topics in heading

Class here do-it-yourself work, home repairs; comprehensive works on maintenance and repair in home economics, on maintenance and repair by members of household

Class renovation, improvement, remodeling of specific areas of the home in 643.3–643.5; class renovation, improvement, remodeling of specific household utilities in 644; class renovation, improvement, remodeling of specific kinds of household furnishings in 645

For maintenance and repair of a specific item in the home, see the item, plus notation 0288 from Table 1, e.g., repair of appliances 643.60288, repair of furniture 645.40288

See Manual at 690 vs. 643.7

[.702 88]	Maintenance and repair

Do not use; class in 643.7

644   Household utilities

Works for owner-occupants or renters covering activities by members of household

Class here home energy conservation

See Manual at 647 vs. 647.068, 658.2, T1—0682

---

*Do not use notation 0284 from Table 1; class in base number

.1	**Heating**
.3	**Lighting**

Class lighting fixtures as furnishings in 645.5

.5	**Ventilation and air conditioning**
.6	**Plumbing**

Class here water fixtures

645 Household furnishings

Works for owner-occupants or renters covering activities by members of household

Class here household furnishings of residential buildings, comprehensive works on household furnishings and interior decoration

Class manufacture of household furnishings in 684

> *For home construction of fabric furnishings, see 646.21; for interior decoration, see 747*

.04	Special topics of household furnishings
.046	Fabrics

Description, selection, purchase, care, use

Class home construction of household articles made of fabric in 646.21

> **645.1–645.5 Specific kinds of interior furnishings**

Class comprehensive works in 645

.1	**Floor covering**
.12	Rugs

Class here carpets

.2	**Wall and ceiling coverings**

Standard subdivisions are added for wall and ceiling coverings together, for wall coverings alone

Including hangings, paint, paneling, wallpaper

.3	**Window furnishings**

Including awnings, blinds, shades

.32	Draperies

Class here curtains

.4   **Furniture and accessories**

> Standard subdivisions are added for furniture and accessories together, for furniture alone

> Including bedclothes, upholstery, slipcovers

> Class home construction of furniture in 684.1; class artistic aspects of furniture and accessories in 749

> > *For outdoor furniture and accessories, see 645.8*

.5   **Lighting fixtures**

.6   **Furnishings for specific rooms**

> Class interior furnishings of specific kinds regardless of room in 645.1–645.5

> > *See also 644 for utilities for specific rooms*

.8   **Outdoor furnishings**

> Including furnishings for balconies, gardens, patios, roofs

> Class here outdoor furniture and accessories

646   Sewing, clothing, management of personal and family life

.1   **Sewing materials and equipment**

> Standard subdivisions are added for sewing materials and equipment together, for sewing materials alone

> Including leathers and furs

> > *See also 646.30284 for materials and equipment used for clothing*

.11   Fabrics

> Class here comprehensive works on fabrics in the home

> > *For fabrics for a specific use, see the use, e.g., use in furnishings 645.046*

.19   Sewing equipment, fasteners

> Standard subdivisions are added for either or both topics in heading

> Including needles, pins, scissors, shears, thimbles, thread

> Class here notions

> > *For sewing machines, see 646.2044*

.2   **Sewing and related operations**

> Standard subdivisions are added for sewing and related operations together, for sewing alone

> Class here mending, sewing for the home

> Class clothing construction in 646.4; class mending clothes in 646.6

> > *For a specific technique in textile arts, see the technique in 746, e.g., weaving 746.14*

[.202 84]	Apparatus, equipment, materials
	Do not use; class in 646.1. Do not use for sewing machines; class in 646.2044
[.202 88]	Maintenance and repair
	Do not use; class in 646.2
.204	Basic sewing operations
	Class here darning
.204 2	Hand sewing
.204 4	Machine sewing
	Including serging
.21	Construction of home furnishings
	Including making bedclothes, curtains, hangings, slipcovers, table linens, towels
	Class basic sewing operations in 646.204; class artistic and decorative aspects of construction of interior furnishings in 746.9
.25	Reweaving
.3	**Clothing and accessories**
	Standard subdivisions are added for clothing and accessories together, for clothing alone
	Description, selection, purchase of clothing and accessories for utility, quality, economy, appearance, style
	Class here casual wear (sportswear)
	Class interdisciplinary works on clothing and accessories in 391
	For clothing and accessories construction, see 646.4; for care of clothing and accessories, see 646.6
	See Manual at 391 vs. 646.3, 746.92
[.302 88]	Maintenance and repair
	Do not use; class in 646.6
[.308 1]	Clothing for men and women
	Do not use; class in 646.32–646.34
.308 3	Clothing for young people
	Do not use for children under twelve; class in 646.36
.308 4	Clothing for people in specific stages of adulthood
	Do not use for clothing for men in specific stages of adulthood; class in 646.32. Do not use for clothing for women in specific stages of adulthood; class in 646.34

.308 7   Clothing for gifted people

> Do not use for clothing for people with disabilities and illnesses; class in 646.31

.31–.36   Clothing for people with disabilities and illnesses; men, women, children

> Add to base number 646.3 the numbers following 646.40 in 646.401–646.406, e.g., women's clothing 646.34

> Class clothing for young people twelve to twenty in 646.30835

.4   **Clothing and accessories construction**

> Standard subdivisions are added for clothing and accessories construction together, for clothing construction alone

> Class here dressmaking, tailoring; construction of casual wear (sportswear)

> *For construction of headwear, see 646.5; for commercial manufacture of clothing, see 687. For clothing construction by a specific technique in textile arts, see the technique in 746, e.g., knitting sweaters 746.4320432*

> *See also 646.47 for construction of activewear (clothing for athletic and outdoor sports)*

.400 1–.400 7   Standard subdivisions

.400 8   Clothing with respect to groups of people

[.400 811]   Clothing for men

> Do not use; class in 646.402

[.400 82]   Clothing for women

> Do not use; class in 646.404

.400 83   Clothing for young people

> Do not use for children under twelve; class in 646.406

.400 84   Clothing for people in specific stages of adulthood

> Do not use for clothing for men in specific stages of adulthood; class in 646.402. Do not use for clothing for women in specific stages of adulthood; class in 646.404

.400 87   Clothing for gifted people

> Do not use for clothing for people with disabilities and illnesses; class in 646.401

.400 9   History, geographic treatment, biography

.401   Clothing for people with disabilities and illnesses

>   **646.402–646.406 Clothing for men, women, children**

Class construction of clothing for people with disabilities and illnesses regardless of age or sex in 646.401; class patterns regardless of groups of people in 646.407; class fitting and alterations regardless of groups of people in 646.408; class comprehensive works in 646.4

.402   Men's clothing

.404   Women's clothing

.406   Children's clothing

From birth through age eleven

Class clothing for young people twelve to twenty in 646.400835

.407   Patterns

.407 2   Pattern design and patternmaking

Standard subdivisions are added for either or both topics in heading

.408   Fitting and alterations

Standard subdivisions are added for either or both topics in heading

>   **646.42–646.48 Specific kinds of clothing**

Add to each subdivision identified by * as follows:

001–007	Standard subdivisions
008	Clothing with respect to groups of people
[00811]	Clothing for men
	Do not use; class in notation 02 from this table
[0082]	Clothing for women
	Do not use; class in notation 04 from this table
0083	Clothing for young people
	Do not use for children under twelve; class in notation 06 from this table
0084	Clothing for people in specific stages of adulthood
	Do not use for clothing for men in specific stages of adulthood; class in notation 02 from this table. Do not use for clothing for women in specific stages of adulthood; class in notation 04 from this table
0087	Clothing for gifted people
	Do not use for clothing for people with disabilities and illnesses; class in notation 01 from this table
009	History, geographic treatment, biography
01–06	Clothing for people with disabilities and illnesses, men, women, children
	Add to 0 the numbers following 646.40 in 646.401–646.406, e.g., clothing for people with physical disabilities 01

Class comprehensive works in 646.4

.42   *Construction of undergarments and hosiery

> Subdivisions are added for construction of undergarments and hosiery together, for construction of undergarments alone

> *See also 646.433 for vests (waistcoats); also 646.436 for pants (trousers)*

.43   *Construction of specific kinds of garments

> Not provided for elsewhere

.432   *Dresses

.433   *Suits

> Class here jackets, sport coats, vests (waistcoats)

> Class pants (trousers) in 646.436; class skirts in 646.437; class outerwear, comprehensive works on coats and jackets in 646.45

> *See also 646.42 for vests (undergarments)*

.435   *Shirts, blouses, tops

> Subdivisions are added for any or all topics in heading

.436   *Pants (Trousers)

.437   *Skirts

.45   *Construction of outerwear

> Including capes, cloaks, stoles, sweaters

> Class here overcoats, topcoats, raincoats; comprehensive works on coats and jackets

> Class garments for special purposes in 646.47

> *For suit jackets, sport coats, see 646.433*

.47   *Construction of garments for special purposes

> Including activewear (clothing for athletic and outdoor sports), maternity garments

> Class accessories for special purposes in 646.48

> *See also 646.4 for casual wear (sportswear)*

.475   *Sleepwear and loungewear

> Subdivisions are added for either or both topics in heading

.476   *Evening and formal dress, wedding clothes

> Subdivisions are added for evening and formal dress, wedding clothes together; for evening and formal dress together; for evening dress alone; for formal dress alone

*Add as instructed under 646.42–646.48

.478   *Costumes

> Including party, period costumes

> Class here theatrical costumes

.48   Accessories construction

> Including aprons, belts, gloves and mittens, handbags, handkerchiefs, neckwear, scarves

> Class hosiery in 646.42; class headwear in 646.5; class footwear in 685.3; class handcrafted costume jewelry in 745.5942

.5   Construction of headwear

> Class here bonnets, caps, hats

> *For construction of headwear by a specific technique in textile arts, see the technique in 746, e.g., crocheting hats 746.4340432*

.500 1–.500 7   Standard subdivisions

.500 8   Construction of headwear with respect to groups of people

[.500 811]   Men

> Do not use; class in 646.502

[.500 82]   Women

> Do not use; class in 646.504

[.500 83]   Young people

> Do not use; class in 646.506

.500 84   People in specific stages of adulthood

> Do not use for headwear for men in specific stages of adulthood; class in 646.502. Do not use for headwear for women in specific stages of adulthood; class in 646.504

.500 9   History, geographic treatment, biography

.502   Men's headwear

.504   Women's headwear

> Class here millinery

.506   Young people's headwear

> Class here children's headwear

.6   Care of clothing and accessories

> Standard subdivisions are added for care of clothing and accessories together, for care of clothing alone

> Including mending, reweaving; packing, storage

> *For laundering and related operations, see 648.1*

*Add as instructed under 646.42–646.48

.7 Management of personal and family life

Class here grooming; life skills, success in personal and family life

Class clothing selection and dressing with style in 646.3; class training children in grooming in 649.63; class interdisciplinary works on success in 650.1

> *For parapsychological and occult means for achievement of well-being, happiness, success, see 131; for psychological means for achievement of personal well-being, happiness, success, see 158; for etiquette, see 395; for care of physique and form, see 613.71; for success in business and other public situations, see 650.1*

> *See also 362.82 for social services to families*

.700 1–.700 7	Standard subdivisions of management of personal and family life
.700 8	Management of personal and family life with respect to groups of people
[.700 846]	Management of personal and family life with respect to people in late adulthood
	Do not use; class in 646.79
.700 9	History, geographic treatment, biography of management of personal and family life
.701–.703	Standard subdivisions of grooming
.704	Grooming for women, men, young people
.704 2	Grooming for women
.704 4	Grooming for men
.704 6	Grooming for young people
	Class here grooming for children
.705–.707	Standard subdivisions of grooming
.708	Grooming for groups of people
[.708 1–.708 3]	Grooming for men, women, young people
	Do not use; class in 646.704
.708 4	Grooming for people in specific stages of adulthood
	Do not use for grooming for women in specific stages of adulthood; class in 646.7042. Do not use for grooming for men in specific stages of adulthood; class in 646.7044
.709	History, geographic treatment, biography of grooming
.72	Care of hair, face, skin, nails
	Class here cosmetology, cosmetics, makeup
	Class cosmetology, cosmetics, makeup limited to face in 646.726

.724	Care of hair

Including care of beard, shaving; dyeing, hairweaving, permanent waving, relaxing

Class here barbering, haircutting, hairdressing, hairstyling

.724 7	Braiding
.724 8	Wigs

Including cleaning, dyeing, selection, styling

.726	Care of face and skin

Standard subdivisions are added for either or both topics in heading

Including care of eyes, lips

Class manicuring and pedicuring in 646.727

.727	Care of nails

Class here manicuring, pedicuring

.76	Social skills

Class social skills in family living in 646.78

For dating and choice of mate, see 646.77

.77	Dating and choice of mate

Standard subdivisions are added for either or both topics in heading

.78	Family life

Regardless of legal status of family

Class here guides to harmonious intrafamily relationships

For child rearing, see 649.1

.782	Spousal relationship

Class here husband-wife relationship, married people

.79	Guides for people in late adulthood

Class here guides to retirement

Class family life in 646.78

See also 362.6 for social services to people in late adulthood

647 Management of public households (Institutional housekeeping)

See Manual at 647 vs. 647.068, 658.2, T1—0682

.068	Management

See Manual at 647 vs. 647.068, 658.2, T1—0682

[.068 3]   Personnel management (Human resource management)

             Do not use; class in 647.2

.2   **Employees**

       Class here personnel management

       Class comprehensive home economics works on household employees in 640.46. Class employees and personnel management in a specific field of institutional housekeeping with the field, e.g., waiters 642.6, personnel management of waiters 642.60683

       For hours and duties, see 647.6

.6   **Employee hours and duties**

.9   **Specific kinds of public households and institutions**

       Class a specific aspect of public households and institutions with the aspect, e.g., grounds keeping 635.9, laundering 648.1

       See Manual at 647 vs. 647.068, 658.2, T1—0682

[.901–.909]   Standard subdivisions

       Do not use; class in 647.01–647.09

.92   Multiple dwellings for long-term residents

       Including apartment hotels, condominiums, cooperatives, public housing, tenements; trailer and mobile home parks

       Class here apartment houses

       Class recreation vehicle (RV), trailer camps in 647.942

       For boarding and rooming houses for temporary residents, see 647.94

.94   Lodging for temporary residents

       Class here household management in hospitality industry, bed and breakfast establishments, hostels, hotels, inns, motels, resorts

       Class interdisciplinary works on hospitality industry in 338.4791; class interdisciplinary works on tourism in 910; class interdisciplinary and descriptive works on lodging for temporary residents, hotels, inns, motels in 910.46; class interdisciplinary and descriptive works on resorts in 910.462; class interdisciplinary and descriptive works on bed and breakfast establishments in 910.464; class interdisciplinary and descriptive works on hostels in 910.466; class interdisciplinary and descriptive works on campsites in 910.468

       For eating and drinking places, see 647.95

       See Manual at 913–919: Add table: 04: Guidebooks

.940 25   Directories of persons and organizations

       Limited to directories of personnel and organizations concerned with household management of lodging for temporary residents

       Do not use for directories of lodging for temporary residents; class in 910.46

.942   Campsites

> Class here recreation vehicle (RV) camps, trailer camps
>
> Class trailer and mobile home parks in 647.92

.95   Eating and drinking places

> Standard subdivisions are added for either or both topics in heading
>
> Class here catering establishments
>
> Class interdisciplinary works on facilities for travelers in 910.46
>
> *See Manual at 913–919: Add table: 04: Guidebooks*

[.950 253–.950 259]   Directories of specific continents, countries, localities

> Do not use; class in 647.953–647.959

[.950 93–.950 99]   Specific continents, countries, localities

> Do not use; class in 647.953–647.959

.953–.959   Specific continents, countries, localities

> Class here directories
>
> Add to base number 647.95 notation 3–9 from Table 2, e.g., restaurants of Hawaii 647.95969

.96   Miscellaneous institutional households

> Not provided for elsewhere
>
> Add to base number 647.96 the numbers following 725 in 725.1–725.9, e.g., office buildings 647.9623

.98   Religious institutions

> Add to base number 647.98 the numbers following 726 in 726.1–726.9, e.g., monasteries 647.987

.99   Educational and research institutions

> Add to base number 647.99 the numbers following 727 in 727.1–727.9, e.g., libraries 647.998

648   Housekeeping

> Class here household sanitation
>
> Use 640 for housekeeping covering activities related to running the home, e.g., preparing meals and doing routine repairs as well as cleaning. Use 648 for housekeeping limited to cleaning
>
> *See Manual at 647 vs. 647.068, 658.2, T1—0682*

.1	**Laundering and related operations**

Standard subdivisions are added for laundering and related operations together, for laundering alone

Including bleaching, drying, dyeing, ironing, spot removal

Class dry cleaning in 667.12; class commercial laundering, interdisciplinary works on laundering in 667.13

.5	**Housecleaning**

Class here cleaning floors, furnishings

.7	**Pest control**
.8	**Storage**
.9	**Moving**

649	**Child rearing; home care of people with disabilities and illnesses**

.1	**Child rearing**

Class here supervision

Unless other instructions are given, class a subject with aspects in two or more subdivisions of 649.1 in the number coming last, e.g., gifted boys 649.155 (*not* 649.132)

Class specific elements of home care of children regardless of age, sex, or other characteristics in 649.3–649.7

For child training, see 649.6

.102	Miscellany and works for specific types of users

Notation 02 from Table 1 as modified below

.102 4	Works for specific types of users

Limited to topics named below

Including child rearing for people in specific occupations

Do not add as instructed in Table 1

See Manual at 649.12–649.15 vs. 649.1024, 649.108

.102 42	Works for expectant parents
.102 43	Works for single parents
.102 45	Works for older children in family
.102 48	Works for babysitters
.108	Child rearing with respect to groups of people

See Manual at 649.12–649.15 vs. 649.1024, 649.108

.108 1	People by gender or sex

Do not use for rearing of children by gender or sex; class in 649.13

.108 3	Young people

.108 32–.108 35	Young people of specific age groups

Do not use for rearing of children of specific age groups; class in 649.12

.108 5	Relatives

Do not use for works for expectant parents; class in 649.10242

.108 54	Progeny

Do not use for rearing of only children; class in 649.142. Do not use for rearing of adopted and foster children; class in 649.145

.108 55	Siblings

Do not use for works for older children in the family; class in 649.10245. Do not use for rearing of siblings; class in 649.143

.108 6	People by miscellaneous social attributes

.108 62	People by social and economic levels

Do not use for rearing of children by social and economic levels; class in 649.1562

.108 65	People by marital status

.108 652	Single people

Do not use for works for single parents; class in 649.10243

.108 66	People by sexual orientation

Do not use for rearing of children by sexual orientation; class in 649.1563

.108 67	Transgender and intersex people

Do not use for rearing of transgender and intersex children; class in 649.1564

.108 69	People by miscellaneous social statuses

.108 691	People with status defined by changes in residence

Do not use for rearing of children with status defined by changes in residence; class in 649.1565

.108 692	Antisocial and asocial people

.108 692 3	Juvenile delinquents and predelinquents

Do not use for rearing of juvenile delinquents and predelinquents; class in 649.153

.108 694	People with social disadvantages

Do not use for rearing of children with social disadvantages; class in 649.1567

.108 694 2		Poor people

Do not use for rearing of poor children; class in 649.15672

.108 7		People with disabilities and illnesses, gifted people

Do not use for rearing of children with disabilities and illnesses, gifted children; class in 649.15

.108 8		Occupational and religious groups

Do not use for works for people in specific occupations; class in 649.1024

.108 82		Religious groups

Do not use for religious aspects of child rearing, religious training of children in the home; class in 204.41

.108 9		Ethnic and national groups

Do not use for rearing of children by ethnic and national groups; class in 649.157

.12   Children of specific age groups

Add to base number 649.12 the numbers following —083 in notation 0832–0835 from Table 1, e.g., preschool children 649.123

See Manual at 649.12–649.15 vs. 649.1024, 649.108

.13   Children by gender or sex

Standard subdivisions are added for either or both topics in heading

Class here gender identity, gender role, sex role

Class children of specific sexes belonging to specific age groups in 649.12

For transgender and intersex children, see 649.1564

See Manual at 649.12–649.15 vs. 649.1024, 649.108

.132   Boys

.133   Girls

.14   Children of specific status and relationships

Add to base number 649.14 the numbers following 155.44 in 155.442–155.446, e.g., the only child 649.142

Class children with status defined by changes in residence in 649.1565

See Manual at 649.12–649.15 vs. 649.1024, 649.108

.15   Exceptional children; children by miscellaneous social attributes; children by ethnic and national origin

Standard subdivisions are added for all topics in heading together, for exceptional children alone

Class here children with learning disabilities

See Manual at 649.12–649.15 vs. 649.1024, 649.108

.151–.155	Specific groups of exceptional children

Add to base number 649.15 the numbers following 371.9 in 371.91–371.95, e.g., home care of gifted children 649.155

.156	Children by social and economic levels; children by sexual orientation; transgender and intersex children; children with status defined by changes in residence; children with social disadvantages

.156 2	Children by social and economic levels

Add to base number 649.1562 the numbers following —0862 in notation 08621–08625 from Table 1, e.g., upper-class children 649.15621

.156 3	Children by sexual orientation

Add to base number 649.1563 the numbers following —0866 in notation 08662–08664 from Table 1, e.g., gay children 649.15634

.156 4	Transgender and intersex children

Standard subdivisions are added for transgender and intersex children together, for transgender children alone

.156 45	Intersex children

.156 5	Children with status defined by changes in residence

Add to base number 649.1565 the numbers following —08691 in notation 086912–086918 from Table 1, e.g., immigrant children 649.15652

.156 7	Children with social disadvantages

Class here children with cultural disadvantages, children of alienated and excluded classes

Class adopted and foster children in 649.145

.156 72	Poor children

.157	Children by ethnic and national origin

.157 001–.157 009	Standard subdivisions

.157 05–.157 09	Ethnic and national groups with ethnic origins from more than one continent, of European descent

Add to base number 649.157 notation 05–09 from Table 5, e.g., American native children of mixed ancestry with ethnic origins from more than one continent 649.1570597

.157 1–.157 9	Specific ethnic and national groups

Add to base number 649.157 notation 1–9 from Table 5, e.g., Japanese children 649.157956, Japanese-American children 649.157956073

> **649.3–649.7 Specific elements of home care of children**

Class comprehensive works in 649.1

.3   **Feeding children**

.33   Breast feeding

         Class here interdisciplinary works on breast feeding

          For nutritional aspects of breast feeding, see 613.269

.4   **Child health care**

         Class feeding in 649.3; class home care of children with disabilities and illnesses in 649.8

.48   Substance abuse

.5   **Children's activities and recreation**

.51   Creative activities

         Including modeling, music, painting, paper work

.55   Play with toys

         Including games

         Class sports games in 649.57

.57   Exercise, gymnastics, sports

         Standard subdivisions are added for any or all topics in heading

.58   Reading and related activities

         Standard subdivisions are added for reading and related activities together, for reading alone

         Including storytelling, reading aloud to children, listening

          For home teaching of reading, see 649.68

.6   **Child training**

         Class religious training of children in the home in 204.41

          For moral and character training, see 649.7

.62   Toilet training

.63   Training in grooming and self-reliance

         Including bathing, dressing, feeding self

.64   Behavior modification, discipline, obedience

         Standard subdivisions are added for any or all topics in heading

         Class a specific application with the application, e.g., behavior modification in dressing habits 649.63

.65   Sex education

.68   Home preschool education

> Development of learning ability, of readiness for school by parents in the home
>
> Including home teaching of reading
>
> Class primary level home schools and schooling in 372.104242; class techniques of study at primary level for parents in 372.130281; class home schools and schooling in reading at primary level in 372.4

.7   **Moral and character training of children**

> Standard subdivisions are added for either or both topics in heading
>
> Class religious training of children in the home in 204.41

.8   **Home care of people with disabilities and illnesses**

> Class social services to people with disabilities and illnesses in 362.1–362.4; class nursing aspects in 610.73
>
> *For home care of children with disabilities, see 649.15*

650   Management and auxiliary services

> Class here business
>
> *See Manual at 330 vs. 650, 658*

.01–.09   Standard subdivisions

.1   **Personal success in business**

> Including creative ability
>
> Class here interdisciplinary works on success
>
> > *For success in personal and family life, see 646.7; for success as an executive, see 658.409. For a specific aspect of success, see the aspect, e.g., techniques of study for success as a student 371.30281*

.11   Time management

> Class here personal efficiency, interdisciplinary works on time management
>
> > *For time management in personal life, see 640.43; for executive time management, see 658.4093*

.12   Financial success

.13   Personal improvement and success in business relationships

> Standard subdivisions are added for either or both topics in heading

.14   Success in obtaining jobs and promotions

> Standard subdivisions are added for either or both topics in heading

.142   Résumés, cover letters, job applications

> Standard subdivisions are added for résumés, cover letters, job applications together; for résumés alone

> Including writing cover letters for job hunting

> Class here résumé writing

.144   Employment interviewing

> Class here employment interviewing from the job seeker's viewpoint, comprehensive works on employment interviewing

> *For employment interviewing from the employer's viewpoint, see 658.31124*

> ## 651–657 Auxiliary services

> Class comprehensive works in 650

> *For advertising and public relations, see 659*

651   Office services

Including problems of security and confidentiality

Class a specific aspect of security and confidentiality in office services with the aspect, e.g., security and confidentiality in records management 651.5

For processes of written communication, see 652; for accounting, see 657

[.028 4]   Apparatus, equipment, materials

> Do not use for apparatus and equipment; class in 651.2. Do not use for materials; class in 651.29

[.028 5]   Computer applications

> Do not use; class in 651.8

.2   Equipment and supplies

Standard subdivisions are added for equipment and supplies together, for equipment alone

Class procurement of office equipment and supplies in 658.72

For a specific type of equipment, see the use of the equipment, e.g., computers 651.8, photocopying machines 652.4

.23   Furniture

.26   Processing equipment

> Class here electronic office machines

.29   Forms and supplies

> Standard subdivisions are added for forms and supplies together, for forms alone

> Including materials

.3   **Office management**

.37   Clerical services

> *For written communication, see 652*
>
> *See also 657 for accounting*

.374   Secretarial and related services

> Class here office practice

.374 1   Secretarial services

> Work of secretaries, stenographers, typists

.374 3   Related services

> Including work of filers, messengers, receptionists
>
> Class work of stenographers, typists in 651.3741

.5   **Records management**

> Class clerical services associated with records management in 651.37
>
> *For creation and transmission of records, see 651.7*

.504   Special topics of records management

.504 2   Records management in specific types of enterprises

[.504 201–.504 209]   Standard subdivisions

> Do not use; class in 651.501–651.509

.504 26   Records management in technical enterprises

.504 261   Medical records management

.51   Retention, maintenance, final disposition of records

> Standard subdivisions are added for any or all topics in heading
>
> Class filing systems and storage in 651.53

.53   Filing systems

> Including comprehensive works on storage of records
>
> Class here filing procedures
>
> *For specific aspects of storage, see 651.54–651.59*

.530 285   Computer applications

> Do not use for digitization of files; class in 651.59

> 651.54–651.59   Specific aspects of storage
>
> Class here space, equipment, control, protection, preservation
>
> Class comprehensive works in 651.53

.54   **Storage of original documents**

Including storage in filing cabinets, visible and rotary files

For storage of inactive files, see 651.56

.56   **Storage of inactive files**

Original documents in permanent (dead) storage

.58   **Microreproduction of files**

Active and inactive

.59   **Digitization of files**

Active and inactive

.7   **Communication**

Class here creation and transmission of records

Class communication as a technique of management in 658.45; class interdisciplinary works on communication in 302.2

See Manual at 658.45 vs. 651.7, 808.06665

.73   **Oral communication**

Including use of telephone, telephone answering machines, voice mail

.74   **Written communication**

Including dictating and use of dictating equipment

For specific types of written communication, see 651.75–651.78; for processes of written communication, see 652

See also 653.14 for recording in shorthand and transcribing shorthand notes

---

>   **651.75–651.78 Specific types of written communication**

Class comprehensive works in 651.74

.75   **Correspondence**

Including layout of letters

.752   Form letters

.755   Memorandums

.759   Mail handling

.77   **Minutes**

.78   **Reports**

.79   Internal communication

        Including electronic mail

        Class interdisciplinary works on electronic mail in 004.692

        For oral internal communication, see 651.73; for written internal communication, see 651.74

.792   Intranets

        Class interdisciplinary works on intranets in 004.682

.8   **Computer applications**

        Use in carrying out office functions

        Unless it is redundant, add to base number 651.8 the numbers following 00 in 004–006, e.g., use of digital personal computers 651.8416, but use of digital computers as a whole 651.8 (*not* 651.84)

        Class interdisciplinary works on data processing in 004

        For computer applications in a specific office activity, see the activity, e.g., digitization of files 651.59

.9   **Office services in specific kinds of enterprises**

        Class specific elements of office services in specific kinds of enterprises in 651.2–651.8

[.900 01–.900 09]   Standard subdivisions

        Do not use; class in 651.01–651.09

.900 1–.999 9   Subdivisions for office services in specific kinds of enterprises

        Add to base number 651.9 notation 001–999, e.g., office services in libraries 651.902

652   **Processes of written communication**

        For word processing, see 005.52; for shorthand, see 653

.1   **Penmanship**

        See also 745.61 for calligraphy

.3   **Keyboarding**

        Class here typing

.300 1–.300 6   Standard subdivisions

.300 7   Education, research, related topics

.300 76   Review and exercise

        Do not use for speed and accuracy tests and drills; class in 652.307

.300 8–.300 9   Standard subdivisions

.302   Specific levels of skill

        Class speed and accuracy tests and drills in 652.307

[.302 01–.302 09]	Standard subdivisions	
	Do not use; class in 652.3001–652.3009	
.302 4	Basic level	
	Class here beginning level	
.302 5	Intermediate level	
.302 6	Advanced level	

.307   **Speed and accuracy**

Standard subdivisions are added for either or both topics in heading

Class here tests, drills

[.307 076]   Review and exercise

Do not use; class in 652.307

.32   **Keyboarding for specific purposes**

Other than general commercial and professional keyboarding

Including keyboarding for personal use

[.320 1–.320 9]   Standard subdivisions

Do not use; class in 652.3001–652.3009

.326   **Keyboarding for specific kinds of enterprises**

Including legal, medical keyboarding

[.326 01–.326 09]   Standard subdivisions

Do not use; class in 652.3001–652.3009

.4   **Copying**

Class here photocopying

Class interdisciplinary works on photocopying in 686.4

.8   **Cryptography**

Class here interdisciplinary works on cryptography

For cryptographic techniques used for a specific purpose, see the purpose, e.g., cryptographic techniques used for security in computer systems 005.82

653   Shorthand

.076   Review and exercise

Do not use for speed and accuracy tests and drills; class in 653.15

.1   **Basic shorthand practice**

Class basic practice in a specific system with the system, e.g., Gregg shorthand transcription 653.4270424

| .14 | Taking dictation, and transcription |

Standard subdivisions are added for either or both topics in heading

See also 651.74 for dictating and use of dictating equipment

| .15 | Speed and accuracy |

Standard subdivisions are added for either or both topics in heading

Class here tests, drills

Class speed and accuracy in transcription in 653.14

| [.150 76] | Review and exercise |

Do not use; class in 653.15

| .18 | Specific uses |

Including court reporting; medical, personal uses

| [.180 1–.180 9] | Standard subdivisions |

Do not use; class in 653.101–653.109

> **653.2–653.4 Systems**

Class comprehensive works in 653

| .2 | **Abbreviated longhand systems** |

Systems using conventional letters

| .3 | **Machine systems** |

Add to base number 653.3 the numbers following 653.1 in 653.14–653.18, e.g., specific uses 653.38

| .4 | **Handwritten systems** |

For abbreviated longhand systems, see 653.2

.41	Multilingual systems
.42	English-language systems
.424	Pitman systems
.424 04	Special topics of Pitman systems
.424 042	Basic shorthand practice

Add to base number 653.424042 the numbers following 653.1 in 653.14–653.18, e.g., speed and accuracy 653.4240425

| .424 07 | Education, research, related topics |
| .424 076 | Review and exercise |

Do not use for speed and accuracy tests and drills; class in 653.4240425

| .427 | Gregg systems |

.427 04	Special topics of Gregg systems
.427 042	Basic shorthand practice

> Add to base number 653.427042 the numbers following 653.1 in 653.14–653.18, e.g., transcription 653.4270424

.427 07	Education, research, related topics
.427 076	Review and exercise

> Do not use for speed and accuracy tests and drills; class in 653.4270425

.428	Script systems

> Including Dewey system (1936)

.43–.49	Systems used in other languages

> Add to base number 653.4 notation 3–9 from Table 6, e.g., French-language systems 653.441

[654]   [Unassigned]

> Most recently used in Edition 14

[655]   [Unassigned]

> Most recently used in Edition 17

[656]   [Unassigned]

> Most recently used in Edition 14

657   Accounting

> Class here financial accounting
>
> Class use of accounting information by management in 658.1511

.04	Levels of accounting
.042	Elementary level
.044	Intermediate level

> Including college-level accounting

.046	Advanced level

> ## 657.1–657.9   Elements of accounting

Unless other instructions are given, observe the following table of preference, e.g., accounting for cost of inventory in a corporation engaged in manufacturing 657.867072 (*not* 657.42, 657.72, 657.95):

Accounting for enterprises engaged in specific kinds of activities	657.8
Financial reports (Financial statements)	657.3
Accounting for specific phases of business activity	657.7
Constructive accounting	657.1
Bookkeeping (Recordkeeping)	657.2
Specific fields of accounting	657.4
Accounting for enterprises of specific sizes or specific kinds of legal or ownership form	657.9
Specific kinds of accounting	657.6

Class comprehensive works in 657

.1   Constructive accounting

Development of accounting systems to fit the needs of individual organizations

.2   Bookkeeping (Recordkeeping)

Including secretarial bookkeeping and accounting

Class elementary accounting in 657.042

.3   Financial reports (Financial statements)

Class here consolidated financial statements

Class use of financial reports by management to improve business performance in 658.1512

.32   Preparing financial statements

.4   Specific fields of accounting

Including human resources accounting

For constructive accounting, see 657.1; for bookkeeping, see 657.2; for payroll accounting, see 657.742

See also 658.1511 for managerial accounting; also 658.4013 for management audits

[.401–.409]   Standard subdivisions

Do not use; class in 657.01–657.09

.42   Cost accounting

Class here activity-based costing

.45   Auditing

See also 658.4013 for management audits

.450 285	Computer applications
	Class auditing of computer-processed accounts in 657.453
.452	Audit reports
	Class here audit reporting
.453	Auditing of computer-processed accounts
.458	Internal auditing
.46	Tax accounting
	Including accounting for social security taxes
.47	Fiduciary accounting
	Accounting for receiverships, estates, trusts
.48	Inflation accounting
.6	**Specific kinds of accounting**
[.601–.609]	Standard subdivisions
	Do not use; class in 657.01–657.09
.61	Public accounting
.63	Private accounting
.7	**Accounting for specific phases of business activity**
	Including accounting for income, for profit
[.701–.709]	Standard subdivisions
	Do not use; class in 657.01–657.09
.72	Current assets
	Including accounts receivable, cash, inventory
.73	Fixed assets
	Including depreciation, valuation and revaluation of land, buildings, equipment; insurance
.74	Current liabilities
	Including accounts payable, notes payable
	For tax accounting, see 657.46
.742	Payroll accounting
.75	Fixed liabilities
	Including bonds payable, leases, mortgages, pension plans, purchase contracts

.76   Capital accounting

         Accounting for ownership equity

         Including accounting for stock and dividends

.8   **Accounting for enterprises engaged in specific kinds of activities**

         Except for modifications shown under specific entries, add to each subdivision identified by * as follows:

         001–009   Standard subdivisions

         01–07   Specific aspects of accounting

                 Add to 0 the numbers following 657 in 657.1–657.7, e.g., auditing 045

[.801–.809]   Standard subdivisions

         Do not use; class in 657.01–657.09

.83   Services and professional activities

         Standard subdivisions are added for services and professional activities together, for services alone

         Class here service industries

.832   Social services

         Including libraries, prisons, religious institutions

.832 2   *Health care facilities

         Class here hospitals

.832 7   *Educational institutions

.833   Finance and real estate

.833 3   *Finance

         For insurance, see 657.836

.833 5   *Real estate

.834   Professions

.835   *Government

         Including military accounting

         Class accounting for government corporations (*except* municipalities) in 657.95. Class accounting for a specific government service other than military with the service in a subdivision of 657.83, e.g., educational institutions 657.8327

.835 045   Government auditing

         Number built according to instructions under 657.8

         Class here manuals of government audit procedure

.836   *Insurance

---

*Add as instructed under 657.8

.837	*Hotels and restaurants

Class here hospitality industry

.837 4	*Hotels
.837 5	*Restaurants
.838	*Public utilities
.839	*Commerce

Class here wholesale trade, retail trade

.84	Communications and entertainment media

Including motion-picture producers and theaters, publishing houses, television and radio networks and stations, theaters

.86	Other activities

See also 657.83 for services and professional activities

.861	*Labor unions
.862	*Mining
.863	*Agriculture
.867	*Manufacturing
.869	*Construction
.9	**Accounting for enterprises of specific sizes or specific kinds of legal or ownership form**
[.901–.903]	Standard subdivisions

Do not use; class in 657.01–657.03

.904	Enterprises of specific sizes
.904 2	Small business
[.905–.909]	Standard subdivisions

Do not use; class in 657.05–657.09

.91	Individual proprietorships
.92	Partnerships

For international partnerships, see 657.96

.95	Corporations

For multinational corporations, see 657.96

.96	Combinations

Class here mergers, multinational organizations

.97	Cooperatives

*Add as instructed under 657.8

.98 Nonprofit organizations

658 General management

Management comprises the conduct of all types of enterprises (for profit and not for profit) except government agencies that do not themselves provide direct services

Class here general business management, general industrial management; management of public agencies that themselves provide direct services (in contrast to public agencies that regulate, support, or control services provided by other organizations)

Class analysis and description of behavior in complex organizations, sociology of management in 302.35; class specific principles of management in 658.401–658.403; class comprehensive works on management and economics in 330

> *For public administration, see 351. For management of enterprises engaged in a specific field of activity, see the field, plus notation 068 from Table 1, e.g., management of commercial banks 332.12068, management of automobile manufacturing 629.222068*

> *See also 306.36 for industrial sociology*

> *See Manual at T1—068 vs. 353–354; also at 330 vs. 650, 658*

.001 Philosophy and theory

[.001 1] Systems

Do not use for systems theory and analysis; class in 658.4032. Do not use for operations research; class in 658.4034. Do not use for models and simulation; class in 658.40352

.002 Miscellany

[.002 85] Computer applications

Do not use; class in 658.05

.003–.009 Standard subdivisions

.02 Management of enterprises of specific sizes and scope

Class management of enterprises of specific forms regardless of size or scope in 658.04

[.020 1–.020 9] Standard subdivisions

Do not use; class in 658.001–658.009

.022 Small enterprises

.022 08 Groups of people

Class here minority enterprises

.023 Big enterprises

.04   **Management of enterprises of specific forms**

> *For initiation of specific forms of ownership organization, management of new enterprises of specific forms, see 658.114*

> *See Manual at 658.04 vs. 658.114, 658.402*

[.040 1–.040 9]   Standard subdivisions

> Do not use; class in 658.001–658.009

> **658.041–658.046 For-profit organizations**

> Class international for-profit organizations in 658.049; class comprehensive works in 658

.041   Individual proprietorships

> Including part-time enterprises

> Class here one-person enterprises, self-employment enterprises

> Class executive management by entrepreneurs in 658.421

> *For one-person corporations, see 658.045*

.041 2   Home-based businesses

.042   Partnerships

> General and limited

> Class partnership associations in 658.044

.044   Unincorporated business enterprises

> Including joint stock companies, joint ventures, partnership associations

> *For individual proprietorships, see 658.041; for partnerships, see 658.042*

.045   Corporations

> Including close, family, one-person corporations

> Class government corporations as part of the public administrative process in 352.266; class general works on management that do not emphasize the organizational form corporation even though the works may be predominently about managing corporations in 658; class combinations in 658.046

.046   Combinations

> Including conglomerates, holding companies, interlocking directorates, subsidiaries, trusts

> Class mergers in 658.16

.047   Cooperatives

.048   Nonprofit organizations

Class international nonprofit organizations in 658.049

See also 658.047 for cooperative organizations

.049   International enterprises

Class organization of international enterprises and activities in 658.18

.05   Computer applications

Unless it is redundant, add to base number 658.05 the numbers following 00 in 004–006, e.g., use of digital personal computers 658.05416, but use of digital computers as a whole 658.05 (*not* 658.054); however, for data security, see 658.478

See also 651.8 for computer applications in clerical operations; also 658.4032 for systems analysis in decision making

.1   **Organization and financial management**

Standard subdivisions are added for organization and finance together, for organization alone

For internal organization, see 658.402

.11   Initiation of business enterprises

Including location

Class here management of new business enterprises

Class capitalization in 658.152; class reorganization and dissolution of business enterprises in 658.16

.114   Initiation of business enterprises by form of ownership organization

Add to base number 658.114 the numbers following 658.04 in 658.041–658.049, e.g., initiation of corporations 658.1145

Class comprehensive works on management of specific forms of ownership organization in 658.04

See Manual at 658.04 vs. 658.114, 658.402

.12   Management for legal compliance

Including use of legal counsel

For management for legal compliance with respect to a specific subject, see the subject in 658, e.g., management for legal compliance with respect to collective bargaining 658.3154

See also 346.06 for law of organizations

.15   **Financial management**

Including insolvency, bankruptcy; valuation of businesses

Class here financial decision making, financial planning

Class reorganization and dissolution of business enterprises because of business failure in 658.16. Class a specific aspect of valuation of businesses with the aspect, e.g., valuation of capital 658.1522

See Manual at 332 vs. 338, 658.15

.151   **Financial control**

For budgeting, see 658.154; for management of income and expense, see 658.155

.151 1   Managerial accounting

Design and use of accounting procedures to provide internal reports needed for day-to-day management

Class accounting in 657; class internal auditing in 657.458; class budgeting in 658.154

See also 658.4013 for management audits

.151 2   Use of reports

Including balance sheets, income and expense statements, profit and loss statements

Class here financial reports made to directors, stockholders, top management

.152   **Management of financial operations**

Class here management of investment, comprehensive works on capital and its management

For capital, see 332.041; for budgeting (including capital budgets), see 658.154; for management of income and expense, see 658.155; for compensation management, see 658.32; for management of credit extended by seller to buyer, see 658.88

>   658.152 2–658.152 4   Capital and its management

Class comprehensive works in 658.152

.152 2   Procurement of capital

Class here costs and valuation of capital

For procurement of specific kinds of capital, see 658.1524

.152 24	External sources

Including conversion of closely held corporations to corporations whose stocks are publicly traded; endowments, grants; issue and sale of stocks and bonds; loans

Class here fund raising

Class debt management in 658.1526

> *For fund raising for enterprises engaged in a specific field of activity, see the field, plus notation 0681 from Table 1, e.g., private charitable and philanthropic fund raising for social welfare 361.70681*

.152 26	Internal sources

Including reserves, savings

.152 4	Procurement and management of specific kinds of capital
[.152 401–.152 409]	Standard subdivisions

Do not use; class in 658.152201–658.152209

.152 42	Fixed capital

Class here long-term capital

Including land, buildings, associated industrial equipment; long-term loans receivable; leasing

> *See also 658.72 for procurement of other kinds of equipment*

.152 44	Working capital

Including accounts receivable, cash, inventory, 30–90 day loans receivable

Class here short-term capital

.152 6	Debt management

Including accounts payable, bonds outstanding, notes payable

.153	Taxes, insurance, charitable donations

Including ways that management can deal with taxes, what insurance is needed for the organization

Class interdisciplinary works on and economic aspects of business taxes in 336.207; class interdisciplinary works on charitable donations in 361.765; class interdisciplinary works on insurance in 368

> *See also 343.068 for law of business taxes*

.154	Budgeting

Including capital budgets, zero-base budgeting

.155   **Management of income and expense**

> Including distribution of profits, dividend policy

> Class here management of profit and loss, risk management

> Class interdisciplinary works on risk management in 368; class increasing profits in 658.1554

>> *For use of income and expense statements, see 658.1512; for taxes, insurance, charitable donations, see 658.153; for health and safety programs, see 658.382; for business security, see 658.47; for pricing, see 658.816*

.155 2   **Cost analysis and control**

> Standard subdivisions are added for cost analysis and control together, for cost control alone

> Class managerial accounting in 658.1511

>> *For cost accounting, see 657.42; for analysis and control of specific kinds of costs, see 658.1553; for cost-benefit analysis, cost-volume-profit analysis, see 658.1554*

.155 3   **Kinds of costs**

> Including fixed and overhead costs; variable costs; labor, material costs

>> *For costs of capital, see 658.1522*

.155 4   **Income (Revenue)**

> Including break-even analysis, cost-benefit analysis, cost-volume-profit analysis

> Class here increasing profits

.159   **Financial management in enterprises of specific sizes, scope, forms**

> Including financial management in nonprofit organizations

>> *For a specific aspect of financial management in enterprises of specific sizes, scope, forms, see the aspect in 658.151–658.155, e.g., budgeting management in small business 658.154*

[.159 01–.159 09]   **Standard subdivisions**

> Do not use; class in 658.1501–658.1509

.159 2   **Small business**

.159 208   **Groups of people**

> Class here minority enterprises

.159 9   **International enterprises**

.16 Reorganization and dissolution of enterprises

> Standard subdivisions are added for reorganization and dissolution of enterprises together, for reorganization of enterprises alone
>
> Class here comprehensive works on reorganization, comprehensive works on reorganization resulting from business failure
>
> Class financial management of insolvency, of bankruptcy in 658.15
>
> *For internal reorganization, see 658.402*

.162 Mergers

> Class here acquisitions, consolidations, take-overs

.164 Sales

> Class here corporate divestiture

.166 Dissolution

> Class here dissolution resulting from business failure
>
> Class reorganization resulting from business failure in 658.16

.18 Organization of international enterprises

> Including foreign licensing
>
> Class here organization of international business activities
>
> Class initiation of international enterprises and activities in 658.1149

.2 Plant management

> Class procurement of land and buildings in 658.15242
>
> *See Manual at 647 vs. 647.068, 658.2, T1—0682*

.200 1–.200 9 Standard subdivisions

.202 Maintenance management

> Including total productive maintenance

.21 Location

> Class location of businesses in 658.11

.23 Layout

.24 Lighting

.25 Heating, ventilating, air conditioning

.26 Utilities

> Including electricity, gas, power and power distribution, water
>
> Class here comprehensive business works on energy management
>
> *For lighting, see 658.24; for heating, ventilating, air conditioning, see 658.25. For a specific aspect of energy management, see the aspect, e.g., energy management to promote efficiency in production 658.515*

.27   Equipment

Class procurement of industrial equipment associated with plants in 658.15242; class procurement of other kinds of equipment in 658.72

For office equipment, see 651.2; for utilities, see 658.26; for equipment for safety and comfort, see 658.28

.28   Equipment for safety and comfort

Including equipment for noise control, for sanitation

.3   **Personnel management (Human resource management)**

Class interdisciplinary works on industrial relations, on labor in 331

For management of executive personnel, see 658.407

.300 1–.300 7   Standard subdivisions

.300 8   Groups of people

Class here affirmative action, discrimination in employment, equal employment opportunity, workplace diversity

.300 9   History, geographic treatment, biography

.301   Personnel planning and policy

Standard subdivisions are added for either or both topics in heading

.302   Supervision

By immediate supervisors

Class employee development in 658.3124; class personnel management of supervisors in 658.4071245

.303   Personnel management in enterprises of specific sizes

[.303 01–.303 09]   Standard subdivisions

Do not use; class in 658.3001–658.3009

.304   Management of personnel occupying specific types of positions and management of problem employees

.304 4   Management of personnel occupying specific types of positions

Including blue collar and professional employees; sales personnel

For management of office personnel, see 651.30683; for management of supervisors, executive personnel, see 658.407

[.304 401–.304 409]   Standard subdivisions

Do not use; class in 658.3001–658.3009

.304 5   Management of problem employees

Class management of problem employees occupying specific types of positions in 658.3044. Class management of a specific type of problem employee provided for elsewhere with the type, e.g., alcoholic employees 658.300874

.306	Job analysis

Including specifications of qualifications required of personnel in each position

Class here job description, job evaluation, position classification

.31	Elements of personnel management
.311	Recruitment and selection of personnel
.311 1	Recruitment
.311 2	Selection

Including drug testing, handwriting analysis, security clearance, background investigation, use of lie detector

Class here comprehensive works on selection and placement

For placement, see 658.3128

See also 658.383 for payment of moving expenses

.311 24	Interviewing

Class employment interviewing from the job seeker's viewpoint, comprehensive works on employment interviewing in 650.144

.311 25	Testing

Class here aptitude testing

.312	Conditions of employment, performance rating, utilization of personnel

Standard subdivisions are added for conditions of employment, performance rating, utilization of personnel together; for conditions of employment alone

---

> 658.312 1–658.312 4 Conditions of employment

Class comprehensive works in 658.312

For compensation management, see 658.32; for personnel health, safety, welfare, see 658.38

.312 1	Hours

Including workday, overtime; flexible hours, shift work, part-time work; compressed workweek; night, holy day, Sunday, holiday work

Class here workweek

For leave and rest periods, see 658.3122

.312 2	Leave and rest periods (breaks)

Standard subdivisions are added for leave and rest periods together, for leave alone

Including lunch periods and breaks; educational, parental, sabbatical, sick leave

Class here annual leave, holidays, paid vacations

Class absenteeism in 658.314

.312 3	Telecommuting
.312 4	Education and training

Standard subdivisions are added for either or both topics in heading

Including mentoring

Class here employee development

.312 404	Development and administration of training programs

Standard subdivisions are added for either or both topics in heading

Including evaluation of training programs, selection and training of training personnel, teaching methods

.312 42	Orientation

Class here induction

.312 43	In-house work training

Training needed to enable an employee to do his or her job

Including retraining, adjustment to automation

.312 44	Other kinds of training

Including attitude training, literacy training, rehabilitation training, safety training, training in human relations

.312 45	Training of personnel occupying specific types of positions

Including blue collar and professional employees; sales personnel

Class induction and orientation of personnel occupying specific types of positions in 658.31242; class in-house work training of personnel occupying specific types of positions in 658.31243; class other kinds of training regardless of type of position occupied by employee in 658.31244

For training of supervisors, see 658.4071245

[.312 450 1–.312 450 9]	Standard subdivisions

Do not use; class in 658.312401–658.312409

.312 5	Performance rating (Evaluation)

Class here performance standards

.312 8   Utilization of personnel

Including allocation of staff to specific responsibilities, staffing patterns; placement, transfer of employees from one position to another

Class training in 658.3124; class performance rating in 658.3125; class motivation in 658.314; class work teams in 658.4022

.313   Separation from service

Including dismissal for cause

.313 2   Retirement

.313 4   Reduction in force

Class here downsizing

.314   Motivation, morale, discipline

Standard subdivisions are added for any or all topics in heading

Including absenteeism, misconduct, retention, turnover

Class here promotion of creativity, productivity

Class performance rating in 658.3125

.314 2   Incentives

For incentive payments, see 658.3225

.314 22   Job satisfaction

Class job enrichment in 658.31423

.314 23   Job enrichment

.314 24   Promotion

See also 650.14 for how to obtain a promotion (employee's viewpoint)

.314 4   Penalties

Including demotion, fines, reprimands

For dismissal for cause, see 658.313

.314 5   Interpersonal relations

Including informal, day-to-day relations between superiors and subordinates; conflict management, prevention of sexual harassment

Class comprehensive works on employer-employee relationships from a management perspective in 658.315

.315   Employer-employee relationships

Class here labor relations

For informal relations, see 658.3145

.315 2	Employee participation in management
	Including open-book management, worker self-management
	Class industrial democracy in 331.0112; class worker control of industry in 338.6
.315 3	Labor unions and other employee organizations
	Standard subdivisions are added for labor unions and other employee organizations together, for labor unions alone
	For collective bargaining, see 658.3154; for role of employee organizations in grievance procedures, see 658.3155
.315 4	Collective bargaining
	Including arbitration, mediation, negotiation of contracts, strikes
.315 5	Grievance procedures
.32	Compensation management
	Class here wage administration, salary administration
	Class management of labor costs in 658.1553
.321	Payroll administration
	Class clerical techniques involved in maintaining payroll records in 651.37; class payroll accounting procedures in 657.74
.322	Compensation plans
.322 2	Wage and salary scales
	Standard subdivisions are added for either or both topics in heading
	Hourly or other periodic scales
	Including locality pay (weighting), longevity pay, overtime pay, severance pay
.322 5	Incentive compensation
	Including merit awards, merit pay; bonuses, piecework rates, profit sharing
	Class comprehensive works on incentives in 658.3142
.322 59	Employee stock ownership plans
	Class here employee stock options
.325	Employee benefits
	For personnel health, safety, welfare programs and services, see 658.38
.325 3	Pensions
.325 4	Insurance and workers' compensation
.38	Employee health, safety, welfare
	Class comprehensive management works on employee benefits in 658.325

.382	Health and safety programs

Including mental health programs

Class safety of plant and equipment in 658.200289; class safety training in 658.31244; class provision of health and accident insurance in 658.3254; class comprehensive works on safety management in 658.408; class interdisciplinary works on industrial safety in 363.11

.382 2	Programs for substance abuse

Including alcohol abuse and drug abuse programs; drug testing

Class drug testing in employee selection in 658.3112

.383	Economic services

Including discounts, housing, moving expenses, transportation

.385	Counseling services

Including retirement counseling services, vocational guidance services

Class mental health programs and services in 658.382

.4   Executive management

Limited to those activities named below

Class here role, function, powers, position of top and middle management

Class supervision in 658.302; class comprehensive works on management for legal compliance in 658.12. Class a specific executive managerial activity not provided for here with the activity in management, e.g., personnel management 658.3; class application of a specific activity named below in another branch of management with the branch, e.g., production planning 658.503

.400 1–.400 9	Standard subdivisions

>   658.401–658.409   Specific executive management activities

Unless other instructions are given, observe the following table of preference, e.g., planning for change 658.406 (*not* 658.4012):

Personal aspects of executive management	658.409
Management of executive personnel	658.407
Internal organization	658.402
Managing change	658.406
Negotiation, conflict management, crisis management, contracting out	658.405
Planning, policy making, control, quality management	658.401
Decision making and information management	658.403
Social responsibility of executive management	658.408
Project management	658.404

Class comprehensive works in 658.4

For communication, see 658.45; for use of consultants, see 658.46; for business intelligence and security, see 658.47

.401	Planning, policy making, control, quality management
.401 2	Planning and policy making

Standard subdivisions are added for either or both topics in heading

Class here management by objectives, strategic management

Class decision making in 658.403; class forecasting in 658.40355

.401 3	Control and quality management

Standard subdivisions are added for either or both topics in heading

Class here management audits (assessments of management effectiveness), total quality management

Class management audits applied to a specific function with the function, e.g., management audits applied to production management 658.5; class total quality management applied to a specific function with the function, e.g., total quality management in marketing 658.8

See also 657.45 for financial audits; also 658.562 for quality control of products

.402	Internal organization

Including line and staff, functional, departmental organization; decentralization, distribution and delegation of authority and responsibility; internal reorganization

Class sociology of economic institutions in 306.3; class comprehensive management works on organization in 658.1; class comprehensive management works on reorganization in 658.16

For allocation of personnel to specific responsibilities, see 658.3128

See also 302.3 for social interaction within groups

See Manual at 658.04 vs. 658.114, 658.402

.402 2	Work teams

Class here work groups

.403	Decision making and information management

Class here problem solving

.403 001–.403 009	Standard subdivisions
.403 01	Philosophy and theory of decision making
[.403 011]	Systems in decision making

Do not use; class in 658.4032

.403 015	Scientific principles
[.403 015 1]	Mathematical techniques of decision making

Do not use; class in 658.4033

.403 02–.403 09	Standard subdivisions of decision making

.403 2	Systems theory and analysis

Standard subdivisions are added for either or both topics in heading

Including critical path method (CPM), network analysis, program evaluation review technique (PERT)

For decision theory, see 658.40301; for operations research, see 658.4034; for simulation, see 658.40352; for decision analysis, see 658.40354; for forecasting, see 658.40355

.403 3	Mathematical techniques of decision making

Including mathematical programming

Class here econometrics as an aid in decision making

For simulation, see 658.40352

.403 4	Operations research

Including probability theory, queuing theory

Class mathematical methods in 658.4033; class simulation in 658.40352; class games in 658.40353

.403 5	Other techniques of decision making
.403 52	Simulation

Class here models

.403 53	Games
.403 54	Decision analysis
.403 55	Forecasting
.403 6	Group decision making

Class specific techniques of group decision making in 658.4032–658.4035

See also 658.4052 for negotiation

.403 8	Information management

Class here gathering of information by management for use in managerial decision making; information resources, knowledge management

Class communication in 658.45

.403 801 1	Systems

Class here information systems

.404	Project management
.405	Negotiation, conflict management, crisis management, contracting out
.405 2	Negotiation

See also 658.4036 for group decision making

.405 3	Conflict management
.405 6	Crisis management
.405 8	Contracting out

Contracting for services

Class here subcontracting

Class contracting out a particular managerial service with the service in 658, e.g., personnel management 658.3; class contracting out a particular nonmanagerial service with the service, plus notation 0684 from Table 1, e.g., contracting out hospital care 362.110684

See also 658.723 for contracting for materials

.406   Managing change

Class here expansion, modernization

Class comprehensive works on reorganization of enterprises in 658.16

For internal reorganization, see 658.402. For managing change in a specific branch of management, see the branch, e.g., changes in production 658.5

.406 2   Externally induced change

Including technological innovations

.406 3   Innovation by management

Including corporate turnarounds

Class here reengineering

.407   Management of executive personnel

Add to base number 658.407 the numbers following 658.3 in 658.31–658.38, e.g., training of supervisors 658.4071245

.408   Social responsibility of executive management

Class here comprehensive works on safety management

Class managing welfare services for employees in 658.38; class managing welfare services for people other than employees in 361.7; class interdisciplinary works on safety in 363.1

For a specific aspect of safety management, see the aspect, e.g., product safety 658.56

See Manual at 363.1

.408 3   Protection of environment

Class interdisciplinary works on protection of environment in 363.7

.409   Personal aspects of executive management

Class here success as an executive

Class general success in business in 650.1

.409 2   Executive leadership

.409 3	Time management

Class here personal efficiency (management by executives of their own time and work)

.409 4	Personal characteristics of executives

Including creative ability

.409 5	The management environment

Including interpersonal relations, job stress, social pressures

.42	Top management

Class initiation of business enterprises in 658.11; class comprehensive works on top and middle management in 658.4

For a specific activity of top management, see the activity, e.g., decision making by top management 658.403

.421	Entrepreneurial management

Class management of small business in 658.022

.422	Boards of directors

Class here boards of trustees

.43	Middle management
.45	Communication

As a technique of management

Class mechanics of communication in 651.7

See Manual at 658.45 vs. 651.7, 808.06665

.452	Oral communication

Class here business presentations

See also 808.51 for techniques of public speaking

.453	Written communication
.455	Informational programs

Including bulletin boards, house organs

Class here communication of information by management in order to guide people and control activities

See also 658.4038 for gathering of information by management for use in managerial decision making

.456	Meetings

Class interdisciplinary works on meetings in 060; class general rules of order in 060.42

.46   **Use of consultants**

Class here techniques of management consulting

For use of consultants in a specific branch of management, see the branch, e.g., use of consultants in market research 658.83

.47   **Business security and intelligence**

Standard subdivisions are added for business security and intelligence together, for business security alone

Class insurance in 658.153

.472   **Business intelligence, and security of information and ideas**

Standard subdivisions are added for any or all topics in heading

Class here industrial espionage, countering industrial espionage, trade secrets

For security of information stored in computers, see 658.478

.473   **Physical security**

Including protection from fraud, theft, violence

Class here crime prevention

For protection against fires and other disasters, see 658.477; for physical security of computers, see 658.478

.477   **Protection against fires and other disasters**

.478   **Computer security**

Class here data security

Class comprehensive works on security of information in 658.472; class interdisciplinary works on computer security in 005.8

.5   **Management of production**

Class here production management in manufacturing enterprises, production management in service industries, comprehensive works on logistics

Class marketing in 658.8; class comprehensive works on energy management in 658.26

For materials handling, see 658.781; for physical distribution, see 658.788; for factory operations engineering, see 670.42. For production management in enterprises engaged in a specific kind of activity other than manufacturing, see the activity, plus notation 0685 from Table 1, e.g., management of agricultural production 630.685

.500 1–.500 9   **Standard subdivisions**

.503   **General production planning**

.503 6   **Decision making and use of information**

Standard subdivisions are added for either or both topics in heading

.503 8	Product planning
	Including diversification
	Class marketing in 658.8
	For new product development, see 658.575
.51	Organization of production
	For sequencing, see 658.53; for work studies, see 658.54
.514	Use of technology
	Including automation, man-machine ratios, modernization, technological innovations
	See also 658.577 for development of technology
.515	Promotion of efficiency
	For use of technology, see 658.514
.53	Sequencing
	Including dispatching, routing
	Class here scheduling, workflow
.533	Kinds of sequences
	Including assembly-line, team methods
.54	Work studies
	Including work load
.542	Time and motion studies
.542 1	Time studies
.542 3	Motion studies
.544	Fatigue and monotony studies
	Standard subdivisions are added for either or both topics in heading
.56	Product control, packaging; waste control and utilization
	Including product liability, recall, safety
	Class product planning in 658.5038; class product design in 658.5752; class comprehensive works on safety management in 658.408
.562	Quality control
	Class comprehensive works on quality control in 658.4013
	For inspection, see 658.568

.564	**Packaging**

Including labeling

Class here interdisciplinary works on packaging

> *For storage containers, see 658.785; for packing for shipment, see 658.7884; for use of packaging in sales promotion, see 658.823; for packaging technology, see 688.8*

.567	**Waste control and utilization**

Standard subdivisions are added for either or both topics in heading

.568	**Inspection**

Class comprehensive works on quality control in production management in 658.562

.57	**Research and development (R and D)**

Standard subdivisions are added for research and development together, for research alone

.571	**Fundamental research**
.575	**New product development**

> *For decisions to develop new products, see 658.5038; for market research on new products, see 658.83*

.575 2	**Product design**
.577	**Equipment and process research**

Standard subdivisions are added for either or both topics in heading

.7	**Management of materials**

Class here management of supplies

Class comprehensive works on energy management in 658.26; class comprehensive works on logistics in 658.5

> *For management of office supplies, see 651.29*

.72	**Procurement**

Acquisition of equipment, materials, parts, subassemblies, supplies, tools

Class here procurement of office equipment and supplies, comprehensive works on procurement

Class management of costs of materials in 658.1553

> *For procurement of land, buildings, associated industrial equipment, see 658.15242*

.722	**Vendor selection**
.723	**Contracts**

Class here negotiation of contracts

Class contracting out, subcontracting for services in 658.4058

.728	Receiving
.78	Internal control of materials and physical distribution
.781	Materials handling
.785	Storage

> Including storage containers
>
> Class here warehouse management
>
> Class location of warehouses in 658.21

.787	Inventory control

> Class here stock control
>
> Class financial control of inventories in 658.15244
>
> *For receiving, see 658.728; for storage, see 658.785*

.788	Physical distribution

> Class here shipment
>
> Class internal movement of materials in 658.781

.788 2	Transportation management

> Selection of carrier and routing

.788 4	Packing for shipment

> Class interdisciplinary works on packaging in 658.564

.788 5	Loading and unloading

> Standard subdivisions are added for either or both topics in heading

.8   Management of marketing

> Class here management of distribution; management of marketing goods, marketing services; management of merchandising
>
> Class product design in 658.5752; class comprehensive works on logistics in 658.5
>
> *For physical distribution, see 658.788; for advertising and public relations, see 659*

.800 1	Philosophy and theory
[.800 11]	Systems

> Do not use; class in 658.802

.800 19	Psychological principles

> *For consumer psychology, see 658.8342*

.800 2–.800 6	Standard subdivisions
.800 7	Education, research, related topics

.800 72	Research

For market research, see 658.83

.800 8–.800 9	Standard subdivisions
.802	General topics of marketing management

Including communication in marketing, green marketing, market segmentation

Class application of general topics to marketing to specific kinds of buyers in 658.804

.804	Marketing to specific kinds of buyers

Including governments and their agencies, hospitals; key accounts

Class here industrial marketing

Class consumer research in 658.834

For marketing to foreign buyers, see 658.84

.804 01–.804 09	Standard subdivisions of industrial marketing

Do not use for marketing to specific kinds of buyers; class in 658.8001–658.8009

.81	Sales management

Class management of sales personnel in 658.3044

For sales promotion, see 658.82

.810 01	Philosophy and theory
.810 011 2	Forecasting and forecasts

Do not use for sales forecasting; class in 658.818

.810 02–.810 09	Standard subdivisions
.810 1	Sales planning

For market research, see 658.83

.810 2	Organization of sales force

Including organization by area, by product, by type of customer, by key accounts

.810 6	Sales meetings

Class comprehensive management works on business meetings in 658.456

.812	Customer relations

Including claims, complaints, returns, servicing of products

.816	Pricing
.818	Sales forecasting

.82	Sales promotion

Including use of coupons, discounts, gifts, prizes, samples, trading stamps

For servicing of products, see 658.812; for use of credit to promote sales, see 658.88

.823	Use of packaging

Class interdisciplinary works on packaging in 658.564

.827	Use of brands and trademarks

Standard subdivisions are added for either or both topics in heading

Including business names; producer and distributor brands

.83	Market research

Class here market analysis, market study; interviewing, use of consultants and research agencies, techniques of consulting in market research

Unless other instructions are given, class a subject with aspects in two or more subdivisions of 658.83 in the number coming first, e.g., research in Germany on consumer preferences 658.83430943 (*not* 658.83943)

Class results of market research in 381–382

For sales forecasting, see 658.818

[.830 9]	History, geographic treatment, biography

Do not use; class in 658.839

.834	Consumer research
.834 019	Psychological principles

Do not use for consumer psychology; class in 658.8342

.834 2	Consumer behavior

Including motivation research

Class here consumer psychology

For consumer attitudes, preferences, reactions, see 658.8343

.834 3	Consumer attitudes, preferences, reactions

Standard subdivisions are added for any or all topics in heading

Including brand preferences, consumer satisfaction

.839	History, geographic treatment, biography
.839 01–.839 05	Historical periods

Add to base number 658.8390 the numbers following —090 in notation 0901–0905 from Table 1, e.g., market research 2000–2009 658.8390511

.839 1–.839 9	Geographic treatment and biography

Add to base number 658.839 notation 1–9 from Table 2, e.g., market research in Germany 658.83943

.84   **Export marketing**

.85   **Personal selling**

> Techniques for the individual, Regardless of channel
>
> Class here personal salesmanship

.86   **Wholesale marketing**

> Class personal selling through wholesale channels in 658.85; class wholesale marketing through specific channels in 658.87. Class management of enterprises doing wholesale marketing of a specific type of product with the product in 381.4, plus notation 068 from Table 1, e.g., management of wholesale food marketing 381.4564130068, financial management of wholesale food marketing 381.45641300681

.87   **Marketing channels**

> Including consumer cooperatives, managing producers' cooperatives; convenience stores, shopping centers; fairs, markets; garage, yard sales
>
> Class here marketing through specific wholesale channels, marketing through retail channels; comprehensive works on marketing channels
>
> Class personal selling through specific channels, e.g., personal selling by telephone, in 658.85; class comprehensive works on wholesale marketing in 658.86; class direct-mail advertising in 659.133. Class management of enterprises selling a specific type of product with the product in 381.4, plus notation 068 from Table 1, e.g., management of bookstores 381.45002068, financial management of bookstores 381.450020681; class a specific aspect of managing chain stores, outlet stores, franchise businesses if there is no emphasis on a specific kind of product with the kind of store or business in 658.8702–658.8708, plus notation 0681–0687 from Table 1, e.g., financial management of chain stores 658.87020681; class a specific aspect of managing enterprises in a specific channel if there is no emphasis on a specific kind of product with the channel in 658.871–658.879, plus notation 0681–0687 from Table 1, e.g., financial management of department stores 658.8710681
>
> *For export marketing, see 658.84*

.870 01–.870 09   Standard subdivisions

.870 2   Chain stores

> Including voluntary retail chains
>
> Class chain department stores in 658.871

.870 5   Outlet stores

> Class here discount stores that are outlet stores, factory outlets, manufacturers' outlets, wholesale outlets

.870 8   Franchise businesses

.871   **Department stores**

> Class department stores that are discount stores or superstores in 658.879

.872 Telemarketing and direct marketing

> Standard subdivisions are added for either or both topics in heading

> Class here catalog, mail-order, online, telephone-order marketing; direct-mail marketing, direct selling, multilevel marketing, pyramid marketing; television selling

>> *See also 659.143 for television advertising; also 659.144 for online advertising*

.877 Auctions

[.877 028 5] Computer applications

> Do not use; class in 658.8777

.877 7 Online auctions

.879 Discount stores

> Including customer, warehouse, wholesale clubs

> Class here supermarkets that are not predominantly food stores; hypermarkets, superstores

> Class discount stores that are outlet stores in 658.8705

>> *For management of food retailing in supermarkets, see 381.4564130068*

.88 Credit management

> Limited to credit extended by seller to buyer

> Including collections, credit investigations

> Class comprehensive works on management of financial operations in 658.152. Class credit management by banks and other financial institutions with the institution or type of credit in 332, plus notation 0685 from Table 1, e.g., management of loans issued by commercial banks 332.17530685

.882 Mercantile credit management

.883 Consumer credit management

> Class here retail credit management

(.9) **Management of enterprises engaged in specific fields of activity**

> (Optional number; prefer specific subject, plus notation 068 from Table 1)

(.91) Enterprises other than those engaged in extraction, manufacturing, construction

> (Optional number; prefer specific subject, plus notation 068 from Table 1)

> Add to base number 658.91 notation 001–999, e.g., management of banks 658.913321; however, for management of election campaigns, see 324.7

(.92–.99)   Enterprises engaged in extraction, manufacturing, construction

> (Optional number; prefer specific subject, plus notation 068 from Table 1)

> Add to base number 658.9 the numbers following 6 in 620–690, e.g., management of mines 658.922

659   Advertising and public relations

> Class here publicity

.1   Advertising

> *See also 658.81 for sales management; also 658.85 for personal selling*

.104   Special topics of advertising

.104 2   Social aspects of advertising

> Class social aspects of use of specific images and themes in advertising in 659.10452–659.10459, e.g., social aspects of images of women in advertising 659.1045522

.104 5   Use of images and themes in advertising

> Standard subdivisions are added for either or both topics in heading

> Class here iconography of advertising

> Add to base number 659.1045 the numbers following —3 in notation 32–39 from Table 3C, e.g., use of images of women in advertising 659.1045522, use of sports themes in advertising 659.1045579

.11   General topics of advertising

> Class application of general topics to advertising in specific media in 659.13; class application of general topics to specific kinds of advertising in 659.131; class application of general topics to advertising specific kinds of organizations, products, services in 659.19

.111   Planning and control

> Standard subdivisions are added for either or both topics in heading

.112   Organization

> Managerial organization only

> *See also 338.7616591 for economics and history of advertising organizations*

.112 2   Advertising departments

.112 5   Advertising agencies

.113   Advertising campaigns

.13   Kinds of advertising and advertising in specific media

> Class advertising of specific kinds of organizations, products, services in a specific kind of medium in 659.19

> *For advertising in electronic media, see 659.14; for display advertising, see 659.15; for contests and lotteries, see 659.17*

.131	Kinds of advertising

Including classified advertising, specialty advertising

Class advertising of specific kinds of organizations, products, services by a specific kind of advertising in 659.19. Class a specific kind of advertising in a specific medium with the medium, e.g., classified advertising in print media 659.132, online classified advertising 659.144

.131 2	National advertising
.131 4	Retail advertising
.131 5	Industrial advertising

Class here business-to-business advertising

See also 659.19 for advertising specific kinds of organizations, products, services

.132	Advertising in print media

Including directory advertising

For direct advertising, see 659.133

.133	Direct advertising

Printed advertising delivered or handed directly to consumer

Including circulars, letters, mail-order catalogs; direct-mail advertising

Class direct-mail marketing in 658.872; class online advertising in 659.144

.134	Advertising by location of media

For point-of-sale advertising, see 659.157

.134 2	Outdoor advertising

Including billboards, roadside signs

Class outdoor transportation advertising in 659.1344

For advertising by electric signs, see 659.136

.134 4	Transportation advertising

Including airplane banners, car cards, traveling displays on exteriors of vehicles, station posters

.136	Advertising by electric signs
.14	Advertising in electronic media

Including advertising in motion pictures

Class advertising of specific kinds of organizations, products, services, issues in a specific electronic medium in 659.19

.142	Radio
.143	Television

See also 658.872 for television selling

.144   Advertising in digital media

> Class here online advertising, advertising in social media

> *See also 658.872 for online marketing, search engine optimization*

.15   Display advertising

.152   Exhibitions and shows

> Standard subdivisions are added for either or both topics in heading

> Including fashion modeling

> Class interdisciplinary works on fashion modeling in 746.92

.157   Point-of-sale advertising

> Including counter, showcase, window displays

.17   Advertising by contests and lotteries

> Standard subdivisions are added for either or both topics in heading

> *See also 659.19790134 for advertising of contests; also 659.1979538 for advertising of lotteries*

.19   Advertising specific kinds of organizations, products, services

> Class here advertising to influence behavior or public opinion with respect to specific subjects; advertising specific kinds of organizations, products, services in a specific kind of medium; advertising specific kinds of organizations, products, services by a specific kind of advertising

[.190 001–.190 009]   Standard subdivisions

> Do not use; class in 659.101–659.109

.190 01–.199 99   Subdivisions for specific kinds of organizations, products, services

> Add to base number 659.19 notation 001–999, e.g., library advertising 659.1902, traffic safety advertising 659.19363125, advertising pharmaceutical drugs 659.196151; however, for advertising for political election campaigns, see 324.73

.2   Public relations

.28   Public relations in enterprises of specific forms

> Class public relations in enterprises producing specific kinds of products and services, or pursuing specific objectives, regardless of form of enterprise in 659.29

[.280 1–.280 9]   Standard subdivisions

> Do not use; class in 659.201–659.209

.281–.289   Subdivisions for enterprises of specific forms

> Add to base number 659.28 the numbers following 658.04 in 658.041–658.049, e.g., corporations 659.285

.29   Public relations in organizations producing specific kinds of products and services, or pursuing specific objectives

[.290 001–.290 009]   Standard subdivisions

> Do not use; class in 659.201–659.209

.290 01–.299 99   Subdivisions for organizations producing specific kinds of products and services, or pursuing specific objectives

> Add to base number 659.29 notation 001–999, e.g., public relations for computer industry 659.29004, public relations for lobbying in general 659.293244, public relations for public welfare lobbying 659.293616; however, for public relations in libraries, see 021.7; for public relations for religion, see 200; for public relations for conduct of political election campaigns, see 324.7; for public relations for government, see 352.748; for public relations for armed forces, see 355.342

660   Chemical engineering and related technologies

> Standard subdivisions are added for chemical engineering and related technologies together, for chemical engineering alone

Class military applications in 623

> *For pharmaceutical chemistry, see 615.19; for pulp and paper technology, see 676; for elastomers and elastomer products, see 678*

.01   Philosophy and theory

.011 5   Theory of communication and control

> Do not use for process control; class in 660.2815

.02   Miscellany

[.028 4]   Apparatus, equipment, materials

> Do not use for materials; class in 660.282. Do not use for apparatus and equipment; class in 660.283

[.028 9]   Safety measures

> Do not use; class in 660.2804

.03   Dictionaries, encyclopedias, concordances

.04   Chemical technologies of specific states of matter

> Add to base number 660.04 the numbers following 530.4 in 530.41–530.44, e.g., plasma technology 660.044

> Class industrial gases in 665.7

.05–.09   Standard subdivisions

.2   General topics in chemical engineering

> *For biochemical engineering, see 660.63; for industrial stoichiometry, see 660.7*

.28   Specific types of chemical plant and specific activities in chemical plants

.280 01–.280 09   Standard subdivisions

.280 4   Safety measures

> *See also 363.179 for interdisciplinary works on hazardous chemicals*

> *See Manual at 604.7 vs. 660.2804*

.280 7   Specific types of chemical plant

.280 71   Bench-scale plants

.280 72   Pilot plants

.280 73   Full-scale plants

>   660.281–660.283   Process and materials

> Class specific applications in unit operations in 660.2842; class specific applications in unit processes in 660.2844; class comprehensive works in 660.28

.281   Process design, assembly, control

.281 2   Process design

.281 5   Process control

> Class here computerized process control

> Unless it is redundant, add to base number 660.2815 the numbers following 00 in 004–006, e.g., use of digital personal computers 660.2815416, but use of digital computers 660.2815 (*not* 660.28154)

> Class interdisciplinary works on computerized process control in 629.895

.282   Materials

.283   Process equipment

> Including piping

> Class computer equipment in process control in 660.2815; class interdisciplinary works on piping in 621.8672; class interdisciplinary works on pressure vessels in 681.76041

.283 04   Control of corrosion

> Class interdisciplinary works on corrosion in 620.11223

.283 2   Chemical reactors

.284   Unit operations and unit processes

.284 2   Unit operations

> Unit operations: operations basically physical

> Class here separation processes; transport phenomena engineering

.284 22   Crushing, grinding, screening

.284 23	Mass transfer

Including absorption, gas chromatography

For precipitation, filtration, solvent extraction, see 660.28424; for fractional distillation, see 660.28425

.284 235	Adsorption
.284 24	Precipitation, filtration, solvent extraction
.284 245	Filtration
.284 248	Solvent extraction
.284 25	Fractional distillation
.284 26	Evaporative and drying processes

For dehumidification of air and gas, see 660.28429

.284 27	Heat transfer

Class a specific heat transfer process with the process, e.g., melting 660.284296

.284 29	Other unit operations

Including dehumidification of air and gas

.284 292	Momentum transfer and fluidization

Including mixing

.284 293	Humidification
.284 296	Melting
.284 298	Crystallization
.284 4	Unit processes

Operations basically chemical

For polymerization, see 668.92

.284 43	Oxidation-reduction reaction (Redox reaction)

Including hydrogenation

Class here oxidation, reduction

.284 49	Fermentation
.29	Applied physical chemistry

Add to base number 660.29 the numbers following 541.3 in 541.33–541.39, e.g., catalytic reactions 660.2995; however, for absorption, see 660.28423; for adsorption, see 660.284235; for synthesis (e.g., addition, condensation, hydrolysis, oxidation, reduction) and name reactions, see 660.2844; for polymerization, see 668.92

.6   **Biotechnology**

> Application of living organisms or their biological systems or processes to the manufacture of useful products

> *See also 620.82 for human factors engineering*

.62   Industrial microbiology

> Class a specific aspect of industrial microbiology with the aspect, e.g., fermentation 660.28449, use of microorganisms in biochemical engineering 660.63

.63   Biochemical engineering

.634   Enzyme technology

.65   Genetic engineering

.7   **Industrial stoichiometry**

661   **Technology of industrial chemicals**

> Production of chemicals used as raw materials or reagents in manufacture of other products

> *For industrial gases, see 665.7*

.001–.009   Standard subdivisions

>   661.03–661.08   Inorganic compounds

> Class acids, bases, salts in 661.2–661.6; class comprehensive works in 661

.03   Metallic compounds

> Class here alkali and alkaline-earth compounds

> Add to base number 661.03 the numbers following 546.3 in 546.38–546.39, e.g., sodium compounds 661.0382

> *For metallic compounds other than those of alkali and alkaline-earth metals, see 661.04–661.07*

.04–.07   Other inorganic compounds

> Add to base number 661.0 the numbers following 546 in 546.4–546.7, e.g., sulfur compounds 661.0723

> *For hydrogen compounds, see 661.08*

.08   Hydrogen compounds

> Including heavy water (deuterium oxide), hydrides

.1   **Nonmetallic elements**

> *For carbon, see 662.9; for gaseous elements, see 665.8*

>   **661.2–661.6 Acids, bases, salts**

      Class organic acids, bases, salts in 661.8; class comprehensive works in 661

.2   **Acids**

.22   Sulfuric acid

.23   Hydrochloric acid

.24   Nitric acid

.25   Phosphoric acid

.3   **Bases**

      Class here alkalis

.32   Sodas

.322   Caustic soda (Sodium hydroxide)

.323   Sodium bicarbonate

.324   Sodium carbonate

.33   Potassium alkalis

.332   Caustic potash (Potassium hydroxide)

.333   Potassium bicarbonate

.334   Potassium carbonate

      Class here comprehensive works on potash

        For a specific potash compound other than potassium carbonate, see the compound, e.g., caustic potash 661.332

.34   Ammonia and ammonium hydroxide

      Standard subdivisions are added for ammonia and ammonium hydroxide together, for ammonia alone

.35   Other alkalis

      Including hydroxides and carbonates of cesium, francium, lithium, rubidium, alkaline-earth metals

.4   **Salts**

      For ammonium salts, see 661.5; for sulfur and nitrogen salts, see 661.6

.42   Halogen salts

      Including chlorides, chlorites, chlorates, corresponding salts of other halogens

.43   Phosphorus and silicon salts

      Including phosphides, phosphites, phosphates, corresponding salts of silicon

.5   **Ammonium salts**

.6   **Sulfur and nitrogen salts**

>   *For ammonium salts, see 661.5*

.63   Sulfur salts

>   Including sulfides, sulfites, sulfates

>   *For plaster of paris, see 666.92*

.65   Nitrogen salts

>   Including nitrides, nitrites, nitrates

.8   **Organic chemicals**

.800 1–.800 9   Standard subdivisions

> 661.802–661.804 Derived chemicals

>   Class derived special-purpose chemicals in 661.806–661.808; class comprehensive works in 661.8

.802   Cellulose derivatives

.803   Coal tar chemicals

.804   Petrochemicals

>   Industrial chemicals produced from petroleum or natural gas

>   Class comprehensive works on petrochemicals in 665.538

>   *For a specific petrochemical, see the chemical, e.g., alcohols 661.82, carbon black 662.93*

.805   Synthetic chemicals

> 661.806–661.808 Special-purpose chemicals

>   Class comprehensive works in 661.8

.806   Essential oils

>   Class essential oils used for manufacture of perfumes in 668.54

.807   Solvents, diluents, extenders

.808   Photographic chemicals and photosensitive surfaces

>   Including sensitometry

>   Class here comprehensive works on chemical engineering of organic and inorganic photographic chemicals

>   *For inorganic photographic chemicals, see 661.1–661.6*

.81   Hydrocarbons

.814   Aliphatic hydrocarbons

.815   Alicyclic hydrocarbons

.816   Aromatic hydrocarbons

>   661.82–661.89 Compounds based on specific elements other than carbon

Add to each subdivision identified by * the numbers following 661.81 in 661.814–661.816, e.g., aliphatic esters 661.834

Unless other instructions are given, observe the following table of preference, e.g., phosphoric acids 661.87 (*not* 661.86):

Sulfur compounds	661.896
Phosphorus compounds	661.87
Silicon compounds	661.88
Organometallic compounds	661.895
Nitrogen compounds	661.894
Oxy and hydroxy compounds	661.82–661.86
Halogenated compounds	661.891

Class comprehensive works in 661.8

>   661.82–661.86 Oxy and hydroxy compounds

Class comprehensive works in 661.8

.82   *Alcohols and phenols

For glycerin, see 668.2

.83   *Esters

.84   *Ethers

.85   *Aldehydes and ketones

Subdivisions are added for either or both topics in heading

.86   *Acids

.87   *Phosphorus compounds

.88   *Silicon compounds

.89   Other organic compounds

.891   *Halogenated compounds

.894   *Nitrogen compounds

.895   *Organometallic compounds

.896   *Sulfur compounds

662   Technology of explosives, fuels, related products

.1   **Fireworks (Pyrotechnics)**

---

*Add as instructed under 661.82–661.89

.2   **Explosives**

> Class nuclear explosives in 621.48
>
> *For fireworks, see 662.1*

.26   Propellants

> Including black powder (gunpowder), cordite, flashless and coated powders, nitrocellulose (guncotton), smokeless powder
>
> Class here low (deflagrating) explosives
>
> *For rocket propellants, see 662.666*

.27   High explosives

> Including dynamite, PETN (pentaerythritol tetranitrate); primary explosives, e.g., mercury fulminate

.4   **Detonators**

> Including boosters, firing mechanisms, fuses, percussion caps, primers
>
> Class explosives used in detonators in 662.27

.5   **Matches**

.6   **Fuels**

> Class industrial oils, fats, waxes, gases as fuels in 665
>
> *For a specific fuel not provided for here, see the fuel, e.g., nuclear fuels 621.48335, biomasss as fuel 662.88, petroleum 665.5*
>
> *See also 621.4023 for combustion of fuels*
>
> *See Manual at 622.22, 622.7 vs. 662.6, 669*

.602 86   Green technology (Environmental technology)

> Class wastes as fuels, comprehensive works on chemical technology of energy from waste materials in 662.87

.62   Coal

> *For coke, see 662.72*

[.620 287]   Testing and measurement

> Do not use; class in 662.622

.622   Properties, tests, analysis

.622 09   History and biography

> Do not use for properties, tests, analysis of coal from specific places; class in 662.6229

.622 1–.622 5   Properties, tests, analysis of specific types of coal

> Add to base number 662.622 the numbers following 553.2 in 553.21–553.25, e.g., analysis of bituminous coal 662.6224

.622 9	Properties, tests, analysis of coal from specific places

Add to base number 662.6229 notation 1–9 from Table 2, e.g., properties of Virginia coal 662.6229755

Class specific types of coal regardless of place in 662.6221–662.6225

.623	Treatment of coal

Including desulfurization, sizing, washing; conversion to slurry, slurry dewatering

.624	Storage, transportation, distribution of coal
.625	Uses of coal

Including as a fuel, as a raw material

Class a specific use with the use, e.g., metallurgical use 669.81

.65	Wood and wood derivatives

Standard subdivisions are added for wood and wood derivatives together, for wood alone

Including sawdust, wood briquettes

For charcoal, see 662.74

.66	Synthetic fuels

Class synthetic fuel gases in 665.77

.662	Synthetic petroleum
.662 2	Production of synthetic petroleum through hydrogenation and liquefaction of coal

Including Bergius process

Class production from coal gas in 662.6623

.662 3	Production of synthetic petroleum through hydrogenation of carbonaceous gases

Including Fischer-Tropsch processes

.666	Rocket fuels (Rocket propellants)

Liquid and solid

.669	Other liquid fuels

Including benzene from waste products

.669 2	Alcohol as fuel

Including ethanol, gasohol, methanol

.7	**Coke and charcoal**
.72	Coke
.74	Charcoal
.8	**Other fuels**

.82   Colloidal and mud fuels

.86   Boron fuels

.87   Wastes as fuels

> Class here comprehensive works on the chemical technology of energy from waste materials
>
> Class waste biomass as fuel in 662.88; class interdisciplinary works on energy from waste materials in 333.7938
>
> > *For a specific form of energy from waste materials, see the form, e.g., benzene made from waste products 662.669*

.88   Biomass as fuel

> Including bagasse
>
> Class here plant biomass as fuel, comprehensive works on the chemical technology of biomass as fuel
>
> Class interdisciplinary works on biomass as fuel in 333.9539
>
> > *For wood and wood derivatives as fuels, see 662.65; for biodiesel fuel, see 665.37*
> >
> > *See also 665.776 for gases manufactured from biological wastes*

.9   **Nonfuel carbons**

.92   Graphite and graphite products

> Standard subdivisions are added for graphite and graphite products together, for graphite alone

.93   Adsorbent carbons

> Including activated carbons, adsorbent charcoals, animal black, bone char, carbon black, decolorizing carbons, lampblack

663   Beverage technology

> Commercial preparation, preservation, packaging
>
> Class household preparation of beverages in 641.87; class interdisciplinary works on beverages in 641.2

.1   **Alcoholic beverages**

> > *For wine, see 663.2; for brewed and malted beverages, see 663.3; for distilled liquor, see 663.5*

.102 84   Apparatus and equipment

> Do not use for materials; class in 663.11

.11   Materials

.12   Preliminary preparations

.13   Fermentation

.14   Packing

.15	Refrigeration and pasteurization
.16	Distillation
.17	Aging
.19	Bottling

.2   Wine

Class here grape wine, comprehensive works on white and red wine, comprehensive works on specific white and red wines (specific brands, estate wines)

See also 663.4 for mead; also 663.49 for rice wine

.200 1	Philosophy and theory
.200 2	Miscellany
.200 284	Apparatus and equipment

Do not use for materials; class in 663.201

| .200 3–.200 9 | Standard subdivisions |
| .201–.209 | Materials, processes, operations |

Add to base number 663.20 the numbers following 663.1 in 663.11–663.19, e.g., fermentation 663.203

.22   Kinds of grape wine

Including ice wine

| [.220 1–.220 9] | Standard subdivisions |

Do not use; class in 663.2001–663.2009

.222   White wine

Class here specific white wines (specific brands, estate wines, varietals)

Class comprehensive works on white and red wine in 663.2; class white ice wine in 663.22

For sparkling white wine, see 663.224; for fortified white wine, see 663.226

.223   Red wine

Class here specific red wines (specific brands, estate wines, varietals)

Class red ice wine in 663.22

For sparkling red wine, see 663.224; for fortified red wine, see 663.226

.223 2   Rosé wine

Class here specific rosé wines (specific brands, estate wines, varietals)

.224   Sparkling wine

> Class here specific sparkling wines (specific brands, estate wines, varietals)

> Class comprehensive works on white wine in 663.222; class comprehensive works on red wine in 663.223

.226   Fortified wine

> Class here specific fortified wines (specific brands, estate wines, varietals)

> Class comprehensive works on white wine in 663.222; class comprehensive works on red wine in 663.223

.29   Nongrape wine

> Including fermented cider

.3   **Brewed and malted beverages**

> Standard subdivisions are added for either or both topics in heading

> *For specific kinds of brewed and malted beverages, see 663.4*

.302 84   Apparatus and equipment

> Do not use for materials; class in 663.31

.31–.39   Materials, processes, operations

> Add to base number 663.3 the numbers following 663.1 in 663.11–663.19, e.g., fermentation 663.33

.4   **Specific kinds of brewed and malted beverages**

> Including mead (honey wine)

> Class malt whiskey in 663.52

.42   Beer and ale

> Standard subdivisions are added for either or both topics in heading

.49   Rice wine; pulque

> Standard subdivisions are added for rice wine and pulque together, for rice wine alone

> Class here specific kinds of rice wine

.5   **Distilled liquor**

> Including mescal, potato whiskey, tequila, vodka

.500 1   Philosophy and theory

.500 2   Miscellany

.500 284   Apparatus and equipment

> Do not use for materials; class in 663.501

.500 3–.500 9   Standard subdivisions

.501–.509	Materials, processes, operations

Add to base number 663.50 the numbers following 663.1 in 663.11–663.19, e.g., distillation 663.506

.52	Whiskey

Including bourbon

Class potato whiskey in 663.5

.53	Brandy

.55	Compound liquors

Distilled spirits flavored with various seeds, roots, leaves, flowers, fruits

Including cordials (liqueurs), gin

.59	Rum

.6	**Nonalcoholic beverages**

Including fruit drinks

For nonalcoholic brewed beverages, see 663.9; for milk, see 637.1

.61	Bottled drinking water

Including carbonated water

Class here potable mineral water

.62	Carbonated and mineralized beverages

Standard subdivisions are added for carbonated and mineralized beverages together, for carbonated beverages alone

Class carbonated and mineralized water in 663.61

.63	Fruit and vegetable juices

Standard subdivisions are added for fruit and vegetable juices together, for fruit juices alone

Class here drinks in which the principal ingredient is juice

Class fermented cider in 663.2; class fruit drinks in 663.6; class carbonated juices in 663.62

.64	Milk substitutes

Including coconut milk, nondairy coffee whiteners, soybean milk

.9   **Nonalcoholic brewed beverages**

Add to each subdivision identified by * as follows:

0284	Apparatus and equipment
	Do not use for materials; class in notation 1 from this table
1	Materials
2	Preliminary preparations
3	Fermentation and oxidation
4	Firing, roasting, curing
5	Blending
7	Specific varieties
8	Concentrates
9	Packaging

.92   *Cocoa and chocolate

Subdivisions are added for either or both topics in heading

.93   *Coffee

.94   *Tea

.96   Herb teas

Including catnip, maté, sassafras

.97   Coffee substitutes

Including acorns, cereal preparations, chicory

664   Food technology

Commercial preparation, preservation, packaging

Class here comprehensive works on commercial food and beverage technology

Class household preservation, storage, cooking in 641.4–641.8; class interdisciplinary works on food in 641.3

For commercial processing of dairy and related products, see 637; for commercial beverage technology, see 663

.001   Philosophy and theory

.001 15   Theory of communication and control

Do not use for process control; class in 664.02

.001 5   Scientific principles

.001 579   Microorganisms, fungi, algae

Class here comprehensive works on microbiology in food technology

Class interdisciplinary works on food microbiology in 641.3001579

For fermentation, food processing with microorganisms, see 664.024

*Add as instructed under 663.9

.002	Miscellany
.002 84	Apparatus and equipment
	Do not use for materials; class in 664.01
[.002 87]	Testing and measurement
	Do not use; class in 664.07
.003–.009	Standard subdivisions
.01	Materials
	For additives, see 664.06
.02	Processes
	Class here process design, control, equipment
.022	Extraction
.023	Refining
.024	Manufacturing processes
	Not provided for elsewhere
	Including fermentation, food biotechnology, food processing with microorganisms
.028	Preservation techniques
	Class here interdisciplinary works on food preservation
	For home preservation of foods, see 641.4
.028 1	Preliminary treatment
	Including peeling
.028 2	Canning
.028 4	Drying and dehydrating
	Standard subdivisions are added for either or both topics in heading
.028 42	Drying and dehydrating by slow, thermal processes
.028 43	Drying and dehydrating through pulverizing and flaking
.028 45	Drying and dehydrating by freeze-drying
.028 5	Low-temperature preservation techniques
	For freeze-drying, see 664.02845
.028 52	Cold storage
.028 53	Deep freezing
.028 6	Chemical preservation
	Including brining, pickling, smoking
	For chemical preservation by use of additives, see 664.0287

.028 7	Chemical preservation by use of additives
.028 8	Irradiation
.06	Additives

Production, properties, use

Class flavoring aids in 664.5

For chemical preservation by use of additives, see 664.0287

.062	Food colors
.07	Tests, analyses, quality controls

For color, contaminants, flavor, odor, texture

Including grading

Class tests, analyses, quality controls of additives in 664.06

.072	Sensory evaluation of food
.08	By-products
.09	Packaging
.1	**Sugars, syrups, their derived products**

Standard subdivisions are added for sugars, syrups, their derived products together; for sugars and syrups together; for sugars alone

Class here sweeteners

For artificial sweeteners, see 664.5

.102 84	Apparatus and equipment

Do not use for materials; class in 664.111

[.102 87]	Testing and measurement

Do not use; class in 664.117

>	664.11–664.13 Sugars and syrups

Class comprehensive works in 664.1

'.11	Materials, techniques, processes, operations, by-products of sugars and syrups

Class materials, techniques, processes, operations, by-products of specific sugars and syrups in 664.12–664.13

.111	Materials
.112	Preliminary preparations
.113	Extraction and purification
.114	Concentration

Production of syrup

.115 Crystallization

> Production of sugar

.116 Additives

.117 Tests, analyses, quality controls

> For color, contaminants, flavor, texture

> Class tests, analyses, quality controls of additives in 664.116

.118 By-products

> Including molasses

> Class utilization in 664.19

.119 Packaging

> 664.12–664.13 Specific sugars and syrups

> Class comprehensive works in 664.1

.12 Cane and beet sugar and syrup

> Standard subdivisions are added for cane and beet sugar and syrup together, for cane and beet sugar alone

.122 Cane sugar and syrup

> Standard subdivisions are added for cane sugar and syrup together, for cane sugar alone

.122 028 4 Apparatus and equipment

> Do not use for materials; class in 664.1221

[.122 028 7] Testing and measurement

> Do not use; class in 664.1227

.122 1–.122 9 Materials, processes, operations, by-products

> Add to base number 664.122 the numbers following 664.11 in 664.111–664.119, e.g., cane molasses 664.1228

.123 Beet sugar and syrup

> Standard subdivisions are added for beet sugar and syrup together, for beet sugar alone

.13 Other sugars and syrups

> *For honey, see 638.16*

.132 Maple sugar and syrup

> Standard subdivisions are added for maple sugar and syrup together, for maple syrup alone

.133 Corn and sorghum sugars and syrups

.139 Jerusalem artichoke sugar and syrup

.15	Sugar products
.152	Jams, jellies, marmalades, preserves

        Standard subdivisions are added for any or all topics in heading

        See also 664.26 for jellies (gelatin desserts)

.153	Candy (Sweets)

        See also 664.6 for chewing gum

.19	By-product utilization

        Class a specific use with the use, e.g., molasses for rum 663.59

.2	**Starches and jellying agents**

        Standard subdivisions are added for starches and jellying agents together, for starches alone

---

>   664.22–664.23 Starches

        Class comprehensive works in 664.2

.22	Cornstarch and potato starch
.23	Cassava and arrowroot starches
.25	Jellying agents

        Class here pectin

        For gelatin, see 664.26

.26	Gelatin
.3	**Fats and oils**

        Class interdisciplinary works on animal fats and oils in 665.2; class interdisciplinary works on vegetable fats and oils in 665.3

        For butter, see 637.2; for peanut butter, see 664.726

.32	Margarine
.34	Lard
.36	Salad and cooking oils
.362	Olive oil
.363	Cottonseed oil
.368	Soy oil
.37	Salad dressings

        Including mayonnaise

.4　　**Food salts**

　　Including monosodium glutamate, table salt, tenderizers, sodium-free and other dietetic salts

　　Class comprehensive works on commercial technology of food flavoring aids in 664.5

.5　　**Flavoring aids**

　　Including artificial sweeteners, chocolate, sugar substitutes

　　Class here condiments

　　Class flavoring aids in a specific kind of food with the kind of food, e.g., chocolate candies 664.153

　　　For food salts, see 664.4. For a specific flavoring aid not provided for here, see the aid, e.g., sugar 664.1

.52–.54　　Essences and spices

　　　Add to base number 664.5 the numbers following 633.8 in 633.82–633.84, e.g., vanilla extract 664.52

.55　　Vinegar

.58　　Complex condiments

　　Including catsup, chutney, miso, sauces

　　Class salad dressings in 664.37

.6　　**Special-purpose food and aids**

　　Including chewing gum, snack food

　　Class special-purpose flavoring aids in 664.5

>　　664.62–664.66 Special-purpose food

　　Class comprehensive works in 664.6. Class a specific food with the food, e.g., vegetables 664.8

.62　　Baby food

.63　　Low-calorie food

.64　　Meatless high-protein food

　　Including synthetic meat

.65　　Complete dishes

　　Including complete meals, packaged ingredients for complete recipes

　　Class packaged ingredients for recipes based on a specific kind of food with the kind, e.g., mixes and prepared doughs for bakery goods 664.753

.66　　Food for animals

　　Class here pet food

　　　For animal feed made from grains and other seeds, see 664.76

.68   Leavening agents and baking aids

            Including baking powder, baking soda, cream of tartar, yeast

.7   **Grains, other seeds, their derived products**

            Class sugars and syrups from grain and other seeds in 664.13; class starches and jellying agents from grain and other seeds in 664.2; class fats and oils from grains and other seeds in 664.3

.72   Milling and milling products

            Standard subdivisions are added for milling and milling products together, for milling alone

            For animal feeds, see 664.76

.720 01   Philosophy and theory

.720 02   Miscellany

[.720 028 7]   Testing and measurement

                  Do not use; class in 664.7204

.720 03–.720 09   Standard subdivisions

.720 1   Preliminary treatment

.720 3   Grinding and deflaking

.720 4   Sifting, grading, quality controls

.720 7   Products

                  Including flour, meal, refined grain

                    See also 664.7208 for by-products

.720 8   By-products

                  Including bran, siftings

.720 9   Packaging

.722   Wheat

.722 7   Products

                    See also 664.7228 for by-products

.722 72   Flour

.722 73   Meal

.722 8   By-products

                  Including bran, siftings

.724   Corn

            Variant names: Indian corn, maize

.725   Rice

.726   Nuts, legumes, other non-cereal seeds and their flours, meals, by-products

> Including cottonseeds, sunflower seeds

> Class comprehensive works on commercial processing of nuts in 664.8045; class comprehensive works on commercial processing of legumes in 664.80565

> *For salad and cooking oils, see 664.36*

.75   Secondary products

.752   Bakery goods

> Including crackers

> Class mixes and prepared doughs for bakery goods in 664.753

.752 3   Breads

> Including biscuits, quick breads

.752 5   Pastries

> Including cakes, cookies (biscuits), pies

.753   Mixes and prepared doughs

> Including biscuit, cake, pancake mixes

.755   Noodles and pastas

> Standard subdivisions are added for either or both topics in heading

.756   Ready-to-eat cereals

.76   Animal feeds

> Class comprehensive works on commercial processing of foods for animals in 664.66

.762   Cereal grains

> Individual grains and mixtures

> Class formula feeds in 664.768

.763   Other seeds

> Individual seeds and mixtures

> Class formula feeds in 664.768

.764   Cereal grain and seed mixtures

.768   Formula feeds

> Cakes, flakes, granules, pellets, powders basically of cereal grains and other seeds and fortified with vitamins and minerals

.8   **Fruits and vegetables**

> Class a specific product derived from fruits and vegetables with the product, e.g., jams 664.152, fats and oils 664.3

.800 1	Philosophy and theory
.800 2	Miscellany
[.800 287]	Testing and measurement
	Do not use; class in 664.807
.800 3–.800 9	Standard subdivisions

.804   **Specific fruits and groups of fruits**

> Add to base number 664.804 the numbers following 634 in 634.1–634.8, e.g., citrus fruits 664.804304, nuts 664.8045

.805   **Specific vegetables and groups of vegetables**

> Add to base number 664.805 the numbers following 635 in 635.1–635.8, e.g., salad greens 664.8055

.806–.809   **Additives, tests, analyses, quality controls, by-products, packaging**

> Add to base number 664.80 the numbers following 664.0 in 664.06–664.09, e.g., packaging vegetables 664.809

> Class additives, tests, analyses, quality controls, by-products, packaging applied to specific fruits and groups of fruits in 664.804; class additives, tests, analyses, quality controls, by-products, packaging applied to specific vegetables and groups of vegetables in 664.805

> *See also 664.81–664.88 for preservation techniques*

.81–.88   **Preservation techniques**

> Add to base number 664.8 the numbers following 664.028 in 664.0281–664.0288, e.g., deep freezing fruits 664.853

> Class preservation techniques applied to specific fruits and groups of fruits in 664.804; class preservation techniques applied to specific vegetables and groups of vegetables in 664.805

.9   **Meats and allied foods**

> Standard subdivisions are added for meats and allied foods together, for meats alone

.900 1	Philosophy and theory
.900 2	Miscellany
[.900 287]	Testing and measurement
	Do not use; class in 664.907
.900 3–.900 9	Standard subdivisions

.902   **Preservation techniques, slaughtering, meat cutting**

.902 8   Preservation techniques

> Add to base number 664.9028 the numbers following 664.028 in 664.0281–664.0288, e.g., canning 664.90282

.902 9   Slaughtering and meat cutting

        Standard subdivisions are added for either or both topics in heading

.906–.909   Additives, tests, analyses, quality controls, by-products, packaging

        Add to base number 664.90 the numbers following 664.0 in 664.06–664.09, e.g., packaging meats and allied foods 664.909

        Class additives, tests, analyses, quality controls, by-products, packaging applied to specific meats or allied foods with the meat or food, e.g., packaging red meats 664.9299

        See also 664.9028 for preservation techniques

.92   Red meat

[.920 287]   Testing and measurement

        Do not use; class in 664.9297

.921–.928   Preservation techniques

        Add to base number 664.92 the numbers following 664.028 in 664.0281–664.0288, e.g., canning red meat 664.922
Subdivisions are added for specific red meats, e.g., canning beef 664.922

.929   Additives, tests, analyses, quality controls, by-products, packaging

        Add to base number 664.929 the numbers following 664.0 in 664.06–664.09, e.g., packaging red meat 664.9299
Subdivisions are added for specific red meats, e.g., packaging beef 664.9299

        See also 664.921–664.928 for preservation techniques

.93   Poultry

[.930 287]   Testing and measurement

        Do not use; class in 664.9397

.931–.938   Preservation techniques

        Add to base number 664.93 the numbers following 664.028 in 664.0281–664.0288, e.g., deep freezing 664.9353
Subdivisions are added for specific kinds of poultry, e.g., deep freezing turkeys 664.9353

.939   Additives, tests, analyses, quality controls, by-products, packaging

        Add to base number 664.939 the numbers following 664.0 in 664.06–664.09, e.g., poultry by-products 664.9398
Subdivisions are added for specific kinds of poultry, e.g., turkey by-products 664.9398

        See also 664.931–664.938 for preservation techniques

.94   Fishes and shellfish

        Standard subdivisions are added for fish and shellfish together, for fishes alone

        Class here seafood

[.940 287]	Testing and measurement
	Do not use; class in 664.9497

.941–.948   Preservation techniques

> Add to base number 664.94 the numbers following 664.028 in 664.0281–664.0288, e.g., canning seafood 664.942
>> Subdivisions are not added for specific kinds of fishes and shellfish, e.g., canning oysters 664.94 (*not* 664.942)

.949   Additives, tests, analyses, quality controls, by-products, packaging

> Add to base number 664.949 the numbers following 664.0 in 664.06–664.09, e.g., quality controls for seafood 664.9497
>> Subdivisions are not added for specific kinds of fishes and shellfish, e.g., quality controls for catfish 664.94 (*not* 664.9497)

> *See also 664.941–664.948 for preservation techniques*

.95   Other meats and allied foods

> Including frogs, turtles, snails, insects

665   Technology of industrial oils, fats, waxes, gases

.028   Auxiliary techniques and procedures; apparatus, equipment, materials

> Notation 028 from Table 1 as modified below

> Class here basic techniques and procedures

.028 2   Extraction

> Including pressurizing, rendering, steam distilling

.028 3   Refining

> Including bleaching, blending, coloring, fractionating, purifying

.028 7   Maintenance and repair

> Do not use for testing and measurement; class in 665.0288

.028 8   Tests, analyses, quality controls

> Do not use for maintenance and repair; class in 665.0287

.1   Waxes

> Class polishing waxes in 667.72

> *For mineral waxes, see 665.4*

.12   Vegetable waxes

> Including bayberry, candleberry, carnauba, laurel, myrtle waxes

.13   Animal waxes

> Including lanolin (wool wax), spermaceti

> *For beeswax, see 638.17*

.19   Blended waxes

.2   **Animal fats and oils**

Standard subdivisions are added for either or both topics in heading

Including fish, neat's-foot, whale oils; tallow; biodiesel fuel from animal fats and oils

Class here interdisciplinary works on animal fats and oils

Class comprehensive works on biodiesel fuel in 665.37

For animal fats and oils used in food or food preparation, see 664.3

See also 665.13 for spermaceti

.3   **Vegetable fats and oils**

Class here interdisciplinary works on vegetable fats and oils

Class interdisciplinary works on specific vegetable oils used primarily as food with the vegetable oil in 641.3, e.g., olive oil 641.3463

For the food technology of vegetable fats and oils used in food and food preparation, see 664.3

.33   Wood oil

Class here comprehensive works on naval stores

For a specific kind of naval store, see the kind, e.g., pitch 665.5388

.332   Crude turpentine

Class turpentine oils in 661.806

.333   Tung oil (Chinese wood oil)

.35   Seed oils

Class biodiesel fuel in 665.37

For tung oil, see 665.333

.352   Linseed oil (Flaxseed oil)

.353   Castor oil

.354   Cocoa butter (Cacao butter)

.355   Coconut oil

.37   Biodiesel fuel

Class here comprehensive works on biodiesel fuel

For biodiesel fuel from animal fats and oils, see 665.2

.4   **Mineral oils and waxes**

Including natural asphalt, shale oil, tar sand

For petroleum, see 665.5

.5   **Petroleum**

Class here comprehensive works on technology of petroleum and natural gas

Class synthetic petroleum in 662.662

For technology of extraction of petroleum and natural gas, see 622.338; for comprehensive works on technology of natural gas, see 665.7

.53   Refinery treatment and products

Standard subdivisions are added for refinery treatment and products together, for refinery treatment alone

Class preliminary refining of oil sands and oil shale to obtain distillable fluids in 665.4

.530 286   Green technology (Environmental technology)

Do not use for pollution control technology, waste technology; class in 665.5389

.532   Fractional distillation

.533   Cracking processes

Including thermal and catalytic cracking, hydrogenation of residual petroleum distillates

.534   Purification and blending of distillates

.538   Refinery products and by-products

Including waste products

Class here petrochemicals

For petrochemicals as a type of industrial chemical, see 661.804

.538 2   Highly volatile products

.538 24   Naphthas

.538 25   Aviation fuel

Including high-octane-rating gasoline, jet and turbojet fuel

Class interdisciplinary works on gasoline in 665.53827

.538 27   Gasoline

For high-octane-rating gasoline, see 665.53825

.538 3   Kerosene

For jet and turbojet fuel, see 665.53825

.538 4   Heavy fuel oil

Including absorber oil, diesel fuel, gas oil, heating oil

See also 665.37 for biodiesel fuel

.538 5   Lubricating oil and grease

Including paraffin wax and petrolatum

.538 8   Residues (Bottoms)

      Including asphalt, bunker and road oils, petroleum coke, pitch

      Class unusable residues (wastes) in 665.538; class asphalt concrete in 666.893

.538 9   Waste control

      Class here pollution control

.54   Storage, transportation, distribution

.542   Storage

.543   Transportation

      Including transportation by tankers

      For pipeline transportation, see 665.544

.544   Pipeline transportation

.55   Uses

      Class a specific use with the use, e.g., automobile engine lubricants 629.255

.7   **Natural gas and manufactured gases**

      Standard subdivisions are added for natural gas and manufactured gases together, for natural gas alone

      Class here comprehensive works on technology of industrial gases

      For technology of extracting natural gas, see 622.3385; for technology of industrial gases not provided for here, see 665.8

.702 86   Green technology (Environmental technology)

      Class production of manufactured gases from biological wastes in 665.776

.73   Processing natural gas

      Including extraction of helium

.74   Storage, transportation, distribution of natural gas and manufactured gases

      Standard subdivisions are added for natural gas, manufactured gases, or both

.742   Storage

      Standard subdivisions are added for natural gas, manufactured gases, or both

.743   Transportation

      Standard subdivisions are added for natural gas, manufactured gases, or both

      For pipeline transportation, see 665.744

.744	Pipeline transportation

Standard subdivisions are added for natural gas, manufactured gases, or both

.75	Uses of natural gas and manufactured gases

Standard subdivisions are added for either or both topics in heading

Class a specific use with the use, e.g., heating buildings 697.043

.77	Production of manufactured gases

Class here comprehensive works on technology of manufactured gases

For storage, transportation, distribution, see 665.74; for uses, see 665.75

.772	Production of manufactured gases from coal and coke

Including blast-furnace, carbureted-blue, city, coke-oven, producer, water gases

Class here coal gasification

.773	Production of manufactured gases from petroleum and natural gas

Including oil, refinery, reformed natural, reformed refinery, liquefied petroleum gases, e.g., butane, butene, pentane, propane, and their mixtures

.776	Production of manufactured gases from biological wastes

Class here biogas

.779	Production of manufactured gases by mixing fuel gases from several sources
.8	**Other industrial gases**

For ammonia, see 661.34

.81	Hydrogen
.82	Gases derived from liquefaction and fractionation of air
.822	Noble gases

Variant names: inert, rare gases

Including argon, helium, krypton, neon, radon, xenon

Class extraction of helium from natural gases in 665.73

.823	Oxygen
.824	Nitrogen
.83	Halogen gases
.84	Sulfur dioxide
.85	Acetylene
.89	Carbon dioxide, ozone, hydrogen sulfide

666   Ceramic and allied technologies

Standard subdivisions are added for ceramic and allied technologies together, for ceramic technologies alone

.04   Special topics of ceramic and allied technologies

.042   Ceramic-to-metal bonding

.1   Glass

[.102 8]   Auxiliary techniques and procedures; apparatus, equipment, materials

> Do not use for auxiliary techniques and procedures; class in 666.13

[.102 84]   Apparatus, equipment, materials

> Do not use; class in 666.12

[.102 86]   Green technology (Environmental technology)

> Do not use; class in 666.14

.104   Special topics of glass

.104 2   Physicochemical phenomena occurring during glassmaking processes

> Including phase and structural transformations

>   666.12–666.14   General topics of glass

Class general topics of specific types of glass in 666.15; class general topics of products in 666.19; class comprehensive works in 666.1

.12   Techniques, procedures, apparatus, equipment, materials

> *For auxiliary techniques and procedures, see 666.13*

.121   Materials

>   666.122–666.129   Specific operations in glassmaking

Class tests, analyses, quality controls in 666.137; class comprehensive works in 666.12

.122   Blowing

.123   Pressing

.124   Drawing

.125   Molding and casting

> Standard subdivisions are added for either or both topics in heading

.126   Multiform processes

> Cold-molding glass powder under pressure, and firing at high temperatures

.129   Annealing and tempering

.13   Auxiliary techniques and procedures

> Add to base number 666.13 the numbers following —028 in notation 0285–0289 from Table 1, e.g., quality control in glassmaking 666.137; however, for green technology, see 666.14

.14   Green technology (Environmental technology)

> Including recycling

> Class here environmental engineering (environmental health engineering, environmental protection engineering), sustainable engineering (sustainable technology); pollution control technology, waste technology

> Class recycling a specific type of glass or glass product with the type of glass or product, e.g., recycling bottles 666.192

.15   Specific types of glass

> *See also 669.94 for metallic glass*

.152   Window glass

> Sheet glass that differs from plate glass primarily in being annealed more quickly and in not being ground and polished

.153   Plate glass

> Class laminated plate glass in 666.154

.154   Laminated glass

.155   Heat-resistant glass

.156   Optical glass

.157   Fiber glass and foam glass

> Class fiberglass-reinforced plastic in 668.4942

.19   Products

.192   Bottles and jars

> Standard subdivisions are added for either or both topics in heading

.2   **Enamels**

.3   **Pottery**

> Class here comprehensive works on clay technology

> Class pottery limited to earthenware or stoneware in 666.6

> *For techniques and procedures, see 666.44; for specific types of pottery, see 666.5–666.6; for structural clay products, see 666.73*

[.301–.309]   Standard subdivisions

> Do not use; class in 666.31–666.39

.31–.39   Standard subdivisions

> Add to base number 666.3 the numbers following —0 in notation 01–09 from Table 1, e.g., auxiliary techniques and procedures 666.328; however, for apparatus, equipment, materials, see 666.4

.4   Pottery materials, equipment, processes

> Add to base number 666.4 the numbers following 738.1 in 738.12–738.15, e.g., kilns 666.436

.44   Techniques and procedures

> Number built according to instructions under 666.4

> *For auxiliary techniques and procedures, see 666.328*

> **666.5–666.6 Specific types of pottery**

> Class comprehensive works in 666.3

.5   Porcelain

.58   Specific products

> Including figurines, tableware, vases

.6   Earthenware and stoneware

> Standard subdivisions are added for either or both topics in heading

.68   Specific products

> Including containers, figurines, industrial products, tableware

.7   Refractories and structural clay products

.72   Refractory materials

> Including alumina, asbestos, chrome, fireclays, mica, talc, zirconia

.73   Structural clay products

.732   Roofing tiles

.733   Tile drains and piping

.737   Bricks

> *For hollow and perforated bricks, see 666.738*

.738   Hollow and perforated bricks

.8   Synthetic and artificial minerals and building materials

.86   Synthetic and artificial minerals

> Standard subdivisions are added for either or both topics in heading

> Including cryolite, feldspar, graphite, mica

> *For synthetic and artificial gems, see 666.88*

.88   Synthetic and artificial gems

> Standard subdivisions are added for either or both topics in heading
>
> Including diamonds, garnets, rubies, sapphires

.89   Synthetic building materials

> Including drywall
>
> *For structural clay products, see 666.73*

.893   Concrete

> Including asphalt concrete, ready-mix concrete
>
> Class concrete blocks in 666.894

.894   Hollow concrete and cinder blocks

> Class here interdisciplinary works on concrete blocks
>
> *For solid concrete blocks, see 666.895*

.895   Solid concrete blocks

.9   **Masonry adhesives**

> Class concrete in 666.893

.92   Gypsum plasters

> Including Keene's cement, plaster of paris

.93   Lime mortars

.94   Portland cement

> Class here comprehensive works on cement
>
> *For Keene's cement, see 666.92; for other cements, see 666.95*

.95   Other cements

> Including high-alumina cement, magnesia

667   Cleaning, color, coating, related technologies

> Standard subdivisions are added for cleaning, color, coating, related technologies together; for color technology alone

.1   **Cleaning and bleaching**

> Of textiles, leathers, furs, feathers
>
> Class household bleaching, cleaning, laundry in 648

.12   Dry cleaning

> Including manufacture of dry-cleaning materials

.13   Laundering and finishing operations

> *For soaps, see 668.12; for detergents, see 668.14*

.14   Bleaching

         Including manufacture of bleaching materials

.2   **Dyes and pigments**

         Standard subdivisions are added for dyes and pigments together, for dyes alone

         Including stains

\>   667.25–667.26   Dyes

         Class comprehensive works in 667.2

.25   Synthetic dyes

.252   Nitro and nitroso dyes

.253   Azo-oxy and azo-tetrazo dyes

.254   Diphenylmethane and triphenylmethane dyes

.256   Hydroxyketone dyes

         Including alizarines, quinoidals

.257   Indigoid dyes

         See also 667.26 for indigo

.26   Natural dyes

         Including indigo

.29   Pigments

.3   **Dyeing and printing**

         Standard subdivisions are added for dyeing and printing together, for dyeing alone

         Class here dyeing and printing of textiles, of textile fibers

         Class dyeing and printing of a specific material not provided for here with the material, e.g., dyeing leather 675.25

         For dyes, see 667.25–667.26

         See also 686.2 for printing of books and related products

.31–.35   Dyeing specific textiles

         Add to base number 667.3 the numbers following 677 in 677.1–677.5, e.g., dyeing nylon 667.3473

.38   Textile printing

.4   **Inks**

         For printing ink, see 667.5

.5   **Printing ink**

.6   **Paints and painting**

> Standard subdivisions are added for either or both topics in heading
>
> Including paint removers, sign painting

.62   Oil-soluble paint

.622   Oils, driers, plasticizers

.623   Pigments and extenders

> *For carbon black, see 662.93*

.624   Diluents (Thinners)

.63   Water-soluble paint

> Including latex paint, whitewash

.69   Special-purpose paints

> Including fire-resistant, luminous, rust-resistant paints

.7   **Polishes, lacquers, varnishes**

> Class here methods of applying polishes, lacquers, varnishes

.72   Polishes and polishing

> Standard subdivisions are added for either or both topics in heading

.75   Lacquers and lacquering

> Standard subdivisions are added for either or both topics in heading
>
> Including japans, japanning

.79   Varnishes and varnishing

> Standard subdivisions are added for either or both topics in heading
>
> Including shellac, spar varnish
>
> Class here spirit varnishes
>
> *For lacquers and lacquering, see 667.75*

.9   **Coatings and coating**

> Standard subdivisions are added for either or both topics in heading
>
> Comprehensive works on methods and materials for producing protective and decorative coatings
>
> *For a coating made of a specific material, see the material, e.g., enamel coatings 666.2, thermoset plastic coatings 668.422; for methods of applying a specific kind of coating, see the kind of coating, e.g., painting 667.6; for coatings applied to a specific thing and methods of applying the coatings, see the thing to which the coating is applied, e.g., coatings for metal 671.73, metal coatings for polymers 668.9, painting a building 698.1, varnishing a violin 787.21923*

668   **Technology of other organic products**

.1   **Surface-active agents (Surfactants)**

.12   Soaps

.124   Soluble soaps

Including liquid concentrates, powders

.125   Insoluble soaps (Metallic soaps)

Including oleates and stearates of aluminum

.127   Scouring compounds

.14   Detergents and wetting agents

Nonsoap materials that manifest surface activity

Standard subdivisions are added for detergents and wetting agents together, for detergents alone

Including fatty-alcohol sulfates, sulfated oils and hydrocarbons

.2   **Glycerin**

.3   **Adhesives and related products**

Standard subdivisions are added for adhesives and related products together, for adhesives alone

For masonry adhesives, see 666.9

>   668.31–668.37   Specific kinds of adhesives

Class products made from specific kinds of adhesives in 668.38; class comprehensive works in 668.3

.31   Synthetic glue

.32   Animal glue

Including casein glue

.33   Vegetable glue

Including mucilage

See also 668.37 for gum

.34   Crude gelatin

.37   Gum and resin

Standard subdivisions are added for either or both topics in heading

.372   Natural gum and resin

Standard subdivisions are added for either or both topics in heading

See also 668.33 for mucilage

.374	Synthetic gum and resin

Standard subdivisions are added for either or both topics in heading

Including epoxy resin

.38	Products made from adhesives

Including tape

Class here sealants

.4	**Plastics**
[.402 8]	Auxiliary techniques and procedures; apparatus, equipment, materials

Do not use; class in 668.41

.404	Special topics of plastics
.404 2	Physicochemical phenomena of plastics manufacture
.41	Techniques, procedures, apparatus, equipment, materials

Class application to specific kinds of plastics in 668.42–668.45; class application to forms and products in 668.49

.411	Materials

Including fillers, plasticizers

>   668.412–668.419 Specific operations

Class comprehensive works in 668.41

.412	Molding and casting

Standard subdivisions are added for either or both topics in heading

.413	Extrusion
.414	Laminating
.415	Welding
.416	Reinforcing
.419	Auxiliary techniques and procedures
.419 2	Waste technology

Class here pollution control

.419 5–.419 9	Miscellaneous auxiliary techniques and procedures

Add to base number 668.419 the numbers following —028 in notation 0285–0289 from Table 1, e.g., quality control in plastics manufacture 668.4197; however, for waste technology, see 668.4192

>   668.42–668.45 Specific kinds of plastics

Class forms and products of specific kinds of plastics in 668.49; class comprehensive works in 668.4

.42	Polymerization plastics
.422	Thermosetting plastics
.422 2	Phenolics
.422 3	Ureas
.422 4	Melamines
.422 5	Polyesters

Including polyurethanes

Class interdisciplinary works on polyurethanes in 668.4239

.422 6	Epoxies
.422 7	Silicones
.423	Thermoplastic plastics

Including acetals, acetates, butyrates, polycarbonates, polyethers

.423 2	Acrylics (Polyacrylics)
.423 3	Styrenes (Polystyrenes)
.423 4	Polyolefins

Including polyethylenes, polyisobutylenes, polypropylenes

.423 5	Polyamides (Nylons)
.423 6	Vinyls (Polyvinyls)
.423 7	Vinylidene chlorides
.423 8	Polyfluoro hydrocarbons
.423 9	Polyurethanes

Class here interdisciplinary works on polyurethanes

For thermosetting polyurethanes, see 668.4225; for polyurethane rubber, see 678.72

.43	Protein plastics

Including plastics derived from casein

.44	Cellulosics

Including celluloid

.45	Plastics from natural resins

Including lignin-derived plastics

For protein plastics, see 668.43

.49	Forms and products

Class plastic fibers and fabrics in 677.4

>   668.492–668.495   Specific forms

          Class comprehensive works in 668.49

.492   Laminated plastic

.493   Plastic foams

            Including structural foam

.494   Reinforced plastic

.494 2   Glass-reinforced plastic

            Class here fiberglass-reinforced plastic

.495   Plastic films

.497   Containers

.5   Perfumes and cosmetics

.54   Perfumes

.542   Natural perfumes

            Including floral oils and waters; potpourris

.544   Synthetic perfumes

.55   Cosmetics

.6   Agricultural chemicals

.62   Fertilizers

            Add to base number 668.62 the numbers following 631.8 in 631.83–631.85, e.g., superphosphates 668.625

            For organic fertilizers, see 668.63

.63   Organic fertilizers

            Add to base number 668.63 the numbers following 631.8 in 631.86–631.87, e.g., manufacture of fertilizers from animal wastes 668.636, converting household garbage 668.6375

.64   Soil conditioners

            Manufactured and organic

.65   Pesticides

            Class interdisciplinary works on pesticides in 632.95

.651   Insecticides, rodenticides, vermicides

.652   Fungicides and algicides

.653   Bactericides

.654   Herbicides (Weed killers)

.9   **Polymers and polymerization**

Standard subdivisions are added for polymers and polymerization together, for polymers alone

Class here synthetic polymers

Class a specific application with the application, e.g., manufacture of nylon hosiery 687.3; class a specific polymer with the polymer, e.g., plastics 668.4

.92   Polymerization

669   **Metallurgy**

Class here alloys, extractive metallurgy, process metallurgy, interdisciplinary works on metals

For a specific aspect of metals, see the aspect, e.g., chemistry 546.3, metalworking and primary metal products 671

See Manual at 669; also at 622.22, 622.7 vs. 662.6, 669

.028   Auxiliary techniques and procedures; apparatus, equipment

Notation 028 from Table 1 as modified below

.028 2   Pyrometallurgy

Extraction by furnace methods, e.g., smelting

Class electrical zone melting in 669.0284

.028 3   Hydrometallurgy

Extraction by leaching methods

.028 4   Electrometallurgy

Do not use for apparatus and equipment; class in 669.028. Do not use for materials; class in 669.042

Including electrical zone melting, vacuum metallurgy

Class here electrorefining, electrowinning

.04   Special topics of metallurgy

.042   Materials

Class here prepared ores and scrap metals

Class furnace materials in 669.8

> **669.1–669.7 Metallurgy of specific metals and their alloys**

Class comprehensive works in 669

For physical and chemical metallurgy of specific metals and their alloys, see 669.96

.1   **Ferrous metals**

.14   **Reduction and refining of ferrous ores**

> Class comprehensive works on production of iron and steel in 669.1

[.140 1–.140 9]   Standard subdivisions

> Do not use; class in 669.101–669.109

.141   **Production of iron**

> *For production of ingot iron, see 669.1423*

.141 3   Blast-furnace practice

> Class here casting as a part of the refining process, production of pig iron and crude cast iron
>
> Class iron casting as a metalworking process in 672.25; class cast iron products in 672.8

.141 4   Puddling furnace practice

> Class here production of wrought iron

.142   **Production of steel**

> Class here stainless steel

.142 2   Open-hearth furnace practice (Siemens process)

.142 3   Bessemer converter practice

> Including production of duplex-process steel, ingot iron

.142 4   Electric furnace practice

> Including arc furnace practice

.142 9   Production of crucible steel

>   **669.2–669.7 Nonferrous metals**
>
> Class comprehensive works in 669

.2   **Precious and group 3 metals**

> Standard subdivisions are added for precious and group 3B metals together, for precious metals alone

---

>   **669.22–669.24 Precious metals**
>
> Class comprehensive works in 669.2

.22   Gold

.23   Silver

.24   Platinum

.29   Group 3 metals

.290 01–.290 09   Standard subdivisions

.290 1	Scandium

.290 3	Yttrium

.291–.294	Rare earth elements (Lanthanide series) and actinide series

Add to base number 669.29 the numbers following 546.4 in 546.41–546.44, e.g., rare earth elements 669.291, actinide series metals 669.292, uranium 669.2931

.3   Copper

Class here brass, Muntz metal; bronze, gunmetal; copper-aluminum alloys; copper-beryllium alloys

.4   Lead

.5   Zinc and cadmium

.52	Zinc

For brass, Muntz metal, see 669.3

.56	Cadmium

.6   Tin

For bronze, gunmetal, see 669.3

.7   Other nonferrous metals

Including iridium, osmium, palladium, rhodium, ruthenium; rhenium

See also 669.24 for platinum

.71	Mercury

.72	Light, alkali, alkaline-earth metals

Standard subdivisions are added for light, alkali, alkaline-earth metals together; for light metals alone

For titanium, see 669.7322; for zirconium, see 669.735

.722	Aluminum

For copper-aluminum alloys, see 669.3

.723	Magnesium

.724	Beryllium

For copper-beryllium alloys, see 669.3

.725	Alkali and alkaline-earth metals

Including barium, calcium, cesium, francium, lithium, potassium, radium, rubidium, sodium, strontium

For magnesium, see 669.723; for beryllium, see 669.724

.73	Metals used in ferroalloys

.732	Titanium, vanadium, manganese

.732 2	Titanium
.733	Nickel and cobalt
.733 2	Nickel
.734	Chromium, molybdenum, tungsten
.735	Zirconium and tantalum
.75	Antimony, arsenic, bismuth
.79	Miscellaneous rare metals and metalloids

Limited to gallium, hafnium, indium, niobium, polonium, thallium; germanium, selenium, tellurium

.8 **Metallurgical furnace technology**

Class metallurgical furnace technology used for a specific metal with the metal, e.g., nickel 669.7332

.802 8   Auxiliary techniques and procedures; apparatus, equipment, materials

Do not use for refractory material; class in 669.82

.81   Fuel

.82   Refractory material

Class comprehensive works on technology of refractory materials in 666.72

.83   Firing and heat control

.84   Fluxes and slag

.85   Physical processes

Including heat exchange

.9 **Physical and chemical metallurgy**

Standard subdivisions are added for either or both topics in heading

Physical and chemical phenomena occurring during metallurgical processes; physical and chemical analyses of metals; formation of alloys

Class metalworking and manufacture of primary metal products in 671–673

.92   Chemical analysis

Including assaying

Class chemical analysis of specific metals and their alloys in 669.96

.94   Physicochemical metallurgical phenomena

Including alloy binary systems, intermetallic compounds, metallic glass, solid solutions, solidification; phase diagrams

Class physicochemical metallurgical phenomena of specific metals and their alloys in 669.96

.95   Metallography

.950 28	Auxiliary techniques and procedures; apparatus, equipment, procedures
	Notation 028 from Table 1 as modified below
.950 282	Microscopical metallography
	Optical and electron metallography
.950 283	X-ray metallography
.951–.957	**Metallography of specific metals and their alloys**

> Add to base number 669.95 the numbers following 669 in 669.1–669.7, e.g., aluminum 669.95722

.96	**Physical and chemical metallurgy of specific metals and their alloys**

> Add to base number 669.96 the numbers following 669 in 669.1–669.7, e.g., titanium 669.967322

> *For metallography of specific metals and their alloys, see 669.951–669.957*

670   Manufacturing

Including planning and design for manufactured products

Class here manufactured products

Class military applications in 623; class planning and design for specific kinds of products in 671–679; class the arts in 700. Class comprehensive works on products made by a specific process with the process, e.g., seasoned wood 674.38; however, if a specific provision is made for the product, class with the product, e.g., coated papers 676.283 (*not* 676.235)

> *For manufacture of products based on specific branches of engineering, see 620; for manufacture of products based on chemical technologies, see 660; for manufacture of final products for specific uses not provided for elsewhere, see 680*

> *See Manual at T1—025 vs. T1—029*

.285	Computer applications

Class here computer-aided design / computer-aided manufacture (CAD/CAM), computer integrated manufacturing systems (CIM), comprehensive works on computer use in the management of manufacturing and computer-aided design or computer-aided manufacture

Class computer-aided design (CAD) in 620.00420285; class computer use in the management of manufacturing in 658.05

> *For computer-aided manufacture (CAM), flexible manufacturing systems limited to factory operations, see 670.427*

.4	**Special topics of manufacturing**

.42	**Factory operations engineering**

Class here shop and assembly-line technology

For tools and fabricating equipment, see 621.9; for packaging technology, see 688.8

[.420 685]	Management of factory operations

Do not use; class in 658.5

.423	**Machine-shop practice**
.425	**Inspection technology**
.427	**Mechanization and automation of factory operations**

Standard subdivisions are added for either or both topics in heading

Class here assembling machines, computer control of factory operations; computer-aided manufacture (CAM), flexible manufacturing systems if limited to factory operations

Class computer-aided design (CAD) in 620.00420285; class computer-aided design / computer-aided manufacture (CAD/CAM), computer integrated manufacturing systems (CIM), computer-aided manufacture (CAM), flexible manufacturing systems if applied to design and production of manufactured products in 670.285; class automated machine-shop practice in 670.423; class automated inspection technology in 670.425; class comprehensive works on computer control in 629.89

.427 2	Robots

Unless it is redundant, add to base number 670.4272 the numbers following 00 in 004–006, e.g., use of digital personal computers 670.4272416, but use of digital computers 670.4272 (*not* 670.42724)

.427 5	Computerized process control

Unless it is redundant, add to base number 670.4275 the numbers following 00 in 004–006, e.g., use of digital personal computers 670.4275416, but use of digital computers 670.4275 (*not* 670.42754)

Class comprehensive works on computerized process control in 629.895 ,

[.685]	Management of production

Do not use; class in 658.5

>	**671–679 Manufacture of products from specific materials**

Class here manufacture of primary products

Class comprehensive works in 670

For manufacture of ceramic products, see 666; for manufacture of plastic products, see 668.49

See Manual at 671–679 vs. 680

671 Metalworking processes and primary metal products

Standard subdivisions are added for metalworking processes and primary metal products together, for metalworking processes alone

Class metallurgy and interdisciplinary works on metals in 669

> *For metalworking processes and primary metal products with iron, steel, other iron alloys as the main metal, see 672; for metalworking processes and primary metal products with nonferrous metals as the main metal, see 673*

> ## 671.2–671.7 Specific metalworking processes

> Class specific processes applied to specific primary products in 671.8; class comprehensive works in 671

.2 **Founding (Casting)**

See also 671.3 for hot-working operations

.202 84   Materials

       Do not use for apparatus and equipment; class in 671.22

.22   Foundry equipment

.23   Patternmaking and moldmaking

.24   Melting

.25   Specific methods of casting

.252   Sand casting

.253   Permanent-mold casting

       Including die casting

.254   Centrifugal casting

.255   Investment casting

       Variant names: cire perdue, lost-wax, precision casting

       Including lost-foam casting

.256   Continuous casting

.3   **Mechanical working and related processes**

Standard subdivisions are added for mechanical working and related processes together, for mechanical working alone

Class here hot-working operations, cold-working operations, high-energy forming

For small forge work, see 682

.32   Rolling

.33   Forging, pressing, stamping

.332   Forging

.334	Stamping
.34	Extruding and drawing
.35	Machining

Including grinding

Class here cutting as a machining process, milling

Class comprehensive works on cutting metal in 671.53

.36	Heat treatment and hardening

Including age-hardening, annealing, quenching, shot peening, tempering

.37	Powder metallurgical processes (Powder metallurgy)
.373	Sintering
.4	**Electroforming of metals**
.5	**Joining and cutting of metals**

Standard subdivisions are added for joining and cutting together, for joining alone

Class ceramic-to-metal bonding in 666.042

.52	Welding

Including laser welding, underwater welding

Class underwater welding of a specific type with the type, e.g., underwater arc welding 671.5212

[.520 287]	Testing and measurement

Do not use; class in 671.520423

.520 4	Special topics of welding
.520 42	Welds (Welded joints)
.520 422	Weldability, weld stability, weld defects
.520 423	Inspection and testing
.521	Electric welding
.521 2	Arc welding
.521 3	Resistance welding

Including flash, projection, seam, spot welding

.521 4	Electron beam welding
.521 5	Induction welding
.522	Gas welding
.529	Pressure and thermit welding

Including diffusion welding, forge welding, ultrasonic welding

.53	Cutting

Class cutting as a machining process in 671.35

.56	Soldering and brazing

Standard subdivisions are added for either or both topics in heading

.58	Bonding
.59	Riveting

.7	**Finishing and surface treatment of metals; metal coating of nonmetals**

Including cleaning, deburring

.72	Polishing and buffing

Standard subdivisions are added for polishing and buffing together, for polishing alone

.73	Coating

Including cladding; coating of various metals with a specific metal and metal coating of nonmetals

Class enameling in 666.2; class coating various metals with a specific metal and metal coating of nonmetals using a specific type or method of coating in 671.732–671.736; class comprehensive works on coating in 667.9. Class metal coating of a specific material with the material, e.g., metal coating of plastics 668.4, metal coating of ferrous metals 672.73

.732	Electroplating

Add to base number 671.732 the numbers following 669 in 669.1–669.7, e.g., nickel plating 671.7327332

.733	Hot-metal dipping
.734	Metal spraying

Class here metallizing

For vacuum metallizing, see 671.735

.735	Vapor plating (Vacuum deposition)

Including vacuum metalizing, vapor-phase deposition

.736	Diffusion coating

.8	**Primary products**

Class here comprehensive works on technology of metal products

For a specific metal product not provided for here, see the product, e.g., metal furniture 684.105

.82	Rolled products
.821	Patternmaking
.823	Strips and sheets
.83	Forged, pressed, stamped products

.832	Pipes
.84	Extruded and drawn products
	Including cables
.842	Wires
.87	Powder metal products

672 Iron, steel, other iron alloys

Metalworking processes and primary products

Add to base number 672 the numbers following 671 in 671.2–671.8, e.g., heat treatment 672.36, galvanizing 672.732
Subdivisions are added for any or all topics in heading

For small forge work, see 682

673 Nonferrous metals

Metalworking processes and primary products

Class here alloys of nonferrous metals

Add to each subdivision identified by * the numbers following 671 in 671.2–671.8, e.g., welding aluminum 673.72252

Class metalworking processes and primary products in which nonferrous metals are not the main metal of the final product with the process or the main metal, e.g., nickel plating of various metals 671.7327332, zinc coating of steel 672.73252

.2	**Precious metals**
.22	*Gold
.23	*Silver
.24	*Platinum
.3	***Copper**

Class here brass, Muntz metal; bronze, gunmetal; copper-aluminum alloys; copper-beryllium alloys

.4	***Lead**
.5	**Zinc and cadmium**
.52	*Zinc

For brass, Muntz metal, see 673.3

.56	*Cadmium
.6	***Tin**

For bronze, gunmetal, see 673.3

.7	**Other nonferrous metals**

*Add as instructed under 673

.72	Light, alkali, alkaline-earth metals

> Standard subdivisions are added for light, alkali, alkaline-earth metals together; for light metals alone

> *For titanium, see 673.7322; for zirconium, see 673.735*

.722	*Aluminum

> *For copper-aluminum alloys, see 673.3*

.723	*Magnesium
.724	*Beryllium

> *For copper-beryllium alloys, see 673.3*

.73	Metals used in ferroalloys
.732	Titanium, vanadium, manganese
.732 2	*Titanium
.733	Nickel and cobalt
.733 2	*Nickel
.734	Chromium, molybdenum, tungsten
.735	Zirconium and tantalum

674   Lumber processing, wood products, cork

.001–.009	Standard subdivisions
.01	Philosophy and theory of lumber technology
.02	Miscellany of lumber technology
.021 2	Tables and formulas

> Do not use for specifications; class in 674.5

.028 6	Green technology (Environmental technology)

> Do not use for pollution control technology, waste technology; class in 674.84

.028 7	Testing and measurement

> Do not use for grading lumber; class in 674.5

.03–.09	Standard subdivisions of lumber technology

>   **674.1–674.5 Lumber technology**

> Class physical properties of lumber in 620.12; class comprehensive works in 674

.1	**Structure, chemical properties, types of lumber**

*Add as instructed under 673

.12   Structure

         Gross and microscopic

.13   Chemical properties

         Including chemical properties of wood extracts

.14   Specific types of lumber

         Class structure of specific types of lumber in 674.12; class chemical properties of specific types of lumber in 674.13

.142   Hardwoods

         Including basswood, beech, chestnut, elm, maple, oak, poplar

.144   Softwoods

         Including cedar, cypress, fir, hemlock, larch, pine, redwood, spruce

.2   **Sawmill operations**

         Class wood waste and residues in 674.84

.28   Rough lumber

         Class here dimension stock (cut stock)

.3   **Storage, seasoning, preservation of lumber**

.32   Storage in lumberyards

.38   Seasoning and preservation

         Standard subdivisions are added for seasoning and preservation together, for seasoning alone

         Class here drying

.382   Use of air

.384   Use of kilns

.386   Use of chemicals

         Class here preservation

.4   **Production of finished lumber**

.42   Production of surfaced lumber

.43   Production of pattern lumber

         Including shiplap, sidings, tongue-and-groove products

.5   **Grading lumber**

         Including inspection and specifications

.8 **Wood products**

Class here comprehensive works on wood-using technologies

For a specific product or wood-using technology not provided for here, see the product or technology, e.g., wood as a fuel 662.65, finished lumber 674.4, pulp and paper technology 676, wooden furniture 684.104, carpentry 694

.82 Containers and pallets

Including barrels, boxes, casks, crates

.83 Composite woods; veneers

Standard subdivisions are added for veneers and composite woods together, for composite woods alone

.833 Veneers

> **674.834–674.836 Composite woods**

Class comprehensive works in 674.83

.834 Plywood

See also 674.835 for specialty plywoods

.835 Laminated wood (Sandwich panels, Specialty plywoods)

.836 Particle board

.84 Wood waste and residues

Standard subdivisions are added for either or both topics in heading

Including excelsior, sawdust, wood flour and shavings

Class here pollution control technology, waste technology

Class utilization of wood waste and residues in making a specific product with the product, e.g., particle board 674.836

.88 Other products

Including picture frames, signs, spools, toothpicks, wood-cased pencils, woodenware

.9 **Cork**

675 Leather and fur processing

Standard subdivisions are added for leather and fur processing together, for leather processing alone

For leather and fur goods, see 685

.2 **Processing of natural leather**

[.202 87] Testing and measurement

Do not use; class in 675.29

.22	Preliminary operations

> Including fleshing, unhairing (liming), bating hides and skins

.23	Tanning
.24	Dressing
.25	Finishing

> Including dyeing, embossing, glazing, production of patent leather

.29	Properties, tests, quality controls
.3	**Fur processing**

> Including manufacture of imitation furs

.4	**Manufacture of imitation leathers**

676   Pulp and paper technology

> Standard subdivisions are added for pulp and paper technology together, for paper technology alone

> Class here comprehensive works on paper and paper products, on the total process of making paper out of logs or other sources of pulp

> Class the process of making pulp, through bleaching, in 676.1; class conversion of pulp into paper or paper products, starting with beating and refining the pulp, in 676.2

.028 6	Green technology (Environmental technology)

> Do not use for pollution control technology, waste technology; class in 676.042

.04	Special topics of pulp and paper technology
.042	Waste technology

> Class here pollution control

> Class paper recycling in 676.142

.1	**Pulp**

> Class here the process of making pulp, through bleaching

> Class conversion of pulp into paper, starting with beating and refining the pulp, in 676.2; class pulp by-products in 676.5

[.102 87]	Testing and measurement

> Do not use; class in 676.17

> 676.12–676.14 Specific pulps

> Class comprehensive works in 676.1

> *For purified pulp, see 676.4*

.12	Wood pulp

[.120 287]		Testing and measurement
		Do not use; class in 676.121
.121		Properties, tests, quality controls

> 676.122–676.127 Specific processes

Class comprehensive works in 676.12

.122		Mechanical process (Ground wood process)
.124		Soda process
.125		Sulfite process
.126		Sulfate process (Kraft process)
.127		Semichemical process
.13	Rag pulp	
.14	Other pulps	

Including bagasse, bamboo, cornstalks, hemp, jute, straw

.142	Wastepaper

Class here paper recycling

.17	Properties, tests, quality controls

Class properties, tests, quality controls of specific pulps in 676.12–676.14

.18	Molded products and pulpboards
.182	Molded products
.183	Pulpboards

Including chip boards, fiberboards, wallboards

See also 666.89 for drywall

> **676.2–676.5 Pulp products**

Class comprehensive works in 676

For molded products and pulpboards, see 676.18

.2	**Conversion of pulp into paper, and specific types of paper and paper products**

Class paper recycling in 676.142

[.202 87]		Testing and measurement
		Do not use; class in 676.27

>   676.22–676.27   General topics of conversion of pulp into paper

      Class general topics of specific types of paper and paper products in 676.28; class comprehensive works in 676.2

.22   Production by hand

.23   Specific processes of machine production

.232   Basic processes

.234   Finishing

      Including calendering, coloring, creping, sizing

      For coating, see 676.235

.235   Coating

.27   Properties, tests, quality controls

.28   Specific types of paper and paper products

      For photographic paper, see 661.808

.280 27   Patents and identification marks

      Including watermarks

.282   Graphic arts paper

.282 3   Stationery

      Including onionskin paper

.282 4   Book paper

      Class coated book paper in 676.283

.282 5   Drawing and art paper

      Standard subdivisions are added for either or both topics in heading

.282 6   Currency paper

      Papers for printing money, bonds, securities

.283   Coated paper

      For specific kinds of coated paper, see the kind, e.g., coated wallpaper 676.2848

.284   Specialty paper

.284 2   Tissue paper

      Including cleansing tissues, toilet paper

      Class onionskin paper in 676.2823

.284 4   Blotting and saturating paper

      Standard subdivisions are added for either or both topics in heading

.284 5		Vulcanized and parchment papers

See also 685 for parchment prepared from the skin of an animal

.284 8		Wallpaper
.286		Unsized paper

Including newsprint

.287		Wrapping and bag papers

Including bogus wrapping, butcher, kraft wrapping, Manila paper

.288		Paperboard

Including bristol board, cardboard, food board, pasteboard

.289		Roofing and building papers
.3		**Paper and paperboard containers**
.32		Boxes and cartons

Standard subdivisions are added for either or both topics in heading

Including corrugated and solid paperboard boxes, folding boxes

For food board containers, see 676.34

.33		Bags
.34		Food board containers

Including food cartons, paper plates and cups

.4		**Purified pulp**

Production of alpha cellulose from wood pulp and cotton linters

.5		**Pulp by-products**

Including fatty acids, lignin, resins, tall oil, turpentine

Class comprehensive works on naval stores in 665.33

.7		**Paper from man-made and noncellulosic fibers**
677		**Textiles**

Production of fibers, fabrics, cordage

Class here comprehensive works on manufacture of textiles and clothing

For manufacture of clothing, see 687

.001		Philosophy and theory
.002		Miscellany
.002 8		Auxiliary techniques and procedures
[.002 84]		Apparatus, equipment, materials

Do not use; class in 677.028

.002 86	Green technology (Environmental technology)
	Class waste and reused wool and hair in 677.36; class waste and reused silk in 677.394
[.002 87]	Testing and measurement
	Do not use; class in 677.0287
.003–.009	Standard subdivisions
.02	General topics of textiles
.022	Designs (Working patterns)
.028	Techniques, procedures, apparatus, equipment, materials, products
	For auxiliary techniques and procedures, see 677.0028
.028 2	Operations
.028 21	Preliminary operations
	Including carding, combing
.028 22	Spinning, twisting, reeling
	Standard subdivisions are added for spinning, twisting, reeling together; for spinning alone
.028 24	Weaving, knitting, felting
.028 242	Weaving
.028 245	Knitting
.028 25	Basic finishing
	Physical and chemical processes
	Including beetling, calendering, creping, mercerizing, pressing, shearing, singeing, tentering
	For dyeing and printing, see 667.3
.028 3	Materials
.028 32	Fibers
.028 35	Textile chemicals
.028 5	Power equipment
.028 52	Spinning machines
.028 54	Looms and loom equipment
	Standard subdivisions are added for looms and loom equipment together, for looms alone
.028 55	Basic finishing machines

.028 6		Products

For tests and quality controls of products, see 677.0287; for cordage, trimmings and allied products, see 677.7; for surgical gauze and cotton, see 677.8

.028 62		Yarns and threads

Standard subdivisions are added for either or both topics in heading

.028 64		Fabrics

For special-process fabrics, see 677.6

.028 7		Testing and measurement

Including tests and quality controls of products

> **677.1–677.5 Textiles of specific composition**

Class here specific kinds of textile fibers

Class special-process fabrics regardless of composition in 677.6; class comprehensive works in 677

.1 Textiles of bast fibers

.11 Flax

[.110 284] Apparatus, equipment, materials

Do not use; class in 677.112–677.117

.112–.117 Techniques, procedures, apparatus, equipment, materials, products

Add to base number 677.11 the numbers following 677.028 in 677.0282–677.0287, e.g., linen fabrics 677.1164

For auxiliary techniques and procedures, see 677.11028

.12 Hemp

.13 Jute

.15 Ramie

.18 Coir

.2 Textiles of seed-hair fibers

.21 Cotton

[.210 284] Apparatus, equipment, materials

Do not use; class in 677.212–677.217

.212–.217 Techniques, procedures, apparatus, equipment, materials, products

Add to base number 677.21 the numbers following 677.028 in 677.0282–677.0287, e.g., cotton ginning, carding, combing 677.2121

For auxiliary techniques and procedures, see 677.21028

.23   Kapok

.3   Textiles of animal fibers

.31   Sheep wool

> Class here comprehensive works on technology of wool textiles
>
> *For llama, alpaca, vicuña, guanaco wool textiles, see 677.32*

[.310 284]   Apparatus, equipment, materials

> Do not use; class in 677.312–677.317

.312–.317   Techniques, procedures, apparatus, equipment, materials, products

> Add to base number 677.31 the numbers following 677.028 in 677.0282–677.0287, e.g., sheep wool fibers 677.3132
>
> *For auxiliary techniques and procedures, see 677.31028*

.32   Llama, alpaca, vicuña, guanaco wools

.33   Goat hair

.34   Camel's hair

.35   Rabbit hair

.36   Waste and reused wool and hair

> Standard subdivisions are added for any or all topics in heading

.39   Silk

.391   Cultivated silk

[.391 028 4]   Apparatus, equipment, materials

> Do not use; class in 677.3912–677.3917

.391 2–.391 7   Techniques, procedures, apparatus, equipment, materials, products

> Add to base number 677.391 the numbers following 677.028 in 677.0282–677.0287, e.g., beetling cultivated silk 677.39125
>
> *For auxiliary techniques and procedures, see 677.391028*

.392   Wild silk (Tussah silk)

.394   Waste and reused silk

> Standard subdivisions are added for either or both topics in heading

.4   Textiles of man-made fibers

.46   Cellulosics (Rayon and acetates)

> *For textiles of paper fibers, see 677.5*

.460 01–.460 09   Standard subdivisions

.460 1–.460 9   Standard subdivisions of rayon

> 677.461–677.463 Rayon

   Class comprehensive works in 677.46

.461   Nitrocellulose

.462   Cuprammonium rayon

.463   Viscose rayon

.464   Cellulose acetate

.47   Noncellulosics

   For fiber glass, see 677.52

.472   Azlon

.473   Polyamides (Nylons)

.474   Other polymerization textiles

.474 2   Acrylics

   Class here polyacrylics

.474 3   Polyesters

.474 4   Vinyls

   Including nytrils, sarans, vinyons

   Class here polyvinyls

.474 5   Olefins

   Including polyethylene, polypropylene

.474 8   Polyfluoro hydrocarbons

.5   Other textiles of specific fibers

.51   Textiles of asbestos fibers

.52   Textiles of fiber glass

.53   Textiles of metal fibers

.54   Textiles of unaltered vegetable fibers

   Including bamboo, cane, raffia, rattan, rush

.55   Textiles of elastic fibers

.6   Special-process fabrics regardless of composition

   Class here nonwoven fabrics

.61   Fancy-weave fabrics

   For tapestries, carpets, rugs, see 677.64; for openwork fabrics, see 677.65

.615	Fabrics in dobby weave

Including bird's-eye, figured madras, huckaback, sharkskin

.616	Fabrics in Jacquard weave

Including brocade, brocatelle, damask, lamé, upholstery fabrics

.617	Fabrics in pile weave

Including chenille, corduroy, frieze, plush, terry cloth, velour, velvet, velveteen

.62	Woven felt

Class comprehensive works on felt in 677.63

.624	Flannel and swanskin yard goods
.626	Blankets, lap robes, coverlets
.63	Felt

For woven felt, see 677.62

.632	Yard goods and carpets
.64	Tapestries, carpets, rugs
.642	Tapestry yard goods
.643	Rugs

Class here carpets

For nonwoven felt carpets, see 677.632

.65	Openwork fabrics

For chain-stitch and knotted fabrics, see 677.66

.652	Fabrics in leno weave

Including grenadines, marquisettes

.653	Laces

Including bobbin, machine, needlepoint laces

.654	Tulles
.66	Chain-stitch and knotted fabrics
.661	Knitted fabrics
.662	Crocheted fabrics
.663	Tatted fabrics
.664	Netted fabrics
.68	Fabrics with functional finishes

Including drip-dry, durable press fabrics

Class specific types of special-process fabrics regardless of finish in 677.61–677.66

.681　　　Crease-resistant and wrinkle-resistant fabrics

　　　　　Standard subdivisions are added for either or both topics in heading

.682　　　Waterproof and water-repellent fabrics

　　　　　Standard subdivisions are added for either or both topics in heading

.688　　　Shrinkage-controlled fabrics

.689　　　Flameproof and flame-resistant fabrics

　　　　　Standard subdivisions are added for either or both topics in heading

.69　　　Bonded and laminated fabrics

　　　　　Standard subdivisions are added for either or both topics in heading

.7　　Cordage, trimmings and allied products

.71　　　Ropes, twines, strings

　　　　　Class here cordage

　　　　　For passementerie, see 677.76

.76　　　Passementerie

　　　　　Including decorative bias bindings, braids, cords, gimps, lacings, ribbons, tapes, tinsel; upholstery trimmings

.77　　　Machine embroidery

　　　　　Including clip spot, lappet, Schiffli, swivel (dotted swiss) embroidery

　　　　　Class laces in 677.653

.8　　Surgical gauze and cotton

　　　　　Including bandages, sanitary napkins

678　Elastomers and elastomer products

Standard subdivisions are added for elastomers and elastomer products together, for elastomers alone

.2　　Rubber

　　　　　For rubber products, see 678.3; for properties of rubber, see 678.4; for natural rubber, see 678.62; for synthetic rubber, see 678.72

.202 84　　　Apparatus and equipment

　　　　　Do not use for materials; class in 678.21

.202 86　　　Green technology (Environmental technology)

　　　　　Do not use for pollution control technology, waste technology; class in 678.29

.21　　　Materials

　　　　　For reclaimed rubber, see 678.29

.22　　　Mastication

.23		Compounding

Including use of accelerators, antioxidants, pigments, solvents

.24		Vulcanization
.27		Molding, extruding, calendering
.29		Reclaimed rubber and waste control

Including devulcanizing

Class here pollution control technology, waste technology

.3   **Rubber products**

Class elastic fiber textiles in 677.55

For natural rubber products, see 678.63; for synthetic rubber products, see 678.723

.32	Tires
.33	Overshoes
.34	Articles molded and vulcanized in presses

Including doorstops, hollow ware, hot-water bottles, tiles

.35	Extruded articles

Including inner tubes, rubber bands, weather stripping, windshield wipers

.36	Articles made by dipping, spreading, electrodeposition

Including conveyor and driving belts, hose, sheeting

.4   **Properties of rubber**

.5   **Latexes**

For natural latexes, see 678.61; for synthetic latexes, see 678.71

[.502 84]	Apparatus, equipment, materials

Do not use; class in 678.52

.52	Techniques, procedures, apparatus, equipment, materials
.521	Materials
.522	Preliminary treatment

Including preservation, concentration, creaming, centrifuging, preparation of latex biscuits

.524	Vulcanization
.527	Other operations

Including casting, coating, dipping, electrodepositing, molding, spreading

.53	Products
.532	Foam articles

.533		Articles made by dipping and casting
		Including feeding-bottle nipples
.538		Articles made by extruding, spreading, spraying, electrodeposition
.54		Properties
.6		**Natural elastomers**
.61		Natural latexes
.62		Natural rubber

For natural rubber products, see 678.63; for properties of natural rubber, see 678.64

.63		Natural rubber products
.64		Properties of natural rubber
.68		Chemical derivatives of natural rubber

Including cyclo and halogenated rubber, rubber hydrochloride

.7		**Synthetic elastomers**
.71		Synthetic latexes
.72		Synthetic rubber and derivatives

Standard subdivisions are added for synthetic rubber and derivatives together, for synthetic rubber alone

Including acrylonitrile rubber (GR-A), butadiene-styrene rubber (GR-S), chloroprene rubber (GR-M), isobutylene rubber (GR-I), polybutadiene rubber, polyurethane rubber

Class comprehensive works on polyurethanes in 668.4239

.720 28   Auxiliary techniques and procedures; apparatus, equipment, materials

Do not use for auxiliary techniques and procedures, apparatus, equipment, materials for synthetic rubber; class in 678.722

.722		Techniques, procedures, apparatus, equipment, materials for synthetic rubber
.723		Synthetic rubber products
.724		Properties of synthetic rubber
.728		Chemical derivatives of synthetic rubber
.73		High-styrene resins (Elastoplastics)

679 Other products of specific kinds of materials

.4		**Products of keratinous and dentinal materials**
.43		Ivory products
.47		Feather products

.6   **Products of fibers and bristles**

         Including brooms, brushes, mops

.7   **Products of tobacco**

         See also 688.4 for tobacco substitutes

.72   Cigars

.73   Cigarettes

680   Manufacture of products for specific uses

Not provided for elsewhere

Class here interdisciplinary works on handicrafts

Class repairs of household equipment by members of household in 643.7. Class manufacture of a product based on a specific branch of engineering with the branch of engineering in 620, e.g., military engineering 623, manufacture of motor vehicles 629.2; except for products provided for in 681–688, class manufacture of products of a specific material with the material in 671–679, e.g., manufacture of steel pipes 672.832, but manufacture of steel toys 688.72

     For artistic handicraft work, see 745.5

     See Manual at 671–679 vs. 680; also at 680 vs. 745.5

681   Precision instruments and other devices

Standard subdivisions are added for precision instruments and other devices together, for precision instruments alone

.1   **Instruments for measuring time, counting and calculating machines and instruments**

     For testing, measuring, sensing instruments, see 681.2

.11   Instruments for measuring time

.111   Ancient and primitive instruments

         Including hourglasses, water clocks

.111 2   Sundials

.112   Constituent parts (Clockwork)

         Including gears, escapements, bearings, regulating devices

.113   Clocks

         Class here interdisciplinary works on clocks

         For constituent parts, see 681.112; for pneumatic clocks, see 681.115; for electric clocks, see 681.116; for chronographs, chronoscopes, chronometers, see 681.118; for clocks considered as works of art, see 739.3

.114   Watches

         Class here interdisciplinary works on watches

           For constituent parts, see 681.112; for chronographs, chronoscopes, chronometers, see 681.118; for watches considered as works of art, see 739.3

.115   Pneumatic clocks

.116   Electric clocks

.118   Chronographs, chronoscopes, chronometers

         Including metronomes, stopwatches, tachometers, time clocks, time and date recorders

.14   Counting and calculating machines and instruments

         Including cash registers, slide rules, sorting machines, voting machines

           For computers, see 621.39

.145   Calculators

.2   **Testing, measuring, sensing instruments**

         Standard subdivisions are added for any or all topics in heading

         Including calorimeters

         Class here testing, measuring, sensing instruments of general application in science or technology; testing, measuring, sensing instruments for nontechnological application; instruments for measuring physical quantities; electrical and electronic instruments for measuring nonelectrical and nonelectronic quantities

         Class testing, measuring, sensing instruments for a specific branch of science (other than instruments for measuring physical quantities) in 681.75. Class testing, measuring, sensing instruments for a specific technological application with the manufacturing number, e.g., aircraft instrumentation 629.135, medical diagnostic equipment 681.761

           For instruments for measuring electrical quantities, see 621.37; for instruments for testing and measuring electronic signals, see 621.381548; for instruments for measuring time, see 681.11

.25   Optical testing, measuring, sensing instruments

         Including polarimeters

         Class here fiber optic sensors

         Class optical testing, measuring, sensing instruments applied to a specific property with the property, e.g., fiber optic sensors to measure flow 681.28

           For spectroscopes, see 681.414; for photometers, see 681.415

.28   Flowmeters

.4   **Optical instruments**

.41	Specific instruments

Including contact lenses

For component parts of specific instruments, see 681.42–681.43

.411	Eyeglasses
.412	Telescopes and binoculars
.412 3	Telescopes
.412 5	Binoculars

Including opera glasses

Class here field glasses

.413	Microscopes
.414	Spectroscopes
.414 2–.414 6	Optical, infrared, ultraviolet spectroscopes

Add to base number 681.414 the numbers following 535.84 in 535.842–535.846, e.g., infrared spectroscopes 681.4142

.414 8	Other spectroscopes

Including magnetic resonance, microwave, radio-frequency, X-ray and gamma-ray spectroscopes

.415	Photometers
.418	Photographic equipment

Including cameras, projectors, accessories

Class film and other chemical photographic supplies in 661.808

For photometers, see 681.415; for photocopying equipment, see 681.65

>   **681.42–681.43 Component parts**

Class comprehensive works in 681.4

.42	Lenses, prisms, mirrors
.423	Lenses
.428	Mirrors
.43	Frames and other housings

.6   **Printing, writing, duplicating machines and equipment**

> Including computer output microform (COM) devices, pens, mechanical pencils, rubber stamps
>
> Class here comprehensive works on manufacturing of office equipment
>
> Class facsimile recorders in 621.38235; class wood-cased pencils in 674.88; class interdisciplinary works on office equipment in 651.2
>
> > *For manufacturing a specific kind of office equipment, see the kind, e.g., calculators 681.145*

.61   Stenographic and composing machines, typewriters

.62   Printers and printing presses

> Class here computer output printers
>
> > *See also 621.988 for three-dimensional printing*

.65   Photocopying equipment

.7   **Other scientific and technological instruments, machinery, equipment**

> Not provided for elsewhere

.75   Scientific instruments and equipment

> Standard subdivisions are added for either or both topics in heading
>
> Class here testing, measuring, sensing equipment for specific branches of science
>
> Class comprehensive works on scientific testing, measuring, sensing instruments in 681.2

.753   Physical instruments and equipment

> Standard subdivisions are added for either or both topics in heading
>
> Including instruments with multiple applications based on physical principles, e.g., gyroscopes
>
> Class instruments for measuring physical quantities in 681.2

.754   Chemical instruments and equipment

> Standard subdivisions are added for either or both topics in heading

.755   Geological instruments and equipment

> Standard subdivisions are added for either or both topics in heading

.757   Biological instruments and equipment

> Standard subdivisions are added for either or both topics in heading

.76	Technological equipment

Including construction, pollution control, mining, surveying equipment

Class here instruments, machinery; testing, measuring, sensing instruments in specific branches of technology not provided for elsewhere

Class comprehensive works on technological testing, measuring, sensing instruments in 681.2

.760 4	Special topics of technological equipment
.760 41	Pressure vessels

Class a specific use of pressure vessels with the use, e.g., nuclear pressure vessels 621.483

.761	Medical and health equipment

Standard subdivisions are added for medical and health equipment together, for medical equipment alone

Including condoms, crutches, diagnostic equipment, exercise equipment, prosthetic devices

Class interdisciplinary works on medical and health equipment in 610.284; class interdisciplinary works on exercise equipment in 613.710284

.763	Agricultural and related equipment

Standard subdivisions are added for agricultural and related equipment together, for agricultural equipment alone

Including subsistence hunting, fishing, shooting equipment

Class comprehensive works on commercial and sports hunting, fishing, shooting equipment in 688.79

.763 1	Equipment for plant culture
.763 6	Equipment for animal culture
.766	Equipment for chemical and related technologies
.766 4	Equipment for food and beverage technology
.766 5	Equipment for petroleum and industrial gas technologies
.766 6	Equipment for ceramic technology
.766 8	Equipment for plastic and elastomer technologies
.766 9	Equipment for metallurgy
.767	Equipment for nonchemical manufactures
.767 1	Equipment for metal manufactures
.767 6	Equipment for wood and paper technologies
.767 7	Equipment for textile and clothing technologies

.8 Musical instruments

Add to base number 681.8 the numbers following 78 in 786–788, e.g., manufacture of pianos 681.862

Class hand construction of specific instruments or groups of instruments in 786–788; class comprehensive works on hand construction in 784.1923

682 Small forge work (Blacksmithing)

.1 Horseshoeing

.4 Ironwork and hand-forged tools

Standard subdivisions are added for ironwork and hand-forged tools together, for ironwork alone

683 Hardware, weapons, household appliances

Standard subdivisions are added for hardware, weapons, household appliances together, for hardware alone

Class here comprehensive works on manufacture of hardware and building supplies

For a specific hardware or building supply product not provided for here, see the product, e.g., tools 621.9, paints 667.6

.3 Locksmithing

.31 Bolts and latches

Standard subdivisions are added for either or both topics in heading

.32 Locks and keys

Standard subdivisions are added for either or both topics in heading

.34 Safes and strongboxes

Standard subdivisions are added for either or both topics in heading

.4 Weapons

Class here nonlethal weapons, small firearms, gunsmithing; comprehensive works on engineering and manufacturing of weapons

For military weapons, see 623.4; for comprehensive works on engineering and manufacturing of small arms of pre-firearm origin, see 623.441

.400 1 Philosophy and theory

.400 2 Miscellany

[.400 288] Maintenance and repair

Do not use; class in 683.403

.400 3–.400 9 Standard subdivisions

> 683.401–683.406 General topics of weapons and small firearms

Class comprehensive works in 683.4

.401	Design
.403	Maintenance and repair
	Standard subdivisions are added for either or both topics in heading
.406	Ammunition
.42	Rifles and shotguns
.422	Rifles
.426	Shotguns
.43	Handguns
.432	Pistols
	Class here single-shot pistols
.432 5	Automatic pistols
.436	Revolvers
.44	Electroshock weapons
	Including tasers
.45	Chemical weapons
	Including pepper spray, tear gas

.8   **Household utensils and appliances**

Including tableware

For nonmetallic household utensils and appliances, see the material from which they are made, e.g., porcelain tableware 666.58, woodenware 674.88

.802 88   Maintenance and repair

For maintenance and repair by members of household, see 643.60288

.82   Kitchen utensils

Including cutlery, pots, pans, pails

.83   Electrical appliances

Class comprehensive works on electrical equipment in 621.31042

For electrical equipment requiring special installation, see 683.88

.88   Heavy equipment

Electrical, gas, other equipment requiring special installation

Including dishwashers, dryers, garbage-disposal units, ranges, stoves, washing machines, water heaters

For refrigerators and freezers, see 621.57; for heating, ventilating, air-conditioning equipment, see 697

684   Furnishings and home workshops

Standard subdivisions are added for furnishings and home workshops together, for furnishings alone

Class here home furnishings

For lighting fixtures, see 621.32

.001–.009	Standard subdivisions
.08	Woodworking

Class here comprehensive works on home (amateur) workshops

For metalworking in home workshops, see 684.09; for furniture making in home workshops, see 684.1

.082	Woodworking with hand tools

Including woodworking with specific hand tools, e.g., planes

.083	Woodworking with power tools

Add to base number 684.083 the numbers following 621.9 in 621.91–621.95, e.g., routers 684.08312, power saws 684.08334

.084	Surface finishing
.09	Metalworking

.1   Furniture

Class here home construction of furniture

.100 1–.100 9	Standard subdivisions

>   684.104–684.106   General topics of furniture

Class comprehensive works in 684.1

.104	Wooden furniture

Class here cabinetmaking

[.104 028 8]	Maintenance and repair

Do not use; class in 684.1044

.104 2	Basic construction
.104 3	Surface finishing
.104 4	Maintenance and repair

Standard subdivisions are added for either or both topics in heading

.104 42	Body restoration
.104 43	Surface refinishing
.105	Metal furniture

.106   **Furniture in other materials**

> Including composite materials, plastics, rattan, tiles

>   **684.12–684.16 Specific kinds of furniture**

> Class outdoor furniture in 684.18; class comprehensive works in 684.1

.12   **Upholstered furniture**

> Including couches, sofas, upholstered chairs

.13   **Chairs and tables**

.132   Chairs

> *For upholstered chairs, see 684.12*

.135   Tables

> *For desks, see 684.14*

.14   **Desks**

.15   **Beds**

> Including frames, springs, mattresses

.16   **Cabinets and built-in furniture**

> Standard subdivisions are added for cabinets and built-in furniture together, for cabinets alone

> Including chests, china cabinets, dressers, file cabinets

> Class here furniture used for storage

> *See also 684.104 for cabinetmaking*

.162   Shelving

> Class here bookcases

> *For built-in wooden shelves, see 694.6*

.18   **Outdoor furniture**

> Including garden, patio, porch furniture

> Class camping furniture in 685.53

.3   **Fabric furnishings**

> Including bedclothes, curtains, draperies, hangings, slipcovers

> Class home construction of fabric furnishings in 646.21

> *For carpets and rugs, see 677.643*

685   Leather and fur goods, and related products

Standard subdivisions are added for leather and fur goods and related products together, for leather goods alone

Including parchment prepared from the skin of an animal

See also 676.2845 for parchment paper made from pulp

.1   Saddlery and harness making

.2   Leather and fur clothing and accessories

Class leather and fur footwear in 685.3; class leather and fur gloves and mittens in 685.4

.22   Leather clothing and accessories

Including aprons, belts, jackets, skirts, trousers

.24   Fur clothing and accessories

Standard subdivisions are added for fur clothing and accessories together, for fur clothing alone

Including coats, hats, jackets, muffs, neckpieces, stoles

.3   Footwear and related products

For overshoes, see 678.33; for hosiery, see 687.3

.31   Boots and shoes

Standard subdivisions are added for either or both topics in heading

Class shoes for specific activities in 685.36; class shoes for people with disabilities in 685.38

For wooden shoes and clogs, see 685.32

.310 01   Philosophy and theory

.310 02   Miscellany

[.310 028 8]   Maintenance and repair

Do not use; class in 685.3104

.310 03–.310 09   Standard subdivisions

.310 2   Design

.310 3   Construction

.310 4   Maintenance and repair

Standard subdivisions are added for either or both topics in heading

.32   Wooden shoes and clogs

.36   Footwear for specific activities

For footwear used as equipment in a specific sport, see the sport, e.g., ice skating 688.7691

.38   Footwear and related products for people with disabilities

> Standard subdivisions are added for footwear and related products together, for footwear alone

> Including orthopedic shoes

.4   Gloves and mittens

> Standard subdivisions are added for either or both topics in heading

> Regardless of material

.41   Conventional gloves

.43   Gloves and mittens for specific activities

> Including protective gloves for industry

>> *For gloves and mittens used as equipment in a specific sport, see the sport in 688.7, e.g., baseball 688.76357*

.47   Conventional mittens

.5   Luggage, handbags, camping equipment

.51   Luggage and handbags

> Including briefcases, attaché cases

.53   Camping equipment

> Including sleeping bags, tents

686   Printing and related activities

> Class here design and manufacture of publications, book arts

> Class interdisciplinary works on the book in 002

>> *For book illustration, see 741.64*

>> *See also 681.6 for manufacture of printing equipment*

.1   Invention of printing

.2   Printing

> Class here printing in the Latin alphabet

> Class works on desktop publishing that emphasize typography in 686.22; class comprehensive works on printing and publishing in 070.5; class interdisciplinary works on print media in 302.232

>> *See also 070.593 for self-publishing; also 621.988 for three-dimensional printing*

.209   History, geographic treatment, biography

> Class invention of printing in 686.1

.21 Printing in non-Latin alphabets and characters

Standard subdivisions are added for either or both topics in heading

Class here typefounding, typecasting, typefaces for non-Latin alphabets and characters

For other specific aspects of printing in non-Latin alphabets and characters, see the aspect, e.g., letterpress printing 686.2312

.218 Greek alphabet

.219 Other non-Latin alphabets and characters

Add to base number 686.219 the numbers following —9 in notation 91–99 from Table 6, e.g., Cyrillic alphabet 686.21918

.22 Typography

.221 Typefounding and typecasting

Standard subdivisions are added for either or both topics in heading

.224 Typefaces

Design, style, specimens of letters, ornaments, other characters and devices

Class here typefaces for the Latin alphabet

Class typefaces for non-Latin alphabets and characters in 686.21; class typefaces for braille and other raised characters in 686.282

.224 7 Specific typefaces and kinds of typefaces for the Latin alphabet

Including Gothic, italic, roman type; Bodoni, Garamond, Times Roman type

.225 Composition (Typesetting)

[.225 028 5] Computer applications

Do not use; class in 686.22544

.225 2 Page design

Including paste-up

Class here layout

.225 3 Hand composition

.225 4 Machine composition

.225 42 Composition by use of human-operated equipment

Including linotype composition

.225 44	Composition by use of automatic equipment

> Including phototypesetting (photocomposition)

> Class here computerized typesetting

> Unless it is redundant, add to base number 686.22544 the numbers following 00 in 004–006, e.g., personal computer software for typesetting 686.22544536, the use of digital personal computers 686.22544416, but the use of digital computers 686.22544 (*not* 686.225444)

.225 6	Imposition and lockup
.23	Presswork (Impression)

> Class interdisciplinary works on use of computer printers as low-volume output devices in 004.77. Class a specific use with the use, e.g., use in typesetting 686.22544477

> *For printing special graphic materials, see 686.28*

> *See also 621.38235 for facsimile transmission; also 681.6 for manufacture of printing equipment*

.230 4	Special topics of presswork
.230 42	Color printing
.231	Mechanical techniques

> *For photomechanical techniques, see 686.232*

.231 2	Printing from type

> Class here comprehensive works on letterpress techniques

> *For printing from plates, see 686.2314*

.231 4	Printing from plates

> Printing from stereotypes, electrotypes, autotypes, engraved plates, paper mats

> *See also 686.2315 for printing from planographic plates*

.231 5	Planographic (Flat-surface)

> Class here lithography and offset (offset lithography)

> *For photolithography, photo-offset, collotype, see 686.2325*

.231 6	Stencil techniques

> Including silk-screen printing

.232	Photomechanical techniques
.232 5	Photolithography, photo-offset, collotype (gelatin process)

> *See also 621.381531 for photolithography in manufacture of printed circuits (microlithography)*

.232 7	Photoengraving (Photointaglio)

> Including line and halftone cuts, photogravure

.233   Nonimpact techniques

> Including electrographic, electrophotographic, laser processes

> *See also 686.44 for electrophotographic processes in photocopying*

.28   Printing special graphic materials

.282   Raised characters

> Class here braille

> Class comprehensive works on braille and other raised-character alphabets in 411

.283   Maps

.284   Music

.288   Materials of direct monetary value

> Including postage stamps, securities

.3   **Bookbinding**

> Processes and materials

.300 1–.300 9   Standard subdivisions

.302   Hand and fine binding

> Standard subdivisions are added for either or both topics in heading

.303   Specific kinds of commercial binding

.303 2   Library binding

.303 4   Edition binding

.34   Types of covers

.342   Leather

.343   Cloth and imitation leather

.344   Paper

.35   Methods of fastening

> Including hand sewing, oversewing, side-sewing, wire-stitching; perfect binding and other kinds of gluing

.36   Ornamentation

> Including gilding, lettering, marbling, tooling

.4   **Photocopying**

> Class here photoduplication, interdisciplinary works on photocopying

> Class facsimile transmission in 621.38235

> *For a specific aspect of photocopying, see the aspect, e.g., library photocopying services 025.12*

> *See also 681.65 for manufacture of photocopying equipment*

.42	Blueprinting
.43	Microphotography

         Production of microforms

         Class here production of microfiche and microfilms

.44	Electrostatic and electrophotographic processes
.442	Xerography
.45	Production of photostats

687   Clothing and accessories

Standard subdivisions are added for clothing and accessories together, for clothing alone

Class here dressmaking, casual wear (sportswear)

Unless other instructions are given, class a subject with aspects in two or more subdivisions of 687 in the number coming last, e.g., military headwear 687.4 (*not* 687.15)

Class interdisciplinary works on clothing in 391; class interdisciplinary works on clothing construction in 646.4

        For leather and fur clothing, see 685.2

.04	General topics of clothing
.042	Patternmaking and grading

         Standard subdivisions are added for patternmaking and grading together, for patternmaking alone

.043	Cutting
.044	Tailoring

.1   Specific kinds of garments

        For footwear, see 685.3; for gloves and mittens, see 685.4; for undergarments, see 687.2; for hosiery, see 687.3; for headwear, see 687.4

.11	Miscellaneous kinds of garments

         Limited to those provided for below

.112	Dresses
.113	Suits

         Class here jackets, sport coats, vests (waistcoats)

         Class pants (trousers) in 687.116; class skirts in 687.117

.115	Shirts, blouses, tops

         Standard subdivisions are added for any or all topics in heading

.116	Pants (Trousers)

        See also 687.2 for pants (undergarments)

.117	Skirts
.14	Outerwear

Class here overcoats, topcoats, raincoats; comprehensive works on coats and jackets

For suit jackets, sport coats, see 687.113

[.140 811]	Outerwear for men

Do not use; class in 687.141

[.140 82]	Outerwear for women

Do not use; class in 687.142

.140 83	Outerwear for young adults

Do not use for outerwear for children; class in 687.143

For outerwear for young adult men aged twenty-one and over, see 687.141; for outerwear for young adult women twenty-one and over, see 687.142

.140 84	Outerwear for people in specific stages of adulthood

Class outerwear for adult men regardless of age in 687.141; class outerwear for adult women regardless of age in 687.142

.141	Outerwear for men

Class outerwear for young adult men in 687.1408351

.142	Outerwear for women

Class outerwear for young adult women in 687.1408352

.143	Outerwear for children
.15	Uniforms and symbolic garments

Including civil and military uniforms, ceremonial and academic robes, ecclesiastical vestments

.16	Garments for special purposes

Including activewear (clothing for athletic and outdoor sports), costumes, evening and formal dress, maternity garments, wedding clothes

For uniforms and symbolic garments, see 687.15

See also 687 for casual wear (sportswear)

.162	Protective clothing

Including fire-resistant clothing

.165	Sleepwear and loungewear

Standard subdivisions are added for either or both topics in heading

.19 Accessories

Including aprons, belts, cuffs, handkerchiefs, muffs, neckwear, scarves

Class interdisciplinary works on accessories in 391.44; class interdisciplinary works on making costume jewelry in 688.2; class interdisciplinary works on making jewelry in 739.27

For gloves and mittens, see 685.4; for handbags, see 685.51; for headwear, see 687.4

.2 **Undergarments**

See also 687.3 for hosiery

[.208 11] Undergarments for men

Do not use; class in 687.21

[.208 2] Undergarments for women

Do not use; class in 687.22

[.208 3] Undergarments for young people

Do not use; class in 687.23

.208 4 Undergarments for people in specific stages of adulthood

Class undergarments for adult men regardless of age in 687.21; class undergarments for adult women regardless of age in 687.22

.208 7 Undergarments for people with disabilities and illnesses

Class supporting undergarments worn for medical or health reasons in 687.25

.21 Men's undergarments

.22 Women's undergarments

Class here comprehensive works on lingerie

For women's sleepwear and loungewear, see 687.165082

.23 Children's undergarments

Class young men's undergarments in 687.21; class young women's undergarments in 687.22

.25 Supporting undergarments worn for medical or health reasons

.3 **Hosiery**

.4 **Headwear**

Including headscarves, helmets, protective headwear

Class here bonnets, caps, hats

For helmets as armor, see 623.441. For headwear used as equipment in a specific sport, see the sport in 688.7, e.g., football 688.76332

[.408 11]	Men's headwear	

Do not use; class in 687.41

[.408 2]	Women's headwear

Do not use; class in 687.42

[.408 3]	Young people's headwear

Do not use; class in 687.43

.408 4	Headwear for people in specific stages of adulthood

Class headwear for adult men regardless of age in 687.41; class headwear for adult women regardless of age in 687.42

.41	Men's headwear
.42	Women's headwear
.43	Children's headwear

Class headwear for young men in 687.41; class headwear for young women in 687.42

.8   Items auxiliary to clothing construction (Notions)

Including buttons

Class here comprehensive works on manufacture of sewing equipment and supplies

Class interdisciplinary works on sewing equipment and supplies in 646.1

For manufacture of sewing machinery and equipment, see 681.7677. For manufacture of a specific kind of sewing supply, see the kind, e.g., thread 677.02862

688   Other final products, and packaging technology

.1   Models and miniatures

Standard subdivisions are added for either or both topics in heading

Class here interdisciplinary works on models and miniatures

Class interdisciplinary works on handcrafted models and miniatures in 745.5928

For models and miniatures of a specific object, see the object, plus notation 0228 from Table 1, e.g., scale models of space stations 629.4420228

See Manual at 745.5928

.2   Costume jewelry

Class here interdisciplinary works on making costume jewelry

Class handcrafted costume jewelry in 745.5942; class interdisciplinary works on costume jewelry in 391.7; class interdisciplinary works on making jewelry in 739.27

.4   **Supplies for tobacco users**

Including ash trays, cigarette holders and cases, hookahs, lighters, tobacco pouches, tobacco substitutes

Class here supplies for smoking tobacco, for chewing tobacco

.42   Pipes

.5   **Accessories for personal grooming**

Including combs, electric shavers, nail-care tools, razors, razor blades, tweezers

For cosmetics, see 668.55; for brushes, see 679.6

.6   **Nonmotor land vehicles**

Including carriages, carts, wagons, wheelbarrows

For cycles, see 629.227

See also 688.7622 for skateboards

See Manual at 629.046 vs. 388

.7   **Recreational equipment**

Including stilts

Class here footwear, gloves and mittens, headwear used as equipment in a specific sport

See also 681.761 for exercise equipment

.72   Toys

Class here interdisciplinary works on mass-produced and handcrafted toys

For handcrafted toys, see 745.592

.722   Dolls, puppets, marionettes

.722 1   Dolls

.722 4   Puppets and marionettes

.723   Dollhouses and furniture

Standard subdivisions are added for either or both topics in heading

.724   Soft toys

Class stuffed dolls in 688.7221

.724 3   Teddy bears

.725   Educational toys

Including construction toys, science sets

.726   Novelties, ornaments, puzzles, tricks

Not provided for elsewhere

.728   Action toys

      Mechanical, electrical, electronic, others

      Class scale-model action toys in 688.1

\>   688.74–688.79 Equipment for sports and games

      Not provided for elsewhere

      Class comprehensive works in 688.7

.74   Equipment for indoor games of skill

      Add to base number 688.74 the numbers following 794 in 794.1–794.8, e.g., chessmen 688.741

.75   Equipment for games of chance

      Add to base number 688.75 the numbers following 795 in 795.1–795.4, e.g., playing cards 688.754

.76   Equipment for outdoor sports and games

      Add to base number 688.76 the numbers following 796 in 796.1–796.9, e.g., tennis rackets 688.76342; however, for camping equipment, see 685.53; for baseball caps, see 687.4

      For equipment for equestrian sports and animal racing, see 688.78; for equipment for fishing, hunting, shooting, see 688.79

.78   Equipment for equestrian sports and animal racing

      Including hurdles

      For saddles and harnesses, see 685.1

.79   Equipment for fishing, hunting, shooting

      Add to base number 688.79 the numbers following 799 in 799.1–799.3, e.g., artificial flies 688.79124

      For small firearms, see 683.4

      See also 681.763 for subsistence hunting, fishing, shooting equipment

.8   **Packaging technology**

      Materials, equipment, techniques

      Class interdisciplinary works on packaging in 658.564. Class manufacture and use of containers made of a specific material with the material, e.g., paper containers 676.3; class artistic aspects of containers with the aspect in 700, e.g., earthenware vases 738.38; class containers for a specific product with the product, e.g., beer cans 663.42

[689]   **[Unassigned]**

      Most recently used in Edition 14

690   **Construction of buildings**

Planning, analysis, engineering design, construction, destruction of habitable structures and their utilities

Class interdisciplinary works on design and construction of buildings in 720

See Manual at 624 vs. 690; also at 690 vs. 643.7

.01	Philosophy and theory
.02	Miscellany
.021 2	Formulas

         Do not use for specifications; class in 692.3

[.022 3]	Maps, plans, diagrams

         Do not use; class in 692.1

.028	Auxiliary techniques and procedures; apparatus, equipment
.028 4	Apparatus and equipment

         Do not use for materials; class in 691

.028 6	Green technology (Environmental technology)

         Do not use for comprehensive works on environmental engineering of buildings; class in 696

         Including pollution control technology; comprehensive works on waste technology

         For water drainage, see 696.13; for chimneys and flues, see 697.8; for air quality components of air conditioning systems, see 697.9324

         See also 696 for comprehensive works on energy engineering of buildings

[.028 8]	Maintenance and repair

         Do not use; class in 690.24

[.028 9]	Safety measures

         Do not use; class in 690.22

.029	Commercial miscellany

         Do not use for estimates of labor, time, materials; class in 692.5

.03–.05	Standard subdivisions
.06	Organizations and management
.068	Management

         Do not use for contracting for materials and services; class in 692.8

.07–.09	Standard subdivisions

\>   **690.1–690.8 Special topics of construction of buildings**

Unless other instructions are given, observe the following table of preference, e.g., maintenance and repair of residential buildings 690.80288 (*not* 690.24):

Specific parts of buildings	690.4
Specific types of buildings	690.5–690.8
Structural elements	690.1
General activities of buildings	690.2
Buildings by shape, buildings with atriums	690.38
Portable and temporary buildings	690.34
Special topics of buildings (without subdivision)	690.3

.1   Structural elements

Add to base number 690.1 the numbers following 721 in 721.1–721.8, e.g., auxiliary roof structures 690.15; however, for fireplaces, see 697.1; for chimneys, see 697.8

Class construction of structural elements in wood in 694

.2   General activities of buildings

Including architectural acoustics

Class interdisciplinary works on architectural acoustics in 729.29

**.21   ** Structural analysis

Including statics, dynamics, stability, strength of buildings

**.22   ** Provision for safety

Engineering for safe buildings, safety during construction

**.24   ** Maintenance and repair

Including remodeling

For home repairs by members of household, see 643.7

See Manual at 690 vs. 643.7

**.26   ** Wrecking and razing

.3   Special topics of buildings

**.34   ** Portable and temporary buildings

**.342   ** Portable buildings

**.344   ** Temporary buildings

**.38   ** Buildings by shape, buildings with atriums

Including circular, single-story buildings

**.383   ** Tall buildings

.4   Specific parts of buildings

Class plumbing in specific parts of buildings in 696.18

.42   Bathrooms and lavatories

> Standard subdivisions are added for either or both topics in heading

> Class interdisciplinary works on bathrooms and lavatories in 643.52

.43   Laundries

> Class interdisciplinary works on laundries in 667.13

.44   Kitchens

> Class interdisciplinary works on kitchens in 643.3

.5–.8   Specific types of buildings

> Add to base number 690 the numbers following 72 in 725–728, e.g., airport terminal buildings 690.539; however, for construction of buildings for defense against military action, see 623.1; for naval facilities, see 623.64; for military air facilities, see 623.66; for port facilities, see 627.3

.879   Mobile homes

> Number built according to instructions under 690.5–690.8

> *See Manual at 643.29, 690.879, 728.79 vs. 629.226*

691   Building materials

> Class here construction properties, selection

> Class construction in a specific type of material in 693

.1   Timber

.12   Prevention of decay

> Including impregnation, painting, spraying with fungicides

.14   Prevention of termite damage

.15   Treatment for fire resistance

.2   Natural stones

> Including granite, limestone, marble, sandstone, serpentine, slate, soapstone

.3   Concrete and artificial stones

> Including concrete blocks, cinder blocks

.4   Ceramic and clay materials

> Including brick, terra-cotta, tile, sun-dried blocks

.5   Masonry adhesives

.6   Glass

.7   Iron and steel (Ferrous metals)

> Standard subdivisions are added for either or both topics in heading

.8   **Metals**

> Add to base number 691.8 the numbers following 669 in 669.2–669.7, e.g., aluminum 691.8722
>
> *For iron and steel, see 691.7*

.9   **Other building materials**

.92   Plastics and their laminates

> Standard subdivisions are added for either or both topics in heading

.95   Insulating materials

> Including asbestos, corkboard, diatomaceous earth, kapok, rock wool

.96   Bituminous materials

> Including asphalts, tar

.97   Prefabricated materials

.99   Adhesives and sealants

> *For masonry adhesives, see 691.5; for plastics and their laminates, see 691.92*

692   Auxiliary construction practices

> Class application of a specific auxiliary practice to a specific subject with the subject, e.g., construction specifications for air conditioning 697.93

.1   **Plans and drawings**

> Interpretation and use of rough sketches, working drawings, blueprints
>
> *For detail drawings, see 692.2*

.2   **Detail drawings**

> Interpretation and use of large-scale drawings of trims, moldings, other details

.3   **Construction specifications**

.5   **Estimates of labor, time, materials**

> Class here interdisciplinary works on quantity surveying
>
> Class estimates for a specific subject in building with the subject, plus notation 029 from Table 1, e.g., estimates for air conditioning 697.93029

.8   **Contracting**

> Provision of construction materials and services in accordance with specifications

693   Construction in specific types of materials and for specific purposes

Class comprehensive works on construction in all types of materials in 690

For selection, preservation, construction properties of building materials, see 691; for wood construction, see 694; for roofing materials, see 695

[.01–.09]   Standard subdivisions

Do not use; class in 690.01–690.09

> ### 693.1–693.7   Construction in specific materials

Class construction in specific materials for specific purposes in 693.8; class comprehensive works in 690

For construction in other materials, see 693.9

.1   Masonry

Including construction in natural stone

For masonry using materials other than natural stone, see 693.2–693.5

> ### 693.2–693.5   Masonry using materials other than natural stone

Class comprehensive works in 693.1

.2   Stabilized earth materials

.21   Bricks

For hollow bricks, see 693.4

.22   Sun-dried blocks

Including adobe, cob, pisé, tabby, tapia

.3   Tiles and terra-cotta

For hollow tiles, see 693.4

.4   Artificial stones and hollow bricks

Including cinder blocks, concrete blocks, hollow tiles

.5   Concrete

For concrete blocks, see 693.4

.52   Concrete without reinforcement

.521   Poured concrete

.522   Precast concrete

.54   Concrete with reinforcement (Ferroconcrete)

.541   Poured concrete

.542   Prestressed concrete

.544   Precast concrete

.6   **Lathing, plastering, stuccowork**

Including drywall construction

.7   **Metals**

.71   Iron and steel (Ferrous metals)

Standard subdivisions are added for either or both topics in heading

.72–.77   Nonferrous metals

Add to base number 693.7 the numbers following 669 in 669.2–669.7, e.g., tin 693.76

.8   **Construction for specific purposes**

.82   Fireproof construction

.83   Insulated construction

.832   Thermal insulation

.834   Acoustical insulation (Soundproofing)

.84   Pest-resistant construction

.842   Termite-resistant construction

.844   Rodent-resistant construction

.85   Shock-resistant construction

.852   Earthquake-resistant construction

.854   Blast-resistant construction

.89   Waterproof, moistureproof, lightning-resistant construction

.892   Waterproof construction

Class moistureproof construction in 693.893

.893   Moistureproof construction

.898   Lightning-resistant construction

.9   **Construction in other materials**

.91   Ice and snow

.92   Sandwich panels

Class sandwich panels in a specific substance with the substance, e.g., wood 694

.96   Glass

.97   Prefabricated materials

Class materials prefabricated in a specific substance with the substance, e.g., precast concrete 693.522

.98   Nonrigid materials

      Including pneumatic construction

.99   Miscellaneous materials

      Add to base number 693.99 the numbers following 620.19 in 620.191–620.199, e.g., plastics 693.9923; however, for nonrigid materials, see 693.98

694   Wood construction

      Class here carpentry

.1   **Planning, analysis, engineering design**

>   **694.2–694.6   Carpentry**

      Class comprehensive works in 694

.2   **Rough carpentry (Framing)**

      Construction of ceilings, floors, foundations, frames, openings, partition frames, posts, roofs, sidings, walls

.6   **Finish carpentry (Joinery)**

      On-site construction of doors, doorways; blinds, shutters, windows; balconies, porches, verandas; balustrades, rails, ramps, stairs; trims, e.g., inlays, moldings, paneling; built-in cases and shelves

      Class off-site manufacture of finishing items in 680

695   Roof covering

      Class wooden roofs in 694.2; class comprehensive works on roofs as structural elements in 690.15

696   Utilities

      Class here comprehensive works on energy and environmental engineering of buildings

      Class interior electric wiring in 621.31924; class comprehensive works on waste technology in buildings in 690.0286; class interdisciplinary works on energy for use in buildings in 333.7962

      For heating, ventilating, air-conditioning engineering, see 697. For a specific aspect of energy engineering, see the aspect, e.g., thermal insulation 693.832; for a specific aspect of environmental engineering not provided for here, see the aspect, plus notation 0286 from Table 1, e.g., environmental engineering of building materials 691.0286, environmental engineering in hot-water heating 697.40286

.1   **Plumbing**

      Design and installation of water fixtures and pipes

.12   Water supply

> Including intake pipes, water receiving fixtures, water-softening equipment

> *For water supply in specific parts of buildings, see 696.18; for hot-water supply, see 696.6*

.13   Water drainage

> *For water drainage in specific parts of buildings, see 696.18*

.18   Plumbing in specific parts of buildings

> Class here water supply in specific parts of buildings, drainage in specific parts of buildings

[.180 1–.180 9]   Standard subdivisions

> Do not use; class in 696.101–696.109

.182   Bathrooms and lavatories

> Standard subdivisions are added for either or both topics in heading

.183   Laundries

.184   Kitchens

> Including installation of dishwashers and garbage-disposal units

.2   **Pipe fitting**

> Including gas pipes (gas fitting)

> *For water pipes, see 696.1; for steam fitting, see 696.3*

.3   **Steam pipes (Steam fitting)**

.6   **Hot-water supply**

> Including pipes, water heaters, water-softening equipment

697   Heating, ventilating, air-conditioning engineering

> Standard subdivisions are added for heating, ventilating, air-conditioning engineering together; for heating alone

.001   Philosophy and theory

.002   Miscellany

.002 8   Auxiliary techniques and procedures; apparatus, equipment, materials

.002 84   Apparatus, equipment, materials

> Do not use for heating apparatus and equipment; class in 697.07

.003–.009   Standard subdivisions

.02   Local heating

> Class local heating by source of heat in 697.1–697.2

.03   **Central heating**

Class here comprehensive works on district heating

For district heating by hot water, see 697.4; for district heating by steam, see 697.54. For a specific type of central heating, see the type in 697.3–697.7, e.g., solar heating 697.78

.04   **Heating with specific sources of energy**

Class here fuels

Class a specific fuel used in local heating in 697.02; class a specific fuel used in central heating in 697.03

For solar heating, see 697.78; for nuclear heating, see 697.79

.042   Coal and coke heating

.043   Gas heating

.044   Oil heating

.045   Electric heating

.07   **Heating equipment**

Including boilers, furnaces, radiators, thermostats

Class here heating apparatus

>   **697.1–697.8 Heating**

Class heating in specific kinds of buildings in 697.95–697.98; class comprehensive works in 697

>   **697.1–697.2 Local heating**

Class chimneys and flues for local heating in 697.8; class comprehensive works in 697.02

.1   **Heating with open fires (Radiative heating)**

Including braziers, fireplaces

Class fireplace-like stoves that have visible fires but which are convective heaters in 697.2

.2   **Heating with space heaters (Convective heating)**

Class comprehensive works on local heating in 697.02

.22   Stationary stoves

Class cooking stoves in 683.88

.24   Portable heaters

> **697.3–697.7   Central heating**

Class chimneys and flues for central heating in 697.8; class comprehensive works in 697.03

.3   Hot-air heating

Class radiant panel hot-air heating in 697.72

.4   Hot-water heating

Class hot-water supply in 696.6; class radiant panel hot-water heating in 697.72; class comprehensive works on district heating in 697.03

.5   Steam heating

Class steam fitting in 696.3; class radiant panel steam heating in 697.72

.500 1   Philosophy and theory

.500 2   Miscellany

.500 28   Auxiliary techniques and procedures; materials

.500 284   Materials

                   Do not use for apparatus and equipment; class in 697.507

.500 3–.500 9   Standard subdivisions

.507   Equipment

          Including boilers, furnaces, radiators

          Class here apparatus

.54   District heating

       Heating a group of buildings from a central station

       Class comprehensive works on steam and hot-water district heating in 697.03

       See also 697.4 for hot-water district heating

.7   Other heating methods

.72   Radiant panel heating

.78   Solar heating

       Class building of solar houses in 690.83704724

.79   Nuclear heating

.8   Chimneys and flues

.9   Ventilation and air conditioning; heating, ventilation, air-conditioning in specific kinds of buildings

.92   Ventilation

       Class ventilation in specific kinds of buildings in 697.95–697.98

.93	Air conditioning

Class heating in 697.1–697.8

.931	General topics of air conditioning

Class general topics applied to specific components in 697.932; class general topics applied to specific systems in 697.933; class general topics applied to specific types of buildings in 697.95–697.98

.931 2	Design principles
.931 5	Psychrometrics

Determination and control of enclosed atmospheric environments for optimum comfort

.931 6	Industrial and commercial applications

Determination and control of enclosed atmospheric environment for effective operations

.932	Components

Class here manufacturing

.932 2	Cooling and heating components

Including cooling and heating coils, thermostats

.932 3	Humidifying and dehumidifying components

Including humidistats

.932 4	Air quality components

Devices for removing particulates, e.g., dust, pollen

Class here filters

.932 5	Air circulation components

Including blowers

.933	Systems

Class system components in 697.932; class systems in specific types of buildings in 697.95–697.98

.933 2	Winter systems
.933 3	Summer systems
.933 4	Year-round systems
.95–.98	Air-conditioning, heating, ventilation in specific types of buildings

Add to base number 697.9 the numbers following 72 in 725–728, e.g., heating, ventilation, air-conditioning of industrial buildings 697.954
Subdivisions are added for any or all topics in heading

Class components of air-conditioning systems for specific types of buildings in 697.932

698   Detail finishing

Including cladding, siding, suspended ceilings

Class roof covering in 695

For lathing, plastering, stuccowork, see 693.6; for wooden moldings, paneling, inlays, see 694.6

.1   Painting

.102   Miscellany

.102 8   Auxiliary techniques and procedures; apparatus, equipment, materials

.102 83   Paint mixing

[.102 88]   Maintenance and repair

Do not use; class in 698.1028

.12   Exteriors

.14   Interiors

Class painting woodwork in 698.35

.142   Walls

.146   Floors

.147   Ceilings

.2   Calcimining and whitewashing

Standard subdivisions are added for either or both topics in heading

.3   Finishing woodwork

.32   Staining

Including graining and marbling

.33   Polishing with wax and oil

.34   Lacquering and varnishing

.35   Painting

.5   Glazing and leading windows

.6   Paperhanging

.9   Floor coverings

Including carpets, rugs; linoleum, tiles

Class comprehensive works on floors in 690.16

[699]   [Unassigned]

Most recently used in Edition 14

700

700   The arts

Description, critical appraisal, techniques, procedures, apparatus, equipment, materials of the fine, decorative, performing, recreational, literary arts

Use 701–770 for the fine and decorative arts; use 780–790 for the performing and recreational arts; use 800 for the literary arts

Class here conceptual art, fine and decorative arts, government policy on the arts, plastic arts (visual arts), visual arts

Use 700 and standard subdivisions 700.1–700.9 for artists' books, performance art covering the arts in general; use 702.81 and 709 for artists' books, performance art limited to fine and decorative arts

Class plastic arts when limited to the three-dimensional arts in 730

For book arts, see 686; for literature, see 800

SUMMARY

700.1–.9	Standard subdivisions of the arts
701–703	Standard subdivisions of fine and decorative arts
704	Special topics in fine and decorative arts
705–706	Standard subdivisions of fine and decorative arts
707	Education, research, related topics of fine and decorative arts
708	Galleries, museums, private collections of fine and decorative arts
709	History, geographic treatment, biography
710	Area planning and landscape architecture
711	Area planning (Civic art)
712	Landscape architecture (Landscape design)
713	Landscape architecture of trafficways
714	Water features in landscape architecture
715	Woody plants in landscape architecture
716	Herbaceous plants in landscape architecture
717	Structures in landscape architecture
718	Landscape design of cemeteries
719	Natural landscapes
720	Architecture
.1–.9	Standard subdivisions and special topics of architecture
721	Architectural materials and structural elements
722	Architecture from earliest times to ca. 300
723	Architecture from ca. 300 to 1399
724	Architecture from 1400
725	Public structures
726	Buildings for religious and related purposes
727	Buildings for educational and research purposes
728	Residential and related buildings
729	Design and decoration of structures and accessories

730	Sculpture and related arts
.1–.9	Standard subdivisions of sculpture and related arts together, of sculpture alone
731	Processes, forms, subjects of sculpture
732	Sculpture from earliest times to ca. 500, sculpture of nonliterate peoples
733	Greek, Etruscan, Roman sculpture
734	Sculpture from ca. 500 to 1399
735	Sculpture from 1400
736	Carving and carvings
737	Numismatics and sigillography
738	Ceramic arts
739	Art metalwork

740	Graphic arts and decorative arts
.1–.9	Standard subdivisions and iconography of graphic arts and decorative arts
741	Drawing and drawings
742	Perspective in drawing
743	Drawing and drawings by subject
745	Decorative arts
746	Textile arts
747	Interior decoration
748	Glass
749	Furniture and accessories

750	Painting and paintings
.1–.8	Standard subdivisions
751	Techniques, procedures, apparatus, equipment, materials, forms
752	Color
753	Symbolism, allegory, mythology, legend
754	Genre paintings
755	Religion
757	Human figures
758	Nature, architectural subjects and cityscapes, other specific subjects
759	History, geographic treatment, biography

760	Printmaking and prints
.1–.8	Standard subdivisions
761	Relief processes (Block printing)
763	Lithographic processes (Planographic processes)
764	Chromolithography and serigraphy
765	Metal engraving
766	Mezzotinting, aquatinting, related processes
767	Etching and drypoint
769	Prints

770	Photography, computer art, cinematography, videography
.1–.9	Standard subdivisions
771	Techniques, procedures, apparatus, equipment, materials
772	Metallic salt processes
773	Pigment processes of printing
774	Holography
776	Computer art (Digital art)
777	Cinematography and videography
778	Specific fields and special kinds of photography
779	Photographic images

780	**Music**	
.000 1–.099 9	Relation of music to other subjects	
.1–.9	Standard subdivisions; analytical guides, program notes; texts; treatises on music scores and recordings; performances	
781	**General principles and musical forms**	
782	**Vocal music**	
783	**Music for single voices**	
784	**Instruments and instrumental ensembles and their music**	
785	**Ensembles with only one instrument per part**	
786	**Keyboard, mechanical, electrophonic, percussion instruments**	
787	**Stringed instruments (Chordophones)**	
788	**Wind instruments (Aerophones)**	
790	**Recreational and performing arts**	
.01–.09	Standard subdivisions of recreation; recreation centers	
.1–.2	[General kinds of recreational activities and the performing arts in general]	
791	**Public performances**	
792	**Stage presentations**	
793	**Indoor games and amusements**	
794	**Indoor games of skill**	
795	**Games of chance**	
796	**Athletic and outdoor sports and games**	
797	**Aquatic and air sports**	
798	**Equestrian sports and animal racing**	
799	**Fishing, hunting, shooting**	

> ## 700.1–700.9 Standard subdivisions of the arts

Use this standard subdivision span for material that includes two or more of the fine and decorative arts and one or more of the other arts, e.g., a work about a painter who is also a sculptor and a poet 700.92. If only one fine or decorative art and one of the other arts is involved, class in the number coming first in the schedule, e.g., a United States painter and poet 759.13

Class comprehensive works in 700

.1   ## Philosophy and theory of the arts

Notation 01 from Table 1 as modified below

Class here effects of other topics on the arts

.103   Effects of social conditions and factors on the arts

.104   Effects of humanities on the arts

.105   Effects of science and technology on the arts

.108   Effects of other concepts on the arts

Including humor, mythology, nature, parapsychology

.2   ## Miscellany

.285   Computer applications

Class here computers used as a technique to support traditional techniques in the arts

Class computer art in 776

See Manual at 776 vs. 006.5–006.7

.3	**Dictionaries, encyclopedias, concordances**
.4	**Special topics in the arts**
.41	Arts displaying specific qualities of style, mood, viewpoint

> Add to base number 700.41 the numbers following —1 in notation 11–18 from Table 3C, e.g., horror in the arts 700.4164
>
> Class arts dealing with specific themes and subjects regardless of quality displayed in 700.42–700.49

.42–.49	Arts dealing with specific themes and subjects

> Add to base number 700.4 the numbers following —3 in notation 32–39 from Table 3C, e.g., historical themes in the arts 700.458

.5–.8	**Standard subdivisions of the arts**
.9	**History, geographic treatment, biography of the arts**
.92	Biography

> Class here the works themselves and critical appraisal and description of works of an artist or artists
>
> *See Manual at 700.92*

> ## 701–708 Standard subdivisions of fine and decorative arts
>
> Other than history, geographic treatment, biography
>
> Class standard subdivisions of specific schools, styles, periods of development in 709.012–709.05; class comprehensive works in 700

701 Philosophy and theory of fine and decorative arts

> Notation 01 from Table 1 as modified below
>
> Class here effects of other topics on fine and decorative arts

.03–.08	Special topics of philosophy and theory of fine and decorative arts

> Add to base number 701.0 the numbers following 700.10 in 700.103–700.108, e.g., effects of social conditions and factors on fine and decorative arts 701.03

.1	**Appreciative aspects**

> Do not use for systems; class in 701
>
> Including use of audiovisual aids
>
> *See also 709 for history of the fine arts*

.15	Psychological principles

> Fine arts as products of creative imagination

.17	Aesthetics

> Class interdisciplinary works in 111.85

.18   Criticism and appreciation

         Class here theory, technique, history

         Class works of critical appraisal in 709

.8   **Inherent features**

         Including composition, decorative values, form, light, movement, space, style, symmetry, time, vision

.82   Perspective

         See also 742 for drawing aspects of perspective

.85   Color

         See also 752 for painting aspects of color

.9   **Methodology**

         Do not use for psychological principles; class in 701.15

702   **Miscellany of fine and decorative arts**

.8   **Auxiliary techniques and procedures; apparatus, equipment, materials**

         Notation 028 from Table 1 as modified below

         Including testing and measurement, use of artists' models

         Class here basic techniques and procedures

.81   Mixed-media and composites

         Including artists' books; performance art

         Class finished works of mixed-media and composite art in 709; class two-dimensional mixed-media art or composites in 740

.812   Collage

         Class decoupage in 745.546

.813   Montage

.814   Assemblage

.85   Computer applications

         Class here computers used as a technique to support traditional techniques in fine and decorative arts

         Class computer art in 776

         See Manual at 776 vs. 006.5–006.7

.87   Techniques of reproduction, execution, identification

         Do not use for testing and measurement; class in 702.8

.872   Reproductions and copies

.874   Forgeries and alterations

.88   Maintenance and repair

        Including expertizing

        Class identification of reproductions, copies, forgeries, alterations in 702.87

.9   Commercial miscellany

        Class auction and sales catalogs in which an exhibition is involved in 707.4

703   Dictionaries, encyclopedias, concordances of fine and decorative arts

704   Special topics in fine and decorative arts

>   704.03–704.08 Groups of people

        Unless other instructions are given, class a subject with aspects in two or more subdivisions of 704.03–704.08 in the number coming last, e.g., women with disabilities 704.87 (*not* 704.042)

        Class description, critical appraisal, works, biography of artists as individuals in 709.2; class comprehensive works in 704

.03   Ethnic and national groups

        Class people by gender or sex of a specific ethnic or national group in 704.04; class groups of miscellaneous specific groups of people of a specific ethnic or national group in 704.08; class ethnic and national groups in places where they predominate in 709.1–709.9

.030 01–.030 09   Standard subdivisions

.030 5–.030 9   Specific ethnic and national groups with ethnic origins from more than one continent, of European descent

        Add to base number 704.03 notation 05–09 from Table 5, e.g., art of ethnic groups of European descent 704.0309

.031–.039   Specific ethnic and national groups

        Add to base number 704.03 notation 1–9 from Table 5, e.g., art of North American native peoples 704.0397

.04   People by gender or sex

        Class groups of miscellaneous specific groups of people of a specific gender or sex in 704.08

        For transgender people, see 704.0867

.041   Men in fine arts

        Works specifically emphasizing male sex

.042   Women in fine arts

.08   **Miscellaneous specific groups of people**

> Add to base number 704.08 the numbers following —08 in notation 083–088 from Table 1, e.g., people with disabilities 704.087; however, for art dealers, see 381.457092; for nonliterate peoples, see 709.011

> *See Manual at 709.2 vs. 381.457092*

.9   **Iconography**

> *See Manual at 704.9 and 753–758*

.94   **Specific subjects**

> A work with two or more subjects is classed with the subject that is the center of interest, e.g., cityscapes with incidental human figures 704.944 (*not* 704.942), church interiors displaying Stations of the Cross 704.9484 (*not* 704.944)

[.940 1–.940 9]   Standard subdivision

> Do not use; class in 704.901–704.909

.942   **Human figures**

> Class here portraits

> Unless other instructions are given, observe the following table of preference, e.g., groups of children 704.9425 (*not* 704.9426):

Erotica	704.9428
Nudes	704.9421
Specific groups of people	704.9423–704.9425
Groups of human figures	704.9426

> Class symbolism of human figures in 704.946. Class human figures engaged in a specific occupation with the occupation, e.g., farmers 704.943092, doctors 704.94961092, circus clowns 704.94979133; class human figures engaged in a specific activity with the activity, e.g., ice skaters 704.94979691092

> *For human figures associated with mythology and legend, see 704.947; for human figures associated with religion, see 704.948*

.942 092   Biography

> Artists and critics

> Class works about the person portrayed in 704.942

.942 1   Nudes

> Class here nudes of men, women, children; groups of nudes

> 704.942 3–704.942 5   Specific groups of people

> Class comprehensive works in 704.942

.942 3   Men

.942 4   Women

.942 5   Children

.942 6	Groups of human figures
.942 8	Erotica

Including pornography

.943	**Nature and still life**

Standard subdivisions are added for nature and still life together, for nature alone

Class here agriculture

Class symbolism of nature and still life in 704.946; class comprehensive works on science in 704.9495

> *For nature and still life associated with mythology and legend, see 704.947; for nature and still life associated with religion, see 704.948*

.943 2	Animals

Class here pets

Add to base number 704.9432 the numbers following 59 in 592–599, e.g., eagles 704.94328942

Class symbolism of animals in 704.946

.943 4	Plants

Class symbolism of plants in 704.946

.943 43	Flowers
.943 5	Still life
.943 6	Landscapes

Add to base number 704.9436 notation 1–9 from Table 2, e.g., landscapes of Utah 704.9436792

.943 7	Marine scenes and seascapes

Standard subdivisions are added for either or both topics in heading

.944	**Architectural subjects and cityscapes**

Standard subdivisions are added for either or both topics in heading

Add to base number 704.944 notation 1–9 from Table 2, e.g., cityscapes of England 704.94442

.946	**Symbolism and allegory**

Standard subdivisions are added for either or both topics in heading

> *For religious symbolism, see 704.948*

.947	**Mythology and legend**

Class religious mythology in 704.948

.948   **Religion**

Class here religious mythology, religious symbolism

Class significance and purpose of art in religion in 203.7; class significance and purpose of art in Christianity in 246; class significance and purpose of art in non-Christian religions in 292–299

(.948 1)   **(Permanently unassigned)**

(Optional number used to provide local emphasis and a shorter number for a specific religion other than Christianity; prefer the number for the specific religion in 704.9489)

.948 2   **Christianity**

Class here icons, santos, votive offerings

For specific Christian subjects, see 704.9484–704.9487

>   704.948 4–704.948 7   Specific Christian subjects

Class comprehensive works in 704.9482

.948 4   **Biblical characters and events**

For Trinity and Holy Family and its members, see 704.9485; for apostles, saints, angels, see 704.9486; for devils, see 704.9487

.948 5   **Trinity and Holy Family and its members**

.948 52   **Trinity**

.948 53   **Jesus Christ**

.948 55   **Madonna and Child**

Class here Mary without Child

.948 56   **Holy Family**

Presented as a group

Class Jesus Christ in 704.94853; class Mary with or without Child in 704.94855; class Saint Joseph in 704.94863

.948 6   **Apostles, saints, angels**

.948 62   **Apostles**

.948 63   **Saints**

For Apostles, see 704.94862

.948 64   **Angels**

.948 7   **Devils**

.948 9	Other religions

Add to base number 704.9489 the numbers following 29 in 292–299, e.g., Buddhism in art 704.948943; however, for Old Testament characters and events, see 704.9484

(Option: To give local emphasis and a shorter number to iconography of a specific religion, class in 704.9481, which is permanently unassigned)

.949	Other specific subjects

Add to base number 704.949 notation 001–999, e.g., technological subjects 704.9496; however, for agriculture, see 704.943

705 Serial publications of fine and decorative arts

706 Organizations and management of fine and decorative arts

707 Education, research, related topics of fine and decorative arts

.4	Temporary and traveling collections and exhibits

Do not use for museums and permanent collections and exhibits; class in 708

Class here permanent collections on tour, temporary exhibits of a private collection, auction and sales catalogs in which an exhibition is involved

For temporary in-house exhibits selected from a museum's or gallery's permanent collection, see 708

708 Galleries, museums, private collections of fine and decorative arts

Do not use for groups of people; class in 704.03–704.08

General art collections

Class here annual reports dealing with acquisitions, activities, programs, projects

For temporary and traveling collections and exhibits, see 707.4

.001–.008	Standard subdivisions
.009	History and biography

Do not use for geographic treatment; class in 708.1–708.9

> **708.1–708.9   Geographic treatment**

Class here guidebooks and catalogs of specific galleries, museums, private collections

Class comprehensive works in 708

(Option: To give local emphasis and a shorter number to galleries, museums, private collections of a specific country, use one of the following:

(Option A: Place them first by use of a letter or other symbol, e.g., galleries, museums, private collections in Japan 708.J [preceding 708.1]

(Option B: Class them in 708.1; in that case class galleries, museums, private collections in North America in 708.97)

.1   North America

For galleries, museums, private collections in Middle America, see 708.972

(Option: To give local emphasis and a shorter number to galleries, museums, private collections of a specific country other than United States and Canada, class them in this number; in that case class galleries, museums, private collections in North America in 708.97)

.11   Canada

Add to base number 708.11 the numbers following —71 in notation 711–719 from Table 2, e.g., galleries, museums, private collections in British Columbia 708.111

.13–.19   United States

Add to base number 708.1 the numbers following —7 in notation 73–79 from Table 2, e.g., galleries, museums, private collections in Pennsylvania 708.148

For galleries, museums, private collections in Hawaii, see 708.9969

> **708.2–708.8   Europe**

Class comprehensive works in 708.94

For galleries, museums, private collections not provided for here, see 708.949, e.g., galleries, museums, private collections in Belgium 708.9493

.2   British Isles

Class here England

.21–.28   England

Add to base number 708.2 the numbers following —42 in notation 421–428 from Table 2, e.g., galleries, museums, private collections in Manchester 708.2733

.29 Scotland, Ireland, Wales

Add to base number 708.29 the numbers following —4 in notation 41–42 from Table 2, e.g., galleries, museums, private collections in Wales 708.2929

.3–.8 **Miscellaneous parts of Europe**

Add to base number 708 the numbers following —4 in notation 43–48 from Table 2, e.g., galleries, museums, private collections in France 708.4

.9 **Other geographic areas**

Add to base number 708.9 notation 1–9 from Table 2, e.g., comprehensive works on galleries, museums, private collections in Islamic areas 708.91767, in European countries 708.94, in Belgium 708.9493, in Middle America 708.972, in Hawaii 708.9969

Class parts of Europe in notation 41–48 from Table 2 in 708.2–708.8

709 History, geographic treatment, biography

Development, description, critical appraisal, works

Class here finished works of experimental and mixed-media art that do not fit easily into a recognized medium

Class two-dimensional experimental and mixed-media art in 740

See also 364.16287 for looting, plundering, theft of art as a crime; also 364.164 for destruction of art as a crime

.01 Arts of nonliterate peoples, and earliest times to 499

Notation 0901 from Table 1 as modified below

.011 Nonliterate peoples

Regardless of time or place, but limited to nonliterate peoples of the past and nonliterate peoples clearly not a part of contemporary society

.011 2 Paleolithic art

.011 3 Rock art

> 709.012–709.015 Periods of development to 499 A.D.

Class here schools and styles not limited by country or locality, comprehensive works on European art limited by period, school, or style

Add to each subdivision identified by † notation 01–08 from Table 1, e.g., exhibits of prehistoric art 709.012074

Class comprehensive works in 709

For European art limited to a specific location, see the location in 709.4, e.g., art of Germany 709.43

See Manual at 704.9 and 753–758; also at 709.012–709.015, 709.02–709.05 vs. 709.3–709.9

.012	†To 4000 B.C.
.013	†3999–1000 B.C.
.014	†999–1 B.C.
.015	†1st–5th centuries, 1–499 A.D.

>   709.02–709.05 Periods of development, 500–

Notation 0902–0905 from Table 1 as modified below

Class here schools and styles not limited by country or locality, comprehensive works on European art limited by period, school, or style

Add to each subdivision identified by * notation 01–08 from Table 1, e.g., exhibits of cubism 709.04032074

Class comprehensive works in 709

> *For European art limited to a specific location, see the location in 709.4, e.g., art of Germany 709.43*

> *See Manual at 704.9 and 753–758; also at 709.012–709.015, 709.02–709.05 vs. 709.3–709.9*

.02	*6th-15th centuries, 500–1499

Class here medieval art

.021	*6th-12th centuries, 500–1199
.021 2	*Early Christian art

> *For early Christian art before 500, see 709.015*

.021 4	*Byzantine art

> *For Byzantine art before 500, see 709.015*

.021 6	*Romanesque art
.022	*13th century, 1200–1299

Class here Gothic art

> *For Gothic art of an earlier or later period, see the specific period, e.g., 500–1199 709.021*

.023	*14th century, 1300–1399
.024	*15th century, 1400–1499

Class here Renaissance art

> *For Renaissance art of an earlier or later period, see the specific period, e.g., 16th century 709.031*

*Add as instructed under 709.02–709.05
†Add as instructed under 709.012–709.015

.03	*Modern period, 1500–

> For 20th century, 1900–1999, see 709.04; for 21st century, 2000–2099, see 709.05

.031	*16th century, 1500–1599
.032	*17th century, 1600–1699

Class here baroque art

> For baroque art of 18th century, see 709.033

.033	*18th century, 1700–1799
.033 2	*Rococo art
.034	*19th century, 1800–1899
.034 1	*Classical revival (Neoclassicism)

> For classical revival of 18th century, see 709.033

.034 2	*Romanticism

> For romanticism of 18th century, see 709.033

.034 3	*Naturalism and realism

> For naturalism and realism of an earlier or later period, see the specific period, e.g., 18th century 709.033

.034 4	*Impressionism

Including luminism, pleinairism

.034 5	*Neo-impressionism

Including divisionism, pointillism

.034 6	*Postimpressionism
.034 7	*Symbolism and synthetism
.034 8	*Kitsch (Trash)

> For kitsch of a later period, see the period, e.g., 20th century 709.04013

.034 9	*Art nouveau

> For art nouveau of a later period, see the period, e.g., 20th century 709.04014

.04	20th century, 1900–1999

Class here modern art

> For 19th century, 1800–1899, see 709.034; for 21st century, 2000–2099, see 709.05; for computer art (Digital art), see 776

.040 01–.040 08	Standard subdivisions

*Add as instructed under 709.02–709.05

[.040 09]	History	
	Do not use; class in 709.04	
.040 1	*Art deco, kitsch, art nouveau	
.040 12	*Art deco	
.040 13	*Kitsch (Trash)	
	Class comprehensive works on kitsch in 709.0348	
.040 14	*Art nouveau	
	Class comprehensive works on art nouveau in 709.0349	
.040 2	*Functionalism	
.040 3	*Cubism and futurism	
	Including geometric design	
.040 32	*Cubism	
.040 33	*Futurism	
.040 4	*Expressionism and fauvism	
.040 42	*Expressionism	
	Class abstract expressionism in 709.04052	
.040 43	*Fauvism	
.040 5	*Abstractionism, nonobjectivity, constructivism	
.040 52	*Abstractionism	
	Including abstract expressionism, geometric abstractionism, neoplasticism	
.040 56	*Nonobjectivity	
	Class here concrete art	
.040 57	*Constructivism	
.040 58	*Minimalism	
.040 6	*Dadaism and surrealism	
.040 62	*Dadaism	
.040 63	*Surrealism	
.040 7	*Composite media and sensations	
	Class techniques of composite media in 702.81	
	For specific composite media, see 709.0408	
.040 71	*Pop art	

*Add as instructed under 709.02–709.05

.040 72	*Optical art (Op art)
	See also 776 for computer art
.040 74	*Happenings, environments, events
	For happenings, environments, events of a later period, see the period, e.g., 21st century 709.05014
.040 75	*Conceptual art
	For happenings, environments, events, see 709.04074. For conceptual art of a later period, see the period, e.g., 21st century 709.05015
.040 752	*Body art
.040 755	*Performance art
	For performance art of a later period, see the period, e.g., 21st century 709.050155
.040 76	*Land art (Earthworks)
	For land art (earthworks) of a later period, see the period, e.g., 21st century 709.05016
.040 8	Specific composite media
	Class techniques of composite media in 702.81
.040 82	*Artists' books
	For artists' books of a later period, see the period, e.g., 21st century 709.05018
.040 84	*Mail art (Correspondence art)
.040 9	*Outsider art (Art brut)
.041–.049	Periods
	Add to base number 709.04 the numbers following —0904 in notation 09041–09049 from Table 1, e.g., arts of 1960–1969 709.046
	Class a specific school or style in a specific period in 709.0401–709.0407
.05	21st century, 2000–2099
.050 01–.050 08	Standard subdivisions
[.050 09]	History
	Do not use; class in 709.05
.050 1	*Composite media and sensations
	Class techniques of composite media in 702.81
.050 14	*Happenings, environments, events
	Class comprehensive works on happenings, environments, events in 709.04074

*Add as instructed under 709.02–709.05

.050 15	*Conceptual art
	Class comprehensive works on conceptual art in 709.04075
	For happenings, environments, events, see 709.05014
.050 155	*Performance art
	Class comprehensive works on performance art in 709.040755
.050 16	*Land art (Earthworks)
	Class comprehensive works on land art (earthworks) in 709.04076
.050 18	*Artists' books
	Class comprehensive works on artists' books in 709.04082
.051	*2000–2019
	Class a specific school or style in a specific period in 709.0501
.051 1	*2000–2009
.051 2	*2010–2019
.052	*2020–2029
	Class a specific school or style in a specific period in 709.0501

.1   Areas, regions, places in general

Class groups of people in 704.03–704.08; class art of nonliterate peoples regardless of place in 709.011

.2   Biography

Class here description, critical appraisal, works of artists not limited to or chiefly identified with a specific form, e.g., painting, or group of forms, e.g., graphic arts

See Manual at 709.2 vs. 381.457092

.22   Collected biography

Class works of more than one artist in the same geographic area not limited by continent, country, locality in 709.1; class works of more than one artist in the same continent, country, locality in 709.3–709.9

.3–.9   Specific continents, countries, localities

Class here art of specific periods, e.g., art of 1800–1899 in Germany 709.4309034

Class groups of people in 704.03–704.08; class art of nonliterate peoples regardless of place in 709.011. Class comprehensive works on European art of specific periods with the period in 709.01–709.05 (*not* 709.4), e.g., art of 1800–1899 in Europe 709.034 (*not* 709.409034)

See Manual at 709.012–709.015, 709.02–709.05 vs. 709.3–709.9

*Add as instructed under 709.02–709.05

710   Area planning and landscape architecture

> Class comprehensive works on area planning, landscape architecture, and architecture in 720

711   Area planning (Civic art)

Design of physical environment for public welfare, convenience, pleasure

Class here plans

Unless other instructions are given, observe the following table of preference, e.g., planning of pedestrian malls in business districts 711.5522 (*not* 711.74):

Specific kinds of areas	711.5
Specific elements	711.6–711.8
Specific levels	711.2–711.4
Procedural and social aspects	711.1

Class comprehensive works on area planning and architecture in 720; class interdisciplinary works on area planning in 307.12

.1   **Procedural and social aspects**

.12   Professional practice and technical procedures

> Including collection of data, preparation and presentation of plans and models

.13   Social factors affecting planning

.14   Economic factors affecting planning

>   **711.2–711.4   Specific levels**

> Class comprehensive works in 711

.2   **International and national planning**

.3   **Interstate, state, provincial, county planning**

> *For urban counties, see 711.4; for metropolitan areas, see 711.43*

.4   **Local community planning (City planning)**

> Class here urban renewal (conservation, rehabilitation, redevelopment)

> Class interdisciplinary works on city planning in 307.1216; class interdisciplinary works on urban renewal in 307.3416

> *For urban renewal of specific kinds of areas, see 711.5*

.409 3–.409 9   Specific continents, countries, localities

> Class here specific types of plans for specific cities

>   **711.41–711.45 Specific types of plans**

     Unless other instructions are given, class a subject with aspects in two or more subdivisions of 711.4 in the number coming last, e.g., plans for small cities in cold climates 711.43 (*not* 711.42)

     Class comprehensive works in 711.4

.41	*Plans based on street patterns

     Including gridiron, radial, studied irregularity plans

.42	*Plans based on environment

     Including plans based on topography and climate

.43	*Plans based on size

     Including plans for villages, small and large cities, metropolitan areas

.45	*Plans based on function

     Including new towns; plans for cities serving primarily as governmental, industrial, residential centers

.5   **Specific kinds of areas**

     Class here planning for urban renewal (conservation, rehabilitation, redevelopment) of specific kinds of areas

     Class interdisciplinary works on urban renewal in 307.3416

.55   Functional areas

     Class here plazas, squares

         For religious centers, see 711.56; for cultural and educational areas, see 711.57; for residential areas, see 711.58; for parking areas, see 711.73

.551   Civic, administrative, governmental areas

     Standard subdivisions are added for any or all topics in heading

.552   Commercial and industrial areas

     Class planning of transportation facilities in 711.7

.552 2   Commercial areas

     Class here business districts, shopping centers

.552 4   Industrial areas

     Class here industrial parks

.554   Agricultural areas

.555   Medical centers

.556   Prison and reformatory areas

---

*Do not use notation 093–099 from Table 1 for specific cities; class in 711.4093–711.4099

.557   Hotel and restaurant areas

                Including trailer camps for temporary residents

.558   Recreational areas

                Including parks, playgrounds, theatrical and performing arts centers

.56   Religious centers

.57   Cultural and educational areas

                Including areas for libraries, museums, colleges and universities

                Class theatrical and performing arts centers in 711.558

.58   Residential areas

                Urban, suburban, rural areas

                Including apartment-house districts, trailer parks for long-term residents

                   For hotel areas, trailer camps for temporary residents, see 711.557; for housing renewal, see 711.59

.59   Housing renewal

                Class interdisciplinary works on housing renewal in 307.34

>   **711.6–711.8 Specific elements**

                Class comprehensive works in 711.6

.6   **Structural elements**

                Adaptation to site and use

                Class here comprehensive works on specific elements

                   For utilities, see 711.7

.7   **Transportation facilities**

                Class here comprehensive works on utilities

                   For nontransportation utilities, see 711.8

.72   Bicycle transportation facilities

.73   Motor vehicle transportation facilities

                Including motorcycle transportation facilities, parking areas

.74   Pedestrian transportation facilities

                Including pedestrian malls

.75   Railroad transportation facilities

                Including rapid transit facilities

.76   Marine transportation facilities

.78   Air transportation facilities

.8   **Nontransportation utilities**

> Including water, gas, electricity transmission and supply; communication lines; sanitation and flood control facilities

712   Landscape architecture (Landscape design)

Class engineering aspects of landscape architecture in 624; class comprehensive works on landscape architecture and architecture in 720

For specific elements in landscape architecture, see 714–717

.01   Philosophy and theory

> Class aesthetics, composition, style in 712.2

> **712.2–712.3 General considerations**

> Class general considerations of design of specific kinds of land tracts in 712.5–712.7; class comprehensive works in 712

.2   **Principles**

> Including aesthetics, composition, effect, style

.3   **Professional practice and technical procedures**

> Including collection of data, preparation and presentation of plans and models, supervision of operations

---

> **712.5–712.7 Specific kinds of land tracts**

> Class comprehensive works in 712

>> *For trafficways, see 713; for cemeteries, see 718; for natural landscapes, see 719*

.5   **Public parks and grounds**

> Class here amusement parks, commons, fairgrounds, zoological and botanical gardens; comprehensive works on parks

>> *For private parks, see 712.6; for parks of public reserved lands, see 719.3*

.6   **Private parks and grounds**

> Class here estates, home gardens, penthouse gardens, yards

.7   **Semiprivate and institutional grounds**

> Class here grounds of churches, country clubs, hospitals, hotels, industrial plants, schools

713   Landscape architecture of trafficways

See also 625.77 for planting and cultivation of roadside vegetation

> ### 714–717   Specific elements in landscape architecture

Class comprehensive works in 712

714   Water features in landscape architecture

Including cascades, fountains

Class here natural and artificial pools

Class comprehensive works on fountains in 731.724

715   Woody plants in landscape architecture

Cultivated for flowers or for other attributes

Class here comprehensive works on plants in landscape architecture

Class comprehensive works on plants cultivated for their flowers in landscape architecture in 716

For herbaceeous plants in landscape architecture, see 716

See also 635.97 for planting and cultivation of woody plants

    .1   **Topiary work**

> #### 715.2–715.4   Specific kinds of plants

Class topiary work on specific kinds of plants in 715.1; class comprehensive works in 715

    .2   **Trees**

    .3   **Shrubs**

    .4   **Vines**

716   Herbaceous plants in landscape architecture

Cultivated for flowers or for other attributes

Including ground cover

Class here comprehensive works on plants cultivated for their flowers in landscape architecture

For woody plants cultivated for their flowers, see 715

See also 635.9 for planting and cultivation of herbaceous plants

717   Structures in landscape architecture

Relationship of buildings, terraces, fences, gates, steps, ornamental accessories to other elements of landscape architecture

Including pedestrian facilities, street furniture

718   Landscape design of cemeteries

.8   **National cemeteries**

719   Natural landscapes

> Class natural water features in 714

.3   **Reserved lands**

.32   Public parks and natural monuments

> Standard subdivisions are added for either or both topics in heading

.33   Forest and water-supply reserves

.36   Wildlife reserves

720   Architecture

> Class here architectural structure; comprehensive works on architecture, area planning, and landscape architecture; on architecture and area planning; on architecture and landscape architecture; on architecture and structural engineering; interdisciplinary works on design and construction of buildings

> *For structural engineering, see 624.1; for engineering design and construction of buildings, see 690; for area planning and landscape architecture, see 710*

.1   **Philosophy and theory**

> Notation 01 from Table 1 as modified below

.103–.108   Special topics of philosophy and theory

> Add to base number 720.10 the numbers following 700.10 in 700.103–700.108, e.g., effects of social conditions and factors on architecture 720.103

.2   **Miscellany**

.22   Illustrations, models, miniatures

> Class architectural drawing in 720.284

.222   Pictures and related illustrations

> Class here architectural drawings

> Add to base number 720.222 notation 1–9 from Table 2, e.g., architectural drawings from England 720.22242

> Class drawings in the vertical plane, e.g., elevations, in 729.1 from this table; class drawings in the horizontal plane, e.g., floor plans in 729.2 from this table. Class architectural drawings for one structure or a specific type of structure with the structure in 725–728, plus notation 0222 from table under 721–729, e.g., architectural drawings of palaces 728.820222

.28   Auxiliary techniques and procedures; apparatus, equipment

> Including site planning

.284   Architectural drawing

>Do not use for apparatus and equipment; class in 720.28. Do not use for materials; class in 721.04
>
>Class drawings, illustrations, models in 720.22

.286   Remodeling

>Do not use for green technology; class in 720.47

.288   Maintenance and repair

>Class here conservation, preservation, restoration
>
>Class interdisciplinary works on conservation, preservation, restoration in 363.69
>
>*See Manual at 930–990: Historic preservation*

.4   **Special topics of architecture**

>Unless other instructions are given, observe the following table of preference, e.g., temporary circular buildings 720.48 (*not* 720.444):

Architecture and the environment	720.47
Buildings by shape, buildings with atriums	720.48
Multiple-purpose buildings	720.49
Portable and temporary buildings	720.44

.44   Portable and temporary buildings

.442   Portable buildings

.444   Temporary buildings

.47   Architecture and the environment

>Including pollution control technology
>
>Class here green technology (environmental technology), sustainable architecture

.472   Energy resources

>Class here energy conservation

.472 4   Use of solar energy

>*For solar heating, see 697.78; for daylighting, see 729.28*

.473   Earth-sheltered buildings

>Class here underground architecture

.475   Waste technology

.48   Buildings by shape, buildings with atriums

>Including circular, single-story buildings

.483   Tall buildings

>Class here skyscrapers

.49   Multiple-purpose buildings

> Class a multiple-purpose building with one primary purpose with the single-purpose buildings of that type, e.g., an apartment building with a floor of commercial space 728.314

.9   History, geographic treatment, biography

> Class here architectural aspects of historic buildings, schools and styles limited to a specific country or locality

> Class architectural drawings in 720.222; class comprehensive works on specific schools and styles not limited to a specific country or locality in 722–724

> *See Manual at 913–919: Historic sites and buildings; also at 930–990: Historic preservation*

[.901–.905]   Historical periods

> Do not use; class in 722–724

[.93]   Ancient world

> Do not use; class in 722

.95   Asia

> Class here Buddhist, Oriental architecture

> Class Buddhist architecture of a national style with the style, e.g., Japanese Buddhist architecture 720.952

.954   India and neighboring south Asian countries

> Class here Hindu, Jain architecture

> **721–729 Specific aspects of architecture**

Add to each subdivision identified by * as follows:

01   Philosophy and theory
           Notation 01 from Table 1 as modified below

0103–0108   Special topics
                Add to 010 the numbers following 700.10 in 700.103–700.108, e.g., effects of social conditions and factors on architecture 0103

02   Miscellany

0222   Pictures and related illustrations
             Class here architectural drawings
             Add to 0222 notation 1–9 from Table 2, e.g., architectural drawings from England 022242

028   Auxiliary techniques and procedures; apparatus, equipment, materials
           Notation 028 from Table 1 as modified below

0286   Remodeling
             Do not use for green technology; class in notation 047 from this table

03   Dictionaries, encyclopedias, concordances

04   Special topics
           Add to 04 the numbers following 720.4 in 720.44–720.49, e.g., energy conservation 0472

05–08   Standard subdivisions

09   History, geographic treatment, biography
           Class architectural drawings in notation 0222 from this table
           See Manual at 913–919: Historic sites and buildings; also at 930–990: Historic preservation

Class comprehensive works in 720

721   Architectural materials and structural elements

[.01–.03]   Standard subdivisions

          Do not use; class in 720.1–720.3

.04   Architectural materials

          For engineering design and construction in specific materials, see 693

.044   Specific materials

.044 1–.044 6   Masonry

          Add to base number 721.044 the numbers following 693 in 693.1–693.6, e.g., architectural construction in reinforced concrete 721.04454

.044 7   Metals

          Add to base number 721.0447 the numbers following 669 in 669.1–669.7, e.g., architectural construction in aluminum 721.0447722

.044 8   Wood

.044 9   Other materials

Add to base number 721.0449 the numbers following 693.9 in 693.91–693.99, e.g., architectural construction in glass 721.04496

[.05–.09]   Standard subdivisions

Do not use; class in 720.5–720.9

>   **721.1–721.8 Structural elements**

Class here decoration; interdisciplinary works on design and construction

Class decoration of structural elements in specific mediums in 729.4–729.8; class comprehensive works in 721

For engineering design and construction, see 690.1

.1   **Foundations**

.2   **Walls**

Including footings, entablatures; colonnades, partitions; bearing and retaining walls

See also 725.96 for free-standing walls

.3   **Columnar constructions**

Including abutments, colonnettes, columns, pedestals, piers, pilasters, posts

For colonnades, entablatures, see 721.2

.36   Architectural orders

.4   **Curved constructions and details**

.41   Arcades and arches

For groined arches, see 721.44

See also 725.96 for free-standing arches

.43   Vaults

For specific types of vaults, see 721.44–721.45

>   **721.44–721.45 Specific types of vaults**

Class comprehensive works in 721.43

.44   Groined vaults

Including groined arches

.45   Other types of vaults

Including expanding, fan, rib, tunnel vaults

.46   Domes

Class cupolated roofs in 721.5

.48   Niches

.5   **Roofs and roof structures**

> Standard subdivisions are added for roofs and roof structures together, for roofs alone

> Including dormers, gables; cornices, pediments; cupolas, pinnacles, spires, towers; chimneys, skylights

.6   **Floors**

.7   **Ceilings**

.8   **Other elements**

> Including balustrades, fastenings, fireplaces

.82   Openings

> Class here blinds

.822   Doors and doorways

> Standard subdivisions are added for either or both topics in heading

.823   Windows

> Class windows as parts of roof structures in 721.5

.83   Means of vertical access

> Including ramps

.832   Stairs

> Including escalators

.833   Elevators

.84   Semi-enclosed and uncovered spaces

> Including balconies, courtyards, decks, patios, porches, verandas

> *For arcades, see 721.41; for decks and patios of residential buildings, see 728.93*

> ## 722–724 Architectural schools and styles

Class architects of specific schools and styles not limited to a specific type of structure in 720.92; class details of construction of specific schools and styles in 721; class specific types of structures regardless of school or style in 725–728; class design and decoration of structures of specific schools and styles in 729; class comprehensive works, schools and styles from ca. 300 limited to a specific country or locality in 720.9

722   **Architecture from earliest times to ca. 300**

.1   ***Ancient Chinese, Japanese, Korean architecture**

Class here ancient Oriental architecture

For ancient south and southeast Asian architecture, see 722.4; for ancient Middle Eastern architecture, see 722.5

.11   *Ancient Chinese architecture

Class ancient Tibetan architecture in 722.4

.12   *Ancient Japanese architecture

.13   *Ancient Korean architecture

.2   ***Ancient Egyptian architecture**

.3   ***Ancient Semitic architecture**

Class comprehensive works on Semitic architecture in 720.8992

.31   *Phoenician architecture

Class here architecture of Tyre, ancient Sidon

For colonial Phoenician, see 722.32

.32   *Colonial Phoenician architecture

Including architecture of Carthage, Utica, ancient Cyprus

.33   *Ancient Palestinian architecture

Including ancient Israelite, Judean, Jewish architecture

.4   ***Ancient south and southeast Asian architecture**

.44   *Ancient Indian architecture

.5   ***Ancient Middle Eastern architecture**

For ancient Egyptian architecture, see 722.2; for ancient Semitic architecture, see 722.3; for ancient Aegean architecture, see 722.61

.51   *Mesopotamian architecture

.52   *Ancient Persian architecture

.6   ***Ancient western architecture**

For Roman architecture, see 722.7; for Greek (Hellenic) architecture, see 722.8; for other ancient western architecture, see 722.9

.61   *Aegean, Minoan, Mycenaean architecture

Subdivisions are added for any or all topics in heading

.62   *Etruscan architecture

.7   ***Roman architecture**

*Add as instructed under 721–729

.709 37	Architecture of Italian Peninsula and adjacent territories

Class architecture of Roman empire in 722.7

.8   ***Greek (Hellenic) architecture**

Class here comprehensive works on Greek and Roman architecture

For Roman architecture, see 722.7

.809 38	Architecture of Greece

Class architecture of Hellenistic world in 722.8

.9   ***Other ancient western architecture**

723   **†Architecture from ca. 300 to 1399**

Class here medieval architecture

.1   **†Early Christian architecture**

.2   **†Byzantine architecture**

.3   **†Saracenic architecture**

Class here Moorish architecture

For Mudéjar architecture, see 720.9460902

.4   **†Romanesque and Norman architecture**

.5   **†Gothic architecture**

724   **†Architecture from 1400**

Class here modern architecture

.1   **†1400–1800**

Class here colonial styles

For colonial styles of a later period, see the period, e.g., 1800–1899 724.5

.12   **†1400–1499**

Class here Renaissance architecture

For Renaissance architecture of an earlier or later period, see the period, e.g., 1500–1599 724.14

.14   **†1500–1599**

.16   **†1600–1699**

Class here comprehensive works on baroque architecture

For baroque architecture of 1700–1799, see 724.19

---

*Add as instructed under 721–729

†Do not use notation 09 from Table 1; class architecture limited to a specific country or locality in 720.9, biography in 720.92

.19   †1700–1799

> Class here Georgian, rococo architecture

.2   †**Classical revival architecture**

> Class here neoclassical architecture

.22   †Roman revival architecture

.23   †Greek revival architecture

.3   †**Gothic revival architecture**

.5   †**1800–1899**

> Class here eclecticism, revivals, Victorian architecture
>
> *For classical revival architecture, see 724.2; for gothic revival architecture, see 724.3. For eclecticism and revivals of another specific period, see the period, e.g., 1700–1799 724.19*

.52   †Italianate revivals

> Including Renaissance revival, Romanesque revival architecture

.6   †**1900–1999**

> Including art nouveau, expressionism, functionalism, international style

.7   †**2000–**

>   **725–728 Specific types of structures**

> Class here development of architectural schools and styles, comprehensive works on specific structures and their interior design and decorations, interdisciplinary works on design and construction
>
> Class comprehensive works in 720. Class structures rehabilitated to a single new use with the new use, e.g., warehouses converted into apartments 728.314; class structures rehabilitated to multiple new uses with the old use, e.g., warehouses converted into retail stores and apartments 725.35
>
> *For structural engineering, see 624.1; for engineering design and construction of specific types of habitable structures, see 690.5–690.8; for interior decoration, see 747*

725   **Public structures*

> *For public structures used primarily for religious and related purposes, see 726; for public structures used primarily for educational and research purposes, see 727; for public structures used primarily for residential and related purposes, see 728*

---

*Add as instructed under 721–729

†Do not use notation 09 from Table 1; class architecture limited to a specific country or locality in 720.9, biography in 720.92

.1 ***Government buildings**

Class here international government, civic center buildings

.11 *Legislative buildings

Class here capitols

.12 *Executive buildings

Class here buildings containing branches of executive department

.13 *Local government buildings

Regardless of specific kind of local jurisdiction

.14 *Customs buildings

.15 *Court, record, archive buildings

Subdivisions are added for any or all topics in heading

.16 *Post offices

.17 *Official residences

Including embassy, legation, consulate buildings

Class here executive mansions, palaces of rulers

.18 *Military and police buildings

Including armories, arsenals, barracks, castles, fortresses, forts

Subdivisions are added for either or both topics in heading

Class engineering of forts and fortresses in 623.1; class comprehensive works on castles in 728.81

.19 *Fire stations

.2 ***Commercial and communications buildings**

Subdivisions are added for commercial and communications buildings together, for commercial buildings alone

For refreshment facilities, see 725.7

.21 *Retail trade buildings

Class here bazaars, shopping malls, shops, stores

.23 *Office and communications buildings

Including medical office buildings and clinics, radio and television buildings and towers

Subdivisions are added for either or both topics in heading

.24 *Financial institutions

For exchanges, see 725.25

*Add as instructed under 721–729

.25   *Exchanges

> Including board of trade, chamber of commerce buildings, stock and commodity exchange

.3   *Transportation, storage, agricultural buildings

> Subdivisions are added for transportation, storage, agricultural buildings together; for transportation buildings alone

.31   *Railroad and rapid transit stations

> Class here passenger stations

> Subdivisions are added for either or both topics in heading

> *For railroad freight stations, see 725.32*

.32   *Railroad freight stations

.33   *Railroad and rapid transit buildings

> Including roundhouses

> Subdivisions are added for either or both topics in heading

> *For railroad and rapid transit stations, see 725.31*

.34   *Marine transportation facilities

> Including docks, piers

> Class engineering of naval facilities in 623.64; class engineering of harbors, ports, roadsteads in 627.2

> *See also 725.4 for shipyards*

.35   *Warehouses

> Class here comprehensive works on storage buildings

> > *For a specific kind of storage building other than warehouse, see the kind, e.g., storage elevators 725.36*

.36   *Storage elevators

.37   *Agricultural buildings

> Including shearing sheds, comprehensive works on greenhouses

> Class here farm buildings, comprehensive works on agricultural structures

> > *For storage elevators, see 725.36; for farmhouses, see 728.6; for agricultural buildings associated with residential buildings, see 728.92*

---

*Add as instructed under 721–729

.372   *Barns and sheds

Class here comprehensive works on barns

Subdivisions are added for either or both topics in heading

Class shearing sheds in 725.37

For barns and sheds associated with residential buildings, see 728.922

.38   *Motor vehicle transportation buildings

Including bus terminals, filling stations, garages, parking facilities

.39   *Air transportation buildings

Including air terminals, hangars

Class engineering of military air facilities in 623.66

.4   **Industrial buildings**

Including factories, mills, plants, shipyards

.5   **Welfare and health buildings**

Subdivisions are added for welfare and health buildings together, for welfare buildings alone

.51   *General hospital and sanatorium buildings

Class here comprehensive works on health buildings

For a specific kind of health building not provided for here, see the kind, e.g., medical office buildings and clinics 725.23, children's hospital buildings 725.57

.52   *Mental health facility buildings

Class here psychiatric hospital buildings

.53   *Buildings of institutions for people with mental disabilities

.54   *Buildings of institutions for people with physical disabilities

.55   *Buildings of institutions for poor people

Class buildings of institutions for poor people in late adulthood in 725.56

.56   *Buildings of institutions for people in late adulthood

.57   *Child welfare institutions and children's hospital buildings

Subdivisions are added for either or both topics in heading

.59   Other types of welfare buildings

.592   *Veterinary hospitals and shelters

Subdivisions are added for either or both topics in heading

.594   *Veterans' homes

*Add as instructed under 721–729

.597   *Morgues and crematories

> Subdivisions are added for either or both topics in heading

.6   ***Correctional institutions**

> Class here prison and reformatory buildings

.7   ***Refreshment facilities and park structures**

.71   *Eating places

> Class here restaurants

.72   *Drinking places

> Class here bars, pubs, taverns

.73   *Bathhouses and saunas

> Class here comprehensive works on public and domestic bathhouses and saunas
>
> Subdivisions are added for either or both topics in heading
>
> *For domestic bathhouses and saunas, see 728.96*

.74   *Swimming pools

> Class here comprehensive works on public and domestic swimming pools
>
> *For domestic swimming pools, see 728.962*

.76   *Amusement park buildings and casinos

> Subdivisions are added for either or both topics in heading

.8   **Recreation buildings**

> *For refreshment facilities and park structures, see 725.7*

.804   General categories of recreation buildings

.804 2   *Multiple-purpose complexes

> Class here cultural centers
>
> Class community centers for adult education in 727.9

.804 3   *Sports complexes (Sports centers, Sports pavilions)

.81   *Concert and music halls

> Subdivisions are added for either or both topics in heading
>
> *For opera houses, see 725.822*

.82   *Buildings for shows and spectacles

.822   *Theaters and opera houses

> Subdivisions are added for either or both topics in heading

*Add as instructed under 721–729

.823	*Motion picture theaters (Cinemas)

.827   *Buildings for outdoor performances and for athletic and outdoor sports and games

> Including grandstands
>
> Class here amphitheaters, stadiums
>
> Subdivisions are added for any or all topics in heading
>
> *For racetrack buildings, see 725.89*

.83   *Auditoriums

> Class here performing arts centers
>
> *For concert and music halls, see 725.81; for theaters and opera houses, see 725.822*

.84   *Buildings for indoor games

> Including bowling alleys; pool halls; halls for card games, checkers, chess
>
> *For gymnasiums, see 725.85*

.85   *Athletic club buildings and gymnasiums

> Subdivisions are added for either or both topics in heading

.86   *Dance halls and rinks

> Subdivisions are added for either or both topics in heading

.87   *Boathouses and recreation pier buildings

> Subdivisions are added for either or both topics in heading

.88   *Riding-club buildings

.89   *Racetrack buildings

.9   Other public structures

> Including fountains with little or no sculptural decoration
>
> Class comprehensive works on fountains in 731.724

.91   *Convention centers

> Class here exhibition buildings

.94   *Memorial buildings

> Class memorial buildings for a specific purpose with the purpose, e.g., memorial library buildings 727.8

.96   Arches, gateways, walls

> Standard subdivisions are added for any or all topics in heading
>
> *See also 721.2 for walls as structural elements; also 721 for arches as structural elements*

*Add as instructed under 721–729

.97   *Towers

           Including bell, clock towers

             See also 726.2 for minarets; also 726.597 for church towers

.98   Bridges, tunnels, moats

           Class engineering of moats in 623.31; class engineering of tunnels in 624.193; class engineering of bridges in 624.2

726   *Buildings for religious and related purposes

>   **726.1–726.3   Buildings associated with non-Christian religions**

           Class comprehensive works in 726. Class a specific kind of building for religious purposes associated with a specific religion with the building, e.g., Buddhist monasteries 726.7843

            See also 726.5 for buildings associated with Christianity

.1   ***Temples and shrines**

           Subdivisions are added for either or both topics in heading

.12–.19   Temples and shrines of a specific non-Christian religion

           Add to base number 726.1 the numbers following 29 in 292–299, e.g., Buddhist temples and shrines 726.143; however, for mosques and minarets, see 726.2; for synagogues and Jewish temples, see 726.3

.2   ***Mosques and minarets**

           Subdivisions are added for either or both topics in heading

.3   ***Synagogues and Jewish temples**

           Subdivisions are added for either or both topics in heading

.4   ***Accessory houses of worship**

           For all religions

           Including chapels, parish houses, Sunday school buildings; comprehensive works on baptistries

           Class Christian chapels in 726.5

            For baptistries as a part of church buildings, see 726.596

            See also 726.9 for residential parish houses

*Add as instructed under 721–729

.5 ***Buildings associated with Christianity**

Class here Christian chapels; church buildings

Class side chapels in 726.595

For mortuary chapels, see 726.8. For a specific kind of building not provided for here, see the building, e.g., cathedrals 726.6, Franciscan monasteries 726.773

.51 Design, decoration, construction of structural elements

Add to base number 726.51 the numbers following 721 in 721.1–721.8, e.g., design, decoration, construction of church vaulting 726.5143

Class decoration of structural elements in specific mediums in 726.524–726.528

.52 Decoration in specific mediums, built-in church furniture, design and decoration of parts

.524–.528 Decoration in specific mediums

Add to base number 726.52 the numbers following 729 in 729.4–729.8, e.g., decoration in relief 726.525

Class decorations of built-in church furniture in 726.529. Class decoration in a specific medium not in an architectural context with the medium, e.g., sculpture 730

.529 Built-in church furniture

Class built-in church furniture in a specific medium not in an architectural context with the medium, e.g., carved pew ends 731.54

.529 1 Sacramental furniture

Including altars, baptismal fonts, confessionals, tabernacles

.529 2 Rostral furniture

Including lecterns, prayer desks, pulpits

.529 3 Seats and canopies

Including baldachins, bishops' thrones, choir stalls, pews

.529 6 Screens and railings

Including altar and rood screens, altar and chancel railings, reredoses

.529 7 Organ cases

.529 8 Lighting fixtures

.58 Buildings of specific denominations

Add to base number 726.58 the numbers following 28 in 281–289, e.g., Anglican church buildings 726.583; however, for geographic treatment of buildings of specific denominations, see 726.509

Class specific parts of church buildings of specific denominations in 726.59

*Add as instructed under 721–729

.59		Parts

Class design and construction of parts in 726.51; class design and decoration of parts in 726.52

.591		Entrances and approaches
.592		Naves and transepts
.593		Chancels, choirs, sanctuaries, choir lofts, pulpit platforms
.594		Clerestories
.595		Side chapels

Class chapels as separate buildings in 726.5

.596		Sacristies and baptistries

Class comprehensive works on baptistries in 726.4

.597		Towers and steeples
.6		***Cathedrals**

For details and parts of cathedrals, see 726.51–726.59

.62		Cathedrals of Eastern churches

For Orthodox cathedrals, see 726.63

.620 9		History and biography

Do not use for geographic treatment; class in 726.609

.63		Orthodox cathedrals
.630 9		History and biography

Do not use for geographic treatment; class in 726.609

.64		Roman Catholic cathedrals
.640 9		History and biography

Do not use for geographic treatment; class in 726.609

.65		Anglican cathedrals
.650 9		History and biography

Do not use for geographic treatment; class in 726.609

.69		*Accessory structures

Including cathedral cloisters, chapter houses

Class comprehensive works on cloisters in 726.796

*Add as instructed under 721–729

.7 ***Monastic buildings**

> Class here abbeys, convents, friaries, monasteries, priories

> Class monastic churches either as a place of public worship or as a separate church building in 726.5

.77 Monastic buildings of specific Christian orders

[.770 1–.770 9] Standard subdivisions

> Do not use; class in 726.701–726.709

.771–.779 Subdivisions of monastic buildings of specific Christian orders

> Add to base number 726.77 the numbers following 271 in 271.1–271.9, e.g., Franciscan monasteries 726.773; however, for geographic treatment of buildings of specific orders, see 726.709

.78 Monastic buildings of orders of other religions

> Add to base number 726.78 the numbers following 29 in 292–299, e.g., Buddhist monasteries 726.7843

.79 Parts and accessory structures

> Including cells, refectories

> Class monastic libraries in 727.8

.796 Cloisters

> Class here comprehensive works on cloisters

> > *For cathedral cloisters, see 726.69; for collegiate cloisters, see 727.38*

.8 ***Mortuary chapels and tombs**

> Subdivisions are added for either or both topics in heading

.9 **Other buildings for religious and related purposes**

> Including episcopal palaces, missions, parsonages, buildings of religious associations, buildings housing roadside shrines

727 ***Buildings for educational and research purposes**

Class here school buildings

Subdivisions are added for buildings for educational and research purposes together, for buildings for educational purposes alone

---

> **727.1–727.3 Buildings for education at specific levels**

> > Class professional and technical school buildings at a specific level in 727.4; class comprehensive works in 727

> > *For buildings for adult education, see 727.9*

*Add as instructed under 721–729

.1   ***Primary school buildings**

.2   ***Secondary school buildings**

.3   ***College and university buildings**

> Subdivisions are added for either or both topics in heading
>
> Class specialized buildings of colleges and universities in 727.4–727.8

.38   Accessory structures

> Including dining halls, dormitories, student unions

.4   **Professional and technical school buildings**

.400 01–.400 09   Standard subdivisions

.400 1–.499 9   Specific types of professional and technical school buildings

> Add to base number 727.4 notation 001–999, e.g., law school buildings 727.434

.5   **Research buildings**

> Class here laboratory, observatory buildings

.500 01–.500 09   Standard subdivisions

.500 1–.599 9   Specific types of research buildings

> Add to base number 727.5 notation 001–999, e.g., physics laboratories 727.553

.6   **Museum buildings**

.600 01–.600 09   Standard subdivisions

.600 1–.699 9   Specific types of museum buildings

> Add to base number 727.6 notation 001–999, e.g., science museum buildings 727.65; however, for art museum buildings, see 727.7

.7   ***Art museum and gallery buildings**

> Subdivisions are added for either or both topics in heading

.8   ***Library buildings**

.82   *General libraries

.820 9   History and biography

> Do not use for geographic treatment; class in 727.809

.821–.828   Specific kinds of general libraries

> Add to base number 727.82 the numbers following 027 in 027.1–027.8, e.g., public library buildings 727.824; then add further as instructed under 721–729, e.g., energy conservation in public library buildings 727.8240472; however, for geographic treatment, see 727.809; for branch libraries, see 727.84

*Add as instructed under 721–729

.83   *Libraries devoted to specific subjects

.830 9   History and biography

> Do not use for geographic treatment; class in 727.809

.84   *Branch libraries

.840 9   History and biography

> Do not use for geographic treatment; class in 727.809

.9   Other buildings for educational and research purposes

> Including community centers for adult education, learned society buildings

728   *Residential and related buildings

Class here domestic architecture, conventional housing

Subdivisions are added for residential and related buildings together, for residential buildings alone

> *For official residences, see 725.17; for episcopal palaces, parsonages, see 726.9; for residential educational buildings, see 727.1–727.3*

.1   *Low-cost housing

Dwellings designed along simple lines to reduce construction costs

Class specific types of low-cost housing in 728.3–728.7

.3   Specific kinds of conventional housing

[.301–.309]   Standard subdivisions

> Do not use; class in 728.01–728.09

.31   *Multiple dwellings

.312   *Duplex houses and row houses

> Class here double houses, semi-detached houses, terrace houses, townhouses

> Subdivisions are added for either or both topics in heading

.314   *Apartment houses

> Including apartment hotels, tenements

.37   *Separate houses

> Class here cottages

> *For farmhouses, see 728.6; for vacation houses, see 728.72; for large and elaborate private dwellings, see 728.8*

.372   *Multistory houses

.373   *Single-story houses

> Class here bungalows, ranch and split-level houses

*Add as instructed under 721–729

> ### 728.4–728.7 Special-purpose housing

Class comprehensive works in 728

.4   ***Clubhouses**

Country, city, fraternal clubs

Class a type of club house not provided for here with the type, e.g., racetrack clubhouses 725.89

.5   ***Hotels and motels**

Subdivisions are added for either or both topics in heading

For apartment hotels, see 728.314

.6   ***Farmhouses**

Class here farm cottages

Class comprehensive works on farm buildings in 725.37

.7   ***Vacation houses, cabins, hunting lodges, houseboats, mobile homes**

.72   *Vacation houses

.73   *Cabins

Class vacation cabins in 728.72

.78   *Houseboats

.79   *Mobile homes

Including campers, trailers

For houseboats, see 728.78

See Manual at 643.29, 690.879, 728.79 vs. 629.226

.8   ***Large and elaborate private dwellings**

Class here chateaux, manor houses, mansions, plantation houses, villas

.81   *Castles

Fortified residences

Class here comprehensive works on architecture of castles

For castles as military structures, see 725.18

.82   *Palaces

Residences of nobility

Class fortified palaces in 728.81

See also 725.17 for palaces of rulers; also 726.9 for episcopal palaces

*Add as instructed under 721–729

.9   ***Miscellaneous structures associated with residential buildings**

Including gatehouses

.92   *Agricultural structures associated with residential buildings

Class comprehensive works on agricultural structures in 725.37

For farmhouses, see 728.6

.922   *Barns and sheds

Subdivisions are added for either or both topics in heading

.924   *Greenhouses

Class here conservatories

Class comprehensive works on greenhouses in 725.37

.927   *Birdhouses

Class here aviaries

.93   *Decks and patios

Subdivisions are added for either or both topics in heading

.96   Swimming pools and related structures

Including bathhouses, saunas

Class comprehensive works on bathhouses and saunas in 725.73

.962   *Swimming pools

Class comprehensive works on swimming pools in 725.74

.98   *Garages

729   Design and decoration of structures and accessories

Class here interior architecture (the art or practice of planning and supervising the design and execution of architectural interiors and their furnishings)

Class design and decoration of structures and accessories of specific types of buildings in 725–728

For interior decoration, see 747

See Manual at 729

>   **729.1–729.2 Design in specific planes**

Class design of structural elements in specific planes in 721.1–721.8; class comprehensive works in 729. Class architectural drawings for one structure or a specific type of structure with the structure in 725–728, plus notation 0222 from table under 721–729, e.g., architectural drawings of palaces 728.820222

*Add as instructed under 721–729

.1   **Design in vertical plane**

> Including facades
>
> Class here elevations, sections

.102 22   Pictures and related illustrations

> > Do not use for architectural drawings; class in 729.1

.11   Composition

.13   Proportion

.19   Inscriptions and lettering

> Standard subdivisions are added for either or both topics in heading

.2   **Design in horizontal plane**

> Class here modular design; floor plans
>
> Class architectural plans as a set of drawings for a project in 720.222

.202 22   Pictures and related illustrations

> > Do not use for architectural drawings; class in 729.2

.23   Proportion

.24   *Interior arrangement

.25   *Lines of interior communication

.28   Lighting

> Including daylighting

.29   Acoustics

> **729.4–729.8 Decoration in specific mediums**

> Class comprehensive works in 729. Class decoration in a specific medium not in an architectural context with the medium, e.g., sculpture 730

.4   **Decoration in paint**

> As an adjunct to architecture

.5   **Decoration in relief**

> Including carved and sculptured decoration and ornament, Gothic tracery

.6   **Decoration in veneer and incrustation**

> Use of wood, stone, metal, enamel in architectural decoration

.7   **Decoration in mosaic**

> Class comprehensive works on mosaics in 738.5

*Add as instructed under 721–729

.8   **Decoration in ornamental glass**

730   Sculpture and related arts

Standard subdivisions are added for sculpture and related arts together, for sculpture alone

Class here plastic arts

Class plastic arts covering all visual arts in 700

.1   **Philosophy and theory of sculpture and related arts together, of sculpture alone**

Notation 01 from Table 1 as modified below

.11   Appreciative aspects

Do not use for systems; class in 730.1

Class psychological principles in 730.19

.117   Aesthetics

.118   Criticism and appreciation

Theory, technique, history

Class works of critical appraisal in 730.9

.18   Inherent features

Including color, composition, decorative values, form, movement, space, style, symmetry, vision

.2   **Miscellany of sculpture and related arts together, of sculpture alone**

.28   Auxiliary techniques and procedures; apparatus, equipment, materials of sculpture and related arts

Notation 028 from Table 1 as modified below

Do not use for auxiliary techniques and procedures of sculpture alone; class in 731.028

Class here basic techniques and procedures, techniques of two or more of the plastic arts, e.g., firing of clays in sculpture and ceramics

.284   Apparatus, equipment, materials of sculpture and related arts

Do not use for materials for sculpture alone; class in 731.2. Do not use for apparatus and equipment for sculpture alone; class in 731.3

.9   **History, geographic treatment, biography of sculpture and related arts together, of sculpture alone**

Class here schools and styles limited to a specific country or locality

Class sculpture of nonliterate peoples regardless of time or place in 732.2; class comprehensive works on specific schools and styles of sculpture not limited to country or locality in 732–735

.901–.905   Historical periods of sculpture and related arts

> Do not use for sculpture alone; class in 732–735

.92   Biography

> Class here description and critical appraisal of sculptors or plastic artists and their works regardless of process, representation, style or school, period, place; sculptors who also work in the other plastic arts

.922   Collected biography

> Including works of sculptors or plastic artists from several geographic areas

> Class works of more than one sculptor or plastic artist in the same geographic area, region, place in general (*not* limited by continent, country, locality) in 730.91

.922 3   Ancient world

> Class here works of more than one plastic artist

> Class works of more than one sculptor in 732–733

.922 4–.922 9   Specific continents, countries, localities in modern world

> Class works of more than one sculptor or plastic artist in 730.94–730.99

.93   Ancient world

> Do not use for sculpture alone; class in 732–733

.95   Asia

> Class here Buddhist, Oriental sculpture

> *For Buddhist sculpture in an area not provided for here, see the area, e.g., Buddhist sculpture in Hawaii 730.9969*

.954   India and neighboring south Asian countries

> Class here Hindu, Jain sculpture

> *For Hindu sculpture in an area not provided for here, see the area, e.g., Hindu sculpture in Indonesia 730.9598*

> ## 731–735 Sculpture

> Class comprehensive works in 730

> *See Manual at 731–735 vs. 736–739*

731   Processes, forms, subjects of sculpture

> Class processes, forms, subjects of specific periods and by specific schools in 732–735

.028   Auxiliary techniques and procedures

> Class comprehensive works on basic and auxiliary techniques and procedures in 731.4

[.028 4]	Apparatus, equipment, materials

Do not use for materials; class in 731.2. Do not use for apparatus and equipment; class in 731.3

[.028 8]	Maintenance and repair

Do not use; class in 731.48

.092	Biography

Do not use for individual sculptors; class in 730.92

> ### 731.2–731.4 Techniques, procedures, apparatus, equipment, materials

Class forms employing techniques, procedures, apparatus, equipment, materials in 731.5; class subjects employing techniques, procedures, apparatus, equipment, materials in 731.8; class comprehensive works in 731.4

.2   ***Materials**

Including ceramic materials, found objects, metals, paper, papier-mâché, plastics, rope, stone, textiles, wax, wire, wood

Class use of materials in specific techniques in 731.4

.3   ***Apparatus and equipment**

Including tools, machines, accessories

Class use of apparatus and equipment in specific techniques in 731.4

.4   ***Techniques and procedures**

Class here comprehensive works on techniques, procedures, apparatus, equipment, materials together

For auxiliary techniques and procedures, see 731.028; for materials, see 731.2; for apparatus and equipment, see 731.3

.41   ***Direct-metal sculpture**

Including beating, bending, cutting, hammering, shaping, soldering, welding metals (including pipe and wire)

Class art metalwork in 739

.42   ***Modeling**

In clay, wax, other plastic materials with and without armatures

.43   ***Molding**

Preparation of molds and models

Class use of molds in 731.45

.45   ***Casting**

Including sand casting

---

*Do not use notation 092 from Table 1 for individual sculptors; class in 730.92

.452	*Cement and plaster casting
.453	*Plastics casting
.456	*Casting in bronze

> Including lost-wax casting
>
> Class here casting in metals
>
> *For casting in metals other than bronze, see 731.457*

.457	*Casting in metals other than bronze

> Class comprehensive works on casting in metals in 731.456

.46	*Carving and chiseling techniques in sculpture

> Standard subdivisions are added for either or both topics in heading

.462	*Sculpturing in wood
.463	*Sculpturing in stone
.47	*Firing and baking

> Standard subdivisions are added for either or both topics in heading
>
> Including firing and baking clay models for molding
>
> Class techniques of firing and baking in ceramics in 738.143

.48	*Maintenance and repair

> Class here conservation, preservation, restoration

.5	***Forms**

> Development, description, critical appraisal, collections of works not limited by time or place
>
> *For sculpture in the round, see 731.7*

.54	*Sculpture in relief

> Class iconography of sculpture in relief in 731.8

.542	*Portals and doors

> Standard subdivisions are added for either or both topics in heading

.549	*Monumental reliefs

> *For monumental brasses, see 739.522*

.55	*Mobiles and stabiles
.7	***Sculpture in the round**

> Development, description, critical appraisal, collections of works
>
> Class iconography of sculpture in the round in 731.8

*Do not use notation 092 from Table 1 for individual sculptors; class in 730.92

.72   *Decorative sculpture

             Including garden sculpture, sculptured vases and urns

.724   *Fountains

             Class here comprehensive works on fountains

             *For fountains as a water feature in landscape architecture, see 714;
             for public fountains with little or no sculptural decoration, see 725.9;
             for tabletop and indoor fountains, see 745.5946*

.74   *Busts

.75   *Masks

.76   *Monuments

             For monumental brasses, see 739.522

.77   *Totem poles

.8   ***Iconography**

             Development, description, critical appraisal, works not limited by time or place

.81   *Equestrian sculpture

.82–.89   Other specific subjects

             Add to base number 731.8 the numbers following 704.94 in
             704.942–704.949, e.g., mythology and legend 731.87; however, for
             individual sculptors, see 730.92; for busts, see 731.74; for masks, see 731.75

>   **732–735 Schools and styles of sculpture**

             Class comprehensive works in 730.9

732   **Sculpture from earliest times to ca. 500, sculpture of
             nonliterate peoples**

[.09]   History, geographic treatment, biography

             Do not use for biography; class in 730.92. Do not use for history and
             geographic treatment; class in 732

.2   **†Sculpture of nonliterate peoples**

             Regardless of time or place

.22   †Paleolithic sculpture

.23   †Rock art (sculpture)

---

*Do not use notation 092 from Table 1 for individual sculptors; class in 730.92
†Do not use notation 092 from Table 1; class biography in 730.92

> **732.3–732.9 Ancient sculpture**

Class comprehensive works in 732

.3 **†Ancient Palestinian sculpture**

Including Israelite, Judean, Jewish sculpture

.4 **†Ancient south and southeast Asian sculpture**

.44 †Ancient Indian sculpture

.5 **†Mesopotamian and ancient Persian sculpture**

.6 **†Ancient British, Celtic, Germanic, Iberian, Slavic sculpture**

.7 **†Ancient Oriental sculpture**

For ancient Oriental sculpture of a specific place not provided for here, see the place, e.g., ancient Indian sculpture 732.44

.71 †Ancient Chinese sculpture

.72 †Ancient Japanese sculpture

.73 †Ancient Korean sculpture

.8 **†Ancient Egyptian sculpture**

.9 **Sculpture of other ancient areas**

Add to base number 732.9 the numbers following —39 in notation 392–398 from Table 2, e.g., Phoenician sculpture 732.944; however, for biography, see 730.92; for ancient sculpture of Greek Archipelago, see 733.309391

For Greek, Etruscan, Roman sculpture, see 733

733   †Greek, Etruscan, Roman sculpture

.3 **†Greek (Hellenic) sculpture**

Class comprehensive works on Greek and Roman sculpture in 733

.309 38 Sculpture of Greece

Class sculpture of Hellenistic world in 733.3

.4 **†Etruscan sculpture**

.5 **†Roman sculpture**

.509 37 Sculpture of Italian Peninsula and adjacent territories

Class sculpture of Roman Empire in 733.5

†Do not use notation 092 from Table 1; class biography in 730.92

734   *Sculpture from ca. 500 to 1399

> Class here medieval sculpture

.2   ***Styles**

.22   *Early Christian and Byzantine sculpture

.222   *Early Christian sculpture

.224   *Byzantine sculpture

.24   *Romanesque sculpture

.25   *Gothic sculpture

735   *Sculpture from 1400

> Class here modern sculpture

.2   **Specific periods**

.21   *1400–1799

> Including baroque, Renaissance sculpture

.22   *1800–1899

> Including classical revival sculpture, romanticism, realism

.23   *1900–1999   .

.230 4   Schools and styles

> Add to base number 735.2304 the numbers following 709.040 in 709.0401–709.0407, e.g., abstractionism in sculpture 735.230452; however, for assemblages, constructions, sound sculpture, land art, mixed media, composites, see 709.04; for geographic treatment, see 730.9; for biography, see 730.92

.231–.239   Periods

> Add to base number 735.23 the numbers following —0904 in notation 09041–09049 from Table 1, e.g., sculpture of 1960–1969 735.236; however, for geographic treatment, see 730.9; for biography, see 730.92

.24   *2000–2099

> **736–739   Other plastic arts**

> Processes and products

> Class comprehensive works in 730. Class a plastic art not provided for here with the art in 745–749, e.g., textile arts 746

> *See also 731–735 for sculpture*

> *See Manual at 731–735 vs. 736–739*

---

*Do not use notation 09 from Table 1; class geographic treatment in 730.9, biography in 730.92

736   Carving and carvings

Standard subdivisions are added for either or both topics in heading

.2   **Precious and semiprecious stones (Glyptics)**

Standard subdivisions are added for either or both topics in heading

Class engraved seals, stamps, signets in 737.6; class setting of precious and semiprecious stones in 739.27

.202 8   Lapidary work

Do not use for auxiliary techniques and procedures; apparatus, equipment, materials; class in 736.202

Including cutting, polishing, engraving gems

.22   Specific forms

Class carving in specific materials regardless of form in 736.23–736.28

For scarabs, see 736.20932

.222   Cameos

.223   Intaglios

.224   Figurines

>   736.23–736.28   Specific stones

Class comprehensive works in 736.2

.23   Diamonds

.24   Jade

See also 731–735 for jade sculpture

.25   Sapphires

.28   Obsidian

.4   **Wood**

Including butter prints and molds, whittling

See also 731–735 for wood sculpture; also 745.51 for wood handicrafts

.5   **Stone**

Including lettering, inscriptions, designs

Class here effigial and sepulchral slabs

See also 731–735 for stone sculpture

.6   **Ivory, bone, horn, shell, amber**

.62   Ivory

> Class netsukes of ivory in 736.68; class scrimshaws of ivory in 736.69
>
> *See also 731–735 for ivory sculpture*

.68   Netsukes

.69   Scrimshaws

.7   **Ornamental fans**

> Class fans of a specific material with the material, e.g., ivory fans 736.62

.9   **Other materials**

.93   Wax

.94   Ice and snow

.95   Soap

.96   Sand sculpture

> Class here sandcastles

.98   Paper cutting and folding

.980 952   Paper cutting and folding of Japan

> *For origami, see 736.982*

.982   Origami

.984   Silhouettes

> Class comprehensive works on drawing and cutting silhouettes in 741.7

737   Numismatics and sigillography

> Standard subdivisions are added for numismatics and sigillography together, for numismatics alone
>
> *For paper money, see 769.55*

.2   **Medals and related objects**

.22   Medals

> Class here medallions

.222   Commemorative medals

.223   Civilian and military medals

> Including decorations, orders

.224   Religious medals

.23   Amulets and talismans

.24   Buttons and pins

> Standard subdivisions are added for either or both topics in heading

.242   Political buttons and pins

>> Standard subdivisions are added for either or both topics in heading

>> Class here campaign buttons and pins

.243   Sports buttons and pins

>> Standard subdivisions are added for either or both topics in heading

.3   Counters and tokens

>> Standard subdivisions are added for either or both topics in heading

.4   Coins

>> Class here counterfeit coins

.409 3–.409 9   Specific continents and localities

>> Do not use for specific countries; class in 737.49

.43   Gold coins

.430 93–.430 99   Specific continents and localities

>> Do not use for specific countries; class in 737.49

.49   Coins of specific countries

>> By place of origin

>> Add to base number 737.49 notation 3–9 from Table 2, e.g., Roman coins minted in Egypt 737.4932

.6   Engraved seals, signets, stamps

>> Standard subdivisions are added for any or all topics in heading

>> Class here sigillography

>> Class interdisciplinary works on sigillography in 929.9

738   Ceramic arts

>> Class here pottery

>> Use 738 for pottery encompassing porcelain and earthenware or porcelain and stoneware. Use 738.3 for pottery limited to earthenware or stoneware. Porcelain, which was invented in China, did not reach other parts of Asia until the 9th century and Europe until the 17th century. Use these dates to determine when pottery of a place, other than China, was only earthenware or stoneware

>> Class ceramic sculpture in 731–735

>> *For glass, see 748*

.028   Auxiliary techniques and procedures

>> Class comprehensive works on techniques and procedures in 738.14

[.028 4]   Apparatus, equipment, materials

>> Do not use for materials; class in 738.12. Do not use for apparatus and equipment; class in 738.13

[.028 8]	Maintenance and repair
	Do not use; class in 738.18
.09	History, geographic treatment, biography
	Class here brands of pottery
.092	Biography
	Regardless of material or product
	Class here ceramic artists
	For enamelers, see 738.4092; for mosaicists, see 738.5092
.1	**Techniques, procedures, apparatus, equipment, materials**
	Class techniques, procedures, apparatus, equipment, materials of specific products in 738.4–738.8
.12	Materials
	Including clays, e.g., kaolin; color materials
	Class use of materials in specific techniques in 738.14
.127	Glazes
.13	Apparatus and equipment
	Including potter's wheels
	Class use of apparatus and equipment in specific techniques in 738.14
.136	Kilns
.14	Techniques and procedures
	For auxiliary techniques and procedures, see 738.028; for decorative treatment, see 738.15; for conservation, preservation, restoration, see 738.18
.142	Modeling and casting
.143	Firing
	Before and after glazing
.144	Glazing
.15	Decorative treatment
	Including sgrafitto decoration, slip tracing, transfer painting, underglaze and overglaze painting
	For glazing, see 738.144
.18	Maintenance and repair
	Including expertizing
	Class here conservation, preservation, restoration

>   **738.2–738.8   Products**

> Development, description, critical appraisal, collections of works

> Class comprehensive works in 738

.2   **Porcelain**

> Class comprehensive works on porcelain, earthenware, stoneware in 738

> *For specialized porcelain products, see 738.4–738.8*

[.202 8]   Auxiliary techniques and procedures; apparatus, equipment, materials

> Do not use for auxiliary techniques and procedures; class in 738.028

[.202 84]   Apparatus, equipment, materials

> Do not use for materials; class in 738.12. Do not use for apparatus and equipment; class in 738.13

.209   History and geographic treatment of porcelain

> Class here brands

[.209 2]   Biography

> Do not use; class in 738.092

.27   Specific types and varieties of porcelain

> Including blue and white transfer ware

[.270 1–.270 8]   Standard subdivisions

> Do not use; class in 738.201–738.208

[.270 9]   History, geographic treatment, biography

> Do not use for history and geographic treatment; class in 738.209. Do not use for biography; class in 738.092

.28   Tableware and vessels

> Standard subdivisions are added for either or both topics in heading

> Class tableware and vessels of specific types or varieties in 738.27

.280 9   History

> Do not use for geographic treatment; class in 738.209

[.280 92]   Biography

> Do not use; class in 738.092

.3   **Earthenware and stoneware**

Standard subdivisions are added for either or both topics in heading

Use 738 for pottery encompassing porcelain and earthenware or porcelain and stoneware. Use 738.3 for pottery limited to earthenware or stoneware. Porcelain, which was invented in China, did not reach other parts of Asia until the 9th century and Europe until the 17th century. Use these dates to determine when pottery of a place, other than China, was only earthenware or stoneware

For specific earthenware and stoneware products, see 738.4–738.8

[.302 8]   Auxiliary techniques and procedures; apparatus, equipment, materials

Do not use for auxiliary techniques and procedures; class in 738.028

[.302 84]   Apparatus, equipment, materials

Do not use for materials; class in 738.12. Do not use for apparatus and equipment; class in 738.13

.309   History and geographic treatment

Class here brands

[.309 2]   Biography

Do not use; class in 738.092

.309 3   Ancient world

For ancient and classical Middle Eastern and western vessels, see 738.382

.37   Specific types and varieties of earthenware and stoneware

Including delftware, faience

[.370 1–.370 8]   Standard subdivisions

Do not use; class in 738.301–738.308

[.370 9]   History, geographic treatment, biography

Do not use for history and geographic treatment; class in 738.309. Do not use for biography; class in 738.092

.372   Majolica

.372 09   History

Do not use for geographic treatment; class in 738.309

[.372 092]   Biography

Do not use; class in 738.092

.38   Tableware and vessels

Standard subdivisions are added for either or both topics in heading

Class tableware and vessels of specific types and varieties in 738.37

.380 9   History

> Do not use for geographic treatment; class in 738.309. Do not use for biography; class in 738.092

.382   Middle Eastern and western vessels

> Standard subdivisions are added for a specific type of vessel, e.g., ancient Egyptian vases 738.3820932

> Ancient and classical

[.382 092]   Biography

> Do not use; class in 738.092

738.4–738.8 Specific products and techniques of making them

Class ceramic sculpture in 731–735; class comprehensive works on porcelain products in 738.28; class comprehensive works on earthenware and stoneware products in 738.38; class comprehensive works in 738

For porcelain tableware and vessels, see 738.28; for earthenware and stoneware tableware and vessels, see 738.38

.4   **Enamels**

Including basse-taille, champlevé, ronde bosse

For nielloing, see 739.15; for jewelry, see 739.27; for enameling glass, see 748.6

.42   Cloisonné

.46   Surface-painted enamels

.5   **Mosaics**

Class here mosaic painting, comprehensive works on mosaics in all materials

For mosaics of a specific material not provided for here, see the material, e.g., mosaic glass 748.5

.52   Mosaics used with architecture

Including floors, pavements, walls; fixed screens and panels

.56   Mosaics applied to portable objects

Including mosaic jewelry, ornaments, ornamental objects, movable panels

.6   **Ornamental bricks and tiles**

Standard subdivisions are added for either or both topics in heading

.8   **Other products**

Including braziers, candlesticks, lamps, lighting fixtures, stoves

.82 Figurines

Including figure groups, animals, plants

See also 738.83 for dolls

.83 Dolls

Class comprehensive works on handicrafting dolls in 745.59221

739 Art metalwork

For numismatics, see 737

.028 Auxiliary techniques and procedures

Class comprehensive works on techniques and procedures in 739.14

[.028 4] Apparatus, equipment, materials

Do not use for materials; class in 739.12. Do not use for apparatus and equipment; class in 739.13

.1 Techniques, procedures, apparatus, equipment, materials

Class techniques, procedures, apparatus, equipment, materials for a specific kind of metalwork with the kind, e.g., goldsmithing 739.22028

.12 Materials

Class use of materials in specific techniques in 739.14

.13 Apparatus and equipment

Including tools, machines, accessories

Class use of apparatus and equipment in specific techniques in 739.14

.14 Techniques and procedures

Including bending, casting, drawing, forging, rolling, shaping metals by hammering and beating (repoussé work), stamping, welding

For auxiliary techniques and procedures, see 739.028; for decorative treatment, see 739.15

.15 Decorative treatment

Including chasing, damascening, nielloing, painting, patinating

.2 Work in precious metals

Class clocks and watches in precious metals in 739.3

.209 2 Biography

Use 739.2092 for goldsmiths who work in gold and other materials, especially silver. Use 739.22092 for goldsmiths who work in gold alone

---

> 739.22–739.24 Work in specific metals

Class jewelry in specific metals in 739.27; class comprehensive works in 739.2

.22   Goldsmithing

       Class comprehensive works on goldsmithing and silversmithing in 739.2

.220 28   Auxiliary techniques and procedures

       Class here comprehensive works on techniques, procedures, apparatus, equipment, materials together

       Class comprehensive works on basic and auxiliary techniques and procedures in 739.224

[.220 284]   Apparatus, equipment, materials

       Do not use for materials; class in 739.222. Do not use for apparatus and equipment; class in 739.223

.220 9   History, geographic treatment, biography

.220 92   Biography

       Use 739.2092 for goldsmiths who work in gold and other materials, especially silver. Use 739.22092 for goldsmiths who work in gold alone

.222–.225   Techniques, procedures, apparatus, equipment, materials

       Add to base number 739.22 the numbers following 739.1 in 739.12–739.15, e.g., decorative treatment 739.225; however, for history, geographic treatment, biography, see 739.2209

       Class techniques, apparatus, equipment, materials for specific products in 739.228; class comprehensive works in 739.22028

.228   *Products

       Gold and gold-plate

.228 2   *Religious articles

.228 3   *Tableware

       Including flatware, hollow ware

       Class tableware for religious use in 739.2282

.228 4   *Receptacles

       Including boxes, loving cups, vases

       Class religious receptacles in 739.2282

.23   Silversmithing

.230 28   Auxiliary techniques and procedures

       Class here comprehensive works on techniques, procedures, apparatus, equipment, materials together

       Class comprehensive works on basic and auxiliary techniques and procedures in 739.234

*Do not use notation 09 from Table 1; class in 739.2209

[.230 284]		Apparatus, equipment, materials

> Do not use for materials; class in 739.232. Do not use for apparatus and equipment; class in 739.233

.232–.238   Techniques, procedures, apparatus, equipment, materials; products

> Add to base number 739.23 the numbers following 739.22 in 739.222–739.228, e.g., silver tableware 739.2383

.24   Platinumwork

.27   Jewelry

> Design of settings, mounting gems, repair work
>
> Class here interdisciplinary works on making fine and costume jewelry
>
> Class interdisciplinary works on jewelry in 391.7; class interdisciplinary works on making costume jewelry in 688.2
>
> *For carving precious and semiprecious stones, see 736.2; for making handcrafted costume jewelry, see 745.5942. For jewelry made with little or no precious metal, see the specific material other than metal elsewhere in 700, e.g., mosaic jewelry 738.56, glass bead necklaces 748.85*

.270 28   Auxiliary techniques and procedures

> Class here comprehensive works on techniques, procedures, apparatus, equipment, materials together
>
> Class comprehensive works on basic and auxiliary techniques and procedures in 739.274

[.270 284]   Apparatus, equipment, materials

> Do not use for materials; class in 739.272. Do not use for apparatus and equipment; class in 739.273

.272–.275   Techniques, procedures, apparatus, equipment, materials

> Add to base number 739.27 the numbers following 739.1 in 739.12–739.15, e.g., decorative treatment 739.275
>
> Class techniques, apparatus, equipment, materials for specific products in 739.278; class comprehensive works in 739.27028

.278   Products

> Including belt buckles, shoe buckles, watch fobs

.278 2   Finger rings

.3   Clocks and watches

> Standard subdivisions are added for either or both topics in heading
>
> Class here clockcases regardless of material
>
> Class clocks as furniture in 749.3; class interdisciplinary works on clocks in 681.113; class interdisciplinary works on watches in 681.114

.302 8   Auxiliary techniques and procedures

> Class here comprehensive works on techniques, procedures, apparatus, equipment, materials together
>
> Class comprehensive works on basic and auxiliary techniques and procedures in 739.34

[.302 84]   Apparatus, equipment, materials

> Do not use for materials; class in 739.32. Do not use for apparatus and equipment; class in 739.33

.32–.35   Techniques, procedures, apparatus, equipment, materials

> Add to base number 739.3 the numbers following 739.1 in 739.12–739.15, e.g., decorative treatment 739.35; however, for history, geographic treatment, biography, see 739.309
>
> Class techniques, apparatus, equipment, materials for specific products in 739.38; class comprehensive works in 739.3028

> **739.4–739.5 Work in base metals**

> Class clocks and watches in base metals in 739.3; class comprehensive works in 739
>
> *For arms and armor, see 739.7*

.4   **Ironwork**

> Class here wrought iron, cast iron, stainless steel

.402 8   Auxiliary techniques and procedures

> Class here comprehensive works on techniques, procedures, apparatus, equipment, materials together
>
> Class comprehensive works on basic and auxiliary techniques and procedures in 739.44

[.402 84]   Apparatus, equipment, materials

> Do not use for materials; class in 739.42. Do not use for apparatus and equipment; class in 739.43

.42–.45   Techniques, procedures, apparatus, equipment, materials

> Add to base number 739.4 the numbers following 739.1 in 739.12–739.15, e.g., decorative treatment 739.45; however, for history, geographic treatment, biography, see 739.409
>
> Class techniques, apparatus, equipment, materials for specific products in 739.48; class comprehensive works in 739.4028

.48   Products

> Including balcony motifs, balustrades, grills, knockers, ornamental nails

[.480 9]   History, geographic treatment, biography

> Do not use; class in 739.409

.5	**Work in metals other than iron**
.51	Copper and its alloys

> *For brass, see 739.52*

.511	Copper
.512	Bronze

> *See also 731–735 for bronze sculpture*

.52	Brass
.522	Monumental brasses

> Class here rubbing and rubbings for study and research of brasses
>
> Class rubbings as art form in 740

.53	Tin and its alloys

> *For bronze, see 739.512*

.532	Tin
.533	Pewter
.54	Lead
.55	Zinc and its alloys

> Subdivisions are added for zinc and its alloys together, for zinc alone
>
> *For brass, see 739.52*

.56	Nickel
.57	Aluminum
.58	Chromium
.7	**Arms and armor**

> Standard subdivisions are added for arms and armor together, for arms alone
>
> Class here decorative treatment of shapes, handles, grips, metalwork
>
> Class interdisciplinary works on arms and armor in 623.44
>
> *See also 623.441 for stone weapons*

> 739.72–739.74 Arms
>
> Class comprehensive works in 739.7

.72	Edged weapons

> Including axes, daggers, dirks, knives, spears
>
> Class edged arrows in 739.73; class interdisciplinary works on knives in 621.932

.722	Swords and sabers

> Standard subdivisions are added for either or both topics in heading

.723	Bayonets
.73	Missile-hurling weapons

> Including air guns, bows and arrows, spring guns
>
> *For firearms, see 739.74*

.74	Firearms

> Add to base number 739.74 the numbers following 623.4 in 623.42–623.44, e.g., pistols 739.74432
>
> Class interdisciplinary works on small firearms in 683.4

.75	Armor
.752	Shields

740   Graphic arts and decorative arts

> Standard subdivisions are added for graphic arts and decorative arts together, for graphic arts alone
>
> Including copy art made with photoduplication equipment, rubbings, typewriter art, typographical designs; two-dimensional mixed-media art and composites
>
> Class here digital images, two-dimensional art
>
> Class comprehensive works on graphic arts and plastic arts in 701–709. Class rubbings used for study and research in a specific field with the field, e.g., monumental brasses 739.522
>
> > *For painting and paintings, see 750; for printmaking and prints, see 760; for photography and photographs, see 770; for cinematography and videography, see 777*

.285	Computer applications

> Do not use for comprehensive works on digital images; class in 740; however use subdivisions of 740.285 for specific computer applications in graphic arts, e.g., application of software to digital images 740.28553

.4	**Iconography of graphic arts and iconography of decorative arts**

> Add to base number 740.4 the numbers following 704.94 in 704.942–704.949, e.g., landscapes in graphic arts 740.436
> Subdivisions are added for either or both topics in heading

.9	**History, geographic treatment, biography of graphic arts and of decorative arts**
.901–.905	Periods of development

> Not limited by country or locality
>
> Add to base number 740.90 the numbers following 709.0 in 709.01–709.05, e.g., graphic arts of the Renaissance 740.9024

741   Drawing and drawings

Class comprehensive works on drawing and painting in 750; class comprehensive works on two-dimensional art in 740

For drawing and drawings by subject, see 743

.01	Philosophy and theory

Notation 01 from Table 1 as modified below

.011	Appreciative aspects

Do not use for systems; class in 741.01

Class psychological principles in 741.019

.011 7	Aesthetics
.011 8	Criticism and appreciation

Including theory, technique, history

Class works of critical appraisal in 741.09

.018	Inherent features

Including color, composition, decorative values, form, light, movement, space, style, symmetry, time

Class perspective in 742

.02	Miscellany
.028	Auxiliary techniques and procedures

Class comprehensive works on basic and auxiliary techniques and procedures in 741.2

[.028 4]	Apparatus, equipment, materials

Do not use; class in 741.2

.028 8	Maintenance and repair

Including expertizing

Class identification of reproductions, copies, forgeries, alterations in 741.217

.07	Education, research, related topics
.074	Museums and exhibits

For collections of drawings, see 741.9

.09	History, geographic treatment, biography
.090 1–.090 5	Historical periods

For collections of drawings from specific periods, see 741.92

.092	Biography

Regardless of medium, process, subject, period, place

Class artists working in special applications in 741.5–741.7; class collections of drawings in 741.9

.093–.099	Specific continents, countries, localities

For collections of drawings from specific continents, countries, localities, see 741.93–741.99

.2	***Techniques, procedures, apparatus, equipment, materials**

Including one-color washes highlighting drawings

Class here comprehensive works on basic and auxiliary techniques and procedures

Class techniques, procedures, apparatus, equipment, materials used in special applications in 741.5–741.7; class techniques, procedures, apparatus, equipment, materials used in drawing specific subjects in 743.4–743.8; class collections of drawings regardless of medium or process in 741.9

For auxiliary techniques and procedures, see 741.028; for perspective, see 742

See also 751.422 for watercolor

.21	*Techniques of reproduction and conservation
.217	*Reproduction

Execution and identification

.217 2	*Reproductions and copies

Standard subdivisions are added for either or both topics in heading

.217 4	*Forgeries and alterations

>	741.22–741.29 Specific mediums

Class comprehensive works in 741.2

.22	*Charcoal
.23	*Chalk and crayon
.235	*Pastel
.24	*Pencil
.25	*Silverpoint
.26	*Ink

Class here brush, marker, pen drawing

.29	*Scratchboard and airbrush drawing

*Do not use notation 092 from Table 1 for individual artists; class in 741.092

> **741.5–741.7 Special applications**

Class here works that began with drawing but use other techniques such as painting, printing, photography to create the final product

Class comprehensive works in 741.6

.5   **Comic books, graphic novels, fotonovelas, cartoons, caricatures, comic strips**

Standard subdivisions are added for comic books, graphic novels, fotonovelas, cartoons, caricatures, comic strips together; for comic books alone; for graphic novels alone; for fotonovelas alone

Variant name for comic books: comics

Class comic books, graphic novels, fotonovelas, cartoons, caricatures, comic strips whose purpose is to inform or persuade with the subject, e.g., political cartoons 320.0207

See Manual at 741.5; also at 741.5 vs. 741.56

.502 8   Auxiliary techniques and procedures

Class comprehensive works on basic and auxiliary techniques and procedures in 741.51

[.502 84]   Apparatus, equipment, materials

Do not use; class in 741.51

.507 4   Museums and exhibits

Do not use for collections; class in 741.59

[.509]   History, geographic treatment, biography

Do not use for cartoons, caricatures, comic strips; class in 741.569. Do not use for comic books, graphic novels, fotonovelas; class in 741.59

.51   Techniques, procedures, apparatus, equipment, materials

Class here comprehensive works on basic and auxiliary techniques and procedures; comprehensive works on drawing and writing comic books, graphic novels, fotonovelas, cartoons, caricatures, comic strips

Class techniques, procedures, apparatus, equipment, materials used for special aspects in 741.53; class techniques, procedures, apparatus, equipment, materials used for cartoon animation in 741.58

For auxiliary techniques and procedures, see 741.5028; for photographic techniques for fotonovelas, see 771; for writing comic books, graphic novels, fotonovelas, cartoons, caricatures, comic strips, see 808.06

.53   **Special aspects of comic books, graphic novels, fotonovelas, cartoons, caricatures, comic strips**

Class here critical appraisal and description of genres, techniques for creating works in specific genres

Class single works and collections of cartoons, caricatures, comic strips regardless of genre in 741.569; class single works and collections of comic books, graphic novels, fotonovelas regardless of genre in 741.59

.531   **Comic books, graphic novels, fotonovelas, cartoons, caricatures, comic strips displaying specific qualities**

Add to base number 741.531 the numbers following —1 in notation 11–17 from Table 3C, e.g., critical appraisal of horror graphic novels 741.53164
Subdivisions are added for any or all topics in heading

.532–.539   **Comic books, graphic novels, fotonovelas, cartoons, caricatures, comic strips dealing with specific themes and subjects**

Add to base number 741.53 the numbers following —3 in notation 32–39 from Table 3C, e.g., history and critical appraisal of superhero graphic novels 741.5352, drawing cartoon animals 741.5362
Subdivisions are added for any or all topics in heading

.56   **Cartoons, caricatures, comic strips**

Standard subdivisions are added for any or all topics in heading

Variant name for comic strips: strip cartoons

See Manual at 741.5 vs. 741.56

.560 28   Auxiliary techniques and procedures

Class comprehensive works on basic and auxiliary techniques and procedures in 741.51

.560 74   Museums and exhibits

Do not use for collections; class in 741.569

[.560 9]   History, geographic treatment, biography

Do not use; class in 741.569

.569   **History, geographic treatment, biography of cartoons, caricatures, comic strips**

Single works or collections of works

Class here development, description, critical appraisal; collections of cartoons, caricatures, comic strips

Class cartoon animation in 741.58; class comprehensive works on history, geographic treatment, biography of comic books, graphic novels, fotonovelas, cartoons, caricatures, comic strips in 741.59. Class works of description and critical appraisal that focus on a specific aspect and are not limited to an individual artist or writer with the aspect in 741.53, e.g., critical appraisal of comic strips about animals 741.5362

.569 1   Treatment by areas, regions, places in general

Add to base number 741.5691 the numbers following —1 in notation 11–19 from Table 2, e.g., caricatures from Western Hemisphere 741.5691812

.569 3–.569 9   Specific continents, countries, localities

Add to base number 741.569 notation 3–9 from Table 2, e.g., a collection of European cartoons 741.5694, a collection of cartoons by multiple artists from London 741.569421, a collection of comic strips by a single author first published in United States 741.56973
Single works, collections by individual artists or writers, biographies and critical appraisal of individual artists or writers are classed at country level only, without further addition. For example, a biography of an individual artist from London is classed in 741.56942 (*not* 741.569421, 741.56942092). Notation from Table 1 is added for works treating more than one artist or writer, e.g., general history of United States comic strips 741.5697309, collected biography of English caricature artists 741.569420922

See Manual at 741.593–741.599 and 741.5693–741.5699

.58   Cartoon animation

Class here animation cels; techniques for creating animated drawings

Class photographic techniques in 777.7; class comprehensive works on animated films in 791.4334; class animated films themselves in 791.437; class comprehensive works on animated television programs in 791.4534; class animated television programs themselves in 791.457

.59   History, geographic treatment, biography

Single works or collections of works

Class here development, description, critical appraisal; comprehensive works on history, geographic treatment, biography of comic books, graphic novels, fotonovelas, cartoons, caricatures, comic strips

Class cartoon animation in 741.58. Class works of description and critical appraisal that focus on a specific aspect and are not limited to a single work or to an individual artist or writer with the aspect in 741.53, e.g., critical appraisal of superhero graphic novels 741.5352

For history, geographic treatment, biography of cartoons, caricatures, comic strips, see 741.569

.591   Treatment by areas, regions, places in general

Add to base number 741.591 the numbers following —1 in notation 11–19 from Table 2, e.g., graphic novels from Western Hemisphere 741.591812

.593–.599	Specific continents, countries, localities

Add to base number 741.59 notation 3–9 from Table 2, e.g., a collection of European comic books 741.594, a collection of comic books by multiple artists from London 741.59421, a single graphic novel first published in Japan 741.5952

> Single works, collections by individual artists or writers, biographies and critical appraisal of individual artists or writers are classed at country level only, without further addition. For example, a biography of an individual graphic novelist from London is classed in 741.5942 (*not* 741.59421, 741.5942092). Notation from Table 1 is added for works treating more than one artist or writer, e.g., general history of Japanese comic books 741.595209, collected biography of Japanese comic artists 741.59520922

See Manual at 741.593–741.599 and 741.5693–741.5699

.6	**Graphic design, illustration, commercial art**

Standard subdivisions are added for any or all topics in heading

Class here comprehensive works on special applications of drawing

Class comprehensive works on graphic arts, comprehensive works on two-dimensional art in 740. Class a specific type of illustration, a specific form of graphic design, a specific form of commercial art, not provided for here with the type or form, e.g., original oil paintings for book jackets 759

See Manual at 741.6 vs. 800

.64	Books and book jackets

Standard subdivisions are added for either or both topics in heading

Class illumination of manuscripts and books in 745.67

.642	Children's books
.65	Magazines and newspapers
.652	Magazines and magazine covers

Standard subdivisions are added for either or both topics in heading

.66	Covers for sheet music and recordings
.67	Advertisements and posters

Standard subdivisions are added for advertisements and posters together, for advertisements alone

.672	Fashion drawing

Class fashion design in 746.92

.674	Commercial posters

Class here comprehensive works on posters

For art posters (posters as a specific form of prints), see 769.5

.68	Calendars, postcards, greeting and business cards
.682	Calendars

.683	Postcards

> Class government-issued postcards without illustration in 769.566

.684	Greeting cards
.685	Business cards (Trade cards)
.69	Labels and match covers
.692	Labels
.694	Match covers

.7   **Silhouettes**

> Class cut-out silhouettes in 736.984

.9   **Collections of drawings**

> Regardless of medium or process

> Class here exhibition catalogs, preliminary drawings as works of art in their own right

> Class collections by artists devoted to special applications in 741.5–741.7; class collections of drawings by subject not from a specific period or place in 743.9. Class preliminary drawings not treated as works of art in their own right with the finished work, e.g., preliminary drawings for frescoes 751.73

.92	Specific periods

> Not limited geographically

.921	Earliest times to 499
.922	500–1399
.923	1400–1799
.924	1800–
.924 1	1800–1899
.924 2	1900–1999
.924 3	2000–2099
.93–.99	Specific continents, countries, localities

> Add to base number 741.9 notation 3–9 from Table 2, e.g., collections of drawings from London 741.9421
>> Collections by individual artists are classed at country level only. Notation 074 from Table 1 for collections is not added. For example, a collection of an individual artist from London is classed in 741.942 (*not* 741.9421, 741.942074421)

742   **Perspective in drawing**

> Theory, principles, methods

> Class perspective in special applications in 741.5–741.7; class perspective in drawing specific subjects in 743.4–743.8; class comprehensive works on perspective in the arts in 701.82

743   ***Drawing and drawings by subject**

> Standard subdivisions are added for drawing and drawings by subject together, for drawing alone

.4   ***Drawing human figures**

> Class here nudes
>
> *For fashion drawing, see 741.672*

.42   *Portraiture

> Class portraiture of specific kinds of people in 743.43–743.45

> **743.43–743.45 Specific kinds of people**
>
> Class anatomy of specific kinds of people in 743.49; class comprehensive works in 743.4

.43   *Men

.44   *Women

.45   *Children

.46   *Bones (Skeletal system)

.47   *Muscles (Muscular system)

.49   *Anatomy for artists

> Including parts and regions of body, e.g., head, abdomen, hands
>
> *For bones, see 743.46; for muscles, see 743.47*

.5   ***Drawing draperies**

.6   ***Drawing animals**

> Add to base number 743.6 the numbers following 59 in 592–599, e.g., drawing birds 743.68; however, for artists, see 741.092

.7   ***Drawing plants**

> Including fruits

.73   *Drawing flowers

.76   *Drawing trees

.8   **Drawing other subjects**

> Add to base number 743.8 the numbers following 704.94 in 704.943–704.949, e.g., landscapes 743.836; however, for artists, see 741.092

---

*Do not use notation 092 from Table 1 for artists; class in 741.092

.9   **Collections of drawings by subject (Iconography)**

Not limited by period or by place of production

Add to base number 743.9 the numbers following 704.94 in 704.942–704.949, e.g., collections of drawings of buildings 743.94

Class collections of drawings by subject from a specific period or place in 741.92–741.99

[744]   **[Unassigned]**

Most recently used in Edition 17

745   **Decorative arts**

Class here folk art

For a decorative art not provided for here, see the art in 736–739, 746–749, e.g., interior decoration 747

.1   **Antiques**

For a specific kind of antique, see the kind, e.g., brasses 739.52, passenger automobiles 629.222

See Manual at 745.1

.102 8   Auxiliary techniques and procedures; apparatus, equipment, materials

Notation 028 from Table 1 as modified below

Class here basic techniques and procedures

.102 87   Techniques of reproduction, execution, identification

Do not use for testing and measurement; class in 745.1028

.102 872   Reproductions and copies

.102 874   Forgeries and alterations

.102 88   Maintenance and repair

Including expertizing

Class identification of reproductions, copies, forgeries, alterations in 745.10287

.2   **Industrial art and design**

Creative design of mass-produced commodities

Standard subdivisions are added for either or both topics in heading

For design of a specific commodity, see the commodity, e.g., automobiles 629.231

.4   **Pure and applied design and decoration**

> Standard subdivisions are added for any or all topics in heading
>
> Class here design source books
>
> > *For industrial design, see 745.2. For design in a specific art form, see the form, e.g., design in architecture 729*

.5   **Handicrafts**

> Creative work done by hand with aid of simple tools or machines
>
> Including work in bread dough
>
> Class home (amateur) workshops in 684.08; class interdisciplinary works on handicrafts in 680. Class the handicraft aspects of another form of art with the art, e.g., printmaking using rubber stamps 761
>
> > *For decorative coloring, see 745.7; for floral arts, see 745.92*
>
> > *See Manual at 680 vs. 745.5*

> 745.51–745.58   Specific materials

> Class specific objects made from specific materials in 745.59; class comprehensive works in 745.5
>
> > *For textile handicrafts, see 746; for glass handicrafts, see 748*

.51   Woods

> Including bamboo; ornamental woodwork
>
> Class treen (woodenware) in 674.88; class woodworking in 684.08; class cabinetmaking (wooden furniture making) in 684.104; class artistic aspects of furniture in 749
>
> > *For ornamental woodwork in furniture, see 749.5*

.512   Marquetry

> Class here inlaying

.513   Scrollwork

> Class here work with jig saws (scroll saws)

.514   Woodburning (Pyrography)

.53   Leathers and furs

> Class construction of clothing in 646.4

.531   Leathers

.537   Furs

.54   Papers

> Including endpapers, paper boxes, tissue papers, wallpapers; gift wrapping, quilling
>
> Class paper cutting and folding in 736.98

.542	Papier-mâché
	Class papier-mâché used in sculpture in 731.2
.546	Decoupage
	Including potichomania
.55	Shells
.56	Metals
	Class art metalwork in 739
.57	Rubber and plastics
.572	Plastics
.572 3	Polymer clay
.58	Beads, found and other objects
	Class specific objects made from other objects in 745.59
.582	Beads
	For bead embroidery, see 746.5
	See also 745.5942 for beaded costume jewelry
.584	Found objects
	Including cattails, hosiery, scrap, stones
.59	Making specific objects
	Class here handicrafts in composite materials
	For textile handicrafts, see 746; for glass handicrafts, see 748
.592	Toys, models, miniatures, related objects
	Standard subdivisions are added for toys, models, miniatures, related objects together; for toys alone
	Including paper airplanes
	Class interdisciplinary works on mass-produced and handcrafted toys in 688.72

>   745.592 2–745.592 4 Toys and related objects

Class comprehensive works in 745.592

For toy soldiers, see 745.59282

.592 2	Dolls, puppets, marionettes
	Class here clothing
.592 21	Dolls
	Class porcelain dolls in 738.83
.592 24	Puppets and marionettes

.592 3	Dollhouses and furniture

Standard subdivisions are added for either or both topics in heading

See also 749.0228 for miniature furniture

.592 4	Soft toys

Class here stuffed toys

For stuffed dolls, see 745.59221

.592 43	Teddy bears
.592 8	Models and miniatures

Standard subdivisions are added for either or both topics in heading

Including ships in bottles

Class here interdisciplinary works on handcrafted models and miniatures

Class models and miniatures produced by assembly-line or mechanized manufacturing, interdisciplinary works on models and miniatures in 688.1; class play with remote-control models in 796.15

> *For handcrafted models and miniatures of a specific object, models for technical and professional use, see the object or use, plus notation 0228 from Table 1, e.g., handcrafted models of space stations 629.4420228; for miniature and model educational exhibits, see the subject illustrated, plus notation 074 from Table 1, e.g., handcrafted miniature physical anthropology exhibits 599.9074*
>
> *See Manual at 745.5928*

.592 82	Military models and miniatures

Standard subdivisions are added for either or both topics in heading

Including toy soldiers

.593	Useful objects

For toys, models, miniatures, related objects, see 745.592

.593 2	Lampshades
.593 3	Candles and candlesticks
.593 32	Candles
.593 4	Snuffboxes
.593 6	Decoys

Class carved birds not used for hunting in 730

.593 8	Scrapbooks
.594	Decorative objects

.594 1	Objects for special occasions
	Including weddings
	Class here greeting cards
.594 12	Christmas
.594 16	Holidays

> Add to base number 745.59416 the numbers following 394.26 in 394.261–394.267, e.g., Halloween 745.5941646, Easter 745.5941667; however, for Christmas, see 745.59412; for Easter eggs, see 745.5944

.594 2	Costume jewelry

> Class interdisciplinary works on costume jewelry in 391.7; class interdisciplinary works on making costume jewelry in 688.2; class interdisciplinary works on making jewelry in 739.27

.594 3	Artificial flowers

> Class arrangement of artificial flowers in 745.92

.594 4	Egg decorating
	Including Easter eggs

> Class comprehensive works on handicrafts for Easter in 745.5941667

.594 6	Fountains
	Class here tabletop fountains

> Class comprehensive works on fountains in 731.724

.6   Calligraphy, heraldic design, illumination

.61	Calligraphy

Class here artistic, decorative lettering

Class penmanship in 652.1; class typography in 686.22

.619	Styles
.619 7	Latin styles (Western styles)
.619 74	Carolingian calligraphy
.619 75	Black-letter and Gothic calligraphy
.619 77	Italic calligraphy
.619 78	Roman calligraphy
.619 8	Greek calligraphy
.619 9	Other styles

> Add to base number 745.6199 the numbers following —9 in notation 91–99 from Table 6, e.g., Chinese calligraphy 745.619951

.66	Heraldic design

.67   Illumination of manuscripts and books

> Standard subdivisions are added for either or both topics in heading
>
> Class here facsimiles of manuscripts reproduced for their illuminations
>
> Class development, description, critical appraisal of manuscripts in 091; class development, description, critical appraisal of illustrated books in 096.1
>
> *See also 741.64 for book illustration*

.674   Illuminated manuscripts and books by language

> Add to base number 745.674 notation 1–9 from Table 6, e.g., illuminated manuscripts in Byzantine Greek 745.67487; however, for illuminated manuscripts in Latin, see 745.67094
>
> Class illuminated manuscripts and books in specific languages produced in specific countries and localities in 745.67093–745.67099

.7   **Decorative coloring**

> Including coloring books
>
> Class printing, painting, dyeing textiles in 746.6

.72   Painting and lacquering

.723   Painting

> Including rosemaling, tolecraft

.726   Lacquering

> Class here japanning

.73   Stenciling

.74   Decalcomania

.75   Gilding

> Class gilding as an aspect of bookbinding in 686.36; class gilding as an aspect of illumination of manuscripts and books in 745.67

.8   **Cycloramas, dioramas, panoramas**

.9   **Other decorative arts**

.92   Floral arts

> Flower arrangement: selection and arrangement of plant materials and appropriate accessories
>
> Class here arrangement of artificial flowers, three-dimensional arrangements
>
> Class making artificial flowers in 745.5943; class potted plants as interior decorations in 747.98

> 745.922–745.925 Three-dimensional arrangements with specific materials

Class arrangements with specific materials for special occasions in 745.926; class comprehensive works in 745.92

.922   Flower arrangements in containers

.922 4   Western flower arrangements

.922 5   Asian flower arrangements

.922 51   Chinese flower arrangements

.922 52   Japanese flower arrangements

.923   Flower arrangements without containers

Including boutonnieres, corsages, set floral pieces

.924   Fruit and vegetable arrangements

Including carving of vegetables to produce artificial flowers

.925   Arrangements with other plant materials

Including driftwood, pods and cones, dried and gilded grasses and leaves

.926   Three-dimensional arrangements for special occasions

Including arrangements for church services, funerals, holidays, weddings

.928   Two-dimensional arrangements

Use of seeds and other dried plant materials in pictures, hangings, trays, for other decorative purposes

746   Textile arts

Class here textile handicrafts

Add to each subdivision identified by * as follows:

028	Auxiliary techniques and procedures; apparatus, equipment, materials
0288	Maintenance and repair
	Including expertizing
	Class here conservation, preservation, restoration
	Class identification of reproductions, copies, forgeries, alterations in notation 048 from this table
04	Special topics
041	Patterns
	Class patterns for specific products in notation 043 from this table
042	Stitches
	Class stitches for specific products in notation 043 from this table
043	Products
	Use only with base numbers for techniques
	For laces and related fabrics, see 746.2; for rugs and carpets, see 746.7
0432	Costume
	Including sweaters
0433	Pictures, hangings, tapestries
	Standard subdivisions are added for any or all topics in heading
0434–0438	Interior furnishings
	Add to 043 the numbers following 746.9 in 746.94–746.98, e.g., bedclothes 0437
048	Reproductions, copies, forgeries, alterations
	Execution and identification

Class domestic sewing and related operations in 646.2. Class a specific textile product not provided for here with the product, e.g., stuffed animals 745.5924

.04   Specific materials

Add to base number 746.04 the numbers following 677 in 677.1–677.7, e.g., silk 746.0439, string art 746.0471

Class products in a specific material with the product, e.g., string pictures 746.3

> ### 746.1–746.9 Products and processes

Unless other instructions are given, observe the following table of preference, e.g., embroidered rugs 746.74 (*not* 746.44):

Laces and related fabrics	746.2
Rugs	746.7
Yarn preparation and weaving	746.1
Needlework and handwork	746.4
Bead embroidery	746.5
Printing, painting, dyeing	746.6
Pictures, hangings, tapestries	746.3
Other textile products	746.9

Class home sewing and clothing in 646; class textile manufacturing in 677; class comprehensive works in 746

.1   Yarn preparation and weaving

.11   Carding and combing

.12   Spinning, twisting, reeling

Standard subdivisions are added for spinning, twisting, reeling together; for spinning alone

.13   Dyeing

.14   *Weaving

Including card weaving

For weaving unaltered vegetable fibers, see 746.41; for nonloom weaving, see 746.42

.2   Laces and related fabrics

.22   *Laces

Including crocheted, darned laces

For tatting, see 746.436

.222   *Bobbin laces

.224   *Needlepoint laces

.226   *Knitted laces

.27   Passementerie

Including braids, cords, fringes

.3   *Pictures, hangings, tapestries

Subdivisions are added for any or all topics in heading

---

*Add as instructed under 746

[.309]		History, geographic treatment, biography

> Do not use; class in 746.39

(.309 2)	Biography

> (Optional number; prefer 746.392)

.39   History, geographic treatment, biography

.390 01–.390 09   Standard subdivisions

> Add to base number 746.3900 the numbers following —00 in notation 001–009 from Table 2, e.g., periodicals of the history of tapestries 746.39005

.390 1–.390 5   Historical periods

> Add to base number 746.390 the numbers following —090 in notation 0901–0905 from Table 1, e.g., tapestries from 20th century 746.3904

.391–.399   Geographic treatment, biography

> Add to base number 746.39 notation 1–9 from Table 2, e.g., artists 746.392
> (Option: Class biography in 746.3092)

.4   **Needlework and handwork**

> Standard subdivisions are added for either or both topics in heading

.41   Weaving, braiding, matting unaltered vegetable fibers

> Including raffia work, rushwork

.412   Basketry

.42   Nonloom weaving and related techniques

> Including braiding, plaiting, twining

> Class nonloom weaving of unaltered vegetable fibers in 746.41

> *For card weaving, see 746.14*

.422   *Knotting

.422 2   *Macramé

.422 4   *Netting

> Including knotless netting, sprang

.43   *Knitting, crocheting, tatting

.432   *Knitting

> Class comprehensive works on knitting and crocheting in 746.43

.434   *Crocheting

.436   *Tatting

---

*Add as instructed under 746

.44   *Embroidery

> Including couching, cutwork, drawn work, hardanger, smocking

.440 28   Auxiliary techniques and procedures; apparatus, equipment, materials

> Including machine embroidery

.442   *Canvas embroidery and needlepoint

> Including bargello

> Subdivisions are added for either or both topics in heading

> Class cross-stitch and counted thread embroidery in 746.443

.443   *Cross-stitch

> Class here counted thread embroidery

.445   *Appliqué

.446   *Crewelwork

.447   *Silk ribbon embroidery

.46   *Patchwork and quilting

> Class here quilts

> Subdivisions are added for either or both topics in heading

.460 437   Bedclothes

> Number built according to instructions under 746

> Class quilts in 746.46

.5   *Bead embroidery

.6   *Printing, painting, dyeing

> Including hand decoration, stenciling

.62   *Printing

> Block and silk-screen

.66   *Resist-dyeing

.662   *Batik

.664   *Tie-dyeing

.7   *Rugs

> Class here carpets

[.709]   History, geographic treatment, biography

> Do not use; class in 746.79

*Add as instructed under 746

(.709 2)		Biography
		(Optional number; prefer 746.792)
.72		*Woven rugs

Class here Navajo rugs; Jacquard, plain, tapestry, twill weaves

For pile rugs, see 746.75

.73		*Crocheted, knitted, braided rugs
.74		*Hooked and embroidered rugs
.75		Pile rugs
.750 95		Asian pile rugs

Class here Oriental-style rugs

For styles from Caucasus region, see 746.759

[.750 951–.750 958]   Asian countries and localities other than southeast Asia

Do not use; class in 746.751–746.758

>   746.751–746.759   Oriental-style rugs

Class comprehensive works in 746.75095

.751–.758   Styles from specific Asian countries and localities other than southeast Asia

Add to base number 746.75 the numbers following —5 in notation 51–58 from Table 2, e.g., Chinese rugs 746.751

See also 746.750959 for styles from southeast Asia

.759   Styles from Caucasus region

.79   History, geographic treatment, biography

.790 01–.790 09   Standard subdivisions

Add to base number 746.7900 the numbers following —00 in notation 001–009 from Table 2, e.g., periodicals of the history of rugs 746.79005

.790 1–.790 5   Historical periods

Add to base number 746.790 the numbers following —090 in notation 0901–0905 from Table 1, e.g., rugs from 20th century 746.7904

.791–.799   Geographic treatment, biography

Add to base number 746.79 notation 1–9 from Table 2, e.g., artists 746.792
(Option: Class biography in 746.7092)

.9   Other textile products

---

*Add as instructed under 746

.92   Costume

Class here fashion design

Class interdisciplinary works on clothing in 391; class interdisciplinary works on clothing construction in 646.4

See Manual at 391 vs. 646.3, 746.92

.94   *Draperies

Class here curtains

.95   *Furniture covers

Class here antimacassars, kneelers, slipcovers, upholstery

.96   *Table linens

Class here doilies, mats, napkins (serviettes), scarves, tablecloths; fair linens

.97   *Bedclothes

Class here bedspreads, blankets; sheets, pillowcases

For afghans, see 746.430437; for quilts, see 746.46

.98   *Towels

Class here toweling

747   Interior decoration

Design and decorative treatment of interior furnishings

Class here interior decoration of residential buildings

Class interior architecture (interior design) in 729; class textile arts and handicrafts in 746; class interior decoration of specific types of residential buildings in 747.88

For furniture and accessories, see 749

.1   **Decoration under specific limitations**

Including decorating on a budget

Class a specific aspect of decoration under limitations with the aspect, e.g., decorating dining rooms on a budget 747.76

>   **747.3–747.4 Decoration of specific elements**

Class decoration of specific elements in specific rooms of residential buildings in 747.7; class decoration of specific elements in specific types of buildings in 747.8; class specific decorations of specific elements in 747.9; class comprehensive works in 747

*Add as instructed under 746

.3   **Ceilings, walls, doors, windows**

> Including decorative hangings, painting, paneling, woodwork

> Class here textile wall coverings, wallpapers

> *For draperies, see 747.5*

.4   **Floors**

> *For rugs and carpets, see 747.5*

.5   **Draperies, upholstery, rugs and carpets**

.7   **Decoration of specific rooms of residential buildings**

> Class specific decorations regardless of room in 747.9

.73   Studies

> Class here home libraries

.75   Living rooms, drawing rooms, parlors

> Standard subdivisions are added for any or all topics in heading

.76   Dining rooms

.77   Bedrooms

.78   Bathrooms

> Including powder rooms

.79   Other rooms

.791   Recreation rooms

> Class here family rooms

.797   Kitchens

.8   **Decoration of specific types of buildings**

> Class specific decorations regardless of type of building in 747.9

.85–.87   Decoration of public, religious, educational, research buildings

> Add to base number 747.8 the numbers following 72 in 725–727, e.g., decoration of theaters 747.85822

.88   Decoration of specific types of residential buildings

> Add to base number 747.88 the numbers following 728 in 728.1–728.9, e.g., decoration of hotels 747.885

> Class decoration of residential buildings of institutions in 747.85–747.87; class comprehensive works on decoration of residential buildings in 747

> *For decoration of specific rooms of residential buildings, see 747.7*

.9   **Specific decorations**

Unless other instructions are given, observe the following table of preference, e.g., decorative lighting for Christmas 747.92 (*not* 747.93):

Decorating with houseplants	747.98
Decorative lighting	747.92
Decorating with color	747.94
Decorations for specific occasions	747.93

See also 747.5 for draperies, upholstery, rugs and carpets

.92   Decorative lighting

.93   Decorations for specific occasions

Including holidays, parties, weddings

.94   Decorating with color

.98   Decorating with houseplants

748   Glass

Class here glassware

For glass sculpture, see 730

.092   Biography

Class here glassmakers

.2   **Blown, cast, decorated, fashioned, molded, pressed glass**

Standard subdivisions are added for any or all topics in heading

Class here comprehensive works on tableware

Class stained glass in 748.5; class comprehensive works on glass made by a specific technique in 748

For methods of decoration, see 748.6; for stained, painted, leaded, mosaic tableware, see 748.5; for specific articles made from blown, cast, decorated, fashioned, molded, pressed glass, see 748.8

.202 8   Auxiliary techniques and procedures; apparatus, equipment, materials

Notation 028 from Table 1 as modified below

Class here basic techniques and procedures

.202 82   Glassblowing

.202 86   Bottle and jar cutting

Do not use for green technology; class in 748.2028

Standard subdivisions are added for either or both topics in heading

.202 87   Reproductions, copies, forgeries, alterations

Do not use for testing and measurement; class in 748.2028

Execution and identification

.202 88   Maintenance and repair

                 Including expertizing

                 Class identification of reproductions, copies, forgeries, alterations in 748.20287

.5   **Stained, painted, leaded, mosaic glass**

                 Standard subdivisions are added for stained, painted, leaded, mosaic glass together; for stained glass alone; for painted glass alone; for leaded glass alone

                 Class comprehensive works on mosaics in 738.5; class comprehensive works on tableware in 748.2

                 For specific articles made from stained, painted, leaded, mosaic glass, see 748.8

.502 8   Auxiliary techniques and procedures; apparatus, equipment, materials

                 Notation 028 from Table 1 as modified below

                 Class here basic techniques and procedures

.502 82   Glass painting and staining

.502 84   Leaded glass craft

                 Do not use for apparatus, equipment, materials of stained, painted, leaded, mosaic glass together; class in 748.5028

.502 85   Mosaic glass craft

                 Do not use for computer applications; class in 748.5028

.6   **Methods of decoration**

                 Including cutting, enameling, sandblasting

                 Class methods of decoration of specific articles in 748.8

                 For painted glass, see 748.5

[.609 2]   Biography

                 Do not use; class in 748.2092

.62   Engraving

.63   Etching

.8   **Specific articles**

                 Including mirrors, ornaments

                 Class mirrors as furniture in 749.3; class glass lamps and lighting fixtures in 749.63

.82   Bottles

                 Bottles of artistic interest Regardless of use

                 Class manufacture of glass bottles in 666.192

.83 Specific articles of tableware

Class here drinking glasses

Class works on more than one type of tableware, comprehensive works on tableware in 748.2

.84 Paperweights

.85 Glass beads

749 Furniture and accessories

Standard subdivisions are added for furniture and accessories together, for furniture alone

For upholstery, see 747.5

.1 Antique furniture

Class specific kinds of antique furniture in 749.3

.102 8 Auxiliary techniques and procedures; apparatus, equipment, materials

Notation 028 from Table 1 as modified below

.102 87 Reproductions, copies, forgeries, alterations

Do not use for testing and measurement; class in 749.1028

Execution and identification

.102 88 Maintenance and repair

Including expertizing

Class identification of reproductions, copies, forgeries, alterations in 749.10287

[.109] History, geographic treatment, biography

Do not use; class in 749.09

.3 Specific kinds of furniture

Including beds, cabinets, chests, clockcases, desks, mirrors, screens, tables

Class outdoor furniture in 749.8

For built-in furniture, see 749.4; for heating and lighting fixtures and furniture, see 749.6; for picture frames, see 749.7

[.301–.309] Standard subdivisions

Do not use; class in 749.01–749.09

.32 Chairs

.4 Built-in furniture

Class built-in church furniture in architectural design in 726.529

For heating and lighting fixtures and furniture, see 749.6

.5	**Ornamental woodwork in furniture**

Including inlay trim, lacquer work, marquetry, scrollwork

Class ornamental woodwork in a specific kind of furniture with the kind, e.g., picture frames 749.7

.6	**Heating and lighting fixtures and furniture**
.62	Heating

Including mantels, fireplace and inglenook fixtures and furniture

.63	Lighting

Including chandeliers, lamps, sconces

Class built-in church lighting fixtures in architectural design in 726.5298

.7	**Picture frames**

Including shadow boxes

Class here picture framing

.8	**Outdoor furniture**

Class furniture used both indoors and outdoors in 749.3

750 Painting and paintings

Class here comprehensive works on painting and drawing

Unless other instructions are given, observe the following table of preference, e.g., an individual Canadian painter of landscapes 759.11 (*not* 758.10971), landscape painting in Canada 758.10971 (*not* 759.11):

Individual painters and their work	759.1–759.9
Techniques, procedures, apparatus, equipment, materials	751.2–751.6
Iconography	753–758
Specific forms	751.7
Geographic treatment	759.1–759.9
Periods of development	759.01–759.07
Color	752

Class comprehensive works on graphic arts, two-dimensional art in 740. Class painting in a specific decorative art with the art, e.g., illumination of manuscripts and books 745.67

For drawing and drawings, see 741

.1	**Philosophy and theory**

Notation 01 from Table 1 as modified below

.11	Appreciative aspects

Do not use for systems; class in 750.1

Class psychological principles in 750.19

.117	Aesthetics

.118   Criticism and appreciation

Including theory, technique, history

Class works of critical appraisal in 759

.18   Inherent features

Including composition, decorative values, form, light, movement, perspective, space, style, symmetry, vision

For color, see 752

.28   Auxiliary techniques and procedures

For comprehensive works on basic and auxiliary techniques and procedures, see 751.4

[.284]   Apparatus, equipment, materials

Do not use for materials; class in 751.2. Do not use for apparatus and equipment; class in 751.3

[.288]   Maintenance and repair

Do not use; class in 751.6

[.9]   **History, geographic treatment, biography**

Do not use; class in 759

(.92)   Biography

(Optional number; prefer 759)

751   *Techniques, procedures, apparatus, equipment, materials, forms

.2   ***Materials**

Including coatings, fixatives, mediums, pigments, surfaces

Class use of materials in specific techniques in 751.4

.3   ***Apparatus, equipment, artists' models**

Class use of apparatus and equipment in specific techniques in 751.4

.4   ***Techniques and procedures**

Class here comprehensive works on basic and auxiliary techniques and procedures

For auxiliary techniques and procedures, see 750.28; for techniques of reproduction, see 751.5; for maintenance and repair, see 751.6

.42   ***Use of water-soluble mediums**

For tempera painting, see 751.43

---

*Do not use notation 092 from Table 1 for individual painters; class in 759.1–759.9

.422	*Watercolor painting

Including casein painting, gouache

Class ink painting in color in 751.425

.422 4	Watercolor painting techniques by subject

Add to base number 751.4224 the numbers following 704.94 in 704.942–704.949, e.g., techniques of landscape painting in watercolor 751.422436; however, for individual painters, see 759.1–759.9

.425	*Ink painting
.425 1	*Chinese ink painting
.425 14	Chinese ink painting techniques by subject

Add to base number 751.42514 the numbers following 704.94 in 704.942–704.949, e.g., techniques of landscape painting in Chinese ink painting 751.4251436; however, for individual painters, see 759.1–759.9

.425 2	*Japanese ink painting
.426	*Acrylic painting
.426 4	Acrylic painting techniques by subject

Add to base number 751.4264 the numbers following 704.94 in 704.942–704.949, e.g., techniques of landscape painting in acrylics 751.426436; however, for individual painters, see 759.1–759.9

.43	*Tempera painting
.44	*Fresco painting
.45	*Oil painting
.454	Oil painting techniques by subject

Add to base number 751.454 the numbers following 704.94 in 704.942–704.949, e.g., techniques of landscape painting in oils 751.45436; however, for individual painters, see 759.1–759.9

.46	*Encaustic painting (Wax painting)
.49	*Other methods

Including finger, polymer, roller (brayer), sand painting

For mosaic painting, see 738.5

.493	*Collage

With painting as the basic technique

.494	*Airbrush

*Do not use notation 092 from Table 1 for individual painters; class in 759.1–759.9

.5	*Techniques of reproduction

Execution, identification, determination of authenticity of reproductions, copies, forgeries, alterations

For printmaking and prints, see 760

.58	*Forgeries and alterations
.6	***Maintenance and repair**
.62	*Conservation, preservation, restoration

Standard subdivisions are added for any or all topics in heading

Including expertizing

Class identification of reproductions, copies, forgeries, alterations in 751.5

.7	***Specific forms**
.73	*Murals and frescoes

Standard subdivisions are added for either or both topics in heading

Class here painted graffiti, street art

.74	*Panoramas, cycloramas, dioramas

Standard subdivisions are added for any or all topics in heading

.75	*Scene paintings

Including theatrical scenery

.76	*Glass underpainting

Class glass underpainting as a technique of glass decoration in 748.6

.77	*Miniatures

Class miniatures done as illuminations in manuscripts and books in 745.67

752	***Color**

Class technology of color in 667; class comprehensive works on color in the fine and decorative arts in 701.85

> ## 753–758 Iconography

Class here development, description, critical appraisal, works regardless of form

A work with two or more subjects is classed with the subject that is the center of interest, e.g., cityscapes with incidental human figures 758.7 (*not* 757), church interiors displaying Stations of the Cross 755.4 (*not* 758.7)

Class comprehensive works in 750

See Manual at 704.9 and 753–758

---

*Do not use notation 092 from Table 1 for individual painters; class in 759.1–759.9

753   *Symbolism, allegory, mythology, legend

.6   ***Symbolism and allegory**

> Standard subdivisions are added for either or both topics in heading

> *For religious symbolism, see 755*

.7   ***Mythology and legend**

> Class religious mythology in 755

754   *Genre paintings

755   *Religion

> Class here religious symbolism

> Add to base number 755 the numbers following 704.948 in 704.9482–704.9489, e.g., paintings of Holy Family 755.56; however, for individual painters, see 759.1–759.9

[756]   [Unassigned]

> Most recently used in Edition 19

757   *Human figures

> Class here portraits

> Unless other instructions are given, observe the following table of preference, e.g., groups of nude women 757.2 (*not* 757.4 or 757.6):

> | | |
> |---|---|
> | Erotica | 757.8 |
> | Nudes | 757.2 |
> | Miniature portraits | 757.7 |
> | Specific groups of people | 757.3–757.5 |
> | Groups of human figures | 757.6 |

> Class symbolism of human figures in 753.6. Class human figures engaged in a specific activity or occupation with the activity or occupation, e.g., farmers 758.5092, doctors 758.961092, circus clowns 758.979133

> *For human figures associated with mythology and legend, see 753.7; for human figures associated with religion, see 755*

.2   ***Nudes**

> Class here nudes of men, nudes of women, nudes of children, groups of nudes

---

> ### 757.3–757.5   Specific groups of people

> Class comprehensive works in 757

.3   ***Men**

.4   ***Women**

*Do not use notation 092 from Table 1 for individual painters; class in 759.1–759.9

.5   ***Children**

.6   ***Groups of human figures**

.7   ***Miniature portraits**

.8   ***Erotica**

> Including pornography

758   ***Nature, architectural subjects and cityscapes, other specific subjects**

> Standard subdivisions are added for nature and other specific subjects together; for nature alone

---

> **758.1–758.5 Nature**

> Class comprehensive works in 758

.1   ***Landscapes**

> Add to base number 758.1 notation 1–9 from Table 2, e.g., landscapes of Utah 758.1792; however, for individual painters, see 759.1–759.9

.2   ***Marine scenes and seascapes**

> Standard subdivisions are added for either or both topics in heading

.3   ***Animals**

> Add to base number 758.3 the numbers following 59 in 592–599, e.g., eagles 758.38942

> Class symbolism of animals in 753.6

>> *For animals associated with mythology and legend, see 753.7; for animals associated with religion, see 755*

.4   ***Still life**

> Class symbolism of still life in 753.6

>> *For still life associated with mythology and legend, see 753.7; for still life associated with religion, see 755*

.42   ***Flowers**

.5   ***Plants**

> Class here agriculture

> Class symbolism of plants in 753.6; class landscapes in 758.1

>> *For plants associated with mythology and legend, see 753.7; for plants associated with religion, see 755; for animals, see 758.3; for flowers, see 758.42*

---

*Do not use notation 092 from Table 1 for individual painters; class in 759.1–759.9

.7   ***Architectural subjects and cityscapes**

Standard subdivisions are added for either or both topics in heading

Add to base number 758.7 notation 1–9 from Table 2, e.g., cityscapes of England 758.742; however, for individual painters, see 759.1–759.9

.9   **Other specific subjects**

Not provided for elsewhere

Add to base number 758.9 notation 001–999, e.g., paintings of scientific subjects 758.95, of historical events 758.99; however, for individual painters, see 759.1–759.9

759   **History, geographic treatment, biography**

Class here development, description, critical appraisal, works

Class exhibitions of paintings not limited by place, period, or subject in 750.74

(Option: Class biography in 750.92)

\>   759.01–759.07   Periods of development

Class here schools and styles not limited by country or locality, works on one or two periods of European painting

Class works on three or more periods of European painting in 759.94; class comprehensive works in 759. Class schools associated with a specific locality with the locality in 759.1–759.9, e.g., Florentine school of Italian painting 759.551

When classifying works of more than one painter, notation 074 and notation 075 from Table 1 for Museums, collections, exhibits and Museum activities, respectively, take preference over notation 0922 for Collected biography

See Manual at 704.9 and 753–758

.01   ***Nonliterate peoples, and earliest times to 499**

.011   ***Nonliterate peoples**

Regardless of time or place

Class paintings of both nonliterate and literate cultures in 759.1–759.9

.011 2   ***Paleolithic painting and paintings**

Standard subdivisions are added for either or both topics in heading

.011 3   ***Rock art (painting and paintings)**

.02   ***500–1399**

Class here medieval painting and paintings

.021   ***500–1199**

---

*Do not use notation 092 from Table 1 for individual painters; class in 759.1–759.9

.021 2   *Early Christian painting and paintings

           Standard subdivisions are added for either or both topics in heading

               For early Christian painting and paintings before 500, see 759.01

.021 4   *Byzantine painting and paintings

           Standard subdivisions are added for either or both topics in heading

               For Byzantine painting and paintings before 500, see 759.01

.021 6   *Romanesque painting and paintings

           Standard subdivisions are added for either or both topics in heading

.022   *1200–1399

           Class here Gothic painting and paintings

               For Gothic painting and paintings of an earlier or later period, see the specific period, e.g., 500–1199 759.021

.03   *1400–1599

           Class here Renaissance painting and paintings

               For Renaissance painting and paintings before 1400, see 759.022

.04   *1600–1799

.046   *1600–1699

           Class here baroque painting and paintings

               For baroque painting and paintings of 1700–1799, see 759.047

.047   *1700–1799

           Including rococo painting and paintings

.05   *1800–1899

           Add to base number 759.05 the numbers following 709.034 in 709.0341–709.0349, e.g., romanticism in painting 759.052; however, for individual painters, see 759.1–759.9

.06   *1900–1999

           Class here modern painting

           Add to base number 759.06 the numbers following 709.040 in 709.0401–709.0407, e.g., surrealist painting 759.0663; however, for individual painters, see 759.1–759.9

               For 1800–1899, see 759.05; for 2000–2099, see 759.07

.07   *2000–2099

*Do not use notation 092 from Table 1 for individual painters; class in 759.1–759.9

> **759.1–759.9 Geographic treatment**

Individual painters are classed in notation at country level only. Standard subdivisions —074, —075, and —092 from Table 1 are not added for individual painters, e.g., an exhibition of the work of a Canadian painter, collecting the person's works, and a biography of the painter 759.11 (*not* 759.11074, 759.11075, or 759.11092, respectively)

Class painting and paintings of nonliterate peoples in 759.011; class western painting of one or two specific periods in 759.02–759.07; class comprehensive works in 759

(Option: To give local emphasis and a shorter number to painting and paintings of a specific country, use one of the following:

(Option A: Place them first by use of a letter or other symbol for the country, e.g., Burmese painting and paintings 759.B [preceding 759.1]

(Option B: Class them in 759.1; in that case class painting and paintings of North America in 759.97)

.1   **North America**

For painting and paintings of Middle America, see 759.972

(Option: To give local emphasis and a shorter number to painting and paintings of a specific country other than United States and Canada, class them in this number; in that case class painting and paintings of North America in 759.97)

.11   Canada

Add to base number 759.11 the numbers following —71 in notation 711–719 from Table 2, e.g., painting and paintings of Toronto 759.113541

.13   United States

Class painting and paintings of specific states in 759.14–759.19

See also 759.97295 for painting and paintings of Puerto Rico

.14–.19   Specific states of United States

Add to base number 759.1 the numbers following —7 in notation 74–79 from Table 2, e.g., painting and paintings of San Francisco 759.19461

Class individual painters in 759.13

For painting and paintings of Hawaii, see 759.9969

> **759.2–759.8 Europe**

Class comprehensive works in 759.94

For countries and localities not provided for here, see the country or locality in 759.949, e.g., painting and paintings of Belgium 759.9493

.2   **British Isles**

Class here England

When classifying individual painters, England, Scotland, Wales, and Northern Ireland are considered to be separate countries. Therefore, an English painter is classed in 759.2, a Scottish painter in 759.2911, a Welsh painter in 759.2929, and a Northern Ireland painter in 759.2916

.21–.28   England

Add to base number 759.2 the numbers following —42 in notation 421–428 from Table 2, e.g., painting and paintings of Manchester 759.2733

.29   Scotland, Ireland, Wales

Add to base number 759.29 the numbers following —4 in notation 41–42 from Table 2, e.g., painting and paintings of Scotland 759.2911

.3–.8   **Miscellaneous parts of Europe**

Add to base number 759 the numbers following —4 in notation 43–48 from Table 2, e.g., painting and paintings of France 759.4

.9   **Other geographic areas**

.91   Areas, regions, places in general

Add to base number 759.91 the numbers following —1 in notation 11–19 from Table 2, e.g., Western Hemisphere 759.91812

Individual painters are classed in the notation for their respective countries, e.g., painters from Canada 759.11

.93–.99   Specific continents, countries, localities

Class here painting and paintings of specific periods, e.g., painting and paintings of 1800–1899 in South America 759.9809034

Add to base number 759.9 notation 3–9 from Table 2, e.g., comprehensive works on painting and paintings of Europe 759.94, Etruscan painting and paintings 759.9375, painting and paintings of Hawaii 759.9969; however, for individual Hawaiian painters, see 759.13

Class works on one or two periods of European painting in 759.02–759.07, e.g., painting and paintings of 1800–1899 in Europe 759.05 (*not* 759.9409034); class painting and paintings from parts of Europe in notation 41–48 from Table 2 in 759.2–759.8

760   Printmaking and prints

For printing, see 686.2

.1   **Philosophy and theory**

Notation 01 from Table 1 as modified below

.11   Appreciative aspects

Do not use for systems; class in 760.1

Class psychological principles in 760.19

.117	Aesthetics
.118	Criticism and appreciation

         Including theory, technique, history

         Class works of critical appraisal in 769.9

.18	Inherent features

         Including color, composition, decorative values, form, light, movement, perspective, space, style, symmetry, vision

.2	**Miscellany**
.28	Auxiliary techniques and procedures; apparatus, equipment, materials

         Class here basic techniques and procedures

         Class techniques, procedures, apparatus, equipment, materials for making specific kinds of prints in 761–767

.7	**Education, research, related topics**
.75	Museum activities and services

         Do not use for collecting; class in 769.12

[.9]	**History, geographic treatment, biography**

         Do not use; class in 769.9

(.92)	Biography

         (Optional number; prefer 769.92)

>   **761–767   Printmaking**

         Fine art of executing a printing block or plate representing a picture or design conceived by the printmaker or copied from another artist's painting or drawing or from a photograph

         Techniques, procedures, equipment, materials

         Class maintenance and repair in 769.0288; class techniques, procedures, apparatus, equipment, materials of reproduction in 769.1; class techniques, procedures, apparatus, equipment, materials employed by individual printmakers in 769.92; class comprehensive works in 760.28

761	**Relief processes (Block printing)**

         Including raw potato printing, rubber-stamp printing

.2	**Wood engraving**
.3	**Linoleum-block printing**
.8	**Metal relief engraving**
[762]	**[Unassigned]**

         Most recently used in Edition 14

763 Lithographic processes (Planographic processes)

For chromolithography, see 764.2

.2	**Surfaces**
.22	Stone lithography
.23	Aluminum lithography
.24	Zinc lithography

764 Chromolithography and serigraphy

.2 Chromolithography

.8 Serigraphy

Class here silk-screen printing

> ## 765–767 Intaglio processes

Class comprehensive works in 765

765 Metal engraving

Class here comprehensive works on metal relief and metal intaglio processes, on intaglio processes

For metal relief engraving, see 761.8; for mezzotinting and aquatinting, see 766; for etching and drypoint, see 767

.2 Line engraving

.5 Stipple engraving

.6 Criblé engraving

766 Mezzotinting, aquatinting, related processes

.2 Mezzotinting

.3 Aquatinting

.7 Composite processes

Use of two or more processes in a single print

767 Etching and drypoint

.2 Etching

.3 Drypoint

[768] [Unassigned]

Most recently used in Edition 14

769   Prints

> Works produced using a printing block, screen, or plate
>
> Class here description, critical appraisal, collections regardless of process

.075   Museum activities and services

> Do not use for collecting; class in 769.12

[.09]   History, geographic treatment, biography

> Do not use; class in 769.9

.1   **Collecting and reproduction of prints**

> Class collecting and reproduction of specific forms of prints in 769.5

.12   Collecting prints

.17   Techniques of reproduction

.172   Reproductions and copies

.174   Forgeries and alterations

.4   *Iconography

> Add to base number 769.4 the numbers following 704.94 in 704.942–704.949, e.g., portrait prints 769.42; however, for individual printmakers, see 769.92
>
> Class postage stamps by subject in 769.564; class printmakers regardless of subject in 769.92; class sports cards in 796.075

.5   *Forms of prints

> Including lettering, inscriptions, designs on name cards, diplomas, decorative prints, art posters
>
> Class prints other than postage stamps on a specific subject regardless of form in 769.4; class comprehensive works on posters in 741.674
>
> *For sports cards, see 796.075*

.52   *Bookplates

.53   *Paper dolls

.55   Paper money

> Class here counterfeit paper money

[.550 9]   History, geographic treatment, biography

> Do not use; class in 769.559

.559   History, geographic treatment, biography

.559 001–.559 009   Standard subdivisions

> Add to base number 769.55900 the numbers following —00 in notation 001–009 from Table 2, e.g., periodicals of the history of paper money 769.559005

*Do not use notation 092 from Table 1 for individual printmakers; class in 769.92

.559 01–.559 05	Historical periods

Add to base number 769.5590 the numbers following —090 in notation 0901–0905 from Table 1, e.g., paper money from 20th century 769.55904

.559 1–.559 9	Geographic treatment, biography

Add to base number 769.559 notation 1–9 from Table 2, e.g., paper money of France 769.55944; however, for individual printmakers, see 769.92

.56	Postage stamps and related devices

Standard subdivisions are added for postage stamps and related devices together, for postage stamps alone

Class here philately (study and collecting of stamps)

Unless other instructions are given, class a subject with aspects in two or more subdivisions of 769.56 in the number coming first, e.g., counterfeit stamps depicting plants 769.562 (*not* 769.56434)

Class stamps other than for prepayment of postage in 769.57

[.560 9]	History, geographic treatment, biography

Do not use; class in 769.569

.561	*United Nations postage stamps, postal stationery, covers
.562	*Counterfeit postage stamps, covers, cancellations
.563	*Postage stamps commemorating persons and events
.564	Postage stamps depicting various specific subjects (Iconography)

Add to base number 769.564 the numbers following 704.94 in 704.943–704.949, e.g., postage stamps of plants of the world 769.56434; however, for individual printmakers, see 769.92

For stamps commemorating persons and events, see 769.563

.565	*Covers
.566	*Postal stationery

Postal-service-issued stationery (e.g., letter sheets, envelopes, postcards) bearing imprinted stamps

Class illustrated postcards in 741.683

.567	*Postmarks, cancellations, cachets

Standard subdivisions are added for any or all topics in heading

See also 769.562 for counterfeit cancellations

.569	History, geographic treatment, biography

*Do not use notation 092 from Table 1 for individual printmakers; class in 769.92

.569 001–.569 009	Standard subdivisions

> Add to base number 769.56900 the numbers following —00 in notation 001–009 from Table 2, e.g., periodicals of the history of postage stamps 769.569005

.569 01–.569 05	Historical periods

> Add to base number 769.5690 the numbers following —090 in notation 0901–0905 from Table 1, e.g., postage stamps from 20th century 769.56904

.569 1–.569 9	Geographic treatment, biography

> Add to base number 769.569 notation 1–9 from Table 2, e.g., postage stamps from San Marino 769.5694549; however, for individual printmakers, see 769.92

.57   *Stamps other than for prepayment of postage

> Including Christmas seals, officially sealed labels, ration coupons; postage-due, postal savings, and savings stamps

.572   *Revenue stamps

.9   **History, geographic treatment, biography of printmaking and prints**

> Class the history of a specific process with the process, e.g., history of lithography 763.09

> *See Manual at 769.9*

.900 1–.900 9	Standard subdivisions

> Add to base number 769.900 the numbers following —00 in notation 001–009 from Table 2, e.g., periodicals of the history of printmaking 769.9005

.901–.905	Historical periods

> Add to base number 769.90 the numbers following —090 in notation 0901–0905 from Table 1, e.g., printmaking in 20th century 769.904

.91–.99	Geographic treatment, biography

> Add to base number 769.9 notation 1–9 from Table 2, e.g., printmaking in England 769.942

.92   Biography

> Number built according to instructions under 769.91–769.99

> Class here engravers, printmakers

> (Option: Class in 760.92)

---

*Do not use notation 092 from Table 1 for individual printmakers; class in 769.92

770　Photography, computer art, cinematography, videography

Standard subdivisions are added for photography, computer art, cinematography, videography together; for photography alone

Class here conventional photography (photography using film), digital photography

Class technological photography in 621.367

.1　Philosophy and theory

> Notation 01 from Table 1 as modified below

.11　Inherent features

> Do not use for systems; class in 770.1

> Including color, composition, decorative values, form, light, movement, perspective, space, style, symmetry, vision

.2　Miscellany

.23　Photography as a profession, occupation, hobby

.232　Photography as a profession and occupation

.233　Photography as a hobby

.28　Auxiliary techniques and procedures

> *For comprehensive works on basic and auxiliary techniques and procedures, see 771*

[.284]　Apparatus, equipment, materials

> Do not use; class in 771

.285　Computer applications

> Do not use for comprehensive works on digital photography; class in 770; however use subdivisions of 770.285 for specific computer applications in photography, e.g., application of computer software to digital photography 770.28553

[.286]　Green technology (Environmental technology)

> Do not use; class in 771.40286

.9　History, geographical treatment, biography

.92　Biography

> Class here photographers regardless of type of artistic photography

> Class photographs in 779. Class photographers associated with a specific application with the application, e.g., photojournalists 070.49092

> *For motion picture, television, video photographers, see 777.092*

> *See Manual at 779 vs. 770.92*

771   ***Techniques, procedures, apparatus, equipment, materials**

> Including techniques of pinhole photography, of photography without camera; comprehensive works on basic and auxiliary techniques and procedures
>
> Class here interdisciplinary works on description, use, manufacture of apparatus, equipment, materials
>
> Class techniques, procedures, apparatus, equipment, materials used in special processes in 772–774; class techniques, procedures, apparatus, equipment, materials used in specific fields and special kinds of photography in 778
>
> > *For auxiliary techniques and procedures, see 770.28. For manufacture of a specific kind of apparatus, equipment, material, see the apparatus, equipment, or material, e.g., cameras 681.418*

.1   **Studios, laboratories, darkrooms**

> Class laboratory and darkroom practice in 771.4

.2   **Furniture and fittings**

.3   **Cameras and accessories**

> Standard subdivisions are added for cameras and accessories, for cameras alone
>
> Class here digital cameras

.31   Specific makes of cameras

> Class here specific brands of cameras, specific makes and brands of digital cameras
>
> (Option: Arrange alphabetically by trade name)

.32   Specific types of cameras

> Including 35mm cameras, automatic cameras, instant cameras, large format cameras, miniature cameras, single-lens reflex cameras, smartphone cameras
>
> Class here specific types of digital cameras
>
> Class specific makes of specific types of cameras in 771.31

.35   Optical parts of cameras

> Class optical parts of specific makes of cameras in 771.31
>
> > *For shutters, see 771.36; for focusing and exposure apparatus, see 771.37*

.352   Lenses

.356   Filters

---

*Do not use notation 0285 from Table 1 for comprehensive works on digital photography; class in 770 and its subdivisions without use of notation 0285, e.g., digital trick photography 778.8; however, use subdivisions of notation 0285 for specific computer applications in photography, e.g., application of computer software to digital trick photography 778.8028553. Do not use notation 092 from Table 1 for photographers; class in 770.92

.36   Camera shutters

> Class shutters of specific makes of cameras in 771.31

.37   Focusing and exposure apparatus

> Including exposure meters, range finders, viewfinders

> Class focusing and exposure apparatus of specific makes of cameras in 771.31

.38   Accessories

> Including carrying cases, tripods

.4   ***Processing of photographic images**

> Photographic images: negatives, positives, digital images, photographs, prints, slides, transparencies

> Class here comprehensive works on laboratory practice of photography and cinematography

> Class comprehensive works on photographic images in 779

> *For chemical materials, see 771.5; for laboratory practice of cinematography, see 777.55*

.43   *Preparation and manipulation of negatives

> Standard subdivisions are added for either or both topics in heading

> Class here comprehensive works on negatives

> Class comprehensive works on darkroom practice in 771.44

> *For preservation and storage of negatives, see 771.45; for organization and distribution of negatives, see 771.48*

.44   *Preparation and manipulation of positives

> Standard subdivisions are added for either or both topics in heading

> Including contact printing, enlarging, developing, mounting; developing and printing apparatus

> Class here preparation and manipulation of photographic digital images, photographs, prints, slides, transparencies; comprehensive works on positives, on darkroom practice, on preparation and manipulation of photographic images

> *For darkroom practice involving negatives, preparation and manipulation of negatives, see 771.43; for preservation and storage of positives, see 771.46; for organization and distribution of positives, see 771.48; for darkroom practice of cinematography, see 777.55*

---

*Do not use notation 0285 from Table 1 for comprehensive works on digital photography; class in 770 and its subdivisions without use of notation 0285, e.g., digital trick photography 778.8; however, use subdivisions of notation 0285 for specific computer applications in photography, e.g., application of computer software to digital trick photography 778.8028553. Do not use notation 092 from Table 1 for photographers; class in 770.92

.45   *Preservation and storage of negatives

         Standard subdivisions are added for either or both topics in heading

         Class here comprehensive works on preservation and storage of photographic images

         For preservation and storage of positives, see 771.46

.46   *Preservation and storage of positives

         Standard subdivisions are added for either or both topics in heading

         Class here preservation and storage of photographic digital images, photographs, prints, slides, transparencies

         For mounting, see 771.44

.48   *Projection, organization, distribution of photographic images

         Standard subdivisions are added for any or all topics in heading

         For motion picture projection, see 777.57; for stereoscopic projection, see 778.4

.5   **Chemical materials**

.52   Support materials

         Including backings of cellulose compounds, ceramics, glass, metal, paper

.53   Photosensitive surfaces

.532   Specific photosensitive surfaces

.532 2   Plates

.532 3   Papers

.532 4   Films

         Class here comprehensive works on film used in photography and cinematography

         For film used in cinematography, see 777.38

.54   Developing and printing supplies

         Including developing, fixing, intensifying, reducing, toning solutions

---

*Do not use notation 0285 from Table 1 for comprehensive works on digital photography; class in 770 and its subdivisions without use of notation 0285, e.g., digital trick photography 778.8; however, use subdivisions of notation 0285 for specific computer applications in photography, e.g., application of computer software to digital trick photography 778.8028553. Do not use notation 092 from Table 1 for photographers; class in 770.92

> ### 772–774 Special photographic processes

Techniques, procedures, apparatus, equipment, materials

Class processing techniques in specific fields and special kinds of photography in 778; class comprehensive works in 771

For photomechanical printing techniques, see 686.232

772   *Metallic salt processes

.1   ***Direct positive and printing-out processes**

Early photographic processes

For platinum printing-out process, see 772.3

.12   *Daguerreotype process

.14   *Ferrotype, tintype, wet-collodion processes

.16   *Kallitype processes

.3   ***Platinotype processes**

Including platinum printing-out process

.4   ***Silver processes**

Use of silver halides in principal light-sensitive photographic emulsions

773   *Pigment processes of printing

Early photographic printing processes

.1   ***Carbon and carbro processes**

Including Mariotype, ozotype, ozobrome

.2   ***Powder processes (Dusting-on processes)**

Class xerography in 686.44

.3   ***Imbibition processes**

.5   ***Gum-bichromate processes**

.6   ***Photoceramic and photoenamel processes**

.7   ***Diazotype processes**

.8   ***Oil processes**

Including bromoil process

*Do not use notation 0285 from Table 1 for comprehensive works on digital photography; class in 770 and its subdivisions without use of notation 0285, e.g., digital trick photography 778.8; however, use subdivisions of notation 0285 for specific computer applications in photography, e.g., application of computer software to digital trick photography 778.8028553. Do not use notation 092 from Table 1 for photographers; class in 770.92

774   *Holography

Class here holographic images

776   Computer art (Digital art)

Art objects produced using computers for display using computer output devices

Including artistic aspects of virtual reality

Class here comprehensive works on computer art and computer applications in the arts

> *For computer applications in the arts, see 700.285; for computer applications in fine and decorative arts, see 702.85; for computer music, see 786.76. For computer design of specific commodity, see the commodity, e.g., computer design of automobiles 629.231*

> *See Manual at 776 vs. 006.5–006.7*

.2   Graphics displayed on computer display devices

.4   Prints of computer graphics

.6   Animation and video

> *For animated cartoon cinematography and videography, see 777.7*

.7   Multimedia computer art

> *For web page design, see 006.7*

777   Cinematography and videography

Standard subdivisions are added for either or both topics in heading

Class here conventional cinematography (cinematography using film), digital cinematography and videography, amateur and professional cinematography and videography; home video systems, television photography, video art

Unless other instructions are given, class a subject with aspects in two or more subdivisions of 777 in the number coming last, e.g., cameras used for special effects 777.9 (*not* 777.34)

Class comprehensive works on motion picture production and cinematography, interdisciplinary works on motion pictures in 791.43; class comprehensive works on television production in 791.45; class interdisciplinary works on television in 384.55. Class a specific application of cinematography, videography, or video art with the application, e.g., use of videography in diagnosis of diseases 616.075028, use of videos in performance art 709.04

> *See also 006.7 for interactive video*

> *See Manual at 791.43, 791.45 vs. 777*

---

*Do not use notation 0285 from Table 1 for comprehensive works on digital photography; class in 770 and its subdivisions without use of notation 0285, e.g., digital trick photography 778.8; however, use subdivisions of notation 0285 for specific computer applications in photography, e.g., application of computer software to digital trick photography 778.8028553. Do not use notation 092 from Table 1 for photographers; class in 770.92

.028 5   Computer applications

> Do not use for comprehensive works on digital cinematography and videography; class in 777; however use subdivisions of notation 0285 for specific computer applications in cinematography and videography, e.g., application of computer software to digital cinematography 777.028553

.028 8   Maintenance and repair

> Do not use for preservation; class in 777.58

.092   Biography

> Class here cinematographers and videographers regardless of type of artistic cinematography and videography

> Class cinematographers and videographers associated with a specific application with the application, e.g., photojournalists 070.49092

.3   †Apparatus, equipment, materials

> Class here interdisciplinary works on use and manufacture of apparatus, equipment, materials

> *For manufacture of a specific kind of apparatus, equipment, materials, see the apparatus, equipment, or material, e.g., cameras 681.418*

.34   †Cameras and camcorders

> Standard subdivisions are added for either or both topic in heading

.36   †Recorders

.38   †Recording formats

> Class here DVDs, film

.5   †Elements and modes

> Including electronic field production (EFP)

> *See also 070.43 for electronic news gathering*

.52   †Lighting

.53   †Sound

.55   †Editing and post-production

> Standard subdivisions are added for either or both topics in heading

> Including titling

> Class here darkroom and laboratory practice

> *For animation, see 777.7; for special effects, see 777.9*

---

†Do not use notation 0285 from Table 1 for comprehensive works on digital cinematography and videography; class in 777 and its subdivisions without use of notation 0285, e.g., digital trick videography 777.9; however, use subdivisions of notation 0285 for specific computer applications in cinematography and videography, e.g., application of computer software to digital trick videography 777.9028553. Do not use notation 092 from Table 1 for photographers; class in 770.92

.57 †Projection and display

.58 †Preservation and storage

> Standard subdivisions are added for either or both topics in heading

> Including restoration

> *See also 025.1773 for archiving of motion picture films and video recordings*

.6 **†Specific kinds and types of cinematography and videography**

> Including aerial, close-up, high-speed, infrared, macrography, micrography, panoramic, space, time-lapse, underwater cinematography and videography

.65 †Stereoscopic cinematography and videography

> Standard subdivisions are added for either or both topics in heading

.7 **†Animation**

> Including stop motion

> Class here animated cartoons

> Class comprehensive works on animated cartoon films in 791.4334; class comprehensive works on animated television programs in 791.4534

.8 **Cinematography and videography of specific subjects**

> Add to base number 777.8 the numbers following 704.94 in 704.942–704.949, e.g., cinematography of animals 777.832, videography of landscapes 777.836; then, for either or both topics in heading, add further as follows:

01	Philosophy and theory
02	Miscellany
0285	Computer applications
	Do not use for comprehensive works on digital cinematography and videography; class in 777.82–777.89 without use of notation 0285 e.g., digital cinematography of animals 777.832; however, use subdivisions of notation 0285 for specific computer applications in cinematography and videography, e.g., application of computer software to digital cinematography of animals 777.832028553
03–08	Standard subdivisions
09	History, geographic treatment, biography
092	Biography
	Do not use for cinematographers and videographers; class in 777.092

.9 **†Special effects**

> Class here trick cinematography and videography

---

†Do not use notation 0285 from Table 1 for comprehensive works on digital cinematography and videography; class in 777 and its subdivisions without use of notation 0285, e.g., digital trick videography 777.9; however, use subdivisions of notation 0285 for specific computer applications in cinematography and videography, e.g., application of computer software to digital trick videography 777.9028553. Do not use notation 092 from Table 1 for photographers; class in 770.92

778   Specific fields and special kinds of photography

Class here interdisciplinary works on use and manufacture of apparatus, equipment, materials of specific fields and specific kinds of photography

Unless other instructions are given, observe the following table of preference, e.g., color aerial photography 778.35 (*not* 778.6):

Special effects and trick photography	778.8
Photography of specific subjects	778.9
Stereoscopic photography and projection	778.4
Special kinds of photography	778.3
Photography under specific conditions	778.7
Color photography	778.6

Class photographs created by a specific field or kind of photography in 779

For manufacture of a specific kind of apparatus, equipment, materials, see the apparatus, equipment, or material, e.g., cameras 681.418

.3   *Special kinds of photography

Not provided for elsewhere

Including Kirlian photography (high-voltage, high-frequency photopsychography)

Class a special kind of photography in relation to cinematography and videography in 777. Class a specific application of photography with the application, e.g., use of photography in astronomy 522.63

For technological photography and photo-optics, see 621.367

See also 133.892 for parapsychological aspects of Kirlian photography

.31   *Photomicrography

.32   *Photography in terms of focus

.322   *Telephotography

For aerial and space photography, see 778.35; for panoramic photography, see 778.36

.324   *Close-up photography

Including photomacrography

.34   *Infrared photography

Interdisciplinary works

For technological infrared photography, see 621.3672

---

*Do not use notation 0285 from Table 1 for comprehensive works on digital photography; class in 770 and its subdivisions without use of notation 0285, e.g., digital trick photography 778.8; however, use subdivisions of notation 0285 for specific computer applications in photography, e.g., application of computer software to digital trick photography 778.8028553. Do not use notation 092 from Table 1 for photographers; class in 770.92

.35   *Aerial and space photography

Including interpretation

For photogrammetry, see 526.982

.36   *Panoramic photography

.37   *High-speed photography

Including use of short-duration electronic flash

Class use of normal photographic electronic flash (flashbulb photography) in 778.72

.4   *Stereoscopic photography and projection

For stereoscopic motion picture projection, see 777.57; for stereoscopic cinematography and videography, see 777.65

> **778.6–778.8 Specific topics in photography**

Class specific topics in relation to cinematography and videography in 777; class comprehensive works in 770

.6   *Color photography

Class here photography of colors

Class color photomicrography in 778.31

.602 8   Auxiliary techniques and procedures; apparatus, equipment, materials

For processing auxiliary techniques and procedures, apparatus, equipment, materials in color photography, see 778.66

.62   *Photography of colors in monochrome

Orthochromatic and panchromatic

.63   *Direct process reproduction in color photography

Including Lippmann process

.65   *Additive processes in color photography

.66   *Processing techniques, procedures, apparatus, equipment, materials in color photography

Class here subtractive processes, production of color films and prints by subtractive analysis and subtractive synthesis, respectively

Class direct process reproduction in color photography in 778.63; class additive processes in color photography in 778.65

---

*Do not use notation 0285 from Table 1 for comprehensive works on digital photography; class in 770 and its subdivisions without use of notation 0285, e.g., digital trick photography 778.8; however, use subdivisions of notation 0285 for specific computer applications in photography, e.g., application of computer software to digital trick photography 778.8028553. Do not use notation 092 from Table 1 for photographers; class in 770.92

.7 ***Photography under specific conditions**

.71   *Outdoor photography

.712   *Photography in sunlight

.719   *Night photography

> *For infrared photography, see 778.34*

.72   *Indoor photography and photography by artificial light

> Class here use of normal photographic electronic flash (flashbulb photography)

> Class short-duration flash in high-speed photography in 778.37

> *For infrared photography, see 778.34*

.73   *Underwater photography

.75   *Photography under extreme climatic conditions

.76   *Available light photography

> Class outdoor available light photography in 778.71; class indoor available light photography in 778.72

.8 ***Special effects and trick photography**

> Standard subdivisions are added for either or both topics in heading

> Including composite, high-contrast, tabletop photography; photomontage; photography of specters, distortions, multiple images, silhouettes

---

*Do not use notation 0285 from Table 1 for comprehensive works on digital photography; class in 770 and its subdivisions without use of notation 0285, e.g., digital trick photography 778.8; however, use subdivisions of notation 0285 for specific computer applications in photography, e.g., application of computer software to digital trick photography 778.8028553. Do not use notation 092 from Table 1 for photographers; class in 770.92

.9   Photography of specific subjects

Class here photography of specific subjects by special kinds of photography; photography of specific subjects under specific conditions; comprehensive works on techniques of photographing, photographs of, and photographers of a specific subject

Add to base number 778.9 the numbers following 704.94 in 704.942–704.949, e.g., portrait photography 778.92; then add further as follows:

01	Philosophy and theory
02	Miscellany
0285	Computer applications

           Do not use for comprehensive works on digital photography in the topic; class in 778.92–778.99 without use of notation 0285, e.g., digital portrait photography 778.92; however, use subdivisions of notation 0285 for specific computer applications in photography, e.g., application of computer software to digital portrait photography 778.92028553

03–08	Standard subdivisions
09	History, geographic treatment, biography
092	Biography

           Do not use for photographers; class in 770.92

779   Photographic images

Collections, history, criticism

Class here filmstrips, slides, transparencies; digital images, photographs, prints

Add to base number 779 the numbers following 704.94 in 704.942–704.949, e.g., photographic images of children 779.25

For processing of photographic images, see 771.4; for holographic images, see 774

See Manual at 779 vs. 770.92

780 Music

After general topics (780 and 781) the basic arrangement of the schedule is based on the voice, instrument, or ensemble making the music. Any tradition of vocal music (e.g., classical, popular) is classed in 782–783; any tradition of instrumental music (e.g., classical, popular) is classed in 784–788

Unless other instructions are given, class a subject with aspects in two or more subdivisions of 780 in the number coming last, e.g., sacred vocal music 782.22 (*not* 781.7)

When instructed, add the indicator 0 or 1 and the notation from the subdivisions coming earlier in the schedule, e.g., rock songs 782.42166 (*not* 781.66). In building numbers, do not add by use of 0 or 1 (alone or in combination) more than twice, e.g., history of rock protest songs 782.421661592 (*not* 782.42166159209)
(Option: Add as many times as desired)

This schedule does not distinguish scores, texts, or recordings
(Option: To distinguish scores, texts, recordings, use one of the following:

(Option A: Prefix a letter or other symbol to the number for treatises, e.g., scores for violin M787.2, violin recordings R787.2 or MR787.2; use a special prefix to distinguish miniature scores from other scores, MM787.2

(Option B: Add to the number for treatises the numbers following 78 in 780.26–780.269, e.g., miniature scores of music for violin 787.20265

(Option C: Class recordings in 789, e.g., recordings of folk music 789.2, recordings of violin folk music 789.2072)

See Manual at 780; also at 781.6 vs. 780, 780.9

.000 1–.099 9	Relation of music to other subjects
	Works in which the focus is music
	Add to base number 780.0 three-digit numbers 001–999 (but stop before any zero that follows a non-zero number), e.g., music and literature 780.08, music and Welsh literature 780.0891 (*not* 780.089166), music and the performing arts 780.079 (*not* 780.07902)
.079	Recreational and performing arts
	Number built according to instructions under 780.0001–780.0999
	See Manual at 780.079 vs. 790.2
.1	**Philosophy and theory, analytical guides, program notes**
	Notation 01 from Table 1 as modified below
	For general principles, theory of music, see 781
.14	Communication, editing
	Notation 014 from Table 1 as modified below
.148	Musical notation, abbreviations, acronyms, symbols
	Including staff notation, neumes, tablature, tonic sol-fa; braille musical notation
	Class transcription from one form of notation to another in 780.149

.149	Editing
.15	Analytical guides and program notes

        Do not use for scientific principles; class in 781.2

(.16)	Bibliographies, catalogs, indexes

        (Optional number; prefer 016.78)

(.162)	†Bibliographies and catalogs of music literature
(.164)	†Bibliographies and catalogs of scores and parts

        Including bibliographies and catalogs of manuscript scores and parts

(.166)	†Discographies

        Bibliographies and catalogs of music recorded on phonorecords (cylinders, discs, wires, tapes, films)

        Including biodiscographies

[.19]	Psychological principles

        Do not use; class in 781.11

.2	**Miscellany; texts; treatises on music scores and recordings**

        Notation 02 from Table 1 as modified below

.202	Synopses and outlines

        For synopses of stories and plots, see 782.00269

.216	Lists, inventories, catalogs of music

        Class here thematic catalogs

        Class bibliographic catalogs of music in 016.78

        For thematic catalogs of individual composers, see 780.92

.26	Texts; treatises on music scores and recordings

        Standard subdivisions are added for a combination of two or more topics in heading, for scores alone

        In schedules other than 780, indicate scores, recordings, texts, and treatises about them by adding the numbers following 78 in 780.262–780.269, e.g., bibliography of music manuscripts 016.780262, bibliography of manuscripts of violin music 016.78720262, discography of violin music 016.78720266

        See Manual at 780.26

        (Option: To distinguish scores and recordings within 780, add to the number for treatises the numbers following 78 in 780.26–780.269, e.g., miniature scores of music for violin 787.20265. Other options are described at 780)

        (Option: Class here law of music; prefer appropriate subdivisions of 340)

†(Optional number; prefer 016.78)

> 780.262–780.265 Scores

Class comprehensive works in 780.26

For words and other vocal sounds to be sung or recited with music, see 780.268

.262 *Manuscripts

Including autograph scores, sketch books

.263 *Printed music

For performance scores, see 780.264; for study scores, see 780.265

See also 070.5794 for music publishing; also 686.284 for music printing

.264 *Performance scores and parts

Standard subdivisions are added for either or both topics in heading

Including full scores, conducting scores, piano-vocal scores

.265 *Study scores (Miniature scores, Pocket scores)

.266 *Sound recordings of music

Class here comprehensive works on music recordings

For video recordings, see 780.267

See also 781.49 for recording of music

.267 *Video recordings of music

.268 Words and other vocal sounds to be sung or recited with music

Including librettos, lyrics, poems, screenplays

Class here texts

The words must be discussed in a musical context. If the words are presented as literature, folklore, or religious text, class the work in 800, 398, or 200, respectively, e.g., hymn texts presented as religious texts 264.23

Use this number only for building other numbers, e.g., lyrics of songs 782.420268, texts of choral symphonies 784.221840268; never use it by itself

Class comprehensive works in 782.00268

For stories, plots, synopses, see 780.269

*(Option: Use this standard subdivision to distinguish scores and recordings; see details in note under 780.26)

.269	**Stories, plots, synopses**

Standard subdivisions are added for any or all topics in heading

Including scenarios

Use this number only for building other numbers, e.g., plots of operas 782.10269, synopses of choral symphonies 784.221840269; never use it by itself

Class comprehensive works in 782.00269

.28   Auxiliary techniques and procedures; apparatus, equipment, materials

See also 781.4 for techniques of music

.284   Apparatus, equipment, materials

Do not use for musical instruments; class in 784.19

See also 780.26 for scores; also 780.266 for recordings

.285   Computer applications

For computer composition, see 781.34; for the computer as a musical instrument, see 786.76

.7   **Education, research, related topics; performances**

Notation 07 from Table 1 as modified below

Including use of apparatus and equipment in study and teaching

.72   Research

.721   Research methods

Class here musicology

.74   Museums, collections, exhibits

Do not use for exhibitions, fairs, festivals; class in 780.78

.76   Review, exercises, examinations, works for self-instruction

.77   Special teaching and learning methods

For techniques for acquiring musical skills and learning a repertoire, see 781.42

.78   Performances (Concerts and recitals)

Do not use for use of apparatus and equipment in study and teaching; class in 780.7

Class here exhibitions, fairs; performances at festivals and competitions

Add to base number 780.78 notation 3–9 from Table 2, e.g., concerts in London 780.78421

See also 781.43 for performance techniques

.79	Competitions, awards, financial support

> Add to base number 780.79 notation 3–9 from Table 2 for geographic eligibility only, e.g., music competitions open to contestants from Italy 780.7945, music awards open to entries from the United States 780.7973, music fellowships limited to residents of California 780.79794

> Class performances at competitions in 780.78

.8   **Groups of people**

.89   Ethnic and national groups

> *For folk music, see 781.62*

> *See Manual at 781.62 vs. 780.89*

.9   **History, geographic treatment, biography**

> No distinction is made between the music of a place and music in a place, e.g., Viennese music and music played in Vienna are both classed in 780.943613

> Class critical appraisal in analytical guides and program notes in 780.15

> *See Manual at 781.6 vs. 780, 780.9*

> 780.901–780.905   Periods of stylistic development of music

> Even though the periods are those of western music, this does not limit the use of these numbers to western or European music only

> Class here schools, styles, time periods not limited ethnically or by country or locality

> Class comprehensive works in 780.9

.901   Ancient times through 499

.902   500–1449

> Including Gothic style, ars antiqua, ars nova, medieval music

> *For 1450–1499, see 780.9031*

.903   1450–

> Class here modern music

> *For 1900–1999, see 780.904; for 2000–2099, see 780.905*

.903 1   Ca. 1450–ca. 1600

> Including Renaissance music

.903 2   Ca. 1600–ca. 1750

> Including baroque music, nuove musiche

.903 3	Ca. 1750–ca. 1825

Including preclassicism, classicism, rococo style

Class here 18th century music

> For rococo style of earlier period, music of 1700–1750, see 780.9032

.903 4   Ca. 1825–ca. 1900

Including nationalism, romanticism

Class here 19th century music

> For music of earlier part of 19th century, see 780.9033; for 20th century nationalism, see 780.904

.904   1900–1999

Including avant-garde music, impressionism, neoclassicism

> For early impressionism, see 780.9034

[.904 1–.904 9]   Individual decades

Do not use; class in 780.904

.905   2000–2099

.92   Biography

Class here composers, performers, critics; thematic catalogs of individual composers

Class general thematic catalogs in 780.216

> See Manual at 780.92; also at 780.92 and 791.092

(Option: Class individual composers in 789)

.94   Music of Europe

Use only for works that stress that they are discussing the European origin and character of music in contrast to music from other sources

---

> ## 781–788 Principles, forms, ensembles, voices, instruments

Class here music of all traditions
(Option: 781–788 may be used for only one tradition of music; in that case, class all other traditions in 789. For example, if it is desired to emphasize western art music, class it here, and class all other traditions of music in 789, e.g., jazz 789.5; or, if it is desired to emphasize jazz, class it here, and class all other traditions of music in 789, e.g., western art music 789.8)

Unless other instructions are given, class a subject with aspects in two or more subdivisions of 781–788 in the number coming last, e.g., jazz mass 782.323165 (*not* 781.65), Johann Sebastian Bach's cello sonatas 787.4183 (*not* 784.183)

Class comprehensive works in 780

781   General principles and musical forms

Class here music theory

Use the subdivisions of 781 only when the subject is not limited to voice, instrument, or ensemble. If voice, instrument, or ensemble is specified, class with voice, instrument, or ensemble; and then add as instructed. For example, rehearsal of music 781.44, rehearsal of opera (a form for the voice) 782.1144, rock music (both vocal and instrumental) 781.66, rock songs 782.42166

> *See Manual at 780.92*

.01–.09   Standard subdivisions

Notation from Table 1 as modified under 780.1–780.9, e.g., music theory during the Renaissance 781.09031

.1   Basic principles of music

.11   Psychological principles

> *For aesthetics, appreciation, taste, see 781.17*

.12   Religious principles

.17   Artistic principles

Class here aesthetics, appreciation, taste

> ### 781.2–781.8 Other principles and musical forms

Add to each subdivision identified by * as follows:
  01–09   Standard subdivisions
                Notation from Table 1 as modified under 780.1–780.9, e.g., performances 078
  1   General principles
                Add to 1 the numbers following 781 in 781.1–781.7, e.g., rock music 166, rehearsing rock music 166144

In building numbers, do not add by use of 0 or 1 (alone or in combination) more than twice, e.g., history of rock protest songs 782.421661592 (*not* 782.42166159209)
  (Option: Add as many times as desired)

Class comprehensive works in 781

.2   *Elements of music

Class here scientific principles

.22   *Time

> *For playing time, see 781.432*

.222   *Pulse

.224   *Rhythm

.226   *Meter

---

*Add as instructed under 781.2–781.8

.23	*Musical sound
.232	*Pitch
.233	*Volume
.234	*Timbre (Tone color)
.235	*Attack and decay

Subdivisions are added for either or both topics in heading

.236	*Silence

Including rests

.237	*Intervals

For consonance, see 781.238; for dissonance, see 781.239

.238	*Consonance
.239	*Dissonance
.24	*Melody
.246	*Scales and scalic formations

Subdivisions are added for either or both topics in heading

Class comprehensive works on modes in 781.263

.247	*Ornaments

Including embellishments, trills

.248	*Themes

Including subject, countersubject, idée fixe, leitmotif

See also 780.216 for thematic catalogs

.25	*Harmony

Class here harmonic organization, comprehensive works on harmony and counterpoint

Class intervals in 781.237; class figured bass in 781.47

For homophony, see 781.285; for counterpoint, see 781.286

.252	*Chords

Including arpeggios

.254	*Cadences
.256	*Harmonic rhythm
.258	*Tonality

Key relationships

For tonal systems, see 781.26

*Add as instructed under 781.2–781.8

.26	*Tonal systems
.262	*Diatonicism
.263	*Medieval church modes

Class here comprehensive works on modes, modes of western folk music

For other modes, see 781.264

.264	Other modes

Including ancient Greek modes, Byzantine echoi, Indian rāgas

Class modes of western folk music in 781.263

.265	*Macrotonality

Tonality based on units larger than the diatonic whole tone

Including pentatonicism

.266	*Whole tonality

Tonality based on scales of diatonic whole tones

.267	*Atonality

Music with no fixed tonic or key center

For dodecaphony, see 781.268

.268	*Dodecaphony (Twelve-tone system, Note rows)

Class comprehensive works on serialism in 781.33

.269	*Microtonality

Tonality based on melodic units smaller than the diatonic semitone

.28	*Texture
.282	*Monody

Music with a single melodic line

.283	*Heterophony

Music with a single melodic line simultaneously varied by two or more performers

.285	*Homophony

A dominant melodic line over chordal accompaniment

.286	*Counterpoint

Two or more independent melodic lines

Class here polyphony

Class comprehensive works on harmony and counterpoint in 781.25

.3	***Composition**

*Add as instructed under 781.2–781.8

.302 85	Computer applications
	Do not use for computer composition; class in 781.34
.32	*Indeterminacy and aleatory composition
	Forms of composition based on chance
.33	Serialism
.330 1–.330 9	Standard subdivisions
	Notation from Table 1 as modified under 780.1–780.9, e.g., performances of serial music 781.33078
.331	Basic principles of serialism
.331 1	Psychological principles
	For aesthetics, appreciation, taste, see 781.3317
.331 2	Religious principles
.331 7	Artistic principles
	Class here aesthetics, appreciation, taste
.332–.338	Specific elements of serialism
	Add to base number 781.33 the numbers following 781.2 in 781.22–781.28, e.g., serialized rhythm 781.3324; however, for atonality, see 781.267
.34	*Computer composition
	See also 786.76 for computers as a musical instrument
.344–.346	Computer science aspects
	Unless it is redundant, add to base number 781.34 the numbers following 00 in 004–006, e.g., use of digital personal computers 781.34416, but use of digital computers 781.34 (*not* 781.344)
.36	*Extemporization (Improvisation)
.37	*Arrangement
	Including transcription
	For arrangements, see 781.38
.374	*Orchestration
.377	*Paraphrase and parody
.38	*Arrangements
	See Manual at 781.38

*Add as instructed under 781.2–781.8

.382–.388	Original voice, instrument, ensemble of the arrangements

Add to base number 781.38 the numbers following 78 in 782–788, e.g., arrangements of violin music 781.3872

Use these numbers only for building other numbers; never use them by themselves

.4   *Techniques of music

For techniques of composition, see 781.3

.42   *Techniques for acquiring musical skills and learning a repertoire

.423   *Sight and score reading

Subdivisions are added for either or both topics in heading

.424   *Listening and ear training

Subdivisions are added for either or both topics in heading

.426   *Memorizing

.43   *Performance techniques

For extemporization, see 781.36; for specific performance techniques, see 781.44–781.48

See also 784.193 for techniques for playing instruments

.432   *Playing time

.434   *Harmonization

.436   *Transposition

.438   *Ensemble technique

>   781.44–781.48 Specific performance techniques

Class comprehensive works in 781.43

.44   *Rehearsal and practice

Subdivisions are added for either or both topics in heading

.45   *Conducting

.46   *Interpretation

Including rubato

.47   *Accompaniment

Including continuo (figured bass, thorough bass)

Class here collaboration

See Manual at 781.47

*Add as instructed under 781.2–781.8

.48	*Breathing and resonance

Subdivisions are added for either or both topics in heading

Class breathing and resonance associated with instrumental performance in 784.1932

.49	*Recording of music

See also 006.5 for computer hardware and software used in digital sound recording; also 621.3893 for sound recording and reproducing equipment; also 780.266 for treatises on music recordings

.5	***Kinds of music**
.52	*Music for specific times
.522	*Music for days of week
.522 2	*Sunday
.522 8	*Saturday
.523	*Music for times of day
.524	*Music for the seasons
.524 2	*Spring
.524 4	*Summer
.524 6	*Fall (Autumn)

Including harvest

.524 8	*Winter
.53	*Music in specific settings
.532	*Outdoor music

Including street music

.534	*Indoor music

For specific indoor settings, see 781.535–781.539

>   781.535–781.539   Specific indoor settings

Class music in religious settings in 781.7; class comprehensive works in 781.534

.535	*Domestic setting
.536	*Court setting
.538	*Theater setting
.539	*Concert hall setting

---

*Add as instructed under 781.2–781.8

.54	*Music for specific media

Background or mood music

Including music for video games

.542	*Film music

See also 777.53 for sound synchronization of motion pictures

.544	*Radio music
.546	*Television music

See also 777.53 for sound synchronization of television programs

.55	*Music accompanying public entertainments
.552	*Dramatic music

Class here incidental music

Class incidental music for specific media in 781.54; class dramatic vocal music in 782.1

.554	*Dance music

For ballet music, see 781.556

.556	*Ballet music
.56	*Program music

Music depicting nonmusical concepts, e.g., music depicting the sea

Class musical forms depicting nonmusical concepts in 784.18, e.g., nocturnes 784.18966

.57	*Music accompanying activities

Including inaugurations, initiations

Class music accompanying stages of the life cycle in 781.58; class music reflecting other themes and subjects regardless of activity in 781.59

See also 781.55 for music accompanying public entertainments

.58	*Music accompanying stages of the life cycle
.582	*Birth and infancy

Including music for infant baptism and circumcision

Class here music for confinement

.583	*Attainment of puberty

Including music for bar or bat mitzvahs

.584	*Attainment of majority

Including music for debuts

.586	*Courtship and engagement

*Add as instructed under 781.2–781.8

.587	*Weddings and marriage

Subdivisions are added for either or both topics in heading

.588	*Dying and death

Including music for burials, cremations, funerals, mourning

.59	*Music reflecting other themes and subjects
.592	*Protest
.593	*Work
.594	*Sports and recreation
.595	*Sea life
.599	*Patriotic, political, military music

Class here music commemorating historical events

Subdivisions are added for any or all topics in heading

.6	***Traditions of music**

Works emphasizing a specific tradition

See Manual at 781.6; also at 781.6 vs. 780, 780.9

(Option: If 781–788 is used for only one tradition of music, class all other traditions in 789)

.62	Folk music

Music originating within and associated with an ethnic or national group

Class folk rock in 781.66172. Class a specific style of music provided for in 781.64–781.66 with the style, e.g., reggae 781.646, Afro-Cuban jazz 781.6572687291

See also 780.9 for music of and performed in a specific location

See Manual at 781.62 vs. 780.89; also at 781.62 vs. 781.63–781.66

.620 01–.620 07	Standard subdivisions

Notation from Table 1 as modified under 780.1–780.7, e.g., performances of folk music 781.620078

.620 08	Groups of people
.620 089	Ethnic and national groups
.620 089 1–.620 089 9	Specific ethnic and national groups

Do not use for folk music of specific ethnic and national groups; class in 781.621–781.629

.620 09	History, geographic treatment, biography

---

*Add as instructed under 781.2–781.8

.620 090 1–.620 090 3	Historical periods to 1900

Add to base number 781.620090 the numbers following 780.90 in 780.901–780.903, e.g., folk music of the Renaissance 781.62009031

.620 090 4–.620 090 5	1900–2099

Add to base number 781.620090 the numbers following —090 in notation 0904–0905 from Table 1, e.g., folk music of the 1970s 781.62009047

.620 091	Areas, regions, places in general

For geographic treatment of folk music of specific ethnic and national groups, see 781.621–781.629

.620 092	Biography

Class here composers, performers, critics; thematic catalogs of individual composers

See Manual at 780.92; also at 780.92 and 791.092

(Option: Class individual composers in 789)

.620 093–.620 099	Specific continents, countries, localities; extraterrestrial worlds

For geographic treatment of folk music of specific ethnic and national groups, see 781.621–781.629

.620 1–.620 5	General principles of folk music

Add to base number 781.620 the numbers following 781 in 781.1–781.5, e.g., folk music for springtime 781.6205242, rehearsing folk music for springtime 781.6205242144

.620 6	Influence of other traditions of music

Add to base number 781.6206 the numbers following 781.6 in 781.63–781.69, e.g., influence of jazz on folk music 781.62065, performances of folk music influenced by jazz 781.62065078

.621–.629   Folk music of specific ethnic and national groups

> Add to base number 781.62 notation 1–9 from Table 5, e.g., Spanish folk music 781.6261; then add further as follows:
>
> 001–008   Standard subdivisions
> > Notation from Table 1 as modified under 780.1–780.9, e.g., performances of Spanish folk music 781.62610078
>
> 009   History, geographic treatment, biography
> 00901–00903   Historical periods to 1900
> > Add to 0090 the numbers following 780.90 in 780.901–780.903, e.g., Spanish folk music of the Renaissance 781.6261009031
>
> 00904–00905   1900–2099
> > Add to 0090 the numbers following —090 in notation 0904–0905 from Table 1, e.g., Spanish folk music of the 1970s 781.6261009047
>
> [0093–0099]   Specific continents, countries, localities
> > Do not use; class in notation 03–09 from this table
>
> 01   General principles
> > Add to 01 the numbers following 781 in 781.1–781.5, e.g., Spanish folk music for springtime 781.6261015242, rhythm in Spanish folk music for springtime 781.62610152421224
>
> 02   Influence of other traditions of music
> > Add to 02 the numbers following 781.6 in 781.63–781.69, e.g., influence of jazz on Spanish folk music 781.6261025, performances of Spanish folk music influenced by jazz 781.6261025078
>
> 03–09   Specific continents, countries, localities
> > Add to 0 notation 3–9 from Table 2, e.g., Spanish folk music in New York City 781.626107471

In building numbers, do not add by use of 0 or 1 (alone or in combination) more than twice, e.g., history of Spanish protest folk-songs 782.421626101592 (*not* 782.42162610159209)
(Option: Add as many times as desired)

>   781.63–781.69 Other traditions of music

Add to each subdivision identified by † as follows:
01–08   Standard subdivisions
            Notation from Table 1 as modified under 780.1–780.8, e.g.,
            performances 078
09   History, geographic treatment, biography
0901–0903   Historical periods to 1900
            Add to 090 the numbers following 780.90 in
            780.901–780.903, e.g., music of the Renaissance 09031
0904–0905   1900–2099
            Add to 090 the numbers following —090 in notation
            0904–0905 from Table 1, e.g., music of the 1970s 09047
1   General principles, influence of other traditions of music, hybrid styles
11–15   General principles
            Add to 1 the numbers following 781 in 781.1–781.5, e.g.,
            springtime music 15242, melody in springtime music 15242124
16   Influence of other traditions of music
            Add to 16 the numbers following 781.6 in 781.62–781.69, e.g.,
            influence of folk music 162, performances of music influenced
            by folk music 162078
            See also 17 for hybrid styles
17   Hybrid styles
            Fusion of two or more styles from different traditions of music
            to create a new style
            Add to 17 the numbers following 781.6 in 781.62–781.69, e.g.,
            fusion with folk music 172, folk rock 781.66172
            See Manual at 781.6: Hybrid styles
            See also 16 for influence of other traditions of music

In building numbers, do not add by use of 0 or 1 (alone or in combination)
more than twice, e.g., history of rock protest songs 782.421661592 (*not*
782.42166159209)
    (Option: Add as many times as desired)

Class comprehensive works in 781.6

.63   †Popular music

      Class popular music originating within and associated with an ethnic or
      national group in 781.62

      For western popular music, see 781.64

      See Manual at 781.62 vs. 781.63–781.66

.64   †Western popular music

      Class western popular music originating within and associated with an ethnic
      or national group in 781.62; class country music in 781.642

      For jazz, see 781.65; for rock, see 781.66

      See Manual at 781.62 vs. 781.63–781.66

---

†Add as instructed under 781.63–781.69

.642   †Country music

> Class here bluegrass music; specific country music styles

.643   †Blues

> Class here traditional rhythm and blues; specific blues styles

> Class comprehensive works on rhythm and blues in 781.644

.644   †Soul

> Class here R&B; specific soul styles; comprehensive works on rhythm and blues

> *For traditional rhythm and blues, see 781.643*

.645   †Ragtime

.646   †Reggae

> Class here specific reggae styles

.648   †Electronica

> Class here specific electronica styles

> Class comprehensive works on electronic music in 786.7

[.648 155 4]   Dance music

> Do not use; class in 781.648

.649   †Rap

> Class here specific rap styles

> Class comprehensive works on rap in 782.421649

.65   †Jazz

> *See Manual at 781.62 vs. 781.63–781.66*

[.651 7]   Hybrid styles

> Do not use; class in 781.657

.652   †Early jazz

> Class here origins of jazz

.653   †Traditional jazz

> Including New Orleans, Dixieland, Southwest and Kansas City, Harlem, white New York styles; Chicago breakdown

.654   †Mainstream jazz

> Including swing

---

†Add as instructed under 781.63–781.69

.655	†Modern jazz

> Including bop (bebop), hard bop, cool jazz, progressive jazz
>
> *For avant-garde jazz, see 781.656*

.656	†Avant-garde jazz
.657	Hybrid styles

> Add to base number 781.657 the numbers following 781.6 in 781.62–781.69, e.g., Afro-Cuban 781.6572687291, Indo-jazz 781.657291411

.66	†Rock (Rock'n' roll)

> Class here specific rock styles
>
> *See Manual at 781.62 vs. 781.63–781.66*

.68	†Western art music (Classical music)

> Limited to classical music as a tradition in contrast to other traditions
>
> Class here comprehensive works on traditions of art music
>
> Class classical music in general in 780
>
> *For nonwestern art music, see 781.69*

.681 75	Hybrid styles

> Number built according to instructions under 781.63–781.69
>
> Class here third stream

.69	†Nonwestern art music
.7	**Sacred music**

> Class sacred music accompanying stages of life cycle in 781.58; class works about church music that are limited to Christian church music in 781.71; class sacred vocal music in 782.22

.700 1–.700 9	Standard subdivisions

> Notation from Table 1 as modified under 780.1–780.9, e.g., performances of sacred music 781.70078

.701–.706	General principles of sacred music

> Add to base number 781.70 the numbers following 781 in 781.1–781.6, e.g., harmonic rhythm in sacred music 781.70256, appreciation of harmonic rhythm in sacred music 781.70256117

.71	Christian sacred music

> *For music of Christian church year, see 781.72*

.710 01–.710 09	Standard subdivisions

> Notation from Table 1 as modified under 780.1–780.9, e.g., performances of Christian sacred music 781.70078

†Add as instructed under 781.63–781.69

.710 1–.710 6	General principles of Christian sacred music

Add to base number 781.710 the numbers following 781 in 781.1–781.6, e.g., harmonic rhythm in Christian sacred music 781.710256, appreciation of harmonic rhythm in Christian sacred music 781.710256117

.711–.719	Christian sacred music of specific denominations and sects

Add to base number 781.71 the numbers following 28 in 281–289 for the denomination or sect only, e.g., Lutheran sacred music 781.7141; then add further as follows:

001–009   Standard subdivisions

Notation from Table 1 as modified under 780.1–780.9, e.g., performances of Lutheran sacred music 781.71410078

01–06   General principles

Add to 0 the numbers following 781 in 781.1–781.6, e.g., harmonic rhythm in Lutheran sacred music 781.71410256, appreciation of harmonic rhythm in Lutheran sacred music 781.71410256117

.72	*Music of Christian church year
.722	*Advent
.723	*Christmas day

Class here Christmas season

For Epiphany, see 781.724

.724	*Epiphany
.725	*Lent
.725 5	*Passiontide

For Holy Week, see 781.726

.726	*Holy Week

Including Palm Sunday, Maundy Thursday, Good Friday

.727	*Easter Sunday

Class here Eastertide (Easter season)

For Ascensiontide, see 781.728

.728	*Ascensiontide
.729	*Pentecost and Trinity Sunday
.729 3	*Pentecost (Whitsunday)
.729 4	*Trinity Sunday
.73	*Sacred music of classical (Greek and Roman) and Germanic religions

*Add as instructed under 781.2–781.8

.74–.79	Sacred music of other religions and sects

Add to base number 781.7 the numbers following 29 in 294–299 for the religion or sect only, e.g., Jewish sacred music 781.76; then add further as follows:

001–009	Standard subdivisions

Notation from Table 1 as modified under 780.1–780.9, e.g., performances of Jewish sacred music 781.760078

01–06	General principles

Add to 0 the numbers following 781 in 781.1–781.6, e.g., harmonic rhythm in Jewish sacred music 781.760256, appreciation of harmonic rhythm in Jewish sacred music 781.760256117

.8	*Musical forms

Class here formal analysis; works that do not specify voice, instrument, or ensemble

Class works for specific voice, instrument, or ensemble with the voice, instrument, or ensemble, e.g., Brahms' Variations on a theme by Schumann 786.21825 (*not* 781.825)

For vocal forms, see 782.1–782.4; for instrumental forms, see 784.183–784.189

.82	Specific musical forms
[.820 1–.820 9]	Standard subdivisions

Do not use; class in 781.801–781.809

.822	*Binary, ternary, da capo forms

Subdivisions are added for a combination of two or more forms

.822 2	*Binary form
.822 3	*Ternary form
.822 5	*Da capo form
.823	*Strophic form
.824	*Rondos

Including sonata-rondos

.825	*Variations

Including theme and variations

.826	*Paraphrase forms

Including musical parody

.827	*Ground bass (Ostinato)

Including chaconnes, passacaglias

.828	*Cantus firmus

*Add as instructed under 781.2–781.8

782   Vocal music

Class orchestral music with vocal parts in 784.22

For music for single voices, see 783

See Manual at 782; also at 782: Flow chart

.001–.009   Standard subdivisions

Notation from Table 1 as modified under 780.1–780.9, e.g., performances of vocal music 782.0078

.01–.07   General principles of vocal music

Add to base number 782.0 the numbers following 781 in 781.1–781.7, e.g., patriotic vocal music 782.0599, rhythm in patriotic vocal music 782.05991224

.08   Musical forms

Add to base number 782.08 the numbers following 784.18 in 784.182–784.189, e.g., vocal music in waltz form 782.08846

For vocal forms, see 782.1–782.4

>   **782.1–782.4   Vocal forms**

Class here treatises about and recordings of vocal forms for specific voices and ensembles

Add to each subdivision identified by * as follows:
    01–09   Standard subdivisions
            Notation from Table 1 as modified under 780.1–780.9, e.g., performances 078
    1   General principles and musical forms
    11–17   General principles
            Add to 1 the numbers following 781 in 781.1–781.7, e.g., rock music 166, rehearsing rock music 166144
    18   Musical forms
            Add to 18 the numbers following 784.18 in 784.182–784.189, e.g., da capo form 1822, composition in da capo form 182213

In building numbers, do not add by use of 0 or 1 (alone or in combination) more than twice, e.g., history of rock protest songs 782.421661592 (*not* 782.42166159209)
    (Option: Add as many times as desired)

Class comprehensive works in 782

.1   ***Operas and related dramatic vocal forms**

> Regardless of type of voice or vocal group
>
> Subdivisions are added for operas and related dramatic vocal forms together, for operas alone
>
> Class here concert versions
>
> *See Manual at 782.1 vs. 792.5, 792.6*

.109 2   Biography

> Class here biographies of singers known equally well as opera and recital singers, of conductors known primarily as opera conductors
>
> Class biographies of singers known primarily as recital singers in 782.42168092; class biographies of conductors known equally well for conducting operas and orchestral music in 784.2092

.109 4   European opera

> Use only for works that stress that they are discussing European opera in contrast to operas from all other sources

.12   ***Operettas**

> Class here zarzuelas

.13   ***Singspiels**

.14   ***Musical plays**

> Musical plays differ from other dramatic musical forms by the fact that in them the action is predominantly outside the music, while in the other dramatic forms the action is predominantly in the music
>
> Class here ballad operas, musicals, revues
>
> *For masques, see 782.15*
>
> *See Manual at 782.1 vs. 792.5, 792.6*

.15   ***Masques**

.2   ***Nondramatic vocal forms**

> *For secular forms, see 782.4*

.22   ***Sacred vocal forms**

> *For specific sacred vocal forms, see 782.23–782.29*

>   **782.23–782.29 Specific sacred vocal forms**
>
> Class comprehensive works in 782.22
>
> *For services, see 782.3*

*Add as instructed under 782.1–782.4

.23   *Oratorios

Including passions

.24   *Large-scale vocal forms

Class here comprehensive works on cantatas

For oratorios, see 782.23; for secular cantatas, see 782.48

.25   *Small-scale vocal forms

Class here anthems, sacred songs

Unless otherwise indicated, if the forms are called motets, class them in 782.26; if called hymns, class them in 782.27; if called carols, class them in 782.28; otherwise, class them here

Class comprehensive works on songs in 782.42

See also 782.421599 for national anthems

.253   *Spirituals

.254   *Gospel music

.26   *Motets

Motets composed after 1600 limited to those using imitative polyphony in the style of Palestrina

.27   *Hymns

For carols, see 782.28

.28   *Carols

.29   *Liturgical forms

.292   *Chant

Including responses, e.g., litanies, suffrages

Class here plainsong

Class Gregorian chant in 782.3222; class Anglican chant in 782.3223

>   782.294–782.298 Specific texts

Class comprehensive works in 782.29

.294   *Psalms

.295   *Biblical texts

Including amens, canticles

For psalms, see 782.294

.296   *Non-Biblical texts

Class parts of the mass in 782.323

*Add as instructed under 782.1–782.4

.297   *Tropes

                Accretions to the liturgy

                For liturgical drama, see 782.298

.298   *Liturgical drama

.3   ***Services (Liturgy and ritual)**

                Musical settings of prescribed texts of specific religions

                Class texts used by a specific religion with the religion, e.g., liturgy and ritual of a Christian church 264

.32   *Christian services

.322   Services of specific denominations

[.322 01–.322 09]   Standard subdivisions

                Do not use; class in 782.3201–782.3209

.322 1–.322 9   Subdivisions for services of specific denominations

                Add to base number 782.322 the numbers following 28 in 281–289, e.g., music for Lutheran services 782.32241; then add further as follows:

                    001–009   Standard subdivisions
                               Notation from Table 1 as modified under 780.1–780.9, e.g., performances of music for Lutheran services 782.322410078

                    01–07   General principles
                               Add to 0 the numbers following 781 in 781.1–781.7, e.g., music for Lutheran Easter Sunday services 782.322410727, composition of music for Lutheran Easter Sunday services 782.32241072713

                    08   Musical forms
                               Add to 08 the numbers following 784.18 in 784.182–784.189, e.g., preludes for Lutheran services 782.3224108928, composition of preludes for Lutheran services 782.322410892813

                Class specific liturgies of specific denominations in 782.323–782.326

>   **782.323–782.326 Specific liturgies**

                Class comprehensive works in 782.32

.323   *Mass (Communion service)

                This number is used for music including both the common and the proper of the mass. Masses written from 1350 to today are usually limited to the common and are thus classed in 782.3232. The major exception is the requiem mass, which is classed in 782.3238. Music for an individual part of the mass is classed with that part, e.g., gradual 782.3235

.323 2	*Common of the mass (Ordinary of the mass)

         Including Kyrie, Gloria, Credo, Sanctus, Benedictus, Agnus Dei

         For common of requiem mass, see 782.3238

.323 5	*Proper of the mass

         Including introit, gradual, tract, sequence, offertory, communion

         For proper of requiem mass, see 782.3238

.323 8	*Requiem mass
.324	*Divine office

         Including matins, lauds, prime, terce, sext, none, vespers, compline

         See also 782.325 for morning prayer; also 782.326 for evening prayer

.325	*Morning prayer

         Including matins of the Anglican church

.326	*Evening prayer

         Including evensong of the Anglican church

.33	*Services of classical (Greek and Roman) and Germanic religions
.34–.39	Services of other specific religions and sects

         Add to base number 782.3 the numbers following 29 in 294–299 for the religion or sect only, e.g., music for Jewish services 782.36; then add further as follows:

001–009	Standard subdivisions
	Notation from Table 1 as modified under 780.1–780.9, e.g., performances of music for Jewish services 782.360078
01–07	General principles
	Add to 0 the numbers following 781 in 781.1–781.7, e.g., music for Jewish spring services 782.3605242, composition of music for Jewish spring services 782.360524213
08	Musical form
	Add to 08 the numbers following 784.18 in 784.182–784.189, e.g., preludes for Jewish services 782.3608928, composition of preludes for Jewish services 782.360892813

.4	***Secular forms**
.42	*Songs

         Class here comprehensive works on songs

         For sacred songs, see 782.25

.421 599	National anthems

         Number built according to instructions under 782.1–782.4

         See also 782.25 for sacred anthems

*Add as instructed under 782.1–782.4

.421 64   Western popular songs

Number built according to instructions under 782.1–782.4

Class comprehensive works on western popular music in 781.64

For jazz songs, see 782.42165; for rock songs, see 782.42166

.421 649   Rap songs

Number built according to instructions under 782.1–782.4

Class here comprehensive works on rap music

For rap music limited to instrumental tracks, see the instrument, e.g., drum rap beats 786.91649

.421 65   Jazz songs

Number built according to instructions under 782.1–782.4

Class comprehensive works on jazz in 781.65; class comprehensive works on western popular songs in 782.42164

.421 66   Rock (Rock'n' roll) songs

Number built according to instructions under 782.1–782.4

Class comprehensive works on rock music in 781.66; class comprehensive works on western popular songs in 782.42164

.421 68   Art songs

Number built according to instructions under 782.1–782.4

Class here lieder

.421 680 92   Biography

Number built according to instructions under 782.1–782.4

Class here biographies of singers known primarily as recital singers

Class biographies of singers known equally well as opera and recital singers in 782.1092

.43   *Forms derived from poetry

Including ballads, balletts, chansons, frottole, villancicos

Class here madrigals

For villancicos that are Christmas carols, see 782.281723

.47   *Song cycles

.48   *Secular cantatas

*Add as instructed under 782.1–782.4

>   **782.5–782.9   Vocal executants**

Add to each subdivision identified by † as follows:
01–09   Standard subdivisions
          Notation from Table 1 as modified under 780.1–780.9, e.g.,
          performances 078
1   General principles and musical forms
11–17   General principles
          Add to 1 the numbers following 781 in 781.1–781.7, e.g., rock
          music 166, rehearsing rock music 166144
18   Musical forms
          Add to 18 the numbers following 784.18 in 784.182–784.189,
          e.g., da capo form 1822, composition in da capo form 182213
          Class dramatic vocal forms in 782.1
              For nondramatic vocal forms, see notation 2–4 from this
              table
2–4   Nondramatic vocal forms
          Add the numbers following 782 in 782.2–782.4, e.g., secular
          cantatas 48

In building numbers, do not add by use of 0 or 1 (alone or in combination) more
than twice, e.g., texts of rock protest songs for mixed voices 782.5421661592
(*not* 782.54216615920268)
     (Option: Add as many times as desired)

Use 782.5–782.9 for scores and parts of vocal forms for specific kinds of
vocal ensembles, e.g., mixed-voice choirs 782.5, children's choirs 782.7. Use
782.1–782.4 for treatises about and recordings of vocal forms for specific kinds
of vocal ensembles. Class performance techniques for a specific ensemble or
form with the ensemble or form, e.g., breathing techniques for choral music
782.5148, for opera 782.1148

Class comprehensive works in 782

     See Manual at 782

.5   **†Mixed voices**

Class here choral music, music intended equally for choral or part-song
performance, choral music with solo parts, unison voices

     For part songs, see 783.1

>   **782.6–782.9   Types of voices**

Class comprehensive works in 782

.6   **†Women's voices**

Class here music intended equally for women's or children's voices

Class music for children's voices in 782.7

.66   †Soprano voices (Treble voices)

.67   †Mezzo-soprano voices

†Add as instructed under 782.5–782.9

.68	†Contralto voices (Alto voices)
.7	**†Children's voices**

Class music intended equally for women's or children's voices in 782.6

.76	†Soprano voices (Treble voices)
.77	†Mezzo-soprano voices
.78	†Contralto voices (Alto voices)
.79	†Changing voices
.8	**†Men's voices**
.86	†Treble and alto voices

Class here countertenor, falsetto, castrato voices

Subdivisions are added for either or both topics in heading

.87	†Tenor voices
.88	†Baritone voices
.89	†Bass voices
.9	**†Other types of voices**
.96	†Speaking voices (Choral speech)
.97	†Sprechgesang
.98	†Whistle

783 Music for single voices

Class here the voice

Use 783 for scores and parts of vocal forms for specific kinds or ensembles of single voice. Use 782.1–782.4 for treatises about and recordings of vocal forms for specific kinds or ensembles of single voice. Class performance techniques for a specific kind or ensemble of single voice or for a specific form with the kind, ensemble, or form, e.g., breathing techniques for part songs 783.1148, for opera 782.1148

See Manual at 782

.001–.009	Standard subdivisions

Notation from Table 1 as modified under 780.1–780.9, e.g., performances of music for single voice 783.0078

.01–.07	General principles of music for single voices

Add to base number 783.0 the numbers following 781 in 781.1–781.7, e.g., patriotic music for single voices 783.0599, rhythm in patriotic music for single voices 783.05991224

---

†Add as instructed under 782.5–782.9

.08   Musical forms

> Add to base number 783.08 the numbers following 784.18 in 784.182–784.189, e.g., vocal music in waltz form for the single voice 783.08846

>> *For dramatic vocal forms, see 782.1; for nondramatic vocal forms, see 783.09*

.09   Nondramatic vocal forms

> Add to base number 783.09 the numbers following 782 in 782.2–782.4, e.g., carols for single voices 783.0928

.1   **Single voices in combination**

> Class here part songs

> Class music intended equally for choral or part-song performance in 782.5

.101–.109   Standard subdivisions

> Notation from Table 1 as modified under 780.1–780.9, e.g., performances of part songs 783.1078

.11   General principles and musical forms

.111–.117   General principles of single voices in combination

> Add to base number 783.11 the numbers following 781 in 781.1–781.7, e.g., patriotic part songs 783.11599, rehearsing patriotic part songs 783.11599144

.118   Musical forms

> Add to base number 783.118 the numbers following 784.18 in 784.182–784.189, e.g., part songs in waltz form 783.118846, rehearsing part songs in waltz form 783.118846144

>> *For dramatic vocal forms, see 782.1; for nondramatic vocal forms, see 783.119*

.119   Nondramatic vocal forms

> Add to base number 783.119 the numbers following 782 in 782.2–782.4, e.g., carols for single voices in combination 783.11928

>   783.12–783.19 Ensembles by size

        Add to each subdivision identified by † as follows:

    01–09   Standard subdivisions

         Notation from Table 1 as modified under 780.1–780.9, e.g., performances 078

    1   General principles and musical forms

    11–17   General principles

         Add to 1 the numbers following 781 in 781.1–781.7, e.g., rock music 166, rehearsing rock music 166144

    18   Musical forms

         Add to 18 the numbers following 784.18 in 784.182–784.189, e.g., da capo form 1822, composition in da capo form 182213

         Class dramatic vocal forms in 782.1

            For nondramatic vocal forms, see notation 2–4 from this table

    2–4   Nondramatic vocal forms

         Add the numbers following 782 in 782.2–782.4, e.g., secular cantatas 48

    6–9   Types of voices

         Add the numbers following 782 in 782.6–782.9, e.g., female voices 6; then add notation 01–09 from this table or notation 1–4 from this table, e.g., secular cantatas for female voice 648

    In building numbers, do not add by use of 0 or 1 (alone or in combination) more than twice, e.g., texts of rock protest songs for two singers 783.12421661592 (*not* 783.124216615920268)

        (Option: Add as many times as desired)

    Class comprehensive works in 783.1

.12   †Duets

.13   †Trios

.14   †Quartets

.15   †Quintets

.16   †Sextets

.17   †Septets

.18   †Octets

.19   †Nonets and larger combinations

†Add as instructed under 783.12–783.19

>   **783.2–783.9 Solo voices**

Add to each subdivision identified by ‡ as follows:

01–09   Standard subdivisions

Notation from Table 1 as modified under 780.1–780.9, e.g., performances 078

1   General principles and musical forms

11–17   General principles

Add to 1 the numbers following 781 in 781.1–781.7, e.g., rock music 166, rehearsing rock music 166144

18   Musical forms

Add to 18 the numbers following 784.18 in 784.182–784.189, e.g., da capo form 1822, composition in da capo form 182213

Class dramatic vocal forms in 782.1

For nondramatic vocal forms, see notation 2–4 from this table

2–4   Nondramatic vocal forms

Add the numbers following 782 in 782.2–782.4, e.g., secular cantatas 48

In building numbers, do not add by use of 0 or 1 (alone or in combination) more than twice, e.g., history of rock protest songs for high voice 783.3421661592 (*not* 783.342166159209)

(Option: Add as many times as desired)

Class comprehensive works in 783.2

.2   **‡Solo voice**

Class here comprehensive works on types of single voices

For specific types of single voices, see 783.3–783.9

>   **783.3–783.9 Specific types of single voices**

Class single voices in ensembles in 783.12–783.19; class comprehensive works in 783.2

.3   **‡High voice**

Class woman's soprano voice in 783.66; class child's soprano voice in 783.76; class man's treble voice and alto voice in 783.86; class tenor voice in 783.87

.4   **‡Middle voice**

Class woman's mezzo-soprano voice in 783.67; class child's mezzo-soprano voice in 783.77; class baritone voice in 783.88

.5   **‡Low voice**

Class woman's contralto voice in 783.68; class child's contralto voice in 783.78; class bass voice in 783.89

‡Add as instructed under 783.2–783.9

.6–.8   **Women's, children's, men's voices**

> Add to base number 783 the numbers following 782 in 782.6–782.8, e.g., bass voice 783.89

.9   ‡**Other types of voice**

.96   ‡Speaking voice

.97   ‡Sprechgesang

.98   ‡Whistle

.99   ‡Voice instruments

> Including didjeridu, mirliton (kazoo), roarers, voice disguisers (sympathetic instruments relying on the human voice for their sound production)

> **784–788   Instruments and their music**

> Add to each subdivision identified by * as follows:
> 01–09   Standard subdivisions
>> Notation from Table 1 as modified under 780.1–780.9, e.g., performances 078
>>> *See Manual at 784–788: Add table: 092*
> 1   General principles, musical forms, instruments
> 11–17   General principles
>> Add to 1 the numbers following 781 in 781.1–781.7, e.g., performance techniques 143
>>> *For techniques for playing instruments, see notation 193 from this table*
> 18–19   Musical forms and instruments
>> Add to 1 the numbers following 784.1 in 784.18–784.19, e.g., sonata form 183, techniques for playing instruments 193
>
> In building numbers, do not add by use of 0 or 1 (alone or in combination) more than twice, e.g., history of atonality in piano sonatas 786.21831267 (*not* 786.2183126709)
>> (Option: Add as many times as desired)
>
> Class comprehensive works in 784
>
> *See Manual at 784–788*

784   **Instruments and instrumental ensembles and their music**

> *For ensembles with only one instrument per part, see 785; for specific instruments and their music, see 786–788*
>
> *See also 787 for music for unspecified melody instrument*
>
> *See Manual at 784–788*

.01–.09   Standard subdivisions

> Notation from Table 1 as modified under 780.1–780.9, e.g., performances 784.078

.1   **General principles, musical forms, instruments**

‡Add as instructed under 783.2–783.9

.11–.17   General principles of instruments and instrumental ensembles and their music

> Add to base number 784.1 the numbers following 781 in 781.1–781.7, e.g., performance techniques 784.143

> *For techniques for playing instruments, see 784.193*

.18   †Musical forms

> 784.182–784.189 Specific musical forms

> Add to each subdivision identified by † as instructed under 781.2–781.8, e.g., composing waltzes 784.1884613

> Class comprehensive works in 784.18

.182   †General musical forms

.182 2   †Binary, ternary, da capo forms

> Subdivisions are added for a combination of two or more forms

.182 3   †Strophic form

.182 4   †Rondos

> Including sonata-rondos

.182 5   †Variations

> Including theme and variations

.182 6   †Paraphrase forms

> Including musical parody

.182 7   †Ground bass (Ostinato)

> Including chaconnes, passacaglias

> 784.183–784.189 Instrumental forms

> Except for concerto form, comprehensive works on an instrumental form regardless of the executant are classed here, e.g., symphony form 784.184. Individual works and works for a specific executant are classed with the executant, e.g., Camille Saint-Saëns' Symphony No. 3 (for full orchestra including an organ) 784.2184, Charles Marie Widor's Symphony No. 5 (for solo organ) 786.5184

> Class comprehensive works in 784.18

.183   †Sonata form and sonatas

> Subdivisions are added for either or both topics in heading

> Class sonata-rondos in 784.1824

.183 2   †Sonatinas

†Add as instructed under 781.2–781.8

.184	†Symphonies

Including sinfoniettas

Class symphonies, sinfoniettas for full orchestras in 784.2184

.184 3	†Symphonic poems

Class symphonic poems for full orchestras in 784.21843

.184 5	†Sinfonia concertantes
.185	†Suites and related forms

Including cassations

Subdivisions are added for a combination of two or more forms

.185 2	†Divertimentos
.185 4	†Partitas
.185 6	†Serenades
.185 8	†Suites
.186	†Concerto form

Including cadenzas, concertantes

Class comprehensive works on concertos in 784.23

.186 2	†Concertinos
.187	†Contrapuntal forms
.187 2	†Fugues
.187 4	†Inventions
.187 5	†Canzonas
.187 6	†Fancies and ricercares

Including innomines, tientos

Subdivisions are added for either or both topics in heading

See also 784.1894 for fantasias (an improvisatory form)

.187 8	†Canons
.188	†Dance forms
.188 2	†European dance forms

Including galliards, saltarellos

For dances of the classical suite, see 784.1883; for European dance forms of the 19th and later centuries, see 784.1884

.188 23	†Pavans

†Add as instructed under 781.2–781.8

.188 3	†Dances of the classical suite
	Including gavottes, sicilianas
.188 35	†Minuets
.188 4	†European dance forms of the 19th and later centuries
	Including galops, mazurkas, polonaises
.188 44	†Polkas
.188 46	†Waltzes
.188 5	†Asian dance forms
.188 6	†African dance forms
.188 7	†North American dance forms
	Including cakewalks, hoedowns, square dances
	For Latin-American dance forms, see 784.1888
.188 8	†Latin-American dance forms
	Including rumbas, sambas
.188 85	†Tangos
.188 9	†Dance forms of the Pacific Ocean islands and other parts of the world
.189	†Other instrumental forms
	Class here small-scale and character instrumental forms
.189 2	†Introductory forms
	Music preceding other music or other activities
.189 24	†Fanfares
.189 26	†Overtures
	Class here concert overtures
	Class overtures for full orchestras in 784.218926
.189 28	†Preludes
.189 3	†Intermediate forms
	Music for between or after other activities
	Including interludes, intermezzos, postludes, voluntaries
	Class voluntaries for organs in 786.51893
	For incidental music, see 781.552

†Add as instructed under 781.2–781.8

.189 4	†Forms of music of an improvisatory or virtuoso nature
	Including arabesques, fantasias, impromptus
	See also 784.1876 for fancies (a contrapuntal form)
.189 45	†Rhapsodies
.189 47	†Toccatas
.189 49	†Artistic études
.189 6	†Romantic and descriptive forms
	Including ballades, meditations, songs without words
.189 64	†Elegies
.189 66	†Nocturnes
.189 68	†Romances
.189 7	†Marches
.189 9	†Forms derived from vocal music
.189 92	†Forms derived from sacred music
	Including chorale preludes
	Class chorale preludes for organs in 786.518992
	For instrumental forms derived from liturgical forms, see 784.18993
.189 925	†Chorales
.189 93	†Instrumental forms derived from liturgical forms
.19	Instruments
	Class here acoustic form of instruments, electric form of instruments
	For specific instruments, see 786–788
.190 28	Auxiliary techniques and procedures
[.190 284]	Apparatus, equipment, materials
	Do not use; class in 784.19
[.190 287]	Testing and measurement
	Do not use; class in 784.1927
[.190 288]	Maintenance and repair
	Do not use; class in 784.1928
[.190 94–.190 99]	Specific continents, countries, localities in modern world
	Do not use; class in 784.194–784.199

†Add as instructed under 781.2–781.8

.192	Techniques and procedures for instruments themselves
	See also 784.193 for techniques for playing instruments
.192 2	Description and design
.192 3	Construction
	For construction by machine, see 681.8
.192 7	Testing, measurement, verification
.192 8	Maintenance, tuning, repair
	Including temperament
.193	†Techniques for playing instruments
	Class comprehensive works on performance techniques in 784.143
.193 2	†Breathing and resonance
.193 4	†Embouchure
	Including lipping, tonguing
.193 6	†Arm techniques
.193 62	†Forearm techniques
.193 64	†Wrist techniques
.193 65	†Hand techniques
	For left-hand techniques, see 784.19366; for right-hand techniques, see 784.19367
.193 66	†Left-hand techniques
.193 67	†Right-hand techniques
.193 68	†Finger techniques
	Including fingering, touch, vibrato
.193 69	†Bowing techniques
.193 8	†Leg techniques
	Including pedaling
.194–.199	Specific continents, countries, localities in modern world
	Add to base number 784.19 notation 4–9 from Table 2, e.g., instruments of Germany 784.1943

†Add as instructed under 781.2–781.8

.2   ***Full orchestra (Symphony orchestra)**

> Class here comprehensive works on orchestral combinations, music intended equally for orchestral or chamber performance

> *For other orchestral combinations, see 784.3–784.9; for chamber music, see 785*

.209 2   Biography

> Class here biographies of conductors known equally well for conducting operas and orchestral music

> Class biographies of conductors known primarily as opera conductors in 782.1092

.22   *Orchestra with vocal parts

.23   *Orchestra with one or more solo instruments

> Class here comprehensive works on concertos

> *For concerto form, see 784.186; for orchestra with more than one solo instrument, see 784.24; for orchestra with one solo instrument, see 784.25*

.24   *Orchestra with more than one solo instrument

> Including concerti grossi

.25   *Orchestra with one solo instrument

> Class here comprehensive works on solo concertos

> *For specific solo instruments, see 784.26–784.28*

.26–.28   Specific solo instruments with orchestra

> Add to base number 784.2 the numbers following 78 in 786–788, e.g., orchestra with solo piano 784.262, rehearsing orchestra with solo piano 784.262144, concertos for orchestra with solo piano 784.262186, fantasias for orchestra with solo piano 784.2621894

---

*Add as instructed under 784–788

> **784.3–784.9 Other orchestral and band combinations**

Add to each subdivision identified by † as follows:

01–09   Standard subdivisions

        Notation from Table 1 as modified under 780.1–780.9, e.g., performances 078

1   General principles, musical forms, instruments

11–17   General principles

        Add to 1 the numbers following 781 in 781.1–781.7, e.g., sacred music 17, rehearsing sacred music 17044

18–19   Musical forms and instruments

        Add to 1 the numbers following 784.1 in 784.18–784.19, e.g., waltz form 18846, bowing techniques 19369

2   Featured voices, instruments, ensembles

        Add to 2 the numbers following 78 in 782–788, e.g., flutes 2832

Class comprehensive works on orchestral and band combinations, on band in 784; class comprehensive works on orchestral combinations in 784.2

.3   **†Chamber orchestra**

        For chamber music, see 785

.4   **†Light orchestra**

        Class here salon orchestra

.44   †School orchestra

.46   †Orchestra with toy instruments

.48   †Dance orchestra (Dance band)

        Class here big bands

.6   **†Keyboard, mechanical, electronic, percussion bands**

.68   †Percussion band

        Class here rhythm band

.7   **†String orchestra**

.8   **†Wind band**

        Band consisting of woodwind instruments, brass instruments, or both

        For brass band, see 784.9

.83   †Marching band

.84   †Military band

.89   †Woodwind band

.9   **†Brass band**

†Add as instructed under 784.3–784.9

785   Ensembles with only one instrument per part

Class here chamber music

Class works for solo melody instrument with keyboard or other accompanying or collaborative instrument in 786–788

See Manual at 784–788

.001–.009   Standard subdivisions

Notation from Table 1 as modified under 780.1–780.9, e.g., performances of chamber music 785.0078

.01–.07   General principles of ensembles with only one instrument per part

Add to base number 785.0 the numbers following 781 in 781.1–781.7, e.g., performance techniques 785.043, jazz ensembles 785.065

For techniques for playing instruments, see 785.093

.08–.09   Musical forms and instruments

Add to base number 785.0 the numbers following 784.1 in 784.18–784.19, e.g., waltz form 785.08846, techniques for playing instruments 785.093

.1   Ensembles by size

These provisions, when applied throughout 785, refer to the number of instruments, except when percussion instruments are involved; in that case they refer to the number of performers

.12   *Duets

.13   *Trios

.14   *Quartets

.15   *Quintets

.16   *Sextets

.17   *Septets

.18   *Octets

.19   *Nonets and larger ensembles

*Add as instructed under 784–788

> **785.2–785.9 Specific kinds of ensembles**

Add to each subdivision identified by † as follows:

01–09   Standard subdivisions

         Notation from Table 1 as modified under 780.1–780.9, e.g., performances 078

1   General principles, musical forms, size of ensemble

11–17   General principles

         Add to 1 the numbers following 781 in 781.1–781.7, e.g., sacred music 17, conducting sacred music 17045

         Class instrumental techniques for mixed ensembles in 784.193.
Class instrumental techniques for a specific instrument with the instrument in 786–788, e.g., bowing techniques for violins 787.219369

18   Musical forms

         Add to 18 the numbers following 784.18 in 784.182–784.189, e.g., waltz form 18846

19   Size of ensemble

         Add to 19 the numbers following 785.1 in 785.12–785.19, e.g., octets 198

In building numbers, do not add by use of 0 or 1 (alone or in combination) more than twice, e.g., history of atonality in piano duets 785.621921267 (*not* 785.62192126709)

     (Option: Add as many times as desired)

Class comprehensive works in 785

> **785.2–785.5 Ensembles consisting of instruments from two or more instrument groups**

Class comprehensive works in 785

See also 785.6–785.9 for ensembles consisting of instruments from only one instrument group

.2   †**Ensembles with keyboard**

For ensembles without electrophones and with percussion and keyboard, see 785.3

.22   †Ensembles of woodwind, brass, strings, keyboard

.23   †Ensembles of woodwind, brass, keyboard

.24   †Ensembles of woodwind, strings, keyboard

.25   †Ensembles of brass, strings, keyboard

.26   †Ensembles of woodwind and keyboard

Three or more instruments

See also 788.2 for ensembles of one woodwind instrument and keyboard

†Add as instructed under 785.2–785.9

.27	†Ensembles of brass and keyboard
	Three or more instruments
	See also 788.9 for ensembles of one brass instrument and keyboard
.28	†Ensembles of strings and keyboard
	Three or more instruments
	See also 787 for ensembles of one stringed instrument and keyboard
.29	†Ensembles with electrophones, percussion, keyboard
.292	†Ensembles of woodwind, brass, strings, electrophones, percussion, keyboard
.293	†Ensembles of woodwind, brass, electrophones, percussion, keyboard
.294	†Ensembles of woodwind, strings, electrophones, percussion, keyboard
.295	†Ensembles of brass, strings, electrophones, percussion, keyboard
.296	†Ensembles of woodwind, electrophones, percussion, keyboard
.297	†Ensembles of brass, electrophones, percussion, keyboard
.298	†Ensembles of strings, electrophones, percussion, keyboard
.299	†Ensembles with electrophones and keyboard
.299 2	†Ensembles of woodwind, brass, strings, electrophones, keyboard
.299 3	†Ensembles of woodwind, brass, electrophones, keyboard
.299 4	†Ensembles of woodwind, strings, electrophones, keyboard
.299 5	†Ensembles of brass, strings, electrophones, keyboard
.299 6	†Ensembles of woodwind, electrophones, keyboard
.299 7	†Ensembles of brass, electrophones, keyboard
.299 8	†Ensembles of strings, electrophones, keyboard
.299 9	†Ensembles of electrophones and keyboard
	Two or more electrophones
	See also 786.7 for ensembles of one electrophone and keyboard
.3	**†Ensembles without electrophones and with percussion and keyboard**
.32	†Ensembles of woodwind, brass, strings, percussion, keyboard
.33	†Ensembles of woodwind, brass, percussion, keyboard
.34	†Ensembles of woodwind, strings, percussion, keyboard
.35	†Ensembles of brass, strings, percussion, keyboard
.36	†Ensembles of woodwind, percussion, keyboard

†Add as instructed under 785.2–785.9

.37	†Ensembles of brass, percussion, keyboard
.38	†Ensembles of strings, percussion, keyboard
.39	†Ensembles of keyboard and percussion

.4   †Ensembles without keyboard

For ensembles without keyboard and with percussion, see 785.5

.42	†Ensembles of woodwind, brass, strings
.43	†Ensembles of woodwind and brass (Wind ensembles)
.44	†Ensembles of woodwind and strings
.45	†Ensembles of brass and strings
.46	†Ensembles with electrophones
.462	†Ensembles of woodwind, brass, strings, electrophones
.463	†Ensembles of woodwind, brass, electrophones
.464	†Ensembles of woodwind, strings, electrophones
.465	†Ensembles of brass, strings, electrophones
.466	†Ensembles of woodwinds and electrophones
.467	†Ensembles of brass and electrophones
.468	†Ensembles of strings and electrophones

.5   †Ensembles without keyboard and with percussion

.52	†Ensembles of woodwind, brass, strings, percussion
.53	†Ensembles of woodwind, brass, percussion
.54	†Ensembles of woodwind, strings, percussion
.55	†Ensembles of brass, strings, percussion
.56	†Ensembles of woodwind and percussion
.57	†Ensembles of brass and percussion
.58	†Ensembles of strings and percussion
.59	†Ensembles with electrophones and percussion
.592	†Ensembles of woodwind, brass, strings, electrophones, percussion
.593	†Ensembles of woodwind, brass, electrophones, percussion
.594	†Ensembles of woodwind, strings, electrophones, percussion
.595	†Ensembles of brass, strings, electrophones, percussion
.596	†Ensembles of woodwind, electrophones, percussion
.597	†Ensembles of brass, electrophones, percussion

†Add as instructed under 785.2–785.9

.598	†Ensembles of strings, electrophones, percussion
.599	†Ensembles of electrophones and percussion

> **785.6–785.9 Ensembles consisting of instruments from only one instrument group**

Unless other instructions are given, when adding from 786–788 to indicate instrument or instruments, use the first higher number that includes all the instruments in the ensemble; prefer numbers for comprehensive works on kinds of instruments. Take into account only which kinds of instruments are in the ensemble, not whether one kind of instrument predominates. For example, a reed quintet consisting of an oboe, a clarinet, an alto saxophone, a bass clarinet, and a bassoon is classed in 785.84195 (*not* in 785.8195); a brass quintet consisting of two trumpets, a French horn, a trombone, and a tuba is classed in 785.9195 (*not* in 785.92195)

After adding from 786–788 to indicate the instrument or instruments only, do not follow the footnote to add as instructed under 784–788. Instead add further as instructed under 785.2–785.9. Do this for all ensembles, whether or not the participating instruments approximate the whole of the number. In the add table under 785.2–785.9, notation 19 is used to indicate size of ensemble. For example, 785.87194 means saxophone quartets, not saxophone instruments of Europe (the meaning that would result from following the footnote instruction under 788.7). The correct number for saxophone quartets of Europe is 785.87194094

Class comprehensive works in 785

See also 785.2–785.5 for ensembles consisting of instruments from two or more instrument groups

.6 †Keyboard, mechanical, aeolian, electrophone, percussion ensembles

Subdivisions are added for ensembles of keyboard, mechanical, aeolian, electrophone, percussion instruments together; for ensembles of keyboard instruments alone

.62–.65 Specific ensembles of keyboard instruments

Add to base number 785.6 the numbers following 786 in 786.2–786.5 for the instrument or instruments only, e.g., music for piano ensembles 785.62; then add further as instructed under 785.2–785.9, e.g., music for three pianos 785.62193

Notation 19 from table under 785.2–785.9 for size of ensemble can mean either number of instruments or, when only one instrument is used, number of performers. For example, 785.62192 can mean either music for two pianos or music for piano (four hands)

.66 †Ensembles of mechanical and aeolian instruments

Subdivisions are added for ensembles of mechanical and aeolian instruments together, for ensembles of mechanical instruments alone

†Add as instructed under 785.2–785.9

.664–.668   Specific ensembles of mechanical instruments

> Add to base number 785.66 the numbers following 786.6 in 786.64–786.68 for the instrument or instruments only, e.g., music for carillon ensembles 785.664

.669   †Aeolian ensembles

.67   †Electrophone ensembles

> *For ensembles of a specific kind or group of electrically amplified or modified standard instruments, see the instrument or group of instruments, e.g., electric guitar ensembles 785.787*
>
> *See also 786.7 for electronic music for one performer*

.673–.676   Specific ensembles of electrophone instruments

> Add to base number 785.67 the numbers following 786.7 in 786.73–786.76 for the instrument or instruments only, e.g., music for synthesizer ensembles 785.674; then add further as instructed under 785.2–785.9, e.g., sextets for synthesizers 785.674196

.68   †Percussion ensembles

> Class here ensembles for more than one performer; see note under 785.1
>
> *See also 786.8 for percussion music for one performer*

.7   †String ensembles

> Class here bowed string ensembles, string ensembles consisting of two or more kinds of instruments from the violin family

.719 4   Quartets

> Number built according to instructions under 785.2–785.9
>
> Class here string quartets

.72–.79   Specific ensembles of stringed instruments

> Add to base number 785.7 the numbers following 787 in 787.2–787.9 for the instrument or instruments only, e.g., music for guitar ensembles 785.787; then add further as instructed under 785.2–785.9, e.g., duets for guitars 785.787192; however, for string ensembles consisting of two or more kinds of instruments from the violin family, see 785.7

.8   †Woodwind ensembles

.83–.88   Specific ensembles of woodwind instruments

> Add to base number 785.8 the numbers following 788 in 788.3–788.8 for the instrument or instruments only, e.g., music for saxophone ensembles 785.87; then add further as instructed under 785.2–785.9, e.g., quartets for saxophones 785.87194

.9   †Brass ensembles

†Add as instructed under 785.2–785.9

.92–.99   Specific ensembles of brass instruments

> Add to base number 785.9 the numbers following 788.9 in 788.92–788.99 for the instrument or instruments only, e.g., music for trombone ensembles 785.93; then add further as instructed under 785.2–785.9, e.g., quartets for trombones 785.93194

> ## 786–788 Specific instruments and their music

> Class here music for solo instrument, music for solo melody instrument with keyboard or other accompanying or collaborative instrument; acoustic form of instruments, electric form of instruments

> Unless the forerunner of a modern instrument has its own notation, class it with the modern instrument. For example, the shawm, a forerunner of the oboe and an instrument without its own number, is classed with the oboe in 788.52; however, the vihuela, the forerunner of the guitar, is classed in 787.86 (its own number), not with the guitar in 787.87

> Class chamber music in 785; class comprehensive works in 784

> *For voice instruments, see 783.99*

786   *Keyboard, mechanical, electrophonic, percussion instruments

> Class here comprehensive works on keyboard instruments, on keyboard stringed instruments; music for unspecified keyboard instrument

> *See Manual at 784–788*

> ### 786.2–786.5 Keyboard instruments

> Class mechanical keyboard instruments in 786.66; class keyboard idiophones in 786.83; class comprehensive works in 786. Class music for more than one performer on one keyboard instrument as an ensemble with the ensemble in 785.62–785.65, e.g., piano (four hands) 785.62192

> ### 786.2–786.4 Keyboard stringed instruments

> Class comprehensive works in 786

.2   ***Pianos**

.28   ***Prepared pianos**

.3   ***Clavichords**

.4   ***Harpsichords**

> Class here spinets, virginals

---

*Add as instructed under 784–788

.5   ***Organs**

> Class here keyboard wind instruments
>
> Class concertinas in 788.84; class accordions in 788.86

.55   ***Reed organs and regals**

> Variant names for reed organs: American organs, cabinet organs, harmoniums
>
> Subdivisions are added for either or both topics in heading

.59   ***Electronic organs**

> Class here comprehensive works on keyboard electrophones
>
> Class a keyboard instrument whose sound is generated by conventional means, even though amplified or modified electronically, with the instrument, e.g., electric piano 786.2
>
> *See also 786.74 for synthesizers*

.6   ***Mechanical and aeolian instruments**

> Subdivisions are added for mechanical and aeolian instruments together, for mechanical instruments alone

>   _____

\>   786.64–786.68   Mechanical instruments

> Class comprehensive works in 786.6

.64   ***Mechanical struck idiophones**

> Including carillons, mechanized bells
>
> Class here comprehensive works on mechanical idiophones
>
> Class comprehensive works on idiophones in 786.82
>
> *For mechanical plucked idiophones, see 786.65*

.65   ***Mechanical plucked idiophones**

> Including music boxes, symphonions
>
> Class comprehensive works on mechanical idiophones in 786.64

.66   ***Mechanical keyboard instruments**

> Mechanical instruments with attached functional keyboard
>
> Including player pianos (pianolas)
>
> Class mechanical wind keyboard instruments in 786.68

.67   ***Mechanical stringed instruments**

> Class mechanical stringed keyboard instruments in 786.66

*Add as instructed under 784–788

.68   *Mechanical wind instruments

    Including fair organs

.69   *Aeolian instruments

    Instruments activated by the blowing of the wind

.7   *Electronic instruments (Electrophones)

    Class here electronic music in the sense of music with a focus on electronically produced or manipulated sounds; comprehensive works on electronic music

    Class keyboard electrophones in 786.59. Class a specific electrically amplified or modified acoustic instrument with the instrument, e.g., electric guitar 787.87

    For electronica, see 781.648

.73   *Monophonic electrophones

    Electronic sound producers capable of producing only one pitch at a time

    Including ondes martenot, theremins

.74   *Synthesizers

    For tapes, see 786.75; for computers, see 786.76

.75   Tapes

    Class here musique concrète (concrete music)

.76   Computers

    See also 781.34 for using computers to compose music

.8   *Percussion instruments

    For drums, see 786.92–786.98; for struck stringed instruments, see 787.7

.82   *Idiophones (Vibrating sonorous solids)

    Class here comprehensive works on percussion instruments of definite pitch

    Class percussion instruments of indefinite pitch in 786.88

        For mechanical idiophones, see 786.64; for keyboard idiophones, see 786.83; for set idiophones, see 786.84–786.87; for single idiophones, see 786.88

.83   *Keyboard idiophones

    Class here celestas

    Class comprehensive works on idiophones in 786.82

>   786.84–786.87 Set idiophones

    Class comprehensive works on idiophones in 786.82; class comprehensive works on set idiophones in 786.84

*Add as instructed under 784–788

.84   *Percussed idiophones

> Sonorous solids struck by or against nonsonorous objects, e.g., sticks struck on ground

> Class here comprehensive works on set idiophones (similar sonorous solids combined to form one instrument)

>> *For plucked idiophones, see 786.85; for friction idiophones, see 786.86; for concussion idiophones, see 786.87*

.842–.848   Sonorous solids of specific shapes

> Add to base number 786.84 the numbers following 786.884 in 786.8842–786.8848, e.g., bar idiophones 786.843, performances on bar idiophones 786.843078

.85   *Plucked idiophones

> Elastic bars or rods, usually of metal, fixed at one end and vibrated by plucking the free end

> Including sanzas (thumb pianos)

> Class comprehensive works on set idiophones in 786.84

.86   *Friction idiophones

> Objects rubbed to produce sounds of definite pitch

> Class comprehensive works on set idiophones in 786.84

.862–.868   Sonorous solids of specific shapes

> Add to base number 786.86 the numbers following 786.884 in 786.8842–786.8848, e.g., vessels 786.866, rehearsing on vessels 786.866144

.87   *Concussion idiophones

> Two or more similar sonorous objects struck together to make both vibrate

> Class comprehensive works on set idiophones in 786.84

.872–.878   Sonorous objects of specific shapes

> Add to base number 786.87 the numbers following 786.884 in 786.8842–786.8848, e.g., blocks 786.873, rehearsing playing of blocks 786.873144

.88   *Single idiophones

> Idiophones consisting of a single sonorous object

> Class here comprehensive works on percussion instruments of indefinite pitch

> Class comprehensive works on idiophones in 786.82

>> *For a specific percussion instrument of indefinite pitch not provided for here, see the instrument, e.g., cymbals 786.873*

*Add as instructed under 784–788

.884	*Percussed idiophones
.884 2	*Sticks and rods

        Including triangles

        Subdivisions are added for either or both topics in heading

.884 3	*Bars, plates, blocks

        Including anvils, gongs

        Subdivisions are added for any or all topics in heading

.884 4	*Troughs
.884 5	*Tubes
.884 6	*Vessels

        For bells, see 786.8848

.884 8	*Bells

        Class comprehensive works on vessels in 786.8846

.884 85	*Hand bells
.885	*Rattled idiophones

        Including maracas, sistrums

.886	*Scraped idiophones

        Idiophones consisting of two objects, a notched one being scraped by the other to create vibrations in one or the other

        Including football rattles, washboards

.887	*Plucked idiophones

        Including jew's harps

.888	*Friction idiophones

        Including musical saws

.9   ***Drums and devices used for percussive effects**

        Subdivisions are added for drums and devices used for percussive effects together, for drums alone

---

>   786.92–786.98 Drums (Membranophones, Vibrating stretched membranes)

        Class comprehensive works on percussion instruments in 786.8; class comprehensive works on drums in 786.9

.92	*Struck drums

        For kettle-shaped drums, see 786.93; for tubular drums, see 786.94; for frame-shaped drums, see 786.95

*Add as instructed under 784–788

.93   *Kettle-shaped drums

             Including timpani (kettledrums), nakers (naqara), tabla

             Class comprehensive works on struck drums in 786.92

.94   *Tubular drums

             Including snare drums (side drums)

             Class comprehensive works on struck drums in 786.92

.95   *Frame-shaped drums

             Drums with depth of body not exceeding radius of membrane

             Including bass drums, tambourines

             Class comprehensive works on struck drums in 786.92

.96   *Rattle drums

             Drums whose membrane or membranes are struck by pellets or pendants

.97   *Plucked drums

             Drums each with a string that when plucked transmits a vibration to the membrane through which the string passes

.98   *Friction drums

             Drums whose membrane is made to vibrate by being rubbed either directly or by an attached stick or cord

             Including quicas, rommelpots

.99   *Devices used for percussion effects

             Including motor horns, popguns, sirens, whips

787   *Stringed instruments (Chordophones)

Class here bowed string instruments, music for unspecified melody instrument, comprehensive works on the lute family (instruments whose strings run from the resonating belly to the neck)

Class keyboard stringed instruments in 786; class mechanical stringed instruments in 786.67; class violin family in 787.2; class lyres in 787.78; class plectral lute family in 787.8

See Manual at 784–788

.2   *Violins

             Class here comprehensive works on violin family

             Class comprehensive works on lute family in 787

             For violas, see 787.3; for cellos, see 787.4; for double basses, see 787.5

.3   *Violas

             Class comprehensive works on violin family in 787.2

*Add as instructed under 784–788

.4   ***Cellos (Violoncellos)**

> Class comprehensive works on violin family in 787.2

.5   ***Double basses**

> Class comprehensive works on violin family in 787.2; class comprehensive works on viols and related instruments in 787.6

.6   ***Viols and related instruments**

> Subdivisions are added for viols and related instruments together, for viols alone
>
> *For double basses, see 787.5*

.62   *Descant viols

.63   *Treble viols

.64   *Tenor viols

.65   *Bass viols (Viola da gambas)

.66   *Viola d'amores

.69   *Hurdy-gurdies (Vielles)

.7   ***Plectral instruments**

> Class here zithers, comprehensive works on struck stringed instruments
>
> Class comprehensive works on percussion instruments in 786.8
>
> *For plectral lute family, see 787.8; for harps and musical bows, see 787.9*

> 787.72–787.75   Zithers

> Class comprehensive works in 787.7

.72   *Stick, tube, trough zithers

> Subdivisions are added for any or all topics in heading

.73   *Frame, ground, harp, raft zithers

> Subdivisions are added for any or all topics in heading

.74   *Board zithers

> Including cimbaloms, dulcimers, santirs, yang ch'ins
>
> Class here struck board zithers
>
> *For plucked board zithers, see 787.75*

*Add as instructed under 784–788

.75   *Plucked board zithers

> Including Appalachian dulcimers, autoharps, concert zithers, psalteries, Tyrolean zithers
>
> Class comprehensive works on board zithers in 787.74

.78   *Lyres

> Class comprehensive works on lute family in 787

.8   *Plectral lute family

> Class here long-necked, short-necked lutes
>
> Class comprehensive works on lute family in 787; class comprehensive works on struck stringed instruments in 787.7

.82   *Round-backed lute family

> Including sitars, tamburas
>
> > *For lutes, see 787.83; for mandolins, see 787.84*

.83   *Lutes

> Class comprehensive works on round-backed lute family in 787.82

.84   *Mandolins

> Class comprehensive works on round-backed lute family in 787.82

.85   *Flat-backed lute family

> Including biwas, citterns, shamisens
>
> > *For vihuelas, see 787.86; for guitars, see 787.87; for banjos, see 787.88; for ukuleles, see 787.89*

.86   *Vihuelas

> Class comprehensive works on flat-backed lute family in 787.85

.87   *Guitars

> Class comprehensive works on flat-backed lute family in 787.85

.875   *Balalaikas

.88   *Banjos

> Class comprehensive works on flat-backed lute family in 787.85

.89   *Ukuleles

> Class comprehensive works on flat-backed lute family in 787.85

.9   *Harps and musical bows

> Subdivisions are added for harps and musical bows together, for harps alone
>
> Class comprehensive works on struck stringed instruments in 787.7

---

*Add as instructed under 784–788

.92   *Musical bows

>Stringed instruments each with one or more strings stretched across a single flexible string bearer

>Class pluriarcs in 787.93

>>*See also 787.19 for the bow of bowed instruments*

.93   *Pluriarcs (Compound musical bows)

>Stringed instruments with strings stretched across several string bearers

---

> 787.94–787.98 Harps

>Class comprehensive works in 787.9

.94   *Bow harps (Arched harps) and angle harps

>Harps with neck forming an arch with the resonator

>Subdivisions are added for either or both topics in heading

.95   *Frame harps

>Harps with pillar joining end of neck to resonator

>Including Celtic harps, orchestral harps

.98   *Bridge harps (Harp-lutes)

>Lute-bodied harps with strings that are perpendicular to body of the harp and that pass through a bridge

>Including koras

788   *Wind instruments (Aerophones)

>Class keyboard wind instruments in 786.5; class mechanical wind instruments in 786.68

>>*See Manual at 784–788*

.2   ***Woodwind instruments and free aerophones**

>Subdivisions are added for woodwind instruments and free aerophones together, for woodwind instruments alone

>>*For specific woodwind instruments, see 788.3–788.8*

.29   *Free aerophones

>Aerophones in which the airstream is not directed into or through a cavity or tube but directly into the outer air, or the air remains static and the instrument when moved vibrates through friction with the air

>Including bull-roarers

>Class free aerophones used for percussion effects in 786.99

---

*Add as instructed under 784–788

> ### 788.3–788.8 Specific woodwind instruments

Class comprehensive works in 788.2

.3   ***Flute family**

Including nose flutes

.32   *Transverse flutes (Side-blown flutes)

Variant name: flutes

For piccolos and fifes, see 788.33; for bass flutes, see 788.34

.33   *Piccolos and fifes

Subdivisions are added for either or both topics in heading

Class comprehensive works on transverse flute family in 788.32

.34   *Bass flutes

Class comprehensive works on transverse flute family in 788.32

.35   *Duct, end-blown, notched flutes

Including flageolets, penny whistles, shakuhachis

Subdivisions are added for any or all topics in heading

For recorders, see 788.36

.36   *Recorders

Class comprehensive works on duct flutes in 788.35

.363   *Sopranino recorders

.364   *Descant recorders (Soprano recorders)

.365   *Treble recorders (Alto recorders)

.366   *Tenor recorders

.367   *Bass recorders

.37   *Multiple flutes

Several flutes formed into one instrument

Class here pan pipes

.38   *Vessel flutes

Including ocarinas

.4   ***Reed instruments**

For double-reed instruments, see 788.5; for single-reed instruments, see 788.6; for free reeds, see 788.8

*Add as instructed under 784–788

.49   *Bagpipes

> Including Northumbrian, uilleann (union) pipes
>
> Class here single-reed and double-reed bagpipes
>
> Class comprehensive works on double-reed instruments in 788.5; class comprehensive works on single-reed instruments in 788.6

.5   ***Double-reed instruments**

> Including crumhorns, racketts
>
> Class comprehensive works on reed instruments in 788.4
>
> *For bagpipes, see 788.49*

.52   *Oboes

.53   *Cors anglais (English horns)

.58   *Bassoons

> *For double bassoons, see 788.59*

.59   *Double bassoons (Contrabassoons)

> Class comprehensive works on bassoons in 788.58

.6   ***Single-reed instruments**

> Class comprehensive works on reed instruments in 788.4
>
> *For bagpipes, see 788.49; for saxophones, see 788.7*

.62   *Clarinets

> *For bass clarinets, see 788.65*

.65   *Bass clarinets

> Class comprehensive works on clarinets in 788.62

.7   ***Saxophones**

> Class comprehensive works on single-reed instruments in 788.6

.72   *Soprano saxophones

.73   *Alto saxophones

.74   *Tenor saxophones

.75   *Bass saxophones

.8   ***Free reeds**

> Instruments consisting of sets of individual free reeds
>
> Class comprehensive works on reed instruments in 788.4

*Add as instructed under 784–788

.82   *Mouth organs

        Including shengs

        Class here harmonicas

.84   *Concertinas

        Including bandoneons

.86   *Accordions

.863   *Button accordions

        Class here melodeons

.865   *Piano accordions

.9   ***Brass instruments (Lip-reed instruments)**

.92   *Trumpets

.93   *Trombones

.94   *French horns (Horns)

        See also 788.53 for English horns

.95   *Bugles

.96   *Cornets

.97   *Flugelhorns (Saxhorns)

.974   *Tenor horns

        Including B-flat horns (also called baritones in United Kingdom and Germany), E-flat horns (also called alto horns in North America and France)

.975   *Euphoniums and baritones (American)

        Subdivisions are added for either or both topics in heading

.98   *Tubas

.99   *Other brass instruments

        Including cornetts, ophicleides, serpents

*Add as instructed under 784–788

(789)   Composers and traditions of music

(Optional number and subdivisions; prefer 780 for music as a whole; prefer 781–788 for principles, forms, ensembles, voices, instruments)

(Option A: Arrange treatises about all composers at 789 plus an alphabeting mark; then to the result add further as follows:

(Option A add table
      01–09   Music as a whole
             Add the numbers following 78 in 780.1–780.9, e.g., manuscripts 0262
      1–8   Principles, forms, ensembles, voices, instruments
             Add the numbers following 78 in 781–788, e.g., vocal music 2

(Option B: Use 789 and its subdivisions for traditions of music

(Option C: Use 789 and its subdivisions for recordings of music

(If option A is used with either option B or C, class comprehensive works on traditions of music in 789.1)

Unless other instructions are given, class a subject with aspects in two or more subdivisions of 789 in the number coming last, e.g., Spanish folk music for springtime 789.261015242 (*not* 789.2015242)

(.1)   †General principles of traditions of music

Add to base number 789.1 the numbers following 781 in 781.1–781.5, e.g., treatment of springtime music in various traditions 789.15242

(If Option A is used with either Option B or C, class here comprehensive works on traditions of music)

(.2)   †Folk music

Music originating within and associated with an ethnic or national group

Class folk rock in 789.6172. Class a specific style of music provided for in 789.4–789.6 with the style, e.g., reggae 789.46, Afro-Cuban jazz 789.572687291

(.200 1–.200 7)   †Standard subdivisions

Notation from Table 1 as modified under 780.1–780.7, e.g., performances of folk music 789.20078

(.200 8)   †Groups of people

(.200 89)   †Ethnic and national groups

(.200 891–.200 899)   †Specific ethnic and national groups

Do not use for folk music of specific ethnic and national groups; class in 789.21–789.29

(.200 9)   †History, geographic treatment, biography

†(Optional number; prefer 781–788)

(.200 901–.200 903)	†Historical periods to 1900

Add to base number 789.20090 the numbers following 780.90 in 780.901–780.903, e.g., folk music of the Renaissance 789.2009031

(.200 904–.200 905)	†1900–2099

Add to base number 789.20090 the numbers following —090 in notation 0904–0905 from Table 1, e.g., folk music of the 1970s 781.62009047

(.200 91–.200 99)	†Geographic treatment and biography

For geographic treatment of folk music of specific ethnic and national groups, see 789.21–789.29

(.201)	†General principles, influence of other traditions, musical forms

(.201 1–.201 5)	†General principles

Add to base number 789.201 the numbers following 781 in 781.1–781.5, e.g., folk music for springtime 789.2015242, rhythm in folk music for springtime 789.20152421224

(.201 6)	†Influence of other traditions of music

Add to base number 789.2016 the numbers following 789 in 789.3–789.9, e.g., influence of jazz on folk music 789.20165, performances of folk music influenced by jazz 789.20165078

(.201 8)	†Musical forms

Add to base number 789.2018 the numbers following 784.18 in 784.182–784.189, e.g., march form in folk music 789.201897

(.202–.208)	†Voices, instruments, ensembles

Add to base number 789.20 the numbers following 78 in 782–788, e.g., folk songs for women singers 789.202642

---

†(Optional number; prefer 781–788)

(.21–.29)   †Folk music of specific ethnic and national groups

> Add to base number 789.2 notation 1–9 from Table 5, e.g., Spanish folk
> music 789.261; then add further as follows:
>
> (001–008)   Standard subdivisions
>> Notation from Table 1 as modified under 780.1–780.9,
>> e.g., performances of Spanish folk music 789.2610078
>
> (009)   History, geographic treatment, biography
> 00901–00903   Historical periods to 1900
>> Add to 0090 the numbers following 780.90 in
>> 780.901–780.903, e.g., Spanish folk music of the
>> Renaissance 789.261009031
> 00904–00905   1900–2099
>> Add to 0090 the numbers following —090 in
>> notation 0904–0905 from Table 1, e.g., Spanish folk
>> music of the 1970s 789.261009047
> [0093–0099]   Specific continents, countries, localities
>> Do not use; class in notation 03–09 from this table
> (01)   General principles, influence of other traditions of music,
>   musical forms
> 011–015   General principles
>> Add to 01 the numbers following 781 in 781.1–781.5, e.g.,
>> Spanish folk music for springtime 789.261015242, rhythm
>> in Spanish folk music for springtime 789.2610152421224
> 016   Influence of other traditions of music
>> Add to 016 the numbers following 789 in 789.3–789.9,
>> e.g., influence of jazz on Spanish folk music 789.2610165,
>> performances of Spanish folk music influenced by jazz
>> 789.2610165078
> 018   Musical forms
>> Add to 018 the numbers following 784.18 in
>> 784.182–784.189, e.g., march form in Spanish folk music
>> 789.26101897
> (02)   Voices, instruments, ensembles
>> Add to 02 the numbers following 78 in 782–788, e.g.,
>> Spanish folk music for the guitar 789.26102787
> (03–09)   Specific continents, countries, localities
>> Add to 0 notation 3–9 from Table 2, e.g., Spanish folk music
>> in New York City 789.26107471

---

†(Optional number; prefer 781–788)

>   **(789.3–789.9) Other traditions of music**

Add to each subdivision identified by * as follows:
(001–008)	Standard subdivisions
	Notation from Table 1 as modified under 780.1–780.8, e.g., performance 0078
(009)	History, geographic treatment, biography
00901–00903	Historical periods to 1900
	Add to 0090 the numbers following 780.90 in 780.901–780.903, e.g., music of the Renaissance 009031
00904–00905	1900–2099
	Add to 0090 the numbers following —090 in notation 0904–0905 from Table 1, e.g., music of the 1970s 009047
(01)	General principles, influence of other traditions of music, hybrid styles, musical forms
011–015	General principles
	Add to 01 the numbers following 781 in 781.1–781.5, e.g., springtime music 015242, melody in springtime music 015242124
016	Influence of other traditions of music
	Add to 016 the numbers following 789 in 789.2–789.9, e.g., influence of folk music 0162, performances of music influenced by folk music 0162078
	See also 017 for hybrid styles
017	Hybrid styles
	Fusion of two or more styles from different traditions of music to create a new style
	Add to 017 the numbers following 789 in 789.2–789.9, e.g., fusion with folk music 0172, folk rock 789.60172
	See also 016 for influence of other traditions of music
018	Musical forms
	Add to 018 the numbers following 784.18 in 784.182–784.189, e.g., march form 01897
(1)	Voices, instruments, ensembles
	Add to 1 the numbers following 78 in 782–788, e.g., guitar music 1787

Class comprehensive works in 789

(.3)   †***Popular music**

Class popular music originating within and associated with an ethnic or national group in 789.2

For western popular music, see 789.4

(.4)   †***Western popular music**

Class western popular music originating within and associated with an ethnic or national group in 789.2; class country music in 789.42

For jazz, see 789.5; for rock, see 789.6

---

*Add as instructed under 789.3–789.9
†(Optional number; prefer 781–788)

(.42)   †*Country music

> Class here bluegrass music; specific country music styles

(.43)   †*Blues

> Class here traditional rhythm and blues; specific blues styles

> Class comprehensive works on rhythm and blues in 789.44

(.44)   †*Soul

> Class here R&B; specific soul styles; comprehensive works on rhythm and blues

> *For traditional rhythm and blues, see 789.43*

(.45)   †*Ragtime

(.46)   †*Reggae

> Class here specific reggae styles

(.48)   †*Electronica

> Class here specific electronica styles

(.49)   †*Rap

> Class here specific rap styles

(.5)   †*Jazz

[.501 7]   Hybrid styles

> Do not use; class in 789.57

(.52)   †*Early jazz

> Class here origins of jazz

(.53)   †*Traditional jazz

> Including New Orleans, Dixieland, Southwest and Kansas City, Harlem, white New York styles; Chicago breakdown

(.54)   †*Mainstream jazz

> Including swing

(.55)   †*Modern jazz

> Including bop (bebop), hard bop, cool jazz, progressive jazz

> *For avant-garde jazz, see 789.56*

(.56)   †*Avant-garde jazz

(.57)   †Hybrid styles

> Add to 789.57 the numbers following 781.6 in 781.62–781.69, e.g., Afro-Cuban 789.572687291, Indo-jazz 789.57291411

---

*Add as instructed under 789.3–789.9
†(Optional number; prefer 781–788)

(.6)   †*Rock (Rock'n' roll)

> Class here specific rock styles

(.7)   †Sacred music

(.700 1–.700 9)   †Standard subdivisions

> Notation from Table 1 as modified under 780.1–780.9, e.g., performances of sacred music 789.70078

(.701)   †General principles, influence of other traditions of music, musical forms

> Add to base number 789.701 the numbers following 01 in notation 011–018 from table under 789.3–789.9, e.g., influence of folk music 789.70162

(.702)   †Voices, instruments, ensembles

> Add to base number 789.702 the numbers following 78 in 782–788, e.g., sacred music for the guitar 789.702787

(.71)   †*Christian sacred music

> *For music of Christian church year, see 789.72*

(.72)   †*Music of Christian church year

(.722–.729)   †Sacred music of specific parts of Christian church year

> Add to base number 789.72 the numbers following 781.72 in 781.722–781.729, e.g., Christmas music 789.723; then add further as instructed under 789.3–789.9, e.g., Christmas music for the guitar 789.7231787

(.73)   †*Sacred music of classical (Greek and Roman) and Germanic religions

(.74–.79)   †Sacred music of other specific religions

> Add to base number 789.7 the numbers following 29 in 294–299, e.g., Jewish sacred music 789.76; then add further as instructed under 789.3–789.9, e.g., Jewish sacred music for the guitar 789.761787

(.8)   †*Western art music (Classical music)

> Limited to classical music as a tradition in contrast to other traditions

> Class here comprehensive works on traditions of art music

> *For nonwestern art music, see 789.9*

(.801 75)   †Hybrid styles

> Number built according to instructions under 789.3–789.9

> Class here third stream

(.9)   †*Nonwestern art music

---

*Add as instructed under 789.3–789.9
†(Optional number; prefer 781–788)

790 Recreational and performing arts

> Class here government policy on recreation; interdisciplinary works on recreation

> *For sociology of recreation, see 306.48; for music, see 780*

.01–.05 Standard subdivisions of recreation

.06 Organizations and management of recreation; recreation centers

> Notation 06 from Table 1 as modified below

.068 Recreation centers

> Do not use for management of recreation; class in 790.069

> Indoor and outdoor

> Including parks and community centers as recreation centers

> Add to base number 790.068 notation 1–9 from Table 2, e.g., recreation centers of California 790.068794

.069 Management of recreation

> Add to base number 790.069 the numbers following —068 in notation 0681–0688 from Table 1, e.g., personnel management 790.0693

.07 Education, research, related topics of recreation

.08 Recreation for groups of people

> Do not use for activities and programs for specific groups of people; class in 790.19

.09 History, geographic treatment, biography of recreation

.1 General kinds of recreational activities

> Class here leisure

> *For a specific activity, see the activity, e.g., paper cutting and folding 736.98, piano playing 786.2143, outdoor sports 796*

[.101–.109] Standard subdivisions

> Do not use; class in 790.01–790.09

.13 Activities generally engaged in by individuals

> Class here interdisciplinary works on hobbies

> *For a hobby, see the subject of the hobby, plus notation 023 from Table 1, e.g., knitting as a hobby 746.432023*

.132 Collecting

> Class collecting a specific kind of object with the object, plus notation 075 from Table 1, e.g., coin collecting 737.4075, sports cards 796.075

.133	Play with toys

Including electric trains

For play with a specific toy not provided for here, see the toy, e.g., flying model airplanes 796.154

.134	Participation in contests

See also 659.17 for advertising by means of contests

.138	Passive activities (Spectator activities)

Including listening, reading, watching

.15	Activities generally engaged in by groups
.18	Travel and tourism

Standard subdivisions are added for either or both topics in heading

.19	Activities and programs for specific groups of people

Class activities generally engaged in by individuals in 790.13; class activities generally engaged in by groups other than families in 790.15

.191	Activities and programs for families
.192	Activities and programs by age level

Class activities for specific sexes regardless of age in 790.194; class activities for people with physical illnesses, people with disabilities regardless of age in 790.196

.192 2	Children
.192 6	Adults aged 65 and over
.194	Activities and programs for groups by sex

Class activities for people with physical illnesses, people with disabilities regardless of sex in 790.196

.196	Activities and programs for people with physical illnesses, people with disabilities

See also 615.85153 for recreational therapy

.2	**The performing arts in general**

Use for works that treat athletic and outdoor sports and games as well as public performances

Class comprehensive works on public performances in 791; class comprehensive works on athletic and outdoor sports and games in 796

For sociology of performing arts, see 306.484. For a specific performing art, see the art, e.g., symphony orchestra performances 784.2078, motion pictures 791.43; for a specific sport, see the sport, e.g., basketball 796.323, swimming 797.21

See Manual at 780.079 vs. 790.2

791   Public performances

Other than sport and game performances

Class here performances at fairs

> *For musical performances other than stage presentations, see 780; for stage presentations, see 792; for musical stage presentations, see 792.5; for magic, see 793.8; for speech as a type of performance, see 808.54*

> *See also 793–796 for sport and game performances*

.06   Organizations and management; amusement parks

Notation 06 from Table 1 as modified below

.068   Amusement parks

Do not use for management; class in 791.069

Add to base number 791.068 notation 1–9 from Table 2, e.g., amusement parks of United States 791.06873

.069   Management

Add to base number 791.069 the numbers following —068 in notation 0681–0688 from Table 1, e.g., marketing 791.0698

.09   History, geographic treatment, biography

.092   Biography

> *See Manual at 780.92 and 791.092*

.1   **Traveling shows**

Including medicine shows

> *For circuses, see 791.3; for showboats, see 792.022*

.12   Minstrel shows and skits

> *See also 792.7 for vaudeville*

.3   **Circuses**

Class here amateur circuses

.32   Animal performances

.33   Clowns

.34   Acrobatics and trapeze work

.35   Freaks and sideshows

.38   Parades

.4	**Motion pictures, radio, television, podcasting**

> Unless other instructions are given, class a subject with aspects in two or more subdivisions of 791.4 in the number coming last, e.g., critical appraisal of a specific film 791.4372 (*not* 791.433)

> *See also 302.234 for social aspects of motion pictures, radio, television, and podcasting as mass media*

> *See Manual at 363.31 vs. 303.376, 791.4; also at 384.54, 384.55, 384.8 vs. 791.4*

.43	**Motion pictures**

> Regardless of distribution medium or method

> Class here direct-to-video and direct-to-DVD releases of motion pictures; dramatic films, entertainment films; films developed originally for Internet transmission; made-for-television movies; video recordings of motion pictures; comprehensive works on dramatic, entertainment, documentary, educational, news films

> Class photographic aspects of motion pictures in 777

> *For documentary, educational, news films, see 070.18*

> *See also 384.8 for communication aspects of motion pictures*

> *See Manual at 780.92 and 791.092; also at 791.43 vs. 791.45; also at 791.43, 791.45 vs. 777*

.430 1–.430 2	**Standard subdivisions**

> Notation from Table 1 as modified under 792.01–792.02, e.g., makeup for motion pictures 791.43027; however, for programming (scheduling), see 384.84; for types of presentation, see 791.433

.430 9	**History, geographic treatment, biography**

> Class here description, critical appraisal of specific companies and studios

> *For description, critical appraisal of specific films, see 791.437*

.430 92	**Biography**

> Do not use for people associated with only one aspect of motion pictures; class in 791.4302, e.g., actors 791.43028092

.433	**Types of presentation**

> Including home and amateur films

> Class a specific genre or type of film with a specific type of presentation in 791.436; class specific films in 791.437

.433 4   Animated films

Including cartoon films, computer animated films, puppet films

Class comprehensive works on puppetry in 791.53

For animation of cartoon films, see 741.58; for time-lapse cinematography, see 776.6; for photographic techniques of cartoon films, see 777.7

.433 402 85   Computer applications

Do not use for computer animated films; class in 791.4334

.436   Special aspects of films

Class here film adaptations, film genres

.436 1   Films displaying specific qualities

Add to base number 791.4361 the numbers following —1 in notation 11–17 from Table 3C, e.g., comedies 791.43617

.436 2–.436 9   Films dealing with specific themes and subjects

Add to base number 791.436 the numbers following —3 in notation 32–39 from Table 3C, e.g., films of the West and westerns 791.4365878

.437   Films

Class here screenplays

Class texts of plays in 800. Class subject-oriented films themselves with the subject, e.g., films on flower gardening 635.9

See Manual at 791.437 and 791.447, 791.457, 792.9; also at 808.82 vs. 791.437, 791.447, 791.457, 792.9

.437 2   Single films

(Option: Arrange alphabetically by title of film)

.437 5   Two or more films

Class here collections of film reviews

Class works which focus on a specific aspect of films with the aspect in 791.436, e.g., westerns 791.4365878; class critical appraisal of films associated with a specific person with the person, e.g., films of a motion-picture photographer 777.092, of a director 791.430233092

.44　　　　　　Radio

Regardless of distribution medium or method

Class here dramatic programs, entertainment programs; radio programs developed originally for Internet transmission; comprehensive works on dramatic, entertainment, documentary, educational, news programs

For documentary, educational, news programs, see 070.194

See also 384.54 for communication aspects of radio

See Manual at 780.92 and 791.092

.440 1–.440 2　　Standard subdivisions

Notation from Table 1 as modified under 792.01–792.02, e.g., value of radio 791.44013; however, for programming (scheduling), see 384.5442; for types of presentation, see 791.443

.440 9　　　　History, geographic treatment, biography

Class here description, critical appraisal of specific companies and stations

For description, critical appraisal of specific programs, see 791.447

.440 92　　　Biography

Do not use for people associated with only one aspect of radio; class in 791.4402 e.g., actors 791.44028092

.443　　　　　Types of presentation

Including commercials, live or recorded programs, network programs

Class a specific genre or type of program with a specific type of presentation in 791.446; class specific programs in 791.447

.446　　　　　Special aspects of radio programs

Class here radio adaptations, radio genres, types of programs

.446 1　　　　Programs displaying specific qualities

Add to base number 791.4461 the numbers following —1 in notation 11–17 from Table 3C, e.g., comedies 791.44617

.446 2–.446 9　Programs dealing with specific themes and subjects

Add to base number 791.446 the numbers following —3 in notation 32–39 from Table 3C, e.g., programs of the West and westerns 791.4465878

.447　　　　　Radio programs

Class here radio plays

Class texts of plays in 800. Class subject-oriented programs themselves with the subject, e.g., programs on flower gardening 635.9

See Manual at 791.437 and 791.447, 791.457, 792.9; also at 808.82 vs. 791.437, 791.447, 791.457, 792.9

.447 2	Single programs

(Option: Arrange alphabetically by name of program)

.447 5	Two or more programs

Class here collections of program reviews

Class works which focus on a specific aspect of programs with the aspect in 791.446, e.g., westerns 791.4465878; class critical appraisal of programs associated with a specific person with the person, e.g., programs of a director 791.440233092

.45	Television

Regardless of distribution medium or method

Class here dramatic programs, entertainment programs; mini-series, extended pilots of television series; television-like programs developed originally for Internet transmission; comprehensive works on dramatic, entertainment, documentary, educational, news programs

Class use of video recordings not provided for here with the use, e.g., video recordings of rock music 781.66

For documentary, educational, news programs, see 070.195

See also 384.55 for communication aspects of television; also 791.43 for direct-to-video and direct-to-DVD releases of motion pictures

See Manual at 780.92 and 791.092; also at 791.43 vs. 791.45; also at 791.43, 791.45 vs. 777

.450 1–.450 2	Standard subdivisions

Notation from Table 1 as modified under 792.01–792.02, e.g., scenery and lighting for television 791.45025; however, for programming (scheduling), see 384.5531; for types of presentation, see 791.453

.450 9	History, geographic treatment, biography

Class here description, critical appraisal of specific companies, stations, networks

For description, critical appraisal of specific programs, see 791.457

.450 92	Biography

Do not use for people associated with only one aspect of television; class in 791.4502, e.g., actors 791.45028092

.453	Types of presentation

Including commercials, live or recorded programs, network programs

Class a specific genre or type of program with a specific type of presentation in 791.456; class specific programs in 791.457

.453 4		Animated television programs

Including cartoon television programs, computer animated television programs, puppet television programs

Class comprehensive works on animated cartoons in 791.4334; class comprehensive works on puppetry in 791.53

For animation of cartoon television programs, see 741.58; for time-lapse cinematography, see 776.6; for photographic techniques of cartoon television programs, see 777.7

.453 402 85   Computer applications

Do not use for computer animated television programs; class in 791.4534

.456   Special aspects of television programs

Class here television adaptations, television genres, types of programs

.456 1   Programs displaying specific qualities

Add to base number 791.4561 the numbers following —1 in notation 11–17 from Table 3C, e.g., comedies 791.45617

.456 2–.456 9   Programs dealing with specific themes and subjects

Add to base number 791.456 the numbers following —3 in notation 32–39 from Table 3C, e.g., programs of the West and westerns 791.4565878

.457   Programs

Class here television plays

Class texts of plays in 800. Class subject-oriented programs themselves with the subject, e.g., programs on flower gardening 635.9

See Manual at 791.437 and 791.447, 791.457, 792.9; also at 808.82 vs. 791.437, 791.447, 791.457, 792.9

.457 2   Single programs

(Option: Arrange alphabetically by name of program)

.457 5   Two or more programs

Class here collections of program reviews

Class works which focus on a specific aspect of programs with the aspect in 791.456, e.g., westerns 791.456278; class critical appraisal of programs associated with a specific person with the person, e.g., programs of a television photographer 777.092, of a director 791.450233092

.46   Podcasting

Class here dramatic podcasting, entertainment podcasting; works on dramatic podcasting, entertainment podcasting, documentary podcasting, educational podcasting, news podcasting

See Manual at 780.92 and 791.092

.460 9	History, geographic treatment, biography

Class here description, critical appraisal of specific podcasting production or distribution companies

For description, critical appraisal of specific podcasts, see 791.467

.466	Special aspects of podcasts

Class here podcast adaptations, podcast genres, types of podcasts

.466 1	Podcasts displaying specific qualities

Add to base number 791.4661 the numbers following —1 in notation 11–17 from Table 3C, e.g., comedies 791.46617

.466 2–.466 9	Podcasts dealing with specific themes and subjects

Add to base number 791.466 the numbers following —3 in notation 32–39 from Table 3C, e.g., podcasts with love themes 791.466543

.467	Podcasts

Class texts of literary podcasts in 800. Class subject-oriented podcasts themselves with the subject, e.g., podcasts on folklore 398

See Manual at 791.437 and 791.447, 791.457, 792.9

.467 2	Specific podcasts

(Option: Arrange alphabetically by name of podcast)

.5	**Puppetry and toy theaters**
.53	Puppetry

Class here marionettes, shadow puppets

Class puppet films in 791.4334

.538	Production scripts of puppet plays

Class texts of plays in 800

.6	**Pageantry**

Including parades, floats for parades

Class interdisplinary works on pageants, processions, parades in 394.5

For circus parades, see 791.38; for water pageantry, see 797.203

See also 794.17 for living chess

.62	Pageants

See also 791.66 for beauty pageants

.622	Religious pageants
.624	Historical and patriotic pageants

.64	Cheerleading

> Add to base number 791.64 the numbers following 796.3 in 796.31–796.35, e.g., cheerleading at American football games 791.6432

.66	Beauty contests

> Class here beauty pageants

.8   **Animal performances**

> Including cockfighting

> *For circus animal performances, see 791.32; for equestrian sports and animal racing, see 798*

.82	Bullfighting
.84	Rodeos

> Class here Wild West shows

792   **Stage presentations**

> Class here dramatic presentation, theater

> Class texts of plays in 800

> *For motion pictures, radio, television, podcasting, see 791.4; for puppetry and toy theaters, see 791.5*

> *See Manual at 780.92 and 791.092*

.01	Philosophy and theory

> Notation 01 from Table 1 as modified below

> Do not use for value; class in 792.013

.013	Value, influence, effect

> Class influence and effect on a specific subject with the subject, e.g., influence and effect on crime 364.254

.015	Criticism and appreciation

> Do not use for scientific principles; class in 792.01

> Standard subdivisions are added for either or both topics in heading

.02	Techniques, procedures, apparatus, equipment, materials, miscellany

> Do not use for miscellany; class in 792.029

>   792.022–792.028 Specific techniques, procedures, apparatus, equipment, materials

> Use notation 01–09 (*except* —028 for apparatus, equipment, materials) from Table 1 under each subdivision identified by *, e.g., periodicals on amateur theater 792.022205, computer applications for special effects 792.0240285

> Class comprehensive works in 792.02

.022	*Types of stage presentation

Including showboats, street theater, tent shows

.022 2	*Amateur theater
.022 3	*Little theater
.022 4	*Summer theater
.022 6	*Children's theater
.022 8	*Arena theater (Theater-in-the-round)
.023	*Supervision
.023 2	*Production
.023 3	*Direction
.023 6	*Programming
.024	*Special effects

Including sound effects, visual effects

.025	*Setting

Including lighting, scenery

.026	*Costuming
.027	*Makeup and hair

Standard subdivisions are added for makeup and hair together, for makeup alone

Including wigs

.028	*Acting and performance

Including impersonation, improvisation, use of expression and gestures

.029	Miscellany

Do not use for commercial miscellany; class in 792.0299

.029 07	Humorous treatment
.029 08	Audiovisual treatment
.029 1–.029 8	Miscellaneous works

Add to base number 792.029 the numbers following —02 in notation 021–028 from Table 1, e.g., stage as a profession 792.0293; however, for specific techniques, procedures, apparatus, equipment, materials, see 792.022–792.028

.029 9	Commercial miscellany

Including price lists, prospectuses, trade catalogs

*Add as instructed under 792.022–792.028

.09   History, geographic treatment, biography

> Class here description, critical appraisal of specific theaters and companies
>
> *For specific productions in specific theaters or by specific companies, see 792.9*

.092   Biography

> Do not use for people associated with only one aspect of stage presentations; class in 792.02, e.g., actors 792.028092

> **792.1–792.8 Specific kinds of performances**
>
> Add to each subdivision identified by † the numbers following 792 in 792.01–792.09, e.g., costuming for ballet 792.8026
>
> Class comprehensive works in 792

.1   **†Tragedy and serious drama**

.12   †Tragedy

.14   †Historical drama

.16   †Religious and morality plays

> Including miracle, mystery, passion plays
>
> *See also 792.09 for treatment of religious concepts in the theater; also 792.27 for modern mystery plays*

.2   **†Comedy and melodrama**

.23   †Comedy

> *For panto, see 792.38; for stand-up comedy, see 792.76*

.27   †Melodrama

> Including modern mystery (suspense) drama
>
> *See also 792.16 for religious mystery-plays*

.3   **†Pantomime**

> Class here mime, silent pantomime

.38   †Panto

> Pantomime in the nonsilent British tradition, usually performed around Christmas time

†Add as instructed under 792.1–792.8

.5   †**Opera**

> Class here dramatic vocal forms
>
> Class interdisciplinary works on dramatic vocal forms, on opera in 782.1
>
> > *For musical plays, see 792.6; for variety shows, see 792.7*
> >
> > *See Manual at 782.1 vs. 792.5, 792.6*

.509   History, geographic treatment, biography

> > Class here description, critical appraisal of specific theaters and companies
> >
> > > *For specific productions in specific theaters or by specific companies, see 792.54*

.54   Opera productions

> Class here production and stage guides

.542   Single operas

> (Option: Arrange alphabetically by title)

.545   Two or more operas

> Class here collections of reviews
>
> Class critical appraisal of operas associated with a specific person other than the composer or librettist with the person, e.g., operas associated with a singer 782.1092, with a director 792.50233092

.6   †**Musical plays**

> Class here ballad operas, musicals, revues
>
> Class interdisciplinary works on musical plays in 782.14
>
> > *See Manual at 782.1 vs. 792.5, 792.6*

.609   History, geographic treatment, biography

> > Class here description, critical appraisal of specific theaters and companies
> >
> > > *For specific productions in specific theaters or by specific companies, see 792.64*

.62   Dancing

> Including choreography
>
> Class comprehensive works on theatrical dancing in 792.78; class comprehensive works on choreography in 792.82

.64   Musical play productions

> Class here production and stage guides

---

†Add as instructed under 792.1–792.8

.642	Single musical plays

> (Option: Arrange alphabetically by name)

.645	Two or more musical plays

Class here collections of reviews

Class critical appraisal of musical plays associated with a specific person other than the composer or librettist with the person, e.g., musical plays associated with a singer 782.14092, with a director 792.60233092

.7	†**Variety shows and theatrical dancing**

Class here burlesque, cabaret, vaudeville, music hall and nightclub presentations

Subdivisions are added for variety shows and theatrical dancing together, for variety shows alone

Class stage productions in 792.9

> *For magic shows, see 793.8; for juggling, see 793.87; for ventriloquism, see 793.89*

> *See also 791.12 for minstrel shows and skits*

.76	†Stand-up comedy
.78	†Theatrical dancing

Including tap dancing

Class stage productions in 792.9

> *For dancing in musical plays, see 792.62*

.8	†**Ballet and modern dance**

Class here comprehensive works on dancing

Subdivisions are added for either or both topics in heading

> *For dancing in musical plays, see 792.62; for theatrical and tap dancing, see 792.78; for social, folk, national dancing, see 793.3*

> *See Manual at 780.92 and 791.092*

.801 48	Abbreviations, acronyms, symbols

> Do not use for dance notation; class in 792.82

.809	History, geographic treatment, biography

Class here description, critical appraisal of specific theaters and companies

> *For specific productions in specific theaters or by specific companies, see 792.84*

.809 2	Biography

> Do not use for people associated with only one aspect of ballet and modern dance; class in 792.802, e.g., dancers 792.8028092

†Add as instructed under 792.1–792.8

.82   Choreography

Class here choreology, e.g., Labanotation, Benesh

For choreography of specific kinds of performances, see the kind, e.g., cheerleading 791.64, dancing in musical plays 792.62

.84   Ballet productions

Class here stories, plots, analyses, librettos, production scripts, stage guides

.842   Single ballets

(Option: Arrange alphabetically by title)

.845   Two or more ballets

Class here collections of reviews

Class critical appraisal of ballets associated with a specific person with the person, e.g., ballets associated with a director 792.80233092

.9   Stage productions

Class here production scripts, stage guides; description, critical appraisal of specific productions in specific theaters and companies

Class description, critical appraisal, production scripts of operas in 792.54; class description, critical appraisal, production scripts of musical plays in 792.64; class description, critical appraisal, production scripts of ballets in 792.84

See Manual at 791.437 and 791.447, 791.457, 792.9; also at 808.82 vs. 791.437, 791.447, 791.457, 792.9

.92   Single productions

(Option: Arrange alphabetically by title)

.95   Two or more productions

Class here collections of reviews

Class critical appraisal of productions associated with a specific person other than the playwright with the person, e.g., productions associated with a director 792.0233092

793   Indoor games and amusements

Class games that originated as electronic games in 794.8

For indoor games of skill, see 794; for games of chance, see 795

.01   Philosophy and theory; activities and programs for specific groups of people

Notation 01 from Table 1 as modified below

.019   Activities and programs for specific groups of people

Do not use for psychological principles; class in 793.01

Add to base number 793.019 the numbers following 790.19 in 790.191–790.196, e.g., indoor games and amusements for children 793.01922

.08	Groups of people

> For activities and programs for specific groups of people, see 793.019

.2	**Parties and entertainments**
.21	Children's parties
.22	Seasonal parties

> Class children's seasonal parties in 793.21

.24	Charades and tableaux
.3	**Social, folk, national dancing**

> Standard subdivisions are added for social, folk, national dancing together; for social dancing alone

> Including belly, jazz dancing

.31	Folk and national dancing

> Standard subdivisions are added for either or both topics in the heading

[.310 9]	History, geographic treatment, biography

> Do not use; class in 793.319

.319	History, geographic treatment, biography
.319 001–.319 009	Standard subdivisions

> Add to base number 793.31900 the numbers following —00 in notation 001–009 from Table 2, e.g., periodicals of the history of folk dancing 793.319005

.319 01–.319 05	Historical periods

> Add to base number 793.3190 the numbers following —090 in notation 0901–0905 from Table 1, e.g., folk dances of 20th century 793.31904

.319 1–.319 9	Geographic treatment, biography

> Add to base number 793.319 notation 1–9 from Table 2, e.g., folk dances of Germany 793.31943

.32	Clog dancing
.33	Ballroom dancing (Round dances)

> Including disco dancing, fox trot, jitterbug, waltz

.34	Square dancing
.35	Dances with accessory features

> Including cotillions, germans, sword dances

.36	Line dancing
.38	Balls

> Class ballroom dancing in 793.33

.4   **Games of action**

.5   **Forfeit and trick games**

.7   **Games not characterized by action**

> *For charades and tableaux, see 793.24*

.73   Puzzles and puzzle games

> Standard subdivisions are added for either or both topics in heading

> Including acrostics, quizzes, rebuses; jigsaw puzzles

> Class puzzles as formal instructional devices for the teaching of a specific subject with the subject, plus notation 07 from Table 1, e.g., puzzles teaching the use of the Bible 220.07

> *For mathematical games and recreations, see 793.74*

.732   Crossword puzzles

.734   Word games

> Including anagrams, palindromes

.735   Riddles

> Class riddles as folk literature in 398.6; class riddles as jokes by known authors, interdisciplinary works on riddles in 808.882

> *See Manual at T3A—8 + 02, T3B—802, T3B—8 + 02 vs. 398.6, 793.735*

.738   Maze puzzles

.74   Mathematical games and recreations

.8   **Magic and related activities**

> Standard subdivisions are added for magic and related activities together, for magic alone

> Including scientific recreations

> Class here conjuring

.85   Card tricks

.87   Juggling

.89   Ventriloquism

.9   **Other indoor diversions**

.92   War games (Battle games)

> *See also 355.48 for military use of war games; also 796.1 for outdoor war games*

.93   Adventure games

> Class here fantasy games, mystery games, role-playing games

>> *See also 793.92 for war games (battle games); also 794.9 for fantasy sports*

.96   String games

> Including making cat's cradles

794   Indoor games of skill

> Class here board games

> Class war games in 793.92; class adventure games, fantasy games, mystery games in 793.93; class games combining skill and chance in 795

>> *For backgammon, see 795.15*

.1   **Chess**

.12   Strategy and tactics

> Including specific strategies and tactics, e.g., combinations, sacrifices, traps, pitfalls, attack, counterattack, defense

> Class specific strategies and tactics applied during a specific portion of a game in 794.122–794.124; class strategy and tactics with individual chessmen in 794.14

.122   Openings

.122 5   Specific openings

> (Option: Arrange by codes from the *Encyclopaedia of Chess Openings* [ECO codes], e.g., Sicilian Defence 794.1225 B20)

.123   Middle games

.124   End games

.14   Individual chessmen

> Including specific attributes, e.g., position, moves, power, value

> Class specific attributes of a specific piece in 794.142–794.147

.142   Pawns

.143   Rooks (Castles)

.144   Knights

.145   Bishops

.146   Queen

.147   King

.15   Collections of games

.152   Master matches

> Class master matches by individual players in 794.159

.157	Tournaments and championships
	Class tournaments and championships of individual players in 794.159
.159	Games, matches, tournaments, championships of individual players
.17	Special forms of chess
	Including living chess, simultaneous play
.18	Variants of chess
	Including fairy chess, shogi

.2   **Checkers (Draughts)**

.3   **Darts**

.4   **Go**

.6   **Bowling**

Class here variants of bowling, e.g., ninepins (skittles), tenpins

See also 796.315 for lawn bowling

.7   **Ball games**

Class athletic ball games, comprehensive works on ball games in 796.3

For bowling, see 794.6

.72	Billiards
	Class here carom billiards
	For pocket billiards, see 794.73
.73	Pocket billiards
	Including English billiards
.733	Pool (American pocket billiards)
.735	Snooker
.75	Pinball games

.8   **Electronic games**

Class here computer games, video games

Unless other instructions are given, class a subject with aspects in two or more subdivisions of 794.8 in the number coming last, e.g., critical appraisal of a specific game 794.85 (*not* 794.8015)

Class electronic games as formal instructional devices for the teaching of a specific subject with the subject, plus notation 07 from Table 1, e.g., video games for teaching astronomy in secondary education 520.712; class computerized forms of a specific indoor game or amusement with the game or amusement in 793–795, e.g., computerized checkers 794.2

.801   Philosophy and theory

Notation from Table 1 as modified under 792.01, e.g., influence of electronic games 794.8013

.802 8   Auxiliary techniques and procedures; apparatus, equipment, materials

Class comprehensive works on basic and auxiliary techniques and procedures in 794.83

[.802 85]   Computer applications

Do not use; class in 794.81

.809   History, geographic treatment, biography

Class here description, critical appraisal of specific companies and studios

For description, critical appraisal of specific games, see 794.85

.81   Computer applications

Class here data processing

Unless it is redundant, add to base number 794.81 the numbers following 00 in 004–006, e.g., software for digital personal computers 794.81536, but use of digital computers as a whole 794.81 (*not* 794.814)

[.810 92]   Biography

Do not use; class in 794.8092

.83   Techniques and procedures

Including design, direction, production, special effects

Class here comprehensive works on basic and auxiliary techniques and procedures

For auxiliary techniques, see 794.8028

[.830 92]   Biography

Do not use; class in 794.8092

.84   Special aspects of electronic games

Class here comprehensive works on electronic game genres

.842–.849   Electronic games dealing with specific themes and subjects

Add to base number 794.84 the numbers following —3 in notation 32–39 from Table 3C, e.g., military games 794.84581; however, for computer athletic and outdoor sports and games, see 794.86–794.89

.85   Specific electronic games

(Option: Arrange alphabetically by title of game)

For specific computer athletic and outdoor sports and games, see 794.86–794.89

.86–.89   Computer athletic and outdoor sports and games

> Add to base number 794.8 the numbers following 79 in 796–799, e.g., computer baseball 794.86357

.9   **Fantasy sports**

> Variant name: Rotisserie sports

> Add to base number 794.9 the numbers following 796 in 796.3–796.9, e.g., fantasy baseball 794.9357

> *See also 793.93 for fantasy games*

795   Games of chance

> Class here gambling

> Class games that originated as electronic games in 794.8. Class gambling on a specific activity with the activity, e.g., on horse racing 798.401. Class interdisciplinary works on gambling in 306.482

.01   Philosophy and theory

> Including betting systems

.015 192   Probabilities

> Class here probabilities of winning

> *See Manual at 795.015192 vs. 519.27*

.1   **Games with dice**

.12   Craps

.15   Backgammon

.2   **Wheel and top games**

.23   Roulette

.27   Slot machines

.3   **Games dependent on drawing numbers or counters**

.32   Dominoes

.34   Mah jong

.36   Bingo

.38   Lotteries

> Including lotto

.4   **Card games**

.41   Games in which skill is a major element

.411   Cribbage

.412   Poker

.413   Whist and bridge whist

.414		Auction bridge
.415		Contract bridge

           Class here comprehensive works on bridge

             For bridge whist, see 795.413; for auction bridge, see 795.414

.415 2		Bidding
.415 3		Play of the hand
.415 4		Scoring systems
.415 8		Collections of games and matches
.416		Pinochle
.418		Rummy and its variants

           Including canasta

.42	Games based chiefly on chance

           Including baccarat, faro

.423	Blackjack (Twenty-one)
.43	Games in which card position is a major element

           Including solitaire, patience

796   Athletic and outdoor sports and games

Standard subdivisions are added for any or all topics in heading

Including modern pentathlon

Class here government policy on sports

Use 796 for athletics covering sports as a whole. Use 796.42 for athletics limited to track and field

Class exercise and sports activities as means of improving physical fitness in 613.71; class computer athletic and outdoor sports and games in 794.86–794.89; class fantasy sports in 794.9

> *For aquatic and air sports, see 797; for equestrian sports and animal racing, see 798; for fishing, hunting, shooting, see 799. For a specific sport of modern pentathlon, see the sport, e.g., pistol shooting 799.312*

> *See also 617.1027 for sports medicine*

.04	General kinds of sports and games

           See Manual at 796.08 vs. 796.04

>   796.042–796.044   Amateur and professional sports

           Class variants of amateur and professional sports in 796.045; class extreme amateur and professional sports in 796.046; class comprehensive works in 796.04

.042   Amateur sports

       Class here intramural sports

       For college sports, see 796.043

.043   College sports

       Intercollegiate and intramural sports

.044   Professional sports

.045   Variant sports and games

       Versions of sports and games developed by modifying the basic version of the original sports and games

       Class variants of extreme sports and games in 796.046

.045 6   Sports and games modified for participation of people with physical disabilities

       Class here wheelchair sports

       See Manual at 796.08 vs. 796.04

.046   Extreme sports

.06   Organizations, facilities, management

       Notation 06 from Table 1 as modified below

.068   Facilities

       Do not use for management; class in 796.069

       Class here field houses, physical education facilities, playgrounds, stadiums

       Add to base number 796.068 notation 1–9 from Table 2, e.g., playgrounds of London 796.068421

       See also 725.8 for architecture of recreational buildings

.069   Management

       Add to base number 796.069 the numbers following —068 in notation 0681–0688 from Table 1, e.g., financial management 796.0691

.07   Education, research, related topics

       Notation 07 from Table 1 as modified below

.071   Education

       Do not use for teaching; class in 796.077

.077   Coaching

       Class here teaching

.08   Groups of people

> Class general kinds of sports and games for specific groups of people in 796.04
>
> *See Manual at 796.08 vs. 796.04*

.087   People with disabilities and illnesses, gifted people

> Class sports and games modified for participation of people with physical disabilities in 796.0456
>
> *See Manual at 796.08 vs. 796.04*

.1   **Miscellaneous games**

> Not provided for elsewhere

.13   Singing and dancing games

.14   Active games

> *For activities and games requiring equipment, see 796.2*

.15   Play with remote-control vehicles; play with kites

> Toy or model vehicles
>
> Standard subdivisions are added for play with remote-control vehicles and play with kites together; for play with remote-control vehicles alone
>
> Class here control line vehicles; comprehensive works on model vehicles
>
> Class comprehensive works on play with toys in 790.133
>
> *See Manual at 796.15 vs. 629.0460228*

>   796.152–796.156   Play with remote-control vehicles
>
> Class comprehensive works in 796.15

.152   Remote-control ships

> Class here comprehensive works on model ships

.154   Remote-control aircraft

> Class here remote-control airplanes; comprehensive works on model aircraft, on model airplanes
>
> Class paper airplanes in 745.592

.156   Remote-control land vehicles

> Including remote-control racing cars
>
> Class here model automobiles; comprehensive works on model land vehicles
>
> *For play with model trains, play with remote-control trains, see 790.133*

.158   Play with kites

.16	Play with robots

.2 **Activities and games requiring equipment**

Not provided for elsewhere

Including flying discs, marbles, Yo-Yos

.21 Roller skating

Class here in-line skating (rollerblading)

Class a specific sport using roller skates or rollerblades with the sport, e.g., roller hockey 796.3566

.22 Skateboarding

.24 Pitching games

Including horseshoes, quoits

.3 **Ball games**

Class here comprehensive works on outdoor and indoor ball games

For indoor ball games, see 794.7

.309 415 Ireland

Class here Gaelic games

For a specific Gaelic game, see the game, e.g., Gaelic football 796.337

.31 Ball thrown or hit by hand

Including boccie, pétanque

For inflated ball thrown or hit by hand, see 796.32

.312 Court handball

Variant name: handball

Class here American handball, Gaelic handball

See also 796.327 for team handball

.315 Lawn bowling

See also 794.6 for indoor bowling

.32 Inflated ball thrown or hit by hand

.323 Basketball

.323 01–.323 09 Standard subdivisions

Notation from Table 1 as modified under 796.33202–796.33207, e.g., basketball courts 796.323068

.323 2 *Strategy and tactics

---

*Do not use notation 092 from Table 1; class biography in 796.323092

.323 3	*Refereeing	
.323 6	Specific types of basketball	

Class strategy and tactics regardless of type in 796.3232; class refereeing of specific types of basketball in 796.3233

See Manual at 796.08 vs. 796.04

[.323 601–.323 609]	Standard subdivisions

Do not use; class in 796.32301–796.32309

.323 62	*Precollege basketball
.323 63	*College basketball
.323 64	*Professional and semiprofessional basketball
.323 8	Variants of basketball

Including wheelchair basketball, women's rules

See also 796.323082 for women playing by standard rules

See Manual at 796.08 vs. 796.04

.324	Netball
.325	Volleyball
.325 01–.325 09	Standard subdivisions

Notation from Table 1 as modified under 796.33202–796.33207, e.g., coaching 796.325077

.325 2	†Strategy and tactics
.325 3	†Refereeing and umpiring
.325 6	Specific types of volleyball

Class strategy and tactics regardless of type in 796.3252; class refereeing and umpiring of specific types of volleyball in 796.3253

See Manual at 796.08 vs. 796.04

[.325 601–.325 609]	Standard subdivisions

Do not use; class in 796.32501–796.32509

.325 62	†Precollege volleyball
.325 63	†College volleyball
.325 64	†Professional and semiprofessional volleyball
.325 8	Variants of volleyball

See Manual at 796.08 vs. 796.04

.325 82	Beach volleyball

*Do not use notation 092 from Table 1; class biography in 796.323092
†Do not use notation 092 from Table 1; class biography in 796.325092

.327	Team handball

Variant names: field handball, fieldball, handball

See also 796.312 for court handball

.33	Inflated ball driven by foot
.332	American football
.332 02	Miscellany

Notation 02 from Table 1 as modified below

.332 020 2	Handbooks and guides

Do not use for synopses and outlines; class in 796.33202

.332 020 22	Official rules
.332 020 24	Spectators' guides
.332 06	Organizations, facilities, management

Notation 06 from Table 1 as modified below

Including clubs, leagues

.332 068	Grounds and their layout

Do not use for management; class in 796.332069

Add to base number 796.332068 notation 1–9 from Table 2, e.g., football fields of Washington, D.C. 796.332068753

.332 069	Management

Add to base number 796.332069 the numbers following —068 in notation 0681–0688 from Table 1, e.g., financial management 796.3320691

.332 07	Education, research, related topics

Notation 07 from Table 1 as modified below

.332 071	Education

Do not use for teaching; class in 796.332077

.332 077	‡Coaching

Class here teaching, training

.332 08	Groups of people

See Manual at 796.08 vs. 796.04

.332 2	‡Strategy and tactics
.332 22	‡Formations
.332 23	‡Line play
.332 24	‡Backfield play

‡Do not use notation 092 from Table 1; class biography in 796.332092

.332 25	‡Passing
.332 26	‡Blocking and tackling
.332 27	‡Kicking
.332 3	‡Refereeing and umpiring
.332 6	Specific types of American football

Class strategy and tactics regardless of type in 796.3322; class refereeing and umpiring of specific types of American football in 796.3323

See Manual at 796.08 vs. 796.04

[.332 601–.332 609]	Standard subdivisions

Do not use; class in 796.33201–796.33209

.332 62	‡Precollege American football
.332 63	‡College American football

Including bowl games

See also 796.332648 for Super Bowl

.332 64	‡Professional and semiprofessional American football
.332 648	‡Super Bowl
.332 8	Variants of American football

Including six-man football, touch football

See Manual at 796.08 vs. 796.04

.333	Rugby

Class here Rugby Union

.333 01–.333 09	Standard subdivisions

Notation from Table 1 as modified under 796.33202–796.33207, e.g., official rules 796.33302022

.333 2	*Strategy and tactics
.333 23	*Forward play
.333 24	*Halfback play
.333 25	*Three-quarter play
.333 26	*Back play
.333 3	*Refereeing and umpiring

*Do not use notation 092 from Table 1; class biography in 796.333092
‡Do not use notation 092 from Table 1; class biography in 796.332092

.333 6	Specific types of rugby

Class strategy and tactics regardless of type in 796.3332; class refereeing and umpiring of specific types of rugby in 796.3333

See Manual at 796.08 vs. 796.04

[.333 601–.333 609]	Standard subdivisions

Do not use; class in 796.33301–796.33309

.333 62	*Clubs

Including college and university

.333 63	*County cup competition
.333 64	*Tours
.333 65	*International rugby
.333 8	Rugby League
.334	Soccer (Association football)

See also 796.337 for Gaelic football

.334 01–.334 09	Standard subdivisions

Notation from Table 1 as modified under 796.33202–796.33207, e.g., coaching 796.334077

.334 2	†Strategy and tactics
.334 22	†Formations
.334 23	†Forward play
.334 24	†Halfback play
.334 25	†Back play
.334 26	†Goalkeeping
.334 3	†Refereeing and umpiring
.334 6	Specific types of soccer

Class strategy and tactics regardless of type in 796.3342; class refereeing and umpiring of specific types of soccer in 796.3343

See Manual at 796.08 vs. 796.04

[.334 601–.334 609]	Standard subdivisions

Do not use; class in 796.33401–796.33409

.334 62	†Amateur soccer
.334 63	†League soccer

---

*Do not use notation 092 from Table 1; class biography in 796.333092
†Do not use notation 092 from Table 1; class biography in 796.334092

.334 64	†Cup competition
	For World Cup competition, see 796.334668
.334 66	†International soccer
.334 668	†World Cup competition
.334 8	Variants of soccer
	See Manual at 796.08 vs. 796.04
.335	Canadian football
.335 01–.335 09	Standard subdivisions
	Notation from Table 1 as modified under 796.33202–796.33207, e.g., coaching 796.335077
.335 2	‡Strategy and tactics
.335 3	‡Refereeing and umpiring
.335 6	Specific types of Canadian football
	Class strategy and tactics regardless of type in 796.3352; class refereeing and umpiring of specific types of Canadian football in 796.3353
	See Manual at 796.08 vs. 796.04
[.335 601–.335 609]	Standard subdivisions
	Do not use; class in 796.33501–796.33509
.335 62	‡Precollege Canadian football
.335 63	‡College Canadian football
.335 64	‡Professional and semiprofessional Canadian football
.335 648	‡Grey Cup
.335 8	Variants of Canadian football
	Including touch football
	See Manual at 796.08 vs. 796.04
.336	Australian-rules football
.337	Gaelic football
	Class here ladies' Gaelic football
.34	Racket games
	Including court tennis (royal tennis), paddle tennis
	See also 796.24 for deck tennis; also 796.362 for lacrosse; also 796.364 for jai alai

†Do not use notation 092 from Table 1; class biography in 796.334092
‡Do not use notation 092 from Table 1; class biography in 796.335092

.342	Tennis (Lawn tennis)
.342 01–.342 09	Standard subdivisions

Notation from Table 1 as modified under 796.33202–796.33207, e.g., layout of tennis courts 796.342068

.342 2	*Strategy and tactics
.342 21	*Service
.342 22	*Forehand
.342 23	*Backhand
.342 27	*Singles
.342 28	*Doubles
.342 3	*Refereeing
.343	Squash

Class here rackets

.344	Racquetball
.345	Badminton
.346	Table tennis
.348	Pickleball
.35	Ball driven by club, mallet, bat
.352	Golf
.352 01–.352 09	Standard subdivisions

Notation from Table 1 as modified under 796.33202–796.33207, e.g., official rules 796.35202022

See also 712.5 for design and construction of golf courses

.352 2	Variants of golf

Including miniature golf

See Manual at 796.08 vs. 796.04

.352 3	†Tactics of play

Class here grip, swing, adapting to specific golf courses

.352 32	†Play with woods
.352 33	†Play with distance irons

Class here comprehensive works on play with irons

For play with chipping or pitching irons, see 796.35234

.352 34	†Play with chipping or pitching irons

*Do not use notation 092 from Table 1; class biography in 796.342092
†Do not use notation 092 from Table 1; class biography in 796.352092

.352 35	†Putting
.352 4	†Refereeing
.352 6	Specific types of golf

         Class tactics of play regardless of type in 796.3523; class refereeing of specific types of golf in 796.3524

         See Manual at 796.08 vs. 796.04

[.352 601–.352 609]	Standard subdivisions

         Do not use; class in 796.35201–796.35209

.352 62	†Amateur golf

         Class open games and matches in 796.35266

.352 64	†Professional golf

         Class open games and matches in 796.35266

.352 66	†Open games and matches

         Including British Open, Masters Tournament

.353	Polo
.354	Croquet
.355	Field hockey

         Including indoor field hockey

         Class comprehensive works on hockey in 796.356

.356	Hockey

         Using ball, puck, or ring

         For field hockey, see 796.355; for hockey games played on ice, see 796.96; for hockey games played underwater, see 797.25

.356 2	Floorball
.356 4	Street hockey

         Class here ball hockey, dek hockey

.356 6	Roller hockey

         Including skater hockey (inline skater hockey)

         See also 796.35662 for inline hockey

.356 62	Inline hockey

         See also 796.3566 for skater hockey

.356 64	Rink hockey

         Variant names: hardball hockey, quad roller hockey

---

†Do not use notation 092 from Table 1; class biography in 796.352092

.357	Baseball

.357 01–.357 09	Standard subdivisions

Notation from Table 1 as modified under 796.33202–796.33207, e.g., coaching 796.357077

.357 2	‡Strategy and tactics
.357 22	‡Pitching
.357 23	‡Catching
.357 24	‡Infield play

Class here comprehensive works on fielding

For outfield play, see 796.35725

.357 25	‡Outfield play
.357 26	‡Batting
.357 27	‡Base running
.357 3	‡Umpiring
.357 6	Specific types of baseball

Class strategy and tactics regardless of type in 796.3572; class umpiring of specific types of baseball in 796.3573

See Manual at 796.08 vs. 796.04

[.357 601–.357 609]	Standard subdivisions

Do not use; class in 796.35701–796.35709

.357 62	‡Precollege baseball

Class here Little league

.357 63	‡College baseball
.357 64	‡Professional and semiprofessional baseball
.357 646	‡World series games
.357 648	‡All-star games
.357 8	Variants of baseball

Including softball

See Manual at 796.08 vs. 796.04

.358	Cricket

.358 01–.358 09	Standard subdivisions

Notation from Table 1 as modified under 796.33202–796.33207, e.g., coaching 796.358077

---

‡Do not use notation 092 from Table 1; class biography in 796.357092

.358 2	*Strategy and tactics
.358 22	*Bowling
.358 23	*Fielding
.358 24	*Wicketkeeping
.358 26	*Batting
.358 3	*Umpiring
.358 6	Specific types of cricket

Class strategy and tactics regardless of type in 796.3582; class umpiring of specific types of cricket in 796.3583

See Manual at 796.08 vs. 796.04

[.358 601–.358 609]	Standard subdivisions

Do not use; class in 796.35801–796.35809

.358 62	*Amateur cricket

Including school, college and university

.358 63	*County cricket
.358 65	*International cricket
.358 8	Variants of cricket

Including single-wicket cricket

See Manual at 796.08 vs. 796.04

.359	Miscellaneous club, mallet, bat games

Not provided for elsewhere

.359 2	Hurling and camogie

Standard subdivisions are added for either or both topics in heading

.359 208 11	Men

Do not use for hurling; class in 796.3592

.359 208 2	Women

Do not use for camogie; class in 796.3592

.36	Ball caught and thrown with same equipment
.362	Lacrosse
.364	Jai alai
.4	**Weight lifting, track and field, gymnastics**
.406	Organizations, facilities, management

Notation 06 from Table 1 as modified below

---

*Do not use notation 092 from Table 1; class biography in 796.358092

.406 8	Gymnasiums and stadiums

Do not use for management; class in 796.4069

Add to base number 796.4068 notation 1–9 from Table 2, e.g., gymnasiums of Japan 796.406852

.406 9	Management

Add to base number 796.4069 the numbers following —068 in notation 0681–0688 from Table 1, e.g., financial management 796.40691

.407	Education, research, related topics

Notation 07 from Table 1 as modified below

.407 1	Education

Do not use for teaching; class in 796.4077

.407 7	Coaching

Class here teaching

.41	Weight lifting

Including bodybuilding for contests

Class weight training for fitness and interdisciplinary works on weight training, bodybuilding for fitness and interdisciplinary works on bodybuilding in 613.713

.42	Track and field

Class here decathlon, heptathlon; running

Use 796 for athletics covering sports as a whole. Use 796.42 for athletics limited to track and field

For field events, see 796.43; for orienteering, see 796.58

See also 613.7172 for running as an exercise

.420 6	Organizations, facilities, management

Notation 06 from Table 1 as modified below

.420 68	Athletic fields

Do not use for management; class in 796.42069

Add to base number 796.42068 notation 1–9 from Table 2, e.g., athletic fields of Russia 796.4206847

.420 69	Management

Add to base number 796.42069 the numbers following —068 in notation 0681–0688 from Table 1, e.g., personnel management 796.420693

.420 92	Biography

Class biography of a specific type of track and field athlete with the type, e.g., sprinter 796.422092

.422	Sprints

Class sprint relays in 796.427

.423	Middle-distance races

Class middle-distance relay races in 796.427

.424	Distance races

Class distance relay races in 796.427

For marathon, see 796.4252; for triathlon, see 796.4257; for cross-country races, see 796.428

.425	Non-track races

Class here road running

For cross-country races, see 796.428; for race walking, see 796.429

.425 2	Marathon
.425 7	Triathlon
.426	Hurdles and steeplechase

Class hurdle and steeplechase relay races in 796.427

.427	Relay races
.428	Cross-country races

Including mountain running

.429	Race walking (Heel-and-toe races)
.43	Jumping and throwing

Class here field events

.432	Jumping

Including long jump (broad jump), triple jump (hop, step, and jump), high jump

For pole vaulting, see 796.434

.434	Pole vaulting

See also 796.442 for gymnastic vaulting

.435	Throwing

Including boomerang and discus throwing, javelin hurling, shot-putting

See also 796.24 for throwing games

.44   **Gymnastics**

Including aerobic gymnastics (sports aerobics)

Class interdisciplinary works on aerobic exercise in 613.71

For trapeze work, rope climbing, tightrope walking, see 796.46; for tumbling, trampolining, acrobatics, contortion, see 796.47

See also 613.714 for gymnastic exercises

.440 92   Biography

Class biography of a specific type of gymnast with the type, e.g., artistic gymnast 796.442092

.442   Artistic gymnastics

Gymnastics whose routines use the following apparatus: balance beam, floor, high bar, parallel bars, pommel horse, still rings, uneven bars, vault

.443   Rhythmic gymnastics

Gymnastics whose routines use the following apparatus: ball, clubs, hoop, ribbon, rope

.46   Trapeze work, rope climbing, tightrope walking

See also 791.34 for trapeze work and tightrope walking as circus acts

.47   Tumbling, trampolining, acrobatics, contortion

.472   Tumbling

Class tumbling as part of artistic gymnastics in 796.442; class tumbling as part of rhythmic gymnastics in 796.443; class tumbling as part of trampolining in 796.474

.474   Trampolining

Class here trampoline, synchronized trampoline, double mini-trampoline

.476   Acrobatics

Class here acrobatic gymnastics (sports acrobatics)

For acrobatics as circus acts, see 791.34

.48   Olympic games

(Option: Arrange specific games chronologically)

Class Paralympics in 796.0456; class Special Olympics in 796.0874. Class a specific activity with the activity, e.g., basketball 796.323, swimming 797.21

For winter Olympic games, see 796.98

.480 93–.480 99   Geographic treatment

Do not use for specific games; class in 796.48

.5   **Outdoor life**

Class a specific activity of outdoor life not provided for here with the activity, e.g., fishing 799.1

.51	Walking

     Class here backpacking, hiking

       For walking by kind of terrain, see 796.52

       See also 796.58 for orienteering

       See Manual at 913–919 vs. 796.51

.510 223	Diagrams

         Do not use for maps and plans; class in 912

.52	Walking and exploring by kind of terrain
.522	Mountains, hills, rocks

     Class here mountaineering, ski mountaineering

       See also 796.428 for mountain running

.522 3	Rock climbing

     Class sport and indoor rock climbing in 796.5224

.522 4	Sport climbing

     Class here indoor climbing

.524	Canyons and other depressions

     Class here a sport regardless of type of depression, e.g., canyoning (canyoneering), gorge walking

.525	Caves

     Class here spelunking

       See also 797.2 for cave swimming

.53	Beach activities

       For aquatic sports, see 797.1–797.3

.54	Camping

     Including snow camping

.542	Kinds of camps

     Class here camps operated for profit

     Class activities in specific kinds of camps in 796.545

.542 2	Institutional camps

       Including church, school, scouts, YMCA camps

     Class institutional day camps in 796.5423

.542 3	Day camps

.545   Activities

Including campfires, games, woodcraft

For beach activities, see 796.53

.56   Dude ranching and farming

.58   Orienteering

Class here ski orienteering

Class orientation in 912.014

.6   **Cycling and related activities**

Use of wheeled vehicles not driven by motor or animal power

Including soapbox racing

For roller skating, see 796.21; for skateboarding, see 796.22

\>   796.62–796.63   Cycling

Class comprehensive works in 796.6

.62   Bicycle racing

Class triathlon in 796.4257; class racing on mountain bikes in 796.63

See also 796.75 for motorcycle racing

.622   BMX (Bicycle motocross)

.624   Cyclo-cross

.626   Road cycling

.628   Track cycling

.63   Mountain biking (All-terrain cycling)

.67   Street luge racing

See also 796.954 for lugeing

.68   Landsailing (Sand yachting)

.7   **Driving motor vehicles**

For snowmobiling, see 796.94

\>   796.72–796.76   Driving for competition

Class comprehensive works in 796.7

.72   Automobile racing

Class here driving sports cars

See also 796.156 for toy car racing

.720 6   Organizations, facilities, management

                             Notation 06 from Table 1 as modified below

.720 68   Racetracks and speedways

                             Do not use for management; class in 796.72069

                             Add to base number 796.72068 notation 1–9 from Table 2, e.g., Indianapolis Motor Speedway 796.7206877252

.720 69   Management

                             Add to base number 796.72069 the numbers following —068 in notation 0681–0688 from Table 1, e.g., financial management 796.720691

.73   Automobile rallies

.75   Motorcycle and motor scooter racing

.756   Motocross and supercross

                             Standard subdivisions are added for either or both topics in heading

.76   Karting and midget car racing

                             Standard subdivisions are added for karting and midget car racing together, for karting alone

.8   **Combat sports**

                             Class here interdisciplinary works on martial arts

                             Class combat with animals in 791.8; class Oriental martial arts forms in 796.815

                             For martial arts as exercises for physical fitness, see 613.7148

.809   History, geographic treatment, biography

                             Class here combat sports and martial arts in general practiced in a specific location, e.g., combat sports practiced in Italy 796.80945, martial arts practiced in Japan 796.80952

                             Class a specific combat sport or martial arts form practiced in a specific location in 796.81–796.86, plus notation 09 from Table 1, e.g., Oriental martial arts forms practiced in Japan 796.8150952, fencing practiced in Italy 796.8620945

.81   Unarmed combat

                             For boxing, see 796.83

.810 95   Asia

                             Do not use for martial arts forms originating in, or in styles characteristic of, Eastern, Southern, and Southeast Asia; class in 796.815

.810 951   China and adjacent areas

                             Do not use for Chinese forms of martial arts; class in 796.8155

.812	Wrestling

Including arm wrestling

.812 2	Greco-Roman wrestling
.812 3	Freestyle wrestling (Catch-as-catch-can wrestling)
.812 5	Sumo
.815	Oriental martial arts forms

Limited to martial arts forms originating in, or in styles characteristic of, Eastern, Southern, and Southeast Asia

Class here comprehensive works on armed and unarmed Oriental martial arts forms

Class comprehensive works on Oriental and other martial arts forms in 796.8 Class martial arts forms originating in, or in styles characteristic of, other parts of Asia in 796.81095

For armed Oriental martial arts forms, see 796.85

.815 2	Judo

Class here jujitsu

.815 3	Karate
.815 4	Aikido
.815 5	Chinese forms of martial arts

Class interdisciplinary works on tai chi in 613.7148155

For kempo and kung fu, see 796.8159

.815 7	Taekwondo
.815 9	Kempo and kung fu
.817	Kickboxing
.83	Boxing

Class kickboxing in 796.817

.85	Armed combat

Class comprehensive works on armed and unarmed Oriental martial arts forms in 796.815

For sword fighting, see 796.86

.852	Knife fighting
.855	Stick fighting

Including bojutsu

For kendo, see 796.86

.86	Sword fighting

Including kendo

.862	Fencing	

.9   **Ice and snow sports**

> *For ski mountaineering, see 796.522; for sled dog racing, see 798.83; for ice fishing, see 799.122*
>
> *See also 796.54 for snow camping; also 798.6 for horse-drawn sleighing*

.91	Ice skating
.912	Figure skating

Including synchronized skating

Class here ice dancing, pair skating

.914	Speed skating

Class here long track speed skating, short track speed skating

.92	Snowshoeing
.93	Skiing and snowboarding

Standard subdivisions are added for skiing and snowboarding together, for skiing alone

.930 92	Biography

Class biography of a specific type of skier or snowboarder with the type, e.g., ski jumper 796.933092

.932	Cross-country skiing

Class here Nordic combination, Nordic skiing

> *For ski orienteering, see 796.58; for jumping, see 796.933*

.932 2	Biathlon
.933	Jumping
.935	Alpine skiing (Downhill skiing)

Class here downhill, giant slalom, slalom, supergiant slalom racing

> *See also 796.937 for ski cross*

.937	Freestyle skiing

Including aerial skiing, mogul skiing; ski cross, ski half-pipe, ski slopestyle

.939	Snowboarding

Including big air, halfpipe, slopestyle snowboarding; snowboard cross (boardercross), parallel giant slalom racing, parallel slalom racing

Class here alpine and freestyle snowboarding

.94	Snowmobiling
.95	Sledding and coasting

Including tobogganing

.952	Bobsleigh	
.954	Luge	

See also 796.67 for street luge racing

.956	Skeleton	
.96	Ice games	
.962	Ice hockey	

Class comprehensive works on hockey in 796.356

.962 01–.962 09   Standard subdivisions

Notation from Table 1 as modified under 796.33202–796.33207, e.g., coaching 796.962077

.962 2   †Strategy and tactics

Including skating

.962 27   †Goalkeeping

.962 3   †Refereeing

.962 6   Specific types of ice hockey

Class strategy and tactics regardless of type in 796.9622

See Manual at 796.08 vs. 796.04

[.962 601–.962 609]   Standard subdivisions

Do not use; class in 796.96201–796.96209

.962 62   †Junior ice hockey

.962 63   †College ice hockey

.962 64   †Professional ice hockey

.962 648   †Stanley Cup

.962 66   †International ice hockey

Class here specific tournaments

.963   Bandy

Including rink bandy

.964   Curling

.965   Broomball

.966   Ringette

See also 796.356 for gym ringette, inline ringette

.97   Iceboating

---

†Do not use notation 092 from Table 1; class biography in 796.962092

.98   Winter Olympic games

> (Option: Arrange specific games chronologically)

> Class a specific activity with the activity, e.g., skating 796.91

.980 93–.980 99   Geographic treatment

> Do not use for specific games; class in 796.98

797   Aquatic and air sports

> Standard subdivisions are added for aquatic and air sports together, for aquatic sports alone

> Class computer aquatic and air sports in 794.87

.028 9   Safety measures

> Class comprehensive works on water safety in aquatic sports in 797.200289

> ## 797.1–797.3   Aquatic sports

> Class comprehensive works in 797

> *For fishing, see 799.1*

.1   **Boating**

.12   Types of vessels

> Class seamanship for specific types of vessels in 623.882; class boat racing with specific types of vessels in 797.14

.121   Rafting

.122   Canoeing

.122 4   Kayaking

.123   Rowing

.124   Sailing

> *See also 796.68 for landsailing; also 797.33 for sailboarding*

.124 6   Yachting

> Class here comprehensive works on yachting

> *For motor yachting, see 797.1256*

> *See also 643.29 for yachts permanently docked as dwellings*

.125   Motorboating

.125 6   Yachting

.129   Houseboating

> *See also 643.29 for houseboats permanently docked as dwellings*

.14   Boat racing and regattas

         Standard subdivisions are added for any type of racing, e.g., yacht racing in Britain 797.140941

.2   **Swimming and diving**

         Standard subdivisions are added for swimming and diving together, for diving alone

         Class here water parks

.200 1–.200 9   Standard subdivisions

.203   Water pageantry

         See also 797.217 for synchronized swimming

.21   Swimming

         Class triathlon in 796.4257

         For underwater swimming, see 797.23

.217   Synchronized swimming

.23   Underwater swimming

         For a specific underwater game, see the game, e.g., underwater hockey 797.25

.232   Skin diving and snorkeling

         Standard subdivisions are added for either or both topics in heading

.234   Scuba diving

.24   Springboard and platform diving

         Standard subdivisions are added for either or both topics in heading

.25   Water games

         Including underwater hockey

.252   Water polo

.3   **Other aquatic sports**

         Including wakeboarding

.32   Surfing (Surf riding)

.33   Windsurfing (Boardsailing, Sailboarding)

.35   Water skiing

.37   Jet skiing

.5   **Air sports**

         Including bungee jumping

.51   Balloon flying

>   797.52–797.54 Flying motor-driven aircraft

Class comprehensive works in 797.5

See also 797.55 for paramotoring

.52   Racing

.53   Flying for pleasure

.54   Stunt flying

Class here display aerobatics

.55   Gliding and soaring

Including hang gliding, paramotoring

.56   Parachuting

Including skysurfing

Class here skydiving

.562   BASE jumping

798   Equestrian sports and animal racing

Standard subdivisions are added for equestrian sports and animal racing together, for equestrian sports alone

Class computer equestrian sports and animal racing in 794.88

>   **798.2–798.6 Equestrian sports**

Class rodeos in 791.84; class hunting with aid of horses in 799.23; class comprehensive works in 798

For polo, see 796.353

See also 636.108971027 for equine sports medicine

.2   **Horsemanship**

For horse racing, see 798.4

.23   Riding

Class here training of both horse and rider, dressage

Class training of only the horse in 636.1088

For jumping, see 798.25

.230 74   Museums, collections, exhibits

Do not use for riding exhibitions; class in 798.24

[.230 79]   Competitions and awards

Do not use; class in 798.24

.24		Riding exhibitions and competitions

Class jumping in 798.25

.242		Eventing

Class here three-day events

.25		Jumping

.4   **Horse racing**

Class here flat racing

.400 1–.400 5   Standard subdivisions

.400 6   Organizations, facilities, management

Notation 06 from Table 1 as modified below

.400 68   Racetracks

Do not use for management; class in 798.40069

Add to base number 798.40068 notation 1–9 from Table 2, e.g., racetracks of England 798.4006842

.400 69   Management

Add to base number 798.40069 the numbers following —068 in notation 0681–0688 from Table 1, e.g., management of marketing 798.400698

.400 7–.400 8   Standard subdivisions

.400 9   History, geographic treatment, biography

Class here specific races

.401   Betting

Including pari-mutuel

.45   Steeplechasing (National Hunt racing)

.46   Harness racing

.6   **Driving and coaching**

Including horse-drawn sleighing

For harness racing, see 798.46

.8   **Dog racing**

.83   Sled dog racing

.85   Greyhound racing

799   **Fishing, hunting, shooting**

Class computer fishing, hunting, shooting games in 794.89

See also 688.79 for the manufacture of both mass-produced and handcrafted equipment

.1   **Fishing**

> Class shellfishing in 799.254; class interdisciplinary works on fishing in 639.2

.11   Freshwater fishing

> Class here coarse fishing
>
> Class fishing for specific kinds of freshwater fishes in 799.17

> **799.12–799.14 Specific methods of fishing**
>
> Class specific methods of freshwater fishing in 799.11; class specific methods of saltwater fishing in 799.16; class specific methods of fishing for specific kinds of fish in 799.17; class comprehensive works in 799.1

.12   Angling

> Class here game, pan fishing
>
> Class game fishing in the sense of fishing for salmon, trout, graylings in 799.1755

.122   Bait fishing

> Variant names: bottom, still fishing
>
> Including ice fishing

.124   Fly fishing

> Class here casting
>
> *For bait-casting, see 799.126*
>
> *See also 688.79124 for making artificial flies*

.126   Bait-casting (Spin-fishing)

.128   Trolling

.13   Net fishing

.14   Other methods of fishing

> Including spearfishing

.16   Saltwater fishing

> Class fishing for specific kinds of saltwater fishes in 799.17

.17   Specific kinds of fishes

> Class comprehensive works on fishing for freshwater fishes in 799.11; class comprehensive works on fishing for saltwater fishes in 799.16

[.170 1–.170 9]   Standard subdivisions

> Do not use; class in 799.101–799.109

.172–.177	Subdivisions for specific kinds of fishes

Add to base number 799.17 the numbers following 597 in 597.2–597.7, e.g., trout fishing 799.1757

Class coarse fishing, game fishing in sense of sports fishing in 799.12; class game fishing in sense of fishing for salmon, trout, graylings in 799.1755

.2	**Hunting**

Class here sports trapping; comprehensive works on hunting and shooting sports, on commercial and sports hunting

For commercial, subsistence hunting, see 639.1; for shooting other than game, see 799.3

.202	Miscellany
.202 8	Auxiliary techniques and procedures; apparatus, equipment, materials

Notation 028 from Table 1 as modified below

Class here basic techniques and procedures

.202 82	Blowpipes, bolas, boomerangs, lassos, nets, slings, spears
.202 83	Guns
.202 832	Rifles
.202 833	Pistols
.202 834	Shotguns
.202 85	Bows and arrows

Do not use for computer applications; class in 799.2028

[.209]	History, geographic treatment, biography

Do not use; class in 799.29

> 799.21–799.23 Methods

Class methods of hunting specific kinds of animals in 799.24–799.27; class comprehensive works in 799.2

.21	Shooting game
.213	Shooting game with guns
.215	Shooting game with bows and arrows
.23	Hunting with aid of animals
.232	Hunting with falcons
.234	Hunting with dogs

> 　　　799.24–799.27　Hunting specific kinds of animals

　　　　　　Class comprehensive works in 799.2

.24　　　　Birds

　　　　　　Including crows

　　　　　　Class here fowling, game birds, wildfowling

　　　　　　Class waterfowling in 799.244

.243　　　Wading birds

　　　　　　Add to base number 799.243 the numbers following 598.3 in 598.32–598.35, e.g., woodcocks 799.2433

　　　　　　Class waterfowl in 799.244

.244　　　Waterfowl

　　　　　　Class here ducks, lowland game birds

　　　　　　Add to base number 799.244 the numbers following 598.41 in 598.412–598.418, e.g., geese 799.2447

　　　　　　Class wading birds in 799.243

.246　　　Landfowl, doves, pigeons

　　　　　　Standard subdivisions are added for landfowl, doves, pigeons together; for landfowl alone

　　　　　　Class here upland game birds

　　　　　　Add to base number 799.246 the numbers following 598.6 in 598.62–598.65, e.g., turkeys 799.24645

.25　　　　Small game hunting

　　　　　　For birds, see 799.24

.252–.259　Specific kinds of small game

　　　　　　Add to base number 799.25 the numbers following 59 in 592–599, e.g., shellfishing 799.254, fox hunting 799.259775

.26　　　　Big game hunting

　　　　　　Class here comprehensive works on hunting big game mammals

　　　　　　For specific kinds, see 799.27

.27　　　　Specific kinds of big game

　　　　　　For birds, see 799.24

[.270 1–.270 9]　Standard subdivisions

　　　　　　Do not use; class in 799.2601–799.2609

.271–.278	Specific kinds of big game mammals

Add to base number 799.27 the numbers following 599 in 599.1–599.8, e.g., white-tailed deer 799.27652; however, for comprehensive works on big game, on big game mammals, see 799.26

.279	Reptiles

Add to base number 799.279 the numbers following 597.9 in 597.92–597.98, e.g., crocodiles 799.27982

.29	History, geographic treatment, biography
.290 01–.290 09	Standard subdivisions

Add to base number 799.2900 the numbers following —00 in notation 001–009 from Table 2, e.g., periodicals of the history of hunting 799.29005

.290 1–.290 5	Historical periods

Add to base number 799.290 the numbers following —090 in notation 0901–0905 from Table 1, e.g., hunting in 20th century 799.2904

.291–.299	Geographic treatment, biography

Add to base number 799.29 notation 1–9 from Table 2, e.g., hunting in Germany 799.2943

.3	**Shooting other than game**

For ballistic devices, see 799.20282–799.20285

.31	Shooting with guns
.312	Shooting at stationary targets

For biathlon, see 796.932

.313	Shooting at moving targets
.313 2	Trapshooting

Class here skeet shooting

.32	Shooting with bow and arrow (Archery)

800

800   Literature (Belles-lettres) and rhetoric

Class here works of literature, works about literature

After general topics (800–809) the basic arrangement is literature by language, then literature of each language by form, then each form by historical period; however, miscellaneous writings are arranged first by historical period, then by form. More detailed instructions are given at the beginning of Table 3

Unless other instructions are given, observe the following table of preference, e.g., collections of drama written in poetry from more than two literatures 808.82 (*not* 808.81):

    Drama
    Poetry
       Class epigrams in verse with miscellaneous writings
    Fiction
    Essays
    Speeches
    Letters
    Miscellaneous writings
    Humor and satire

Class folk literature in 398.2; class librettos, poems, words written to be sung or recited with music in 780.268; class interdisciplinary works on language and literature in 400; class interdisciplinary works on the arts in 700

> *See Manual at 800; also at 080 vs. 800; also at 741.6 vs. 800; also at 800 vs. 398.2; also at 800, T3C—362 vs. 398.245, 590, 636*

SUMMARY

801–807	Standard subdivisions
808	Rhetoric and collections of literary texts from more than two literatures
809	History, description, critical appraisal of more than two literatures
810	American literature in English
.1–.9	Standard subdivisions; collections in more than one form; history, description, critical appraisal of works in more than one form of American literature in English
811	American poetry in English
812	American drama in English
813	American fiction in English
814	American essays in English
815	American speeches in English
816	American letters in English
817	American humor and satire in English
818	American miscellaneous writings in English

820	**English and Old English (Anglo-Saxon) literatures**
.1–.9	Standard subdivisions; collections in more than one form; history, description, critical appraisal of works in more than one form of English literature
821	English poetry
822	English drama
823	English fiction
824	English essays
825	English speeches
826	English letters
827	English humor and satire
828	English miscellaneous writings
829	Old English (Anglo-Saxon) literature
830	**German literature and literatures of related languages**
.01–.09	Standard subdivisions of literatures of Germanic languages
.1–.9	Standard subdivisions; collections in more than one form; history, description, critical appraisal of works in more than one form of German literature
831	German poetry
832	German drama
833	German fiction
834	German essays
835	German speeches
836	German letters
837	German humor and satire
838	German miscellaneous writings
839	Other Germanic literatures
840	**French literature and literatures of related Romance languages**
.01–.09	Standard subdivisions of literatures of Romance languages
.1–.9	Standard subdivisions; collections in more than one form; history, description, critical appraisal of works in more than one form of French literature
841	French poetry
842	French drama
843	French fiction
844	French essays
845	French speeches
846	French letters
847	French humor and satire
848	French miscellaneous writings
849	Occitan, Catalan, Franco-Provençal literatures
850	**Literatures of Italian, Dalmatian, Romanian, Rhaetian, Sardinian, Corsican languages**
.1–.9	Standard subdivisions; collections in more than one form; history, description, critical appraisal of works in more than one form of Italian literature
851	Italian poetry
852	Italian drama
853	Italian fiction
854	Italian essays
855	Italian speeches
856	Italian letters
857	Italian humor and satire
858	Italian miscellaneous writings
859	Literatures of Romanian, Rhaetian, Sardinian, Corsican languages

860	**Literatures of Spanish, Portuguese, Galician languages**
.01–.09	Standard subdivisions of literatures of Spanish, Portuguese, Galician languages
.1–.9	Standard subdivisions; collections in more than one form; history, description, critical appraisal of works in more than one form of Spanish literature
861	**Spanish poetry**
862	**Spanish drama**
863	**Spanish fiction**
864	**Spanish essays**
865	**Spanish speeches**
866	**Spanish letters**
867	**Spanish humor and satire**
868	**Spanish miscellaneous writings**
869	**Literatures of Portuguese and Galician languages**
870	**Latin literature and literatures of related Italic languages**
.01–.09	Standard subdivisions of literatures of Italic languages
.1–.9	Standard subdivisions; collections in more than one form; history, description, critical appraisal of works in more than one form of Latin literature
871	**Latin poetry**
872	**Latin dramatic poetry and drama**
873	**Latin epic poetry and fiction**
874	**Latin lyric poetry**
875	**Latin speeches**
876	**Latin letters**
877	**Latin humor and satire**
878	**Latin miscellaneous writings**
879	**Literatures of other Italic languages**
880	**Classical Greek literature and literatures of related Hellenic languages**
.01–.09	Standard subdivisions of classical (Greek and Latin) literatures
.1–.9	Standard subdivisions; collections in more than one form; history, description, critical appraisal of works in more than one form of classical Greek literature
881	**Classical Greek poetry**
882	**Classical Greek dramatic poetry and drama**
883	**Classical Greek epic poetry and fiction**
884	**Classical Greek lyric poetry**
885	**Classical Greek speeches**
886	**Classical Greek letters**
887	**Classical Greek humor and satire**
888	**Classical Greek miscellaneous writings**
889	**Modern Greek literature**
890	**Literatures of other specific languages and language families**
891	**East Indo-European and Celtic literatures**
892	**Afro-Asiatic literatures**
893	**Non-Semitic Afro-Asiatic literatures**
894	**Literatures of Altaic, Uralic, Hyperborean, Dravidian languages; literatures of miscellaneous languages of south Asia**
895	**Literatures of East and Southeast Asia**
896	**African literatures**
897	**Literatures of North American native languages**
898	**Literatures of South American native languages**
899	**Literatures of non-Austronesian languages of Oceania, of Austronesian languages, of miscellaneous languages**

801   Philosophy and theory

Notation 01 from Table 1 as modified below

Do not use for value; class in 801.3. Do not use for techniques and principles of criticism; class in 801.95

.3   **Value, influence, effect**

.9   **Nature and character**

Notation 019 from Table 1 as modified below

Do not use for psychological principles; class in 801.92

.92   Psychology

Including literature as a product of imagination

.93   Aesthetics

.95   Criticism

Class here theory, technique, history of literary criticism

Class textual criticism of specific literary forms in 801.959; class theory, technique, history of literary criticism of specific literary forms in 808.1–808.7; class works of critical appraisal in 809

See Manual at 800: Literary criticism

.959   Textual criticism

802   Miscellany

803   Dictionaries, encyclopedias, concordances

[804]   [Unassigned]

Most recently used in Edition 16

805   Serial publications

Class collections of literary texts in serial form in 808.80005; class history, description, critical appraisal in serial form in 809.005

806   Organizations and management

807   Education, research, related topics

808   **Rhetoric and collections of literary texts from more than two literatures**

> Rhetoric: effective use of language
>
> Standard subdivisions are added for rhetoric and collections of literary texts from more than two literatures, for rhetoric alone
>
> Do not use for literature with respect to groups of people; class in 808.89
>
> Class here composition, creative writing
>
> Class general treatment of standard usage of language (prescriptive linguistics) in 418; class theory, technique, history of literary criticism in 801.95. Class treatment of standard usage in a specific language with the specific language, plus notation 8 from Table 4, e.g., English usage 428

.001–.009   Standard subdivisions

>   808.02–808.06   General topics in rhetoric
>
>   Class comprehensive works in 808

.02   Authorship techniques, plagiarism, editorial techniques

> Writing in publishable form
>
> Class here comprehensive works on preparation and submission of manuscripts, on preparation and submission of scholarly manuscripts
>
> Class authorship and editorial techniques for a specific kind of composition with the kind in 808.06, e.g., 808.066378 academic theses and dissertations
>
> *For submission of manuscripts to agents and publishers, see 070.52*
>
> *See also 001.4 for research*

.025   Plagiarism

> Class here works that focus on avoiding unintentional plagiarism, interdisciplinary works on plagiarism
>
> Class citation style in 808.027
>
> > *For a specific aspect of plagiarism, see the aspect, e.g., plagiarism in the context of copyright law 346.0482, plagiarism as a kind of student cheating 371.58, plagiarism in the work of an American fiction writer of the late 20th century 813.54*

.027   Editorial techniques

> Preparation of manuscripts in publishable form
>
> Including proofreading
>
> Class here style manuals

.03   Specific elements of rhetoric

> Class preparation of manuscripts using specific elements in 808.02; class specific kinds of writing using specific elements in 808.06

.032   Figures of speech

                 Including metaphor, metonymy, simile

                 Class interdisciplinary works on metaphor, on metonymy in 401.43

.036   Narration

.04   Rhetoric in specific languages

                 Class preparation of manuscripts in specific languages in 808.02; class specific elements of rhetoric in specific languages in 808.03; class rhetoric of specific kinds of composition in specific languages in 808.06

.042   Rhetoric in English

.042 7   Study of rhetoric through critical reading

                 Including collections and single works for critical reading

                 Class here readers used in the study of composition

                 For readers limited to a particular literary form, see the form, e.g., short stories 808.31

.042 8   Rhetoric in English for those whose native language is different

.043–.049   Rhetoric in other languages

                 Add to base number 808.04 notation 3–9 from Table 6, e.g., German rhetoric 808.0431; then to the result add the numbers following 808.042 in 808.04201–808.0428, e.g., study of German rhetoric through critical reading 808.04317

.06   Rhetoric of specific kinds of writing

                 Class rhetoric in specific literary forms in 808.1–808.7

.062   Abstracts and summaries

.066   Professional, technical, expository literature

                 Add to base number 808.066 three-digit numbers 001–999 (but stop before any zero that follows a non-zero number), e.g., legal writing 808.06634, writing about natural history 808.0665 (*not* 808.066508), writing on bridge engineering 808.066624 (*not* 808.0666242); then, for writing in a foreign language, add 0 and to the result add notation 2–9 from Table 6, e.g., legal writing in Spanish for speakers of another language 808.06634061; however, for résumé writing, writing cover letters for job hunting, see 650.142

                 For abstracts and summaries, see 808.062; for expository adult easy literature, see 808.067; for expository writing for children, see 808.0688

                 See Manual at 005.15 vs. 808.066005; also at 340 vs. 808.06634; also at 658.45 vs. 651.7, 808.06665

.066 378		Writing for and about higher education

Number built according to instructions under 808.066

Class here authorship and editorial techniques for academic theses and dissertations

Class comprehensive works on authorship and editorial techniques for scholarly writing in 808.02. Class authorship and editorial techniques for academic theses and dissertations about a specific subject other than higher education with the subject in 808.066, e.g., psychology 808.06615

.067   **Adult easy literature**

Works for adults learning to read or for adult beginners in foreign languages

.068   **Children's literature**

.068 1–.068 7   Specific literary forms

Add to base number 808.068 the numbers following 808 in 808.1–808.7, e.g., drama 808.0682

.068 8   Expository writing

>   **808.1–808.7   Rhetoric in specific literary forms**

Class here aesthetics, appreciation, character and nature, composition, theory of specific literary forms; technique, theory, history of criticism of specific literary forms

Observe table of preference under 800

Class theory, technique, history of textual criticism of specific literary forms in 801.959; class specific forms for children in 808.0681–808.0687; class works of critical appraisal of specific literary forms in 809.1–809.7; class comprehensive works on theory, technique, history of literary criticism in 801.95; class comprehensive works on rhetoric in specific literary forms in 808

See Manual at 800: Literary criticism

.1   **Rhetoric of poetry**

Class here prosody

Add to base number 808.1 the numbers following —10 in notation 102–107 from Table 3B, e.g., lyric poetry 808.14

Class linguistic studies of prosody across several languages and from the linguist's viewpoint in 414.6. Class prosodic studies of a particular language as a whole from the linguist's viewpoint with the intonation for the specific language, plus notation 16 from Table 4, e.g., prosodic studies of the Italian language 451.6

.2   **Rhetoric of drama**

Add to base number 808.2 the numbers following —20 in notation 202–205 from Table 3B, e.g., one-act plays 808.241

.3 **Rhetoric of fiction**

Class here rhetoric of novelettes and novels

.31–.38 Fiction of specific scope and kinds

Add to base number 808.3 the numbers following —30 in notation 301–308 from Table 3B, e.g., science fiction 808.38762

.39 Fiction displaying specific elements

Add to base number 808.39 the numbers following —2 in notation 22–27 from Table 3C, e.g., characters in fiction 808.397

Class fiction of specific scope and kinds displaying specific elements in 808.31–808.38

.4 **Rhetoric of essays**

.5 **Rhetoric of speech**

Art or technique of oral expression

Class here voice, expression, gesture

.51 Public speaking (Oratory)

Including public speaking for broadcast media

For preaching, see 251; for debating, see 808.53

.512 Toasts and after-dinner speeches

Standard subdivisions are added for either or both topics in heading

.53 Debating

Class here public discussion of opposing views regardless of format

.54 Recitation

Class here oral interpretation

Class choral speaking in 808.55

.543 Storytelling

.545 Oral interpretation of poetry

Class here poetry slams

.55 Choral speaking

.56 Conversation

.6 **Rhetoric of letters**

.7 **Rhetoric of humor and satire**

Class here rhetoric of parody

.8   **Collections of literary texts from more than two literatures**

> Texts by more than one author in more than two languages not from the same language family

> Class here texts in more than two literatures from two or more language families

> Class works that are limited to a specific topic found in subdivisions of 808.8 and consist equally of literary texts and history, description, critical appraisal of literature with the topic in 808.8, e.g., texts and criticism of literature of the 18th century 808.80033, texts and criticism of drama 808.82; class collections of texts from more than two literatures in the same language with the literature of that language, e.g., collections of works from English, American, and Australian literatures in English (more than one literary form) 820.8; class collections of texts from literatures in more than two languages from the same family with the literature of that family, e.g., French, Italian, and Spanish literatures 840

> *See Manual at 808.8; also at 080 vs. 800*

.800 01–.800 07   Standard subdivisions

[.800 08]   Groups of people

> Do not use; class in 808.89

[.800 09]   History, geographic treatment, biography

> Do not use for collections of literature for and by residents of specific regions, continents, countries, localities; class in 808.89. Do not use for history, description, critical appraisal; class in 809

.800 1–.800 5   Collections from specific periods

> Add to base number 808.800 the numbers following —090 in notation 0901–0905 from Table 1, e.g., collections of 18th century literature 808.80033

.801–.803   Collections displaying specific features

> Add to base number 808.80 notation 1–3 from Table 3C, e.g., collections of literature featuring classicism 808.80142, on death 808.803548

>   808.81–808.88 Collections in specific forms

> Observe table of preference under 800

> Class comprehensive works in 808.8

> *See Manual at 808.81–808.88 and 809.1–809.7*

.81   Collections of poetry

> Class here folk poetry

>> *For anonymous nursery rhymes and related rhymes and rhyming games from the oral tradition, see 398.8*

.810 01–.810 07   Standard subdivisions

[.810 08]   Groups of people

> Do not use; class in 808.81 without adding notation from Table 1

[.810 089]	Poetry for and by ethnic and national groups

Do not use; class in 808.8198

.810 09	History and geographic treatment

[.810 090 1–.810 090 5]	Historical periods

Do not use; class in 808.8101–808.8105

.810 091	Areas, regions, places in general

Do not use for poetry for and by residents of specific regions; class in 808.81991

[.810 092]	Biography

Do not use; class in 808.81 without adding notation from Table 1

.810 093–.810 099	Specific continents, countries, localities

Do not use for poetry for and by residents of specific continents, countries, localities; class in 808.81993–808.81999

.810 1–.810 5	Historical periods

Add to base number 808.810 the numbers following —090 in notation 0901–0905 from Table 1, e.g., 18th century poetry 808.81033

.812–.817	**Specific kinds of poetry**

Add to base number 808.81 the numbers following —10 in notation 102–107 from Table 3B, e.g., collections of narrative poetry 808.813

.819	**Poetry displaying specific features, poetry for and by specific groups of people**

Class poetry of specific kinds displaying specific features, poetry of specific kinds for and by specific groups of people in 808.812–808.817

.819 1–.819 3	Poetry displaying specific features

Add to base number 808.819 notation 1–3 from Table 3C, e.g., collections of poetry about animals 808.819362

.819 8	Poetry for and by ethnic and national groups

Observe table of preference under —8–9 in Table 3C

.819 800 1–.819 800 9	Standard subdivisions

.819 805–.819 809	Poetry for and by ethnic and national groups with ethnic origins from more than one continent, of European descent

Add to base number 808.8198 notation 05–09 from Table 5, e.g., poetry by people of mixed African and European descent 808.81980596009

.819 81–.819 89	Poetry for and by specific ethnic and national groups

Add to base number 808.8198 notation 1–9 from Table 5, e.g., poetry by people of African ancestry 808.819896

.819 9	Poetry for and by groups of people with specific attributes, residents of specific areas

Add to base number 808.8199 the numbers following —9 in notation 91–99 from Table 3C, e.g., poetry for and by residents of specific continents, countries, localities 808.81993–808.81999

Observe table of preference under —8–9 in Table 3C

.82	Collections of drama

Class here folk drama

See Manual at 808.82 vs. 791.437, 791.447, 791.457, 792.9

.820 01–.820 07	Standard subdivisions
[.820 08]	Groups of people

Do not use; class in 808.82 without adding notation from Table 1

[.820 081–.820 088]	Drama for and by groups of people with specific attributes

Do not use; class in 808.82992

[.820 089]	Drama for and by ethnic and national groups

Do not use; class in 808.8298

.820 09	History and geographic treatment
[.820 090 1–.820 090 5]	Historical periods

Do not use; class in 808.8201–808.8205

.820 091	Areas, regions, places in general

Do not use for drama for and by residents of specific regions; class in 808.82991

[.820 092]	Biography

Do not use; class in 808.82 without adding notation from Table 1

.820 093–.820 099	Specific continents, countries, localities

Do not use for drama for and by residents of specific continents, countries, localities; class in 808.82993–808.82999

.820 1–.820 5	Historical periods

Add to base number 808.820 the numbers following —090 in notation 0901–0905 from Table 1, e.g., 18th century drama 808.82033

.822–.825	Specific media, scope, kinds of drama

Add to base number 808.82 the numbers following —20 in notation 202–205 from Table 3B, e.g., collections of tragedies 808.82512

.829	Drama displaying specific features, drama for and by specific groups of people

Class drama of specific media, scope, kinds displaying specific features, drama of specific media, scope, kinds for and by specific groups of people in 808.822–808.825

.829 1–.829 3	Drama displaying specific features

Add to base number 808.829 notation 1–3 from Table 3C, e.g., collections of plays about Faust 808.829351

.829 8	Drama for and by ethnic and national groups

Observe table of preference under —8–9 in Table 3C

.829 800 1–.829 800 9	Standard subdivisions

.829 805–.829 809	Drama for and by ethnic and national groups with ethnic origins from more than one continent, of European descent

Add to base number 808.8298 notation 05–09 from Table 5, e.g., drama by people of mixed Asian and European descent 808.82980595009

.829 81–.829 89	Drama for and by specific ethnic and national groups

Add to base number 808.8298 notation 1–9 from Table 5, e.g., drama by people of Asian ancestry 808.829895

.829 9	Drama for and by groups of people with specific attributes, residents of specific areas

Add to base number 808.8299 the numbers following —9 in notation 91–99 from Table 3C, e.g., drama for and by residents of specific continents, countries, localities 808.82993–808.82999

Observe table of preference under —8–9 in Table 3C

.83   Collections of fiction

.830 01–.830 07	Standard subdivisions

[.830 08]	Groups of people

Do not use; class in 808.83 without adding notation from Table 1

[.830 081–.830 088]	Fiction for and by groups of people with specific attributes

Do not use; class in 808.83992

[.830 089]	Fiction for and by ethnic and national groups

Do not use; class in 808.8398

.830 09	History and geographic treatment

[.830 090 1–.830 090 5]	Historical periods

Do not use; class in 808.8301–808.8305

.830 091	Areas, regions, places in general

Do not use for fiction for and by residents of specific regions; class in 808.83991

[.830 092]	Biography

Do not use; class in 808.83 without adding notation from Table 1

.830 093–.830 099	Specific continents, countries, localities
	Do not use for fiction for and by residents of specific continents, countries, localities; class in 808.83993–808.83999
.830 1–.830 5	Historical periods
	Add to base number 808.830 the numbers following —090 in notation 0901–0905 from Table 1, e.g., 18th century fiction 808.83033

.831–.838   Specific scope and types of fiction

Add to base number 808.83 the numbers following —30 in notation 301–308 from Table 3B, e.g., collections of love stories 808.8385

.839   Fiction displaying specific features, fiction for and by specific groups of people

Class fiction of specific scope and types displaying specific features, fiction of specific scope and types for and by specific groups of people, in 808.831–808.838

.839 1–.839 3	Fiction displaying specific features
	Add to base number 808.839 notation 1–3 from Table 3C, e.g., collections of fiction about animals 808.839362
.839 8	Fiction for and by ethnic and national groups
	Observe table of preference under —8–9 in Table 3C
.839 800 1–.839 800 9	Standard subdivisions
.839 805–.839 809	Fiction for and by ethnic and national groups with ethnic origins from more than one continent, of European descent
	Add to base number 808.8398 notation 05–09 from Table 5, e.g., fiction by people of mixed African and European descent 808.83980596009
.839 81–.839 89	Fiction for and by specific ethnic and national groups
	Add to base number 808.8398 notation 1–9 from Table 5, e.g., fiction by people of African ancestry 808.839896
.839 9	Fiction for and by groups of people with specific attributes, residents of specific areas
	Add to base number 808.8399 the numbers following —9 in notation 91–99 from Table 3C, e.g., fiction for and by residents of specific continents, countries, localities 808.83993–808.83999
	Observe table of preference under —8–9 in Table 3C

.84   Collections of essays

.840 01–.840 07	Standard subdivisions
[.840 08]	Groups of people
	Do not use for groups of people; class in 808.84 without adding notation from Table 1

[.840 081–.840 088]	Essays for and by groups of people with specific attributes
	Do not use; class in 808.84992
[.840 089]	Essays for and by ethnic and national groups
	Do not use; class in 808.8498
.840 09	History and geographic treatment
[.840 090 1–.840 090 5]	Historical periods
	Do not use; class in 808.8401–808.8405
.840 091	Areas, regions, places in general
	Do not use for essays for and by residents of specific regions; class in 808.84991
[.840 092]	Biography
	Do not use; class in 808.84 without adding notation from Table 1
.840 093–.840 099	Specific continents, countries, localities
	Do not use for essays for and by residents of specific continents, countries, localities; class in 808.84993–808.84999
.840 1–.840 5	Historical periods
	Add to base number 808.840 the numbers following —090 in notation 0901–0905 from Table 1, e.g., 18th century essays 808.84033
.849	**Essays displaying specific features, essays for and by specific groups of people**
.849 1–.849 3	Essays displaying specific features
	Add to base number 808.849 notation 1–3 from Table 3C, e.g., collections of descriptive essays 808.84922
.849 8	Essays for and by ethnic and national groups
	Observe table of preference under —8–9 in Table 3C
.849 800 1–.849 800 9	Standard subdivisions
.849 805–.849 809	Essays for and by ethnic and national groups with ethnic origins from more than one continent, of European descent
	Add to base number 808.8498 notation 05–09 from Table 5, e.g., essays by people of mixed African and European descent 808.84980596009
.849 81–.849 89	Essays for and by specific ethnic and national groups
	Add to base number 808.8498 notation 1–9 from Table 5, e.g., essays by people of African ancestry 808.849896

.849 9   Essays for and by groups of people with specific attributes, residents of specific areas

> Add to base number 808.8499 the numbers following —9 in notation 91–99 from Table 3C, e.g., essays for and by residents of specific continents, countries, localities 808.84993–808.84999

> Observe table of preference under —8–9 in Table 3C

.85   Collections of speeches

.850 01–.850 07   Standard subdivisions

[.850 08]   Groups of people

> Do not use; class in 808.85 without adding notation from Table 1

[.850 081–.850 088]   Speeches for and by groups of people with specific attributes

> Do not use; class in 808.85992

[.850 089]   Speeches for and by ethnic and national groups

> Do not use; class in 808.8598

.850 09   History and geographic treatment

[.850 090 1–.850 090 5]   Historical periods

> Do not use; class in 808.8501–808.8505

.850 091   Areas, regions, places in general

> Do not use for speeches for and by residents of specific regions; class in 808.85991

[.850 092]   Biography

> Do not use; class in 808.85 without adding notation from Table 1

.850 093–.850 099   Specific continents, countries, localities

> Do not use for speeches for and by residents of specific continents, countries, localities; class in 808.85993–808.85999

.850 1–.850 5   Historical periods

> Add to base number 808.850 the numbers following —090 in notation 0901–0905 from Table 1, e.g., 18th century speeches 808.85033

.851–.856   Specific kinds of speeches

> Add to base number 808.85 the numbers following —50 in notation 501–506 from Table 3B, e.g., debates 808.853

.859   Speeches displaying specific features, speeches for and by specific groups of people

> Class speeches of specific kinds displaying specific features, speeches of specific kinds for and by specific groups of people in 808.851–808.856

.859 1–.859 3   Speeches displaying specific features

> Add to base number 808.859 notation 1–3 from Table 3C, e.g., collections of descriptive speeches 808.85922

.859 8	Speeches for and by ethnic and national groups

Observe table of preference under —8–9 in Table 3C

.859 800 1–.859 800 9	Standard subdivisions

.859 805–.859 809	Speeches for and by ethnic and national groups with ethnic origins from more than one continent, of European descent

Add to base number 808.8598 notation 05–09 from Table 5, e.g., speeches by people of mixed Asian and European descent 808.85980595009

.859 81–.859 89	Speeches for and by specific ethnic and national groups

Add to base number 808.8598 notation 1–9 from Table 5, e.g., speeches by people of African ancestry 808.859896

.859 9	Speeches for and by groups of people with specific attributes, residents of specific areas

Add to base number 808.8599 the numbers following —9 in notation 91–99 from Table 3C, e.g., speeches for and by residents of specific continents, countries, localities 808.85993–808.85999

Observe table of preference under —8–9 in Table 3C

.86	Collections of letters

.860 01–.860 07	Standard subdivisions

[.860 08]	Groups of people

Do not use; class in 808.86 without adding notation from Table 1

[.860 081–.860 088]	Letters for and by groups of people with specific attributes

Do not use; class in 808.86992

[.860 089]	Letters for and by ethnic and national groups

Do not use; class in 808.8698

.860 09	History and geographic treatment

[.860 090 1–.860 090 5]	Historical periods

Do not use; class in 808.8601–808.8605

.860 091	Areas, regions, places in general

Do not use for letters for and by residents of specific regions; class in 808.86991

[.860 092]	Biography

Do not use; class in 808.86 without adding notation from Table 1

.860 093–.860 099	Specific continents, countries, localities

Do not use for letters for and by residents of specific continents, countries, localities; class in 808.86993–808.86999

.860 1–.860 5   Historical periods

> Add to base number 808.860 the numbers following —090 in notation 0901–0905 from Table 1, e.g., 18th century letters 808.86033

.869   Letters displaying specific features, letters for and by specific groups of people

.869 1–.869 3   Letters displaying specific features

> Add to base number 808.869 notation 1–3 from Table 3C, e.g., collections of letters displaying classicism 808.869142

.869 8   Letters for and by ethnic and national groups

> Observe table of preference under —8–9 in Table 3C

.869 800 1–.869 800 9   Standard subdivisions

.869 805–.869 809   Letters for and by ethnic and national groups with ethnic origins from more than one continent, of European descent

> Add to base number 808.8698 notation 05–09 from Table 5, e.g., letters by people of mixed African and European descent 808.86980596009

.869 81–.869 89   Letters for and by specific ethnic and national groups

> Add to base number 808.8698 notation 1–9 from Table 5, e.g., letters by people of African ancestry 808.869896

.869 9   Letters for and by groups of people with specific attributes, residents of specific areas

> Add to base number 808.8699 the numbers following —9 in notation 91–99 from Table 3C, e.g., letters for and by residents of specific continents, countries, localities 808.86993–808.86999

> Observe table of preference under —8–9 in Table 3C

.87   Collections of humor and satire

> Limited to collections (or texts and criticism) of works in two or more literary forms including both verse and prose

> Class here parody

> *See also 808.888 for humor and satire in two or more prose forms*

> (Option: Give preference to humor and satire over all other literary forms)

.870 01–.870 07   Standard subdivisions

[.870 08]   Groups of people

> Do not use; class in 808.87 without adding notation from Table 1

[.870 081–.870 088]   Humor and satire for and by groups of people with specific attributes

> Do not use; class in 808.87992

[.870 089]   Humor and satire for and by ethnic and national groups

> Do not use; class in 808.8798

.870 09	History and geographic treatment
[.870 090 1–.870 090 5]	Historical periods
	Do not use; class in 808.8701–808.8705
.870 091	Areas, regions, places in general
	Do not use for humor and satire for and by residents of specific regions; class in 808.87991
[.870 092]	Biography
	Do not use; class in 808.87 without adding notation from Table 1
.870 093–.870 099	Specific continents, countries, localities
	Do not use for humor and satire for and by residents of specific continents, countries, localities; class in 808.87993–808.87999

.870 1–.870 5   Historical periods

> Add to base number 808.870 the numbers following —090 in notation 0901–0905 from Table 1, e.g., 18th century literary humor 808.87033

.879   **Humor and satire displaying specific features, humor and satire for and by specific groups of people**

.879 1–.879 3   Humor and satire displaying specific features

> Add to base number 808.879 notation 1–3 from Table 3C, e.g., collections of literary humor about holidays 808.879334

.879 8   Humor and satire for and by ethnic and national groups

> Observe table of preference under —8–9 in Table 3C

.879 800 1–.879 800 9   Standard subdivisions

.879 805–.879 809   Humor and satire for and by ethnic and national groups with ethnic origins from more than one continent, of European descent

> Add to base number 808.8798 notation 05–09 from Table 5, e.g., humor and satire by people of mixed African and European descent 808.87980596009

.879 81–.879 89   Humor and satire for and by specific ethnic and national groups

> Add to base number 808.8798 notation 1–9 from Table 5, e.g., humor and satire by people of African ancestry 808.879896

.879 9   Humor and satire for and by groups of people with specific attributes, residents of specific areas

> Add to base number 808.8799 the numbers following —9 in notation 91–99 from Table 3C, e.g., humor and satire for and by residents of specific continents, countries, localities 808.87993–808.87999

> Observe table of preference under —8–9 in Table 3C

.88   Collections of miscellaneous writings

> Limited to kinds of miscellaneous writings provided for below

.880 01–.880 08	Standard subdivisions
.880 09	History and geographic treatment
[.880 090 1–.880 090 5]	Historical periods

Do not use; class in 808.8801–808.8805

[.880 092]	Biography

Do not use; class in 808.88 without adding notation from Table 1

.880 1–.880 5	Historical periods

Add to base number 808.880 the numbers following —090 in notation 0901–0905 from Table 1, e.g., 18th century miscellaneous writings 808.88033

.882   **Anecdotes, epigrams, graffiti, jokes, jests, quotations, riddles, tongue twisters**

Standard subdivisions are added for any or all topics in heading

Class here interdisciplinary works on riddles; interdisciplinary works on tongue twisters; riddles as jokes by known authors; tongue twisters by known authors; jokes and jests by known authors, interdisciplinary works on jokes and jests

Class humor and satire in two or more literary forms, including both verse and prose, in 808.87

> *For anonymous riddles from the oral tradition, see 398.6; for anonymous jokes and jests from the oral tradition, see 398.7; for anonymous tongue twisters from the oral tradition, see 398.8; for riddles as a type of puzzle similar to logic puzzles, see 793.735*

.883   **Diaries, journals, notebooks, reminiscences**

Class interdisciplinary collections of diaries in 900. Class diaries, journals, notebooks, reminiscences of nonliterary authors with the appropriate subject, e.g., diaries of astronomers 520.922

.887   **Works without identifiable form**

Class here experimental and nonformalized works

Class experimental works with an identifiable literary form with the form, e.g., experimental novels 808.83

.888   **Prose literature**

Class prose without identifiable form in 808.887. Class a specific form of prose literature with the form, e.g., essays 808.84

.89   Collections for and by groups of people

Class here comprehensive works consisting equally of literary texts and history, description, critical appraisal of literature with respect to groups of people

Add to base number 808.89 notation 8–9 from Table 3C, e.g., collections of literature in more than one language by people of African descent 808.89896

Class literature displaying specific features for and by groups of people in 808.801–808.803; class literature in specific forms for and by groups of people in 808.81–808.88; class literatures of specific languages for and by groups of people in 810–890

For history, description, critical appraisal of literature with respect to groups of people, see 809.8

809   History, description, critical appraisal of more than two literatures

Notation 09 from Table 1 as modified below

Do not use for geographic treatment; class in 809.89

History, description, critical appraisal of works by more than one author in more than two languages not from the same language family

Class here collected biography of authors, individual and collected biography of critics; history, description, critical appraisal of works in more than two literatures from two or more language families

Class theory, technique, history of literary criticism in 801.95. Class history, description, critical appraisal of more than two literatures in the same language with the literature of that language, e.g., history of English, American, and Australian literatures in English (more than one literary form) 820.9; class history, description, critical appraisal of literatures in more than two languages from the same family with the literature of that family, e.g., French, Italian, and Spanish literatures 840

See Manual at 808.8

.001–.007   Standard subdivisions

[.008]   Groups of people

Do not use; class in 809.8

[.009]   History, geographic treatment, biography

Do not use for history without subdivision, biography; class in 809. Do not use for historical periods; class in 809.01–809.05. Do not use for geographic treatment; class in 809.89

.01–.05   Literature from specific periods

Add to base number 809.0 the numbers following —090 in notation 0901–0905 from Table 1, e.g., history, description, critical appraisal of 18th century literature 809.033

.1–.7   **Literature in specific forms other than miscellaneous writings**

Add to base number 809 the numbers following 808.8 in 808.81–808.87, e.g., history, description, critical appraisal of poetry 809.1, of poetry about animals 809.19362

Class theory, technique, history of literary criticism of specific literary forms other than miscellaneous writings in 808.1–808.7; class miscellaneous writings in 809.98

See Manual at 800: Literary criticism; also at 808.81–808.88 and 809.1–809.7

.8   **Literature for and by groups of people**

Class here history and description of literature with respect to groups of people

Unless other instructions are given, observe the following table of preference, e.g., history, description, critical appraisal of literature for or by American Roman Catholic girls 809.892827 (*not* 809.813, 809.8921282, or 809.8973):

People by age group	809.89282–809.89285
People by gender or sex	809.89286–809.89287
People by relationships, people by miscellaneous social attributes, people with disabilities and illnesses, gifted people	809.89205–809.89207
Occupational and religious groups	809.8921
Ethnic and national groups except for groups with ethnic origins from more than one continent, of European descent	809.81–809.88
Ethnic and national groups with ethnic origins from more than one continent, of European descent	809.805–809.809
Residents of specific continents, countries, localities	809.893–809.899
Residents of specific regions	809.891

Class literature in specific forms for and by groups of people in 809.1–809.7; class literature displaying specific features for and by groups of people in 809.9; class literatures of specific languages for and by groups of people in 810–890

.800 1–.800 9   Standard subdivisions

.805–.809   **Literature for and by ethnic and national groups with ethnic origins from more than one continent, of European descent**

Add to base number 809.80 the numbers following —0 in notation 05–09 from Table 5, e.g., Europeans 809.809

>   **809.81–809.88 Literature for and by ethnic and national groups except for groups with ethnic origins from more than one continent, of European descent**

Class comprehensive works in 809.8

.81–.87   **Literature for and by larger western ethnic and national groups**

Add to base number 809.8 notation 1–7 from Table 5, e.g., North Americans 809.81

.88   **Literature for and by ancient Greeks, modern Greeks and Cypriots, other ethnic and national groups**

.881   Ancient Greeks

.888   Modern Greeks and Cypriots

.889   Other ethnic and national groups

> Add to base number 809.889 the numbers following —9 in notation 91–99 from Table 5, e.g., Jewish literature 809.88924

.89   Literature for and by other groups of people

> Add to base number 809.89 the numbers following —9 in notation 91–99 from Table 3C, e.g., literature in more than one language by painters 809.892175, literature by residents of Canada 809.8971

.9   Literature displaying specific features, miscellaneous writings

> Class literature in specific forms other than miscellaneous writings displaying specific features in 809.1–809.7

.91–.92   Literature displaying specific qualities and elements

> Add to base number 809.9 notation 1–2 from Table 3C, e.g., history, description, critical appraisal of literature displaying tragedy and horror 809.916

> Class literature dealing with specific themes and subjects and displaying specific qualities and elements in 809.933

.93   Literature displaying other aspects

.933   Literature dealing with specific themes and subjects

> Add to base number 809.933 the numbers following —3 in notation 32–39 from Table 3C, e.g., history, description, critical appraisal of literature dealing with marriage 809.933543

.935   Literature emphasizing subjects

> Works not basically belletristic discussed as literature, in which the real interest is in the literary quality of the text rather than the subject of the text

> Add to base number 809.935 notation 001–999, e.g., religious works as literature 809.9352, biography and autobiography as literature 809.93592

> Class literary examination of texts in which the real interest is in the subject of the texts with the texts, e.g., literary examination of sacred books in order to reach conclusions about meaning, structure, authorship, date 208.2

.98   Miscellaneous writings

> Add to base number 809.98 the numbers following 808.88 in 808.882–808.887, e.g., history, description, critical appraisal of jokes 809.982

> Class theory, technique, history of literary criticism of miscellaneous writings in 808

> ## 810–890 Literatures of specific languages and language families

Literature is classed by the language in which originally written
(Option: Class translations into a language requiring local emphasis with the literature of that language)

Class here collections of texts from literatures of two languages; history, description, critical appraisal of literatures of two languages

Unless there is a specific provision for a dialect, literature in a dialect is classed with the literature of the basic language. Subdivisions are added for literature in a dialect if subdivisions can be added for literature of the basic language, e.g., poetry by early 20th-century author writing in Swiss German dialect 831.912

Literature in a pidgin or creole is classed with the source language from which more of its vocabulary comes than from its other source language(s). Subdivisions are added for literature in a pidgin or creole if subdivisions can be added for literature of the source language, e.g., poetry by late 20th-century author writing in French creole 841.914

Under each literature identified by *, add to designated base number notation 1–8 from Table 3A for works by or about individual authors, notation 01–09 or notation 1–8 from Table 3B for works by or about more than one author. If the base number is not identified in a note, it is the number given for the literature, e.g., for Dutch 839.31. Full instructions for building numbers are given at the start of Table 3

Use the same literary period table for all works of or about literature in the same language, regardless of country of origin, except for special provisions for American literature in English under 810. If option C below is followed, optional period tables may be used for affiliated literatures (literatures in the same language, but from countries other than the traditional homeland)

The numbers used in this schedule for literatures of individual languages do not necessarily correspond exactly with those in 420–490 or with the notation in Table 6. Use notation from Table 6 only when so instructed, e.g., at 899

Unless other instructions are given, class a work containing or discussing literatures of two languages in 810–890 in the number coming first, e.g., a collection of English and French texts 820.8 (*not* 840.8), but a collection of classical Greek and Latin texts 880

Class texts by more than one author in more than two languages not from the same language family in 808.8; class history, description, critical appraisal of works by more than one author in more than two languages not from the same language family in 809; class comprehensive works in 800

(Option: For any group of literatures, add notation 04 from Table 1 and then add notation 01–09 or notation 1–8 from Table 3B, e.g., collections of literary texts written in Ethiopian languages 892.80408. Other options for specific groups of literatures are found at 891.4, 894.8, 896, 897, 898)

(Option: To give preferred treatment to, or make available more and shorter numbers for the classification of, literature of any specific language that it is desired to emphasize, use one of the following options:

(Option A: Class in 810, where full instructions appear

> ## 810–890 Literatures of specific languages and language families

> (Option B: Give preferred treatment by placing before 810 through use of a letter or other symbol, e.g., literature of Arabic language 8A0, for which the base number is 8A

> (Option C: Where two or more countries share the same language, either [1] use initial letters to distinguish the separate countries, or [2] use the special number designated for literatures of those countries that are not preferred. Full instructions appear under 811–818, 819, 821–828, 828.99, 841–848, 848.99, 861–868, 868.99, 869, 869.899)

810 American literature in English

English-language literature of North America, South America, Hawaii, and geographically associated islands

Class comprehensive works on American literature in English and English literature in 820

(Option: To give local emphasis and a shorter number to a specific literature other than American literature in English, e.g., Afrikaans literature, class it here; in that case class American literature in English in 820. Other options are described under 810–890)

.1–.9 Standard subdivisions; collections in more than one form; history, description, critical appraisal of works in more than one form of American literature in English

Add to base number 810 the numbers following —0 in notation 01–09 from Table 3B, e.g., a collection of American literature in English 810.8

Use period table under 811–818

> ### 811–818   Subdivisions for specific forms of American literature in English

Except for modifications shown below, add to base number 81 as instructed at beginning of Table 3, e.g., American poetry in English 811

Use the following period table for English-language literature from any part of North America, South America, Hawaii, and geographically associated islands; for comprehensive works on English-language literature from all these areas

PERIOD TABLE FOR AMERICAN LITERATURE IN ENGLISH

1	Colonial period, 1607–1776
2	1776–1829
3	1830–1861
	Class here 19th century
	For 1800–1829, see notation 2 from this table; for 1861–1899, see notation 4 from this table
4	1861–1899
5	1900–1999
52	1900–1945
54	1945–1999
6	2000–

Class comprehensive works in 810

(Option: Distinguish English-language literatures of specific countries by initial letters, e.g., literature of Canada C810, of Jamaica J810, of United States U810; or class literatures not requiring local emphasis in 819. Other options are described under 810–890)

(OPTIONAL PERIOD TABLE FOR AMERICAN LITERATURE IN ENGLISH

(For Canada

(3	Colonial period to 1867 in Canada
	Class here 19th century
	For 1867–1899, see notation 4 from this table
(4	1867–1899 in Canada
(5	1900–1999 in Canada
(52	1900–1945 in Canada
(54	1945–1999 in Canada
(6	2000 to present in Canada)

811   American poetry in English

Number built according to instructions under 811–818 and at beginning of Table 3

812   American drama in English

Number built according to instructions under 811–818 and at beginning of Table 3

813   American fiction in English

Number built according to instructions under 811–818 and at beginning of Table 3

814   American essays in English

Number built according to instructions under 811–818 and at beginning of Table 3

815   American speeches in English

Number built according to instructions under 811–818 and at beginning of Table 3

816   American letters in English

Number built according to instructions under 811–818 and at beginning of Table 3

817   American humor and satire in English

Number built according to instructions under 811–818 and at beginning of Table 3

818   American miscellaneous writings in English

Number built according to instructions under 811–818 and at beginning of Table 3

(819)   American literatures in English not requiring local emphasis

(Optional number; prefer 810 for all American literatures in English. Other options are described under 810–890)

Class here English-language literatures of specific American countries other than the country requiring local emphasis, e.g., libraries emphasizing United States literature may class here Canadian literature, and libraries emphasizing Canadian literature may class here United States literature

(.1)   *†**Canada**

(.3)   *†**United States**

(.5)   *†**Mexico**

(.7)   **Central America**

(Optional number; prefer 810)

(.700 1–.700 9)   Standard subdivisions; collections in more than one form; history, description, critical appraisal of works in more than one form of Central American literature in English

(Optional numbers; prefer 810.1–810.9)

Add to base number 819.700 the numbers following —0 in notation 01–09 from Table 3B, e.g., a collection of Central American literature in English 819.7008

(.701–.708)   Subdivisions for specific forms of Central American literature in English

(Optional numbers; prefer 811–818)

Add to base number 819.70 as instructed at beginning of Table 3, e.g., Central American poetry in English 819.701

*Add to base number as instructed at beginning of Table 3
†(Optional number; prefer 810 for comprehensive works; prefer 810.1–810.9 for standard subdivisions; collections in more than one form; history, description, critical appraisal of works in more than one form; prefer 811–818 for specific forms)

(.71–.77)	Specific countries	

          (Optional numbers; prefer 810)

          Add to base number 819.7 the numbers following —728 in notation 7281–7287 from Table 2, e.g., English-language literature of Costa Rica 819.76; then add further as instructed at beginning of Table 3, e.g., a collection of English-language literature of Costa Rica 819.7608

(.8)   **West Indies (Antilles) and Bermuda**

          (Optional number; prefer 810)

(.800 1–.800 9)   Standard subdivisions; collections in more than one form; history, description, critical appraisal of works in more than one form of English-language literatures of West Indies (Antilles) and Bermuda

          (Optional numbers; prefer 810.1–810.9)

          Add to base number 819.800 the numbers following —0 in notation 01–09 from Table 3B, e.g., a collection of English-language literature of West Indies 819.8008

(.801–.808)   Subdivisions for specific forms of English-language literatures of West Indies (Antilles) and Bermuda

          (Optional numbers; prefer 811–818)

          Add to base number 819.80 as instructed at beginning of Table 3, e.g., English-language poetry of West Indies 819.801

(.81)   *†Cuba

(.82)   *†Jamaica

(.83)   *†Dominican Republic

(.84)   *†Haiti

(.85)   *†Puerto Rico

(.86)   *†Bahama Islands

(.87)   *†Leeward Islands

(.88)   *†Windward and other southern islands

(.89)   *†Bermuda

(.9)   **South America**

          (Optional number; prefer 810)

---

*Add to base number as instructed at beginning of Table 3
†(Optional number; prefer 810 for comprehensive works; prefer 810.1–810.9 for standard subdivisions; collections in more than one form; history, description, critical appraisal of works in more than one form; prefer 811–818 for specific forms)

(.900 1–.900 9)	Standard subdivisions; collections in more than one form; history, description, critical appraisal of works in more than one form of English-language literatures of South America

(Optional numbers; prefer 810.1–810.9)

Add to base number 819.900 the numbers following —0 in notation 01–09 from Table 3B, e.g., a collection of English-language literature from South America 819.9008

(.901–.908)	Subdivisions for specific forms of English-language literatures of South America

(Optional numbers; prefer 811–818)

Add to base number 819.90 as instructed at beginning of Table 3, e.g., English-language poetry from South America 819.901

(.91–.99)	Specific countries

(Optional numbers; prefer 810)

Add to base number 819.9 the numbers following —8 in notation 81–89 from Table 2, e.g., English-language literature of Brazil 819.91; then add further as instructed at beginning of Table 3, e.g., a collection of English-language literature of Brazil 819.9108

820   English and Old English (Anglo-Saxon) literatures

Subdivisions are added for English literature alone

For American literature in English, see 810

.1–.9   Standard subdivisions; collections in more than one form; history, description, critical appraisal of works in more than one form of English literature

Add to base number 820 the numbers following —0 in notation 01–09 from Table 3B, e.g., a collection of English literature 820.8

Use period table under 821–828

> **821–828 Subdivisions for specific forms of English literature**

Except for modifications shown under specific entries, add to base number 82 as instructed at beginning of Table 3, e.g., a collection of English literature 820.8

Use the following period table for literature from all countries and continents except North America, South America, Hawaii, and associated islands; for comprehensive works on literature in English language

PERIOD TABLE FOR ENGLISH

1	Early English period, 1066–1400
	Class here medieval period
2	1400–1558
3	Elizabethan period, 1558–1625
	Class here 16th century; Renaissance and Jacobean periods
	For 1500–1558, the pre-Elizabethan part of the Renaissance, see notation 2 from this table
4	1625–1702
	Class here Caroline and Restoration periods
5	Queen Anne period, 1702–1745
	Class here 18th century
	For 1700–1702, see notation 4 from this table; for 1745–1799, see notation 6 from this table
6	1745–1799
7	1800–1837
	Class here romantic period
8	Victorian period, 1837–1899
	Class here 19th century
	For 1800–1837, see notation 7 from this table
9	1900–
91	1900–1999
912	1900–1945
914	1945–1999
92	2000–

Class comprehensive works in 820

(Option: Distinguish English-language literatures of specific countries by initial letters, e.g., literature of England E820, of Ireland Ir820, of Scotland S820, of Wales W820, or of all British Isles B820, of Australia A820, of India In820; or class literatures not requiring local emphasis in 828.99. If literatures are identified by one of these methods, assign optional period numbers given below for literature of Ireland, Africa, Asia, Australia, and New Zealand; otherwise, assign the period numbers given above for all English-language literatures except American literature. Other options are described under 810–890

(OPTIONAL PERIOD TABLES FOR ENGLISH

  (For Ireland

(1	Medieval and early modern to 1659 in Ireland
	Class here 17th century
	For 1660–1699, see notation 2 from this table
(2	1660–1799 in Ireland
(3	1800–1899 in Ireland

> **821–828 Subdivisions for specific forms of English literature**

   (4   1900–1945 in Ireland
            Class here Irish literary revival, 20th century
            For Irish literary revival in 19th century, see notation 3 from this table; for 1945–1999, see notation 5 from this table
   (5   1945–1999 in Ireland
   (6   2000 to present in Ireland

(For African countries other than South Africa
   (1   Early period to 1959 in African countries other than South Africa
   (2   1960–1999 in African countries other than South Africa
            Class here 20th century
            For 1900–1959, see notation 1 from this table
   (3   2000 to present in African countries other than South Africa

(For Asian countries
   (1   Early period to 1858 in Asian countries
            Class here 19th century
            For 1858–1899, see notation 2 from this table
   (2   1858–1947 in Asian countries
   (3   1947–1999 in Asian countries
            Class here 20th century
            For 1900–1947, see notation 2 from this table
   (4   2000 to present in Asian countries

(For Australia
   (1   Early period to 1889 in Australia
   (2   1890–1945 in Australia
   (3   1945–1999 in Australia
            Class here 20th century
            For 1900–1945, see notation 2 from this table
   (4   2000 to present in Australia

(For New Zealand
   (1   Early period to 1907 in New Zealand
   (2   1907–1999 in New Zealand
   (3   2000 to present in New Zealand

(For South Africa
   (1   Early period to 1909 in South Africa
   (2   1909–1961 in South Africa
            Class here 20th century
            For 1900–1909, see notation 1 from this table; for 1961–1994, see notation 3 from this table; for 1994–1999, see notation 4 from this table
   (3   1961–1994 in South Africa
   (4   1994 to present in South Africa)

821   English poetry

Number built according to instructions under 821–828 and at beginning of Table 3

822   English drama

> Number built according to instructions under 821–828 and at beginning of Table 3

.3   Drama of Elizabethan period, 1558–1625

> Number built according to instructions under 821–828 and at beginning of Table 3

.33   William Shakespeare

(Option: Subarrange works about and by Shakespeare according to the
following table, which may be adapted for use with any specific author:

A   Authorship controversies
         (Option: Class here bibliography; prefer 016.82233)
B   Biography
D   Critical appraisal
         Class critical appraisal of individual works in notation O-Z
         from this table
E   Textual criticism
         Class textual criticism of individual works in notation O-Z
         from this table
F   Sources, allusions, learning
G   Societies, concordances, miscellany
H   Quotations, condensations, adaptations
I   Complete works in English without notes
J   Complete works in English with notes
K   Complete works in translation
L   Partial collections in English without notes
M   Partial collections in English with notes
N   Partial collections in translation
>O-Z   Individual works
         Use the first number of each pair for texts, the second for
         description and critical appraisal
         Class poems in 821.3
>O-R   Comedies
O1–2   All's well that ends well
O3–4   As you like it
O5–6   The comedy of errors
O7–8   Love's labour's lost
P1–2   Measure for measure
P3–4   The merchant of Venice
P5–6   The merry wives of Windsor
P7–8   A midsummer night's dream
Q1–2   Much ado about nothing
Q3–4   The taming of the shrew
Q5–6   The tempest
Q7–8   Twelfth night
R1–2   The two gentlemen of Verona
R3–4   The winter's tale
>S-V   Tragedies
S1–2   Antony and Cleopatra
S3–4   Coriolanus
S5–6   Cymbeline
S7–8   Hamlet
T1–2   Julius Caesar
T3–4   King Lear
T5–6   Macbeth
T7–8   Othello
U1–2   Pericles
U3–4   Romeo and Juliet
U5–6   Timon of Athens
U7–8   Titus Andronicus
V1–2   Troilus and Cressida
>W-X   Histories
W1–2   Henry IV, parts 1–2

.33	William Shakespeare	
	W3–4	Henry V
	W5–6	Henry VI, parts 1–3
	W7–8	Henry VIII
	X1–2	King John
	X3–4	Richard II
	X5–6	Richard III
	Y	Poems
		(Optional numbers; prefer 821.3)
	Y1–2	General works
	Y3–4	Venus and Adonis
	Y5–6	The rape of Lucrece
	Y7–8	Sonnets
	Z	Spurious and doubtful works)

823 English fiction

Number built according to instructions under 821–828 and at beginning of Table 3

824 English essays

Number built according to instructions under 821–828 and at beginning of Table 3

825 English speeches

Number built according to instructions under 821–828 and at beginning of Table 3

826 English letters

Number built according to instructions under 821–828 and at beginning of Table 3

827 English humor and satire

Number built according to instructions under 821–828 and at beginning of Table 3

828 English miscellaneous writings

Number built according to instructions under 821–828 and at beginning of Table 3

(.99) English-language literatures not requiring local emphasis

(Optional number; prefer 820 for all non-American English-language literatures. Other options are described under 810–890)

Class here English-language literatures of specific non-American countries other than the country requiring local emphasis, e.g., libraries emphasizing British literature may class here Australian, Indian, other literatures, and libraries emphasizing Indian literature may class here British literature

(.991) †Scotland and Ireland

(Option: Class here all English-language literature of United Kingdom, of Great Britain, of British Isles. Add to base number 828.991 as instructed at beginning of Table 3 for United Kingdom, for Great Britain, for British Isles, e.g., a collection of English-language literature from the British Isles 828.99108)

†(Optional number; prefer 820 for comprehensive works; prefer 820.1–820.9 for standard subdivisions; collections in more than one form; history, description, critical appraisal of works in more than one form; prefer 821–828 for specific forms)

(.991 1)	*†Scotland
(.991 5)	*†Ireland
(.992)	*†England and Wales
(.992 9)	*†Wales
(.993)	†New Zealand, Australia, India, South Africa
(.993 3)	*†New Zealand
(.993 4)	*†Australia
(.993 5)	*†India
(.993 6)	*†South Africa
(.994–.999)	Other parts of the world

> (Optional numbers; prefer 820)
>
> English-language literature except of British Isles, North America, South America, Hawaii, New Zealand, Australia, India, South Africa, and associated islands
>
> Add to base number 828.99 notation 4–9 from Table 2, e.g., English-language literature of Israel 828.995694; then add 0 and to the result add further as instructed at beginning of Table 3, e.g., English-language poetry of Israel 828.99569401

829   Old English (Anglo-Saxon) literature

.01–.09   Standard subdivisions; collections in more than one form; history, description, critical appraisal of works in more than one form of Old English (Anglo-Saxon) literature

> Limited to works by or about more than one author
>
> Add to base number 829 notation 01–09 from Table 3B, e.g., history, description, critical appraisal of works in more than one form 829.09

.1   Poetry

> *For Caedmon, see 829.2; for Beowulf, see 829.3; for Cynewulf, see 829.4*

.100 1–.100 9   Standard subdivisions; collections; history, description, critical appraisal

> Limited to works by or about more than one author
>
> Add to base number 829.100 the numbers following —100 in notation 1001–1009 from Table 3B, e.g., collections of Old English poetry 829.1008

.2   Caedmon

.3   Beowulf

---

*Add to base number as instructed at beginning of Table 3
†(Optional number; prefer 820 for comprehensive works; prefer 820.1–820.9 for standard subdivisions; collections in more than one form; history, description, critical appraisal of works in more than one form; prefer 821–828 for specific forms)

.4   **Cynewulf**

.8   **Prose literature**

.800 1–.800 9   Standard subdivisions; collections; history, description, critical appraisal

> Limited to works by or about more than one author
>
> Add to base number 829.800 the numbers following —100 in notation 1001–1009 from Table 3B, e.g., collections of Old English prose 829.8008

830   German literature and literatures of related languages

> Class here literatures of Germanic languages
>
> *For English and Old English (Anglo-Saxon) literatures, see 820*

.01–.09   Standard subdivisions of literatures of Germanic languages

.1–.9   **Standard subdivisions; collections in more than one form; history, description, critical appraisal of works in more than one form of German literature**

> Class here literature in Alsatian, Franconian, Pennsylvania Dutch (Pennsylvania German), Swabian, Swiss-German dialects
>
> Add to base number 830 the numbers following —0 in notation 01–09 from Table 3B, e.g., a collection of German literature 830.8
>
> Use period table under 831–838
>
> *See also 839.1 for Yiddish (Judeo-German) literature; also 839.4 for low German (Plattdeutsch) literature*

> ## 831–838 Subdivisions for specific forms of German literature

Class here specific forms of literature in Alsatian, Franconian, Pennsylvania Dutch (Pennsylvania German), Swabian, Swiss-German dialects

Add to base number 83 as instructed at beginning of Table 3, e.g., German poetry 831

PERIOD TABLE

1	Early period to 1099
	Class here Old High German literature
2	1100–1349
	Class here medieval period, 750–1349; Middle High German literature
	For 750–1099, see notation 1 from this table
21	1100–1249
	Class here 13th century, Blütezeit
	For 1250–1299, see notation 22 from this table
22	1250–1349
	Class here 14th century
	For 1350–1399, see notation 3 from this table
3	1350–1517
4	Reformation period, 1517–1625
5	1625–1749
	Class here baroque period
6	1750–1832
	Class here 18th century, classical period, romantic period
	For 1700–1749, see notation 5 from this table; for later romantic period, see notation 7 from this table
7	1832–1856
	Class here 19th century
	For 1800–1832, see notation 6 from this table; for 1856–1899, see notation 8 from this table
8	1856–1899
9	1900–
91	1900–1990
912	1900–1945
914	1945–1990
92	1990–

Class comprehensive works in 830

See also 839.1 for Yiddish (Judeo-German) literature; also 839.4 for low German (Plattdeutsch) literature

831   German poetry

Number built according to instructions under 831–838 and at beginning of Table 3

832   German drama

Number built according to instructions under 831–838 and at beginning of Table 3

833   German fiction

Number built according to instructions under 831–838 and at beginning of Table 3

834   German essays

> Number built according to instructions under 831–838 and at beginning of Table 3

835   German speeches

> Number built according to instructions under 831–838 and at beginning of Table 3

836   German letters

> Number built according to instructions under 831–838 and at beginning of Table 3

837   German humor and satire

> Number built according to instructions under 831–838 and at beginning of Table 3

838   German miscellaneous writings

> Number built according to instructions under 831–838 and at beginning of Table 3

839   Other Germanic literatures

.1   *Yiddish literature

PERIOD TABLE
1	Early period to 1699
2	Period of enlightenment, 1700–1859
	Class here 19th century
	For 1860–1899, see notation 3 from this table
3	1860–1945
	Class here 20th century
	For 1945–1999, see notation 4 from this table
4	1945–

> **839.2–839.4   Low Germanic literatures**

> Class comprehensive works in 839

.2   *Frisian literature

Including Old Frisian literature

PERIOD TABLE
1	Early period to 1609
2	1609–1799
3	1800–1899
4	1900–1999
5	2000–

.3   Netherlandish literatures

*Add to base number as instructed at beginning of Table 3

.31   *Dutch literature

Including Old Low Franconian literature

Class here Flemish literature

PERIOD TABLE
1		Medieval period to 1449
		Class here 15th century
		For 1450–1499, see notation 2 from this table
2		Renaissance period, 1450–1599
3		1600–1699
4		1700–1799
5		1800–1899
6		1900–1999
62		1900–1945
64		1945–1999
7		2000–

.36   *Afrikaans literature

PERIOD TABLE
1	Early period to 1875
2	1875–1904
3	1904–1924
4	1924–1961
	Class here 20th century
	For 1900–1904, see notation 2 from this table; for 1904–1924, see notation 3 from this table; for 1961–1994, see notation 5 from this table; for 1994–1999, see notation 6 from this table
5	1961–1994
6	1994–

.4   ***Low German (Plattdeutsch) literature**

Including Old Low German literature, Old Saxon literature

PERIOD TABLE
1	Early period to 1599
2	1600–1899
3	1900–1999
4	2000–

.5   **North Germanic literatures**

Class here comprehensive works on east Scandinavian literatures, comprehensive works on west Scandinavian literatures, comprehensive works on modern west Scandinavian literatures; comprehensive works on literatures of the Nordic countries

For specific North Germanic literatures, see 839.6–839.8; for Finnic literatures, see 894.54; for Sámi literatures, see 894.57

---

*Add to base number as instructed at beginning of Table 3

>   **839.6–839.8 Specific North Germanic literatures**

         Class comprehensive works in 839.5

.6   **Old Norse (Old Icelandic), Icelandic, Faroese literatures**

.600 1–.600 9   Standard subdivisions of comprehensive works on Old Norse (Old Icelandic), Icelandic, Faroese literatures

.601–.609   Standard subdivisions; collections in more than one form; history, description, critical appraisal of works in more than one form of Old Norse (Old Icelandic) literature

         Add to base number 839.60 the numbers following —0 in notation 01–09 from Table 3B, e.g., a collection of Old Norse literature 839.608

.61–.68   Subdivisions for specific forms of Old Norse (Old Icelandic) literature

         Add to base number 839.6 as instructed at beginning of Table 3, e.g., Old Norse poetry 839.61

.69   Icelandic and Faroese literatures

.690 01–.690 09   Standard subdivisions of comprehensive works on Icelandic and Faroese literatures

.690 1–.690 9   Standard subdivisions; collections in more than one form; history, description, critical appraisal of works in more than one form of Icelandic literature

         Add to base number 839.690 the numbers following —0 in notation 01–09 from Table 3B, e.g., a collection of Icelandic literature 839.6908

         Use period table under 839.691–839.698

.691–.698   Subdivisions for specific forms of Icelandic literature

         Add to base number 839.69 as instructed at beginning of Table 3, e.g., Icelandic poetry 839.691

         PERIOD TABLE
           1   Early period, 1500–1719
           2   Age of enlightenment, 1720–1835
           3   1835–1899
              Class here 19th century
                 For 1800–1835, see notation 2 from this table
           4   1900–1999
           5   2000–

.699   *Faroese literature

*Add to base number as instructed at beginning of Table 3

.7   **Swedish literature**

PERIOD TABLE

1	Medieval period to 1519
2	Reformation period, 1520–1639
3	1640–1739

    Class here 17th century

      For 1600–1639, see notation 2 from this table

4   1740–1779

    Class here 18th century

      For 1700–1739, see notation 3 from this table; for
      1780–1799, see notation 5 from this table

5   Age of Gustavus, 1780–1809

    Including 1800–1809 [*formerly* 6]

6   1809–1909

62   1809–1830

    Class here period of romanticism

64   1830–1879

    Class here period of liberalism

67   1879–1909

    Including 1900–1909 [*formerly* 72]
    Class here period of realism

7   1909–1999

72   1909–1945

74   1945–1999

8   2000–

.8   **Danish and Norwegian literatures**

.81   *Danish literature

PERIOD TABLE

1   Medieval period to 1499

2   Reformation period, 1500–1559

    Class here 16th century

      For 1560–1599, see notation 3 from this table

3   Learned period, 1560–1699

4   Age of Holberg, 1700–1749

    Class here 18th century

      For 1750–1799, see notation 5 from this table

5   Period of enlightenment, 1750–1799

6   1800–1899

7   1900–1999

72   1900–1945

74   1945–1999

8   2000–

Class Dano-Norwegian literature in 839.82

*Add to base number as instructed at beginning of Table 3

.82   *Norwegian literature

             Class here Dano-Norwegian, New Norwegian, Bokmål, Landsmål, Riksmål
             literature

             PERIOD TABLE
             1   Medieval period to 1499
             2   Reformation period, 1500–1559
                         Class here 16th century
                             For 1560–1599, see notation 3 from this table
             3   Learned period, 1560–1699
             4   1700–1749
                         Class here 18th century
                             For 1750–1799, see notation 5 from this table
             5   Period of enlightenment, 1750–1799
             6   1800–1899
             7   1900–1999
             72   1900–1945
             74   1945–1999
             8   2000–

.9   **East Germanic literatures**

840   French literature and literatures of related Romance languages

             Class here literatures of Romance languages

             Class comprehensive works on literatures of Italic languages in 870

             *For literatures of Italian, Dalmatian, Romanian, Rhaetian, Sardinian, Corsican
             languages, see 850; for literatures of Spanish, Portuguese, Galician languages,
             see 860*

.01–.09   Standard subdivisions of literatures of Romance languages

.1–.9   **Standard subdivisions; collections in more than one form; history,
             description, critical appraisal of works in more than one form of
             French literature**

             Add to base number 840 the numbers following —0 in notation 01–09 from
             Table 3B, e.g., a collection of French literature 840.8

             Use period table under 841–848

             See also 849 for Occitan literature

---

*Add to base number as instructed at beginning of Table 3

> ## 841–848 Subdivisions for specific forms of French literature

Except for modifications shown under specific entries, add to base number 84 as instructed at beginning of Table 3, e.g., French poetry 841

Use the following period table for literature in French language from all countries and continents, for comprehensive works on literature in French language

PERIOD TABLE FOR FRENCH

1	Early period to 1399
	Class here medieval period
2	1400–1499
3	Renaissance period, 1500–1599
4	Classical period, 1600–1715
5	1715–1789
	Class here 18th century, Enlightenment, Age of Reason
	For 1700–1715, see notation 4 from this table; for 1789–1799, see notation 6 from this table
6	Revolution and Empire, 1789–1815
7	Constitutional monarchy, 1815–1848
	Class here 19th century
	For 1800–1815, see notation 6 from this table; for 1848–1899, see notation 8 from this table
8	1848–1899
9	1900–
91	1900–1999
912	1900–1945
914	1945–1999
92	2000–

Class comprehensive works in 840

See also 849 for Occitan literature

(Option: Distinguish French-language literatures of specific countries by initial letters, e.g., literature of Canada C840, of France F840; or class literatures not requiring local emphasis in 848.99. If literatures are identified by one of these methods, assign the optional period numbers given below for Belgium and non-European countries; otherwise, assign the period numbers given above for all French-language literatures. Other options are described under 810–890

(OPTIONAL PERIOD TABLES FOR FRENCH

    (For Asian and African countries

(1	Early period to 1959 in Asian and African countries
(2	1960–1999 in Asian and African countries
	Class here 20th century
	For 1900–1959, see notation 1 from this table
(3	2000 to present in Asian and African countries

    (For Belgium

(1	Early period to 1829 in Belgium
(2	1830–1899 in Belgium
	Class here 19th century
	For 1800–1829, see notation 2 from this table
(3	1900–1999 in Belgium

> **841–848 Subdivisions for specific forms of French literature**

    (32   1900–1945 in Belgium
    (34   1945–1999 in Belgium
    (4   2000 to present in Belgium

(For Canada
    (3   Colonial period to 1867 in Canada
           Class here 19th century
              For 1867–1899, see notation 4 from this table
    (4   1867–1899 in Canada
    (5   1900–1999 in Canada
    (52   1900–1945 in Canada
    (54   1945–1999 in Canada
    (6   2000 to present in Canada)

841   French poetry

Number built according to instructions under 841–848 and at beginning of Table 3

842   French drama

Number built according to instructions under 841–848 and at beginning of Table 3

843   French fiction

Number built according to instructions under 841–848 and at beginning of Table 3

844   French essays

Number built according to instructions under 841–848 and at beginning of Table 3

845   French speeches

Number built according to instructions under 841–848 and at beginning of Table 3

846   French letters

Number built according to instructions under 841–848 and at beginning of Table 3

847   French humor and satire

Number built according to instructions under 841–848 and at beginning of Table 3

848   French miscellaneous writings

Number built according to instructions under 841–848 and at beginning of Table 3

(.99)   French-language literatures not requiring local emphasis

(Optional number; prefer 840 for all French-language literatures. Other options are described under 810–890)

Class here literatures of specific countries, e.g., libraries emphasizing literature of France may class here Belgian and Canadian literatures, libraries emphasizing Canadian literature may class here literature of France

(.991)   *†France

(.992)   *†Canada

(.993)   *†Belgium

(.994–.999)   Other parts of the world

> (Optional numbers; prefer 840)
>
> French-language literature except of France, Belgium, Canada
>
> Add to base number 848.99 notation 4–9 from Table 2, e.g., French-language literature of Tahiti 848.9996211; then add 0 and to the result add further as instructed at beginning of Table 3, e.g., French-language drama of Tahiti 848.999621102

849   Occitan, Catalan, Franco-Provençal literatures

Subdivisions are added for Occitan literature alone

.01–.09   Standard subdivisions; collections in more than one form; history, description, critical appraisal of works in more than one form of Occitan literature

> Class here Langue d'oc literature; literature in Auvergnat, Gascon, Languedocien, Limousin, Vivaro-Alpine dialects; literature in Provençal, Nissart dialects
>
> Add to base number 849.0 the numbers following —0 in notation 01–09 from Table 3B, e.g., a collection of Occitan literature 849.08
>
> Use period table under 849.1–849.8
>
> Class Franco-Provençal literature in 849 without further addition

.1–.8   **Subdivisions for specific forms of Occitan literature**

> Class here specific forms of Langue d'oc literature; specific forms of literature in Auvergnat, Gascon, Languedocien, Limousin, Vivaro-Alpine dialects; specific forms of literature in Provençal, Nissart dialects
>
> Add to base number 849 as instructed at beginning of Table 3, e.g., Occitan poetry 849.1
>
> PERIOD TABLE
> | | |
> |---|---|
> | 1 | Early period to 1099 |
> | 2 | Golden age, 1100–1299 |
> | 3 | 1300–1499 |
> | 4 | 1500–1899 |
> | 5 | 1900–1999 |
> | 52 | 1900–1945 |
> | 54 | 1945–1999 |
> | 6 | 2000– |
>
> Class Franco-Provençal literature in 849 without further addition

*Add to base number as instructed at beginning of Table 3

†(Optional number; prefer 840 for comprehensive works; prefer 840.1–840.9 for standard subdivisions; collections in more than one form; history, description, critical appraisal of works in more than one form; prefer 841–848 for specific forms)

.9 ***Catalan literature**

PERIOD TABLE
1   Early period to 1349
      Class here 14th century
        For 1350–1399, see notation 2 from this table
2   1350–1449
3   Golden age, 1450–1499
      Class here 15th century
        For 1400–1449, see notation 2 from this table
4   1500–1899
5   1900–1999
52   1900–1945
54   1945–1999
6   2000–

850 Literatures of Italian, Dalmatian, Romanian, Rhaetian, Sardinian, Corsican languages

Subdivisions are added for Italian literature alone

Class comprehensive works on literatures of Romance languages in 840; class comprehensive works on literatures of Italic languages in 870

.1–.9 **Standard subdivisions; collections in more than one form; history, description, critical appraisal of works in more than one form of Italian literature**

Add to base number 850 the numbers following —0 in notation 01–09 from Table 3B, e.g., a collection of Italian literature 850.8

Use period table under 851–858

> ### 851–858 Subdivisions for specific forms of Italian literature

Add to base number 85 as instructed at beginning of Table 3, e.g., Italian poetry 851

PERIOD TABLE

1	Early period to 1375
2	Period of classical learning, 1375–1492
	Class here Renaissance period
	For later Renaissance period, see notation 3 from this table
3	1492–1542
4	1542–1585
	Class here 16th century
	For 1500–1542, see notation 3 from this table; for 1585–1599, see notation 5 from this table
5	1585–1748
6	1748–1814
	Class here 18th century
	For 1700–1748, see notation 5 from this table
7	1814–1859
	Class here 19th century, romantic period
	For 1800–1814, see notation 6 from this table; for 1859–1899, see notation 8 from this table
8	1859–1899
9	1900–
91	1900–1999
912	1900–1945
914	1945–1999
92	2000–

Class comprehensive works in 850

851 Italian poetry

Number built according to instructions under 851–858 and at beginning of Table 3

852 Italian drama

Number built according to instructions under 851–858 and at beginning of Table 3

853 Italian fiction

Number built according to instructions under 851–858 and at beginning of Table 3

854 Italian essays

Number built according to instructions under 851–858 and at beginning of Table 3

855 Italian speeches

Number built according to instructions under 851–858 and at beginning of Table 3

856 Italian letters

Number built according to instructions under 851–858 and at beginning of Table 3

857   Italian humor and satire

> Number built according to instructions under 851–858 and at beginning of Table 3

858   Italian miscellaneous writings

> Number built according to instructions under 851–858 and at beginning of Table 3

859   Literatures of Romanian, Rhaetian, Sardinian, Corsican languages

> Subdivisions are added for Romanian literature alone

.01–.09   Standard subdivisions; collections in more than one form; history, description, critical appraisal of works in more than one form of Romanian literature

> Add to base number 859.0 the numbers following —0 in notation 01–09 from Table 3B, e.g., a collection of Romanian literature 859.08

> Use period table under 859.1–859.8

.1–.8   **Subdivisions for specific forms of Romanian literature**

> Add to base number 859 as instructed at beginning of Table 3, e.g., Romanian poetry 859.1

> PERIOD TABLE
> 1   Early period to 1799
> 2   1800–1899
> 3   1900–
> 32   1900–1945
> 34   1945–1989
> 35   1989–

.9   **Literatures of Rhaetian, Sardinian, Corsican languages**

.92   *Friulian literature

.94   *Ladin literature

.96   *Romansch literature

.98   Sardinian and Corsican literatures

.982   *Sardinian literature

.984   *Corsican literature

860   Literatures of Spanish, Portuguese, Galician languages

> Class comprehensive works on literatures of Romance languages in 840

.01–.09   Standard subdivisions of literatures of Spanish, Portuguese, Galician languages

---

*Add to base number as instructed at beginning of Table 3

.1–.9   **Standard subdivisions; collections in more than one form; history, description, critical appraisal of works in more than one form of Spanish literature**

Class here Judeo-Spanish (Ladino), Papiamento literature

Add to base number 860 the numbers following —0 in notation 01–09 from Table 3B, e.g., a collection of Spanish literature 860.8

Use period table under 861–868

See also 849.9 for Catalan literature

> ## 861–868 Subdivisions for specific forms of Spanish literature

Except for modifications shown under specific entries, add to base number 86 as instructed at beginning of Table 3, e.g., Spanish poetry 861

Class here specific forms of Judeo-Spanish (Ladino), Papiamento literature

Use the following period table for literature in Spanish language from all countries and continents, for comprehensive works on literature in Spanish language

PERIOD TABLE FOR SPANISH

1		Early period to 1369
		Class here 14th century
		For 1369–1399, see notation 2 from this table
2		1369–1516
3		Golden Age, 1516–1699
4		1700–1799
5		1800–1899
6		1900–1999
62		1900–1945
64		1945–1999
7		2000–

Class comprehensive works in 860

See also 849.9 for Catalan literature

(Option: Distinguish Spanish-language literatures of specific countries by initial letters, e.g., literature of Chile Ch860, of Colombia Co860, of Mexico M860 [or, of all American countries A860], of Spain S860; or class literatures not requiring local emphasis in 868.99. If literatures are identified by one of these methods, assign the optional period numbers given below for literature of American countries; otherwise, assign the period numbers given above for all Spanish-language literatures. Other options are described under 810–890

(OPTIONAL PERIOD TABLE FOR SPANISH

(For American countries

(1		Colonial and revolutionary period, 1519–1826, in American countries
(2		1826–1888 in American countries
		Class here 19th century
		For 1800–1826, see notation 1 from this table; for
		1888–1899, see notation 3 from this table
(3		1888–1909 in American countries
(4		1910–1999 in American countries
(42		1910–1945 in American countries
(44		1945–1999 in American countries
(5		2000 to present in American countries)

861   Spanish poetry

Number built according to instructions under 861–868 and at beginning of Table 3

862   Spanish drama

Number built according to instructions under 861–868 and at beginning of Table 3

863   Spanish fiction

Number built according to instructions under 861–868 and at beginning of Table 3

864   Spanish essays

Number built according to instructions under 861–868 and at beginning of Table 3

865   Spanish speeches

Number built according to instructions under 861–868 and at beginning of Table 3

866   Spanish letters

Number built according to instructions under 861–868 and at beginning of Table 3

867   Spanish humor and satire

Number built according to instructions under 861–868 and at beginning of Table 3

868   Spanish miscellaneous writings

Number built according to instructions under 861–868 and at beginning of Table 3

(.99)   Spanish-language literatures not requiring local emphasis

(Optional number; prefer 860 for all Spanish-language literatures. Other options are described under 810–890)

Class here literatures of specific countries other than the country requiring local emphasis, e.g., libraries emphasizing literature of Spain may class here Hispanic-American literatures, and libraries emphasizing literature of Mexico may class here literatures of other Hispanic-American countries and of Spain

(.991)   *†Spain

(.992)   Hispanic North America

(Optional number; prefer 860)

Class here comprehensive works on Spanish-language literature of Hispanic America

For Hispanic South America, see 868.993

(.992 001–.992 009)   Standard subdivisions; collections in more than one form; history, description, critical appraisal of works in more than one form of Spanish-language literatures of Hispanic North America

(Optional numbers; prefer 860.1–860.9)

Add to base number 868.99200 the numbers following —0 in notation 01–09 from Table 3B, e.g., a collection of Spanish-language literature of Hispanic North America 868.992008

---

*Add to base number as instructed at beginning of Table 3
†(Optional number; prefer 860 for comprehensive works; prefer 860.1–860.9 for standard subdivisions; collections in more than one form; history, description, critical appraisal of works in more than one form; prefer 861–868 for specific forms)

(.992 01–.992 08)	Subdivisions for specific forms of Spanish-language literatures of Hispanic North America

          (Optional numbers; prefer 861–868)

          Add to base number 868.9920 as instructed at beginning of Table 3, e.g., Spanish-language poetry of Hispanic North America 868.99201

(.992 1)	*†Mexico
(.992 2)	Central America

          (Optional number; prefer 860)

(.992 200 1–.992 200 9)	Standard subdivisions; collections in more than one form; history, description, critical appraisal of works in more than one form of Spanish-language literatures of Central America

          (Optional numbers; prefer 860.1–860.9)

          Add to base number 868.992200 the numbers following —0 in notation 01–09 from Table 3B, e.g., a collection of Spanish-language literature of Central America 868.9922008

(.992 201–.992 208)	Subdivisions for specific forms of Spanish-language literatures of Central America

          (Optional numbers; prefer 861–868)

          Add to base number 868.99220 as instructed at beginning of Table 3, e.g., Spanish-language poetry of Central America 868.992201

(.992 21–.992 27)	Specific countries

          (Optional numbers; prefer 860)

          Add to base number 868.9922 the numbers following —728 in notation 7281–7287 from Table 2, e.g., Spanish-language literature of Costa Rica 868.99226; then add further as instructed at beginning of Table 3, e.g., collections of Spanish-language literature of Costa Rica 868.9922608

(.992 3)	West Indies (Antilles)

          (Optional number; prefer 860)

---

*Add to base number as instructed at beginning of Table 3

†(Optional number; prefer 860 for comprehensive works; prefer 860.1–860.9 for standard subdivisions; collections in more than one form; history, description, critical appraisal of works in more than one form; prefer 861–868 for specific forms)

(.992 300 1–.992 300 9)	Standard subdivisions; collections in more than one form; history, description, critical appraisal of works in more than one form of Spanish literatures of West Indies

        (Optional numbers; prefer 860.1–860.9)

        Add to base number 868.992300 the numbers following —0 in notation 01–09 from Table 3B, e.g., a collection of Spanish-language literature of West Indies 868.9923008

(.992 301–.992 308)	Subdivisions for specific forms of Spanish-language literatures of West Indies

        (Optional numbers; prefer 861–868)

        Add to base number 868.99230 as instructed at beginning of Table 3, e.g., Spanish-language poetry of West Indies 868.992301

(.992 31)	*†Cuba
(.992 33)	*†Dominican Republic
(.992 35)	*†Puerto Rico
(.993)	**Hispanic South America**

        (Optional number; prefer 860)

(.993 001–.993 009)	Standard subdivisions; collections in more than one form; history, description, critical appraisal of works in more than one form of Spanish-language literatures of Hispanic South America

        (Optional numbers; prefer 860.1–860.9)

        Add to base number 868.99300 the numbers following —0 in notation 01–09 from Table 3B, e.g., a collection of Spanish-language literature of Hispanic South America 868.993008

(.993 01–.993 08)	Subdivisions for specific forms of Spanish-language literatures of Hispanic South America

        (Optional numbers; prefer 861–868)

        Add to base number 868.9930 as instructed at beginning of Table 3, e.g., Spanish-language poetry of Hispanic South America 868.99301

---

*Add to base number as instructed at beginning of Table 3
†(Optional number; prefer 860 for comprehensive works; prefer 860.1–860.9 for standard subdivisions; collections in more than one form; history, description, critical appraisal of works in more than one form; prefer 861–868 for specific forms)

(.993 2–.993 7)   Argentina, Chile, Bolivia, Peru, Colombia, Ecuador, Venezuela

(Optional numbers; prefer 860)

Add to base number 868.993 the numbers following —8 in notation 82–87 from Table 2, e.g., Spanish-language literature of Chile 868.9933; then add further as instructed at beginning of Table 3, e.g., history and critical appraisal of Spanish-language literature of Chile 868.993309

(.993 9)   Paraguay and Uruguay

(Optional numbers; prefer 860)

Add to base number 868.9939 the numbers following —89 in notation 892–895 from Table 2, e.g., Spanish-language literature of Uruguay 868.99395; then add further as instructed at beginning of Table 3, e.g., history and critical appraisal of Spanish-language literature of Uruguay 868.9939509

(.994–.999)   Other parts of the world

(Optional numbers; prefer 860)

Spanish-language literature except of Spain, Hispanic America

Add to base number 868.99 notation 4–9 from Table 2, e.g., Spanish-language literature of the United States 868.9973; then add 0 and to the result add further as instructed at beginning of Table 3, e.g., Spanish-language poetry of the United States 868.997301

869   *Literatures of Portuguese and Galician languages

Subdivisions are added for literature of Portuguese language alone

Use the following period table for literature in Portuguese language from all countries and continents, for comprehensive works on literature in Portuguese language

PERIOD TABLE FOR PORTUGUESE
1	Early period to 1499
2	1500–1799
	Class here classical period
3	1800–1899
4	1900–1999
41	1900–1945
42	1945–1999
5	2000–

> *See also 860 for Papiamento literature*

(Option: Distinguish Portuguese-language literatures of specific countries by initial letters, e.g., literature of Brazil B869, of Portugal P869; or class literatures not requiring local emphasis in 869.899. If literatures are identified by one of these methods, assign the optional period numbers given below for literature of Brazil; otherwise, assign the period numbers given above for all Portuguese-language literatures. Other options are described under 810–890)

(OPTIONAL PERIOD TABLE FOR PORTUGUESE
  (For Brazil
(1	Period of formation, 1500–1749, in Brazil
	Class here 18th century
	For 1750–1799, see notation 2 from this table
(2	Period of transformation, 1750–1829, in Brazil
(3	1830–1921 in Brazil
	Class here 19th century
	For 1800–1829, see notation 2 from this table
(4	1921–1999 in Brazil
(5	2000 to present in Brazil)

(.899)	Portuguese-language literatures not requiring local emphasis

(Optional number; prefer 869 for all Portuguese-language literatures. Other options are described under 810–890)

Class here literatures of specific countries other than the country requiring local emphasis, e.g., libraries emphasizing literature of Portugal may class here Brazilian literature, and libraries emphasizing Brazilian literature may class here literature of Portugal

(.899 1)	*‡Portugal
(.899 2)	*‡Brazil

---

*Add to base number as instructed at beginning of Table 3

‡(Optional number; prefer 869 for comprehensive works; prefer 869.01–869.09 for standard subdivisions; collections in more than one form; history, description, critical appraisal of works in more than one form; prefer 869.1–869.8 for specific forms)

(.899 4–.899 9)   ‡Other parts of world

> Portuguese-language literature except of Portugal, Brazil
>
> Add to base number 869.899 notation 4–9 from Table 2, e.g., Portuguese-language literature of India 869.89954; then add 0 and to the result add further as instructed at beginning of Table 3, e.g., Portuguese-language drama of India 869.8995402

.9   ***Galician literature**

> Class here Gallegan literature
>
> Use the following period table for literature in Galician language from all countries and continents, for comprehensive works on literature in Galician language
>
> PERIOD TABLE
> | | |
> |---|---|
> | 1 | Early period to 1499 |
> | 2 | 1500–1799 |
> | 3 | 1800–1899 |
> | | Class here period of revival |
> | 4 | 1900–1999 |
> | 5 | 2000– |

870   Latin literature and literatures of related Italic languages

> Class here literatures of Italic languages
>
> Class comprehensive works of or on literatures of classical (Greek and Latin) languages in 880
>
> *For literatures of Romance languages, see 840*

.01–.09   Standard subdivisions of literatures of Italic languages

.1–.9   **Standard subdivisions; collections in more than one form; history, description, critical appraisal of works in more than one form of Latin literature**

> Add to base number 870 the numbers following —0 in notation 01–09 from Table 3B, e.g., a collection of Latin literature 870.8
>
> Use period table under 871–878

---

*Add to base number as instructed at beginning of Table 3

‡(Optional number; prefer 869 for comprehensive works; prefer 869.01–869.09 for standard subdivisions; collections in more than one form; history, description, critical appraisal of works in more than one form; prefer 869.1–869.8 for specific forms)

> **871–878 Subdivisions for specific forms of Latin literature**

Use the following period table for literature in Latin language

PERIOD TABLE
1   Roman period to ca. 499
2   Pre-Carolingian period, ca. 500–ca. 749
      Class here 8th century
         For 750–799, see notation 3 from this table
3   Medieval period, ca. 750–1349
      Class here 14th century
         For 1350–1399, see notation 4 from this table
4   Modern period, 1350–

Class comprehensive works in 870

871   Latin poetry

For dramatic poetry, see 872; for epic poetry, see 873; for lyric poetry, see 874

.001–.009   Standard subdivisions; collections; history, description, critical appraisal

For works by or about more than one author, add to base number 871.00 the numbers following —100 in notation 1001–1009 from Table 3B, e.g., critical appraisal of Latin poetry from more than one period 871.009

.01–.04   Specific periods

Add to base number 871.0 notation 1–4 from the period table under 871–878, e.g., Latin poetry of the Roman period 871.01; then, for works by or about more than one author, add the numbers following —10 in notation 1001–1009 from Table 3B, e.g., collections of Latin poetry from the Roman period 871.0108

872   Latin dramatic poetry and drama

.001–.009   Standard subdivisions; collections; history, description, critical appraisal

For works by or about more than one author, add to base number 872.00 the numbers following —100 in notation 1001–1009 from Table 3B, e.g., critical appraisal of Latin drama from more than one period 872.009
      Subdivisions are added for Latin dramatic poetry, for Latin drama, or both

.01–.04   Specific periods

Add to base number 872.0 notation 1–4 from the period table under 871–878, e.g., Latin drama of the Roman period 872.01; then, for works by or about more than one author, add the numbers following —10 in notation 1001–1009 from Table 3B, e.g., collections of Latin drama from the Roman period 872.0108
      Subdivisions are added for Latin dramatic poetry, for Latin drama, or both

873   Latin epic poetry and fiction

.001–.009   Standard subdivisions; collections; history, description, critical appraisal

> For works by or about more than one author, add to base number 873.00 the numbers following —100 in notation 1001–1009 from Table 3B, e.g., critical appraisal of Latin epic poetry from more than one period 873.009
> > Subdivisions are added for Latin epic poetry, for Latin fiction, or both

.01–.04   Specific periods

> Add to base number 873.0 notation 1–4 from the period table under 871–878, e.g., Latin epic poetry of the Roman period 873.01; then, for works by or about more than one author, add the numbers following —10 in notation 1001–1009 from Table 3B, e.g., collections of Latin epic poetry from the Roman period 873.0108
> > Subdivisions are added for Latin epic poetry, for Latin fiction, or both

874   Latin lyric poetry

.001–.009   Standard subdivisions; collections; history, description, critical appraisal

> For works by or about more than one author, add to base number 874.00 the numbers following —100 in notation 1001–1009 from Table 3B, e.g., critical appraisal of Latin lyric poetry from more than one period 874.009

.01–.04   Specific periods

> Add to base number 874.0 notation 1–4 from the period table under 871–878, e.g., Latin lyric poetry of the Roman period 874.01; then, for works by or about more than one author, add the numbers following —10 in notation 1001–1009 from Table 3B, e.g., collections of Latin lyric poetry from the Roman period 874.0108

875   Latin speeches

.001–.009   Standard subdivisions; collections; history, description, critical appraisal

> For works by or about more than one author, add to base number 875.00 the numbers following —100 in notation 1001–1009 from Table 3B, e.g., critical appraisal of Latin speeches from more than one period 875.009

.01–.04   Specific periods

> Add to base number 875.0 notation 1–4 from the period table under 871–878, e.g., Latin speeches of the Roman period 875.01; then, for works by or about more than one author, add the numbers following —10 in notation 1001–1009 from Table 3B, e.g., collections of Latin speeches from the Roman period 875.0108

876   Latin letters

.001–.009   Standard subdivisions; collections; history, description, critical appraisal

> For works by or about more than one author, add to base number 876.00 the numbers following —100 in notation 1001–1009 from Table 3B, e.g., critical appraisal of Latin letters from more than one period 876.009

.01–.04   Specific periods

> Add to base number 876.0 notation 1–4 from the period table under
> 871–878, e.g., Latin letters of the Roman period 876.01; then, for works by
> or about more than one author, add the numbers following —10 in notation
> 1001–1009 from Table 3B, e.g., collections of Latin letters from the Roman
> period 876.0108

877   Latin humor and satire

.001–.009   Standard subdivisions; collections; history, description, critical
appraisal

> For works by or about more than one author, add to base number 877.00
> the numbers following —100 in notation 1001–1009 from Table 3B, e.g.,
> critical appraisal of Latin satire from more than one period 877.009
>> Subdivisions are added for Latin humor, for Latin satire, or both

.01–.04   Specific periods

> Add to base number 877.0 notation 1–4 from the period table under
> 871–878, e.g., Latin humor and satire of the Roman period 877.01; then, for
> works by or about more than one author, add the numbers following —10
> in notation 1001–1009 from Table 3B, e.g., collections of Latin humor and
> satire from the Roman period 877.0108
>> Subdivisions are added for Latin humor, for Latin satire, or both

878   Latin miscellaneous writings

.000 1–.000 9   Standard subdivisions; collections; history, description, critical appraisal

> For more than one author, add to base number 878.000 the numbers
> following —100 in notation 1001–1009 from Table 3B, e.g., critical
> appraisal of Latin miscellaneous writings from more than one period
> 878.0009

.002–.008   Specific kinds of miscellaneous writings

> Add to base number 878.0 the numbers following —8 in —802–808
> from Table 3B, e.g., Latin prose literature in more than one literary form
> 878.008

.01–.04   Specific periods

> Add to base number 878.0 notation 1–4 from the period table under
> 871–878, e.g., Latin miscellaneous writings of the Roman period 878.01;
> then add further as follows:

>> For works by or about an individual author, follow the instructions
>> for adding further at —81–89 in Table 3A, e.g., collected works of an
>> individual author not identified with a specific form who wrote in the
>> Roman period 878.0109

>> For works by or about more than one author, follow the instructions
>> for adding further at —81–89 in Table 3B, e.g., collected epigrams of
>> authors who wrote in the Roman period 878.010208

879   Literatures of other Italic languages

.4   **Latinian literatures other than Latin**

.7   **Literatures of Sabellian languages**

.9   **Osco-Umbrian literatures**

880   Classical Greek literature and literatures of related Hellenic languages

Class here literatures of Hellenic languages, comprehensive works of or on literatures of classical (Greek and Latin) languages

For Latin literature, see 870

.01–.09   Standard subdivisions of classical (Greek and Latin) literatures

.1–.9   **Standard subdivisions; collections in more than one form; history, description, critical appraisal of works in more than one form of classical Greek literature**

Add to base number 880 the numbers following —0 in notation 01–09 from Table 3B, e.g., a collection of Greek literature 880.8

Use period table under 881–888

> ## 881–888   Subdivisions for specific forms of classical Greek literature

Use the following period table for literature in classical Greek language

PERIOD TABLE
1   Ancient period to ca. 499
2   Medieval and Byzantine periods, ca. 500–1599
3   Modern period, 1600–

Class comprehensive works in 880

881   Classical Greek poetry

For dramatic poetry, see 882; for epic poetry, see 883; for lyric poetry, see 884

.001–.009   Standard subdivisions; collections; history, description, critical appraisal

For works by or about more than one author, add to base number 881.00 the numbers following —100 in notation 1001–1009 from Table 3B, e.g., critical appraisal of classical Greek poetry from more than one period 881.009

.01–.03   Specific periods

Add to base number 881.0 notation 1–3 from the period table under 881–888, e.g., classical Greek poetry of the ancient period 881.01; then, for works by or about more than one author, add the numbers following —10 in notation 1001–1009 from Table 3B, e.g., collections of classical Greek poetry of the ancient period 881.0108

882   Classical Greek dramatic poetry and drama

.001–.009   Standard subdivisions; collections; history, description, critical appraisal

> For works by or about more than one author, add to base number 882.00 the numbers following —100 in notation 1001–1009 from Table 3B, e.g., critical appraisal of classical Greek drama from more than one period 882.009
>> Subdivisions are added for classical Greek dramatic poetry, for classical Greek drama, or both

.01–.03   Specific periods

> Add to base number 882.0 notation 1–3 from the period table under 881–888, e.g., classical Greek drama of the ancient period 882.01; then, for works by or about more than one author, add the numbers following —10 in notation 1001–1009 from Table 3B, e.g., collections of classical Greek drama of the ancient period 882.0108
>> Subdivisions are added for classical Greek dramatic poetry, for classical Greek drama, or both

883   Classical Greek epic poetry and fiction

.001–.009   Standard subdivisions; collections; history, description, critical appraisal

> For works by or about more than one author, add to base number 883.00 the numbers following —100 in notation 1001–1009 from Table 3B, e.g., critical appraisal of classical Greek epic poetry from more than one period 883.009
>> Subdivisions are added for classical Greek epic poetry, for classical Greek fiction, or both

.01–.03   Specific periods

> Add to base number 883.0 notation 1–3 from the period table under 881–888, e.g., classical Greek epic poetry of the ancient period 883.01; then, for works by or about more than one author, add the numbers following —10 in notation 1001–1009 from Table 3B, e.g., collections of classical Greek epic poetry of the ancient period 883.0108
>> Subdivisions are added for classical Greek epic poetry, for classical Greek fiction, or both

884   Classical Greek lyric poetry

.001–.009   Standard subdivisions; collections; history, description, critical appraisal

> For works by or about more than one author, add to base number 884.00 the numbers following —100 in notation 1001–1009 from Table 3B, e.g., critical appraisal of classical Greek lyric poetry from more than one period 884.009

.01–.03   Specific periods

> Add to base number 884.0 notation 1–3 from the period table under 881–888, e.g., classical Greek lyric poetry of the ancient period 884.01; then, for works by or about more than one author, add the numbers following —10 in notation 1001–1009 from Table 3B, e.g., collections of classical Greek lyric poetry of the ancient period 884.0108

885   Classical Greek speeches

.001–.009   Standard subdivisions; collections; history, description, critical appraisal

> For works by or about more than one author, add to base number 885.00 the numbers following —100 in notation 1001–1009 from Table 3B, e.g., critical appraisal of classical Greek speeches from more than one period 885.009

.01–.03   Specific periods

> Add to base number 885.0 notation 1–3 from the period table under 881–888, e.g., classical Greek speeches of the ancient period 885.01; then, for works by or about more than one author, add the numbers following —10 in notation 1001–1009 from Table 3B, e.g., collections of classical Greek speeches of the ancient period 885.0108

886   Classical Greek letters

.001–.009   Standard subdivisions; collections; history, description, critical appraisal

> For works by or about more than one author, add to base number 886.00 the numbers following —100 in notation 1001–1009 from Table 3B, e.g., critical appraisal of classical Greek letters from more than one period 886.009

.01–.03   Specific periods

> Add to base number 886.0 notation 1–3 from the period table under 881–888, e.g., classical Greek letters of the ancient period 886.01; then, for works by or about more than one author, add the numbers following —10 in notation 1001–1009 from Table 3B, e.g., collections of classical Greek letters of the ancient period 886.0108

887   Classical Greek humor and satire

.001–.009   Standard subdivisions; collections; history, description, critical appraisal

> For works by or about more than one author, add to base number 887.00 the numbers following —100 in notation 1001–1009 from Table 3B, e.g., critical appraisal of classical Greek satire from more than one period 887.009
>> Subdivisions are added for classical Greek humor, for classical Greek satire, or both

.01–.03   Specific periods

> Add to base number 887.0 notation 1–3 from the period table under 881–888, e.g., classical Greek humor and satire of the ancient period 887.01; then, for works by or about more than one author, add the numbers following —10 in notation 1001–1009 from Table 3B, e.g., collections of classical Greek humor and satire of the ancient period 887.0108
>> Subdivisions are added for classical Greek humor, for classical Greek satire, or both

888   Classical Greek miscellaneous writings

.000 1–.000 9   Standard subdivisions; collections; history, description, critical appraisal

> Add to base number 888.000 the numbers following —100 in notation 1001–1009 from Table 3B, e.g., critical appraisal of classical Greek miscellaneous writings from more than one period 888.0009

.002–.008   Specific kinds of miscellaneous writings

> Add to base number 888.0 the numbers following —8 in —802–808 from Table 3B, e.g., classical Greek prose literature in more than one literary form 888.008

.01–.03   Specific periods

> Add to base number 888.0 notation 1–3 from the period table under 881–888, e.g., classical Greek miscellaneous writings of the ancient period 888.01; then add further as follows:
>
> For works by or about an individual author, follow the instructions for adding further at —81–89 in Table 3A, e.g., collected works of an individual author not identified with a specific form who wrote in the ancient period 888.0109
>
> For works by or about more than one author, follow the instructions for adding further at —81–89 in Table 3B, e.g., collected epigrams of authors who wrote in the ancient period 888.010208

889   *Modern Greek literature

Class here Katharevusa and Demotic literature

PERIOD TABLE
1	Early period to 1821
2	1821–1899
3	1900–1999
32	1900–1945
34	1945–1999
4	2000–

890   Literatures of other specific languages and language families

Class texts by more than one author in more than two languages not from the same language family in 808.8; class history, description, critical appraisal of works by more than one author in more than two languages not from the same language family in 809

891   East Indo-European and Celtic literatures

Standard subdivisions are added for East Indo-European and Celtic literatures together, for East Indo-European literatures alone

.1   **Indo-Iranian literatures**

> *For Indo-Aryan literatures, see 891.2–891.4; for Iranian literatures, see 891.5*

---

*Add to base number as instructed at beginning of Table 3

>   **891.2–891.4 Indo-Aryan literatures**

        Class comprehensive works in 891.1

.2   ***Sanskrit literature**

        Class here classical Sanskrit literature

.29   Vedic (Old Indo-Aryan) literature

.3   **Middle Indo-Aryan literatures**

        Class here comprehensive works on Prakrit literatures

        For modern Prakrit literatures, see 891.4

.37   *Pali literature

.4   **Modern Indo-Aryan literatures**

        PERIOD TABLE FOR SPECIFIC MODERN INDO-ARYAN LITERATURES

     1   Early period to 1345

     2   1345–1645

         Class here 14th century

          For 1300–1345, see notation 1 from this table

     3   1645–1845

         Class here 17th century

          For 1600–1645, see notation 2 from this table

     4   1845–1895

         Class here 19th century

          For 1800–1845, see notation 3 from this table; for 1895–1899, see notation 5 from this table

     5   1895–1919

     6   1920–1939

     7   1940–

     71   1940–1999

         Class here 20th century

          For 1900–1919, see notation 5 from this table; for 1920–1939, see notation 6 from this table

     72   2000–

        Class comprehensive works on Prakrit literatures in 891.3

        (Option: Treat literatures of all modern Indo-Aryan languages as literature of one language, with base number 891.4. Add to base number 891.4 as instructed at beginning of Table 3, e.g., a collection of literary texts in modern Indo-Aryan languages 891.408)

.41   Sindhi and Lahnda literatures

        Subdivisions are added for Sindhi literature alone

---

*Add to base number as instructed at beginning of Table 3

.410 1–.410 9	Standard subdivisions; collections in more than one form; history, description, critical appraisal of works in more than one form of Sindhi literature

> Add to base number 891.410 the numbers following —0 in notation 01–09 from Table 3B, e.g., a collection of Sindhi literature 891.4108

> Use period table under 891.4

.411–.418	Subdivisions for specific forms of Sindhi literature

> Add to base number 891.41 as instructed at beginning of Table 3, e.g., Sindhi poetry 891.411

> Use period table under 891.4

.419	*Lahnda literature

> Use period table under 891.4

.42	*Panjabi literature

> Use period table under 891.4

.43	Hindi literature and related Western Hindi literatures

Class here Western Hindi literatures

For languages of east central zone of Indo-Aryan languages (Eastern Hindi languages), see 891.492

.430 01–.430 09	Standard subdivisions of Western Hindi literatures
.430 1–.430 9	Standard subdivisions; collections in more than one form; history, description, critical appraisal of works in more than one form of Hindi literature

> Add to base number 891.430 the numbers following —0 in notation 01–09 from Table 3B, e.g., a collection of Hindi literature 891.4308

> Use period table under 891.4

.431–.438	Subdivisions for specific forms of Hindi literature

> Add to base number 891.43 as instructed at beginning of Table 3, e.g., Hindi poetry 891.431

> Use period table under 891.4

.439	*Urdu literature

> Use period table under 891.4

.44	*Bengali literature

> Use period table under 891.4

.45	Assamese, Bihari, Oriya literatures
.451	*Assamese literature

> Use period table under 891.4

---

*Add to base number as instructed at beginning of Table 3

.454   *Bihari literature

> Class here literatures in Bhojpuri, Magahi, Maithili

> Use period table under 891.4

.456   *Oriya literature

> Class here Odia literature

> Use period table under 891.4

.46   Marathi and Konkani literatures

> Subdivisions are added for Marathi literature alone

.460 1–.460 9   Standard subdivisions; collections in more than one form; history, description, critical appraisal of works in more than one form of Marathi literature

> Add to base number 891.460 the numbers following —0 in notation 01–09 from Table 3B, e.g., a collection of Marathi literature 891.4608

> Use period table under 891.4

.461–.468   Subdivisions for specific forms of Marathi literature

> Add to base number 891.46 as instructed at beginning of Table 3, e.g., Marathi poetry 891.461

> Use period table under 891.4

.469   *Konkani literature

> Use period table under 891.4

.47   Gujarati, Bhili, Rajasthani literatures

> Subdivisions are added for Gujarati literature alone

.470 1–.470 9   Standard subdivisions; collections in more than one form; history, description, critical appraisal of works in more than one form of Gujarati literature

> Add to base number 891.470 the numbers following —0 in notation 01–09 from Table 3B, e.g., a collection of Gujarati literature 891.4708

> Use period table under 891.4

.471–.478   Subdivisions for specific forms of Gujarati literature

> Add to base number 891.47 as instructed at beginning of Table 3, e.g., Gujarati poetry 891.471

> Use period table under 891.4

.479   *Rajasthani literature

> Class here Jaipuri, Marwari literatures

> Use period table under 891.4

*Add to base number as instructed at beginning of Table 3

.48   Sinhalese-Maldivian literatures

Class here Sinhalese (Sinhala) literature

.480 1–.480 9   Standard subdivisions; collections in more than one form; history, description, critical appraisal of works in more than one form of Sinhalese (Sinhala) literature

Add to base number 891.480 the numbers following —0 in notation 01–09 from Table 3B, e.g., a collection of Sinhalese literature 891.4808

Use period table under 891.4

.481–.488   Subdivisions for specific forms of Sinhalese (Sinhala) literature

Add to base number 891.48 as instructed at beginning of Table 3, e.g., Sinhalese poetry 891.481

Use period table under 891.4

.489   *Divehi (Maldivian) literature

Use period table under 891.4

.49   Other Indo-Aryan literatures

Including Nuristani (Kafiri) literature

See also 894.8 for Dravidian literatures; also 895.4 for Tibeto-Burman literatures; also 895.95 for Munda literatures

.492   Literatures of east central zone of Indo-Aryan languages (Eastern Hindi literatures)

Including Awadhi, Bagheli, Chattisgarhi, Fijian Hindustani (Fiji Hindi) literatures

Class comprehensive works on Hindi literatures in 891.43

.495   *Nepali literature

.496   Pahari literatures

Including Garhwali literature

Class here literatures of northern zone of Indo-Aryan languages

For Nepali literature, see 891.495

.497   *Romani literature

.499   Dardic (Pisacha) literatures

Including Kashmiri, Khowar, Kohistani, Shina literatures

.5   Iranian literatures

.51   *Old Persian literature

Class here ancient West Iranian literatures

See also 891.52 for Avestan literature

*Add to base number as instructed at beginning of Table 3

.52	*Avestan literature

        Class here ancient East Iranian literatures

.53	Middle Iranian literatures

        Including Khotanese (Saka), Pahlavi (Middle Persian), Sogdian literatures

.55	*Modern Persian (Farsi) literature

        PERIOD TABLE

1	Period of formal development, ca. 1000–1389
2	1389–1899
3	1900–1999
4	2000–

See also 891.56 for Dari literature; also 891.57 for Tajik literature

.56	*Dari literature
.57	*Tajik literature
.59	Other modern Iranian literatures

        Including Pamir literatures, Ossetic literature

.593	*Pashto (Afghan) literature
.597	Kurdish literatures and literatures of related languages

        Including central and southern Kurdish

        Class here Kurdish (Kurmanji, northern Kurdish) literature

.597 01–.597 09	Standard subdivisions; collections in more than one form; history, description, critical appraisal of works in more than one form of Kurdish (Kurmanji, northern Kurdish) literature

        Add to base number 891.5970 the numbers following —0 in notation 01–09 from Table 3B, e.g., a collection of Kurdish literature 891.59708

.597 1–.597 8	Subdivisions for specific forms of Kurdish (Kurmanji, northern Kurdish) literature

        Add to base number 891.597 as instructed at beginning of Table 3, e.g., Kurdish poetry 891.5971

.598	*Baluchi literature
.6	**Celtic literatures**

        Including Gaulish

*Add to base number as instructed at beginning of Table 3

.62   *Irish Gaelic literature

        PERIOD TABLE
           1   Early period to 1171
                  Class here 12th century
                      For 1171–1199, see notation 2 from this table
           2   1171–1599
           3   1600–1875
           4   1875–1999
           42   1875–1922
                  Class here Irish literary revival
           43   1922–1999
           5   2000–

.63   *Scottish Gaelic literature

        PERIOD TABLE
           1   Early period to 1599
           2   1600–1829
           3   1830–1999
           32   1830–1899
                  Class here 19th century
                      For 1800–1829, see notation 2 from this table
           34   1900–1999
           4   2000–

.64   *Manx literature

.66   *Welsh (Cymric) literature

        PERIOD TABLE
           1   Early period to 1599
           12   Early period to 1299
           14   1300–1599
           2   1600–1999
            22   1600–1799
           24   1800–1899
           26   1900–1945
                  Class here 20th century
                      For 1945–1999, see notation 28 from this table
           28   1945–1999
           3   2000–

.67   *Cornish literature

.68   *Breton literature

        PERIOD TABLE
           1   Early period to 1799
           2   1800–1899
           3   1900–1999
           4   2000–

*Add to base number as instructed at beginning of Table 3

.7   **Russian literature and related East Slavic literatures**

Class here East Slavic literatures

Class comprehensive works on Slavic (Slavonic) literatures in 891.8

.700 1–.700 9   Standard subdivisions of East Slavic literatures

.701–.709   Standard subdivisions; collections in more than one form; history, description, critical appraisal of works in more than one form of Russian literature

Add to base number 891.70 the numbers following —0 in notation 01–09 from Table 3B, e.g., a collection of Russian literature 891.708

Use period table under 891.71–891.78

.71–.78   Subdivisions for specific forms of Russian literature

Add to base number 891.7 as instructed at beginning of Table 3, e.g., Russian poetry 891.71

PERIOD TABLE
1	Early period to 1699
2	1700–1799
3	1800–1917
4	1917–1991
	Class here 20th century
	For 1900–1917, see notation 3 from this table; for 1991–1999, see notation 5 from this table
42	1917–1945
44	1945–1991
5	1991–

.79   Ukrainian and Belarusian literatures

Subdivisions are added for Ukrainian literature alone

.790 1–.790 9   Standard subdivisions; collections in more than one form; history, description, critical appraisal of works in more than one form of Ukrainian literature

Add to base number 891.790 the numbers following —0 in notation 01–09 from Table 3B, e.g., a collection of Ukrainian literature 891.7908

Use period table under 891.791–891.798

.791–.798   Subdivisions for specific forms of Ukrainian literature

Add to base number 891.79 as instructed at beginning of Table 3, e.g., Ukrainian poetry 891.791

PERIOD TABLE
1	Early period to 1798
2	1798–1917
3	1917–1991
	Class here 20th century
	For 1900–1917, see notation 2 from this table; for 1991–1999, see notation 4 from this table
32	1917–1945
34	1945–1991
4	1991–

.799   *Belarusian literature

PERIOD TABLE
1	Early period to 1798
2	1798–1917
3	1917–1991
	Class here 20th century
	For 1900–1917, see notation 2 from this table; for 1991–1999, see notation 4 from this table
4	1991–

.8   Slavic (Slavonic) literatures

Class here comprehensive works on literatures of Balto-Slavic languages

For East Slavic literatures, see 891.7; for Baltic literatures, see 891.91–891.93

.81   Bulgarian literature and related South Slavic literatures

Class here South Slavic literatures

For Serbian literature, see 891.82; for Croatian and Bosnian literatures, see 891.83; for Slovenian literature, see 891.84

.810 01–.810 09   Standard subdivisions of South Slavic literatures

.810 1–.810 9   Standard subdivisions; collections in more than one form; history, description, critical appraisal of works in more than one form of Bulgarian literature

Add to base number 891.810 the numbers following —0 in notation 01–09 from Table 3B, e.g., a collection of Bulgarian literature 891.8108

Use period table under 891.811–891.818

*Add to base number as instructed at beginning of Table 3

813

.811–.818   Subdivisions for specific forms of Bulgarian literature

Add to base number 891.81 as instructed at beginning of Table 3, e.g., Bulgarian poetry 891.811

PERIOD TABLE

1	Early period to 1849
	Class here 19th century
	For 1850–1899, see notation 2 from this table
2	1850–1899
3	1900–1991
4	1991–

.819   *Macedonian literature

.82   *Serbian literature and Montenegrin literature

Subdivisions are added for Serbian literature alone

Class here Serbo-Croatian literature; comprehensive works on Serbian, Croatian, Bosnian, Montenegrin literatures

For Croatian literature, see 891.83; for Bosnian literature, see 891.839

.820 1–.820 9   Standard subdivisions; collections in more than one form; history, description, critical appraisal of works in more than one form of Serbian literature

Add to base number 891.820 the numbers following —0 in notation 01–09 from Table 3B, e.g., a collection of Serbian literature 891.8208

Use period table under 891.821–891.828

.821–.828   Subdivisions for specific forms of Serbian literature

Add to base number 891.82 as instructed at beginning of Table 3, e.g., Serbian poetry 891.821

PERIOD TABLE

1	Early period to ca. 1549
	Class here 16th century
	For 1550–1599, see notation 2 from this table
2	Period of Renaissance, ca. 1550–1699
3	1700–1799
4	1800–1899
5	1900–1991
52	1900–1945
54	1945–1991
6	1991–

*Add to base number as instructed at beginning of Table 3

.829   *Montenegrin literature

      PERIOD TABLE
       1   Early period to ca. 1549
          Class here 16th century
           For 1550–1599, see notation 2 from this table
       2   Period of Renaissance, ca. 1550–1699
       3   1700–1799
       4   1800–1899
       5   1900–1991
       52   1900–1945
       54   1945–1991
       6   1991–

.83   Croatian literature and Bosnian literature

      Subdivisions are added for Croatian literature alone

.830 1–.830 9   Standard subdivisions; collections in more than one form; history, description, critical appraisal of works in more than one form of Croatian literature

      Add to base number 891.830 the numbers following —0 in notation 01–09 from Table 3B, e.g., a collection of Croatian literature 891.8308

      Use period table under 891.831–891.838

.831–.838   Subdivisions for specific forms of Croatian literature

      Add to base number 891.83 as instructed at beginning of Table 3, e.g., Croatian poetry 891.831

      PERIOD TABLE
       1   Early period to ca. 1549
          Class here 16th century
           For 1550–1599, see notation 2 from this table
       2   Period of Renaissance, ca. 1550–1699
       3   1700–1799
       4   1800–1899
       5   1900–1991
       52   1900–1945
       54   1945–1991
       6   1991–

*Add to base number as instructed at beginning of Table 3

.839   *Bosnian literature

             PERIOD TABLE

1	Early period to ca. 1549	
	Class here 16th century	
	For 1550–1599, see notation 2 from this table	
2	Period of Renaissance, ca. 1550–1699	
3	1700–1799	
4	1800–1899	
5	1900–1991	
52	1900–1945	
54	1945–1991	
6	1991–	

.84   *Slovenian literature

             PERIOD TABLE

1	Early period to ca. 1549	
	Class here 16th century	
	For 1550–1599, see notation 2 from this table	
2	Period of Renaissance, ca. 1550–1699	
3	1700–1799	
4	1800–1899	
5	1900–1991	
6	1991–	

.85   Polish literature and related West Slavic literatures

         Including Kashubian literature

         Class here West Slavic literatures

         For Czech literature, see 891.86; for Slovak literature, see 891.87; for Wendish literature, see 891.88; for Polabian literature, see 891.89

.850 01–.850 09   Standard subdivisions of West Slavic literatures

.850 1–.850 9   Standard subdivisions; collections in more than one form; history, description, critical appraisal of works in more than one form of Polish literature

         Add to base number 891.850 the numbers following —0 in notation 01–09 from Table 3B, e.g., a collection of Polish literature 891.8508

         Use period table under 891.851–891.858

*Add to base number as instructed at beginning of Table 3

.851–.858 Subdivisions for specific forms of Polish literature

     Add to base number 891.85 as instructed at beginning of Table 3, e.g., Polish poetry 891.851

     PERIOD TABLE
1	Early period to 1399
2	1400–1499
3	Golden age, 1500–1599
4	1600–1699
5	1700–1795
6	1795–1919
7	1919–1989

       Class here 20th century
        For 1900–1919, see notation 6 from this table; for 1989–1999, see notation 8 from this table

72	1919–1945
73	1945–1989
8	1989–

.86   *Czech literature

    Class here literature in Moravian dialects

    PERIOD TABLE
1	Early period to 1399
2	1400–1449

       Class here 15th century
        For 1450–1499, see notation 3 from this table

3	Humanist period, 1450–1620
4	1620–1899

       Class here 17th century
        For 1600–1620, see notation 3 from this table

5	1900–1989
52	1900–1945
54	1945–1989
6	1989–

.87   *Slovak literature

.88   *Wendish (Lusatian, Sorbian) literature

.89   *Polabian literature

.9   **Baltic and other Indo-European literatures**

>   891.91–891.93 Baltic literatures

    Class comprehensive works in 891.9

.91   Old Prussian literature

---

*Add to base number as instructed at beginning of Table 3

.92   *Lithuanian literature

PERIOD TABLE
1   Early period to 1799
2   1800–1899
3   1900–1991
4   1991–

.93   *Latvian (Lettish) literature

PERIOD TABLE
1   Early period to 1799
2   1800–1899
3   1900–1991
4   1991–

.99   Other Indo-European literatures

Add to base number 891.99 the numbers following —9199 in notation 91991–91998 from Table 6, e.g., Albanian literature 891.991, Hittite literature 891.998; then to the number given for each literature listed below add further as instructed at beginning of Table 3, e.g., a collection of Albanian literature 891.99108

891.991 Albanian

891.992 Armenian

Use period table under 891.992

.992   *Armenian literature

Number built according to instructions under 891.99

PERIOD TABLE
1   Early period to 599
2   600–999
3   1000–1399
4   1400–1849
5   1850–1991
      Class here 19th century
        For 1800–1849, see notation 4 from this table
6   1991–

892   Afro-Asiatic literatures

Class here Semitic literatures

For non-Semitic Afro-Asiatic literatures, see 893

---

*Add to base number as instructed at beginning of Table 3

.1   Akkadian (Assyro-Babylonian) literature

Class here East Semitic literatures; literatures in Assyrian, Babylonian dialects of Akkadian

For Eblaite literature, see 892.6

See also 899.95 for Sumerian literature

\>   **892.2–892.9 West Semitic literatures**

Class comprehensive works in 892

.2   Aramaic literatures

For Eastern Aramaic literatures, see 892.3

.29   Western Aramaic literatures

Including Samaritan literature

.3   Eastern Aramaic literatures

Class here Syriac literature

.4   *Hebrew literature

PERIOD TABLE
1	Early period to 699
2	700–1699
	Class here medieval period
3	1700–1819
4	1820–1885
	Class here 19th century
	For 1800–1819, see notation 3 from this table; for 1885–1899, see notation 5 from this table
5	1885–1947
6	1947–1999
	Class here 20th century
	For 1900–1947, see notation 5 from this table
7	2000–

Class comprehensive works on Canaanitic literatures in 892.6

.6   Canaanite literatures

Including Eblaite literature

Class here comprehensive works on Canaanitic literatures

For Hebrew, see 892.4

.67   Ugaritic literature

---

*Add to base number as instructed at beginning of Table 3

.7   Arabic and Maltese literatures

Class here classical Arabic literature, modern standard Arabic literature, Judeo-Arabic literature; literatures of Arabic and Maltese languages

See also 892.9 for South Arabian literatures

.701–.709   Standard subdivisions; collections in more than one form; history, description, critical appraisal of works in more than one form of Arabic literatures

Add to base number 892.70 the numbers following —0 in notation 01–09 from Table 3B, e.g., a collection of Arabic literature 892.708

Use period table under 892.71–892.78

.71–.78   Subdivisions for specific forms of Arabic literatures

Add to base number 892.7 as instructed at beginning of Table 3, e.g., Arabic poetry 892.71

PERIOD TABLE

1	Pre-Islamic period to 622	
2	Early Islamic and Mukhadrami period, 622–661	
	Class here 7th century	
	For 600–622, see notation 1 from this table; for 661–699, see notation 32 from this table	
3	661–1258	
32	Umayyad period, 661–749	
	Class here 8th century	
	For 750–799, see notation 34 from this table	
34	Abbasid period, 750–1258	
	Class here 13th century	
	For 1258–1299, see notation 4 from this table	
4	1258–1799	
5	1800–1945	
6	1945–1999	
	Class here 20th century	
	For 1900–1945, see notation 5 from this table	
7	2000–	

.79   *Maltese literature

.8   Ethiopian literatures

Including Gurage, Harari literatures

Class here comprehensive works on South Semitic literatures

For South Arabian literatures, see 892.9

.81   Ge'ez literature

.82   *Tigré literature

.83   *Tigrinya (Tigrigna) literature

.87   *Amharic literature

*Add to base number as instructed at beginning of Table 3

.9   **South Arabian literatures**

Including Mahri, Sokotri literatures

Class comprehensive works on South Semitic literatures in 892.8

See also 892.7 for North Arabic literatures

893   **Non-Semitic Afro-Asiatic literatures**

Add to base number 893 the numbers following —93 in notation 931–937 from Table 6, e.g., Berber literatures 893.3, Somali literature 893.54; then to the number given for each literature listed below add further as instructed at beginning of Table 3, e.g., a collection of Somali literature 893.5408

893.1 Egyptian

893.2 Coptic

893.33 Tamazight

893.34 Kabyle

893.38 Tamashek

893.54 Somali

893.55 Oromo

893.72 Hausa

894   **Literatures of Altaic, Uralic, Hyperborean, Dravidian languages; literatures of miscellaneous languages of south Asia**

.1–.3   **Altaic literatures**

Add to base number 894 the numbers following —94 in notation 941–943 from Table 6, e.g., Mongolian literature 894.23, Altai literature 894.33; then to the number given for each literature listed below add further as instructed at beginning of Table 3, e.g., a collection of Mongolian literature 894.2308

> 894.23 Mongolian proper, Halh Mongolian (Khalkha Mongolian)
>
> 894.315 Chuvash
>
> 894.323 Uighur
>
> 894.325 Uzbek
>
> 894.332 Yakut
>
> 894.345 Kazakh
>
> 894.347 Kyrgyz
>
> 894.35 Turkish (Osmanli), Ottoman Turkish
>
> > Use period table under 894.35
>
> 894.361 Azerbaijani
>
> 894.364 Turkmen
>
> 894.387 Tatar
>
> 894.388 Crimean Tatar

Class comprehensive works in 894

> *For Ainu literature, see 894.6; for Japanese literature, see 895.6; for Korean literature, see 895.7*

.35   **Turkish (Osmanli) literature*

Number built according to instructions under 894.1–894.3

Class here Ottoman Turkish literature

PERIOD TABLE
     1   Early period to 1499
     2   1500–1849
     3   1850–1999
           Class here 19th century, 20th century
             For 1800–1849, see notation 2 from this table
     4   2000–

.4   **Samoyedic literatures**

---

*Add to base number as instructed at beginning of Table 3

.5 Finno-Ugric literatures

Class here comprehensive works on Uralic literatures, on Uralic and Yukaghir literatures

For Samoyedic literatures, see 894.4; for Yukaghir literatures, see 894.6

.51 Ugric literatures

Including Ostyak (Khanty), Vogul literatures

.511 *Hungarian (Magyar) literature

PERIOD TABLE
1	Early period to 1799
2	1800–1899
3	1900–1989
32	1900–1945
34	1945–1989
4	1989–

.53 Permic literatures

Including Votyak (Udmurt), Zyrian (Komi) literatures

.54 Finnic literatures

Including Karelian, Livonian, Tornedalen Finnish, Veps literatures

For Permic literatures, see 894.53; for Middle Volga literatures, see 894.56; for Sámi literatures, see 894.57

.541 *Finnish (Suomi) literature

PERIOD TABLE
1	Early period to 1799
2	1800–1899
3	1900–1999
4	2000–

Class Tornedalen Finnish literature in 894.54; class Kven Finnish literature in 894.543

.543 *Kven Finnish literature

.545 *Estonian literature

PERIOD TABLE
1	Early period to 1861
	Class here 19th century
	For 1861–1899, see notation 2 from this table
2	1861–1991
3	1991–

.56 Middle Volga literatures

Including Mari, Mordvin literatures

*Add to base number as instructed at beginning of Table 3

.57   Sámi (Saami) literatures

> Add to base number 894.57 the numbers following —9457 in notation 94572–94576 from Table 6, e.g., Eastern Sámi literatures 894.576, North Sámi literature 894.5745; then to the number given for each literature listed below add further as instructed at beginning of Table 3, e.g., a collection of North Sámi literature 894.574508

> 894.5722 South Sámi

> 894.5743 Lule Sámi

> 894.5745 North Sámi

.6   **Hyperborean (Paleosiberian) literatures**

> Including Ainu literature, Yukaghir literatures

> Class comprehensive works on Uralic and Yukaghir literatures in 894.5

.8   **Dravidian literatures and literatures of miscellaneous languages of south Asia**

> Standard subdivisions are added for Dravidian literatures and literatures of miscellaneous languages of south Asia together, for Dravidian literatures alone

PERIOD TABLE FOR SPECIFIC DRAVIDIAN LITERATURES

1	Early period to 1345
2	1345–1645
	Class here 14th century
	For 1300–1345, see notation 1 from this table
3	1645–1845
	Class here 17th century
	For 1600–1645, see notation 2 from this table
4	1845–1895
	Class here 19th century
	For 1800–1845, see notation 3 from this table; for 1895–1899, see notation 5 from this table
5	1895–1919
6	1920–1939
7	1940–
71	1940–1999
	Class here 20th century
	For 1900–1919, see notation 5 from this table; for 1920–1939, see notation 6 from this table
72	2000–

> (Option: Treat literatures of all Dravidian languages as literature of one language, with base number 894.8. Add to base number 894.8 as instructed at beginning of Table 3, e.g., a collection of literature in Dravidian languages 894.808)

.81   South Dravidian literatures

> Including Kota, Toda literatures

> Class here literatures of the Dravida group

.811   *Tamil literature

    Use period table under 894.8

.812   *Malayalam literature

    Use period table under 894.8

.814   *Kannada (Kanarese) literature

    Use period table under 894.8

.82   Central Dravidian literatures

.823   *Gondi literature

    Use period table under 894.8

.824   *Kui (Khond, Kandh) literature

    Use period table under 894.8

.827   *Telugu literature

    Use period table under 894.8

.83   Brahui literature and related North Dravidian literatures

    Class here North Dravidian literatures

.830 01–.830 09   Standard subdivisions of North Dravidian literatures

.830 1–.830 9   Standard subdivisions; collections in more than one form; history, description, critical appraisal of works in more than one form of Brahui literature

    Add to base number 894.830 the numbers following —0 in notation 01–09 from Table 3B, e.g., a collection of Brahui literature 894.8308

    Use period table under 894.8

.831–.838   Subdivisions for specific forms of Brahui literature

    Add to base number 894.83 as instructed at beginning of Table 3, e.g., Brahui poetry 894.831

    Use period table under 894.8

.89   Literatures of miscellaneous languages of south Asia

    Only those literatures provided for below

    Class literatures of languages of south Asia closely related to languages of east and southeast Asia in 895; class literatures of Indo-Iranian languages of south Asia and comprehensive works on literatures of south Asia in 891.1

.892   *Burushaski literature

---

*Add to base number as instructed at beginning of Table 3

895   Literatures of East and Southeast Asia

Class here Sino-Tibetan literatures

Here are classed literatures of South Asian languages closely related to the languages of East and Southeast Asia

For literature of Austronesian languages of East and Southeast Asia, see 899.2

.1   ***Chinese literature**

PERIOD TABLE

1	Origins, 15th century to 221 B.C.
	Class here classical age
2	221 B.C.–618 A.D.
	Class here middle epoch
22	Period of Qin (Ch'in) and Han dynasties, 221 B.C.–220 A.D.
24	Period of Six dynasties and Sui dynasty, 220–618 A.D.
3	Period of Tang dynasty, Five dynasties, Ten kingdoms, 618–960
	Class here renaissance and neoclassicism
4	960–1912
42	Period of Song dynasty, 960–1279
44	Period of Yuan (Mongol) dynasty, 1271–1368
	For period of Yuan dynasty during 1271–1279, see notation 42 from this table
46	Period of Ming dynasty, 1368–1644
48	Period of Qing (Manchu) dynasty, 1644–1912
5	1912–2009
51	1912–1949
52	1949–2009
6	2010–

.4   **Tibetan literature and related Tibeto-Burman literatures**

Class here Tibeto-Burman literatures

For Burmese literature, see 895.8

.400 1–.400 9   Standard subdivisions of Tibeto-Burman literatures

.401–.409   Standard subdivisions; collections in more than one form; history, description, critical appraisal of works in more than one form of Tibetan literature

Add to base number 895.40 the numbers following —0 in notation 01–09 from Table 3B, e.g., a collection of Tibetan literature 895.408

.41–.48   Subdivisions for specific forms of Tibetan literature

Add to base number 895.4 as instructed at beginning of Table 3, e.g., Tibetan poetry 895.41

.49   Literatures of Eastern Himalayan languages

Including Newari literature

Class here literatures of Kiranti languages, of Mahakiranti languages

See also 891.495 for Nepali literature

*Add to base number as instructed at beginning of Table 3

.6   ***Japanese literature**

PERIOD TABLE

1	Early period to 1185
14	Heian period, 794–1185
2	Medieval period, 1185–1603
22	Kamakura period, 1185–1334
24	1334–1603

      Class here 14th century, Muromachi period
        For 1300–1334, see notation 22 from this table

3	Tokugawa (Edo) period, 1603–1868
32	1603–1769

      Class here 18th century, Genroku period
        For 1770–1799, see notation 34 from this table

34	1770–1868

      Class here Bunka-Bunsei period (1804–1829), 19th century
        For 1868–1899, see notation 4 from this table

4	1868–1945
42	Meiji period, 1868–1912
44	1912–1945

      Class here 20th century
        For 1900–1912, see notation 42 from this table; for
        1945–1999, see notation 5 from this table

5	1945–1999
6	2000–

.7   ***Korean literature**

PERIOD TABLE

1	Early period to 1392
2	Yi period, 1392–1910
28	1894–1910
3	1910–1945
4	1945–1999

      Class here 20th century
        For 1900–1910, see notation 28 from this table; for
        1910–1945, see notation 3 from this table

5	2000–

.8   ***Burmese literature**

PERIOD TABLE

1	Early period to 1799
2	1800–1899
3	1900–1999
4	2000–

*Add to base number as instructed at beginning of Table 3

.9   **Literatures of miscellaneous languages of Southeast Asia; Munda literatures**

Limited to the literatures provided for below

Including literatures of Kadai languages, Kam-Sui languages

Class here literatures of Daic languages

Class literatures in Austroasiatic languages in 895.93

For literatures in Austronesian languages, see 899.2

.91   Thai (Siamese) literature and Tai literatures

Class here Tai literatures

.910 01–.910 09   Standard subdivisions of literatures of Tai languages

.910 1–.910 9   Standard subdivisions; collections in more than one form; history, description, critical appraisal of works in more than one form of Thai (Siamese) literature

Add to base number 895.910 the numbers following —0 in notation 01–09 from Table 3B, e.g., a collection of Thai literature 895.9108

Use period table under 895.911–895.918

.911–.918   Subdivisions for specific forms of Thai (Siamese) literature

Add to base number 895.91 as instructed at beginning of Table 3, e.g., Thai poetry 895.911

PERIOD TABLE
1	Early period to 1799
2	1800–1899
3	1900–1999
4	2000–

.919   Other Tai literatures

Including Shan literature

For Viet-Muong literatures, see 895.92

.919 1   *Lao literature

---

*Add to base number as instructed at beginning of Table 3

.92–.97   Viet-Muong, Austroasiatic, Munda, Hmong-Mien (Miao-Yao) literatures

Add to base number 895.9 the numbers following —959 in notation 9592–9597 from Table 6, e.g., Khmer literature 895.932, Mundari literature 895.95; then to the number given for each literature listed below add further as instructed at beginning of Table 3, e.g., a collection of Khmer literature 895.93208

895.922 Vietnamese

Use period table under 895.922

895.932 Khmer (Cambodian)

895.972 Hmong (Miao)

895.978 Yao

.922   *Vietnamese literature

Number built according to instructions under 895.92–895.97

PERIOD TABLE
1	Early period to 1799
2	1800–1899
3	1900–1999
32	1900–1945
	Class here 20th century
	For 1945–1999, see notation 34 from this table
34	1945–1999
4	2000–

---

*Add to base number as instructed at beginning of Table 3

896   African literatures

Add to base number 896 the numbers following —96 in notation 961–965 from Table 6, e.g., Swahili literature 896.392, Songhai literatures 896.58; then to the number given for each literature listed below add further as instructed at beginning of Table 3, e.g., a collection of Swahili literature 896.39208

896.3214 Wolof

896.322 Fula (Fulani)

896.332 Ibo (Igbo)

896.333 Yoruba

896.3374 Ewe

896.3378 Gã

896.3385 Akan, Fante, Twi

896.3452 Bambara

896.348 Mende

896.3616 Sango

896.3642 Efik

896.3915 Bemba

896.3918 Nyanja, Chichewa (Chewa)

896.392 Swahili

896.3931 Kongo (Koongo)

896.3932 Mbundu (Kimbundu)

896.39461 Rwanda (Kinyarwanda)

896.39465 Rundi

896.3954 Kikuyu

896.3957 Ganda (Luganda)

896.3962 Duala

896.39686 Lingala

896.3975 Shona

896.3976 Venda (Tshivenda)

896.39771 Northern Sotho

896.39772 Southern Sotho

896   African literatures

896.39775 Tswana

896.3978 Tsonga

896.3985 Xhosa

896.3986 Zulu

896.3987 Swazi (siSwati)

896.3989 Ndebele (South Africa)

896.55226 Maasai

896.55842 Dholuo (Luo of Kenya and Tanzania)

PERIOD TABLE FOR SPECIFIC AFRICAN LITERATURES
1   Early period to 1959
2   1960–1999
       Class here 20th century
         For 1900–1959, see notation 1 from this table
3   2000–

Class Afrikaans literature in 839.36; class Malagasy literature in 899.3. Class literature in an African creole having a non-African primary source language with the source language, e.g., Krio literature 820

> *For Ethiopian literatures, see 892.8; for non-Semitic Afro-Asiatic literatures, see 893*

(Option: Treat literatures of all African languages as literature of one language, with base number 896. Add to base number 896 as instructed at beginning of Table 3, e.g., a collection of literature in African languages 896.08)

897   Literatures of North American native languages

Class here comprehensive works on literatures of North and South American native languages

Add to base number 897 the numbers following —97 in notation 971–979 from Table 6, e.g., Zoque literature 897.43, Nahuatl literature 897.452; then to the number given for each literature listed below add further as instructed at beginning of Table 3, e.g., a collection of Nahuatl literature 897.45208

897.124 Eastern Canadian Inuktitut

897.19 Aleut

897.26 Navajo (Diné)

897.28 Haida

897.323 Cree

897.333 Ojibwa, Chippewa

897.422 Cakchikel

897.423 Quiché

897.427 Maya, Yucatec Maya

897.4287 Tzotzil

897.452 Nahuatl (Aztec)

897.4542 Yaqui

897.4544 Huichol

897.4552 Tohono O'odham

897.45529 Akimel O'odham

897.4574 Shoshoni

897.458 Hopi

897.492 Kiowa

897.494 Tewa

897.5243 Dakota

897.557 Cherokee

897.68 Zapotec

897.83 San Blas Kuna (San Blas Cuna)

897.933 Pawnee

897.9435 Kalispel, Pend d'Oreille

897   Literatures of North American native languages

897.994 Zuni

For literatures of South American native languages, see 898

(Option: Treat literatures of all North American native languages as literature of one language, with base number 897. Add to base number 897 as instructed at beginning of Table 3, e.g., a collection of literary texts in North American native languages 897.08)

898   Literatures of South American native languages

Add to base number 898 the numbers following —98 in notation 982–989 from Table 6, e.g., Quechua literature 898.323, Tucano literature 898.35; then to the number given for each literature listed below add further as instructed at beginning of Table 3, e.g., a collection of Quechua literature 898.32308

898.323 Quechua (Kechua)

898.324 Aymara

898.372 Shuar

898.3822 Paraguayan Guaraní

898.3832 Tupí (Nhengatu)

898.72 Mapudungun (Mapuche)

Class comprehensive works on literatures of North and South American native languages in 897

(Option: Treat literatures of all South American native languages as literature of one language, with base number 898. Add to base number 898 as instructed at beginning of Table 3, e.g., a collection of literature in South American Native languages 898.08)

899   **Literatures of non-Austronesian languages of Oceania, of Austronesian languages, of miscellaneous languages**

Add to base number 899 the numbers following —99 in notation 991–999 from Table 6, e.g., Polynesian literatures 899.4, Maori literature 899.442, literature originally composed and presented in sign languages 899.98, American Sign Language literature 899.987; then to the number given for each literature listed below add further as instructed at beginning of Table 3, e.g., a collection of Maori literature 899.44208

899.211 Tagalog (Filipino)

     Use period table under 899.211

899.221 Indonesian (Bahasa Indonesia)

     Use period table under 899.221

899.222 Javanese

899.2232 Sunda (Sundanese)

899.2234 Madura (Madurese)

899.2238 Bali (Balinese)

899.2242 Aceh (Achinese)

899.2244 Minangkabau

899.22462 Batak Toba

899.22466 Batak Dairi

899.2248 Lampung

899.2256 Banjar (Banjarese)

899.2262 Bugis (Buginese)

899.2264 Makasar

899.28 Malay (Bahasa Malaysia, Standard Malay)

899.3 Malagasy

899.42 Hawaiian

899.442 Maori

899.444 Tahitian

899.462 Samoan

899.482 Tongan (Tonga)

899.484 Niue (Niuean)

899.59 Fijian

899   Literatures of non-Austronesian languages of Oceania, of Austronesian languages, of miscellaneous languages

899.92 Basque

899.95 Sumerian

899.9623 Abkhaz

899.9625 Adyghe

899.969 Georgian

899.992 Esperanto

.211   *Tagalog (Filipino) literature

       Number built according to instructions under 899

       PERIOD TABLE
1	Early period to 1799
2	1800–1899
3	1900–1999
4	2000–

.221   *Indonesian (Bahasa Indonesia) literature

       Number built according to instructions under 899

       PERIOD TABLE
1	Early period to 1899
2	1900–1999
3	2000–

       Class comprehensive works on Indonesian (Bahasa Indonesia) and Malay (Bahasa Malaysia, standard Malay) literatures in 899.28

*Add to base number as instructed at beginning of Table 3

900

900   History, geography, and auxiliary disciplines

Class here social situations and conditions; general political history; military, diplomatic, political, economic, social, welfare aspects of specific wars

Class interdisciplinary works on ancient world, on specific continents, countries, localities in 930–990. Class history and geographic treatment of a specific subject with the subject, plus notation 09 from Table 1, e.g., history and geographic treatment of natural sciences 509, of economic situations and conditions 330.9, of purely political situations and conditions 320.9, history of military science 355.009

See also 303.49 for future history (projected events other than travel)

See Manual at 900

SUMMARY

900.1–.9	**Standard subdivisions of history and geography**
901–903	**Standard subdivisions of history**
904	**Collected accounts of events**
905–908	**Standard subdivisions of history**
909	**World history**
910	**Geography and travel**
.01–.02	**[Philosophy and theory of geography and travel; the earth (physical geography)]**
.2–.9	**Standard subdivisions, world travel guides, accounts of travel and facilities for travelers**
911	**Historical geography**
912	**Maps and plans of surface of earth and of extraterrestrial worlds**
913–919	**Geography of and travel in specific continents, countries, localities; extraterrestrial worlds**
920	**Biography, genealogy, insignia**
.001–.009	**Standard subdivisions of biography as a discipline**
.02–.09	**[General collections of biography not limited by period, group, or subject]**
.7	**People by gender or sex**
929	**Genealogy, names, insignia**
930	**History of ancient world to ca. 499**
.01–.09	**Standard subdivisions**
.1–.5	**[Archaeology and historical periods]**
931	**China to 420**
932	**Egypt to 640**
933	**Palestine to 70**
934	**South Asia to 647**
935	**Mesopotamia to 637 and Iranian Plateau to 637**
936	**Europe north and west of Italian Peninsula to ca. 499**
937	**Italian Peninsula to 476 and adjacent territories to 476**
938	**Greece to 323**
939	**Other parts of ancient world**

940	History of Europe
.01–.09	Standard subdivisions
.1–.5	[Historical periods]
941	British Isles
942	England and Wales
943	Germany and neighboring central European countries
944	France and Monaco
945	Italy, San Marino, Vatican City, Malta
946	Spain, Andorra, Gibraltar, Portugal
947	Russia and neighboring east European countries
948	Scandinavia and Finland
949	Other parts of Europe
950	History of Asia
.01–.09	Standard subdivisions
.1–.4	[Historical periods]
951	China and adjacent areas
952	Japan
953	Arabian Peninsula and adjacent areas
954	India and neighboring south Asian countries
955	Iran
956	Middle East (Near East)
957	Siberia (Asiatic Russia)
958	Central Asia
959	Southeast Asia
960	History of Africa
.01–.09	Standard subdivisions
.1–.3	[Historical periods]
961	Tunisia and Libya
962	Egypt, Sudan, South Sudan
963	Ethiopia and Eritrea
964	Morocco, Ceuta, Melilla, Western Sahara, Canary Islands
965	Algeria
966	West Africa and offshore islands
967	Central Africa and offshore islands
968	Republic of South Africa and neighboring southern African countries
969	South Indian Ocean islands
970	History of North America
.001–.009	Standard subdivisions
.01–.05	Historical periods
971	Canada
972	Mexico, Central America, West Indies, Bermuda
973	United States
974	Northeastern United States (New England and Middle Atlantic states)
975	Southeastern United States (South Atlantic states)
976	South central United States
977	North central United States
978	Western United States
979	Great Basin and Pacific Slope region of United States

980		**History of South America**
.001–.009		**Standard subdivisions**
.01–.04		**Historical periods**
981		**Brazil**
982		**Argentina**
983		**Chile**
984		**Bolivia**
985		**Peru**
986		**Colombia and Ecuador**
987		**Venezuela**
988		**Guiana**
989		**Paraguay and Uruguay**

990   **History of Australasia, Pacific Ocean islands, Atlantic Ocean islands, Arctic islands, Antarctica, extraterrestrial worlds**

       .01–.09   **Standard subdivisions of Australasia, Pacific Ocean islands, Atlantic Ocean islands, Arctic islands, Antarctica, extraterrestrial worlds together; of Australasia alone; of Pacific Ocean islands alone**

993	**New Zealand**
994	**Australia**
995	**New Guinea and neighboring countries of Melanesia**
996	**Polynesia and other Pacific Ocean islands**
997	**Atlantic Ocean islands**
998	**Arctic islands and Antarctica**
999	**Extraterrestrial worlds**

     .1–.9   **Standard subdivisions of history and geography**

901   Philosophy and theory of history

902   Miscellany of history

     [.23]   Maps, plans, diagrams

                Do not use; class in 911

903   Dictionaries, encyclopedias, concordances of history

904   Collected accounts of events

            Class here adventure

            Class travel in 910; class collections limited to a specific period in 909; class collections limited to a specific area or region but not limited by continent, country, locality in 909.09; class collections limited to a specific continent, country, locality in 930–990. Class history of a specific kind of event with the event, e.g., geological history of California earthquakes 551.2209794

             See Manual at 900: Historic events vs. nonhistoric events

     .5   **Events of natural origin**

     .7   **Events induced by human activity**

905   Serial publications of history

906   Organizations and management of history

907   Education, research, related topics of history

.2   Historical research

Including oral history

Class here historiography, interdisciplinary works on historical research

Class writing of history in 808.0669

.201–.209   Geographic treatment and biography

Add to base number 907.20 notation 1–9 from Table 2, e.g., historians and historiographers 907.202

Class historians and historiographers who specialize in a specific area with the area in 930–990, plus notation 007202 from table under 930–990, e.g., the biography of a German who specializes in French history in general 944.007202; class historians and historiographers who specialize in specific historical periods of a specific area with the historical period for the area studied, plus notation 092 from Table 1, e.g., biography of a German historian who specializes in the French Revolutionary period 944.04092

908   History with respect to groups of people

[.9]   Ethnic and national groups

Do not use; class in 909.04

909   World history

Civilization and events not limited by continent, country, locality

Class collected accounts of events not limited by period, area, region, subject in 904

See Manual at 306 vs. 305, 909, 930–990; also at 324 vs. 320.5, 320.9, 909, 930–990; also at 909, 930–990 vs. 320; also at 909, 930–990 vs. 320.4, 321, 321.09; also at 909, 930–990 vs. 910

(Option: Class primary textbooks on general history in 372.89045)

[.001–.008]   Standard subdivisions

Do not use; class in 901–908

[.009]   History

Do not use for historiography; class in 907.2. Do not use for general works on history; class in 909

[.009 01–.009 05]   Historical periods

Do not use; class in 909.1–909.8

[.009 1]   Areas, regions, places in general

Do not use; class in 909.09

[.009 2]   Biography

Do not use; class in 920

[.009 3–.009 9]   Specific continents, countries, localities; extraterrestrial worlds

                  Do not use; class in 930–990

.04   History with respect to ethnic and national groups

           See also 920.0092 for general collections of biography of members of a specific ethnic or national group

           See Manual at 920.008 vs. 305–306, 362

.040 01–.040 09   Standard subdivisions

.040 5–.040 9   People of mixed ancestry with ethnic origins from more than one continent, people of European descent

           Add to base number 909.04 notation 05–09 from Table 5 for the group only, e.g., world history of people of European descent 909.0409; then add 0* and to the result add the numbers following 909 in 909.1–909.8, e.g., world history of people of European descent in 18th century 909.040907

           (Option: Class here general history of specific ethnic and national groups with ethnic origins from more than one continent, of European descent in a specific continent, country, locality; prefer subdivision 004 from table under 930–990. If option is chosen, add notation 05–09 from Table 5 as above; then add 00 instead of 0 as above for world history by period, e.g., world history of people of European descent in 18th century 909.0409007; for specific areas add 0 and to the result add notation 3–9 from Table 2, e.g., history of people of European descent in United States 909.0409073)

.041–.049   Specific ethnic and national groups

           Add to base number 909.04 notation 1–9 from Table 5 for the group only, e.g., world history of Jews 909.04924; then add 0* and to the result add the numbers following 909 in 909.1–909.8, e.g., world history of Jews in 18th century 909.0492407

           (Option: Class here general history of specific ethnic and national groups in a specific continent, country, locality; prefer subdivision 004 from table under 930–990. If option is chosen, add notation 1–9 from Table 5 as above; then add 00 instead of 0 as above for world history by period, e.g., world history of Jews in 18th century 909.04924007; for specific areas add 0 and to the result add notation 3–9 from Table 2, e.g., history of Jews in Germany 909.04924043)

>   909.07–909.08   General historical periods

           Class here general histories covering three or more continents (or three or more countries if not on the same continent)

           Class specific historical periods in 909.1–909.8; class comprehensive works in 909

           For ancient history, see 930

---

*Add 00 for standard subdivisions; see instructions at beginning of Table 1

.07   Ca. 500–1450/1500

Including comprehensive works on Crusades

Class here Middle Ages

Class history of a place during the period of the Crusades with the history of the place, e.g., history of Europe during the period of Crusades 940.18

> *For comprehensive works on a specific Crusade, see the history of the country or region in which most of the fighting took place, e.g., First Crusade 956.014, Fourth Crusade 949.503*

> *See also 940.1 for history of Europe during Middle Ages*

.08   Modern history, 1450/1500–

.09   Areas, regions, places in general

Not limited by continent, country, locality

Class here interdisciplinary works on areas, regions, places in general (other than landforms, oceans, seas)

Class general collections of biography by areas, regions, places in general in 920.0091; class interdisciplinary works on landforms, oceans, seas in 551.4

> *For geography of and travel in areas, regions, places in general, see 910.91*

> *See Manual at T1—092: Comprehensive biography: Public figures; also at 920.009, 920.03–920.09 vs. 909.09, 909.1–909.8, 930–990; also at 930–990: Biography*

.090 1–.090 9   Standard subdivisions

.091–.099   Specific areas, regions, places in general

Add to base number 909.09 the numbers following —1 in notation 11–19 from Table 2, e.g., history of tropical regions 909.093, of Caribbean Sea 909.096365, of western civilization 909.09821; then add 0* and to the result add the numbers following 909 in 909.1–909.8, e.g., history of tropical regions in 20th century 909.093082

>   **909.1–909.8 Specific historical periods**

Class general historical periods in 909.07–909.08; class general biographies limited to a specific historical period in 920.00901–920.00905; class comprehensive works in 909

> *For historical periods through 5th century, see 930.1–930.5*

> *See Manual at T1—092: Comprehensive biography: Public figures; also at 920.009, 920.03–920.09 vs. 909.09, 909.1–909.8, 930–990; also at 930–990: Biography*

---

*Add 00 for standard subdivisions; see instructions at beginning of Table 1; however, class historical atlases in 911.1

.1	**6th-12th centuries, 500–1199**

Class comprehensive works on Middle Ages in 909.07

.2	**13th century, 1200–1299**
.3	**14th century, 1300–1399**
.4	**15th century, 1400–1499**
.5	**16th century, 1500–1599**
.6	**17th century, 1600–1699**
.7	**18th century, 1700–1799**
.8	**1800–**
.81	19th century, 1800–1899

Class here industrial revolution

.82	20th century, 1900–1999
.821	1900–1919

Class here early 20th century

For World War I, see 940.3. For a part of early 20th century not provided for here, see the part, e.g., 1930–1939 909.823

.822	1920–1929
.823	1930–1939
.824	1940–1949

For World War II, see 940.53

.825	1950–1959

Class here late 20th century, post World War II period

For a part of late 20th century, post World War II period not provided for here, see the part, e.g., 1980–1989 909.828

.826	1960–1969
.827	1970–1979
.828	1980–1989
.829	1990–1999
.83	21st century, 2000–2099

See also 303.49 for futurology

.831	2000–2019
.831 1	2000–2009
.831 2	2010–2019
.832	2020–2029

910 Geography and travel

Class here travel by specific kind of vehicle, e.g., travel by automobile, travel by bicycle; interdisciplinary works on tourism, on travel

Class general works on civilization, other than accounts of travel, in 909; class works on civilization, other than accounts of travel, in ancient world and specific places in modern world in 930–990. Class geographic treatment of a specific subject with the subject, plus notation 09 from Table 1, e.g., geographic treatment of religion 200.9, of geomorphology 551.4109

> *For mathematical geography, see 526. For a specific aspect of tourism, see the aspect, e.g., tourist industry 338.4791, travel and tourism in Mexico 917.204*
>
> *See Manual at 550 vs. 910; also at 578 vs. 304.2, 508, 910; also at 909, 930–990 vs. 910*

(Option: Class primary textbooks on general geography in 372.891045)

.01	Philosophy and theory of geography and travel
.014	Communication

Class here discursive works on place names and their origin, history, meaning

Class dictionaries and gazetteers of place names in 910.3

.02	The earth (Physical geography)

Class physical geography of a specific geological feature with the feature in 550, e.g., glaciers 551.312

> *See also 551.41 for geomorphology*
>
> *See Manual at 550 vs. 910*

.020 9	History and biography
[.020 91]	Areas, regions, places in general

Do not use; class in 910.021

[.020 93–.020 99]	Specific continents, countries, localities; extraterrestrial worlds

Do not use; class in 913–919, plus notation 02 from table under 913–919

.021	Physical geography of areas, regions, places in general

Add to base number 910.021 the numbers following —1 in notation 11–18 from Table 2, e.g., physical geography of forests 910.02152

(.1)   **Topical geography**

(Optional number; prefer specific subject, e.g., economic geography 330.91–330.99)

Do not use for philosophy and theory of geography and travel; class in 910.01

Add to base number 910.1 notation 001–899, e.g., economic geography 910.133; then add 0* and to the result add notation 1–9 from Table 2, e.g., economic geography of British Isles 910.133041

.2   **Miscellany; world travel guides**

Notation 02 from Table 1 as modified below

.202   World travel guides

Do not use for synopses and outlines; class in 910.2

Class here guidebooks and tour books providing tourists updated information about places in many areas of the globe: how to travel, what to see, where to stay, how to plan a vacation

Class guides to areas, regions, places in general in 910.91; class guides to specific continents, countries, localities in 913–919, plus notation 04 from table under 913–919

.22   Illustrations, models, miniatures

.223   Diagrams

Do not use for maps and plans; class in 912

.25   Directories of persons and organizations

Class here city directories, telephone books

Class city directories, telephone books of a specific place in 913–919, plus notation 0025 from table under 913–919

See also 910.46 for directories of facilities for travelers

See Manual at T1—025 vs. T1—029

.28   Auxiliary techniques and procedures; apparatus, equipment, materials

.285   Computer applications

Class here interdisciplinary works on geographic information systems (GIS), global positioning systems (GPS), real-time locating systems (RTLS)

Class real-time locating systems that use radio frequency identification in 910.2856245

For an application of geographic information systems (GIS), global positioning systems (GPS), or real-time locating systems (RTLS) to a subject, see the subject, plus notation 0285 from Table 1, e.g., GIS applications in mathematical geography 526.0285

*Add 00 for standard subdivisions; see instructions at beginning of Table 1

.3   **Dictionaries, encyclopedias, concordances, gazetteers**

Class here works on place names systematically arranged for ready reference

Class discursive works on place names in 910.014; class historical material associated with place names in general in 909; class historical material associated with place names of specific places in 930–990

.4   **Accounts of travel and facilities for travelers**

Standard subdivisions are added for accounts of travel and facilities for travelers together, for accounts of travel alone

Not geographically limited

For travel accounts that emphasize civilization of places visited, see 909; for discovery and exploration, see 910.9; for accounts of space travel near Earth, see 910.919

See also 508 for scientific exploration and travel; also 910.202 for world travel guides

.41   Trips around the world

.45   Ocean travel and seafaring adventures

Including pirates' expeditions

Class how to plan a cruise vacation in 910.202; class ocean trips around the world in 910.41; class travel in specific oceans in 910.9163–910.9167

.452   Shipwrecks

Class here comprehensive works on ocean and inland waterway shipwrecks

Class water transportation safety in 363.123

For ocean shipwrecks, see the location of the wrecks in 910.9163–910.9167, e.g., sinking of Titanic 910.91634, shipwrecks of Alaskan waters of the Pacific Ocean 910.916434; for inland waterway shipwrecks, see the location of the wrecks in 913–919, plus notation 04 from table under 913–919, e.g., shipwrecks of Mississippi River 917.704, shipwrecks of Lake Superior 917.74904

See Manual at 900: Historic events vs. nonhistoric events

.46   Facilities for travelers

Class here directories of lodging for temporary residents; interdisciplinary and descriptive works on lodging for temporary residents, hotels, inns, motels

For a specific kind of facility for travelers other than lodging, see the kind of facility, e.g., transportation facilities 388.04, eating and drinking places 647.95; for a specific aspect of lodging for temporary residents, see the aspect, e.g., household management 647.94

[.460 25]	Directories of persons and organizations

> Do not use for general directories of persons and organizations; class in 910.46. Do not use for directories of persons and organizations limited to specific continents, countries, localities; class in 913–919, plus notation 06 from table under 913–919

.460 9	History and biography
[.460 93–.460 99]	Specific continents, countries, localities

> Do not use; class in 913–919, plus notation 06 from table under 913–919

.462	Resorts

> Class here park and safari lodges, directories

[.462 025]	Directories of persons and organizations

> Do not use for general directories of persons and organizations; class in 910.462. Do not use for directories of persons and organizations limited to specific continents, countries, localities; class in 913–919, plus notation 062 from table under 913–919

.462 09	History and biography
[.462 093–.462 099]	Specific continents, countries, localities

> Do not use; class in 913–919, plus notation 062 from table under 913–919

.464	Bed and breakfast accommodations

> Class here boarding and rooming houses, directories

[.464 025]	Directories of persons and organizations

> Do not use for general directories of persons and organizations; class in 910.464. Do not use for directories of persons and organizations limited to specific continents, countries, localities; class in 913–919, plus notation 064 from table under 913–919

.464 09	History and biography
[.464 093–.464 099]	Specific continents, countries, localities

> Do not use; class in 913–919, plus notation 064 from table under 913–919

.466	Hostels

> Class here elder, youth hostels; directories

[.466 025]	Directories of persons and organizations

> Do not use for general directories of persons and organizations; class in 910.466. Do not use for directories of persons and organizations limited to specific continents, countries, localities; class in 913–919, plus notation 066 from table under 913–919

.466 09	History and biography

[.466 093–.466 099]	Specific continents, countries, localities

> Do not use; class in 913–919, plus notation 066 from table under 913–919

.468   Campsites

> Class here recreation vehicle (RV), trailer camps; directories

> Class trailer camps for long-term residents in 647.92; class travel by motor homes, recreational vehicles, trailers in 910

[.468 025]   Directories of persons and organizations

> Do not use for general directories of persons and organizations; class in 910.468. Do not use for directories of persons and organizations limited to specific continents, countries, localities; class in 913–919, plus notation 068 from table under 913–919

.468 09   History and biography

[.468 093–.468 099]   Specific continents, countries, localities

> Do not use; class in 913–919, plus notation 068 from table under 913–919

.5–.8   Standard subdivisions

.9   History, geographic treatment, biography

> Class here discovery, exploration, growth of geographic knowledge

.91   Geography of and travel in areas, regions, places in general

> Class physical geography of areas, regions, places in general in 910.02; class interdisciplinary works on landforms, oceans, seas in 551.4

> (Option: Class primary geography textbooks on specific areas, regions, places in general in 372.8911)

.919   Space travel near Earth

> Do not use for travel to or on extraterrestrial worlds, for comprehensive works on space travel; class in 919.904. Do not use for travel to or on Earth's moon; class in 919.9104

> Class here space travel in Earth's orbit, suborbital space tourism; near-Earth space travelers

> *See Manual at 629.43, 629.45 vs. 559.9, 919.904, 910.919*

.92   Geographers, travelers, explorers regardless of country of origin

> Do not use for near-Earth space travelers; class in 910.919

.93–.99   Discovery and exploration by specific countries

> Do not use for geography of and travel in specific continents, countries, localities; extraterrestrial worlds; class in 913–919
>
> Add to base number 910.9 notation 3–9 from Table 2 for the country responsible, e.g., explorations by Great Britain 910.941
>
> Class discovery and exploration by a specific country in areas, regions, places in general in 910.91; class discovery and exploration by a specific country in specific continents, countries, localities, extraterrestrial worlds in 913–919, plus notation 04 from table under 913–919; class periods of discovery and exploration in history in 930–990

911   Historical geography

> Growth and changes in political divisions
>
> Class here historical atlases

.09   History

[.091–.099]   Geographic treatment and biography

> Do not use; class in 911.1–911.9

.1–.9   Geographic treatment and biography

> Add to base number 911 notation 1–9 from Table 2, e.g., historical geography of China 911.51

912   Maps and plans of surface of earth and of extraterrestrial worlds

> Standard subdivisions are added for either or both topics in heading
>
> Class here atlases, charts; road maps, cycling maps, pedestrian maps, hiking maps
>
> *For cartography (map making), see 526. For maps and plans of a specific subject other than geography and travel, see the subject, plus notation 0223 from Table 1, e.g., maps of routes of bicycle racing 796.620223, cross-country ski trails 796.9320223, maps of military operations of American Revolution 973.330223; for maps and plans associated with a type of vehicle other than motor land vehicles and cycles, see the type, plus notation 0223 from Table 1, e.g., railroad atlases 385.0223*
>
> *See Manual at 526 vs. 912*

.01   Philosophy and theory; map reading

> Notation 01 from Table 1 as modified below

.014   Map reading

> Do not use for communication; class in 912.01
>
> Class here orientation
>
> Class orienteering in 796.58

.014 8   Map scales, symbols, abbreviations, acronyms

.09   History and biography of maps

[.091]	Maps and map making of specific areas, regions, places in general

Do not use; class in 912.19

.092	Biography

Do not use for map makers; class in 526.092

[.093–.099]	Maps and map making of specific continents, countries, localities, extraterrestrial worlds

Do not use; class in 912.3–912.9

.1   **Areas, regions, places in general**

.19   Specific areas, regions, places in general

Add to base number 912.19 the numbers following —1 in notation 11–19 from Table 2, e.g., maps of Western Hemisphere 912.19812

.3–.9   **Specific continents, countries, localities; extraterrestrial worlds**

Class here land atlases of countries, tax maps that provide general descriptions of assessed land and structures

Add to base number 912 notation 3–9 from Table 2, e.g., maps of DuPage County, Illinois 912.77324

913–919   Geography of and travel in specific continents, countries, localities; extraterrestrial worlds

Class here comprehensive works on ancient and modern geography of and travel in specific continents, countries, localities

Add to base number 91 notation 3–9 from Table 2, e.g., geography of England 914.2, of Norfolk, England 914.261; then add further as follows:

001	Philosophy and theory
0014	Communication
	Class here discursive works on place names and their origin, history, and meaning
	Class dictionaries and gazetteers of place names in notation 003 from this table
002	Miscellany
0022	Illustrations, models, miniatures
00222	Pictures and related illustrations
	Including aerial photographs
	Class photographs reflecting the civilization of places in 930–990
00223	Diagrams
	Do not use for maps and plans; class in 912
0025	Directories of persons and organizations
	Class here city directories, telephone books
0028	Auxiliary techniques and procedures; apparatus, equipment, materials
00285	Computer applications
	Class here geographic information systems (GIS), global positioning systems (GPS), real-time locating systems (RTLS)
	Class real-time locating systems that use radio frequency identification in notation 002856245 from this table
003	Dictionaries, encyclopedias, concordances, gazetteers
	Class here works on place names systematically arranged for ready reference
	Class discursive works on place names in notation 0014 from this table; class historical material associated with place names in 930–990
005–008	Standard subdivisions
[009]	History, geographic treatment, biography
	Do not use; class in 913–919 without adding from this table
01	Prehistoric geography
	Do not add to notation 4–6 from Table 2 if there is a corresponding notation 3 from Table 2, e.g., prehistoric geography of Greece 913.801 (*not* 914.9501), of Russia 914.701
	Class prehistoric physical geography in notation 02 from this table; class prehistoric geography of areas, regions, places in general in notation 09 from this table
02	The earth (Physical geography)
	Class physical geography of a specific geological feature with the feature in 550, e.g., glaciers of Canada 551.3120971
	See also 551.41 for geomorphology
	See Manual at 550 vs. 910

913–919   Geography of and travel in specific continents, countries, localities; extraterrestrial worlds

04   Travel

Class here discovery, exploration; guidebooks

Class world travel guides in 910.202; class travel accounts that emphasize the civilization of country visited in 930–990

For facilities for travelers, see notation 06 from this table

See Manual at 913–919: Add table: 04; also at 913–919 vs. 796.51

040223   Maps, plans, diagrams

Do not use for road maps, cycling maps, pedestrian maps, hiking maps; class in 912

040901–040905   Historical periods for regions

Do not use for historical periods of continents countries, localities; for historical periods for regions sharing the same historical period numbers as a country; class in notation 041–049 from this table

Limited to regions not sharing the same historical period numbers as a country, e.g., travel in central Europe during 19th century 914.30409034

041–049   Historical periods

Add to 04 the historical period numbers following 0 that appear in subdivisions of 930–990, e.g., travel in England during period of House of Tudor 914.2045; however, for historical periods of United States as a whole, see 917.3041–917.3049

For historical periods for regions not sharing the same historical period numbers as a country, see notation 040901–040905 from this table

06   Facilities for travelers

Class here lodging for travelers; directories of facilities for travelers; interdisciplinary and descriptive works on lodging for temporary residents, hotels, motels, inns in specific continents, countries, localities

For a specific kind of facility for travelers other than lodging, see the kind of facility, e.g., transportation facilities 388.04, eating and drinking places 647.953–647.959; for a specific aspect of lodging for temporary residents, see the aspect, e.g., household management 647.94093–647.94099

[06025]   Directories of persons and organizations

Do not use; class in notation 06 from this table

0609   History and biography

060901–060905   Historical periods for regions

Do not use for historical periods of continents countries, localities; for historical periods for regions sharing the same historical period numbers as a country; class in notation 061 from this table

Limited to regions not sharing the same historical period numbers as a country, e.g., facilities for travelers in central Europe during 19th century 914.30609034

913–919 Geography of and travel in specific continents, countries, localities; extraterrestrial worlds

061   Historical periods

Add to 061 the historical period numbers following 0 that appear in subdivisions of 930–990, e.g., facilities for travelers in England in 2011 914.20618612; however, for historical periods of United States as a whole, see 917.3061

For historical periods for regions not sharing the same historical period numbers as a country, see notation 060901–060905 from this table

062   Resorts

Class here park and safari lodges

06201–06209   Standard subdivisions

As modified under 0602–0609

0621–0629   Historical periods

Add to 062 the historical period numbers following 0 that appear in subdivisions of 930–990, e.g., resorts in England in 2011 914.20628612; however, for historical periods of United States as a whole, see 917.30621–917.30629

For historical periods for regions not sharing the same historical period numbers as a country, see notation 0620901–0620905 from this table

064   Bed and breakfast accommodations

Class here boarding and rooming houses, directories

06401–06409   Standard subdivisions

As modified under 0602–0609

0641–0649   Historical periods

Add to 064 the historical period numbers following 0 that appear in subdivisions of 930–990, e.g., bed and breakfast accommodations in England in 2011 914.20648612; however, for historical periods of United States as a whole, see 917.30641–917.30649

For historical periods for regions not sharing the same historical period numbers as a country, see notation 0640901–0640905 from this table

066   Hostels

Class here elder, youth hostels; directories

06601–06609   Standard subdivisions

As modified under 0602–0609

0661–0669   Historical periods

Add to 066 the historical period numbers following 0 that appear in subdivisions of 930–990, e.g., hostels in England in 2011 914.20668612; however, for historical periods of United States as a whole, see 917.30661–917.30669

For historical periods for regions not sharing the same historical period numbers as a country, see notation 0660901–0660905 from this table

068   Campsites

Class here recreation vehicle (RV), trailer camps; directories; interdisciplinary and descriptive works on lodging for campsites in specific continents, countries, localities

Class trailer camps for long-term residents in 647.92

06801–06809   Standard subdivisions

As modified under 0602–0609

913–919 Geography of and travel in specific continents, countries, localities; extraterrestrial worlds

0681–0689	Historical periods
	Add to 068 the historical period numbers following 0 that appear in subdivisions of 930–990, e.g., campsites in England in 2011 914.20688612; however, for historical periods of United States as a whole, see 917.30681–917.30689
	For historical periods for regions not sharing the same historical period numbers as a country, see notation 0680901–0680905 from this table
09	Areas, regions, places in general
	Add to 09 the numbers following —1 in notation 11–18 from Table 2, e.g., geography of urban regions of England 914.209732 Class physical geography of areas, regions, places in notation 02 from this table; class travel in notation 04 from this table; class civilization in 930–990, plus notation 0091–0098 from table under 930–990

Class historical geography in 911; class graphic representations in 912; class area studies in 940–990; class comprehensive works, geography of and travel in more than one continent in 910; class interdisciplinary works on geography and history of ancient world, of specific continents, countries, localities in 930–990

> See Manual at 913–919; also at 333.7–333.9 vs. 508, 913–919, 930–990; also at 629.43, 629.45 vs. 559.9, 919.904, 910.919

(Option: Class primary geography textbooks on ancient world, on specific continents, countries, localities in 372.8913–372.8919)

913 Geography of and travel in ancient world

Number built according to instructions under 913–919

914 Geography of and travel in Europe

Number built according to instructions under 913–919

915 Geography of and travel in Asia

Number built according to instructions under 913–919

916 Geography of and travel in Africa

Number built according to instructions under 913–919

917 Geography of and travel in North America

Number built according to instructions under 913–919

.3 Geography of and travel in United States

Number built according to instructions under 913–919

> *For geography of and travel in specific states of United States, see 917.4–917.9*

.304 Travel

Number built according to instructions under 913–919

.304 1–.304 9	Historical periods

Add to base number 917.304 the numbers following 973 in 973.1–973.9, e.g., travel in United States during the Obama administration 917.304932

.306	Facilities for travelers

Number built according to instructions under 913–919

.306 1	Historical periods

Add to base number 917.3061 the numbers following 973 in 973.1–973.9, e.g., facilities for travelers in United States in 1993–2001 917.3061929

.306 2	Resorts

Number built according to instructions under 913–919

.306 21–.306 29	Historical periods

Add to base number 917.3062 the numbers following 973 in 973.1–973.9, e.g., resorts in United States in 1993–2001 917.3062929

.306 4	Bed and breakfast accommodations

Number built according to instructions under 913–919

.306 41–.306 49	Historical periods

Add to base number 917.3064 the numbers following 973 in 973.1–973.9, e.g., bed and breakfast accommodations in United States in 1993–2001 917.3064929

.306 6	Hostels

Number built according to instructions under 913–919

.306 61–.306 69	Historical periods

Add to base number 917.3066 the numbers following 973 in 973.1–973.9, e.g., hostels in United States in 1993–2001 917.3066929

.306 8	Campsites

Number built according to instructions under 913–919

.306 81–.306 89	Historical periods

Add to base number 917.3068 the numbers following 973 in 973.1–973.9, e.g., campsites in United States in 1993–2001 917.3068929

.4–.9	**Geography of and travel in specific states of United States**

Add to base number 91 notation 74–79 from Table 2, e.g., geography of and travel in California 917.94; then add further as instructed under 913–919, e.g., travel in California 917.9404, travel in California in 2001 917.940454

For geography of and travel in Hawaii, see 919.69

918   **Geography of and travel in South America**

        Number built according to instructions under 913–919

919   **Geography of and travel in Australasia, Pacific Ocean islands, Atlantic Ocean islands, Arctic islands, Antarctica and on extraterrestrial worlds**

        Number built according to instructions under 913–919

.904   Travel to or on extraterrestrial worlds

           Number built according to instructions under 913–919

           Class here accounts of projected flights; comprehensive works on space travel

              For space travel near Earth, see 910.919

              See Manual at 629.43, 629.45 vs. 559.9, 919.904, 910.919

.920 4   Travel in planets of solar system and their satellites

           Number built according to instructions under 913–919

           Class here accounts of projected planetary flights

           Class accounts of projected flights to a specific planet with the planet in 919.921–919.929, plus notation 04 from table under 913–919, e.g., projected accounts of flights to Mars 919.92304

920   Biography, genealogy, insignia

        Class here autobiographies, correspondence, diaries, reminiscences; biography as a discipline

        Class biography of people associated with a specific subject with the subject, plus notation 092 from Table 1, e.g., biography of chemists 540.92

           For personal improvement and analysis through diary keeping, see 158.16

        (Option A: For biography of people associated with a specific subject, use subdivisions identified by *, then, for each number identified by †, add notation 3–9 from Table 2, e.g., Baptists from Louisiana 922.6763

        (Option B: Class individual biography in 92 or B; class collected biography in 92 or 920 undivided

        (Option C: Class individual biography of men in 920.71; class individual biography of women in 920.72)

           See Manual at T1—092

.001–.002   Standard subdivisions of biography as a discipline

.003   Dictionaries, encyclopedias, concordances of biography as a discipline

           See also 920.02 for biographical dictionaries

.005–.007   Standard subdivisions of biography as a discipline

.008	Biography as a discipline with respect to groups of people; general collections of biography by groups of people with specific attributes

> *See Manual at 920.008 vs. 305–306, 362*

[.008 1]	People by gender or sex

> Do not use; class in 920.7

[.008 2]	Women

> Do not use; class in 920.72

[.008 8]	Occupational and religious groups

> Do not use; class with the specific group, plus notation 092 from Table 1, e.g., biography of Lutherans 284.1092

[.008 9]	Ethnic and national groups

> Do not use; class in 920.0092

.009	History and geographic treatment of biography as a discipline; general collections of biography by period, region, group

> Subdivisions are added for biography as a discipline, for general collections of biography, or for both

> *See Manual at T1—092: Comprehensive biography: Public figures; also at 920.009, 920.03–920.09 vs. 909.09, 909.1–909.8, 930–990; also at 930–990: Biography*

.009 01–.009 05	Historical periods

> Add to base number 920.0090 the numbers following —090 in notation 0901–0905 from Table 1, e.g., general biography of 19th century 920.009034

.009 1	Areas, regions, places in general

> Add to base number 920.0091 the numbers following —1 in notation 11–19 from Table 2, e.g., biographies of suburbanites 920.0091733

.009 2	Ethnic and national groups

> Do not use for biography of biography as a discipline; class in 920 without subdivision

> *See Manual at 920.008 vs. 305–306, 362*

.009 205–.009 209	People of mixed ancestry with ethnic origins from more than one continent, people of European descent

> Add to base number 920.0092 notation 05–09 from Table 5, e.g., biographies of people of European descent 920.009209

.009 21–.009 29	Specific ethnic and national groups

> Add to base number 920.0092 notation 1–9 from Table 5, e.g., biographies of Swedes 920.0092397

.009 3–.009 9	Biography as a discipline by specific continents, countries, localities

> Do not use for general collections of biography by specific continents, countries, localities; class in 920.03–920.09

.02	General collections of biography

> *For a collection limited by period, place, group, or subject, see the period, place, group, or subject, e.g., collections of biographies of people resident in England 920.042, collections of biographies of scientists 509.22*

[.020 3]	Dictionaries, encyclopedias, concordances

Do not use; class in 920.02

[.020 8]	General collections of biography with respect to groups of people

Do not use; class in 920.008

[.020 81]	People by gender or sex

Do not use; class in 920.7

[.020 82]	Women

Do not use; class in 920.72

[.020 88]	Occupational and religious groups

Do not use; class with the specific group, plus notation 092 from Table 1, e.g., biography of Lutherans 284.1092

[.020 89]	Ethnic and national groups

Do not use; class in 920.0092

.03–.09	General collections of biography by specific continents, countries, localities

Not associated with a specific subject

Add to base number 920.0 notation 3–9 from Table 2, e.g., collections of biographies of people resident in England 920.042

Class collections by sex regardless of continent, country, locality in 920.7

> *For collected biography of public figures who had a significant impact upon general history of a specific continent, country, or locality, see the history of the continent, country, or locality in 930–990, plus notation 0099 from table under 930–990, e.g., collected biography of kings and queens of England 942.0099*

> *See Manual at T1—092: Comprehensive biography: Public figures; also at 920.009, 920.03–920.09 vs. 909.09, 909.1–909.8, 930–990; also at 930–990: Biography*

(.1)	***Bibliographers**
(.2)	***Librarians and book collectors**
(.3)	***Encyclopedists**

Class lexicographers in 924

(.4)	***Publishers and booksellers**

*(Optional number; prefer specific subject, as described under 920)

(.5)	***Journalists and news commentators**
.7	**People by gender or sex**

Class here individual biography of people not associated with a specific subject, collected biography of people by gender or sex

Class general collections of biography in 920.02

> *For collected biography of transgender or intersex people, see 920.00867*

(Option: Class here all individual biography; prefer specific subject, plus notation 092 from Table 1, e.g., biography of a female scientist 509.2)

.71	Men

> *See Manual at 920.008 vs. 305–306, 362*

.72	Women

> *See Manual at 920.008 vs. 305–306, 362*

(.9)	***People associated with other subjects**

Not provided for in 920.1–920.5, 921–928

Add to base number 920.9 notation 001–999, e.g., astrologers 920.91335

(921)   *Philosophers and psychologists

>	**(921.1–921.8) Modern western philosophers and psychologists**

Class comprehensive works in 921

(.1)	***United States and Canadian philosophers and psychologists**
(.2)	***British philosophers and psychologists**

Including English, Scottish, Irish, Welsh philosophers and psychologists

(.3)	***German and Austrian philosophers and psychologists**
(.4)	***French philosophers and psychologists**
(.5)	***Italian philosophers and psychologists**
(.6)	***Spanish and Portuguese philosophers and psychologists**
(.7)	***Russian philosophers and psychologists**
(.8)	***†Other modern western philosophers and psychologists**
(.9)	***Ancient, medieval, eastern philosophers and psychologists**

Add to base number 921.9 the numbers following 18 in 181–189, e.g., Aristotelian philosophers 921.95

---

*(Optional number; prefer specific subject, as described under 920)
†Add as instructed under 920

(922) *Religious leaders, thinkers, workers

> ### (922.1–922.8) Christians

Class comprehensive works in 922

(.1) *†Early church and Eastern churches

Subdivisions are added for either or both topics in heading

(.2) *Roman Catholics

(.21) *Popes

(.22) *Saints

(.24–.29) *Roman Catholics from specific continents, countries, localities in modern world

Add to base number 922.2 notation 4–9 from Table 2, e.g., Roman Catholics from the City of Montréal 922.271428

For popes, see 922.21; for saints, see 922.22

(.3) *†Anglicans

(.4) *†Lutherans, Huguenots, continental Protestants

Subdivisions are added for any or all topics in heading

(.5) *†Presbyterians, Congregationalists, American Reformed

Subdivisions are added for any or all topics in heading

(.6) *†Baptists, Disciples of Christ, Adventists

Subdivisions are added for any or all topics in heading

(.7) *†Methodists

(.8) *Members of other Christian denominations and sects

(.81) *†Unitarians and Universalists

Subdivisions are added for either or both topics in heading

(.83) *†Latter-Day Saints

(.84) *†Swedenborgians

(.85) *†Christian Scientists

(.86) *†Friends (Quakers)

(.87) *†Mennonites

(.88) *†Shakers

*(Optional number; prefer specific subject, as described under 920)
†Add as instructed under 920

(.89)	*Other Christian denominations and sects

     Not provided for elsewhere

(.9)	***Adherents of other religions**
(.91)	*Atheists and Deists
(.94)	*Adherents of Indic religions
(.943)	*Buddhists
(.944)	*Jains
(.945)	*Hindus
(.946)	*Sikhs
(.95)	*Zoroastrians (Parsees)
(.96)	*Adherents of Judaism
(.97)	*Adherents of Islam
(.99)	*Other religions

     Not provided for elsewhere

(923) *People in social sciences

(.1)	***†Heads of state**

     Class here kings, queens, presidents

(.2)	***†People in political science and politics**

     Class here legislators, governors, politicians, statesmen, diplomats, nobility; political scientists

     For heads of state, see 923.1

(.3)	***People in economics**
(.31)	*†Labor leaders
(.33–.39)	*People in economics from specific continents, countries, localities

     Add to base number 923.3 notation 3–9 from Table 2, e.g., people in economics from Chicago 923.377311

     For labor leaders, see 923.31

(.4)	***Criminals and people in law**
(.41)	*†Criminals
(.43–.49)	*People in law

     Add to base number 923.4 notation 3–9 from Table 2, e.g., people in law from Sydney 923.49441

---

*(Optional number; prefer specific subject, as described under 920)
†Add as instructed under 920

| (.5) | *†Public administrators and military personnel |

Class here government workers

Subdivisions are added for either or both topics in heading

For heads of state, see 923.1; for governors, politicians, statesmen, see 923.2

| (.6) | *†Philanthropists, humanitarians, social reformers |

Subdivisions are added for any or all topics in heading

| (.7) | *†Educators |

| (.8) | *†People in commerce, communications, transportation |

Subdivisions are added for any or all topics in heading

| (.9) | *Explorers, geographers, pioneers |

(924) *Philologists and lexicographers

Add to base number 924 notation 1–9 from Table 6, e.g., lexicographers of Chinese 924.951

(925) *Scientists

Add to base number 925 the numbers following 5 in 510–590, e.g., botanists 925.8

(926) *People in technology

Add to base number 926 the numbers following 6 in 610–690, e.g., engineers 926.2

See also 920.4 for booksellers

(927) *People in the arts and recreation

Add to base number 927 the numbers following 7 in 710–790, e.g., baseball players 927.96357

For people in literature, see 928

(928) *People in literature, history, biography, genealogy

Including historians, writers and critics of belles-lettres

See also 923.9 for explorers, geographers, pioneers

| (.1) | *Americans |

| (.2–.9) | *Writers in literature, history, biography, genealogy by language |

Add to base number 928 notation 2–9 from Table 6 for language in which person has written, e.g., writers in Italian 928.51

Class Americans in 928.1

929 Genealogy, names, insignia

*(Optional number; prefer specific subject, as described under 920)
†Add as instructed under 920

.1   Genealogy

For family histories, see 929.2; for sources, see 929.3

[.102 84]   Apparatus, equipment, materials

             Do not use; class in 929.3

.107 2   Research

             Class here the specific techniques and procedures involved in doing genealogical research in a specific area

             Class comprehensive works on genealogical research in 929.1

[.109 4–.109 9]   Specific continents, countries, localities in modern world

             Do not use; class in 929.107204–929.107209

.2   Family histories

Class family histories emphasizing the contributions of the members of the family to a specific occupation with the occupation, e.g., the Rothschilds as a family of bankers 332.10922; class family histories of a prominent person that emphasize the person's life with the biography number for the person, e.g., forebears, family, and life of John Fitzgerald Kennedy 973.922092

For royal houses, peerage, see 929.7

See Manual at 929.2

(Option: Arrange alphabetically by name)

.202 8   Auxiliary techniques and procedures; apparatus, equipment, materials

             Do not use for the techniques of compiling family histories; class in 929.1

.3   Genealogical sources

Standard subdivisions are added for miscellaneous collections and individual sources

Class here census records, court records, tax lists, wills

Use only for sources published by a genealogical organization or compiled by a genealogist. Sources published or compiled by other agencies are normally classed with the subject of the publication, e.g., United States population census records 304.60973; however, if the source has been either enhanced or rearranged to emphasize the genealogical content, the source is classed here, e.g., United States population census records with name indexes added 929.373

Class how to use sources in 929.1; class cemetery records used as genealogical sources in 929.5

For epitaphs, see 929.5

[.309 3–.309 9]   Specific continents, countries, localities

             Do not use; class in 929.33–929.39

.33–.39   Specific continents, countries, localities

         Regardless of form

         Add to base number 929.3 notation 3–9 from Table 2, e.g., sources from New York 929.3747

.4   **Personal names**

         See also 929.97 for names of houses, pets, ships

.42   Surnames

.44   Forenames

         Class here lists of names for babies

.5   **Cemetery records**

         Regardless of form

         Including epitaphs

.6   **Heraldry**

         Including crests

         Class here armorial bearings, coats of arms

         For royal houses, peerage, orders of knighthood, see 929.7

.7   **Royal houses, peerage, orders of knighthood**

         Class here rank, precedence, titles of honor; genealogies tracing or establishing titles of honor; works emphasizing lineage or descent with respect to royalty or the peerage; history and genealogy of royal families

         Class histories of a royal family that include general historical events or biographies of members of the royal family in 930–990. Class family histories of a prominent person that emphasize the person's life with the biography number for the person, e.g., forebears, family, and life of Winston Churchill 941.084092

[.709 41–.709 49]   Specific countries of Europe

         Do not use; class in 929.72–929.79

.71   Orders of knighthood

         Class Christian orders of knighthood in 255.791; class Christian orders of knighthood in church history in 271.791

\>   929.72–929.79 Treatment of royal houses, peerage, gentry by specific countries of Europe

         Class comprehensive works in 929.7094

.72   Great Britain and Ireland

.73–.79   Other countries of Europe

         Add to base number 929.7 the numbers following —4 in notation 43–49 from Table 2, e.g., royal houses of France 929.74

.8   **Orders, decorations, autographs**

.81   Orders and decorations

> Add to base number 929.81 notation 1–9 from Table 2, e.g., orders of Germany 929.8143
>> Subdivisions are added for either or both topics in heading

> *For armorial bearings, see 929.6*

.88   Autographs

> Class autographs associated a specific subject with the subject, plus notation 075 from Table 1, e.g., American football autographs 796.332075

.9   **Forms of insignia and identification**

> Including identification cards, motor vehicle registration plates, seals

> Class seals with armorial bearings in 929.6. Class forms of insignia and identification not provided for here with the form, e.g., coats of arms 929.6; class a specific aspect of identification cards not provided for here with the aspect, e.g., forgery of identification cards 364.163; class identification marks in a specific subject with the subject, plus notation 027 from Table 1, e.g., airline insignia 387.70275

> *See also 737.6 for artistic aspects of seals*

.92   Flags and banners

> Standard subdivisions are added for either or both topics in heading

> Including ship, ownership flags and banners

> Class here national, state, provincial flags and banners

> Class military use in 355.15

.95   Service marks and trademarks

> Standard subdivisions are added for either or both topics in heading

.97   Names

> Including names of houses, ships, pets

> Class here interdisciplinary works on onomastics (study of origin, history, use of proper names)

> *For place names, see 910.014; for personal names, see 929.4*

.970 14   Communication

> Do not use for etymology; class in 412

> ## 930–990 History of specific continents, countries, localities; extraterrestrial worlds

Civilization and events

Class here interdisciplinary works on geography and history of ancient world, of specific continents, countries, localities

Add to base number 9 notation 3–9 from Table 2, e.g., general history of Europe 940, of England 942, of Norfolk, England 942.61; then add further as follows:

001	Philosophy and theory
002	Miscellany
00223	Maps, plans, diagrams
	Do not use for historical atlases; class in 911.1–911.9
003	Dictionaries, encyclopedias, concordances
004	Ethnic and national groups
	(Option: Class in 909.04)
004001–004009	Standard subdivisions
00405–00409	Specific ethnic and national groups with ethnic origins from more than one continent, of European descent

Add to 0040 the numbers following —0 in notation 05–09 from Table 5, e.g., history and civilization of people of European descent in New York 974.700409, history and civilization of people of European descent in New York during 1980–1989 974.700409009048 Class relation of ethnic and national groups with ethnic origins from more than one continent, of European descent to a war with the war, plus notation 089 from Table 1, e.g., relation of Europeans to World War II 940.5308909

0041–0049	Specific ethnic and national groups

Add to 004 notation 1–9 from Table 5, e.g., history and civilization of North American native peoples in New York 974.700497, history and civilization of North American native peoples in New York during 1980–1989 974.700497009048

Class indigenous groups in the prehistoric period with the period, e.g., Inca empire before Spanish conquest 985.019; class relation of ethnic and national groups to a war with the war, plus notation 089 from Table 1, e.g., relation of Arabs to World War II 940.53089927

005–006	Standard subdivisions
007	Education, research, related topics
0072	Historical research
007202	Historians and historiographers

Class historians and historiographers specializing in a specific historical period of a specific area with the historical period for the area studied, plus notation 092 from Table 1, e.g., the biography of a Canadian historian who specializes in United States Revolutionary War 973.3092

See also notation 0090909 from this table for archaeologists

See Manual at 930–990: Biography

008	Groups of people

> ## 930–990   History of specific continents, countries, localities; extraterrestrial worlds

[0089]	Ethnic and national groups
	Do not use; class in notation 004 from this table
009	Areas, regions places in general; collected biography
	Notation 09 from Table 1 as modified below
	Do not use for history, geographic treatment, biography together; class in 930–990 without adding from this table. Do not use for historical periods; class in notation 01–09 from this table. Do not use for individual biography; class in notation 01–09 from this table, plus notation 092 from Table 1. Do not use for specific continents, countries, localities; class in 930–990 without adding from this table
00909	Archaeology
	Unless other instructions are given, observe the following table of preference, e.g., a periodical of statistics 00909021 (*not* 0090905):

Biography	0090909
Museums, collections, exhibits	00909074
Collecting objects	00909075
Illustrations	00909022
Statistics	00909021
Dictionaries, encyclopedias, concordances	0090903
Serial publications	0090905

Class archaeology of a specific period with the period in notation 01–09 from this table, plus notation 09009 from Table 1, e.g., archaeology of period of 1815–1874 in Austrian history 04209009

0090902	Statistics and illustrations
00909021	Statistics
00909022	Illustrations
	Including cartoons, drawings, pictures, pictorial charts and designs, sketches; graphs; maps, plans, diagrams
	Class statistical graphs in notation 00909021 from this table; class humorous cartoons in 930–990 without adding from this table
0090903	Dictionaries, encyclopedias, concordances
	Including thesauri (synonym dictionaries)
0090905	Serial publications
	Regardless of form (print or electronic) or frequency
	Class here house organs, magazines, newspapers, yearbooks
0090907	Museums, collections, exhibits; collecting objects
00909074	Museums, collections, exhibits
	Class here exhibitions, fairs, festivals; catalogs, lists regardless of whether or not articles are offered for sale; guidebooks, history and description
	Add to 00909074 notation 4–9 from Table 2, e.g., collections in Pennsylvania 00909074748, collections of Brazilian objects in Pennsylvania 981.00909074748

> ## 930–990 History of specific continents, countries, localities; extraterrestrial worlds

00909075		Collecting objects

00909075   Collecting objects
     Class here collectibles, memorabilia, price trends for collectors

0090909   Biography
     Class here archaeologists
     Class archaeologists specializing in a specific historical period of a specific area with the historical period for the area studied, plus notation 092 from Table 1, e.g., the biography of a Canadian archaeologist who specializes in United States Revolutionary War 973.3092
       See also notation 007202 from this table for historians and historiographers
       See Manual at 930–990: Biography

0091–0098   Areas, regions, places in general
     Add to 009 the numbers following —1 in notation 11–18 from Table 2, e.g., urban regions 009732

0099   Collected biography
     Description, critical appraisal, biography of people associated with the history of the continent, country, locality but limited to no specific period
     Class collected biography of a specific period in notation 01–09 from this table, plus notation 0922 from Table 1; class historians and historiographers in notation 007202 from this table; class archaeologists in notation 0090909 from this table; class comprehensive works on collected biography of a specific continent, country, or locality in 920.03–920.09
       See Manual at T1—092: Comprehensive biography: Public figures; also at 920.009, 920.03–920.09 vs. 909.09, 909.1–909.8, 930–990; also at 930–990: Biography

01–09   Historical periods
     Class here indigenous groups in the prehistoric period, e.g., Inca empire before Spanish conquest 985.019 (*not* 985.00498323)
     Add to 0 the historical period numbers following 0 from the appropriate continent, country, locality in 930–990, e.g., period of 1760–1820 in British history 073 (from 941.073), period of 1815–1847 in German history 073 (from 943.073), period of 1815–1847 in Austrian history 042 (from 943.6042)
     Unless other period notation is specified, add to each geographic subdivision of an area the period notation for the area as a whole, e.g., period of Ottoman Empire in Saudi Arabia 953.803 (based on period of Ottoman Empire in Arabian Peninsula 953.03)
     Class areas, regions, places in general in a specific period in notation 0091–0098 from this table; class ethnic and national groups in a specific period in notation 004 from this table. Class relation of ethnic and national groups to a war with the war, plus notation 089 from Table 1, e.g., relation of Arabs to World War II 940.53089927
       See Manual at 930–990: Biography; also at 930–990: Add table: 01–09

> ## 930–990   History of specific continents, countries, localities; extraterrestrial worlds

The schedules that follow do not enumerate all the countries and localities that appear in Table 2; however, the foregoing instructions apply to history of any place in notation 3–9 from Table 2, e.g., period of 1815–1847 in Viennese history 943.613042

Class sociology of war in 303.66; class sociology of military institutions in 306.27; class social factors affecting war in 355.02; class social causes of war in 355.0274; class historical geography in 911; class geography of ancient world, of specific continents, countries, localities in 913–919; class comprehensive works in 909

> *See Manual at 930–990; also at 306 vs. 305, 909, 930–990; also at 324 vs. 320.5, 320.9, 909, 930–990; also at 333.7–333.9 vs. 508, 913–919, 930–990; also at 909, 930–990 vs. 320; also at 909, 930–990 vs. 320.4, 321, 321.09; also at 909, 930–990 vs. 910; also at 930–990 vs. 355.009, 355–359*

(Option: Class primary history textbooks on ancient world, on specific continents, countries, localities in 372.893–372.899)

930   History of ancient world to ca. 499

.01–.09   Standard subdivisions

> As modified in notation 001–009 from table under 930–990; however, for archaeology, see 930.1

.1   **Archaeology**

> Class here early history to 4000 B.C.; prehistoric archaeology; interdisciplinary works on archaeology

> *For archaeology of specific oceans and seas, see 909.0963–909.0967; for archaeology of continents, countries, localities provided for in notation 3 from Table 2, see 931–939; for archaeology of modern period, ancient and prehistoric archaeology of continents, countries, localities not provided for in notation 3 from Table 2, see 940–990. For archaeology of a specific subject, see the subject, plus notation 09009 from Table 1, e.g., industrial archaeology 609.009*

> *See also 700 for artistic aspects of archaeological objects*

.102   Miscellany

.102 8   Auxiliary techniques and procedures; apparatus, equipment, materials

> Notation 028 from Table 1 as modified below

> Class here basic techniques and procedures

.102 804   Underwater archaeology

> *For archaeology of specific oceans and seas, see 909.0963–909.0967*

.102 82   Discovery of remains

.102 83   Excavation of remains

.102 85	Interpretation of remains

Do not use for computer applications; class in 930.1028

Including dating techniques

.109 2	Biography

Class archaeologists who specialize in a specific area with the area in 930–990, plus notation 0090909 from table under 930–990, e.g., biography of a German who specializes in the archaeology of France in general 944.0090909; class archaeologists who specialize in specific historical periods of a specific area with the historical period for the area studied, plus notation 092 from Table 1, e.g., biography of a German archaeologist who specializes in the Medieval period of France 944.02092

>   930.12–930.16   Specific prehistoric ages

Class comprehensive works in 930.1

.12	Paleolithic Age (Old Stone Age)

Class here comprehensive works on Stone Ages

For Mesolithic Age, see 930.13; for Neolithic Age, see 930.14

.124	Lower Paleolithic Age

Including Acheulian culture

Class here Eolithic Age

.126	Middle Paleolithic Age

Including Mousterian culture

.128	Upper Paleolithic Age

Including Aurignacian culture, Solutrean culture

.13	Mesolithic Age (Middle Stone Age)
.14	Neolithic Age (New Stone Age)
.15	Copper Age and Bronze Age
.153	Copper Age (Chalcolithic Age)
.156	Bronze Age
.16	Iron Age
.5	**1st-5th centuries, 1–499**

>   **931–939   Specific places**

Class archaeology and history of specific oceans and seas in 909.0963–909.0967; class archaeology and history of modern period, ancient and prehistoric archaeology and history of continents, countries, localities not provided for in notation 3 from Table 2 in 940–990; class comprehensive works in 930

931   ***China to 420**

      (Option: Class in 951.01)

.01   Early history to ca. 1523 B.C.

.02   Period of Shang (Yin) dynasty, ca. 1523–ca. 1028 B.C.

.03   Period of Zhou (Chou) dynasty and warring states, ca. 1028–221 B.C.

.04   Period of Qin (Ch'in) to Jin (Chin) dynasties, 221 B.C.–420 A.D.

          Including Han dynasty, 202 B.C.–220 A.D.

.1–.6   **Localities of China to 420**

      Add to base number 931 the numbers following —51 in notation 511–516 from
Table 2, e.g., Sichuan Province 931.38; then add further as follows:

        001–009   Standard subdivisions

                 Add to 00 the numbers following 00 in notation 001–009
from table under 930–990, e.g., ethnic and national groups
004, ethnic and national groups in Sichuan Province
931.38004

        01–04   Historical periods

                 Add to 0 the numbers following 931.0 in 931.01–931.04, e.g.,
Sichuan Province during period of Qin (Ch'in) to Jin (Chin)
dynasties, 221 B.C.–420 A.D. 931.3804

932   ***Egypt to 640**

      (Option: Class in 962.01)

.01   Early history to 332 B.C.

.011   Prehistoric period to ca. 3100 B.C.

.012   Protodynastic, Old Kingdom, first intermediate periods,
ca. 3100–2052 B.C.

          Including 1st-11th dynasties

.013   Middle Kingdom and second intermediate periods, 2052–1570 B.C.

          Including 12th-17th dynasties

.014   Period of New Kingdom, 1570–1075 B.C.

          Including 18th-20th dynasties

.015   Late and Saite periods, 1075–525 B.C.

          Including 21st-26th dynasties, period of sovereignty of Cush

.016   Persian periods and last Egyptian kingdom, 525–332 B.C.

          Including 27th-31st dynasties

.02   Hellenistic, Roman, Byzantine periods, 332 B.C.–640 A.D.

.021   Hellenistic period, 332–30 B.C.

.022   Roman period, 30 B.C.–324 A.D.

*Add as instructed under 930–990

.023	Byzantine (Coptic) period, 324–640

.1–.3   Localities of Egypt to 640

Add to base number 932 the numbers following —62 in notation 621–623 from Table 2, e.g., Alexandria 932.1; then add further as follows:

    001–009   Standard subdivisions

                 Add to 00 the numbers following 00 in notation 001–009 from table under 930–990, e.g., ethnic and national groups 004, ethnic and national groups in Alexandria 932.1004

    01–02   Historical periods

                 Add to 0 the numbers following 932.0 in 932.01–932.02, e.g., Alexandria during Hellenistic, Roman, Byzantine periods, 332 B.C.–640 A.D. 932.102

933   *Palestine to 70

See also 220.93 for Biblical archaeology; also 220.95 for history of Biblical events

(Option: Class Palestine, Israel in 956.9401; class West Bank in 956.94201; class Gaza Strip in 956.94301)

.01	Early history to return of Jews from bondage in Egypt, ca. 1225 B.C.
.02	Great age of Twelve Tribes, ca. 1225–922 B.C.

Including rule of Judges, Saul, David, Solomon

.03	Periods of partition, conquest, foreign rule, 922–168 B.C.

Including periods of Assyrian, Babylonian, Persian, Hellenistic rule

.04	168–63 B.C.

Including Hasmonean (Maccabean) period

.05	Period of Roman protectorate and rule to destruction of Jerusalem, 63 B.C.–70 A.D.

.2–.5   Localities of Palestine to 70

Add to base number 933 the numbers following —33 in notation 332–335 from Table 2, e.g., Israel to 70 933.4; then add further as follows:

    001–009   Standard subdivisions

                 Add to 00 the numbers following 00 in notation 001–009 from table under 930–990, e.g., ethnic and national groups 004, ethnic and national groups in Israel to 70 933.4004

    01–05   Historical periods

                 Add to 0 the numbers following 933.0 in 933.01–933.05, e.g., Israel during period of Roman protectorate and rule to destruction of Jerusalem, 63 B.C.–70 A.D. 933.405

934   *South Asia to 647

Class here India to 647

(Option: Class in 954.01)

.01	Pre-Aryan civilizations to ca. 1500 B.C.

*Add as instructed under 930–990

.02	Indo-Aryan (Vedic) period, ca. 1500–ca. 600 B.C.
	Including Iron Age culture in south India
.03	Ca. 600–ca. 322 B.C.
.04	Period of Maurya dynasty, ca. 322–185 B.C.
.043	Ca. 322–ca. 274 B.C.
.045	Reign of Aśoka, ca. 274–ca. 237 B.C.
.047	Ca. 237–185 B.C.
.05	Period of changing dynasties, 185 B.C.–318 A.D.
.06	Period of Gupta dynasty, 318–500
.07	500–647
	Including reign of Harsha, 606–647

.1–.9   Localities of South Asia to 647

Add to base number 934 the numbers following —54 in notation 541–549 from
Table 2, e.g., western India 934.7; then add further as follows:
    001–009   Standard subdivisions
                 Add to 00 the numbers following 00 in notation 001–009
                 from table under 930–990, e.g., ethnic and national groups
                 004, ethnic and national groups in western India 934.7004
    01–07   Historical periods
                 Add to 0 the numbers following 934.0 in 934.01–934.07, e.g.,
                 western India during 500–647 934.707

.9   Other jurisdictions to 647

Class here Pakistan (West and East, 1947–1971) to 647

(Option: Class in 954.901)

.91	*Pakistan to 647
	(Option: Class in 954.9101)
.92	*Bangladesh to 647
	(Option: Class in 954.9201)

935   *Mesopotamia to 637 and Iranian Plateau to 637

Subdivisions are added for Mesopotamia and Iranian Plateau together, for
Mesopotamia alone

(Option: Class in 956.701)

.01	Early history to ca. 1900 B.C.
.02	Ca. 1900–ca. 900 B.C.
.03	Period of Assyrian Empire, ca. 900–625 B.C.

*Add as instructed under 930–990

.04	625–539 B.C.
	Including reign of Nebuchadnezzar II, 605–562 B.C.
	Class here Neo-Babylonian (Chaldean) Empire
.05	Period of Persian Empire, 539–332 B.C.
	For Persian Wars, see 938.03
.06	Hellenistic period, 332 B.C.–226 A.D.
.062	332–ca. 250 B.C.
	Class here period of Seleucid Empire, 323–ca. 250 B.C.
.064	Period of Parthian Empire, ca. 250 B.C.–226 A.D.
.07	Period of Neo-Persian (Sassanian) Empire, 226–637

> **935.2–935.5 Mesopotamia to 637**

Class here Iraq to 637

Class comprehensive works in 935

.2   **Kurdish Autonomous Region of Iraq to 637**

Add to base number 935.2 the numbers following 935 in 935.01–935.07, e.g., period of Persian Empire 935.205

(Option: Class in 956.7201)

.4   **Upper Mesopotamia to 637**

Including Upper Mesopotamian portion of Arabia Deserta to 637

Add to base number 935.4 the numbers following 935 in 935.01–935.07, e.g., Kingdom of Mitanni 935.402

(Option: Class in 956.7401)

.5   **Lower Mesopotamia to 637**

Including Lower Mesopotamian portion of Arabia Deserta to 637

Class here Babylonia

(Option: Class in 956.7501)

.501   Early history to ca. 1900 B.C.

Class here Akkadian, Sumerian, Ur periods

.502   Period of Babylonian Empire, ca. 1900–ca. 900 B.C.

Including reign of Hammurabi, ca. 1792–ca. 1750 B.C.

.503–.507   Ca. 900 B.C.–637 A.D.

Add to base number 935.5 the numbers following 935 in 935.03–935.07, e.g., period of Neo-Babylonian Empire 935.504

.7   **Iranian Plateau to 637**

Class here Iran to 637, Persia to 637

(Option: Class in 955.01)

.701–.707   Historical periods of Iranian Plateau to 637

Add to base number 935.7 the numbers following 935 in 935.01–935.07, e.g., period of Persian Empire 935.705

.71–.79   Provinces of Iran to 637

Add to base number 935.7 the numbers following —55 in notation 551–559 from Table 2, e.g., Media 935.75, Elam 935.764; then add 0† and to the result add the numbers following 935.0 in 935.01–935.07, e.g., Median Empire 935.7504, Media province of Persian Empire 935.7504, Elamite Kingdom 935.76401, Elam province of Persian Empire 935.76405

(Option: Class Media in 955.501; class Ecbatana in 955.5201; class Elam, Susa in 955.6401; class Persis, Pasargadae, Persepolis in 955.7201)

936   *Europe north and west of Italian Peninsula to ca. 499

Including western Mediterranean region

Class here Europe, western Europe

For a specific part of ancient Europe not provided for here, see the part, e.g., Italy 937; Eastern Europe 947.000901, Russia 947.01

(Option: Class western Mediterranean region in 909.098221; class Europe, Europe north and west of Italian Peninsula, western Europe in 940.11)

.01   Early history to ca. 1000 B.C.

Add to base number 936.01 the numbers following 930.1 in 930.12–930.15, e.g., Bronze Age 936.0156; however, for Bronze Age from ca. 1000 to ca. 800 B.C., see 936.02

(Option: Class in 940.111)

.02   Ca. 1000–ca. 200 B.C.

Including La Tène period

Class here Hallstatt period

For Hallstatt period from ca. 1200 to ca. 1000 B.C., see 936.0156; for La Tène period from ca. 200 B.C. to period of Roman conquest, see 936.03

(Option: Class in 940.112)

.03   Ca. 200 B.C.–ca. 499 A.D.

(Option: Class in 940.113)

---

*Add as instructed under 930–990

†Add 00 for standard subdivisions; see instructions at beginning of Table 1

.1   ***British Isles to 410**

> *For England to 410 and Wales to 410, see 936.2*

> (Option: Class in 941.012)

.101–.104   Historical periods of British Isles to 410

> Add to base number 936.10 the numbers following 936.20 in 936.201–936.204, e.g., Roman period 936.104

.11   *Scotland to 410

> (Option: Class in 941.1012)

.110 1   Early history to ca. 600 B.C.

> (Option: Class in 941.10121)

.110 2   Ca. 600–79 B.C.

> Class here Celtic period

> (Option: Class in 941.10122)

.110 3   79 B.C.–410 A.D.

> Class here period of Roman contacts

> (Option: Class in 941.10123)

.111–.115   Localities of northern Scotland to 410

> Add to base number 936.1 the numbers following —41 in notation 4111–4115 from Table 2, e.g., Inner Hebrides 936.1154; then add further as follows:
> 001–009   Standard subdivisions
> > Add to 00 the numbers following 00 in notation 001–009 from table under 930–990, e.g., ethnic and national groups 004, ethnic and national groups in Inner Hebrides 936.1154004
> 01–03   Historical periods
> > Add to 0 the numbers following 936.110 in 936.1101–936.1103, e.g., Inner Hebrides during 79 B.C.–410 A.D. 936.115403

.12   *Northeastern Scotland to 410

> (Option: Class in 941.2012)

.120 1   Early history to ca. 600 B.C.

> (Option: Class in 941.20121)

.120 2   Ca. 600–79 B.C.

> (Option: Class in 941.20122)

.120 3   79 B.C.–410 A.D.

> (Option: Class in 941.20123)

*Add as instructed under 930–990

.122–.129   Localities of northeastern Scotland to 410

> Add to base number 936.1 the numbers following —41 in notation 4122–4129 from Table 2, e.g., Angus 936.126; then add further as follows:
>
> 001–009   Standard subdivisions
>> Add to 00 the numbers following 00 in notation 001–009 from table under 930–990, e.g., ethnic and national groups 004, ethnic and national groups in Angus 936.126004
>
> 01–03   Historical periods
>> Add to 0 the numbers following 936.120 in 936.1201–936.1203, e.g., Angus during 79 B.C.–410 A.D. 936.12603

.13   *Southeastern Scotland to 410

> (Option: Class in 941.3012)

.130 1   Early history to ca. 600 B.C.

> (Option: Class in 941.30121)

.130 2   Ca. 600–79 B.C.

> (Option: Class in 941.30122)

.130 3   79 B.C.–410 A.D.

> (Option: Class in 941.30123)

.131–.137   Localities of southeastern Scotland to 410

> Add to base number 936.1 the numbers following —41 in notation 4131–4137 from Table 2, e.g., Edinburgh 936.134; then add further as follows:
>
> 001–009   Standard subdivisions
>> Add to 00 the numbers following 00 in notation 001–009 from table under 930–990, e.g., ethnic and national groups 004, ethnic and national groups in Edinburgh 936.134004
>
> 01–03   Historical periods
>> Add to 0 the numbers following 936.130 in 936.1301–936.1303, e.g., Edinburgh during 79 B.C.–410 A.D. 936.13403

.14   *Southwestern Scotland to 410

> (Option: Class in 941.4012)

.140 1   Early history to ca. 600 B.C.

> (Option: Class in 941.40121)

.140 2   Ca. 600–79 B.C.

> (Option: Class in 941.40122)

.140 3   79 B.C.–410 A.D.

> (Option: Class in 941.40123)

*Add as instructed under 930–990

.142–.147   Localities of southwestern Scotland to 410

> Add to base number 936.1 the numbers following —41 in notation
> 4142–4147 from Table 2, e.g., Glasgow 936.144; then add further as
> follows:
>> 001–009   Standard subdivisions
>>> Add to 00 the numbers following 00 in notation
>>> 001–009 from table under 930–990, e.g., ethnic and
>>> national groups 004, ethnic and national groups in
>>> Glasgow 936.144004
>> 01–03   Historical periods
>>> Add to 0 the numbers following 936.140 in
>>> 936.1401–936.1403, e.g., Glasgow during 79 B.C.–410
>>> A.D. 936.14403

.15   *Ireland to 433

> (Option: Class in 941.5012)

.150 1   Early history to ca. 400 B.C.

> (Option: Class in 941.50121)

.150 2   Celtic period, ca. 400 B.C.–433 A.D.

> (Option: Class in 941.50122)

.16   *Northern Ireland to 433; Donegal, Monaghan, Cavan counties of
             Republic of Ireland to 433

> Subdivisions are added for Northern Ireland, Donegal, Monaghan, Cavan
> counties together; for Northern Ireland alone

.160 1   Early history to ca. 400 B.C.

> (Option: Class in 941.60121)

.160 2   Celtic period, ca. 400 B.C.–433 A.D.

> (Option: Class in 941.60122)

.161–.169   Localities of Northern Ireland to 433; Donegal County, Monaghan
                   County, Cavan County of Republic of Ireland to 433

> Add to base number 936.1 the numbers following —41 in notation
> 4161–4169 from Table 2, e.g., Derry (Londonderry) 936.1621; then add
> further as follows:
>> 001–009   Standard subdivisions
>>> Add to 00 the numbers following 00 in notation
>>> 001–009 from table under 930–990, e.g., ethnic and
>>> national groups 004, ethnic and national groups in
>>> Derry (Londonderry) 936.1621004
>> 01–02   Historical periods
>>> Add to 0 the numbers following 936.160 in
>>> 936.1601–936.1602, e.g., Derry (Londonderry) during
>>> Celtic period, ca. 400 B.C.–433 A.D. 936.162102

.17   *Republic of Ireland to 433

> (Option: Class in 941.7012)

*Add as instructed under 930–990

.170 1	Early history to ca. 400 B.C.

(Option: Class in 941.70121)

.170 2	Celtic period, ca. 400 B.C.–433 A.D.

(Option: Class in 941.70122)

.171–.176	**Localities of Republic of Ireland (Eire) to 433**

Add to base number 936.1 the numbers following —41 in notation 4171–4176 from Table 2, e.g., Roscommon County 936.175; then add further as follows:

     001–009   Standard subdivisions

                 Add to 00 the numbers following 00 in notation 001–009 from table under 930–990, e.g., ethnic and national groups 004, ethnic and national groups in Roscommon County 936.175004

     01–02   Historical periods

                 Add to 0 the numbers following 936.170 in 936.1701–936.1702, e.g., Roscommon County during Celtic period, ca. 400 B.C.–433 A.D. 936.17502

.18	***Leinster to 433**

(Option: Class in 941.8012)

.180 1	Early history to ca. 400 B.C.

(Option: Class in 941.80121)

.180 2	Celtic period, ca. 400 B.C.–433 A.D.

(Option: Class in 941.80122)

.181–.189	**Localities of Leinster to 433**

Add to base number 936.1 the numbers following —41 in notation 4181–4189 from Table 2, e.g., Drogheda 936.18256; then add further as follows:

     001–009   Standard subdivisions

                 Add to 00 the numbers following 00 in notation 001–009 from table under 930–990, e.g., ethnic and national groups 004, ethnic and national groups in Drogheda 936.18256004

     01–02   Historical periods

                 Add to 0 the numbers following 936.180 in 936.1801–936.1802, e.g., Drogheda during Celtic period, ca. 400 B.C.–433 A.D. 936.1825602

.19	***Munster to 433**

(Option: Class in 941.9012)

.190 1	Early history to ca. 400 B.C.

(Option: Class in 941.90121)

.190 2	Celtic period, ca. 400 B.C.–433 A.D.

(Option: Class in 941.90122)

*Add as instructed under 930–990

.191–.196   Localities of Munster to 433

> Add to base number 936.1 the numbers following —41 in notation
> 4191–4196 from Table 2, e.g., Limerick 936.1945; then add further as
> follows:
>> 001–009   Standard subdivisions
>>> Add to 00 the numbers following 00 in notation
>>> 001–009 from table under 930–990, e.g., ethnic and
>>> national groups 004, ethnic and national groups in
>>> Limerick 936.1945004
>> 01–02   Historical periods
>>> Add to 0 the numbers following 936.190 in
>>> 936.1901–936.1902, e.g., Limerick during Celtic period,
>>> ca. 400 B.C.–433 A.D. 936.194502

.2   ***England to 410 and Wales to 410**

> Subdivisions are added for England to 410 and Wales to 410 together, for
> England to 410 alone
>
> (Option: Class England to 410 in 942.012)

.201   Early history to ca. 600 B.C.

.201 2–.201 5   Early history to ca. 1000 B.C.

> Add to base number 936.201 the numbers following 930.1 in
> 930.12–930.15, e.g., Bronze Age 936.20156

.201 6   Ca. 1000–ca. 600 B.C.

.202   Celtic period, ca. 600–55 B.C.

.203   Period of early Roman contacts, 55 B.C.–43 A.D.

.204   Roman period, 43–410

.21–.28   Localities of England to 410

> Add to base number 936.2 the numbers following —42 in notation 421–428
> from Table 2, e.g., Cheshire 936.271; then add further as follows:
>> 001–009   Standard subdivisions
>>> Add to 00 the numbers following 00 in notation 001–009
>>> from table under 930–990, e.g., ethnic and national groups
>>> 004, ethnic and national groups in Cheshire 936.271004
>> 01–04   Historical periods
>>> Add to 0 the numbers following 936.20 in 936.201–936.204,
>>> e.g., Cheshire during Roman period, 43–410 936.27104

.29   *Wales to 410

> (Option: Class Wales to 410 in 942.9012)

.290 1   Early history to ca. 600 B.C.

.290 12–.290 15   Early history to ca. 1000 B.C.

> Add to base number 936.2901 the numbers following 930.1 in
> 930.12–930.15, e.g., Bronze Age 936.290156

*Add as instructed under 930–990

.290 16	Ca. 1000–ca. 600 B.C.
.290 2	Celtic period, ca. 600 B.C.–48 A.D.
.290 4	Roman period, 48–410
.291–.299	Localities of Wales to 410

Add to base number 936.2 the numbers following —42 in notation 4291–4299 from Table 2, e.g., Cardiff 936.2987; then add further as follows:

    001–009   Standard subdivisions

          Add to 00 the numbers following 00 in notation 001–009 from table under 930–990, e.g., ethnic and national groups 004, ethnic and national groups in Cardiff 936.2987004

    01–04   Historical periods

          Add to 0 the numbers following 936.290 in 936.2901–936.2904, e.g., Cardiff during Roman period, 48–410 936.298704

.3   *Germanic regions to 481 and Pannonia

Class here Germany to 481

For a specific area of Germanic regions not provided for here, see the area, e.g., British Isles 936.1

(Option: Class Germanic regions, Germany in 943.012)

.301	Early history to 113 B.C.

(Option: Class in 943.0121)

.301 2–.301 5	Early history to ca. 800 B.C.

Add to base number 936.301 the numbers following 930.1 in 930.12–930.15, e.g., Bronze Age 936.30156

.301 56	Bronze Age

Number built according to instructions under 936.3012–936.3015

.301 6	Ca. 800–113 B.C.
.301 63	Ca. 800–ca. 450 B.C.

Class here Hallstatt period, Hallstatt C, Hallstatt D

For Hallstatt A, Hallstatt B, see 936.30156

.301 66	Ca. 450–113 B.C.

Class here La Tène period

.302	Period of contacts with Roman Republic and Empire, 113 B.C.–481 A.D.

(Option: Class in 943.0122)

---

*Add as instructed under 930–990

.31–.35   Localities of Germanic regions to 481

> Add to base number 936.3 the numbers following —43 in notation 431–435
> from Table 2, e.g., Vindelicia 936.33; then add further as follows:
> 001–009   Standard subdivisions
>> Add to 00 the numbers following 00 in notation 001–009
>> from table under 930–990, e.g., ethnic and national groups
>> 004, ethnic and national groups in Vindelicia 936.33004
> 01–02   Historical periods
>> Add to 0 the numbers following 936.30 in 936.301–936.302,
>> e.g., Vindelicia during period of contacts with Roman
>> Republic and Empire, 113 B.C.–481 A.D. 936.3302

.36   *Austria and Liechtenstein to 476

> Class here Noricum

> Subdivisions are added for Austria and Liechtenstein together, for Austria
> alone

> (Option: Class in 943.601)

.360 1   Early history to ca. 390 B.C.

> (Option: Class in 943.6011)

.360 12–.360 15   Early history to ca. 800 B.C.

> Add to base number 936.3601 the numbers following 930.1 in
> 930.12–930.15, e.g., Bronze Age 936.360156

.360 16   Ca. 800–ca. 390 B.C.

> Class here Hallstatt period, Hallstatt C, Hallstatt D

> *For Hallstatt A, Hallstatt B, see 936.360156*

.360 2   Celtic period, ca. 390–15 B.C.

> Class here La Tène period

> (Option: Class in 943.6012)

.360 3   Roman period, ca. 15 B.C.–476 A.D.

> (Option: Class in 943.6013)

.361–.366   Localities of Austria

> Add to base number 936.3 the numbers following —43 in notation
> 4361–4366 from Table 2, e.g., Vienna 936.3613; however, for
> Liechtenstein, see 936.3648; then add further as follows:
> 001–009   Standard subdivisions
>> Add to 00 the numbers following 00 in notation
>> 001–009 from table under 930–990, e.g., ethnic and
>> national groups 004, ethnic and national groups in
>> Vienna 936.3613004
> 01–03   Historical periods
>> Add to 0 the numbers following 936.360 in
>> 936.3601–936.3603, e.g., Vienna during Celtic period, ca.
>> 390–15 B.C. 936.361302

*Add as instructed under 930–990

.364	*Western Austria, and Liechtenstein

Subdivisions are added for Western Austria and Liechtenstein together, for Western Austria alone

.364 8	*Liechtenstein to 476

(Option: Class in 943.648)

.364 801	Early history to ca. 390 B.C.
.364 801 2–.364 801 5	Early history to ca. 800 B.C.

Add to base number 936.364801 the numbers following 930.1 in 930.12–930.15, e.g., Bronze Age 936.36480156

.364 801 6	Ca. 800–ca. 390 B.C.

Class here Hallstatt period, Hallstatt C, Hallstatt D

For Hallstatt A, Hallstatt B, see 936.360156

.364 802	Celtic period, ca. 390–15 B.C.

Class here La Tène period

.364 803	Roman period, ca. 15 B.C.–476 A.D.
.39	*Pannonia

Class here Hungary to ca. 640

(Option: Class in 943.9011)

.4	***Celtic regions to 486**

Class here France to 486

For a specific area of Celtic regions to 486 not provided for here, see the area, e.g., British Isles 936.1

(Option: Class Celtic regions to 486, France in 944.012)

.401	Early history to 125 B.C.

(Option: Class in 944.0121)

.401 2–.401 5	Early history to ca. 800 B.C.

Add to base number 936.401 the numbers following 930.1 in 930.12–930.15, e.g., Bronze Age 936.40156

.401 56	Bronze Age

Number built according to instructions under 936.4011–936.4015

.401 6	Ca. 800–125 B.C.
.401 63	Ca. 800–ca. 450 B.C.

Class here Hallstatt period, Hallstatt C, Hallstatt D

For Hallstatt A, Hallstatt B, see 936.40156

*Add as instructed under 930–990

.401 66   Ca. 450–125 B.C.

              Class here La Tène period

.402   Gallo-Roman period, 125 B.C.–486 A.D.

             (Option: Class in 944.0122)

.41–.49   Localities of Celtic regions to 486

             Add to base number 936.4 the numbers following —44 in notation 441–449
             from Table 2, e.g., Germania Superior 936.439; then add further as follows:
                001–009   Standard subdivisions
                          Add to 00 the numbers following 00 in notation 001–009
                          from table under 930–990, e.g., ethnic and national groups
                          004, ethnic and national groups in Germania Superior
                          936.439004
                01–02   Historical periods
                          Add to 0 the numbers following 936.40 in 936.401–936.402,
                          e.g., Germania Superior during Gallo-Roman period, 125
                          B.C.–486 A.D. 936.43902

.6   ***Iberian Peninsula to 415 and adjacent islands to 415**

             (Option: Class Iberian Peninsula and adjacent islands in 946.000901; class
             Spain in 946.012)

.601   Early history to ca. 1000 B.C.

             (Option: Class Iberian Peninsula and adjacent islands to 4000 B.C. in
             946.0009012; Iberian Peninsula and adjacent islands, 3999–1000 B.C., in
             946.0009013; class Spain in 946.0121)

.602   Period of Greek, Phoenician, and early Celtic and Germanic
             contacts, ca. 1000–218 B.C.

             (Option: Class Iberian Peninsula and adjacent islands in 946.0009014;
             class Spain in 946.0122)

.603   Roman period, 218 B.C.–415 A.D.

             (Option: Class Iberian Peninsula and adjacent islands to 999–1 B.C.
             in 946.0009014; Iberian Peninsula and adjacent islands, 1–415, in
             946.0009015; class Spain in 946.0123)

.61–.68   Localities of Iberian Peninsula to 415 and adjacent islands to 415

             Add to base number 936.6 the numbers following —46 in notation 461–468
             from Table 2, e.g., Toledo to 415 936.643; then add further as follows:
                001–009   Standard subdivisions
                          Add to 00 the numbers following 00 in notation 001–009
                          from table under 930–990, e.g., ethnic and national
                          groups 004, ethnic and national groups in Toledo to 415
                          936.643004
                01–03   Historical periods
                          Add to 0 the numbers following 936.60 in 936.601–936.603,
                          e.g., Toledo during Roman period, 218 B.C.–415 A.D.
                          936.64303

---

*Add as instructed under 930–990

.69	*Portugal to 415
	(Option: Class in 946.9012)
.690 1	Early history to ca. 1000 B.C.
	(Option: Class in 946.90121)
.690 2	Period of Greek, Phoenician, and early Celtic and Germanic contacts, ca. 1000–218 B.C
	(Option: Class in 946.90122)
.690 3	Roman period, 218 B.C.–415 A.D.
	(Option: Class in 946.90123)
.691–.699	Localities of Portugal to 415

         Add to base number 936.6 the numbers following —46 in notation
         4691–4699 from Table 2, e.g., Lisbon to 415 and adjacent islands to 415
         936.6942; then add further as follows:

            001–009   Standard subdivisions
                         Add to 00 the numbers following 00 in notation
                         001–009 from table under 930–990, e.g., ethnic and
                         national groups 004, ethnic and national groups in
                         Lisbon to 415 936.6942004
            01–03   Historical periods
                         Add to 0 the numbers following 936.690 in
                         936.6901–936.6903, e.g., Lisbon during Roman period,
                         218 B.C.–415 A.D. 936.69903

.8	***Scandinavia to 481**
	See also 948.9701 for Finland to 481
	(Option: Class in 948.012)
.81	*Norway to 481
	(Option: Class in 948.1012)
.85	*Sweden to 481
	(Option: Class in 948.5012)
.89	*Denmark to 481
	(Option: Class in 948.9012)
.9	**†Netherlands to 486, Belgium to 486, Luxembourg to 486, Switzerland to 486**

---

*Add as instructed under 930–990
†Add as instructed under 930–990; however, do not add historical periods

.92   *Netherlands to 486

Class here Celtic regions of Netherlands to 486, comprehensive works on Low Countries to 486

For southern Low Countries to 486, see 936.93

(Option: Class in 949.2012)

.920 1   Early history to 125 B.C.

(Option: Class in 949.20121)

.920 12–.920 15   Early history to ca. 800 B.C.

Add to base number 936.9201 the numbers following 930.1 in 930.12–930.15, e.g., Bronze Age 936.920156

.920 16   Ca. 800–125 B.C.

.920 163   Ca. 800–ca. 450 B.C.

Class here Hallstatt period, Hallstatt C, Hallstatt D

For Hallstatt A, Hallstatt B, see 936.920156

.920 166   Ca. 450–125 B.C.

Class here La Tène period

.920 2   Gallo-Roman period, 125 B.C.–486 A.D.

(Option: Class in 949.20122)

.921   *Northeastern provinces of Netherlands to 481

Class here Germanic regions of Netherlands to 481

For Flevoland to 481, see 936.922

(Option: Class in 949.21012)

.921 01   Early history to 113 B.C.

(Option: Class in 949.210121)

.921 012–.921 015   Early history to ca. 800 B.C.

Add to base number 936.92101 the numbers following 930.1 in 930.12–930.15, e.g., Bronze Age 936.9210156

.921 016   Ca. 800–113 B.C.

.921 016 3   Ca. 800–ca. 450 B.C.

Class here Hallstatt period, Hallstatt C, Hallstatt D

For Hallstatt A, Hallstatt B, see 936.9210156

.921 016 6   Ca. 450–113 B.C.

Class here La Tène period

*Add as instructed under 930–990

.921 02	Period of contacts with Roman Republic and Empire, 113 B.C.–481 A.D.

                              (Option: Class in 949.210122)

.921 2–.921 8	Localities of northeastern provinces of Netherlands to 481

Add to base number 936.9 the numbers following —49 in notation 49212–49218 from Table 2, e.g., Friesland 936.9213; then add further as follows:

      001–009   Standard subdivisions

                Add to 00 the numbers following 00 in notation 001–009 from table under 930–990, e.g., ethnic and national groups 004, ethnic and national groups in Friesland 936.9213004

      01–02   Historical periods

                Add to 0 the numbers following 936.9210 in 936.92101–936.92102, e.g., Friesland during period of contacts with Roman Republic and Empire, 113 B.C.–481 A.D. 936.921302

.922–.924	**Localities of Flevoland (Zuidelijke IJsselmeerpolders) and Markerwaard to 486, northwestern provinces of Netherlands to 486, southern provinces of Netherlands to 486**

Add to base number 936.9 the numbers following —49 in notation 4922–4924 from Table 2, e.g., South Holland (Zuid-Holland) 936.9238; then add further as follows:

      001–009   Standard subdivisions

                Add to 00 the numbers following 00 in notation 001–009 from table under 930–990, e.g., ethnic and national groups 004, ethnic and national groups in South Holland (Zuid-Holland) 936.9238004

      01–02   Historical periods

                Add to 0 the numbers following 936.920 in 936.9201–936.9202, e.g., South Holland (Zuid-Holland) during Gallo-Roman period, 125 B.C.–486 A.D. 936.923802

.93	***Belgium to 486**

                                (Option: Class in 949.3012)

.930 1	Early history to 125 B.C.

                                (Option: Class in 949.30121)

.930 12–.930 15	Early history to ca. 800 B.C.

                Add to base number 936.9301 the numbers following 930.1 in 930.12–930.15, e.g., Bronze Age 936.930156

.930 16	Ca. 800–125 B.C.
.930 163	Ca. 800–ca. 450 B.C.

                Class here Hallstatt period, Hallstatt C, Hallstatt D

                For Hallstatt A, Hallstatt B, see 936.930156

*Add as instructed under 930–990

.930 166	Ca. 450–125 B.C.

Class here La Tène period

.930 2	Gallo-Roman period, 125 B.C.–486 A.D.

(Option: Class in 949.30122)

.931–.934	Localities of Belgium to 486

Add to base number 936.9 the numbers following —49 in notation
4931–4934 from Table 2, e.g., East Flanders (Oost-Vlaanderen)
936.9314; then add further as follows:

    001–009   Standard subdivisions

                 Add to 00 the numbers following 00 in notation
                 001–009 from table under 930–990, e.g., ethnic and
                 national groups 004, ethnic and national groups in East
                 Flanders (Oost-Vlaanderen) 936.9314004

    01–02   Historical periods

                 Add to 0 the numbers following 936.930
                 in 936.9301–936.9302, e.g., East Flanders
                 (Oost-Vlaanderen) during Gallo-Roman period, 125
                 B.C.–486 A.D. 936.931402

.935	*Luxembourg to 486

(Option: Class in 949.35012)

.935 01	Early history to 125 B.C.

(Option: Class in 949.350121)

.935 012–.935 015	Early history to ca. 800 B.C.

Add to base number 936.93501 the numbers following 930.1 in
930.12–930.15, e.g., Bronze Age 936.9350156

.935 016	Ca. 800–125 B.C.
.935 016 3	Ca. 800–ca. 450 B.C.

Class here Hallstatt period, Hallstatt C, Hallstatt D

For Hallstatt A, Hallstatt B, see 936.9350156

.935 016 6	Ca. 450–125 B.C.

Class here La Tène period

.935 02	Gallo-Roman period, 125 B.C.–486 A.D.

(Option: Class in 949.350122)

.94	*Switzerland to 486

(Option: Class in 949.4012)

.940 1	Early history to 125 B.C.

(Option: Class in 949.40121)

---

*Add as instructed under 930–990

.940 12–.940 15	Early history to ca. 800 B.C.
	Add to base number 936.9401 the numbers following 930.1 in 930.12–930.15, e.g., Bronze Age 936.940156
.940 16	Ca. 800–125 B.C.
.940 163	Ca. 800–ca. 450 B.C.
	Class here Hallstatt period, Hallstatt C, Hallstatt D
	For Hallstatt A, Hallstatt B, see 936.940156
.940 166	Ca. 450–125 B.C.
	Class here La Tène period
.940 2	Gallo-Roman period, 125 B.C.–486 A.D.
	(Option: Class in 949.40122)
.943–.945	Localities of Jura region cantons to 486, Mittelland cantons to 486
	Add to base number 936.9 the numbers following —49 in notation 4943–4945 from Table 2, e.g., Geneva 936.94516; then add further as follows:

           001–009   Standard subdivisions

                    Add to 00 the numbers following 00 in notation 001–009 from table under 930–990, e.g., ethnic and national groups 004, ethnic and national groups in Geneva 936.94516004

           01–02   Historical periods

                    Add to 0 the numbers following 936.940 in 936.9401–936.9402, e.g., Geneva during Gallo-Roman period, 125 B.C.–486 A.D. 936.9451602

.947	*Alpine region cantons to 481
	Class here Germanic regions of Switzerland to 481
	(Option: Class in 949.47012)
.947 01	Early history to 113 B.C.
	(Option: Class in 949.470121)
.947 012–.947 015	Early history to ca. 800 B.C.
	Add to base number 936.94701 the numbers following 930.1 in 930.12–930.15, e.g., Bronze Age 936.9470156
.947 016	Ca. 800–113 B.C.
.947 016 3	Ca. 800–ca. 450 B.C.
	Class here Hallstatt period, Hallstatt C, Hallstatt D
	For Hallstatt A, Hallstatt B, see 936.9470156
.947 016 6	Ca. 450–113 B.C.
	Class here La Tène period

*Add as instructed under 930–990

| .947 02 | Period of contacts with Roman Republic and Empire, 113 B.C.–481 A.D. |

(Option: Class 949.47012)

| .947 1–.947 9 | Localities of Alpine region cantons to 481 |

Add to base number 936.9 the numbers following —49 in notation 49471–49479 from Table 2, e.g., Sion 936.9479644; then add further as follows:

| 001–009 | Standard subdivisions |

Add to 00 the numbers following 00 in notation 001–009 from table under 930–990, e.g., ethnic and national groups 004, ethnic and national groups in Sion 936.9479644004

| 01–02 | Historical periods |

Add to 0 the numbers following 936.9470 in 936.94701–936.94702, e.g., Sion during period of contacts with Roman Republic and Empire, 113 B.C.–481 A.D. 936.947964402

937   *Italian Peninsula to 476 and adjacent territories to 476

Class here Mediterranean region

Subdivisions are added for Italian Peninsula and adjacent territories together, for Italian Peninsula alone

(Option: Class Mediterranean region in 909.09822; class Italian Peninsula and adjacent territories in 945.012)

| .01 | Early history to 510 B.C. |

Class here Roman Kingdom, 753–510 B.C.

| .02 | Period of Roman Republic, 510–31 B.C. |

For specific periods, see 937.03–937.05

> 937.03–937.05 Specific periods under the Republic

Class comprehensive works in 937.02

.03	Period of unification of Italy, 510–264 B.C.
.04	Period of Punic Wars, 264–146 B.C.
.05	Period of civil strife, 146–31 B.C.
.06	Period of Roman Empire, 31 B.C.–476 A.D.

For specific periods, see 937.07–937.09

> 937.07–937.09 Specific periods under the Empire

Class comprehensive works in 937.06

| .07 | Early and middle periods, 31 B.C.–284 A.D. |

*Add as instructed under 930–990

.08   Period of absolutism, 284–395

.09   Final period, 395–476

.1–.7   Localities of Italian Peninsula to 476

Add to base number 937 the numbers following —37 in notation 371–377 from Table 2, e.g., Liguria 937.1; then add further as follows:

     001–009   Standard subdivisions

              Add to 00 the numbers following 00 in notation 001–009 from table under 930–990, e.g., ethnic and national groups 004, ethnic and national groups in Liguria 937.1004

     01–09   Historical periods

              Add to 0 the numbers following 937.0 in 937.01–937.09, e.g., Liguria during final period under the Empire, 395–476 937.109

.9   *Sardinia to 453 and Corsica to 453

Subdivisions are added for Sardinia and Corsica together; for Sardinia alone

(Option: Class in 945.9012)

.901–.908   Early history to 395

       Add to base number 937.90 the numbers following 937.0 in 937.01–937.08, e.g., Sardinia during period of Roman Empire 937.906

.909   Final period of Roman Empire, 395–453

.91–.98   Localities of Sardinia to 453

       Add to base number 937.9 the numbers following —459 in notation 4591–4598 from Table 2, e.g., Cagliari Metropolitan City to 453 937.91; then add further as follows:

     001–009   Standard subdivisions

              Add to 00 the numbers following 00 in notation 001–009 from table under 930–990, e.g., ethnic and national groups 004, ethnic and national groups in Cagliari Metropolitan City to 453 937.91004

     01–09   Historical periods

              Add to 0 the numbers following 937.90 in 937.901–937.909, e.g., Cagliari Metropolitan City during final period of Roman Empire, 395–476 937.9109

.99   *Corsica to 453

(Option: Class in 944.99012)

.990 1–.990 8   Early history to 395

       Add to base number 937.990 the numbers following 937.0 in 937.01–937.08, e.g., Corsica during period of Roman Empire 937.9906

.990 9   Final period of Roman Empire, 395–453

---

*Add as instructed under 930–990

.992–.996   Localities of Corsica to 453

> Add to base number 937.99 the numbers following —3799 in notation 37992–37996 from Table 2, e.g., Corse-du-Sud department to 453 937.992; then add further as follows:
> 001–009   Standard subdivisions
>> Add to 00 the numbers following 00 in notation 001–009 from table under 930–990, e.g., ethnic and national groups 004, ethnic and national groups in Corse-du-Sud department to 453 937.992004
> 01–09   Historical periods
>> Add to 0 the numbers following 937.0 in 937.01–937.09, e.g., Corse-du-Sud department during final period of Roman Empire, 395–453 937.99209

938   *Greece to 323

> Class here the Hellenistic World; the eastern Mediterranean region; southern Europe
>
> (Option: Class eastern Mediterranean region in 909.098224; class southern Europe in 940.11; class Greece in 949.5012)

.01   Early history to 775 B.C.

.02   775–500 B.C.

.03   Persian Wars, 500–479 B.C.

.04   Period of Athenian supremacy, 479–431 B.C.

.05   Period of Peloponnesian War, 431–404 B.C.

.06   Period of Spartan and Theban supremacy, 404–362 B.C.

.07   Period of Macedonian supremacy, 362–323 B.C.

.08   Hellenistic period, 323–146 B.C.

.09   Roman era, 146 B.C.–323 A.D.

.1–.9   Localities of Greece to 323

> Add to base number 938 the numbers following —38 in notation 381–389 from Table 2, e.g., Macedonia to 323 938.1; then add further as follows:
> 001–009   Standard subdivisions
>> Add to 00 the numbers following 00 in notation 001–009 from table under 930–990, e.g., ethnic and national groups 004, ethnic and national groups in Macedonia to 323 938.1004
> 01–09   Historical periods
>> Add to 0 the numbers following 938.0 in 938.01–938.09, e.g., Macedonia during Roman era, 146 B.C.–323 A.D. 938.109

939   *Other parts of ancient world

.1   *Aegean Islands to 323

> (Option: Class in 949.58012)

*Add as instructed under 930–990

.101–.109	Historical periods

Add to base number 939.10 the numbers following 938.0 in 938.01–938.09, e.g., Hellenistic period 939.108

.11–.18	Localities of Aegean Islands to 323

Add to base number 939.1 the numbers following —391 in notation 3911–3918 from Table 2, e.g., Northern Aegean Islands to 323 939.11; then add further as follows:

001–009	Standard subdivisions

Add to 00 the numbers following 00 in notation 001–009 from table under 930–990, e.g., ethnic and national groups 004, ethnic and national groups in Northern Aegean Islands to 323 939.11004

01–09	Historical periods

Add to 0 the numbers following 938.0 in 938.01–938.09, e.g., Northern Aegean Islands during Hellenistic period, 323–146 B.C. 939.1108

.18	*Crete to 323

(Option: Class in 949.59012)

.2	†Diocese of Asia (Dioecesis Asiana)

Class here western Asia Minor to 640, comprehensive works on Asia Minor to 640

For eastern Asia Minor to 640, see 939.3

(Option: Class in 956.1012)

.3	†Eastern Asia Minor to 640 and Cyprus to 640

(Option: Class eastern Asia Minor in 956.1012)

.37	†Cyprus to 640

(Option: Class in 956.93012)

.4	*Middle East to 640

Class a specific part of Middle East not provided for here with the part, e.g., Egypt 932, Palestine 933

(Option: Class in 956.012)

.401	Early history to ca. 1900 B.C.
.402	Period of Babylonian and Assyrian Empires, ca. 1900–539 B.C.
.403	Period of Persian Empire, 539–332 B.C.
.404	Hellenistic period, 332–30 B.C.
.405	Roman period, 30 B.C.–ca. 640 A.D.

---

*Add as instructed under 930–990
†Add as instructed under 930–990; however, do not add historical periods

| .42–.49 | Localities of Middle East to 640 |

Add to base number 939.4 the numbers following —394 in notation 3942–3949 from Table 2, e.g., southeast central Turkey to 640 939.42; then add further as follows:

001–009   Standard subdivisions

Add to 00 the numbers following 00 in notation 001–009 from table under 930–990, e.g., ethnic and national groups 004, ethnic and national groups in southeast central Turkey to 640 939.42004

01–05   Historical periods

Add to 0 the numbers following 939.40 in 939.401–939.405, e.g., southeast central Turkey during Roman period, 30 B.C.–ca. 640 A.D. 939.4205

| .43 | *Syria to 640 |

(Option: Class in 956.9101)

| .431 | *Hatay Province of modern Turkey to 640 |

Including Antioch

(Option: Class in 956.48)

| .44 | *Phoenicia |

Class here Lebanon to 640

(Option: Class in 956.9202)

| .46 | Moab and Edom |
| .462 | *Moab |

(Option: Class in 956.95601)

| .464 | *Edom |

(Option: Class in 956.94901)

| .48 | *Arabia Petraea |

Including Sinai Peninsula to 622; Petra

(Option: Class Arabia Petraea in 953.01; class Sinai Peninsula in 953.101; class Petra in 956.957701)

*Add as instructed under 930–990

.49   *Arabian Peninsula to 622

> Including Bahrain to 622, Kuwait to 622, Oman to 622, Persian Gulf States to 622, Qatar to 622, Saudi Arabia to 622, United Arab Emirates to 622, Yemen to 622
>
> Class here Arabia Deserta to 622, Arabia Felix
>
> > *For Upper Mesopotamian portion of Arabia Deserta to 637, see 935.4; for Lower Mesopotamian portion of Arabia Deserta to 637, see 935.5; for Arabia Petraea, see 939.48*
>
> (Option: Class Arabia Felix, Arabia to 622 in 953.01; class Yemen to 622 in 953.301; class Oman to 622 in 953.53; class United Arab Emirates to 622 in 953.57; class Persian Gulf States to 622 in 953.6; class Qatar to 622 in 953.63; class Bahrain to 622 in 953.65; class Kuwait to 622 in 953.67; class Saudi Arabia to 622 in 953.801)

.5   †**Black Sea region to 640 and Caucasus to 640**

> Subdivisions are added for Black Sea region to 640 and Caucasus to 640 together, for Black Sea region to 640 alone
>
> (Option: Class Black Sea region to 640 in 909.098229)

.51   †Scythia

> Class here Black Sea area of Romania to 640
>
> (Option: Class in 949.83)

.52   †Sarmatia

> Class here Ukraine to 640
>
> (Option: Class in 947.7)

.53   †Caucasus to 640

> (Option: Class in 947.5)

.534   †Albania

> (Option: Class in 947.54)

.536   †Iberia

> Class here Georgia to 640
>
> (Option: Class in 947.58)

.538   †Colchis

> (Option: Class in 947.58)

.55   †Armenia

> Class here Armenia region to 640
>
> (Option: Class modern country of Armenia in 947.56; class Armenia region to 640, Armenia [ancient kingdom] in 956.62012)

---

*Add as instructed under 930–990
†Add as instructed under 930–990; however, do not add historical periods

.6	†Central Asia to ca. 640

Including Afghanistan to ca. 640, Māzandarān province of Iran to 637, Tajikistan to ca. 640, Turkmenistan to ca. 640, Uzbekistan to ca. 640; Ariana, Bactria, Hyrcania, Margiana, Parthia, Sogdiana

For Kyrgyzstan to ca. 640, see 958.43; for Kazakhstan to ca. 640, see 958.45

(Option: Class Māzandarān province of Iran to 637, Hyrcania in 955.23; class Central Asia to ca. 640 in 958; class Afghanistan to ca. 640, Ariana, Bactria, Parthia in 958.101; class Turkmenistan to ca. 640, Margiana in 958.507; class Tajikistan to ca. 640 in 958.607; class Uzbekistan to ca. 640, Sogdiana in 958.707)

.7	*North Africa to ca. 640

For Egypt to 640, see 932

(Option: Class in 961.01)

.701	Early history to ca. 800 B.C.
.702	Carthaginian period, ca. 800–146 B.C.
.703	Roman period, 146 B.C.–429 A.D.
.704	Vandal period, 429–534
.705	Byzantine period, 534–ca. 640

.71–.78	Localities of North Africa to ca. 640

Add to base number 939.7 the numbers following —397 in notation 3971–3978 from Table 2, e.g., Mauretania to ca. 640 939.71; then add further as follows:
001–009   Standard subdivisions
            Add to 00 the numbers following 00 in notation 001–009 from table under 930–990, e.g., ethnic and national groups 004, ethnic and national groups in Mauretania to ca. 640 939.71004
01–05   Historical periods
            Add to 0 the numbers following 939.70 in 939.701–939.705, e.g., Mauretania during Byzantine period, 534–ca. 640 939.7105

.71	*Mauretania

(Option: Class in 965.01)

.710 1	Early history to ca. 800 B.C.

(Option: Class in 965.011)

.710 2	Carthaginian period, ca. 800–146 B.C.

(Option: Class in 965.012)

*Add as instructed under 930–990
†Add as instructed under 930–990; however, do not add historical periods

.710 3	Period of Kingdom of Mauretania, 146 B.C.–42 A.D.
	(Option: Class in 965.013)
.710 4	Roman period, 42–ca. 435 A.D.
	(Option: Class in 965.014)
.710 5	Vandal period, ca. 435–534
	(Option: Class in 965.015)
.710 6	Byzantine period, 534–647
	(Option: Class in 965.016)
.712	*Mauretania Tingitana
	Class here Morocco to 647
	(Option: Class in 964.01)
.712 01	Early history to ca. 800 B.C.
	(Option: Class in 964.011)
.712 02	Carthaginian period, ca. 800–146 B.C.
	(Option: Class in 964.012)
.712 03	Period of Kingdom of Mauretania, 146–25 B.C.
	(Option: Class in 964.013)
.712 04	Roman period, 25 B.C.–429 A.D.
	(Option: Class in 964.014)
.712 05	Vandal period, 429–534
	(Option: Class in 964.015)
.712 06	Byzantine period, 534–647
	(Option: Class in 964.016)
.714	*Mauretania Caesariensis
	Class here Algeria to 647
	(Option: Class in 965.01)
.714 01–.714 06	Historical periods of Mauretania Caesariensis
	Add to base number 939.7140 the numbers following 939.710 in 939.7101–939.7106, e.g., Roman period 939.71404
.72	*Numidia
	Class here northeastern provinces of Algeria to 647
	(Option: Class in 965.501)

*Add as instructed under 930–990

.720 1	Early history to ca. 800 B.C.
	(Option: Class in 965.5011)
.720 2	Carthaginian period, ca. 800–146 B.C.
	(Option: Class in 965.5012)
.720 3	Period of Kingdom of Numidia, 146–46 B.C.
	(Option: Class in 965.5013)
.720 4	Roman period, 46 B.C.–439 A.D.
	(Option: Class in 965.5014)
.720 5	Vandal period, 439–534
	(Option: Class in 965.5015)
.720 6	Byzantine period, 534–647
	(Option: Class in 965.5016)
.73	*Carthage
	Class here Tunisia to 647
	(Option: Class in 961.101)
.730 1	Early history to ca. 800 B.C.
	(Option: Class in 961.1011)
.730 2	Carthaginian period, ca. 800–146 B.C.
	(Option: Class in 961.1012)
.730 3	Roman period, 146 B.C.–439 A.D.
	(Option: Class in 961.1013)
.730 4	Vandal period, 439–534
	(Option: Class in 961.1014)
.730 5	Byzantine period, 534–647
	(Option: Class in 961.1015)
.74	*Tripolis to 644
	(Option: Class in 961.201)
.740 1	Early history to ca. 800 B.C.
	(Option: Class in 961.2011)
.740 2	Carthaginian period, ca. 800–146 B.C.
	(Option: Class in 961.2012)
.740 3	Roman period, 146 B.C.–439 A.D.
	(Option: Class in 961.2013)

*Add as instructed under 930–990

.740 4	Vandal period, 439–534
	(Option: Class in 961.2014)
.740 5	Byzantine period, 534–644
	(Option: Class in 961.2015)
.75	*Cyrenaica
	(Option: Class in 961.201)
.750 1	Early history to ca. 940 B.C.
	(Option: Class in 961.201)
.750 2	Egyptian period, ca. 940–ca. 630 B.C.
	(Option: Class in 961.201)
.750 3	Greek period, ca. 630–ca. 500 B.C.
	(Option: Class in 961.201)
.750 4	Persian period, ca. 500–323 B.C.
	(Option: Class in 961.201)
.750 5	Hellenistic period, 323–96 B.C.
	(Option: Class in 961.201)
.750 6	Roman period, 96 B.C.–330 A.D.
	(Option: Class in 961.201)
.750 7	Byzantine period, 330–642
	(Option: Class in 961.201)
.76	*Marmarica to 642
	(Option: Class in 961.201)
.760 1	Early history to ca. 940 B.C.
	(Option: Class in 961.201)
.760 2	Egyptian period, ca. 940–ca. 630 B.C.
	(Option: Class in 961.201)
.760 3	Greek period, ca. 630–ca. 500 B.C.
	(Option: Class in 961.201)
.760 4	Persian period, ca. 500–323 B.C.
	(Option: Class in 961.201)
.760 5	Hellenistic period, 323–96 B.C.
	(Option: Class in 961.201)

*Add as instructed under 930–990

.760 6	Roman period, 96 B.C.–330 A.D.
	(Option: Class in 961.201)
.760 7	Byzantine period, 330–642
	(Option: Class in 961.201)
.77	*Gaetulia

Class here Sahara provinces of Algeria to 647

(Option: Class in 965.701)

.78	*Nubia

Class here northern states of Sudan to 500, Ethiopia (a part of what is now modern Sudan, not modern Ethiopia), Kush

Class comprehensive works on the Sudan to 500 in 962.401

(Option: Class in 962.501)

.8   †Southeastern Europe to ca. 640

See also 939.5 for Black Sea region to 640

(Option: Class Thrace to 323 in 949.57012; class southeastern Europe to ca. 640 in 949.601; class Turkey in Europe [Eastern Thrace] to 323 in 949.61012; class İstanbul Province to 323, Constantinople to 323 in 949.618012; class Albania to 640 in 949.65012; class former Yugoslavia to ca. 640, Illyria, Illyricum in 949.7012; class Serbia to ca. 640 in 949.71011; class Croatia to ca. 640 in 949.72012; class Slovenia to ca. 640 in 949.73012; class Bosnia and Hercegovina to ca. 640 in 949.742012; class Montenegro to ca. 640 in 949.745012; class North Macedonia to ca. 640 in 949.76012; class Bulgaria to ca. 640, Moesia in 949.9012)

.88	Dacia

Number built according to instructions under 939.8

Including Moldova to ca. 640

Class here Romania to ca. 640

(Option: Class Moldova to ca. 640 in 947.6; class Romania to ca. 640, Dacia in 949.8012)

---

*Add as instructed under 930–990

†Add as instructed under 930–990; however, do not add historical periods

> ## 940–990 History of specific continents, countries, localities in modern world; extraterrestrial worlds

Class here area studies; comprehensive works on ancient and modern history of specific continents, countries, localities

Except for modifications shown under specific entries, add to each subdivision identified by ‡ as follows:

08   Groups of people

            Do not use for enemy sympathizers, pacifists; class in notation 1 from this table

[086914]   Displaced persons

                Do not use; class in 1

09   History, geographic treatment, biography

            Do not use for participation of specific groups of countries; class in notation 3 from this table

[094–099]   Specific continents, countries, localities

            Do not use for specific continents; class in notation 3 from this table. Do not use for specific countries and localities; class in notation 34–39 from this table

1   Social, political, economic history

        Standard subdivisions are added for any or all topics in heading

        Including consequences, e.g., movement of people; causes, results, efforts to preserve or restore peace; displaced persons

        Class general diplomatic history in notation 2 from this table; class prisoner-of-war camps in notation 7 from this table. Class results in and effects on a specific country with the history of the country, e.g., effect of Vietnamese War on United States 973.923 (*not* 959.70431)

2   Diplomatic history

        Class diplomatic causes, efforts to preserve or restore peace, diplomatic results in notation 1 from this table

3   Participation of specific groups of countries and of specific countries, localities

        Class military participation of specific groups of countries, of specific countries, localities in notation 409 from this table. Class participation in a specific activity with the activity, e.g., efforts to preserve or restore peace 1

34–39   Participation of specific countries and localities

            Add to 3 notation 4–9 from Table 2, e.g., participation by France 344

4   Military operations and units

        Standard subdivisions are added for either or both topics in heading

        Class here military history

        Class units engaged in a specific type of service with the service, e.g., medical units 7

           For an aspect of military history not provided for here, see the aspect, e.g., prisoner-of-war camps 7

42   Land operations

45   Naval operations

48   Air operations

6   Celebrations, commemorations, memorials

        Including decorations and awards, rolls of honor, cemeteries, monuments

> **940–990 History of specific continents, countries, localities in modern world; extraterrestrial worlds**

     7   Prisoners of war, medical and social services

           Including prisoner-of-war camps

     8   Other military topics

           Including deserters; military life and customs; military personnel missing in action; unconventional warfare, propaganda

Class comprehensive works in 909

For general history of ancient world, see 930

See Manual at 930–990: Wars

940   History of Europe

.01–.09   Standard subdivisions

         As modified in notation 001–009 from table under 930–990

.1   **Early history to 1453**

         Class here Middle Ages, 476–1453

         For ancient history to ca. 499, see 936

(.11)   Early history to ca. 499

         (Optional number; prefer 936)

(.111)   Early history to ca. 1000 B.C.

         (Optional number; prefer 936.01)

(.112)   Ca. 1000–ca. 200 B.C.

         (Optional number; prefer 936.02)

(.113)   Ca. 200 B.C.–ca. 499 A.D.

         (Optional number; prefer 936.03)

.12   Ca. 500–799

         Class here Early Middle Ages (Dark Ages), 476–999

         For 800–899, see 940.142; for 900–999, see 940.144

.14   Age of feudalism, 800–1099

.142   800–899

.144   900–999

.146   1000–1099

         For period of First Crusade, see 940.18

.17   1100–1453

         For period of Crusades, 1100–1299, see 940.18; for 1300–1453, see 940.19

.18	Period of Crusades, 1100–1299

Including period of First Crusade, 1096–1099

Class here High Middle Ages, 1000–1299

Class comprehensive works on Crusades in 909.07. Class comprehensive works on a specific Crusade with the history of the country or region in which most of the fighting took place, e.g., First Crusade 956.014

For 1000–1099, see 940.146

.182	1100–1199
.184	1200–1299
.19	1300–1453

Class here Late Middle Ages

.192	1300–1399

Including period of Black Death

.193	1400–1453
.2	**1453–**

For World War I, see 940.3; for 1918 to present, see 940.5

.21	Renaissance period, 1453–1517

Class here 15th century

For 1400–1453, see 940.193

See also 945.05 for Renaissance period in Italy

.22	1517–1789

For Reformation period, 1517–1648, see 940.23; for 1648–1789, see 940.25

.23	Reformation period, 1517–1648

For Thirty Years' War, see 940.24

.232	1517–1618
.24	‡Thirty Years' War, 1618–1648
.25	1648–1789
.252	1648–1715

Class here 17th century

For 1600–1648, see 940.23

.252 3	1648–1688

‡Add as instructed under 940–990

.252 5	1688–1701

Class here War of the League of Augsburg (War of the Grand Alliance), 1688–1697

For North American aspects of War of the League of Augsburg, see 973.25

.252 6	1701–1715

Class here War of the Spanish Succession, 1701–1714

For North American aspects of War of the Spanish Succession, see 973.25

.253	1715–1789

Class here 18th century

For 1700–1715, see 940.252; for 1789–1799, see 940.27

.253 1	1715–1740
.253 2	War of the Austrian Succession, 1740–1748

Class Silesian Wars in 943.054

For North American aspects of War of the Austrian Succession, see 973.26

.253 3	1748–1756
.253 4	Seven Years' War, 1756–1763

For North American aspects of Seven Years' War, see 973.26

.253 5	1763–1789
.27	‡Period of French Revolution and Napoleon I, 1789–1815

Class here Napoleonic Wars in specific European countries, e.g., war in Spain (Peninsular War), 1807–1814

.271	Social, political, economic history

Number built according to instructions under 940–990

.271 4	Congress of Vienna

Class results in and effects on a specific country with the history of the country, e.g., effect on France 944.061

.28	1815–1914

Class here comprehensive works on 19th-20th centuries

For comprehensive works on 20th century, see 940.5

.282	1815–1829
.283	1830–1848

For revolutions of 1848, see 940.284

‡Add as instructed under 940–990

.284	Revolutions of 1848
.285	1849–1859
.286	1860–1869
.287	1870–1899
.288	1900–1914

.3   **World War I, 1914–1918**

> *For military history, see 940.4*

.308   Groups of people

> Do not use for noncombatants, pacifists, enemy sympathizers; class in 940.316

[.308 691 4]   Displaced persons

> Do not use; class in 940.3145

.308 991 992   Armenians

> Do not use for Armenian Genocide, 1915–1916; class in 956.620154

.309   History, geographic treatment, biography

> Do not use for participation of specific groups of countries; class in 940.33

[.309 4–.309 9]   Specific continents, countries, localities in modern world

> Do not use; class in 940.34–940.39

.31   Social, political, economic history

> Add to base number 940.31 the numbers following 940.531 in 940.5311–940.5317, e.g., internment camps 940.317

> *For diplomatic history, see 940.32*

.32   Diplomatic history

> *For diplomatic causes, see 940.3112; for efforts to preserve or restore peace, see 940.312; for diplomatic results, see 940.314*

.322   Allies and associated powers

[.322 094–.322 099]   Specific continents, countries, localities in modern world

> Do not use; class in 940.3224–940.3229

.322 4–.322 9   Specific continents, countries, localities in modern world

> Add to base number 940.322 notation 4–9 from Table 2, e.g., diplomatic history of Great Britain 940.32241

.324   Central Powers

[.324 094–.324 099]   Specific continents, countries, localities in modern world

> Do not use; class in 940.3244–940.3249

.324 4–.324 9	Specific continents, countries, localities in modern world

Add to base number 940.324 notation 4–9 from Table 2, e.g., diplomatic history of Germany 940.32443

.325	Neutrals

[.325 094–.325 099]	Specific continents, countries, localities in modern world

Do not use; class in 940.3254–940.3259

.325 4–.325 9	Specific continents, countries, localities in modern world

Add to base number 940.325 notation 4–9 from Table 2, e.g., diplomatic history of Switzerland 940.325494

.33	Participation of specific groups of countries

Class a specific activity with the activity, e.g., diplomatic history among neutrals 940.325

For participation of specific countries and localities, see 940.34–940.39

.332	Allies and associated powers
.334	Central Powers
.335	Neutrals
.34–.39	Participation of specific countries and localities

Class here mobilization in specific countries and localities

Add to base number 940.3 notation 4–9 from Table 2, e.g., participation of Great Britain 940.341

Class a specific activity with the activity, e.g., efforts by a specific country to preserve or restore peace 940.312

.4	**Military history of World War I**
.400 1–.400 8	Standard subdivisions
.400 9	History, geographic treatment, biography

Do not use for military campaigns; class in 940.41–940.45

.400 92	Biography

Do not use for personal narratives; class in 940.481–940.482

[.400 94–.400 99]	Specific continents, countries, localities in modern world

Do not use for military participation of specific countries; class in 940.4094–940.4099. Do not use for land operations; class in 940.41

.401	Strategy
.401 2	Allies and associated powers
.401 3	Central Powers
.402	Mobilization

[.402 094–.402 099]	Specific continents, countries, localities in modern world

                           Do not use; class in 940.34–940.39

.403   Ethnic minorities as troops

.405   Repressive measures and atrocities

                           Class internment camps in 940.317; class Armenian Genocide, 1915–1916, in 956.620154

.409   Military participation of specific countries

                           Add to base number 940.409 notation 4–9 from Table 2, e.g., military participation of Germany 940.40943

.41   Operations and units

                           Standard subdivisions are added for either or both topics in heading

                           Class here land operations

                           For land campaigns and battles of 1914–1916, see 940.42; for land campaigns and battles of 1917–1918, see 940.43; for air operations, see 940.44; for naval operations, see 940.45

[.410 94–.410 99]	Specific continents, countries, localities in modern world

                           Do not use for operations of specific countries; class in 940.412–940.413. Do not use for operations by continent; class in 940.414–940.416

>   940.412–940.413   Military units and their operations

                   Class here organization, history, rosters, service records

                   Class comprehensive works in 940.41. Class units engaged in a special service with the service, e.g., ambulance companies 940.4753

                   For operations in Europe, see 940.414; for operations in Asia, see 940.415; for operations in Africa, see 940.416; for rolls of honor and lists of dead, see 940.467

.412   Military units of Allies and associated powers

[.412 094–.412 099]	Specific continents, countries, localities in modern world

                           Do not use; class in 940.4124–940.4129

.412 4–.412 9   Specific continents, countries, localities in modern world

                           Add to base number 940.412 notation 4–9 from Table 2, e.g., French units 940.41244

.413   Military units of Central Powers

[.413 094–.413 099]	Specific continents, countries, localities in modern world

                           Do not use; class in 940.4134–940.4139

.413 4–.413 9   Specific continents, countries, localities in modern world

                           Add to base number 940.413 notation 4–9 from Table 2, e.g., Austrian units 940.413436

.414	Operations in Europe
.414 4	Western front
	Class here German western front, French front
.414 5	Austro-Italian front
.414 7	Eastern front
	Class here German eastern front, Russian front
.415	Operations in Asia
.416	Operations in Africa
.42	Land campaigns and battles of 1914–1916
.421	1914, western front
.422	1914, eastern front
.423	1914, other areas
.424	1915, western and Austro-Italian fronts
.425	1915, eastern front
.426	1915, other areas
	Including Gallipoli Campaign
.427	1916, European fronts
.427 2	Western and Austro-Italian fronts
.427 5	Eastern front
.429	1916, other areas
.429 1	Asia Minor
.43	Land campaigns and battles of 1917–1918
.431	1917, western and Austro-Italian fronts
.432	1917, eastern front
.433	1917, other areas
.434	1918, western and Austro-Italian fronts
	Including final German offensives
	Class final allied offensives in 940.435–940.436

>	940.435–940.436 **Final allied offensives**
	Class comprehensive works in 940.434
.435	Allied offensives of July 18–September 24, 1918
.436	Allied offensives of September 25–November 11, 1918
.437	1918, eastern front

.438	1918, other areas
.439	Armistice, November 11, 1918
.44	Air operations

> Including antiaircraft defenses
>
> Class here combined air and naval operations
>
> *For naval operations, see 940.45*

[.440 94–.440 99]	Specific continents, countries, localities in modern world

> Do not use; class in 940.449

.442	Air raids

> Class specific events by year in 940.444–940.448

.443	Air bases

> ## 940.444–940.448 Events by year
>
> Class comprehensive works in 940.44

.444	Events of 1914
.445	Events of 1915
.446	Events of 1916
.447	Events of 1917
.448	Events of 1918
.449	Operations of specific countries

> Class here aircraft, crews, units
>
> Add to base number 940.449 notation 4–9 from Table 2, e.g., air operations of Germany 940.44943
>
> Class events by year regardless of country in 940.444–940.448

.45	Naval operations
[.450 94–.450 99]	Specific continents, countries, localities in modern world

> Do not use; class in 940.459

.451	Submarine warfare
.451 2	German use

> Class events by year in 940.4514

.451 3	Allied use

> Class events by year in 940.4514

[.451 309 4–.451 309 9]	Specific continents, countries, localities in modern world

> Do not use; class in 940.45134–940.45139

.451 34–.451 39	Specific continents, countries, localities in modern world

Add to base number 940.4513 notation 4–9 from Table 2, e.g., United States use of submarines 940.451373

.451 4	Specific events
.451 6	Antisubmarine warfare

Class events by year in 940.4514

.452	**Blockades and blockade running**

Class events by year in 940.454–940.458

.453	Naval bases

>   940.454–940.458 Events by year

Class events in submarine warfare by year in 940.4514; class comprehensive works in 940.45

.454	Events of 1914
.455	Events of 1915
.456	Events of 1916
.457	Events of 1917
.458	Events of 1918
.459	Naval operations of specific countries

Class here ships, crews, units

Add to base number 940.459 notation 4–9 from Table 2, e.g., naval operations of Italy 940.45945

Class events by year regardless of country in 940.454–940.458

.46–.48	Celebrations, commemorations, memorials; prisoners of war; medical and social services; other military topics

Add to base number 940.4 the numbers following 940.54 in 940.546–940.548, e.g., prisoners of war 940.472

.5	**1918–**
.51	1918–1929
.52	1930–1939

Class Holocaust in 940.5318

.53	World War II, 1939–1945

Class here Sino-Japanese Conflict, 1937–1945

For military history, see 940.54; for Sino-Japanese Conflict during 1937–1941, see 951.042

.530 8	Groups of people
	Do not use for noncombatants, pacifists, enemy sympathizers; class in 940.5316
	See also 940.5318 for Holocaust
[.530 869 14]	Displaced persons
	Do not use; class in 940.53145
.530 9	History, geographic treatment, biography
	Do not use for participation of specific groups of countries; class in 940.533
[.530 94–.530 99]	Specific continents, countries, localities in modern world
	Do not use; class in 940.534–940.539
.531	Social, political, economic history; Holocaust
	For diplomatic history, see 940.532
.531 1	Causes
.531 12	Political and diplomatic causes
.531 13	Economic causes
.531 14	Social and psychological causes
.531 2	Efforts to preserve or restore peace
.531 4	Political, diplomatic, economic results
	Class here consequences
	Class results in and effects on a specific country with the history of the country, e.g., on Norway 948.1043
.531 41	Conferences and treaties
	For consequences of conferences and treaties, see 940.53142
.531 42	Consequences of conferences and treaties
	For movement of people, see 940.53145
.531 422	Reparations
.531 424	Territorial questions
.531 425	Establishment of new nations
.531 426	Establishment of mandates
.531 44	Reconstruction
.531 45	Movement of people
	Class here displaced persons, forced repatriation, population transfers
	For emigration of Jews in relation to Holocaust, see 940.5318142

.531 6	Noncombatants, pacifists, enemy sympathizers
.531 61	Noncombatants
	Including children
.531 62	Pacifists
.531 63	Enemy sympathizers
.531 7	Concentration and related camps

Class here internment camps

Class camps as a part of the Holocaust in 940.53185; class prisoner-of-war camps in 940.5472

.531 709	History, geographic treatment, biography

Use area notation to indicate country maintaining the camps, e.g., internment camps maintained by the United States 940.53170973

For camps by location, see 940.53174–940.53179

.531 709 4	Camps maintained by countries in Europe

Do not use for camps maintained by Axis Powers; class in 940.53185

.531 74–.531 79	Camps by location

Add to base number 940.5317 notation 4–9 from Table 2, e.g., Manzanar internment camp for Japanese-Americans 940.531779487; however, for specific European concentration camps maintained by Axis Powers, see 940.531853–940.531859

Class extermination camps in 940.53185

.531 8	Holocaust

Class here Holocaust, 1933–1945; Holocaust with respect to Jews

[.531 808 992 4]	Holocaust with respect to Jews

Do not use; class in 940.5318

.531 809 2	Biography

Class here life of persons in a specific ghetto or extermination camp

.531 81	General topics of Holocaust
[.531 810 1–.531 810 9]	Standard subdivisions

Do not use; class in 940.531801–940.531809

.531 811	Causes
.531 813	Economic history

.531 813 2	Economic actions against businesses and property
	Class here boycott, confiscation
	Class indemnification and restitution of confiscated and stolen property in 940.5318144
.531 813 4	Forced labor
	Class general works on forced labor during World War II in 940.5405
.531 814	Consequences
	Class long-term welfare services to Holocaust survivors and their descendants in 362.87
	For war crime trials, see 341.690268
.531 814 2	Emigration of Jews
	Class here emigration to Palestine
	For emigration of Jews to Palestine as part of the history of Israel, see 956.9404
.531 814 4	Indemnification and restitution of confiscated and stolen property
	Standard subdivisions are added for any or all topics in heading
	Class comprehensive works on confiscated and stolen property in 940.5318132
	See also 341.67 for law of enemy aliens and their property, war victims
.531 818	Holocaust denial
	Class here denial of extermination camps
.531 83	Resistance movements and rescue operations
.531 832	Resistance movements
	Class resistance movements associated with a specific ghetto or extermination camp in 940.53185; class general works on resistance movements during World War II in 940.5336
.531 835	Rescue operations
	Class here Righteous Gentiles
.531 84	Specific events
	Class a specific event associated with a specific ghetto or extermination camp in 940.53185
.531 842	Events of 1933–1938
	Class here Nuremberg laws, Kristallnacht
.531 844	Events of 1939–1945
	Class here Wannsee-Konferenz

.531 844 5	Babi Yar Massacre
.531 846	Events of 1945

           Class here liberation of extermination camps

.531 85	Ghettos and extermination camps maintained by Axis Powers

           Standard subdivisions are added for either or both topics in heading

           Class here European concentration camps maintained by Axis Powers

           Class denial of extermination camps in 940.531818; class Wannsee-Konferenz in 940.531844; class comprehensive works on concentration camps in 940.5317

[.531 850 92]	Biography

           Do not use; class in 940.5318092

[.531 850 943–.531 850 949]	Geographic treatment

           Do not use; class in 940.531853–940.531859

.531 853–.531 859	Specific ghettos and extermination camps

           Class here specific European concentration camps maintained by Axis Powers

           Add to base number 940.53185 the numbers following —4 in notation 43–49 from Table 2, e.g., Warsaw Ghetto 940.531853841, Auschwitz 940.531853862; however, do not add notation 092 from Table 1 for biography; class in 940.5318092

           Subdivisions are added for either or both topics in heading

.531 86	Commemorations and memorials

           Class commemorations and memorials associated with a specific ghetto or extermination camp in 940.53185

.531 862	Commemorations

           Class here remembrance days

.531 864	Memorials

           Class museums that are also memorials in 940.5318074

.531 87	Welfare services to Holocaust victims

           Services provided during and immediately after the Holocaust

           Class long-term welfare services to Holocaust survivors and their descendants in 362.87; class rescue operations in 940.531835

.532	Diplomatic history

           For diplomatic causes, see 940.53112; for efforts to preserve or restore peace, see 940.5312; for diplomatic results, see 940.5314

.532 2	Allies

[.532 209 4–.532 209 9]	Specific continents, countries, localities in modern world
	Do not use; class in 940.53224–940.53229
.532 24–.532 29	Specific continents, countries, localities in modern world
	Add to base number 940.5322 notation 4–9 from Table 2, e.g., diplomatic history of Great Britain 940.532241
.532 4	Axis Powers
[.532 409 4–.532 409 9]	Specific continents, countries, localities in modern world
	Do not use; class in 940.53244–940.53249
.532 44–.532 49	Specific continents, countries, localities in modern world
	Add to base number 940.5324 notation 4–9 from Table 2, e.g., diplomatic history of Japan 940.532452
.532 5	Neutrals
[.532 509 4–.532 509 9]	Specific continents, countries, localities in modern world
	Do not use; class in 940.53254–940.53259
.532 54–.532 59	Specific continents, countries, localities in modern world
	Add to base number 940.5325 notation 4–9 from Table 2, e.g., diplomatic history of Switzerland 940.5325494

.533   **Participation of specific groups of countries**

Class here national groups, anti-Axis and pro-Axis national groups, mobilization

Class a specific activity with the activity, e.g., diplomatic history among Axis Powers 940.5324

For participation of specific countries, see 940.534–940.539

.533 2	Allies
.533 4	Axis Powers
.533 5	Neutrals
.533 6	Occupied countries

Class here governments-in-exile; resistance, underground movements

Class resistance movements as part of Holocaust in 940.531832

For countries occupied by Axis Powers, see 940.5337; for countries occupied by Allies, see 940.5338

.533 7	Countries occupied by Axis Powers
.533 8	Countries occupied by Allies

.534–.539	Participation of specific countries and localities

Add to base number 940.53 notation 4–9 from Table 2, e.g., participation of Great Britain 940.5341

Class a specific activity with the activity, e.g., efforts by a specific country to preserve or restore peace 940.5312

.54	Military history of World War II

.540 01–.540 08	Standard subdivisions

.540 09	History, geographic treatment, biography

Do not use for military campaigns; class in 940.541–940.545

.540 092	Biography

Do not use for personal narratives; class in 940.5481–940.5482

[.540 094–.540 099]	Specific continents, countries, localities in modern world

Do not use for military participation of specific countries; class in 940.54094–940.54099. Do not use for land operations; class in 940.541

.540 1	Strategy

.540 12	Allies

.540 13	Axis Powers

.540 2	Mobilization

[.540 209 4–.540 209 9]	Specific continents, countries, localities in modern world

Do not use; class in 940.534–940.539

.540 3	African Americans and American native peoples as troops

.540 4	Ethnic minorities as troops

For African Americans and American native peoples as troops, see 940.5403

.540 5	Repressive measures and atrocities

Including forced labor

Class concentration and related camps in 940.5317; class Holocaust in 940.5318; class forced labor as part of Holocaust in 940.5318134

.540 9	Military participation of specific countries

Add to base number 940.5409 notation 4–9 from Table 2, e.g., military participation of Germany 940.540943

.541	Operations and units

For air operations, see 940.544; for naval operations, see 940.545

[.541 094–.541 099]	Specific continents, countries, localities in modern world

Do not use for operations of specific countries; class in 940.5412–940.5413. Do not use for specific campaigns and battles by theater; class in 940.542

>   940.541 2–940.541 3   Military units and their operations

Class here organization, history, rosters, service records; comprehensive works on units whose operations were limited to a specific theater

Class comprehensive works in 940.541. Class units engaged in a special service with the service, e.g., ambulance companies 940.54753

For units engaged in a specific campaign or battle not equal to a theater, see 940.542; for rolls of honor and lists of dead, see 940.5467

.541 2   Military units of Allies

[.541 209 4–.541 209 9]   Specific continents, countries, localities in modern world

Do not use; class in 940.54124–940.54129

.541 24–.541 29   Specific continents, countries, localities in modern world

Add to base number 940.5412 notation 4–9 from Table 2, e.g., French units 940.541244

.541 3   Military units of Axis Powers

[.541 309 4–.541 309 9]   Specific continents, countries, localities in modern world

Do not use; class in 940.54134–940.54139

.541 34–.541 39   Specific continents, countries, localities in modern world

Add to base number 940.5413 notation 4–9 from Table 2, e.g., Japanese units 940.541352

.542   Campaigns and battles by theater

.542 1   European theater

Add to base number 940.5421 the numbers following —4 in notation 41–49 from Table 2, e.g., battles in France 940.54214

.542 3   African theater

Add to base number 940.5423 the numbers following —6 in notation 61–69 from Table 2, e.g., battles in North Africa 940.54231

.542 4   Middle East theater

Class African countries of the Middle East in 940.5423

.542 5   East and South Asian theaters

Standard subdivisions are added for East and South Asian theaters together, for East Asian theater alone

.542 51–.542 52   Battles in China, Korea, Japan, adjacent areas

Add to base number 940.5425 the numbers following —5 in notation 51–52 from Table 2, e.g., battles in China 940.54251

Class Sino-Japanese Conflict during 1937–1941 in 951.042

.542 59	Southeast Asian theater

Add to base number 940.54259 the numbers following —59 in notation 591–599 from Table 2, e.g., battles in Philippines 940.542599

For battles in western New Guinea, see 940.542651

.542 6	Pacific Ocean theater

Add to base number 940.5426 the numbers following —9 in notation 93–96 from Table 2, e.g., battles in western New Guinea 940.542651, battle of Midway 940.5426699, attack on Pearl Harbor 940.5426693

For Southeast Asian theater, see 940.54259

See also 940.54252 for Japan; also 940.542599 for Philippines

.542 8	American theater
.542 9	Other areas
.542 93	Atlantic Ocean

Class here battle of the Atlantic, 1939–1945

.544	Air operations

Including antiaircraft defenses

Class here combined air and naval operations

For naval operations, see 940.545

[.544 094–.544 099]	Specific continents, countries, localities in modern world

Do not use for campaigns and battles by theater; class in 940.542. Do not use for operations of specific countries; class in 940.5449

.544 2	Campaigns and battles
.544 209 4–.544 209 9	Specific continents, countries, localities in modern world

Class here comprehensive works on campaigns and battles by a specific country

Do not use for a specific campaign or battle; class in 940.542, e.g., battle of Britain 940.54211, attack on Pearl Harbor 940.5426693

.544 3	Air bases
[.544 309 4–.544 309 9]	Specific continents, countries, localities in modern world

Do not use; class in 940.54434–940.54439

.544 34–.544 39	Specific continents, countries, localities in modern world

Add to base number 940.5443 notation 4–9 from Table 2, e.g., air bases in England 940.544342

.544 9   Operations of specific countries

                 Class here aircraft, crews, units

                 Add to base number 940.5449 notation 4–9 from Table 2, e.g., operations of Germany 940.544943

                 For comprehensive works on campaigns and battles by a specific country, see 940.5442. For a specific campaign or battle, see the campaign or battle in 940.5421–940.5429, e.g., battle of Britain 940.54211, attack on Pearl Harbor 940.5426693

.545   Naval operations

                 Class here campaigns and battles

[.545 094–.545 099]   Specific continents, countries, localities in modern world

                 Do not use for campaigns and battles by theater; class in 940.542. Do not use for operations of specific countries; class in 940.5459

.545 1   Submarine warfare

.545 16   Antisubmarine warfare

.545 2   Blockades and blockade running

                 Standard subdivisions are added for either or both topics in heading

.545 3   Naval bases

.545 9   Operations of specific countries

                 Class here ships, crews, units; comprehensive works on campaigns and battles by a specific country

                 Add to base number 940.5459 notation 4–9 from Table 2, e.g., Australian naval operations 940.545994

                 Class a specific kind of operation with the operation, e.g., blockades 940.5452

                 For a specific campaign or battle, see the campaign or battle in 940.5421–940.5429, e.g., battle of Midway 940.5426699, battle of the Atlantic 940.54293

.546   Celebrations, commemorations, memorials

                 Standard subdivisions are added for any or all topics in heading

                 Including commemorative meetings, decorations and awards

                 For celebrations, commemorations, memorials of a specific event, see the event, e.g., Normandy Invasion 940.5421421

.546 5   Monuments and cemeteries

                 Standard subdivisions are added for either or both topics in heading

[.546 509 4–.546 509 9]   Specific continents, countries, localities in modern world

                 Do not use; class in 940.54654–940.54659

.546 54–.546 59	Specific continents, countries, localities in modern world

Add to base number 940.5465 notation 4–9 from Table 2, e.g., monuments and cemeteries in France 940.546544

.546 7	Rolls of honor and lists of dead

Standard subdivisions are added for either or both topics in heading

[.546 709 4–.546 709 9]	Specific continents, countries, localities in modern world

Do not use; class in 940.54674–940.54679

.546 74–.546 79	Specific continents, countries, localities in modern world

Add to base number 940.5467 notation 4–9 from Table 2, e.g., lists of Japanese dead 940.546752

.547	**Prisoners of war; medical and social services**
.547 2	Prisoner-of-war camps

Class here prisoners of war

For prisoners exchange, see 940.5473

[.547 209 4–.547 209 9]	Specific continents, countries, localities in modern world

Do not use; class in 940.54724–940.54729

.547 24–.547 29	Specific continents, countries, localities in modern world

Add to base number 940.5472 notation 4–9 from Table 2, e.g., prisoner-of-war camps maintained by Germany 940.547243, prisoner-of-war camps maintained by Germany in Poland 940.54724309438

.547 3	Prisoners exchange
.547 5	Medical services

For hospitals, see 940.5476

.547 509 4–.547 509 9	Specific continents and localities in modern world

Do not use for services of specific countries; class in 940.54754–940.54759

.547 52	Sanitary affairs
.547 53	Ambulance services
.547 54–.547 59	Services of specific countries

Add to base number 940.5475 notation 4–9 from Table 2, e.g., French medical services 940.547544

.547 6	Hospitals
[.547 609 4–.547 609 9]	Specific continents, countries, localities in modern world

Do not use for hospitals in specific places; class in 940.54763. Do not use for hospitals maintained by specific countries; class in 940.54764–940.54769

.547 63   Hospitals in specific places

> Add to base number 940.54763 notation 4–9 from Table 2, e.g., hospitals in Rome 940.5476345632

> Class hospitals maintained in specific places by specific countries in 940.54764–940.54769

.547 64–.547 69   Hospitals maintained by specific countries

> Add to base number 940.5476 notation 4–9 from Table 2, e.g., hospitals maintained by Italy 940.547645

.547 7   Relief and welfare services

> Standard subdivisions are added for either or both topics in heading

[.547 709 4–.547 709 9]   Specific continents, countries, localities in modern world

> Do not use for activities conducted by specific countries; class in 940.54778. Do not use for activities in specific places; class in 940.54779

.547 71   Activities of Red Cross

.547 78   Activities conducted by specific countries

> Add to base number 940.54778 notation 4–9 from Table 2, e.g., activities conducted by Switzerland 940.54778494

> Class Red Cross activities conducted by specific countries in 940.54771

.547 79   Activities in specific places

> Add to base number 940.54779 notation 4–9 from Table 2, e.g., welfare activities in Paris 940.5477944361

> Class activities of Red Cross in specific places in 940.54771; class welfare activities conducted in specific places by specific countries in 940.54778

.547 8   Religious life and chaplain services

> Standard subdivisions are added for either or both topics in heading

.548   Other military topics

> Including deserters, military personnel missing in action

.548 1   Personal narratives of individuals from Allies

> Class here comprehensive works on personal narratives

> Class personal narratives on a specific subject with the subject, plus notation 092 from Table 1, e.g., on blockade running 940.5452092

> *For personal narratives of individuals from Axis Powers, see 940.5482*

[.548 109 4–.548 109 9]   Specific continents, countries, localities in modern world

> Do not use; class in 940.54814–940.54819

.548 14–.548 19	Specific continents, countries, localities in modern world
	Add to base number 940.5481 notation 4–9 from Table 2, e.g., personal narratives of Britons 940.548141
.548 2	Personal narratives of individuals from Axis Powers
	Class personal narratives on a specific subject with the subject, plus notation 092 from Table 1, e.g., on blockade running 940.5452092
[.548 209 4–.548 209 9]	Specific continents, countries, localities in modern world
	Do not use; class in 940.54824–940.54829
.548 24–.548 29	Specific continents, countries, localities in modern world
	Add to base number 940.5482 notation 4–9 from Table 2, e.g., personal narratives of Germans 940.548243
.548 3	Military life and customs of Allies
	Class here comprehensive works on military life and customs
	For celebrations, commemorations, memorials, see 940.546; for military life and customs of Axis Powers, see 940.5484
[.548 309 4–.548 309 9]	Specific continents, countries, localities in modern world
	Do not use; class in 940.54834–940.54839
.548 34–.548 39	Specific continents, countries, localities in modern world
	Add to base number 940.5483 notation 4–9 from Table 2, e.g., military life in United States Navy 940.548373
.548 4	Military life and customs of Axis Powers
	For celebrations, commemorations, memorials, see 940.546
[.548 409 4–.548 409 9]	Specific continents, countries, localities in modern world
	Do not use; class in 940.54844–940.54849
.548 44–.548 49	Specific continents, countries, localities in modern world
	Add to base number 940.5484 notation 4–9 from Table 2, e.g., military life in Luftwaffe 940.548443
.548 5	Unconventional warfare
	Class here counterintelligence, intelligence, psychological warfare, sabotage, subversion
	For propaganda, see 940.5488
.548 509 4–.548 509 9	Specific continents, countries, localities in modern world
	Do not use for unconventional warfare of Allies; class in 940.5486. Do not use for unconventional warfare of Axis Powers; class in 940.5487
.548 6	Unconventional warfare of Allies
[.548 609 4–.548 609 9]	Specific continents, countries, localities in modern world
	Do not use; class in 940.54864–940.54869

.548 64–.548 69   Specific continents, countries, localities in modern world

> Add to base number 940.5486 notation 4–9 from Table 2, e.g., intelligence operation of United States 940.548673

.548 7   Unconventional warfare of Axis Powers

[.548 709 4–.548 709 9]   Specific continents, countries, localities in modern world

> Do not use; class in 940.54874–940.54879

.548 74–.548 79   Specific continents, countries, localities in modern world

> Add to base number 940.5487 notation 4–9 from Table 2, e.g., intelligence operations of Germany 940.548743

.548 8   Propaganda

[.548 809 4–.548 809 9]   Specific continents, countries, localities in modern world

> Do not use for propaganda by Allies; class in 940.54886. Do not use for propaganda by Axis Powers; class in 940.54887. Do not use for propaganda in specific places; class in 940.54889

.548 86   Propaganda by Allies

[.548 860 94–.548 860 99]   Specific continents, countries, localities in modern world

> Do not use; class in 940.548864–940.548869

.548 864–.548 869   Specific continents, countries, localities in modern world

> Add to base number 940.54886 notation 4–9 from Table 2, e.g., propaganda by United States 940.5488673

.548 87   Propaganda by Axis Powers

[.548 870 94–.548 870 99]   Specific continents, countries, localities in modern world

> Do not use; class in 940.548874–940.548879

.548 874–.548 879   Specific continents, countries, localities in modern world

> Add to base number 940.54887 notation 4–9 from Table 2, e.g., propaganda by Germany 940.5488743

.548 89   Propaganda in specific places

> Add to base number 940.54889 notation 4–9 from Table 2, e.g., propaganda in United States 940.5488973

> Class propaganda by one side or one country regardless of location in 940.54886–940.54887

.55   1945–1999

.554   1945–1949

.555   1950–1959

.556   1960–1969

.557   1970–1979

.558   1980–1989

.559	1990–1999
.56	2000–
.561	2000–2019
.561 1	2000–2009
.561 2	2010–2019
.562	2020–2029

941   *British Isles

Class here Great Britain, United Kingdom; Celtic regions, 487 to present

For a specific area of Celtic regions from 487 to present not provided for here, see the area, e.g., Brittany 944.1

See Manual at 941

.01   Early history to 1066

For ancient history to 410, see 936.1

(.012)   Ancient history to 410

(Optional number; prefer 936.1)

Add to base number 941.012 the numbers following 936.20 in 936.201–936.204, e.g., 4th century 941.0124

.013–.019   Pre-Anglo-Saxon period through reign of Saxon kings, 410–1066

Add to base number 941.01 the numbers following 942.01 in 942.013–942.019, e.g., period of Danish kings 941.018

.02–.05   Norman period through House of Tudor period, 1066–1603

Add to base number 941.0 the numbers following 942.0 in 942.02–942.05, e.g., reign of Henry VIII 941.052

.06   House of Stuart and Commonwealth periods, 1603–1714

(Option: Class here Anglo-Dutch Wars; prefer 949.204)

.061   Reign of James I, 1603–1625

.062   Reign of Charles I, 1625–1649

Class Civil War in 942.062

.063   Period as Commonwealth and Protectorate, 1649–1660

For Protectorate of Oliver Cromwell, see 941.064; for Protectorate of Richard Cromwell, see 941.065

.064   Protectorate of Oliver Cromwell, 1653–1658

.065   Protectorate of Richard Cromwell, 1658–1659

.066   Reign of Charles II, 1660–1685 (Restoration)

*Add as instructed under 930–990

.067	1685–1689
	Class here reign of James II, 1685–1688
.068	Reigns of William III (of Orange) and Mary II, 1689–1702
.069	Reign of Anne, 1702–1714
.07	Period of House of Hanover, 1714–1837
.071	Reign of George I, 1714–1727
.072	Reign of George II, 1727–1760
	(Option: Class here War of Jenkins' Ear; prefer 946.055)
.073	Reign of George III, 1760–1820
	Including formation of United Kingdom
.074	Reign of George IV, 1820–1830
.075	Reign of William IV, 1830–1837
.08	Period of Victoria and House of Windsor, 1837–
.081	Reign of Victoria, 1837–1901
	Class here 19th century
	For 1800–1820, see 941.073; for 1820–1830, see 941.074; for 1830–1837, see 941.075
	(Option: Class here Crimean War; prefer 947.0738. Class here South African [Second Anglo-Boer] War; prefer 968.048)
.082	1901–1999
	For reign of George V, see 941.083; for 1936–1945, see 941.084; for 1945–1999, see 941.085
.082 3	Reign of Edward VII, 1901–1910
.083	Reign of George V, 1910–1936
.084	1936–1945
	Class here reigns of Edward VIII, 1936, and George VI, 1936–1952; period of World War II, 1939–1945
	For reign of George VI during 1945–1949, see 941.0854; for reign of George VI during 1950–1952, see 941.0855
.085	1945–1999
	Class here reign of Elizabeth II, 1952 to present
	For 2000 to present, see 941.086
.085 4	1945–1949
.085 5	1950–1959
.085 6	1960–1969
.085 7	1970–1979

.085 8	1980–1989
.085 9	1990–1999
.086	2000–
.086 1	2000–2019
.086 11	2000–2009
.086 12	2010–2019
.086 2	2020–2029

.1   ***Scotland**

> *For northeastern Scotland, see 941.2; for southeastern Scotland, see 941.3; for southwestern Scotland, see 941.4*

.101   Early history to 1057

Including 11th century

> *For ancient history to 410, see 936.11; for 1057–1099, see 941.102*

(.101 2)   Ancient history to 410

(Optional number; prefer 936.11)

(.101 21)   Early history to ca. 600 B.C.

(Optional number; prefer 936.11)

(.101 22)   Celtic period, ca. 600–79 B.C.

(Optional number; prefer 936.1102)

(.101 23)   Period of Roman contacts, 79 B.C.–410 A.D.

(Optional number; prefer 936.1103)

.102   1057–1314

Including Battle of Bannockburn, 1314

.103   1314–1424

.104   Reigns of James I through James V, 1424–1542

.105   Reformation period, 1542–1603

Class here 16th century

> *For 1500–1542, see 941.104*

.106–.108   Personal union with England to present, 1603–

Add to base number 941.10 the numbers following 941.0 in 941.06–941.08, e.g., reign of Edward VII 941.10823

---

*Add as instructed under 930–990

.11–.15   Localities of northern Scotland

> Add to base number 941.1 the numbers following —411 in notation
> 4111–4115 from Table 2, e.g., Orkney Islands 941.132; then add further as
> follows:
>> 001–009   Standard subdivisions
>>> Add to 00 the numbers following 00 in notation 001–009
>>> from table under 930–990, e.g., ethnic and national
>>> groups 004, ethnic and national groups in Orkney Islands
>>> 941.132004
>> 01–08   Historical periods
>>> Add to 0 the numbers following 941.10 in 941.101–941.108,
>>> e.g., Orkney Islands during Reformation period, 1542–1603
>>> 941.13205

.2–.4   **Localities of northeastern Scotland, southeastern Scotland, southwestern Scotland**

> Add to base number 941 the numbers following —41 in notation 412–414 from
> Table 2, e.g., Moray 941.22; then add further as follows:
>> 001–009   Standard subdivisions
>>> Add to 00 the numbers following 00 in notation 001–009
>>> from table under 930–990, e.g., ethnic and national groups
>>> 004, ethnic and national groups in Moray 941.22004
>> 01–08   Historical periods
>>> Add to 0 the numbers following 941.10 in 941.101–941.108,
>>> e.g., Moray during Reformation period, 1542–1603 941.2205

.2   ***Northeastern Scotland**

.201–.208   Historical periods

> Add to base number 941.20 the numbers following 941.10 in
> 941.101–941.108, e.g., Reformation period 941.205

.3   ***Southeastern Scotland**

.301–.308   Historical periods

> Add to base number 941.30 the numbers following 941.10 in
> 941.101–941.108, e.g., Reformation period 941.305

.4   ***Southwestern Scotland**

.401–.408   Historical periods

> Add to base number 941.40 the numbers following 941.10 in
> 941.101–941.108, e.g., Reformation period 941.405

.5   ***Ireland**

.501   Early history to 1086

> Including Battle of Clontarf, 1014

> *For ancient history to 433, see 936.15*

---

*Add as instructed under 930–990

(.501 2)	Ancient history to 433
	(Optional number; prefer 936.15)
(.501 21)	Early history to ca. 400 B.C.
	(Optional number; prefer 936.1501)
(.501 22)	Celtic period, ca. 400 B.C.–433 A.D.
	(Optional number; prefer 936.1502)
.502	1086–1171
.503	Period under House of Plantagenet, 1171–1399
.504	Period under Houses of Lancaster and York, 1399–1485
.505	Period under House of Tudor, 1485–1603
.506	Period under House of Stuart, 1603–1691
.507	1691–1799
.508	1800–
.508 1	1800–1899
.508 2	1900–1999
.508 21	1900–1921
	Including Sinn Fein Rebellion (Easter Rebellion), 1916; Anglo-Irish War, 1919–1921
.508 22	1921–1949
.508 23	1950–1969
.508 24	1970–1999
.508 3	2000–

.6   ***Northern Ireland; Donegal County, Monaghan County, Cavan County of Republic of Ireland**

> Subdivisions are added for Northern Ireland, Donegal County, Monaghan County, Cavan County of Republic of Ireland together; for Northern Ireland alone

.601–.607	Early history to 1800
	Add to base number 941.60 the numbers following 941.50 in 941.501–941.507, e.g., period under House of Tudor 941.605
.608	1800–
.608 1	1800–1899
.608 2	1900–1999

---

*Add as instructed under 930–990

.608 21	1900–1920
	Including Government of Ireland Act, 1920
.608 22	1921–1949
.608 23	1949–1968
.608 24	1969–1999
.608 3	2000–

.61–.69   Localities of Northern Ireland; Donegal County, Monaghan County, Cavan County of Republic of Ireland

> Add to base number 941.6 the numbers following —416 in notation 4161–4169 from Table 2, e.g., northeast area of Northern Ireland 941.61; then add further as follows:
> 001–009   Standard subdivisions
> > Add to 00 the numbers following 00 in notation 001–009 from table under 930–990, e.g., ethnic and national groups 004, ethnic and national groups in northeast area of Northern Ireland 941.61004
> 01–08   Historical periods
> > Add to 0 the numbers following 941.60 in 941.601–941.608, e.g., northeast area of Northern Ireland during House of Tudor 941.6105

.7   ***Republic of Ireland (Eire)**

> *For Leinster, see 941.8; for Munster, see 941.9*

.701–.707   Early history to 1800

> Add to base number 941.70 the numbers following 941.50 in 941.501–941.507, e.g., period under House of Tudor 941.705

.708	1800–
.708 1	1800–1899
.708 2	1900–1999
.708 21	1900–1921
.708 22	1922–1949
	Including period as Irish Free State, 1922–1937; as Eire, 1937–1949
.708 23	1949–1969
.708 24	1970–1999
.708 3	2000–

---

*Add as instructed under 930–990

.71–.76   Localities of Republic of Ireland (Eire)

> Add to base number 941.7 the numbers following —417 in notation 4171–4176 from Table 2, e.g., Connacht 941.71; then add further as follows:
> 001–009   Standard subdivisions
> > Add to 00 the numbers following 00 in notation 001–009 from table under 930–990, e.g., ethnic and national groups 004, ethnic and national groups in Connacht 941.71004
> 01–08   Historical periods
> > Add to 0 the numbers following 941.70 in 941.701–941.708, e.g., Connacht during period under House of Tudor, 1485–1603 941.7105

.8   *Leinster

.801–.807   Early history to 1800

> Add to base number 941.80 the numbers following 941.50 in 941.501–941.507, e.g., period under House of Tudor 941.805

.808   1800–

> Add to base number 941.808 the numbers following 941.708 in 941.7081–941.7083, e.g., 1949–1969 941.80823

.81–.89   Localities of Leinster

> Add to base number 941.8 the numbers following —418 in notation 4181–4189 from Table 2, e.g., northwest Leinster 941.81; then add further as follows:
> 001–009   Standard subdivisions
> > Add to 00 the numbers following 00 in notation 001–009 from table under 930–990, e.g., ethnic and national groups 004, ethnic and national groups in northwest Leinster 941.81004
> 01–08   Historical periods
> > Add to 0 the numbers following 941.80 in 941.801–941.808, e.g., northwest Leinster during period under House of Tudor 941.8105

.9   *Munster

.901–.907   Early history to 1800

> Add to base number 941.90 the numbers following 941.50 in 941.501–941.507, e.g., period under House of Tudor 941.905

.908   1800–

> Add to base number 941.908 the numbers following 941.708 in 941.7081–941.7083, e.g., 1949–1969 941.90823

*Add as instructed under 930–990

.91–.96   Localities of Munster

> Add to base number 941.9 the numbers following —419 in notation 4191–4196 from Table 2, e.g., Waterford County 941.91; then add further as follows:
>
> 001–009   Standard subdivisions
>
> > Add to 00 the numbers following 00 in notation 001–009 from table under 930–990, e.g., ethnic and national groups 004, ethnic and national groups in Waterford County 941.91004
>
> 01–08   Historical periods
>
> > Add to 0 the numbers following 941.90 in 941.901–941.908, e.g., Waterford County during period under House of Tudor, 1485–1603 941.9105

942   *England and Wales

Subdivisions are added for England and Wales together, for England alone

See Manual at 941

> 942.01–942.08   Historical periods of England and Wales together, of England alone

Class comprehensive works in 942

.01   Early history to 1066

For ancient history to 410, see 936.2

(.012)   Ancient history of southern Britain to 410

(Optional number; prefer 936.2)

Add to base number 942.012 the numbers following 936.20 in 936.201–936.204, e.g., Celtic period 942.0122

.013   Pre-Anglo-Saxon period, 410–449

.014   449–ca. 600

Including reign of King Arthur

.015   Period of Heptarchy, ca. 600–829

Class supremacy of Wessex in 942.016

.015 3   Supremacy of Northumbria, 603–685

.015 7   Supremacy of Mercia, 757–796

.016   Supremacy of Wessex, 829–924

Class here 9th century

For 800–829, see 942.015

.016 1   Reign of Egbert, 829–839

.016 2   Reign of Ethelwulf, 839–858

---

*Add as instructed under 930–990

.034	Reign of Henry III, 1216–1272

Class here 13th century

For 1200–1216, see 942.033; for 1272–1299, see 942.035

.035	Reign of Edward I, 1272–1307
.036	Reign of Edward II, 1307–1327
.037	Reign of Edward III, 1327–1377

Class here 14th century

For 1300–1307, see 942.035; for 1307–1327, see 942.036; for 1377–1399, see 942.038

(Option: Class here Hundred Years' War; prefer 944.025)

.038	Reign of Richard II, 1377–1399
.04	Period of Houses of Lancaster and York, 1399–1485

Class here Wars of the Roses, 1455–1485

.041	Reign of Henry IV, 1399–1413
.042	Reign of Henry V, 1413–1422
.043	Reign of Henry VI, 1422–1461
.044	Reign of Edward IV, 1461–1483
.045	Reign of Edward V, 1483
.046	Reign of Richard III, 1483–1485
.05	Period of House of Tudor, 1485–1603
.051	Reign of Henry VII, 1485–1509
.052	Reign of Henry VIII, 1509–1547
.053	Reign of Edward VI, 1547–1553
.054	Reign of Mary I, 1553–1558
.055	Reign of Elizabeth I, 1558–1603

Including Spanish Armada, 1588

.06–.08	House of Stuart and Commonwealth periods to present, 1603–

Add to base number 942.0 the numbers following 941.0 in 941.06–941.08, e.g., reign of Victoria 942.081

.062	‡Reign of Charles I, 1625–1649

Number built according to instructions under 942.06–942.08

Class here Civil War, 1642–1649

‡Add as instructed under 940–990

.1–.8   Localities of England

Add to base number 942 the numbers following —42 in notation 421–428 from Table 2, e.g., northeastern England 942.8; then add further as follows:

001–009   Standard subdivisions

Add to 00 the numbers following 00 in notation 001–009 from table under 930–990, e.g., ethnic and national groups 004, ethnic and national groups in northeastern England 942.8004

01–08   Historical periods

Add to 0 the numbers following 942.0 in 942.01–942.08, e.g., northeastern England during period of House of Tudor, 1485–1603 942.805

.9   *Wales

.901   Early history to 1066

For ancient history to 410, see 936.29

(.901 2)   Ancient history of Wales to 410

(Optional number; prefer 936.29)

Add to base number 942.9012 the numbers following 936.290 in 936.2901–936.2904, e.g., Celtic period 942.90122

943   Germany and neighboring central European countries

Class here central Europe

.000 1–.000 8   Standard subdivisions of central Europe

As modified in notation 001–008 from table under 930–990

.000 9   Archaeology; historical periods; areas, regions, places in general; collected biography of central Europe

.000 900 9   Archaeology

Notation 09009 from Table 1 as modified below

.000 900 902–.000 900 909   Specific subdivisions of archaeology

Add to base number 943.00090090 the numbers following 009090 in notation 0090902–0090909 from table under 930–990, e.g., serials treating archaeology of central Europe 943.000900905

.000 901–.000 905   Historical periods

Add to base number 943.00090 the numbers following —090 in notation 0901–0905 from Table 1, e.g., central Europe during the Middle Ages 943.000902

.000 91–.000 99   Areas, regions, places in general; collected biography

As modified in notation 0091–0099 from table under 930–990

---

*Add as instructed under 930–990

.001–.009	Standard subdivisions of Germany

As modified in notation 001–009 from table under 930–990

>   943.01–943.08   Historical periods of Germany

Class comprehensive works in 943

.01   Early history to 843

For ancient history to 481, see 936.3

(.012)   Ancient history to 481

(Optional number; prefer 936.3)

(.012 1)   Early history to 113 B.C.

(Optional number; prefer 936.301)

(.012 2)   Period of contacts with Roman Republic and Empire, 113 B.C.–481 A.D.

(Optional number; prefer 936.302)

.013   Period of Merovingian dynasty in Germany, 481–751

Including 8th century

Class comprehensive works on Merovingian dynasty in France and Germany in 944.013

For 751–800, see 943.014

.014   751–843

Class here Carolingian dynasty in Germany, 751–911; reign of Charlemagne in Germany, 768–814

Class comprehensive works on Carolingian dynasty in 944.014; class comprehensive works on reign of Charlemagne in France and Germany in 944.0142

For 843–911, see 943.021

>   943.02–943.05   Specific periods of Holy Roman Empire

Class comprehensive works in 943.02

.02   843–1519

After Treaty of Verdun, 843

Class here medieval period; comprehensive works on period of Holy Roman Empire, 962–1806

For later part of period of Holy Roman Empire, see 943.03–943.06

.021   843–911

Class here 9th century

For 800–843, see 943.014

.022   Period of Conrad I and House of Saxony, 911–1024

.023   1024–1137

         Including reign of Lothair II, Holy Roman Emperor, 1125–1137

         Class here period of Salian (Franconian) emperors, 1024–1125

.024   1138–1198

         Class here period of Hohenstaufen dynasty, 1138–1254; reign of Frederick I Barbarossa, 1152–1190; 12th century

         For 1100–1137, see 943.023; for later period of Hohenstaufen dynasty, see 943.025

.025   Later period of Hohenstaufen dynasty and Interregnum, 1198–1273

         Including reign of Frederick II, 1215–1250

         Class here 13th century

         For 1273–1299, see 943.026

.026   1273–1346

.027   1346–1438

         Including reign of Charles IV, 1346–1378; 14th century

         Class here period of House of Luxemburg

         For 1300–1346, reign of Henry VII, 1273–1313, see 943.026

.028   Reigns of Albert II and Frederick III, 1438–1493

         Class here 15th century

         For 1400–1438, see 943.027; for 1493–1499, see 943.029

.029   Reign of Maximilian I, 1493–1519

.03   Period of Reformation and Counter-Reformation, 1519–1618

         Class here period of House of Habsburg, 1493–1806

         For the reign of a specific Habsburg not provided for here, see the reign, e.g., reign of Leopold I 943.044

.031   Reign of Charles V, 1519–1556

         Including Peasants' War, 1524–1525; Schmalkaldic War, 1546–1547

         Class campaigns and battles of wars between France and Holy Roman Empire fought outside of Italy, 1521–1599 in 944.028; class campaigns and battles of wars between France and Holy Roman Empire fought in Italy, comprehensive works on campaigns and battles of wars between France and Holy Roman Empire, 1521–1599 in 945.06

.032   Reign of Ferdinand I, 1556–1564

.033   Reign of Maximilian II, 1564–1576

.034   Reign of Rudolf II, 1576–1612

.035   Reign of Matthias, 1612–1619

.04	1618–1705
.041	Period of Thirty Years' War, 1618–1648

Class comprehensive works on Thirty Years' War in 940.24

For reign of Matthias during Thirty Years' War, see 943.035; for reign of Ferdinand II during Thirty Years' War, see 943.042; for reign of Ferdinand III during Thirty Years' War, see 943.043

.042	Reign of Ferdinand II, 1619–1637
.043	Reign of Ferdinand III, 1637–1657
.044	Reign of Leopold I, 1658–1705
.05	1705–1790
.051	Reign of Joseph I, 1705–1711
.052	Reign of Charles VI, 1711–1740
.053	1740–1786

Class here reign of Frederick the Great, King of Prussia, 1740–1786

For 1742–1745, see 943.054; for 1745–1765, see 943.055; for 1765–1786, see 943.057

.054	Period of First and Second Silesian Wars, 1740–1745

Class here First Silesian War, 1740–1742; Second Silesian War, 1744–1745; reign of Charles VII, 1742–1745

Class War of the Austrian Succession in 940.2532

See also 940.2534 for Seven Years' War (Third Silesian War)

.055	Reign of Francis I, 1745–1765

Including period of Seven Years' War, 1756–1763

Class comprehensive works on Seven Years' War in 940.2534

.057	Reign of Joseph II, 1765–1790
.06	Period of Napoleonic Wars, 1790–1815

Including Confederation of the Rhine

Class comprehensive works on Napoleonic Wars in 940.27

.07	Period of German Confederation, 1815–1866

Class here 19th century, comprehensive works on Prussia

For 1800–1815, see 943.06; for 1866–1899, see 943.08. For a specific period of history of Prussia not provided for here, see the period, e.g., reign of Frederick the Great 943.053

.073	1815–1847
.074	Revolution of 1848–1849

.076	1849–1866

Including Schleswig-Holstein War, 1864; Austro-Prussian War (Seven Weeks' War), 1866
(Option: Class Schleswig-Holstein War in 948.904)

.08	1866–
.081	1866–1871

Class here period of North German Confederation

For Franco-German War, see 943.082

.082	‡Franco-German War, 1870–1871

(Option: Class in 944.07)

.083	Reign of William I, 1871–1888

Class here comprehensive works on administrations of Otto von Bismarck, 1862–1890; German Empire, 1871–1918

For reigns of Frederick III and William II, see 943.084. For a specific part of administrations of Otto von Bismarck not provided for here, see the part, e.g., administration during period of North German Confederation 943.081

.084	Reigns of Frederick III and William II, 1888–1918
.084 9	Period of World War I, 1914–1918
.085	Period of Weimar Republic, 1918–1933
.085 1	Revolution of 1918
.086	Period of Third Reich, 1933–1945

Class Holocaust in 940.5318

.086 2	1933–1939
.086 4	Period of World War II, 1939–1945
.087	1945–1990

Class here 20th century; Federal Republic, 1949 to present; comprehensive works on Federal and Democratic Republics

For 1900–1918, see 943.084; for period of Weimar Republic, see 943.085; for period of Third Reich, 1933–1945, see 943.086; for 1990 to present, see 943.088; for German Democratic Republic, see 943.1087

.087 4	1945–1949
.087 5	Administration of Konrad Adenauer, 1949–1962
.087 6	1962–1969

Including administrations of Ludwig Erhard, 1962–1966; Kurt Georg Kiesinger, 1966–1969

‡Add as instructed under 940–990

.087 7	1969–1982
	Including administrations of Willy Brandt, 1969–1974; Helmut Schmidt, 1974–1982
.087 8	1982–1990
	Class here administration of Helmut Kohl, 1982–1998
	Including period of reunification, 1989–1990
	For administration of Helmut Kohl during 1990–1998, see 943.0881
.088	1990–
.088 1	Later half of administration of Helmut Kohl, 1990–1998
.088 2	Administration of Gerhard Schröder, 1998–2005
.088 3	Administration of Angela Merkel, 2005–

.1   *Northeastern Germany

For Saxony and Thuringia, see 943.2

.101–.107	Early history to 1866
	Add to base number 943.10 the numbers following 943.0 in 943.01–943.07, e.g., northeastern Germany during period of German Confederation 943.107
.108	1866–
.108 1–.108 6	1866–1945
	Add to base number 943.108 the numbers following 943.08 in 943.081–943.086, e.g., northeastern Germany during period of German Empire 943.1083
.108 7	Period of East Germany, 1945–1990
	Class here period of German Democratic Republic, 1949–1990
.108 74	1945–1949
.108 75	Administration of Walter Ulbricht, 1949–1971
.108 77	Administration of Erich Honecker, 1971–1989
.108 79	1989–1990
	Class comprehensive works on reunification of Germany in 943.0878
	Class here fall of Berlin Wall, 1989
.108 8	Period as part of Federal Republic, 1990–
.108 81	1990–1998
.108 82	1998–2005

*Add as instructed under 930–990

.108 83	2005–

.15–.18   Localities of northeastern Germany

> Add to base number 943.1 the numbers following —431 in notation
> 4315–4318 from Table 2, e.g., Brandenburg and Berlin 943.15; then add
> further as follows:
>> 001–009   Standard subdivisions
>>> Add to 00 the numbers following 00 in notation 001–009
>>> from table under 930–990, e.g., ethnic and national groups
>>> 004, ethnic and national groups in Brandenburg and Berlin
>>> 943.15004
>> 01–08   Historical periods
>>> Add to 0 the numbers following 943.10 in 943.101–943.108,
>>> e.g., Brandenburg and Berlin during period of German
>>> Confederation 943.1507

.2   *Saxony and Thuringia

.201–.208   Historical periods

> Add to base number 943.20 the numbers following 943.10 in
> 943.101–943.108, e.g., period as part of East Germany 943.2087

.21–.22   Localities of Saxony and Thuringia

> Add to base number 943.2 the numbers following —432 in notation
> 4321–4322 from Table 2, e.g., Saxony (Sachsen) 943.21; then add further as
> follows:
>> 001–009   Standard subdivisions
>>> Add to 00 the numbers following 00 in notation 001–009
>>> from table under 930–990, e.g., ethnic and national groups
>>> 004, ethnic and national groups in Saxony (Sachsen)
>>> 943.21004
>> 01–08   Historical periods
>>> Add to 0 the numbers following 943.10 in 943.101–943.108,
>>> e.g., Saxony (Sachsen) during period as part of East
>>> Germany 943.21087

.3–.5   Localities of Bavaria (Bayern), southwestern Germany, northwestern Germany

> Add to base number 943 the numbers following —43 in notation 433–435 from
> Table 2, e.g., Bonn 943.5518; then add further as follows:
>> 001–009   Standard subdivisions
>>> Add to 00 the numbers following 00 in notation 001–009
>>> from table under 930–990, e.g., ethnic and national groups
>>> 004, ethnic and national groups in Bonn 943.5518004
>> 01–08   Historical periods
>>> Add to 0 the numbers following 943.0 in 943.01–943.08, e.g.,
>>> Bonn during period of German Confederation, 1815–1866
>>> 943.551807

.6   *Austria and Liechtenstein

> Subdivisions are added for Austria and Liechtenstein together, for Austria alone

> *For ancient history to 476, see 936.36*

---

*Add as instructed under 930–990

(.601)	Ancient history to 476

(Optional number; prefer 936.36)

> 943.602–943.605 Historical periods of Austria and Liechtenstein together, of Austria alone

Class comprehensive works in 943.6

.602	Medieval period, 476–1526
.602 2	476–976
.602 3	Period of House of Babenberg, 976–1246

Including 13th century

For 1246–1273, see 943.6024; for 1273–1299, see 943.6025

.602 4	1246–1273
.602 5	1273–1526
.603	1526–1815

Class here comprehensive works on period of House of Habsburg, 1273–1919

For a specific part of the period of House of Habsburg, see the part, e.g., period of Austro-Hungarian Monarchy 943.6044, period of House of Habsburg in Spain 946.04

.603 1	1526–1740
.603 2	1740–1815

Class here 18th century

For 1700–1740, see 943.6031

See also 940.2532 for War of the Austrian Succession

.604	1815–1918

Class here Austrian Empire, 1804–1918

For Austrian Empire during 1804–1815, see 943.6032

.604 2	1815–1848
.604 3	1848–1867
.604 4	Period of Austro-Hungarian Monarchy, 1867–1918
.604 41	1867–1914
.604 42	Period of World War I, 1914–1918
.605	1918–
.605 1	Period of First Republic, 1918–1938
.605 11	1918–1933
.605 12	1933–1938

.605 2	1938–1955
.605 22	Anschluss and World War II periods, 1938–1945
	Standard subdivisions are added for either or both topics in heading
.605 23	1945–1955
.605 3	1955–
	Class here period of Second Republic, 1945–
	For 1945–1955, see 943.60523
.605 32	1955–1970
.605 33	1970–1983
.605 34	1983–1999
.605 35	2000–
.61–.66	Localities of Austria

Add to base number 943.6 the numbers following —436 in notation 4361–4366 from Table 2, e.g., eastern Austria 943.61; however, for Liechtenstein, see 943.648; then add further as follows:

    001–009   Standard subdivisions

            Add to 00 the numbers following 00 in notation 001–009 from table under 930–990, e.g., ethnic and national groups 004, ethnic and national groups in eastern Austria 943.61004

    (01)   Ancient history to 476

            (Optional number; prefer 936.361–936.366)

    02–05   476 to present

            Add to 0 the numbers following 943.60 in 943.602–943.605, e.g., eastern Austria during 1918 to present 943.6105

.64	*Western Austria, and Liechtenstein

Subdivisions are added for Western Austria and Liechtenstein together, for Western Austria alone

.648	†Liechtenstein

For ancient history to 476, see 936.3648

.7   *Czech Republic and Slovakia

.702	Early history to 1918
.702 1	Early history to 907
	Including Great Moravian Empire
.702 2	907–1526
.702 23	Period of Přemyslid dynasty, 907–1306

---

*Add as instructed under 930–990

†Add as instructed under 930–990; however, do not add historical periods

.702 24	Period of House of Luxemburg, 1306–1526
	Including Hussite Wars, 1419–1436
.702 3	1526–1815
.702 32	1526–1620
.702 33	1620–1800
.702 34	1800–1815
.702 4	1815–1918
.703	1918–1992
	Class here Czechoslovakia
	For 1945–1992, see 943.704
.703 2	Period of Czechoslovak Republic, 1918–1939
.703 3	1939–1945
	Class here Protectorate of Bohemia and Moravia
.704	1945–1992
.704 2	1945–1968
	Including reform and repression, 1968
.704 3	1968–1992
.705	1993–
	Period of two sovereign nations
.71	*Czech Republic
	For Moravia, see 943.72
.710 2–.710 4	Early history to 1992
	Add to base number 943.710 the numbers following 943.70 in 943.702–943.704, e.g., Kingdom of Bohemia 943.7102
.710 5	Period of Republic, 1993–
.710 51	1993–
.710 511	Administration of Václav Havel, 1993–2003
.710 512	Administration of Václav Klaus, 2003–2013
.710 513	Administration of Miloš Zeman, 2013–

*Add as instructed under 930–990

.711–.719   Localities of Czech Republic

> Add to base number 943.71 the numbers following —4371 in notation 43711–43719 from Table 2, e.g., Středočeský Region (Středočeský Kraj) 943.711; then add further as follows:
> 001–009   Standard subdivisions
>> Add to 00 the numbers following 00 in notation 001–009 from table under 930–990, e.g., ethnic and national groups 004, ethnic and national groups in Středočeský Region (Středočeský Kraj) 943.711004
> 02–05   Historical periods
>> Add to 0 the numbers following 943.710 in 943.7102–943.7105, e.g., Středočeský Region (Středočeský Kraj) during period of Republic, 1993 to present 943.71105

.72   *Moravia

.720 2–.720 5   Historical periods

> Add to base number 943.720 the numbers following 943.70 in 943.702–943.705, e.g.; period as a part of Czech Republic 943.7205

.722–.728   Localities of Moravia

> Add to base number 943.72 the numbers following —4372 in notation 43722–43728 from Table 2, e.g., Vysočina Region (Vysočina Kraj) 943.722; then add further as follows:
> 001–009   Standard subdivisions
>> Add to 00 the numbers following 00 in notation 001–009 from table under 930–990, e.g., ethnic and national groups 004, ethnic and national groups in Vysočina Region (Vysočina Kraj) 943.722004
> 02–05   Historical periods
>> Add to 0 the numbers following 943.70 in 943.702–943.705, e.g., Vysočina Region (Vysočina Kraj) during period as a part of Czech Republic 943.72205

.73   *Slovakia

.730 2–.730 4   Early history to 1992

> Add to base number 943.730 the numbers following 943.70 in 943.702–943.704, e.g., Slovak Republic, 1939–1945, 943.73033

.730 5   Period of Slovak Republic, 1993–

.730 51   1993–

.730 511   1993–1999

> Class here administration of Michal Kováč, 1993–1998

.730 512   Administration of Rudolf Schuster, 1999–2004

.730 513   Administration of Ivan Gašparovič, 2004–2014

.730 514   Administration of Andrej Kiska, 2014–

*Add as instructed under 930–990

.731–.738	Localities of Slovakia

Add to base number 943.73 the numbers following —4373 in notation 43731–43738 from Table 2, e.g., Bratislava Region (Bratislava Kraj) 943.731; then add further as follows:

    001–009   Standard subdivisions

                  Add to 00 the numbers following 00 in notation 001–009 from table under 930–990, e.g., ethnic and national groups 004, ethnic and national groups in Bratislava Region (Bratislava Kraj) 943.731004

    02–05   Historical periods

                  Add to 0 the numbers following 943.730 in 943.7302–943.7305, e.g., Bratislava Region (Bratislava Kraj) during period of Slovak Republic, 1993 to present 943.73105

.8	***Poland**
.802	Early history to 1795
.802 2	Early history to 1370

          Including period of Piast dynasty

.802 3	Period of Jagellon dynasty, 1370–1572

          Including 16th century

          For 1572–1599, see 943.8024

.802 4	Period of elective kings, 1572–1697
.802 5	1697–1795

          Including partitions of 1772, 1793, 1795

.803	Period of foreign rule, 1795–1918
.803 2	1795–1862
.803 3	1863–1918
.804	Period of Republic, 1918–1939
.805	1939–

          Class here 20th century

          For 1900–1918, see 943.8033; for 1918–1939, see 943.804

.805 3	1939–1945
.805 4	1945–1956
.805 5	1956–1980
.805 6	1980–1989
.805 7	1989–

*Add as instructed under 930–990

.805 71	1989–1995
	Class here administration of Lech Wałęsa, 1990–1995
.805 72	Administration of Aleksander Kwaśniewski, 1995–2005
.805 73	Administration of Lech Kaczyński, 2005–2010
.805 74	Administration of Bronisław Komorowski, 2010–2015
.805 75	Administration of Andrzej Duda, 2015–

.81–.86   Localities of Poland

> Add to base number 943.8 the numbers following —438 in notation 4381–4386 from Table 2, e.g., northwestern Poland 943.81; then add further as follows:
> 001–009   Standard subdivisions
> > Add to 00 the numbers following 00 in notation 001–009 from table under 930–990, e.g., ethnic and national groups 004, ethnic and national groups in Northwestern Poland 943.81004
> 02–05   Historical periods
> > Add to 0 the numbers following 943.80 in 943.802–943.805, e.g., northwestern Poland during 1939 to present 943.8105

.9   *Hungary

.901   Early history to 894

> *For ancient history to ca. 640, see 939.8*

(.901 1)   Ancient history to ca. 640

> (Optional number; prefer 939.8)

.902   Period of House of Árpád, 894–1301

.903   Period of elective kings, 1301–1526

.904   Turkish and House of Habsburg periods, 1526–1918

.904 1   Turkish period, 1526–1686

> Including 16th century

> *For 1500–1526, see 943.903*

.904 2   Period of House of Habsburg, 1686–1918

> *For period of Austro-Hungarian Monarchy, see 943.9043*

.904 3   Period of Austro-Hungarian Monarchy, 1867–1918

.905   1918–

.905 1   1918–1941

.905 2   1942–1956

> Including uprising and suppression, 1956

*Add as instructed under 930–990

.905 3	1956–1989
.905 4	1989–
.905 41	1989–2000
	Class here administration of Árpád Göncz, 1990–2000
.905 42	Administration of Ferenc Mádl, 2000–2005
.905 43	Administration of László Sólyom, 2005–2010
.905 44	Administration of Pál Schmitt, 2010–2012
.905 45	2012–
	Class here administration of János Áder, 2012–

.91–.99   Localities of Hungary

> Add to base number 943.9 the numbers following —439 in notation
> 4391–4399 from Table 2, e.g., Pest county and Budapest 943.91; then add
> further as follows:
>
> 001–009   Standard subdivisions
> Add to 00 the numbers following 00 in notation 001–009
> from table under 930–990, e.g., ethnic and national
> groups 004, ethnic and national groups in Pest county and
> Budapest 943.91004
>
> 01–05   Historical periods
> Add to 0 the numbers following 943.90 in 943.901–943.905,
> e.g., Pest county and Budapest during 1918 to present
> 943.9105

944   *France and Monaco

Subdivisions are added for France and Monaco together, for France alone

---

>   944.01–944.08 Historical periods of France and Monaco together, of
>   France alone

Class comprehensive works in 944

.01   Early history to 987

For ancient history to 486, see 936.4

(.012)   Ancient history to 486

(Optional number; prefer 936.4)

(.012 1)   Early history to 125 B.C.

(Optional number; prefer 936.401)

(.012 2)   Gallo-Roman period, 125 B.C.–486 A.D.

(Optional number; prefer 936.402)

---

*Add as instructed under 930–990

.013	Period of Merovingian dynasty, 486–751

Including 8th century

Class here comprehensive works on Merovingian dynasty in France and Germany

For Merovingian dynasty in Germany, see 943.013; for 751–800, see 944.014

.014	Period of Carolingian dynasty, 751–987

Class here comprehensive works on Carolingian dynasty in France, Germany, and Italy

For Carolingian dynasty in Germany, see 943.014; for Carolingian dynasty in Italy, see 945.02

.014 2	Reign of Charlemagne, 768–814
.02	Medieval period, 987–1589
.021	Period of Capetian dynasty, 987–1328

Including reigns of Hugh Capet, Robert II, Henry I, 987–1060; 11th century

For reigns of other Capetian kings, see 944.022–944.024; for 1060–1099, see 944.022

.022	Reigns of Philip I, Louis VI, Louis VII, 1060–1180
.023	Reigns of Philip II, Louis VIII, Louis IX, 1180–1270

Class here 13th century

For 1270–1299, see 944.024

.024	Reigns of Philip III, Philip IV, Louis X, Jean I, Philip V, Charles IV, 1270–1328
.025	‡Period of House of Valois, 1328–1589

Including reigns of Philip VI, Jean II, Charles V, 1328–1380

Class here Hundred Years' War, 1337–1453; 14th century (Option: Class Hundred Years' War in 942.037)

For 1300–1328, see 944.024; for reigns of other Valois kings, see 944.026–944.029

.026	Reigns of Charles VI and Charles VII, 1380–1461

Class here 15th century

For 1461–1499, see 944.027

.027	Reigns of Louis XI, Charles VIII, Louis XII, 1461–1515

Class French invasions of Italy, 1494–1559 in 945.06

‡Add as instructed under 940–990

.028   **Period of House of Angoulême, 1515–1589**

       Including reigns of Francis I and Henry II, 1515–1559

       Class here campaigns and battles of wars between France and Holy Roman Empire fought outside of Italy, 1521–1599; 16th century

       Class French invasions of Italy during period of House of Angoulême in 945.06

       For 1500–1515, see 944.027; for reigns of Francis II, Charles IX, Henry III, see 944.029; for 1589–1600, see 944.031

.029   **Reigns of Francis II, Charles IX, Henry III, 1559–1589**

.03   **Period of House of Bourbon, 1589–1789**

.031   **Reign of Henry IV, 1589–1610**

.032   **Reign of Louis XIII, 1610–1643**

.033   **Reign of Louis XIV, 1643–1715**

       Including War of Devolution, 1667–1668

       Class here 17th century

       For 1600–1610, see 944.031; for 1610–1643, see 944.032

.034   **Reign of Louis XV, 1715–1774**

       Class here 18th century

       For a specific part of 18th century not provided for here, see the part, e.g., Reign of Terror 944.044

.035   **1774–1789**

       Class here period of Louis XVI, 1774–1792

       For period of Louis XVI during 1789–1792, see 944.041

.04   **Revolutionary period, 1789–1804**

.041   **Period of Estates-General, National Assembly, Legislative Assembly, 1789–1792**

.042   **Period of First Republic, 1792–1799**

       Including Vendean War, 1793–1800

       For period of National Convention, see 944.043; for period of Directory, see 944.045

.043   **Period of National Convention, 1792–1795**

       For Reign of Terror, see 944.044

.044   **Period of Reign of Terror, 1793–1794**

.045   **Period of Directory, 1795–1799**

.046   **Period of Consulate, 1799–1804**

.05	Period of First Empire, 1804–1815

    Including reign of Louis XVIII, 1814–1815; Hundred Days, 1815

    Class here reign of Napoleon I, 1804–1814

    Class Napoleonic Wars in 940.27

.06	Period of Restoration, 1815–1848

    Class here 19th century

    For a specific part of 19th century not provided for here, see the part, e.g., Second Empire 944.07

.061	Reign of Louis XVIII, 1815–1824
.062	Reign of Charles X, 1824–1830
.063	Period of Louis Philippe, 1830–1848 (July Monarchy)
.07	Period of Second Republic and Second Empire (period of Napoleon III), 1848–1870

    (Option: Class here Franco-German War; prefer 943.082)

.08	1870–
.081	Period of Third Republic, 1870–1945

    Class here 20th century

    For 1945–1958, see 944.082; for 1958–1999, see 944.083

.081 2	1870–1899

    Including Paris Commune, 1871

.081 3	1900–1914
.081 4	Period of World War I, 1914–1918
.081 5	1918–1939
.081 6	Period of World War II, 1939–1945
.082	Period of Fourth Republic, 1945–1958
.083	Period of Fifth Republic, 1958–

    For 2000 to present, see 944.084

.083 6	1958–1969
.083 7	1970–1979
.083 8	1980–1989
.083 9	1990–1999
.084	2000–
.084 1	2000–2019
.084 11	2000–2009

.084 12	2010–2019
.084 2	2020–2029

.1–.9   Localities of France

> Add to base number 944 the numbers following —44 in notation 441–449 from Table 2, e.g., Brittany (Bretagne) and Pays de la Loire 944.1; however, for Monaco, see 944.949; for Corsica (Corse), see 944.99; then add further as follows:
>
>   001–009   Standard subdivisions
>
>   Add to 00 the numbers following 00 in notation 001–009 from table under 930–990, e.g., ethnic and national groups 004, ethnic and national groups in Brittany (Bretagne) and Pays de la Loire 944.1004
>
>   01–08   Historical periods
>
>   Add to 0 the numbers following 944.0 in 944.01–944.08, e.g., Brittany (Bretagne) and Pays de la Loire during 1870 to present 944.108

.9   *Provence-Alpes-Côte d'Azur, Monaco, Corsica

> Subdivisions are added for Provence-Alpes-Côte d'Azur, Monaco, Corsica together; for Provence-Alpes-Côte d'Azur alone

.94   *Alpes-Maritimes department and Monaco

.949   †Monaco

> *For ancient history to 486, see 936.4*

.99   *Corsica (Corse)

.990 1   Early history to 1077

> *For ancient history to 453, see 937.99*

(.990 12)   Ancient history to 453

> (Optional number; prefer 937.99)

.990 2   Pisan period, 1077–1347

> Including assumption of sovereignty by Pope Gregory VII, 1077

.990 3   Genoan period, 1347–1768

> Including 14th century, 18th century
>
> *For 1300–1347, see 944.9902; for 1768–1799, see 944.9904*

.990 4   1768–1804

> Including British period, 1794–1796
>
> Class here periods as part of France, 1768–1794, 1796–1804

---

*Add as instructed under 930–990

†Add as instructed under 930–990; however, do not add historical periods

.990 5–.990 8	1804–

Add to base number 944.990 the numbers following 944.0 in 944.05–944.08, e.g., period of Third Republic 944.99081

.992–.996	Localities of Corsica (Corse)

Add to base number 944.99 the numbers following —4499 in notation 44992–44996 from Table 2, e.g., Corse-du-Sud department 944.992; then add further as follows:

001–009	Standard subdivisions

Add to 00 the numbers following 00 in notation 001–009 from table under 930–990, e.g., ethnic and national groups 004, ethnic and national groups in Corse-du-Sud department 944.992004

01–08	Historical periods

Add to 0 the numbers following 944.990 in 944.9901–944.9908, e.g., Corse-du-Sud department during 1768–1804 944.99204

945   *Italy, San Marino, Vatican City, Malta

Subdivisions are added for Italy, San Marino, Vatican City, Malta together; for Italy alone

---

>   945.01–945.09 Historical periods of Italy, San Marino, Vatican City, Malta together; of Italy alone

Class comprehensive works in 945

.01	Early history to 774

Including Ostrogothic and Lombard kingdoms, 476–774

Class here comprehensive works on medieval period (Middle Ages)

For ancient history to 476, see 937; for Early Middle Ages, see 945.02; for Late Middle Ages, see 945.04

(.012)	Ancient history to 476

(Optional number; prefer 937)

Add to base number 945.012 the numbers following 937.0 in 937.01–937.09, e.g., Punic Wars 945.0124

.02	Period of Carolingian dynasty, 774–962

Including 10th century

Class here comprehensive works on Early Middle Ages (Dark Ages)

Class comprehensive works on Carolingian dynasty in 944.014

For Early Middle Ages during 476–774, see 945.01; for Early Middle Ages during 962–1122, see 945.03

.03	Period of German emperors, 962–1122

*Add as instructed under 930–990

.04	1122–1348

Class here comprehensive works on Late Middle Ages

For Late Middle Ages during 1348–1492, see 945.05

.05	Period of Black Death to invasion of Charles VIII, 1348–1494

Including 14th century

Class here Renaissance period

.06	1494–1527

Class here French invasions of Italy, 1494–1559; comprehensive works on Italian Wars, 1494–1559; campaigns and battles of wars between France and Holy Roman Empire fought in Italy, comprehensive works on campaigns and battles of wars between France and Holy Roman Empire, 1521–1599;

For campaigns and battles of wars between France and Holy Roman Empire fought outside of Italy, 1521–1599, see 944.028; for Italian Wars during 1527–1559, see 945.07

.07	Spanish and Austrian period, 1527–1796

Including 16th century

For 1500–1527, see 945.06

.08	1796–1900
.082	Napoleonic period, 1796–1815

Including Kingdom of Italy, 1805–1814

.083	Period of Risorgimento, 1815–1861
.084	Reigns of Victor Emmanuel II and Umberto I, 1861–1900

Class here Roman question; period of House of Savoy in Kingdom of Italy, 1861–1946; comprehensive works on period of House of Savoy in Italy, 1343–1946

For comprehensive works on period of House of Savoy in Piedmont, see 945.105; for reign of Victor Emmanuel III, see 945.091

.09	1900–
.091	Reign of Victor Emmanuel III, 1900–1946

Including Fascist period, 1922–1943

Class here 20th century

For 1946–1999, see 945.092

.092	Period of Republic, 1946–

For 2000 to present, see 945.093

.092 4	1946–1949
.092 5	1950–1959
.092 6	1960–1969

.092 7	1970–1979
.092 8	1980–1989
.092 9	1990–1999
.093	2000–
.093 1	2000–2019
.093 11	2000–2009
.093 12	2010–2019
.093 2	2020–2029

.1   ***Northwestern Italy**

> Class here Piedmont (Piemonte) region

.101   Early history to 774

> Class here comprehensive works on medieval period (Middle Ages)

>>*For ancient history to 476, see 937.222; for Early Middle Ages, see 945.102; for Late Middle Ages, see 945.104*

(.101 2)   Ancient history to 476

> (Optional number; prefer 937.222)

> Add to base number 945.1012 the numbers following 937.0 in 937.01–937.09, e.g., Punic Wars 945.10124

.102   Period of Carolingian dynasty, 774–962

> Including 10th century

> Class here comprehensive works on Early Middle Ages (Dark Ages)

>>*For Early Middle Ages during 476–774, see 945.101; for Early Middle Ages during 962–1122, see 945.103*

.103   Period of German emperors, 962–1122

> Class here Margravate of Ivrea

.104   1122–1343

> Class here comprehensive works on Late Middle Ages

>>*For Late Middle Ages during 1343–1492, see 945.105*

*Add as instructed under 930–990

.105   **Period of House of Savoy to death of Philibert II, 1343–1504**

             Including 14th century

             Class here comprehensive works on period of House of Savoy in Piedmont, 1343–1861

             Class comprehensive works on period of House of Savoy in Italy, 1343–1946, in 945.084

                For a specific part of the period of House of Savoy in Piedmont, see the part, e.g., House of Savoy during Napoleonic period 945.1082

.106   **Period of Charles III, 1504–1553**

             Class here 16th century

                For 1553–1600, see 945.107

.107   **Period of Emmanuel Philibert through Victor Amadeus III, 1553–1796**

             Including comprehensive works on Kingdom of Sardinia, 1718–1861

                For Kingdom of Sardinia during 1796–1815, see 945.1082; for Kingdom of Sardinia during 1815–1861, see 945.1083; for Kingdom of Sardinia in Sardinia, see 945.907

.108   **1796–1900**

.108 2   Napoleonic period, 1796–1815

             Class here reign of Victor Emmanuel I, 1802–1821

                For reign of Victor Emmanuel I during 1815–1821, see 945.1083

.108 3   Period of Risorgimento, 1815–1861

.108 4   Reigns of Victor Emmanuel II and Umberto I, 1861–1900

.109   1900–

             Add to base number 945.109 the numbers following 945.09 in 945.091–945.093, e.g., Piedmont during the Fascist period 945.1091

.11   *Valle d'Aosta region

.110 1–.110 9   Historical periods

             Add to base number 945.110 the numbers following 945.0 in 945.01–945.09, e.g., Valle d'Aosta during the Fascist period 945.11091

                For ancient history to 476, see 937.221

.111   *Aosta

.111 01–.111 09   Historical periods

             Add to base number 945.1110 the numbers following 945.0 in 945.01–945.09, e.g., Aosta during the Fascist period 945.111091

---

*Add as instructed under 930–990

.12–.17	Localities of Piedmont (Piemonte) region

Add to base number 945.1 the numbers following —451 in notation 4512–4517 from Table 2, e.g., Turin 945.121; then add further as follows:
- 001–009   Standard subdivisions

         Add to 00 the numbers following 00 in notation 001–009 from table under 930–990, e.g., ethnic and national groups 004, ethnic and national groups in Turin 945.121004

- 01–09   Historical periods

         Add to 0 the numbers following 945.10 in 945.101–945.109, e.g., Turin during 1900 to present 945.12109

.18	*Liguria region

Class here period of Republic of Genoa, 1056–1797

.180 1–.180 9	Historical periods

Add to base number 945.180 the numbers following 945.0 in 945.01–945.09, e.g., Ligurian Republic, 1797–1805 945.18082

For ancient history to 476, see 937.1

.182–.187	Localities of Liguria region

Add to base number 945.18 the numbers following —4518 in notation 45182–45187 from Table 2, e.g., Genoa (Genova) Metropolitan City 945.182; then add further as follows:
- 001–009   Standard subdivisions

         Add to 00 the numbers following 00 in notation 001–009 from table under 930–990, e.g., ethnic and national groups 004, ethnic and national groups in Genoa (Genova) Metropolitan City 945.182004

- 01–09   Historical periods

         Add to 0 the numbers following 945.0 in 945.01–945.09, e.g., Genoa (Genova) Metropolitan City during Ligurian Republic, 1797–1805 945.182082

.2	***Lombardy (Lombardia) region**
.201	Early history to 774

Class here comprehensive works on medieval period (Middle Ages)

For ancient history to 476, see 937.22; for Early Middle Ages, see 945.202; for Late Middle Ages, see 945.204

(.201 2)	Ancient history to 476

(Optional number; prefer 937.22)

Add to base number 945.2012 the numbers following 937.0 in 937.01–937.09, e.g., Punic Wars 945.20124

---

*Add as instructed under 930–990

.202	Period of Carolingian dynasty, 774–962

Including 10th century

Class here comprehensive works on Early Middle Ages (Dark Ages)

For Early Middle Ages during 476–774, see 945.201; for Early Middle Ages during 962–1122, see 945.203

.203	Period of German emperors, 962–1122
.204	1122–1277
.205	Period of House of Visconti, 1277–1447

Class here comprehensive works on Late Middle Ages

.206	Period of House of Sforza, 1447–1535

Including 15th century

For 1400–1447, see 945.205

.207	Spanish and Austrian period, 1535–1796

Including 16th century

For 1500–1527, see 945.206

.208	1796–1900
.208 2	Napoleonic period, 1796–1815

Including Cisalpine Republic, 1797–1802

.208 3	Period of Risorgimento, 1815–1861
.208 4	Reigns of Victor Emmanuel II and Umberto I, 1861–1900
.209	1900–

Add to base number 945.209 the numbers following 945.09 in 945.091–945.093, e.g., Lombardy during the Fascist period 945.2091

.21–.29	Localities of Lombardy (Lombardia) region

Add to base number 945.2 the numbers following —452 in notation 4521–4529 from Table 2, e.g., Pavia province 945.29; then add further as follows:

    001–009   Standard subdivisions
                  Add to 00 the numbers following 00 in notation 001–009 from table under 930–990, e.g., ethnic and national groups 004, ethnic and national groups in Pavia province 945.29004

    01–09   Historical periods
                  Add to 0 the numbers following 945.20 in 945.201–945.209, e.g., Pavia province during 1900 to present 945.2909

.3   ***Northeastern Italy**

Class here Veneto region; period of Republic of Venice, 810–1797

*Add as instructed under 930–990

.301	Early history to 774

Class here comprehensive works on medieval period (Middle Ages)

For ancient history to 476, see 937.3; for Early Middle Ages, see 945.302; for Late Middle Ages, see 945.304

(.301 2)	Ancient history to 476

(Optional number; prefer 937.3)

Add to base number 945.3012 the numbers following 937.0 in 937.01–937.09, e.g., Punic Wars 945.30124

.302	Period of Carolingian dynasty, 774–962

Including 10th century

Class here comprehensive works on Early Middle Ages (Dark Ages)

For Early Middle Ages during 476–774, see 945.301; for Early Middle Ages during 962–1122, see 945.303

.303	Period of German emperors, 962–1122
.304	1122–1339

Including period of House of Scaliger, 1259–1339

Class here comprehensive works on Late Middle Ages

For Late Middle Ages during 1339–1494, see 945.305

.305	Period after defeat of House of Scaliger to invasion of Charles VIII, 1339–1494

Including 14th century

.306	Period of invasion of Charles VIII to Treaty of Noyon, 1494–1516
.307	Period after Treaty of Noyon to Treaty of Campo Formio, 1516–1797

For wars between Venice and Ottoman Empire, see 949.505

.308	1797–1900
.308 2	Napoleonic period, 1797–1815
.308 3	Period of Risorgimento, 1815–1866

Including Venetian Republic, 1849

.308 4	Reigns of Victor Emmanuel II and Umberto I, 1866–1900
.309	1900–

Add to base number 945.309 the numbers following 945.09 in 945.091–945.093, e.g., Veneto region during the Fascist period 945.3091

.31–.37   Localities of Veneto region

> Add to base number 945.3 the numbers following —453 in notation
> 4531–4537 from Table 2, e.g., Venice (Venezia) Metropolitan City 945.31;
> then add further as follows:
>> 001–009   Standard subdivisions
>>> Add to 00 the numbers following 00 in notation 001–009
>>> from table under 930–990, e.g., ethnic and national groups
>>> 004, ethnic and national groups in Venice (Venezia)
>>> Metropolitan City 945.31004
>> 01–09   Historical periods
>>> Add to 0 the numbers following 945.30 in 945.301–945.309,
>>> e.g., Venice (Venezia) Metropolitan City during 1900 to
>>> present 945.3109

.38   *Trentino-Alto Adige region

.380 1–.380 9   Historical periods

> Add to base number 945.380 the numbers following 945.0 in
> 945.01–945.09, e.g., Trentino-Alto Adige region during the Fascist
> period 945.38091

> *For ancient history to 476, see 937.37*

.383–.385   Localities of Trentino-Alto Adige region

> Add to base number 945.38 the numbers following —4538 in notation
> 45383–45385 from Table 2, e.g., Bolzano province 945.383; then add
> further as follows:
>> 001–009   Standard subdivisions
>>> Add to 00 the numbers following 00 in notation
>>> 001–009 from table under 930–990, e.g., ethnic and
>>> national groups 004, ethnic and national groups in
>>> Bolzano province 945.383004
>> 01–09   Historical periods
>>> Add to 0 the numbers following 945.0 in 945.01–945.09,
>>> e.g., Bolzano province during the Fascist period
>>> 945.383091

.39   *Friuli-Venezia Giulia region

.390 1–.390 9   Historical periods

> Add to base number 945.390 the numbers following 945.0 in
> 945.01–945.09, e.g., Friuli-Venezia Giulia region during the Fascist
> period 945.39091

> *For ancient history to 476, see 937.38*

*Add as instructed under 930–990

.391–.394   Localities of Friuli-Venezia Giulia region

> Add to base number 945.39 the numbers following —4539 in notation 45391–45394 from Table 2, e.g., Udine province 945.391; then add further as follows:
>> 001–009   Standard subdivisions
>>> Add to 00 the numbers following 00 in notation 001–009 from table under 930–990, e.g., ethnic and national groups 004, ethnic and national groups in Udine province 945.391004
>> 01–09   Historical periods
>>> Add to 0 the numbers following 945.0 in 945.01–945.09, e.g., Udine province during the Fascist period 945.391091

.4   *Emilia-Romagna region and San Marino

> Subdivisions are added for Emilia-Romagna region and San Marino together, for Emilia-Romagna region alone

.41–.48   Localities of Emilia-Romagna region

> Add to base number 945.4 the numbers following —454 in notation 4541–4548 from Table 2, e.g., Bologna Metropolitan City 945.41; then add further as follows:
>> 001–009   Standard subdivisions
>>> Add to 00 the numbers following 00 in notation 001–009 from table under 930–990, e.g., ethnic and national groups 004, ethnic and national groups in Bologna Metropolitan City 945.41004
>> 01–09   Historical periods
>>> Add to 0 the numbers following 945.0 in 945.01–945.09, e.g., Bologna Metropolitan City during 1900 to present 945.4109

.49   †San Marino

> *For ancient history to 476, see 937.269*

.5   *Tuscany (Toscana) region

> Class here period of city-state of Florence, ca. 1100–1569

.501   Early history to 774

> Class here comprehensive works on medieval period (Middle Ages)

> *For ancient history to 476, see 937.5; for Early Middle Ages, see 945.502; for Late Middle Ages, see 945.504*

(.501 2)   Ancient history to 476

> (Optional number; prefer 937.5)

> Add to base number 945.5012 the numbers following 937.0 in 937.01–937.09, e.g., Punic Wars 945.50124

---

*Add as instructed under 930–990
†Add as instructed under 930–990; however, do not add historical periods

.502   **Period of Carolingian dynasty, 774–962**

       Including 10th century

       Class here comprehensive works on Early Middle Ages (Dark Ages)

       For Early Middle Ages during 476–774, see 945.501; for Early Middle Ages during 962–1122, see 945.503

.503   **Period of House of Attoni, 962–1115**

.504   **1115–1348**

       Class here comprehensive works on Late Middle Ages

       For Late Middle Ages during 1348–1492, see 945.505

.505   **Period of Black Death to invasion of Charles VIII, 1348–1494**

       Including 14th century

       Class here period of House of Medici during 1434–1494; comprehensive works on period of House of Medici

       For period of House of Medici during 1512–1527, see 945.506; for period of Ducal Medici, see 945.507

.506   **1494–1531**

       Including period of invasion of Charles VIII, 1494–1495; period of House of Medici during 1512–1527

       Class here periods of Florence as a republic, 1494–1512 and 1527–1530

       Class comprehensive works on period of House of Medici in 945.505

.507   **1531–1801**

       Including period of Ducal Medici, 1531–1737; 16th century; period of House of Lorraine, 1737–1801, comprehensive works on House of Lorraine

       Class here Grand Duchy of Tuscany during 1569–1801, comprehensive works on Grand Duchy of Tuscany

       For 1500–1531, see 945.506; for Grand Duchy of Tuscany and House of Lorraine during 1814–1860, see 945.5083

.508   **1801–1900**

.508 2   **Napoleonic period, 1801–1814**

       Class here Kingdom of Etruria, 1801–1807

.508 3   **Period of Risorgimento, 1814–1861**

       Class here Grand Duchy of Tuscany and House of Lorraine during 1814–1860

       Class comprehensive works on Grand Duchy of Tuscany and House of Lorraine in 945.507

.508 4   **Reigns of Victor Emmanuel II and Umberto I, 1861–1900**

.509	1900–

Add to base number 945.509 the numbers following 945.09 in 945.091–945.093, e.g., Tuscany during the Fascist period 945.5091

.51–.59   Localities of Tuscany (Toscana) region

Add to base number 945.5 the numbers following —455 in notation 4551–4559 from Table 2, e.g., Florence (Firenze) Metropolitan City and Prato province 945.51; then add further as follows:
001–009   Standard subdivisions
Add to 00 the numbers following 00 in notation 001–009 from table under 930–990, e.g., ethnic and national groups 004, ethnic and national groups in Florence (Firenze) Metropolitan City and Prato province 945.51004
01–09   Historical periods
Add to 0 the numbers following 945.50 in 945.501–945.509, e.g., Florence (Firenze) Metropolitan City and Prato province during 1900 to present 945.5109

.6   *Central Italy and Vatican City

Class here Papal States (States of the Church), 728–1870

Subdivisions are added for central Italy and Vatican City together, for central Italy alone

For a specific part of Papal States, see the part, e.g., Tuscany 945.5, Marches 945.67

.601–.609   Historical periods

Add to base number 945.60 the numbers following 945.0 in 945.01–945.09, e.g., Central Italy during the Fascist period 945.6091

For ancient history to 476, see 937.6

.62–.67   Localities of central Italy

Add to base number 945.6 the numbers following —456 in notation 4562–4567 from Table 2, e.g., Lazio region 945.62; however, for Vatican City, see 945.634; then add further as follows:
001–009   Standard subdivisions
Add to 00 the numbers following 00 in notation 001–009 from table under 930–990, e.g., ethnic and national groups 004, ethnic and national groups in Lazio region 945.62004
01–09   Historical periods
Add to 0 the numbers following 945.0 in 945.01–945.09, e.g., Lazio region during the Fascist period 945.62091

.63   *Rome Capital (Roma Capitale) Metropolitan City and Vatican City

Subdivisions are added for Rome Capital (Roma Capitale) Metropolitan City and Vatican City together, for Rome (Roma Capitale) Metropolitan City alone

.634   †Vatican City

---

*Add as instructed under 930–990
†Add as instructed under 930–990; however, do not add historical periods

.7   ***Southern Italy**

> Class here period of Kingdom of Naples, 1266–1815
>
> *For ancient history to 476, see 937.7; for Sicily, see 945.8*

.701   Early history to 774

> Including comprehensive works on Byzantine period, 553–1071, on Lombardic period, 568–1076
>
> Class here comprehensive works on medieval period (Middle Ages)
>
> > *For ancient history to 476, see 937.7; for Early Middle Ages, see 945.702; for Late Middle Ages, see 945.704. For a part of Byzantine or Lombardic period not provided for here, see the part, e.g., Byzantine or Lombardic period during 1030–1071 945.703*

(.701 2)   Ancient history to 476

> (Optional number; prefer 937.7)
>
> Add to base number 945.7012 the numbers following 937.0 in 937.01–937.09, e.g., Punic Wars 945.70124

.702   Period of conflict between Byzantines and Arabs to start of Norman period, 774–1030

> Class here comprehensive works on Early Middle Ages (Dark Ages)
>
> > *For Early Middle Ages during 476–774, see 945.701; for Early Middle Ages during 962–1111, see 945.703*

.703   Norman period, 1030–1186

> Including 11th century

.704   Period of Swabian dynasties, 1186–1266

> Class here 13th century; period of House of Hohenstaufen, 1194–1266; comprehensive works on Late Middle Ages
>
> > *For Late Middle Ages during 1266–1442, see 945.705; for Late Middle Ages during 1442–1492, see 945.706*

.705   Period of House of Anjou, 1266–1442

.706   Period as part of Kingdom of Aragon, 1442–1516

> Class here 15th century
>
> > *For 1400–1442, see 945.705*

.707   Spanish and Austrian period to Parthenopaean Republic, 1516–1799

> Including comprehensive works on period of House of Bourbon
>
> > *For period of House of Bourbon during 1815–1860, see 945.7083*

.708   1799–1900

.708 2   Napoleonic period, 1799–1815

---

*Add as instructed under 930–990

.708 3	1815–1861

        Class here period of Kingdom of the Two Sicilies, 1816–1860

        For period of Kingdom of the Two Sicilies in Sicily, see 945.8083

.708 4	Reigns of Victor Emmanuel II and Umberto I, 1861–1900
.709	1900–

        Class here questione meridionale (Southern question)

        Add to base number 945.709 the numbers following 945.09 in
        945.091–945.093, e.g., Southern Italy during the Fascist period 945.7091

.71–.78	Localities of southern Italy

        Add to base number 945.7 the numbers following —457 in notation
        4571–4578 from Table 2, e.g., Abruzzo region and Molise region 945.71;
        then add further as follows:

        001–009   Standard subdivisions

                Add to 00 the numbers following 00 in notation 001–009
                from table under 930–990, e.g., ethnic and national groups
                004, ethnic and national groups in Abruzzo region and
                Molise region 945.71004

        01–09   Historical periods

                Add to 0 the numbers following 945.70 in 945.701–945.709,
                e.g., Abruzzo region and Molise region during 1900 to
                present 945.7109

.8   *Sicily and adjacent islands

        Standard subdivisions are added for Sicily and adjacent islands together, for
        Sicily alone

        Class here period of Kingdom of Sicily, 1130–1815

.801	Early history to 827

        Including period of Ostrogothic kingdom, 476–535; period of Byzantine
        Empire, 535–827

        Class here comprehensive works on medieval period (Middle Ages)

        For ancient history to 476, see 937.8; for Early Middle Ages, see
        945.802; for Late Middle Ages, see 945.804

(.801 2)	Ancient history to 476

        (Optional number; prefer 937.8)

        Add to base number 945.8012 the numbers following 937.0 in
        937.01–937.09, e.g., Punic Wars 945.80124

*Add as instructed under 930–990

.802   Arabic period, 827–1061

           Including 9th century, 11th century

           Class here comprehensive works on Early Middle Ages (Dark Ages)

           For Early Middle Ages during 476–827, see 945.801; for Early Middle Ages during 1061–1189, see 945.803

.803   Norman period, 1061–1189

.804   Period of Swabian dynasties and House of Anjou, 1189–1302

           Including period of House of Hohenstaufen, 1194–1266

           Class here comprehensive works on Late Middle Ages

           For Late Middle Ages during 1302–1412, see 945.805; for Late Middle Ages during 1412–1492, see 945.806

.805   Period as part of Kingdom of Aragon, 1302–1412

.806   Spanish period, 1412–1712

.807   First period of House of Bourbon, 1712–1799

           Class here comprehensive works on period of House of Bourbon

           For period of House of Bourbon during 1815–1860, see 945.8083

.808   1799–1900

.808 2   Napoleonic period, 1799–1815

.808 3   1815–1861

           Class here period of Kingdom of the Two Sicilies in Sicily, 1816–1860

           Class comprehensive works on Kingdom of the Two Sicilies in 945.7083

.808 4   Reigns of Victor Emmanuel II and Umberto I, 1861–1900

.809   1900–

           Add to base number 945.809 the numbers following 945.09 in 945.091–945.093, e.g., Sicily during the Fascist period 945.8091

.81–.82   Localities of Sicily

           Add to base number 945.8 the numbers following —458 in notation 4581–4582 from Table 2, e.g., eastern Sicily 945.81; then add further as follows:

           001–009   Standard subdivisions

                         Add to 00 the numbers following 00 in notation 001–009 from table under 930–990, e.g., ethnic and national groups 004, ethnic and national groups in eastern Sicily 945.81004

           01–09   Historical periods

                         Add to 0 the numbers following 945.80 in 945.801–945.809, e.g., eastern Sicily during 1900 to present 945.8109

.85	*Malta
.850 1	Early history to 1530

                 For ancient history to 476, see 937.85

(.850 12)	Ancient history to 476

                 (Optional number; prefer 937.85)

                 Add to base number 945.85012 the numbers following 937.0 in 937.01–937.09, e.g., early period of Roman Empire 945.850127

.850 2	Period of Knights of Malta, 1530–1798

                 Including 16th century

                 For 1500–1530, see 945.8501

.850 3	1798–1964

                 Including French period, 1798–1800

                 Class here British period, 1800–1964; 20th century

                 For 1964 to present, see 945.8504

.850 4	1964–
.9	***Sardinia**
.901	Early history to 534

                 Including Vandal kingdom, 476–534, 5th century

                 For ancient history to 453, see 937.9

(.901 2)	Ancient history to 453

                 (Optional number; prefer 937.9)

                 Add to base number 945.9012 the numbers following 937.0 in 937.01–937.09, e.g., Punic Wars 945.90124

.902	Byzantine period, 534–900

                 Including 6th century

                 Class here comprehensive works on medieval period (Middle Ages), on Early Middle Ages (Dark Ages)

                 For Early Middle Ages during 453–534, see 945.901; for Late Middle Ages, see 945.903

.903	Period of Giudicati, 900–1323

                 Class here comprehensive works on Late Middle Ages

                 For Late Middle Ages during 1323–1479, see 945.905; for Late Middle Ages during 1479–1492, see 945.906

.905	Period as part of Kingdom of Aragon, 1323–1479

---

*Add as instructed under 930–990

.906   Spanish period, 1479–1717

.907   1717–1793

               Class here Kingdom of Sardinia in Sardinia, 1718–1861

               Class comprehensive works on Kingdom of Sardinia in 945.107

> *For Kingdom of Sardinia in Sardinia during 1793–1848, see 945.9082; for Kingdom of Sardinia in Sardinia during 1848–1861, see 945.9083*

.908   1793–1900

.908 2   Period of antifeudal movements prior to Albertine Statute, 1793–1848

.908 3   Period of proclamation of Albertine Statute to the start of Kingdom of Italy, 1848–1861

.908 4   Reigns of Victor Emmanuel II and Umberto I, 1861–1900

.909   1900–

               Add to base number 945.909 the numbers following 945.09 in 945.091–945.093, e.g., Sardinia during the Fascist period 945.9091

.91–.98   Localities of Sardinia

               Add to base number 945.9 the numbers following —459 in notation 4591–4598 from Table 2, e.g., South Sardinia province 945.98; then add further as follows:
               001–009   Standard subdivisions
                         Add to 00 the numbers following 00 in notation 001–009 from table under 930–990, e.g., ethnic and national groups 004, ethnic and national groups in South Sardinia province 945.98004
               01–09   Historical periods
                         Add to 0 the numbers following 945.90 in 945.901–945.909, e.g., South Sardinia province during 1900 to present 945.9809

946   Spain, Andorra, Gibraltar, Portugal

.000 1–.000 8   Standard subdivisions of Spain, Andorra, Gibraltar, Portugal together

               As modified in notation 001–008 from table under 930–990

.000 9   Archaeology; historical periods; areas, regions, places in general; collected biography of Spain, Andorra, Gibraltar, Portugal together

.000 900 9   Archaeology

               Notation 09009 from Table 1 as modified below

.000 900 902–.000 900 909   Specific subdivisions of archaeology

               Add to base number 946.00090090 the numbers following 009090 in notation 0090902–0090909 from table under 930–990, e.g., serials treating archaeology of Spain, Andorra, Gibraltar, Portugal together 946.000900905

.000 901–.000 905	Historical periods

Add to base number 946.00090 the numbers following —090 in notation 0901–0905 from Table 1, e.g., Spain, Andorra, Gibraltar, Portugal together during the Middle Ages 946.000902

.000 91–.000 99	Areas, regions, places in general; collected biography

As modified in notation 0091–0099 from table under 930–990

.001–.009	Standard subdivisions of Spain

As modified in notation 001–009 from table under 930–990

>   **946.01–946.08 Historical periods of Spain**

Class comprehensive works in 946

.01	Early history to 711

Class here period of Visigothic domination, 415–711

For ancient history to 415, see 936.6

(.012)	Ancient history to 415

(Optional number; prefer 936.6)

(.012 1)	Early history to ca. 1000 B.C.

(Optional number; prefer 936.601)

(.012 2)	Period of Greek, Phoenician, early Celtic and Germanic contacts, ca. 1000–218 B.C.

(Optional number; prefer 936.602)

(.012 3)	Roman period, 218 B.C.–415 A.D.

(Optional number; prefer 936.603)

.02	Period of Moorish dynasties and reconquest, 711–1479
.03	Reign of Ferdinand V and Isabella I, 1479–1516

Including union of Castile and Aragon

.04	Period of House of Habsburg, 1516–1700

Class here 16th century

For 1500–1516, see 946.03; for 1598–1599, later period of House of Habsburg, see 946.051

.042	Reign of Charles I, 1516–1556
.043	Reign of Philip II, 1556–1598
.05	Later period of House of Habsburg and period of House of Bourbon, 1598–1808

.051	Later period of House of Habsburg, 1598–1700

Including reign of Philip III, 1598–1621

For reign of Philip IV, see 946.052; for reign of Charles II, see 946.053

.052	Reign of Philip IV, 1621–1665
.053	Reign of Charles II, 1665–1700
.054	1700–1808

Class here comprehensive works on House of Bourbon in Spain

For the reign of a specific Bourbon ruler, see the reign, e.g., reign of Isabella II 946.072

.055	Reign of Philip V, 1700–1746

Including Anglo-Spanish War (War of Jenkins' Ear), 1739–1741 (Option: Class War of Jenkins' Ear in 941.072)

See also 940.2526 for War of the Spanish Succession

.056	Reign of Ferdinand VI, 1746–1759
.057	Reign of Charles III, 1759–1788
.058	Reign of Charles IV, 1788–1808
.06	Period of Peninsular War and rule of Joseph Bonaparte, 1808–1814

Class comprehensive works on Peninsular War in 940.27

.07	1814–1931
.072	Reigns of Ferdinand VII and Isabella II, 1814–1868

Including first Bourbon Restoration

(Option: Class here Spanish-Moroccan War; prefer 964.03)

.073	1868–1874

Including revolution 1868–1871; second Bourbon Restoration, 1871–1873; First Republic, 1873–1874

.074	Reigns of Alfonso XII and Alfonso XIII, 1874–1931

(Option: Class here Spanish-American War; prefer 973.89)

.08	1931–

Class here 20th century

For 1900–1931, see 946.074

.081	‡Period of Second Republic, 1931–1939

Class here Civil War, 1936–1939

.082	Period of Francisco Franco, 1939–1975

‡Add as instructed under 940–990

.082 4	1939–1949
.082 5	1950–1959
.082 6	1960–1969
.082 7	1970–1975
.083	Reign of Juan Carlos I, 1975–2014
.084	Reign of Felipe VI, 2014–

.1–.8   Localities of Spain

> Add to base number 946 the numbers following —46 in notation 461–468 from Table 2, e.g., northwestern Spain 946.1; however, for Andorra, see 946.79; for Gibraltar, see 946.89; then add further as follows:
>
> 001–009   Standard subdivisions
>
> > Add to 00 the numbers following 00 in notation 001–009 from table under 930–990, e.g., ethnic and national groups 004, ethnic and national groups in northwestern Spain 946.1004
>
> 01–08   Historical periods
>
> > Add to 0 the numbers following 946.0 in 946.01–946.08, e.g., northwestern Spain during 1931 to present 946.108

.7   *Eastern Spain and Andorra

> Subdivisions are added for eastern Spain and Andorra together, for eastern Spain alone

.79   †Andorra

> *For ancient history to 415, see 936.6*

.8   *Andalusia autonomous community and Gibraltar

> Subdivisions are added for Andalusia autonomous community and Gibraltar together, for Andalusia autonomous community alone

.89   †Gibraltar

> *For ancient history to 415, see 936.6*

.9   *Portugal

.901   Early history to 1143

> *For ancient history to 415, see 936.6*

(.901 2)   Ancient history to 415

> (Optional number; prefer 936.6)
>
> Add to base number 946.9012 the numbers following 946.012 in 946.0121–946.0123, e.g., period of Greek contacts 946.90122

---

*Add as instructed under 930–990

†Add as instructed under 930–990; however, do not add historical periods

.902	1143–1640

Including 12th century

For 1100–1143, see 946.901

.903	Period of House of Braganza, 1640–1910
.903 2	1640–1750

Including restoration of Portuguese monarchy; 17th century, 18th century

For 1600–1640, see 946.902; for 1750–1799, see 946.9033

.903 3	1750–1807

Including Pombaline reforms

.903 4	Period of monarchy in exile, 1807–1820

Including period of Peninsular War

Class comprehensive works on Peninsular War in 940.27

.903 5	1820–1847
.903 6	1847–1910

Class here 19th century

For a specific part of 19th century not provided for here, see the part, e.g., 1807–1820 946.9034

.904	1910–
.904 1	Period of Republic, 1910–1926
.904 2	1926–1968

Including period of Salazar, 1933–1968

Class here Estado Novo, 1933–1974

For Estado Novo during 1968–1974, see 946.9043

.904 3	1968–1974
.904 4	1974–
.91–.99	Localities of Portugal

Add to base number 946.9 the numbers following —469 in notation 4691–4699 from Table 2, e.g., Minho region and Douro region 946.91; then add further as follows:

    001–009   Standard subdivisions

             Add to 00 the numbers following 00 in notation 001–009 from table under 930–990, e.g., ethnic and national groups 004, ethnic and national groups in Minho region and Douro region 946.91004

    01–04   Historical periods

             Add to 0 the numbers following 946.90 in 946.901–946.904, e.g., Minho region and Douro region during 1910 to present 946.9104

947   Russia and neighboring east European countries

Class here eastern Europe

Subdivisions are added for Russia and neighboring east European countries together, for Russia alone

.000 1–.000 8   Standard subdivisions of eastern Europe

As modified in notation 001–008 from table under 930–990

.000 9   Archaeology; historical periods; areas, regions, places in general; collected biography of eastern Europe

.000 900 9   Archaeology

Notation 09009 from Table 1 as modified below

.000 900 902–.000 900 909   Specific subdivisions of archaeology

Add to base number 947.00090090 the numbers following 009090 in notation 0090902–0090909 from table under 930–990, e.g., serials treating archaeology of eastern Europe 947.000900905

.000 901–.000 905   Historical periods

Add to base number 947.00090 the numbers following —090 in notation 0901–0905 from Table 1, e.g., eastern Europe during the Middle Ages 947.000902

.000 91–.000 99   Areas, regions, places in general; collected biography

As modified in notation 0091–0099 from table under 930–990

.001–.009   Standard subdivisions of Russia

As modified in notation 001–009 from table under 930–990

>   947.01–947.08 Historical periods of Russia

Class comprehensive works in 947

.01   Early history to 862

Including 9th century

For 862–899, see 947.02

.02   Period of Kievan Rus, 862–1240

.03   Period of Tatar suzerainty, 1240–1462

Including 13th century, 15th century

Class here 14th century

For 1200–1240, see 947.02; for 1462–1499, see 947.041

.04   1462–1689

.041   Reign of Ivan III, 1462–1505

.042   Reign of Basil III, 1505–1533

.043   **Reign of Ivan IV (the Terrible), 1533–1584**

        Including Livonian War, 1557–1582
          (Option: Class Livonian War in 948.50322)

        Class here 16th century

          *For a specific part of 16th century not provided for here, see the part,
e.g., 1505–1533 947.042*

.044   **Reigns of Theodore I and Boris Godunov, 1584–1605**

.045   **Time of Troubles, 1605–1613**

        Including reigns of False Dmitri I and False Dmitri II

.046   **Period of House of Romanov, 1613–1917**

          For reigns of specific Romanovs, see 947.047–947.083

.047   **Reign of Michael, 1613–1645**

        Class here 17th century

          *For a specific part of 17th century not provided for here, see the part,
e.g., 1689–1699 947.05*

.048   **Reign of Alexis, 1645–1676**

.049   **Reigns of Theodore III and regent Sophia, 1676–1689**

.05   **Reign of Peter I (the Great), 1689–1725**

        Including Great Northern War, 1700–1721
          (Option: Class Great Northern War in 948.04 or 948.50345)

.06   **1725–1796**

        Class here 18th century

          For 1700–1725, see 947.05; for 1796–1799, see 947.071

.061   **Reigns of Catherine I, Peter II, Anna, Ivan VI, 1725–1741**

.062   **Reigns of Elizabeth and Peter III, 1741–1762**

.063   **Reign of Catherine II (the Great), 1762–1796**

.07   **1796–1855**

        Class here 19th century

          For 1855–1900, see 947.08

.071   **Reign of Paul I, 1796–1801**

.072   **Reign of Alexander I, 1801–1825**

        Including period of invasion by Napoleon, 1812

.073   **Reign of Nicholas I, 1825–1855**

.073 8	‡Crimean War, 1853–1856
	(Option: Class in 941.081)
.08	1855–
.081	Reign of Alexander II, 1855–1881
	Class Russo-Turkish War, 1877–1878, in 949.60387
.082	Reign of Alexander III, 1881–1894
.083	Reign of Nicholas II, 1894–1917
	(Option: Class here Russo-Japanese War; prefer 952.031)
.084	1917–1991

Class here 20th century; Communist period; comprehensive works on Union of Soviet Socialist Republics, 1923–1991

For 1900–1917, see 947.083; for 1953–1991, see 947.085. For a specific part of Union of Soviet Socialist Republics, see the part, e.g., Ukraine 947.7085

.084 1	Period of revolutions, Alexander Kerensky, Vladimir Il´ich Lenin, 1917–1924
.084 2	Period of Joseph Stalin, 1924–1953
	(Option: Class here Russo-Finnish War; prefer 948.97032)
.085	1953–1991
.085 2	Periods of Georgi Malenkov, Nikolay Aleksandrovich Bulganin, Nikita Sergeevich Khrushchev, 1953–1964
.085 3	Period of Leonid Il´ich Brezhnev and Aleksey Nikolayevich Kosygin, 1964–1982
.085 4	Periods of ĪU. V. Andropov, K. U. Chernenko, and Mikhail Sergeevich Gorbachev, 1982–1991
.086	1991–

Class here comprehensive works on Commonwealth of Independent States, 1991–

For a specific part of Commonwealth of Independent States, see the part, e.g., Ukraine 947.7086

.086 1	Administration of Boris Nikolayevich Yeltsin, 1991–1999
.086 2	First administration of Vladimir Vladimirovich Putin, 1999–2008
.086 3	Administration of Dmitry Medvedev, 2008–2012
.086 4	Second administration of Vladimir Vladimirovich Putin, 2012–

‡Add as instructed under 940–990

.1–.4   Localities of Russia

Add to base number 947 the numbers following —47 in notation 471–474 from Table 2, e.g., Moscow 947.31; then add further as follows:
     001–009   Standard subdivisions
                     Add to 00 the numbers following 00 in notation 001–009
                     from table under 930–990, e.g., ethnic and national groups
                     004, ethnic and national groups in Moscow 947.31004
     01–08   Historical periods
                     Add to 0 the numbers following 947.0 in 947.01–947.08, e.g.,
                     Moscow during 1855 to present 947.3108

> **947.5–947.9   European countries of former Soviet Union other than Russia; Caucasus area of Russia**

Except for modifications shown under specific entries, add to each subdivision identified by † as follows:
     07   1796–1855
               Class here period as part of Russia
               Add to 07 the numbers following 947.07 in 947.071–947.073,
               e.g., reign of Paul I 071
                   For a period as part of Russia not provided for here, see the
                   period, e.g., period during reign of Alexander II 081
     08   1855–
     081   Reign of Alexander II, 1855–1881
     082   Reign of Alexander III, 1881–1894
     083   Reign of Nicholas II, 1894–1917
     084   1917–1953
               Class here 20th century
                   For 1900–1917, see notation 083 from this table;
                   for 1953–1991, see notation 085 from this table; for
                   1991–1999, see notation 086 from this table
     0841   1917–1940
               Class here period of independent countries, ca. 1917–ca.
               1920
     0842   Period of Joseph Stalin, 1940–1953
     085   1953–1991
               Class here period as part of Soviet Union, ca. 1920–1991
                   For ca. 1920–1940, see notation 0841 from this table; for
                   period of Joseph Stalin, 1940–1953, see notation 0842
                   from this table
     0852   Periods of Georgi Malenkov, Nikolay Aleksandrovich
               Bulganin, Nikita Sergeevich Khrushchev, 1953–1964
     0853   Period of Leonid Il'ich Brezhnev and Aleksey Nikolayevich
               Kosygin, 1964–1982
     0854   Periods of ĨU. V. Andropov, K. U. Chernenko, and Mikhail
               Sergeevich Gorbachev, 1982–1991
     086   1991–

Class comprehensive works in 947

.5   *†**Caucasus**

> (Option: Class here ancient Caucasus; prefer 939.53)

.52   *Caucasus area of Russia

.520 1–.520 8   Historical periods

> Add to base number 947.520 the numbers following 947.0 in 947.01–947.08, e.g., later 20th century 947.52085

.54   *†Azerbaijan

> (Option: Class here ancient Albania; prefer 939.534)

.56   *†Armenia

> Class comprehensive works on Armenia region in 956.62

.58   *†Georgia

> (Options: Class here ancient Iberia; prefer 939.536. Class here ancient Colchis; prefer 939.538)

.6   *†**Moldova**

> *For Moldova to ca. 640, see 939.88*

.7   *†**Ukraine**

> (Options: Class here ancient Black Sea region; prefer 939.5. Class here ancient Sarmatia; prefer 939.52)

.71–.79   Localities of Ukraine

> Add to base number 947.7 the numbers following —477 in notation 4771–4779 from Table 2, e.g., Odessa 947.72; then add further as follows:
>> 001–009   Standard subdivisions
>>> Add to 00 the numbers following 00 in notation 001–009 from table under 930–990, e.g., ethnic and national groups 004, ethnic and national groups in Odessa 947.72004
>> 07–08   Historical periods
>>> Add to 947.70 the numbers following 0 in notation 07–08 from table under 947.5–947.9, e.g., Odessa during 1855 to present 947.7208

.8   *†**Belarus**

---

*Add as instructed under 930–990
†Add historical periods as instructed under 947.5–947.9

.81–.89　　　Localities of Belarus

> Add to base number 947.8 the numbers following —478 in notation
> 4781–4789 from Table 2, e.g., Minsk 947.86; then add further as follows:
>
> 001–009　　Standard subdivisions
> > Add to 00 the numbers following 00 in notation 001–009
> > from table under 930–990, e.g., ethnic and national groups
> > 004, ethnic and national groups in Minsk 947.86004
>
> 07–08　　Historical periods
> > Add to 947.80 the numbers following 0 in notation 07–08
> > from table under 947.5–947.9, e.g., Minsk during 1855 to
> > present 947.8608

.9　　***†Lithuania, Latvia, Estonia**

> Class here Baltic States

.93　　　***Lithuania**

.930 6　　　　Period of union with Poland, 1569–1795

.930 7–.930 8　　†1795–

.96　　　***Latvia**

.960 5–.960 6　　1721–1796

> > Add to base number 947.960 the numbers following 947.0 in
> > 947.05–947.06, e.g., reign of Peter I 947.9605

.960 7–.960 8　　†1796–

.98　　　***Estonia**

.980 5–.980 6　　1721–1796

> > Add to base number 947.980 the numbers following 947.0 in
> > 947.05–947.06, e.g., reign of Peter I 947.9805

.980 7–.980 8　　†1796–

948　　***Scandinavia and Finland**

> Class here Nordic countries, northern Europe

> Subdivisions are added for Scandinavia and Finland together, for Scandinavia
> alone

>　　948.01–948.07　Historical periods

> Class comprehensive works in 948

.01　　　Early history to ca. 800

> *For ancient history to 481, see 936.8*

(.012)　　　Ancient history to 481

> (Optional number; prefer 936.8)

---

*Add as instructed under 930–990
†Add historical periods as instructed under 947.5–947.9

.02	Medieval period, ca. 800–1523

For 1387–1523, see 948.03

.022	Viking period, ca. 800–ca. 1050

Including 11th century

For ca. 1050–1099, see 948.023

.023	Ca. 1050–1387
.03	1387–1523

Class here period of Union of Kalmar, 1397–1523

.04	1523–1814

(Option: Class here Great Northern War; prefer 947.05)

.05	1814–1905
.06	1905–1999
.061	1905–1939
.062	1940–1945
.063	1945–1969
.064	1970–1999
.07	2000–
.071	2000–2019
.071 1	2000–2009
.071 2	2010–2019
.072	2020–2029
.1	***Norway**

For southeastern Norway, see 948.2; for southwestern Norway, see 948.3; for central and northern Norway, see 948.4

.101	Early history to 1536

Class here medieval period (Middle Ages)

For ancient history to 481, see 936.81

(.101 2)	Ancient history to 481

(Optional number; prefer 936.81)

.101 4	Viking period, ca. 800–ca. 1050

Including 11th century

For ca. 1050–1099, see 948.1015

.101 5	Ca. 1050–1130

*Add as instructed under 930–990

.101 6	High Middle Ages, 1130–1349
	Including 12th century, 14th century
	Class here 13th century
	For 1100–1130, see 948.1015; for 1349–1399, see 948.1017
.101 7	Late Middle Ages, 1349–1536
	Class here period of Union of Kalmar, 1397–1523
.102	Period of union with Denmark, 1536–1814, and Independence, 1814
	Standard subdivisions are added for period of union with Denmark, 1536–1814, and Independence, 1814, together; for period of union with Denmark, 1536–1814, alone
.102 2	1536–1660
	Including 16th century, 17th century
	For 1500–1536, see 948.1017; for 1660–1699, see 948.1023
.102 3	1660–1720
.102 4	1720–1814
.102 5	Independence, 1814
.103	Period of union with Sweden, 1814–1905
.103 1	1814–1884
.103 6	1884–1905
.104	1905–1999
.104 1	1905–1945
.104 12	1905–1918
.104 13	1918–1940
.104 14	1940–1945
.104 3	1945–1969
.104 4	1970–1999
.105	2000–
.105 1	2000–2019
.105 11	2000–2009
.105 12	2010–2019
.105 2	2020–2029

.2–.4   Localities of Norway

Add to base number 948 the numbers following —48 in notation 482–484 from Table 2, e.g., Oslo county (Oslo fylke) 948.21; then add further as follows:

001–009   Standard subdivisions

Add to 00 the numbers following 00 in notation 001–009 from table under 930–990, e.g., ethnic and national groups 004, ethnic and national groups in Oslo county (Oslo fylke) 948.21004

01–05   Historical periods

Add to 0 the numbers following 948.10 in 948.101–948.105, e.g., Oslo county (Oslo fylke) during Viking period 948.21014

.2   *Southeastern Norway (Østlandet)

.201–.205   Historical periods

Add to base number 948.20 the numbers following 948.10 in 948.101–948.105, e.g., Viking period 948.2014

.3   *Sørlandet and Vestlandet

Subdivisions are added for Sørlandet and Vestlandet together, for Sørlandet alone

.301–.305   Historical periods

Add to base number 948.30 the numbers following 948.10 in 948.101–948.105, e.g., Viking period 948.3014

.4   *Trøndelag and Nord-Norge

Subdivisions are added for Trøndelag and Nord-Norge together, for Trøndelag alone

.401–.405   Historical periods

Add to base number 948.40 the numbers following 948.10 in 948.101–948.105, e.g., Viking period 948.4014

.5   *Sweden

For southern Sweden, see 948.6; for central Sweden, see 948.7; for northern Sweden, see 948.8

.501   Early history to 1523

Class here medieval period

For ancient history to 481, see 936.85

(.501 2)   Ancient history to 481

(Optional number; prefer 936.85)

.501 4   Viking period, ca. 800–ca. 1050

Including 11th century

For ca. 1050–1099, see 948.5018

---

*Add as instructed under 930–990

.501 8	Ca. 1050–1523
.501 81	Ca. 1050–1397
.501 82	Period of Union of Kalmar, 1397–1523
.503	1523–1809
.503 2	Period of Vasa dynasty, 1523–1611

                 Class here comprehensive works on period of House of Vasa, 1523–1654

                 For 1611–1654, see 948.5034

.503 21	Reign of Gustav I Vasa, 1523–1560
.503 22	Reign of Erik XIV, 1560–1568

                 (Option: Class here Livonian War; prefer 947.043)

.503 23	Reign of John III, 1568–1592
.503 24	Reign of Sigismund III, 1592–1599
.503 25	Reign of Charles IX, 1599–1611
.503 4	Period of Swedish Empire (Age of Greatness), 1611–1718
.503 41	Reign of Gustav II Adolf, 1611–1632
.503 42	Reign of Christina, 1632–1654
.503 43	Reign of Charles X Gustav, 1654–1660
.503 44	Reign of Charles XI, 1660–1697
.503 45	Reign of Charles XII, 1697–1718

                 (Option: Class here Great Northern War; prefer 947.05)

.503 6	Age of Freedom, 1718–1772

                 Class here 18th century

                 For 1700–1718, see 948.5034; for 1772–1799, see 948.5038

.503 61	Reign of Ulrika Eleonora, 1719–1720
.503 62	Reign of Fredrik I, 1720–1751
.503 63	1751–1772

                 Class here reign of Adolf Fredrik, 1751–1771

.503 8	Gustavian period, 1772–1809
.503 81	Reign of Gustav III, 1772–1792
.503 82	Reign of Gustav IV Adolf, 1792–1809
.504	1809–1905

.504 1	1809–1872

Including reigns of Charles XIII, 1809–1818; Charles XIV John, 1818–1844; Oscar I, 1844–1859; Charles XV, 1859–1872; Riksdag Act, 1866

.504 2	Reign of Oscar II, 1872–1907

For reign of Oscar II during 1905–1907, see 948.5051

.505	1905–1999
.505 1	1905–1945

Class here reign of Gustav V, 1907–1950

For reign of Gustav V during 1945–1950, see 948.5053

.505 3	1945–1969

Class here reign of Gustav VI Adolf, 1950–1973

For reign of Gustav VI Adolf during 1970–1973, see 948.5054

.505 4	1970–1999

Class here reign of Carl XVI Gustaf, 1973 to present

For reign of Carl XVI Gustaf, 2000 to present, see 948.506

.506	2000–
.506 1	2000–2019
.506 11	2000–2009
.506 12	2010–2019
.506 2	2020–2029

.6–.8   Localities of Sweden

Add to base number 948 the numbers following —48 in notation 486–488 from Table 2, e.g., Skåne County (Skåne län) 948.61; then add further as follows:

001–009   Standard subdivisions

Add to 00 the numbers following 00 in notation 001–009 from table under 930–990, e.g., ethnic and national groups 004, ethnic and national groups in Skåne County (Skåne län) 948.61004

01–06   Historical periods

Add to 0 the numbers following 948.50 in 948.501–948.506, e.g., Skåne County (Skåne län) during period of House of Vasa 948.61032

.6   *Southern Sweden (Götaland)

.601–.606	Historical periods

Add to base number 948.60 the numbers following 948.50 in 948.501–948.506, e.g., period of House of Vasa 948.6032

.7   *Central Sweden (Svealand)

*Add as instructed under 930–990

.701–.706	Historical periods

Add to base number 948.70 the numbers following 948.50 in 948.501–948.506, e.g., period of House of Vasa 948.7032

.8 *Northern Sweden (Norrland)

.801–.806	Historical periods

Add to base number 948.80 the numbers following 948.50 in 948.501–948.506, e.g., period of House of Vasa 948.8032

.9 Denmark and Finland

.900 1–.900 9	Standard subdivisions of Denmark

As modified in notation 001–009 from table under 930–990

> 948.901–948.906 Historical periods of Denmark

Class comprehensive works in 948.9

.901	Early history to 1387

Class here medieval period

For ancient history to 481, see 936.89; for 1387–1536, see 948.902

(.901 2)	Ancient history to 481

(Optional number; prefer 936.89)

.901 3	481–ca. 800

.901 4	Viking period, ca. 800–ca. 1050

Including 11th century

For ca. 1050–1099, see 948.9015

.901 5	Ca. 1050–1387

Class here period of Estrith dynasty, 1047–1448

For 1387–1448, see 948.902

.902	Period of union with Norway and Sweden, 1387–1536

Class here period of Union of Kalmar, 1397–1523

.903	Period of union with Norway, 1536–1814

For 1500–1536, see 948.902

.903 2	1536–1660

Including 16th century, 17th century

For 1500–1536, see 948.902; for 1660–1699, see 948.9033

---

*Add as instructed under 930–990

.903 3	1660–1720	

For Great Northern War, see 947.05

.903 4	1720–1814
.904	1814–1906

(Option: Class here Schleswig-Holstein War; prefer 943.076)

.905	1906–1999
.905 1	1906–1945
.905 3	1945–1969
.905 4	1970–1999
.906	2000–
.906 1	2000–2019
.906 11	2000–2009
.906 12	2010–2019
.906 2	2020–2029
.91–.95	Localities of Denmark

Add to base number 948.9 the numbers following —489 in notation 4891–4895 from Table 2, e.g., Zealand (Sjælland) island 948.91; then add further as follows:

001–009   Standard subdivisions
Add to 00 the numbers following 00 in notation 001–009 from table under 930–990, e.g., ethnic and national groups 004, ethnic and national groups in Zealand (Sjælland) island 948.91004

01–06   Historical periods
Add to 0 the numbers following 948.90 in 948.901–948.906, e.g., Zealand (Sjælland) island during 2000 to present 948.9106

.97	*Finland
.970 1	Early history to end of Swedish rule, 1809
.970 11	Early history to ca. 1050
.970 12	Ca. 1050–1523

Including period of Union of Kalmar, 1397–1523

.970 13	1523–1809
.970 132	Period of Vasa dynasty, 1523–1611

Class here comprehensive works on period of House of Vasa, 1523–1654

For 1611–1654, see 948.970134

*Add as instructed under 930–990

.970 134	Period of Swedish Empire (Age of Greatness of Sweden), 1611–1718

For Great Northern War, see 947.05

.970 134 9	Period of Isoviha (period of Russian occupation), 1713–1721

For 1718–1721, see 948.970136

.970 136	Age of Freedom, 1718–1772

Class here 18th century

For 1700–1718, see 948.970134; for 1772–1799, see 948.970138

.970 138	Gustavian period, 1772–1809
.970 2	Period of Russian rule, 1809–1917
.970 3	1917–1999
.970 31	1917–1939
.970 311	1917–1918

Class here Finnish Civil War, 1918

.970 32	1939–1945

Class here Russo-Finnish War, 1939–1940
(Option: Class Russo-Finnish War in 947.0842)

.970 33	1945–1982

Class here administration of Urho Kekkonen, 1956–1981

.970 34	1982–1999
.970 4	2000–
.971–.977	Localities of Finland

Add to base number 948.97 the numbers following —4897 in notation 48971–48977 from Table 2, e.g., Lappi region (Lapin maakunta, Lapland) 948.977; then add further as follows:
001–009   Standard subdivisions
Add to 00 the numbers following 00 in notation 001–009 from table under 930–990, e.g., ethnic and national groups 004, ethnic and national groups in Lappi region (Lapin maakunta, Lapland) 948.977004
01–04   Historical periods
Add to 0 the numbers following 948.970 in 948.9701–948.9704, e.g., Lappi region (Lapin maakunta, Lapland) during 2000 to present 948.97704

949   Other parts of Europe

.1	***Northwestern islands**
.12	*Iceland

*Add as instructed under 930–990

.120 1	Early history to 1262
	Including 13th century
	For 1262–1299, see 949.1202
.120 2	Medieval period, 1262–1550
	Including 16th century
	For 1550–1599, see 949.1203
.120 3	1550–1874
	Including 19th century
	For 1874–1899, see 949.1204
.120 4	Period of Governors, 1874–1904
.120 5	1904–1999
	Including independence under Danish crown, 1918–1944; period of Republic, 1944–1999
.120 6	2000–
	Class here comprehensive works on period of Republic, 1944 to present
	For period of Republic, 1944–1999, see 949.1205
.15	†Faeroes

.2   *Netherlands

Class here comprehensive works on Low Countries, on Benelux countries

For southern Low Countries, see 949.3

.201	Early history to 1477
	For ancient history to 486, see 936.92
(.201 2)	Ancient history to 486
	(Optional number; prefer 936.92)
.202	Period of House of Habsburg, 1477–1568
	Including 16th century
	For 1568–1599, see 949.203
.203	Period of struggle for independence, 1568–1648

---

*Add as instructed under 930–990
†Add as instructed under 930–990; however, do not add historical periods

.204	Period of Dutch Republic, 1648–1795

Including Anglo-Dutch Wars, 1652–1653, 1665–1667; Great Wars against England, France, and allies, 1672–1678; Coalition War, 1690–1697; 17th century
> (Option: Class Anglo-Dutch Wars in 941.06)

For 1600–1648, see 949.203

.205	1795–1830

Including Batavian Republic, 1795–1806; Kingdom of Holland, 1806–1813

Class here Napoleonic era

.206	1830–1901

Class here 19th century

For 1800–1830, see 949.205

.207	1901–
.207 1	Reign of Wilhelmina, 1890–1948

For reign of Wilhelmina during 1890–1901, see 949.206

.207 2	Reign of Juliana, 1948–1980
.207 3	Reign of Beatrix, 1980–2013
.207 4	Reign of Willem-Alexander, 2013–
.21–.24	Localities of Netherlands

Add to base number 949.2 the numbers following —492 in notation 4921–4924 from Table 2, e.g., northeastern provinces of Netherlands 949.21; then add further as follows:

    001–009   Standard subdivisions
                Add to 00 the numbers following 00 in notation 001–009 from table under 930–990, e.g., ethnic and national groups 004, ethnic and national groups in northeastern provinces of Netherlands 949.21004

    01–07   Historical periods
                Add to 0 the numbers following 949.20 in 949.201–949.207, e.g., northeastern provinces of Netherlands during 1901 to present 949.2107

.3	***Belgium and Luxembourg**

Subdivisions are added for Belgium and Luxembourg together, for Belgium alone

.301	Early history to 1477

For ancient history to 486, see 936.93

(.301 2)	Ancient history to 486

(Optional number; prefer 936.93)

---

*Add as instructed under 930–990

.302	Period of foreign rule, 1477–1830
.303	1830–1909

Class here 19th century

For 1800–1830, see 949.302

.304	1909–
.304 1	Reign of Albert I, 1909–1934
.304 2	Reign of Léopold III, 1934–1951
.304 3	Reign of Baudouin I, 1951–1993
.304 4	Reign of Albert II, 1993–2013
.304 5	Reign of Philippe, 2013–
.31–.34	Localities of Belgium

Add to base number 949.3 the numbers following —493 in notation 4931–4934 from Table 2, e.g., northwestern provinces of Belgium 949.31; then add further as follows:
- 001–009   Standard subdivisions

  Add to 00 the numbers following 00 in notation 001–009 from table under 930–990, e.g., ethnic and national groups 004, ethnic and national groups in northwestern provinces of Belgium 949.31004
- 01–04   Historical periods

  Add to 0 the numbers following 949.30 in 949.301–949.304, e.g., northwestern provinces of Belgium during 1909 to present 949.3104

.35	*Luxembourg
.350 1	Early history to 1482

For ancient history to 486, see 936.935

(.350 12)	Ancient history to 486

(Optional number; prefer 936.935)

.350 2	Period of foreign rule, 1482–1830
.350 3	1830–1890

Class here 19th century

For 1800–1830, see 949.3502; for 1890–1899, see 949.35041

.350 4	1890–
.350 41	1890–1918
.350 42	1918–1945

---

*Add as instructed under 930–990

.350 43		1945–1999
		Class here 20th century
		For 1900–1918, see 949.35041; for 1918–1945, see 949.35042
.350 44		2000–
.4	***Switzerland**	
.401		Early history to 1291
		For ancient history to 486, see 936.94
(.401 2)		Ancient history to 486
		(Optional number; prefer 936.94)
.402		1291–1499
.403		1499–1648
.404		1648–1798
		Including 17th century
		For 1600–1648, see 949.403
.405		Napoleonic period, 1798–1815
		Class here Helvetic Republic, 1798–1803
.406		1815–1900
.406 2		Period of restoration, 1815–1848
.406 3		1848–1900
.407		1900–
.407 1		1900–1918
.407 2		1918–1945
.407 3		1945–1999
		Class here 20th century
		For 1900–1918, see 949.4071; for 1918–1945, see 949.4072
.407 4		2000–

*Add as instructed under 930–990

.43–.47   Localities of Switzerland

> Add to base number 949.4 the numbers following —494 in notation 4943–4947 from Table 2, e.g., Jura region cantons 949.43; then add further as follows:
>
> 001–009   Standard subdivisions
>> Add to 00 the numbers following 00 in notation 001–009 from table under 930–990, e.g., ethnic and national groups 004, ethnic and national groups in Jura region cantons 949.43004
>
> 01–07   Historical periods
>> Add to 0 the numbers following 949.40 in 949.401–949.407, e.g., Jura region cantons during 1900 to present 949.4307

.5   *Greece

.501   Early history to 717

> *For ancient history to 323, see 938*

(.501 2)   Ancient history to 323

> (Optional number; prefer 938)

> Add to base number 949.5012 the numbers following 938.0 in 938.01–938.09, e.g., Persian Wars 949.50123

.501 3   Early Byzantine period, 323–717

> Including wars against Avars and Persians

> Class here Eastern Roman (Byzantine) Empire, 323–717

.502   Middle Byzantine period, 717–1081

> Class here comprehensive works on Byzantine Empire

> *For early Byzantine period, see 949.5013; for late Byzantine period, see 949.503. For a specific part of Byzantine Empire, see the part, e.g., Byzantine Empire in Egypt 932.023*

.503   Late Byzantine period, 1081–1204

> Including Fourth Crusade, 1202–1204

.504   Period of Latin and Greek states and Turkish conquest, 1204–1453

> Including 15th century

> *For 1453–1499, see 949.505*

.505   Period of Turkish domination, 1453–1821

.506   War of Independence, 1821–1830

.507   1830–

.507 1   1830–1833

---

*Add as instructed under 930–990

.507 2	Period of monarchy, 1833–1924

        Including Greco-Turkish War, 1896–1897

        Class here 19th century

        For Balkan Wars, see 949.6039. For a specific part of 19th century not provided for here, see the part, e.g., 1821–1830 949.506

.507 3	Period of Republic, 1924–1935
.507 4	The period of the restoration of the monarchy, 1935–1967

        Class here 20th century

        For a specific part of 20th century not provided for here, see the part, e.g., 1974–1999 949.5076

.507 5	Period of military junta, 1967–1974
.507 6	Period of restoration of democratic rule, 1974–
.51–.58	Localities of Greece

        Add to base number 949.5 the numbers following —495 in notation 4951–4958 from Table 2, e.g., Attica region, Central Greece region, regional unit of Aetolia and Acarnania 949.51; then add further as follows:

        001–009   Standard subdivisions

                Add to 00 the numbers following 00 in notation 001–009 from table under 930–990, e.g., ethnic and national groups 004, ethnic and national groups in Attica region, Central Greece region, regional unit of Aetolia and Acarnania 949.51004

        01–07   Historical periods

                Add to 0 the numbers following 949.50 in 949.501–949.507, e.g., Attica region, Central Greece region, regional unit of Aetolia and Acarnania during 1830 to present 949.5107

.58	*Aegean Islands (Aigaio Nēsoi)
.580 1	Early history to 717

        Number built according to instructions under 930–990

        For ancient history to 323, see 939.1

(.580 12)	Ancient history to 323

        (Optional number; prefer 939.1)

        Add to base number 949.58012 the numbers following 938.0 in 938.01–938.09, e.g., mythical age to 775 B.C. 949.580121

.59	*Crete region (Krētē periphereia)
.590 1	Early history to 827

        For ancient history to 323, see 939.18

*Add as instructed under 930–990

(.590 12)	Ancient history to 323
	(Optional number; prefer 939.18)
	Add to base number 949.59012 the numbers following 938.0 in 938.01–938.09, e.g., mythical age to 775 B.C. 949.590121
.590 13	First Byzantine period, 323–827
.590 2	Period of Arab rule, 827–961
	Including 9th century, 10th century
	For 800–827, see 949.59013; for 961–999, see 949.5903
.590 3	Second Byzantine period, 961–1206
.590 4	Period of Venetian rule, 1206–1669
	Including 17th century
	For 1669–1699, see 949.5905
.590 5	Period of Turkish domination, 1669–1898
.590 6	Period of autonomy, 1898–1913
.590 7	1913–
.590 72	Period of incorporation into Greece, 1913–1924
.590 73–.590 76	1924–
	Add to base number 949.5907 the numbers following 949.507 in 949.5073–949.5076, e.g., restoration of monarchy 949.59074

.6 *Balkan Peninsula

For ancient history to ca. 640, see 939.8

(.601)	Ancient history to ca. 640
	(Optional number; prefer 939.8)
.602	Ca. 640–1362
	Class here 14th century
	For 1362–1399, see 949.6031
.603	Period of Ottoman Empire, 1362–1913
.603 1	Period of conquest by Ottoman Empire, 1362–1529
.603 8	Period of national liberation, 1804–1912
.603 87	‡Russo-Turkish War, 1877–1878
.603 9	‡Balkan Wars, 1912–1913
.604	1913–1991

*Add as instructed under 930–990
‡Add as instructed under 940–990

.604 8   Communist period, 1945–1991

.605   1991–

.61   *Turkey in Europe (Eastern Thrace)

.610 1   Early history to 1918

.610 11–.610 14   Early history to 1453

> Add to base number 949.6101 the numbers following 949.50 in 949.501–949.504, e.g., period of Byzantine prosperity, 717–1081 949.61012
>
> *For ancient history to 323, see 939.8*

.610 15   1453–1918

> Class here period of Ottoman empire, 1453–1922
>
> *For 1918–1922, see 949.61023*

.610 2–.610 4   1918–

> Add to base number 949.610 the numbers following 956.10 in 956.102–956.104, e.g., 1918–1923 949.61023

.612–.618   Localities of Turkey in Europe (Eastern Thrace)

> Add to base number 949.61 the numbers following —4961 in notation 49612–49618 from Table 2, e.g., İstanbul Province (İstanbul İli) 949.618; then add further as follows:
> 001–009   Standard subdivisions
>   Add to 00 the numbers following 00 in notation 001–009 from table under 930–990, e.g., ethnic and national groups 004, ethnic and national groups in İstanbul Province (İstanbul İli) 949.618004
> 01–04   Historical periods
>   Add to 0 the numbers following 949.610 in 949.6101–949.6104, e.g., İstanbul Province (İstanbul İli) during early history to 1918 949.61801

.65   *Albania

.650 1   Early history to 1912

> *For ancient history to 323, see 939.8*

(.650 12)   Ancient history to 323

> (Optional number; prefer 939.8)

.650 2   1912–1946

.650 3   1946–1992

> Class here period of People's Republic, 1946–1991; 20th century
>
> *For a specific part of 20th century not provided for here, see the part, e.g., 1912–1946 949.6502*

.650 4   1992–

*Add as instructed under 930–990

.7	***Serbia, Croatia, Slovenia, Bosnia and Hercegovina, Montenegro, North Macedonia**
.701	Early history to 1918

For ancient history to ca. 640, see 939.87; for Balkan Wars, see 949.6039

(.701 2)	Ancient history to ca. 640

(Optional number; prefer 939.87)

.702	Yugoslavia, 1918–1991

Class here comprehensive works on former Yugoslavia, 20th century

For 1900–1918, see 949.701; for 1991–1999, see 949.703; for Yugoslavia (1991–2003), see 949.7103

.702 1	Period of Kingdom, 1918–1939

Class 1939–1941 in 949.7022

.702 2	Period of World War II, 1939–1945
.702 3	Administration of Josip Broz Tito, 1945–1980
.702 4	1980–1991
.703	Period as sovereign nations, 1991–

See also 949.71031 for Yugoslavia (1991–2003)

.71	*Serbia
.710 1	Early history to 1918

For ancient history to ca. 640, see 939.87

(.710 11)	Ancient history to ca. 640

(Optional number; prefer 939.87)

.710 12	Ca. 640–1389
.710 13	Turkish period, 1389–1878

For 1804–1878, see 949.71014

.710 14	Period of revolt and autonomy, 1804–1878

Class here 19th century

For 1800–1804, see 949.71013; for 1878–1899, see 949.71015

.710 15	Period of independence, 1878–1918

---

*Add as instructed under 930–990

.710 2	1918–1991

Class here 20th century

Add to base number 949.7102 the numbers following 949.702 in 949.7021–949.7024, e.g., period of World War II 949.71022

For 1900–1918, see 949.71015; for 1991–1999, see 949.7103

.710 3	1991–
.710 31	1991–2006

Class here Yugoslavia (1991–2003), Serbia and Montenegro (2003–2006)

Class Yugoslavia (1918–1991) in 949.702

For Montenegro, see 949.745

.710 315	‡Kosovo Civil War, 1998–1999
.710 32	2006–
.72	*Croatia
.720 1–.720 3	Historical periods

Add to base number 949.720 the numbers following 949.70 in 949.701–949.703, e.g., period of World War II 949.72022

.73	*Slovenia
.730 1–.730 3	Historical periods

Add to base number 949.730 the numbers following 949.70 in 949.701–949.703, e.g., period of World War II 949.73022

.74	*Bosnia and Hercegovina, Montenegro
.742	*Bosnia and Hercegovina
.742 01–.742 03	Historical periods

Add to base number 949.7420 the numbers following 949.70 in 949.701–949.703, e.g., period of World War II 949.742022

.745	*Montenegro
.745 01–.745 02	Historical periods

Add to base number 949.7450 the numbers following 949.70 in 949.701–949.702, e.g., period of World War II 949.745022

.745 03	1991–

*Add as instructed under 930–990
‡Add as instructed under 940–990

.745 031	1991–2006

Class here period as part of Yugoslavia (1991–2003), Serbia and Montenegro (2003–2006)

Class comprehensive works on Yugoslavia (1991–2003), on Serbia and Montenegro (2003–2006) in 949.71031

.745 032	2006–
.76	*North Macedonia
.760 1–.760 3	Historical periods

Add to base number 949.760 the numbers following 949.70 in 949.701–949.703, e.g., period of World War II 949.76022

.8 *Romania

.801	Early history to 1861

For ancient history to ca. 640, see 939.88

(.801 2)	Ancient history to ca. 640

(Optional number; prefer 939.88)

.801 3	Ca. 640–1250

Including 13th century

For 1250–1299, see 949.8014

.801 4	Period of Wallachia and Moldavia principalities, 1250–ca. 1500
.801 5	Turkish period, ca. 1500–1821

Including reign of Michael the Brave, 1593–1601; Phanarist period, 1711–1821

.801 6	1821–1861

Class here 19th century

For 1800–1821, see 949.8015; for 1861–1899, see 949.802

.802	Period of monarchy, 1861–1947

Class here period of Kingdom, 1881–1947; 20th century

For Balkan Wars, see 949.6039; for 1947–1999, see 949.803

.803	1947–
.803 1	Period of People's Republic, 1947–1989
.803 2	1989–

*Add as instructed under 930–990

.81–.84	Localities of Romania

     Add to base number 949.8 the numbers following —498 in notation 4981–4984 from Table 2, e.g., northeast Romania 949.81; then add further as follows:

     001–009 Standard subdivisions

         Add to 00 the numbers following 00 in notation 001–009 from table under 930–990, e.g., ethnic and national groups 004, ethnic and national groups in northeast Romania 949.81004

     01–03   Historical periods

         Add to 0 the numbers following 949.80 in 949.801–949.803, e.g., northeast Romania during 1947 to present 949.8103

.83	*Black Sea area

     For early history to 640, see 939.51

.9	***Bulgaria**
.901	Early history to 1878

     For ancient history to ca. 640, see 939.89

(.901 2)	Ancient history to ca. 640

     (Optional number; prefer 939.89)

.901 3	Ca. 640–1018

     Class here First Bulgarian Empire, ca. 680–1014

.901 4	Period of Byzantine rule and Second Bulgarian Empire, 1018–1396
.901 5	Turkish period, 1396–1878
.902	1878–1946

     Class here 20th century

     For 1946–1999, see 949.903

.902 2	1878–1918

     For Balkan Wars, see 949.6039

.902 3	1918–1946
.903	1946–
.903 1	Period of People's Republic, 1946–1991
.903 2	1991–

*Add as instructed under 930–990

.91–.99   Localities of Bulgaria

> Add to base number 949.9 the numbers following —499 in notation
> 4991–4999 from Table 2, e.g., Montana region (Montana oblast) 949.91;
> then add further as follows:
>> 001–009   Standard subdivisions
>>> Add to 00 the numbers following 00 in notation 001–009
>>> from table under 930–990, e.g., ethnic and national
>>> groups 004, ethnic and national groups in Montana region
>>> (Montana oblast) 949.91004
>> 01–03   Historical periods
>>> Add to 0 the numbers following 949.90 in 949.901–949.903,
>>> e.g., Montana region (Montana oblast) during 1946 to present
>>> 949.9103

950   History of Asia

.01–.09   Standard subdivisions

> As modified in notation 001–009 from table under 930–990

.1   Early history to 1162

> Including 12th century

> *For 1162–1199, see 950.21*

.2   1162–1480

> Class here Mongol Empire

.21   1162–1227

> Class here reign of Genghis Khan, ca. 1200–1227

.22   1227–1294

> Class here reign of Kublai Khan, ca. 1259–1294; 13th century

> *For 1200–1227, see 950.21; for 1294–1299, see 950.23*

.23   1294–1336

.24   1336–1405

> Class here reign of Timur (Tamerlane), ca. 1358–1405; 14th century

> *For 1300–1336, see 950.23*

.25   1405–1480

> Class here 15th century

> *For 1400–1405, see 950.24; for 1480–1499, see 950.3*

.3   Period of European exploration and penetration, 1480–1905

.4   1905–

.41   1905–1945

.42	1945–1999

Class here 20th century

For 1900–1905, see 950.3; for 1905–1945, see 950.41

.424	1945–1949
.425	1950–1959
.426	1960–1969
.427	1970–1979
.428	1980–1989
.429	1990–1999
.43	2000–
.431	2000–2019
.431 1	2000–2009
.431 2	2010–2019
.432	2020–2029

951   *China and adjacent areas

Subdivisions are added for China and adjacent areas together, for China alone

---

>   951.01–951.06 Historical periods of China and adjacent areas together, of China alone

Class comprehensive works in 951

.01	Early history to 960

For ancient history to 420, see 931

(.011–.014)	Ancient history to 420

(Optional numbers; prefer 931)

Add to base number 951.01 the numbers following 931.0 in 931.01–931.04, e.g., Shang dynasty 951.012

.015	Period of Northern and Southern dynasties, 420–581
.016	Period of Sui dynasty, 581–618
.017	Period of Tang dynasty, 618–907
.018	Period of Five dynasties and Ten kingdoms, 907–960

Class here 10th century

For 900–907, see 951.017; for 960–999, see 951.024

.02	960–1644

*Add as instructed under 930–990

.024	Period of Song dynasty, 960–1279
.025	1279–1368

Class here period of Yuan (Mongol) dynasty, 1271–1368; 14th century

For period of Yuan dynasty during 1271–1279, see 951.024; for 1368–1399, see 951.026

.026	Period of Ming dynasty, 1368–1644
.03	Period of Qing (Manchu) dynasty, 1644–1912
.032	1644–1795

Including 17th century

For 1600–1644, see 951.026

.033	1796–1850

Including Opium War, 1840–1842

Class here 19th century

For 1850–1864, see 951.034; for 1864–1899, see 951.035

.034	Period of Taiping Rebellion, 1850–1864
.035	1864–1911

Including Sino-Japanese War, 1894–1895; Boxer Rebellion, 1899–1901 (Option: Class Sino-Japanese War in 952.031)

.036	Period of Revolution of 1911–1912
.04	Period of Republic, 1912–1949
.041	1912–1927
.042	Period of nationalist government, 1927–1949

Including Sino-Japanese Conflict during 1937–1941 (Option: Class Sino-Japanese Conflict during 1937–1941 in 952.033)

Class here administration of Chiang Kai-shek, 1928–1949

Class comprehensive works on Sino-Japanese Conflict, 1937–1945, in 940.53

See also 951.24905 for administration of Taiwan by Chiang Kai-shek

.05	Period of People's Republic, 1949–

Class here 20th century; administration of Mao Zedong, 1949–1976

For 2000 to present, see 951.06. For a specific part of 20th century not provided for here, see the part, e.g., Revolution of 1911–1912 951.036

.055	1949–1959
.056	1960–1969

Class here Cultural Revolution, 1966–1976

For Cultural Revolution during 1970–1976, see 951.057

.057	1970–1979
.058	1980–1989
.059	1990–1999
.06	2000–
.061	2000–2019
.061 1	2000–2009
.061 2	2010–2019
.062	2020–

.1–.8   **Localities of China**

> Add to base number 951 the numbers following —51 in notation 511–518 from Table 2, e.g., northeastern China 951.1; however, for Hong Kong, see 951.25; for Macau, see 951.26; for Outer Mongolia, Mongolian People's Republic, see 951.73; then add further as follows:
>
> 001–009   Standard subdivisions
>> Add to 00 the numbers following 00 in notation 001–009 from table under 930–990, e.g., ethnic and national groups 004, ethnic and national groups in northeastern China 951.1004
>
> 01–06   Historical periods
>> Add to 0 the numbers following 951.0 in 951.01–951.06, e.g., northeastern China during 2000 to present 951.106

.2   ***Southeastern China and adjacent areas**

.24   *East China Sea area

.249   *Taiwan (Formosa) and adjacent islands

.249 02   Early history to 1683

> *For ancient history to 420, see 931.249*

.249 03   Chinese period, 1683–1895

.249 04   Japanese period, 1895–1945

.249 05   Period of Republic of China (Nationalist China), 1945–

> Class here 20th century; administration of Chiang Kai-shek, 1950–1975
>
> *For 1900–1945, see 951.24904; for 2000 to present, see 951.24906*
>
> *See also 951.042 for administration of China by Chiang Kai-shek*

.249 055   1949–1959

.249 056   1960–1969

.249 057   1970–1979

---

*Add as instructed under 930–990

.249 058	1980–1989

                        Class here administration of Chiang Ching-kuo, 1978–1988

                        For administration of Chiang Ching-kuo during 1978–1979, see 951.249057

.249 059	1990–1999
.249 06	2000–
.249 061	2000–2019
.249 061 1	2000–2009
.249 061 2	2010–2019
.249 062	2020–

.25   *Hong Kong

.250 1–.250 3   Chinese period to 1843

                       Add to base number 951.250 the numbers following 951.0 in 951.01–951.03, e.g., period of Ming dynasty 951.25026

.250 4   Period as a British dependency, 1843–1997

                       Including 19th century

                       For 1800–1843, see 951.25033; for 1945–1997, see 951.2505

.250 5	1945–1997
.250 6	Period as part of People's Republic, 1997–
.250 61	1997–2019
.250 611	1997–2009
.250 612	2010–2019
.250 62	2020–

.26   *Macau

                       For ancient history to 420, see 931

.260 1–.260 3   Chinese period to 1849

                       Add to base number 951.260 the numbers following 951.0 in 951.01–951.03, e.g., period of Ming dynasty 951.26026

.260 4	Period as an overseas territory of Portugal, 1849–1999
.260 6	Period as part of People's Republic, 1999–
.260 61	1999–2019
.260 611	1999–2009
.260 612	2010–2019
.260 62	2020–

*Add as instructed under 930–990

.7	***Mongolia**
.73	†Outer Mongolia (Mongolian People's Republic)
.9	***Korea**
.901	Early history to 1392
.902	Period of Yi dynasty, 1392–1910
.903	Japanese period, 1910–1945
.904	1945–1999

        Class here 20th century

          For 1900–1910, see 951.902; for 1910–1945, see 951.903

.904 1	1945–1950
.904 2	‡Korean War, 1950–1953
.904 3	1953–1999
.905	2000–
.93	*North Korea (People's Democratic Republic of Korea)
.930 1	Early history to 1392
.930 2	Period of Yi dynasty, 1392–1910
.930 3	Japanese period, 1910–1945
.930 4	1945–1994

        Class here 20th century

          For 1900–1910, see 951.9302; for 1910–1945, see 951.9303; for 1994–1999, see 951.93051

.930 41	1945–1950
.930 42	Period of Korean War, 1950–1953
.930 43	Administration of Kim Il-sŏng, 1948–1994

          For administration of Kim Il-sŏng during 1948–1950, see 951.93041; for administration of Kim Il-sŏng during 1950–1953, see 951.93042

.930 5	1994–
.930 51	Administration of Kim Chŏng-il, 1994–2011
.930 52	Administration of Kim Chŏng-ŭn, 2011–
.95	*South Korea (Republic of Korea)
.950 1	Early history to 1392

*Add as instructed under 930–990
†Add as instructed under 930–990; however, do not add historical periods
‡Add as instructed under 940–990

.950 2	Period of Yi dynasty, 1392–1910
.950 3	Japanese period, 1910–1945
.950 4	1945–1998

Class here 20th century

> *For 1900–1910, see 951.9502; for 1910–1945, see 951.9503; for 1998–1999, see 951.9505*

.950 41	1945–1950
.950 42	Period of Korean War, 1950–1953
.950 43	1953–1979

Class here administration of Park Chung Hee, 1962–1979

.950 44	1979–1998
.950 5	1998–

Including administration of Kim Dae Jung, 1998–2003

952   *Japan

.01	Early history to 1185
.02	Feudal period, 1185–1868

Class here chūsei period

.021	Kamakura period, 1185–1334
.022	Namboku period, 1334–1392

Class here 14th century

> *For 1300–1334, see 952.021; for 1392–1399, see 952.023*

.023	Muromachi period, 1392–1573

Including 16th century

> *For 1573–1599, see 952.024*

.024	Momoyama period, 1573–1603
.025	Tokugawa (Edo) period, 1603–1868

Including 19th century

Class here kinsei period

> *For 1868–1899, see 952.031. For a specific part of kinsei period not provided for here, see the part, e.g., 1945–1999 952.04*

.03	1868–1945

*Add as instructed under 930–990

.031   Meiji period, 1868–1912

> Including Russo-Japanese War, 1904–1905
> (Option: Class Russo-Japanese War in 947.083)

> (Option: Class here Sino-Japanese War, 1894–1895; prefer 951.035)

.032   Taishō period, 1912–1926

.033   Shōwa period, 1926–1989

> Class here 20th century

> *For Shōwa period during 1945–1989, see 952.04. For a specific part of 20th century not provided for here, see the part, e.g., Russo-Japanese War, 1904–1905 952.031*

> (Option: Class here Sino-Japanese Conflict, 1937–1941; prefer 951.042)

.04   1945–1999

.044   1945–1949

.045   1950–1959

.046   1960–1969

.047   1970–1979

.048   1980–1989

.049   1990–1999

> Class here Heisei period, 1989–2019

> *For Heisei period in 1989, see 952.048; for 2000–2019, see 952.051*

.05   2000–

.051   2000–2019

.051 1   2000–2009

.051 2   2010–2019

.052   2020–2029

> Class here Reiwa period, 2019 to present

> *For Reiwa period in 2019, see 952.0512*

.1–.8   **Localities of Japan**

> Add to base number 952 the numbers following —52 in notation 521–528 from Table 2, e.g., Honshū (Honsyū) 952.1; then add further as follows:
>
> 001–009   Standard subdivisions
> > Add to 00 the numbers following 00 in notation 001–009 from table under 930–990, e.g., ethnic and national groups 004, ethnic and national groups in Honshū (Honsyū) 952.1004
>
> 01–05   Historical periods
> > Add to 0 the numbers following 952.0 in 952.01–952.05, e.g., Honshū (Honsyū) during 2000 to present 952.105

953   *Arabian Peninsula and adjacent areas

For ancient history to 622, see 939.49

(.01)   Ancient history to 622

(Optional number; prefer 939.49)

>   953.02–953.05 Historical periods of Arabian Peninsula and adjacent areas together, of Arabian Peninsula alone

Class comprehensive works in 953

.02   622–1517

Including Arabia Deserta, 622–637

.03   Period of Ottoman Empire, 1517–1740

Class period of struggles to overthrow Turks in 953.04

.04   1740–1926

Including 18th century

Class here period of struggles to overthrow Turks, 1740–1918

For 1700–1740, see 953.03

.05   1926–

.052   1926–1964

Class here 20th century

For 1900–1926, see 953.04; for 1964–1999, see 953.053

.053   1964–1999

.054   2000–

.1   *Sinai Peninsula

.101–.105   Historical periods

Add to base number 953.10 the numbers following 962.0 in 962.01–962.05, e.g., period of Ottoman Empire 953.103

For ancient history to 622, see 939.48

.3   *Yemen

For ancient history to 622, see 939.49

(.301)   Ancient history to 622

(Optional number; prefer 939.49)

.302   622–1517

---

*Add as instructed under 930–990

.303	Period of Ottoman Empire, 1517–1740
	Class period of struggles to overthrow Turks in 953.304
.304	1740–1918
	Including 18th century
	For 1700–1740, see 953.303
.305	1918–
.305 2	1918–1990
	Class here 20th century
	For 1900–1918, see 953.304; for 1990–1999, see 953.3053
.305 3	Period as Republic of Yemen, 1990–
.32	*Northern Yemen
	For ancient history to 622, see 939.49
(.320 1)	Ancient history to 622
	(Optional number; prefer 939.49)
.320 2–.320 4	622–1918
	Add to base number 953.320 the numbers following 953.30 in 953.302–953.304, e.g., 1740–1918 953.3204
.320 5	1918–
.320 52	1918–1990
	Including Yemen Arab Republic, 1962–1990
	Class here 20th century
	For 1900–1918, see 953.3204; for 1990–1999, see 953.32053
.320 53	Period as part of Republic of Yemen, 1990–
.35	*Southern Yemen
	For ancient history to 622, see 939.49
(.350 1)	Ancient history to 622
	(Optional number; prefer 939.49)
.350 2	622–1517
.350 3	1517–1839
.350 4	British period, 1839–1967
	Including 19th century, 20th century
	For 1800–1839, see 953.3503; for 1967–1990, see 953.35052; for 1900–1999, see 953.35053

*Add as instructed under 930–990

.350 5	1967–
.350 52	1967–1990
	Class here People's Democratic Republic of Yemen, 1970–1990
.350 53	Period as part of Republic of Yemen, 1990–

.5 †Oman and United Arab Emirates

> *For ancient history to 622, see 939.49*

.53 †Oman

> *For ancient history to 622, see 939.49*

> (Option: Class here Oman to 622; prefer 939.49)

.57 †United Arab Emirates

> *For ancient history to 622, see 939.49*

> (Option: Class here United Arab Emirates to 622; prefer 939.49)

.6 †Persian Gulf States

> *For ancient history to 622, see 939.49; for Oman and United Arab Emirates, see 953.5*

> (Option: Class here Persian Gulf States to 622; prefer 939.49)

.63 †Qatar

> *For ancient history to 622, see 939.49*

> (Option: Class here Qatar to 622; prefer 939.49)

.65 †Bahrain

> *For ancient history to 622, see 939.49*

> (Option: Class here Bahrain to 622; prefer 939.49)

.67 †Kuwait

> *For ancient history to 622, see 939.49*

> (Options: Class here Kuwait to 622; prefer 939.49. Class here Persian Gulf Crisis and War, 1990–1991; prefer 956.70442)

.8 *Saudi Arabia

> *For ancient history to 622, see 939.49*

(.801) History to 622

> (Optional number; prefer 939.49)

.802–.805 622–

> Add to base number 953.80 the numbers following 953.0 in 953.02–953.05, e.g., 1740–1926 953.804

*Add as instructed under 930–990

†Add as instructed under 930–990; however, do not add historical periods

.805 3	1964–1999

Number built according to instructions under 953.802–953.805

Class military operations in Saudia Arabia during Persian Gulf Crisis and War, 1990–1991, in 956.704424

954 *India and neighboring south Asian countries

Class here south Asia

Subdivisions are added for India and neighboring south Asian countries together, for India alone

For history of India to 647, see 934

(.01)	Ancient history to 647

(Optional number; prefer 934)

Add to base number 954.01 the numbers following 934.0 in 934.01–934.07, e.g., reign of Aśoka 954.0145

.02	647–1785
.021	647–997

Including 7th century

For 600–647, see 934.07

.022	Period of Muslim conquests, 997–1206
.022 3	Period of Ghazni dynasty, 997–1196
.022 5	Period of Ghor dynasty, 1196–1206
.023	1206–1414
.023 2	Period of slave kings of Delhi, 1206–1290
.023 4	Period of Khalji dynasty, 1290–1320
.023 6	Period of Tughluk dynasty, 1320–1414
.024	1414–1526
.024 2	Period of Sayyid dynasty, 1414–1451
.024 5	Period of Lodi dynasty, 1451–1526
.025	Period of Mogul Empire, 1526–1707
.025 2	Reign of Babur, 1526–1530
.025 3	Reign of Humayun, 1530–1556
.025 4	Reign of Akbar, 1556–1605

Class here 16th century

For a specific part of 16th century not provided for here, see the part, e.g., 1500–1526 954.0236

*Add as instructed under 930–990

.025 6	Reign of Jahangir, 1605–1627
.025 7	Reign of Shahjahan, 1628–1658
.025 8	Reign of Aurangzeb, 1658–1707

Class here 17th century

> *For a specific part of 17th century not provided for here, see the part, e.g., 1605–1627 954.0256*

.029	Period of European penetration, 1707–1785
.029 2	1707–1744
.029 4	Period of Anglo-French conflict, 1744–1757

Including Battle of Plassey, 1757

.029 6	1757–1772

Including governorship of Lord Clive, 1757–1767

.029 8	Governorship of Warren Hastings, 1772–1785
.03	Period of British rule, 1785–1947

> *For governorship of Lord Clive, see 954.0296; for governorship of Warren Hastings, see 954.0298*

.031	Period of East India Company, 1785–1858

Class here 19th century

> *For 1858–1899, see 954.035*

.031 1	Governorships of Sir John Macpherson, Marquis Cornwallis (first term), John Shore (Lord Teignmouth), 1785–1798
.031 2	Governorships of Marquess Wellesley, Marquess Cornwallis (second term), Sir George Barlow, 1798–1807
.031 3	Governorships of 1st Earl of Minto, Marquess of Hastings, Earl Amherst, 1807–1828
.031 4	Governorships of Lord Bentinck, Baron Metcalfe, Earl of Auckland, 1828–1842
.031 5	Governorships of Earl of Ellenborough and Viscount Hardinge, 1842–1848
.031 6	Governorship of Marquis of Dalhousie, 1848–1856
.031 7	Governorship of Earl Canning, 1856–1862

Including Sepoy Mutiny, 1857–1858

> *For governorship of Earl Canning during 1858–1862, see 954.0351*

.035	Period of control by crown, 1858–1947

Class here period of Indian national movement, 1885–1947; 20th century

> *For 1947–1971, see 954.04; for 1971–1999, see 954.05*

.035 1	Governorships of Earl Canning, 8th Earl of Elgin, Baron Lawrence, 1858–1868
.035 2	Governorships of Earl of Mayo and Earl of Northbrook, 1869–1876
.035 3	Governorships of Earl of Lytton and Marquess of Ripon, 1876–1884
.035 4	Governorships of Marquis of Dufferin and Marquess of Lansdowne, 1884–1894
.035 5	Governorships of 9th Earl of Elgin and Marquis of Curzon, 1894–1905
.035 6	Governorships of 4th Earl of Minto and Baron Hardinge, 1905–1916
.035 7	Governorships of Viscount Chelmsford and Marquess of Reading, 1916–1926
.035 8	Governorships of Earl of Halifax and Marquess of Willingdon, 1926–1936
.035 9	Governorships of Marquess of Linlithgow, Earl of Wavell, Earl Mountbatten, 1936–1947

.04   **1947–1971**

.042   **Prime ministership of Jawaharlal Nehru, 1947–1964**

.043   **Prime ministership of Lal Bahadur Shastri, 1964–1966**

> (Option: Class here Indo-Pakistan War, 1965; prefer 954.9045)

.045   **First prime ministership of Indira Gandhi, 1966–1977**

> *For first prime ministership of Indira Gandhi during 1971–1977, see 954.051*

.05   **1971–**

.051   **Later half of first prime ministership of Indira Gandhi, 1971–1977**

> (Option: Class here Indo-Pakistan War, 1971; prefer 954.92051)

.052   **1977–1999**

> Including prime ministerships of Morarji Desai, 1977–1979; of Charan Singh, 1979; of Rajiv Gandhi, 1984–1989; of Vishwanath Pratap Singh, 1989–1990; of Chandra Shekhar, 1990–1991; of P. V. Narasimha Rao, 1991–1999; second prime ministership of Indira Gandhi, 1980–1984

.053   **1999–**

.053 1   Prime ministership of Atal Bihari Vajpayee, 1999–2004

.053 2   Prime ministership of Manmohan Singh, 2004–2014

.053 3   Prime ministership of Narendra Modī, 2014–

.1–.8   Localities of India

Add to base number 954 the numbers following —54 in notation 541–548 from Table 2, e.g., northeastern India 954.1; then add further as follows:
001–009   Standard subdivisions
Add to 00 the numbers following 00 in notation 001–009 from table under 930–990, e.g., ethnic and national groups 004, ethnic and national groups in northeastern India 954.1004
(01)   Ancient history to 647
(Optional number; prefer 934.1–934.8)
Add to 01 the numbers following 934.0 in 934.01–934.07, e.g., northeastern India during reign of Aśoka 954.10145
02–05   647 to present
Add to 0 the numbers following 954.0 in 954.02–954.05, e.g., northeastern India during 1971 to present 954.105

.9   Other jurisdictions

Class here Pakistan (West and East, 1947–1971)

.900 1–.900 9   Standard subdivisions of Pakistan (West and East, 1947–1971)

As modified in notation 001–009 from table under 930–990

(.901)   History of Pakistan (West and East, 1947–1971) to 647

(Optional number; prefer 934.9)

Add to base number 954.901 the numbers following 934.0 in 934.01–934.07, e.g., reign of Aśoka 954.90145

\>   954.902–954.905 Historical periods of Pakistan (West and East, 1947–1971)

Class comprehensive works in 954.9

For ancient history to 647, see 934.9

(Option: Class early history to 647 in 954.901; prefer 934.9)

.902–.903   647–1947

Add to base number 954.90 the numbers following 954.0 in 954.02–954.03, e.g., period of East India Company 954.9031

.904   1947–1971

.904 2   Administration of Mahomed Ali Jinnah, 1947–1948

.904 3   1948–1958

.904 5   Administration of Mohammad Ayub Khan, 1958–1969

Including Indo-Pakistan War, 1965
(Option: Class Indo-Pakistan War, 1965, in 954.043)

.904 6   Administration of Aga Muhammad Yahya Khan, 1969–1971

.905   1971–

.91   *Pakistan

(.910 1)   Ancient history to 647

(Optional number; prefer 934.91)

Add to base number 954.9101 the numbers following 934.0 in 934.01–934.07, e.g., reign of Aśoka 954.910145

>   954.910 2–954.910 5 Historical periods of Pakistan

Class comprehensive works in 954.91

For ancient history to 647, see 934.91

(Option: Class early history to 647 in 954.9101; prefer 934.91)

.910 2–.910 3   647–1947

Add to base number 954.910 the numbers following 954.0 in 954.02–954.03, e.g., period of East India Company 954.91031

.910 4   1947–1971

Add to base number 954.9104 the numbers following 954.904 in 954.9042–954.9046, e.g., administration of Mahomed Ali Jinnah 954.91042

.910 5   1971–

For Indo-Pakistan War, 1971, see 954.9205

.910 51   1971–1988

.910 52   1988–1999

.910 53   1999–

.910 531   Administration of Pervez Musharraf, 1999–2008

.910 532   2008–

Including administrations of Āṣif ʿAlī Zardārī, 2008–2013; of Mamnoon Hussain, 2013 to present

*Add as instructed under 930–990

.911–.918   Localities of Pakistan

> Add to base number 954.91 the numbers following —5491 in notation 54911–54918 from Table 2, e.g., Federally Administered Tribal Areas 954.911; then add further as follows:
>
> 001–009   Standard subdivisions
>> Add to 00 the numbers following 00 in notation 001–009 from table under 930–990, e.g., ethnic and national groups 004, ethnic and national groups in Federally Administered Tribal Areas 954.911004
>
> (01)   Ancient history to 647
>> (Optional number; prefer 934.911–934.918)
>> Add to 01 the numbers following 934.0 in 934.01–934.07, e.g., Federally Administered Tribal Areas during reign of Aśoka 954.9110145
>
> 02–05   647 to present
>> Add to 0 the numbers following 954.91 in 954.9102–954.9105, e.g., Federally Administered Tribal Areas during 1971 to present 954.91105

.92   *Bangladesh

(.920 1)   Ancient history to 647

> (Optional number; prefer 934.92)

> Add to base number 954.9201 the numbers following 934.0 in 934.01–934.07, e.g., reign of Aśoka 954.920145

>   954.920 2–954.920 5   Historical periods of Bangladesh

> Class comprehensive works in 954.92

> *For ancient history to 647, see 934.92*

> (Option: Class early history to 647 in 954.9201; prefer 934.92)

.920 2–.920 3   647–1947

> Add to base number 954.920 the numbers following 954.0 in 954.02–954.03, e.g., period of East India Company 954.92031

.920 4   1947–1971

> Add to base number 954.9204 the numbers following 954.904 in 954.9042–954.9046, e.g., administration of Mahomed Ali Jinnah 954.92042

.920 5   1971–

.920 51   ‡Indo-Pakistan War, 1971

> (Option: Class Indo-Pakistan War, 1971, in 954.051)

.920 52   Administration of Mujibur Rahman, 1971–1975

.920 53   1975–1991

---

*Add as instructed under 930–990
‡Add as instructed under 940–990

.920 54	1991–

.922–.929   Localities of Bangladesh

> Add to base number 954.92 the numbers following —5492 in notation 54922–54929 from Table 2, e.g., Dhaka Division 954.922; then add further as follows:
>
> 001–009   Standard subdivisions
>> Add to 00 the numbers following 00 in notation 001–009 from table under 930–990, e.g., ethnic and national groups 004, ethnic and national groups in Dhaka Division 954.922004
>
> (01)   Ancient history to 647
>> (Optional number; prefer 934.922–934.929)
>> Add to 01 the numbers following 934.0 in 934.01–934.07, e.g., Dhaka Division during reign of Aśoka 954.9220145
>
> 02–05   647 to present
>> Add to 0 the numbers following 954.92 in 954.9202–954.9205, e.g., Dhaka Division during 1971 to present 954.92205

.93   *Sri Lanka

.930 1   Early history to 1795

.930 2   British period, 1795–1948

> Including 20th century

> *For 1948–1972, see 954.93031; for 1972–1999, see 954.93032*

.930 3   1948–

.930 31   Period as independent Commonwealth state, 1948–1972

.930 32   Period as republic, 1972–

.95   †Maldives

.96   †Nepal

.98   †Bhutan

955   *Iran

> *For early history to 637, see 935.7*

(.01)   Early history to 637

> (Optional number; prefer 935.7)

> Add to base number 955.01 the numbers following 935.0 in 935.01–935.07, e.g., period of Sassanian Empire 955.017

.02   637–1499

---

*Add as instructed under 930–990
†Add as instructed under 930–990; however, do not add historical periods

.022	Period of Arab domination, 637–1055
	Including 7th century, 11th century
	For 600–637, see 935.07; for 1055–1099, see 955.024
	See Manual at 930–990: Add table: Centuries
.024	Period of Turkish domination, 1055–1219
.026	Period of Mongol domination, 1219–1335
.028	1335–1499
	Including 14th century
	Class here period of Turkoman domination, 1405–1499
	For 1300–1335, see 955.026
.03	Period of Persian dynasties, 1499–1794
.04	1794–1906
.05	1906–2005
.051	1906–1925
.052	Reign of Reza Shah Pahlavi, 1925–1941
.053	Reign of Mohammed Reza Pahlavi, 1941–1979
.054	1979–2005
.054 2	‡Period of Ruhollah Khomeini, 1979–1989
	Class here Iraqi-Iranian Conflict, 1980–1988
	(Option: Class Iraqi-Iranian Conflict in 956.70441)
.054 3	1989–1997
.054 4	Administration of Muḥammad Khātamī, 1997–2005
.06	2005–
.061	Administration of Mahmoud Ahmadinejad, 2005–2013
.062	Administration of Hassan Rouhani, 2013–

‡Add as instructed under 940–990

.1–.9   **Localities of Iran**

> Add to base number 955 the numbers following —55 in notation 551–559 from Table 2, e.g., Ardabīl province 955.12; then add further as follows:
>
> 001–009   Standard subdivisions
>> Add to 00 the numbers following 00 in notation 001–009 from table under 930–990, e.g., ethnic and national groups 004, ethnic and national groups in Ardabīl province 955.12004
>
> (01)   Early history to 637
>> (Optional number; prefer 935.71–935.79)
>> Add to 01 the numbers following 935.0 in 935.01–935.07, e.g., Ardabīl province during period of Sassanian Empire 955.12017
>
> 02–06   637 to present
>> Add to 0 the numbers following 955 in 955.02–955.06, e.g., Ardabīl province during 2005 to present 955.1206

.23   ***Māzandarān province**

> *For early history to 637, see 939.6*

(.230 1)   Early history to 637

> (Optional number; prefer 939.6)

> Class here Hyrcania

956   *Middle East (Near East)

.01   Early history to 1900

> *For ancient history to ca. 640, see 939.4*

(.012)   Ancient history to ca. 640

> (Optional number; prefer 939.4)

> Add to base number 956.012 the numbers following 939.40 in 939.401–939.405, e.g., Hellenistic period 956.0124

.013   640–1000

> Including 7th century

> *For 600–640, see 939.405*

.014   Period of Seljuk supremacy, 1000–1300

> Including First Crusade, 1096–1099; Second Crusade, 1147–1149; Third Crusade, 1189–1192

.015   1300–1900

> Class here Ottoman Empire, ca. 1300–1922

>> *For 1900–1918, see 956.02; for 1918–1922, see 956.03. For a specific part of the Ottoman Empire, see the part, e.g., Ottoman Empire in Turkey 956.1015*

.02   1900–1918

*Add as instructed under 930–990

.03	1918–1945
.04	1945–1980

Class here 20th century

For 1900–1918, see 956.02; for 1918–1945, see 956.03; for 1980–1999, see 956.05

.042	‡Israel-Arab War, 1948–1949
.044	‡Sinai Campaign, 1956
.046	‡Israel-Arab War, 1967 (Six Days' War)
.048	‡Israel-Arab War, 1973 (Yom Kippur War)
.05	1980–
.052	‡Israel-Lebanon-Syria Conflict, 1982–1985
.053	1985–1999
.054	2000–

.1   ***Turkey**

For divisions of Turkey, see 956.2–956.6

.101	Early history to 1918

For ancient history to ca. 640, see 939.2

(.101 2)	Ancient history to ca. 640

(Optional number; prefer 939.2)

.101 3	640–1100

Including 7th century

For 600–640, see 939.2

.101 4	Period of Seljuk dynasty, 1100–1300
.101 5	1300–1918

Class here period of Ottoman Empire, 1300–1922

For 1918–1922, see 956.1023

.101 51	1300–1451

Including 15th century

For 1451–1499, see 956.10152

.101 52	1451–1566

Including 16th century

For 1566–1599, see 956.10153

---

*Add as instructed under 930–990
‡Add as instructed under 940–990

.101 53	1566–1774

Including 18th century

For 1774–1799, see 956.10154

.101 54	1774–1918

For Russo-Turkish War, 1877–1878, see 949.60387

.102	1918–1950

Class here 20th century; period of Republic, 1923 to present

For 1900–1918, see 956.1015; for 1950–1999, see 956.103

.102 3	1918–1923
.102 4	Administration of Kemal Atatürk, 1923–1938
.102 5	Administration of İsmet İnönü, 1938–1950
.103	1950–1999
.103 5	1950–1959
.103 6	1960–1969
.103 7	1970–1979
.103 8	1980–1989
.103 9	1990–1999
.104	2000–
.104 1	2000–2019
.104 11	2000–2009
.104 12	2010–2019
.104 2	2020–2029

> **956.2–956.6 Divisions of Turkey**

Class comprehensive works in 956.1

For Turkey in Europe, see 949.61

.2   ***Western Turkey**

For history of western Turkey to 640, see 939.2. For history of a specific part of western Turkey to 640, see the part in 939, e.g., history of Troy 939.21

(Option: Class history of a specific part of western Turkey to 640 with the part in 956.2, e.g., history of Troy 956.22)

*Add as instructed under 930–990

.201–.204   Historical periods

> Add to base number 956.20 the numbers following 956.10 in 956.101–956.104, e.g., period of Ottoman Empire 956.2015

.22–.28   Localities of western Turkey

> Add to base number 956.2 the numbers following —562 in notation 5622–5628 from Table 2, e.g., Çanakkale Province (Çanakkale İli) 956.22; then add further as follows:
>
> 001–009   Standard subdivisions
>> Add to 00 the numbers following 00 in notation 001–009 from table under 930–990, e.g., ethnic and national groups 004, ethnic and national groups in Çanakkale Province (Çanakkale İli) 956.22004
>
> 01–04   Historical periods
>> Add to 0 the numbers following 956.10 in 956.101–956.104, e.g., Çanakkale Province (Çanakkale İli) during period of Ottoman Empire 956.22015

.3   *North central Turkey

> *For history of north central Turkey to 640, see 939.3. For history of a specific part of western Turkey to 640, see the part in 939, e.g., history of Paphlagonia 939.317*

> (Option: Class history of a specific part of north central Turkey to 640 with the part in 956.3, e.g., history of Paphlagonia 956.37)

.301–.304   Historical periods

> Add to base number 956.30 the numbers following 956.10 in 956.101–956.104, e.g., period of Ottoman Empire 956.3015

.31–.38   Localities of north central Turkey

> Add to base number 956.3 the numbers following —563 in notation 5631–5638 from Table 2, e.g., Bursa Province (Bursa İli) 956.31; then add further as follows:
>
> 001–009   Standard subdivisions
>> Add to 00 the numbers following 00 in notation 001–009 from table under 930–990, e.g., ethnic and national groups 004, ethnic and national groups in Bursa Province (Bursa İli) 956.31004
>
> 01–04   Historical periods
>> Add to 0 the numbers following 956.10 in 956.101–956.104, e.g., Bursa Province (Bursa İli) during period of Ottoman Empire 956.31015

.4   *South central Turkey

> *For history of south central Turkey to 640, see 939.2. For history of a specific part of south central Turkey to 640, see the part in 939, e.g., history of Cappadocia to 640 939.34*

> (Option: Class history of a specific part of south central Turkey to 640 with the part in 956.4, e.g., history of Cappadocia to 640 956.41)

---

*Add as instructed under 930–990

.401–.404   Historical periods

> Add to base number 956.40 the numbers following 956.10 in 956.101–956.104, e.g., period of Ottoman Empire 956.4015

.41–.49   Localities of south central Turkey

> Add to base number 956.4 the numbers following —564 in notation 5641–5649 from Table 2, e.g., Aksaray Province (Aksaray İli), Kayseri Province (Kayseri İli), Kırşehir Province (Kırşehir İli), Nevşehir Province (Nevşehir İli), Niğde Province (Niğde İli) 956.41; then add further as follows:
>
> 001–009   Standard subdivisions
>> Add to 00 the numbers following 00 in notation 001–009 from table under 930–990, e.g., ethnic and national groups 004, ethnic and national groups in Aksaray Province (Aksaray İli), Kayseri Province (Kayseri İli), Kırşehir Province (Kırşehir İli), Nevşehir Province (Nevşehir İli), Niğde Province (Niğde İli) 956.41004
>
> 01–04   Historical periods
>> Add to 0 the numbers following 956.10 in 956.101–956.104, e.g., Aksaray Province (Aksaray İli), Kayseri Province (Kayseri İli), Kırşehir Province (Kırşehir İli), Nevşehir Province (Nevşehir İli), Niğde Province (Niğde İli) during period of Ottoman Empire 956.41015

.5   *East central Turkey

> *For history of east central Turkey to 640, see 939.33. For history of a specific part of east central Turkey to 640, see the part in 939, e.g., history of Commagene 939.36*

> (Option: Class history of a specific part of east central Turkey to 640 with the part in 956.5, e.g., history of Commagene 956.52)

.501–.504   Historical periods

> Add to base number 956.50 the numbers following 956.10 in 956.101–956.104, e.g., period of Ottoman Empire 956.5015

.51–.58   Localities of east central Turkey

> Add to base number 956.5 the numbers following —565 in notation 5651–5658 from Table 2, e.g., Şanlıurfa Province (Şanlıurfa İli) 956.51; then add further as follows:
>
> 001–009   Standard subdivisions
>> Add to 00 the numbers following 00 in notation 001–009 from table under 930–990, e.g., ethnic and national groups 004, ethnic and national groups in Şanlıurfa Province (Şanlıurfa İli) 956.51004
>
> 01–04   Historical periods
>> Add to 0 the numbers following 956.10 in 956.101–956.104, e.g., Şanlıurfa Province (Şanlıurfa İli) during period of Ottoman Empire 956.51015

*Add as instructed under 930–990

.6 ***Eastern Turkey**

> *For history of eastern Turkey to 640, see 939.42. For history of a specific part of eastern Turkey to 640, see the part in 939, e.g., history of ancient kingdom of Armenia 939.55*

> (Option: Class history of a specific part of eastern Turkey to 640 with the part in 956.6, e.g., history of ancient kingdom of Armenia 956.62012)

.601–.604 Historical periods

> Add to base number 956.60 the numbers following 956.10 in 956.101–956.104, e.g., period of Ottoman Empire 956.6015

.62–.67 Localities of eastern Turkey

> Add to base number 956.6 the numbers following —566 in notation 5662–5667 from Table 2, e.g., northeastern Turkey 956.62; then add further as follows:
>
> 001–009   Standard subdivisions
> > Add to 00 the numbers following 00 in notation 001–009 from table under 930–990, e.g., ethnic and national groups 004, ethnic and national groups in northeastern Turkey 956.62004
>
> 01–04   Historical periods
> > Add to 0 the numbers following 956.10 in 956.101–956.104, e.g., northeastern Turkey during period of Ottoman Empire 956.62015

.62 Northeastern Turkey

Number built according to instructions under 930–990

Class here comprehensive works on Armenia region

For country of Armenia, see 947.56

(.620 12) Ancient history to 640

(Optional number; prefer 939.55)

.620 154 1774–1918

Number built according to instructions under 930–990

Class here Armenian massacres, 1894–1896; Armenian Genocide, 1915–1916

.620 23 1918–1923

Number built according to instructions under 930–990

Class here Republic of Armenia, 1918–1920

.7 ***Iraq**

> *For history to 637, see 935*

*Add as instructed under 930–990

(.701)	Ancient history to 637

(Optional number; prefer 935)

Add to base number 956.701 the numbers following 935.0 in 935.01–935.07, e.g., Hellenistic period 956.7016

.702	637–1553

Including 7th century, 16th century

For 600–637, see 935.07; for 1553–1600, see 956.703

See Manual at 930–990: Add table: Centuries

.703	Period of Ottoman Empire, 1553–1920
.704	1920–
.704 1	Period of mandate, 1920–1932

Class here reign of Faysal I, 1921–1933

For reign of Faysal I during 1932–1933, see 956.7042

.704 2	Period of independent monarchy, 1932–1958

Including reigns of Ghazi I, Faisal II

.704 3	Period of Republic, 1958–

For administration of Saddam Hussein, see 956.7044

.704 4	1979–

Class here administration of Saddam Hussein, 1979–2003

.704 41	1979–1990

(Option: Class here Iraqi-Iranian Conflict, 1980–1988; prefer 955.0542)

.704 42	‡Persian Gulf Crisis and War, 1990–1991

Class here Iraq-Kuwait Crisis, 1990–1991, Persian Gulf War, 1991

(Option: Class in 953.67)

.704 423 1	Participation of specific groups of countries

Number built according to instructions under 940–990

For participation of specific countries, see 956.7044234–956.7044239

.704 423 12	Participation of Arab countries
.704 43	‡1991–

Class here Iraq War, 2003–2011; Iraq Civil War, 2014–2017; period of occupation and reconstruction, 2003 to present

‡Add as instructed under 940–990

.72–.75   Localities of Iraq

> Add to base number 956.7 the numbers following —567 in notation 5672–5675 from Table 2, e.g., Kurdish Autonomous Region 956.72; then add further as follows:
>
> 001–009   Standard subdivisions
>> Add to 00 the numbers following 00 in notation 001–009 from table under 930–990, e.g., ethnic and national groups 004, ethnic and national groups in Kurdish Autonomous Region 956.72004
>
> (01)   Ancient history to 637
>> (Optional number; prefer 935.2–935.5)
>> Add to 01 the numbers following 935.0 in 935.01–935.07, e.g., Kurdish Autonomous Region during Hellenistic period 956.72016
>
> 02–04   637 to present
>> Add to 0 the numbers following 956.7 in 956.702–956.704, e.g., Kurdish Autonomous Region during 1920 to present 956.7204

.9   *Syria, Lebanon, Cyprus, Israel, Jordan*

.901–.905   Early history to present

> Add to base number 956.90 the numbers following 956.0 in 956.01–956.05, e.g., 1945–1980 956.904

.91   *Syria

> *For early history to ca. 640, see 939.43*

(.910 1)   Early history to ca. 640

> (Optional number; prefer 939.43)

.910 2   640–1516

> Including 7th century
>
> *For 600–640, see 939.43*

.910 3   Period of Ottoman Empire, 1516–1920

.910 4   1920–

.910 41   Period of mandate, 1920–1945

.910 42   Period of Republic, 1945–

.910 421   1945–1970

> Including period as a part of United Arab Republic, 1958–1961
>
> Class Israel-Arab War, 1948–1949, in 956.042; class Israel-Arab War, 1967, in 956.046; class comprehensive works on United Arab Republic in 962.053

.910 422   Administration of Hafez al-Assad, 1970–2000

> Class Israel-Arab War, 1973, in 956.048; class Israel-Lebanon-Syria Conflict, 1982–1985, in 956.052

---

*Add as instructed under 930–990

.910 423	‡Administration of Bashar al-Assad, 2000–
	Class here Civil War, 2011 to present

.912–.914   Localities of Syria

> Add to base number 956.91 the numbers following —5691 in notation 56912–56914 from Table 2, e.g., city of Damascus 956.9144; then add further as follows:
> 001–009   Standard subdivisions
>> Add to 00 the numbers following 00 in notation 001–009 from table under 930–990, e.g., ethnic and national groups 004, ethnic and national groups in city of Damascus 956.9144004
> (01)   Early history to ca. 640
>> (Optional number; prefer 939.432–939.434)
> 02–04   Ca. 640 to present
>> Add to 0 the numbers following 956.91 in 956.9102–956.9104, e.g., city of Damascus during period of mandate 956.9144041

.92   *Lebanon

> *For early history to ca. 640, see 939.44*

(.920 2)   Early history to ca. 640

> Class here Phoenicia

> (Optional number; prefer 939.44)

.920 3   640–1926

.920 32   640–1517

> Including 7th century

> *For 600–640, see 939.44*

.920 34   Period of Ottoman Empire, 1517–1920

> Including period of autonomy, 1861–1918

.920 35   Period of mandate, 1920–1941

> *For 1926–1941, see 956.92042*

.920 4   1926–

> Class here 20th century

> *For 1900–1920, see 956.92034; for 1920–1926, see 956.92035*

.920 42   1926–1941

.920 43   1941–

> Class Israel-Arab War, 1948–1949, in 956.042

> *For 1975–1990, see 956.92044; for 1990 to present, see 956.92045*

*Add as instructed under 930–990
‡Add as instructed under 940–990

.920 44	‡Period of civil war and religious strife, 1975–1990
	Class here Civil War, 1975–1990
	Class Israel-Lebanon-Syria Conflict, 1982–1985, in 956.052
.920 45	1990–
.920 451	1990–2006
.920 452	‡Lebanon War, 2006
.920 453	2006–
.925	Beirut
.925 001–.925 009	Standard subdivisions

Add to 956.92500 the numbers following 00 in notation 001–009 from table under 930–990, e.g., ethnic and national groups 004, ethnic and national groups in Beirut 956.925004

(.925 02)	Early history to ca. 640

(Optional number; prefer 939.445)

.925 03–.925 04	Ca. 640 to present

Add to 956.9250 the numbers following 956.92 in 956.9203–956.9204, e.g., Beirut during 1926 to present 956.92504

.93	*Cyprus
.930 1	Early history to 1571

Including 16th century

For ancient history to ca. 640, see 939.37; for 1571–1599, see 956.9302

(.930 12)	Ancient history to ca. 640

(Optional number; prefer 939.37)

.930 2	1571–1878
.930 3	British period, 1878–1960

Class here 20th century

For 1960–1999, see 956.9304

.930 4	1960–
.94	*Palestine; Israel

For early history of Palestine to 70, see 933; for early history of Israel to 70, see 933.4

See also 320.54095694 for Zionism; also 909.04924 for world history of Jews

---

*Add as instructed under 930–990
‡Add as instructed under 940–990

(.940 1)	Early history to 70
	(Optional number; prefer 933 for Palestine to 70; prefer 933.4 for Israel to 70)
	Add to base number 956.9401 the numbers following 933.0 in 933.01–933.05, e.g., age of Solomon 956.94012
.940 2	Mishnaic and Talmudic periods, 70–640
.940 3	640–1917
.940 31	640–1096
	Including 7th century
	For 600–640, see 956.9402
.940 32	Period of Crusades, 1096–1291
.940 33	Mameluke period, 1291–1517
.940 34	Period of Ottoman Empire, 1517–1917
.940 4	Period of British control, 1917–1948
.940 5	1948–
	Class here 20th century
	For 1900–1917, see 956.9403; for 1917–1948, see 956.9404
.940 52	1948–1967
	Class Israel-Arab War, 1948–1949, in 956.042; class Sinai Campaign, 1956, in 956.044; class Israel-Arab War, 1967, in 956.046
.940 53	1967–1974
	Class Israel-Arab War, 1973, in 956.048
.940 54	1974–2001
	Class Israel-Lebanon-Syria Conflict, 1982–1985, in 956.052
.940 55	2001–

.942–.949	Localities of Palestine; Israel

Add to base number 956.94 the numbers following —5692 in notation 56942–56949 from Table 2, e.g., Jerusalem district 956.944; then add further as follows:

	001–009	Standard subdivisions

Add to 00 the numbers following 00 in notation 001–009 from table under 930–990, e.g., ethnic and national groups 004, ethnic and national groups in Jerusalem district 956.944004

	(01)	Early history to 70

(Optional number; prefer 933.2–933.5 for localities of Palestine to 70; prefer 933.4 for localities of Israel to 70) Add to 01 the numbers following 933.0 in 933.01–933.05, e.g., Jerusalem district during age of Solomon 956.944012

	02–05	70 to present

Add to 0 the numbers following 956.940 in 956.9402–956.9405, e.g., Jerusalem district during 1948 to present 956.94405

.949	*Darom district

For early history of Arabia Petraea portion of Darom district to 70, see 933.48; for early history of Judah, Judaea portion of Darom district to 70, see 933.49; for early history of Edom portion of Darom district to 70, see 939.464

(.949 01)	Early history to 70

(Optional number; prefer 933.49 for Judah, Judaea; prefer 939.464 for Edom)

Including Edom, Judah, Judaea

.95	*Jordan

For early history to 70, see 933.5

(.950 1)	Early history to 70

(Optional number; prefer 933.5)

Add to base number 956.9501 the numbers following 933.0 in 933.01–933.05, e.g., Roman period 956.95015

.950 2	70–640
.950 3	640–1923

Including 7th century, period of Ottoman Empire

For 600–640, see 956.9502

.950 4	1923–
.950 42	Period of mandate, 1923–1946

*Add as instructed under 930–990

.950 43	Period of Hashemite Kingdom, 1946–
	Including reign of Hussein during 1953–1967
	Class Israel-Arab War, 1948–1949, in 956.042

> *For 1967–1999, comprehensive works on reign of Hussein, 1953–1999, see 956.95044; for reign of Abdullah II, 1999 to present, see 956.95045*

.950 44	1967–1999
	Class here reign of Hussein, 1953–1999

> *For reign of Hussein during 1953–1967, see 956.95043*

.950 45	Reign of Abdullah II, 1999–
.954–.959	Localities of Jordan

Add to base number 956.95 the numbers following —5695 in notation 56954–56959 from Table 2, e.g., Amman Province 956.958; then add further as follows:

001–009   Standard subdivisions
                Add to 00 the numbers following 00 in notation 001–009 from table under 930–990, e.g., ethnic and national groups 004, ethnic and national groups in Amman Province 956.958004

(01)   Early history to 70
                (Optional number; prefer 933.54–933.59)
                Add to 01 the numbers following 933.0 in 933.01–933.05, e.g., Amman Province during Roman period 956.958015

02–04   70 to present
                Add to 0 the numbers following 956.950 in 956.9502–956.9504, e.g., Amman Province during 1923 to present 956.95804

.956 3	*Karak Province

> *For early history to 70, see 939.462*

(.956 301)	Early history to 70

> (Optional number; prefer 939.462)

> Class here Moab

.957 7	*Ma'ān Province

> *For early history to 70, see 939.48*

(.957 701)	Early history to 70

> (Optional number; prefer 939.48)

> Class here Petra

957   *Siberia (Asiatic Russia)

.03	Pre-Russian period to 1581

---

* Add as instructed under 930–990

.07	1581–1855
.08	1855–

> Add to base number 957.08 the numbers following 947.08 in 947.081–947.086, e.g., period of Siberia under Stalin 957.0842

.3–.7   Localities of Siberia (Asiatic Russia)

> Add to base number 957 the numbers following —57 in notation 573–577 from Table 2, e.g., western Siberia 957.3; then add further as follows:
> 001–009   Standard subdivisions
> > Add to 00 the numbers following 00 in notation 001–009 from table under 930–990, e.g., ethnic and national groups 004, ethnic and national groups in western Siberia 957.3004
> 03–08   Historical periods
> > Add to 0 the numbers following 957.0 in 957.03–957.08, e.g., Western Siberia during 1855 to present 957.308

958   *Central Asia

> *For early history to ca. 640, see 939.6*

> (Option: Class here early history to ca. 640; prefer 939.6)

.01–.04	Historical periods

> Add to base number 958.0 the numbers following 950 in 950.1–950.4, e.g., period of Mongol Empire 958.02

.1   *Afghanistan

.101	Early history to 1221

> *For early history to ca. 640, see 939.6*

> (Option: Class here early history to ca. 640; prefer 939.6)

.102	1221–1709
.103	1709–1919
.104	1919–
.104 2	1919–1933
.104 3	Reign of Muhammad Zahir Shah, 1933–1973
.104 4	Period of Republic, 1973–1978
.104 5	Period of Democratic Republic, 1978–1992
.104 6	1992–2001

> Class here Taliban period, 1996–2001

.104 7	‡2001–

> Class here Afghan War, 2001 to present

---

*Add as instructed under 930–990
‡Add as instructed under 940–990

.4   *Turkestan

> *For Turkmenistan, see 958.5; for Tajikistan, see 958.6; for Uzbekistan, see 958.7*

.407   Pre-Russian period to 1855

> Including 19th century

> *For early history to ca. 640, see 939.6; for 1855–1899, see 958.408*

> (Option: Class here early history to ca. 640; prefer 939.6)

.408   1855–

> Add to base number 958.408 the numbers following 947.08 in 947.081–947.086, e.g., later 20th century 958.4085

.43   *Kyrgyzstan

.430 7   Pre-Russian period to 1855

> Including 19th century

> *For 1855–1899, see 958.4308*

.430 8   1855–

> Add to base number 958.4308 the numbers following 947.08 in 947.081–947.086, e.g., later 20th century 958.43085

.45   *Kazakhstan

.450 7   Pre-Russian period to 1855

> Including 19th century

> *For 1855–1899, see 958.4508*

.450 8   1855–

> Add to base number 958.4508 the numbers following 947.08 in 947.081–947.086, e.g., later 20th century 958.45085

.5   *Turkmenistan

.507   Pre-Russian period to 1855

> Including 19th century

> *For early history to ca. 640, see 939.6; for 1855–1899, see 958.508*

> (Option: Class here early history to ca. 640; prefer 939.6)

.508   1855–

.508 1–.508 5   1855–1991

> Add to base number 958.508 the numbers following 947.08 in 947.081–947.085, e.g., later 20th century 958.5085

.508 6   1991–

*Add as instructed under 930–990

.508 61	Administration of Saparmurad Niyazov, 1991–2006
.508 62	Administration of Gurbanguly Berdimuhamedow, 2006–

.6   *Tajikistan

.607   Pre-Russian period to 1855

Including 19th century

For early history to ca. 640, see 939.6; for 1855–1899, see 958.608

(Option: Class here early history to ca. 640; prefer 939.6)

.608   1855–

Add to base number 958.608 the numbers following 947.08 in 947.081–947.086, e.g., later 20th century 958.6085

.7   *Uzbekistan

.707   Pre-Russian period to 1855

Including 19th century

For early history to ca. 640, see 939.6; for 1855–1899, see 958.708

(Option: Class here early history to ca. 640; prefer 939.6)

.708   1855–

Add to base number 958.708 the numbers following 947.08 in 947.081–947.086, e.g., later 20th century 958.7085

959   *Southeast Asia

.01   Early history to 1499

.02   1500–1699

.03   1700–1799

.04   1800–1899

.05   1900–

.051   1900–1941

Class here 20th century

For 1941–1945, see 959.052; for 1945–1999, see 959.053

.052   Period of Japanese occupation, 1941–1945

.053   1945–1999

.054   2000–

.1   *Myanmar

.102   Early history to 1826

---

*Add as instructed under 930–990

.103		Period of British conquest, 1826–1885

Class here 19th century

For 1800–1826, see 959.102; for 1886–1899, see 959.104

.104		Period of British rule, 1886–1948

Class here 20th century

For 1948–1999, see 959.105

.105		1948–
.105 1		1948–1962
.105 2		1962–1989
.105 3		1989–2016
.105 4		2016–
.3	***Thailand**	
.302		Early history to 1782
.302 1		Early history to 1219
.302 2		Period as Sukhothai, 1219–1350

Including 14th century

For 1350–1399, see 959.3023

.302 3		Period as Ayutthaya, 1350–1767

Including 18th century

For 1767–1782, see 959.3024; for 1782–1799, see 959.3031

.302 4		Reign of Tāk Sin, 1767–1782
.303		1782–1910
.303 1		Reign of Phutthayǭtfā Čhulālōk (Rama I), 1782–1809
.303 2		Reign of Phutthalœtlā Naphālai (Rama II), 1809–1824
.303 3		Reign of Nangklao (Rama III), 1824–1851
.303 4		Reign of Mongkut (Rama IV), 1851–1868
.303 5		Reign of Chulalongkorn (Rama V), 1868–1910
.304		1910–
.304 1		Reign of Vajiravudh (Rama VI), 1910–1925
.304 2		Reign of Prajadhipok (Rama VII), 1925–1935
.304 3		Reign of Ananda Mahidol (Rama VIII), 1935–1946
.304 4		Reign of Bhumibol Adulyadej (Rama IX), 1946–2016

*Add as instructed under 930–990

.304 5	Reign of Wachirālongkǫn (Vajiralongkorn, Rama X), 2016–
.4	***Laos**
.403	Early history to 1949

Including period as a part of French Indochina, 1893–1954

For 1949–1954, see 949.4041

.404	1949–

Class here 20th century

For 1900–1949, see 959.403

.404 1	1949–1975

Class military operations in Laos during Vietnamese War in 959.70434

.404 2	Period as People's Democratic Republic, 1975–
.5	***Malaysia, Brunei, Singapore**

Subdivisions are added for Malaysia, Brunei, Singapore together; for Malaysia alone

.503	Early history to 1946
.504	1946–1963
.505	Period of federation, 1963–

Class here 20th century

For 1900–1946, see 959.503; for 1946–1963, see 959.504; for 2003 to present, see 959.506

.505 1	Prime ministership of Tunku Abdul Rahman Putra Al-Haj, 1963–1970

Including separation of Singapore, 1965

.505 2	Prime ministership of Tun Haji Abdul Razak bin Dato' Hussein, 1971–1976
.505 3	Prime ministership of Datuk Hussein Onn, 1976–1981
.505 4	First prime ministership of Mahathir bin Mohamad, 1981–2003
.506	2003–
.506 1	Prime ministership of Datuk Abdullah bin Haji Ahmad Badawi, 2003–2009
.506 2	Prime ministership of Datuk Najib Tun Razak, 2009–2018
.506 3	Second prime ministership of Mahathir bin Mohamad, 2018–

*Add as instructed under 930–990

.51–.54   Localities of Malaysia

> Add to base number 959.5 the numbers following —595 in notation
> 5951–5954 from Table 2, e.g., Sarawak 959.54; then add further as follows:
>> 001–009   Standard subdivisions
>>> Add to 00 the numbers following 00 in notation 001–009
>>> from table under 930–990, e.g., ethnic and national groups
>>> 004, ethnic and national groups in Sarawak 959.54004
>> 03–06   Historical periods
>>> Add to 0 the numbers following 959.50 in 959.503–959.506,
>>> e.g., Sarawak during 2003 to present 959.5406

.55   *Brunei

.550 3   Early history to 1888

.550 4   Period as British protectorate, 1888–1983

.550 5   1984–

.57   *Singapore

.570 3   Early history to 1946

.570 4   1946–1963

.570 5   1963–

> Class here 20th century; period as separate nation, 1965–

>> *For 1900–1946, see 959.5703; for 1946–1963, see 959.5704*

.570 51   1963–1990

> Including period of federation with Malaysia, 1963–1965

> Class here prime ministership of Lee Kuan Yew, 1959–1990

>> *For prime ministership of Lee Kuan Yew during 1959–1963,*
>> *see 959.5704*

.570 52   Prime ministership of Goh Chok Tong, 1990–2004

.570 53   Prime ministership of Lee Hsien Loong, 2004–

.6   ***Cambodia**

.601   Early history to 802

.602   Period of Khmer Empire, 802–1431

.603   1431–1949

> Including period as a part of French Indochina, 1863–1949; 15th century

.604   1949–

> Class here 20th century

>> *For 1900–1949, see 959.603*

*Add as instructed under 930–990

.604 1	1949–1970
	Class military operations in Cambodia during Vietnamese War in 959.70434
.604 2	1970–1993
	Including period as Khmer Republic, 1970–1979
	Class here period as Kampuchea, 1979–1993
.604 3	1993–

.7   *Vietnam

.701	Early history to 939
.702	939–1883
.703	French period, 1883–1945
	Class here comprehensive works on French Indochina
	For Laos as a part of French Indochina, see 959.403; for Cambodia as a part of French Indochina, see 959.603; for Indochinese War, 1946–1954, see 959.7041
.704	1945–
	Class here 20th century
	For 1900–1945, see 959.703
.704 1	‡1945–1954
	Class here Indochinese War, 1946–1954
.704 2	1954–1961
	Class comprehensive works on period of North Vietnam and South Vietnam, 1954–1975, in 959.7043
.704 3	‡Vietnamese War, 1961–1975
	Class here comprehensive works on period of North Vietnam and South Vietnam, 1954–1975
	For 1954–1961, see 959.7042
.704 33	Participation of specific groups of countries, of specific countries, localities, groups
	Number built according to instructions under 940–990
	Class military participation of specific countries, localities, groups in 959.70434. Class a specific activity with the activity, e.g., efforts to preserve or restore peace 959.70431
.704 331	North Vietnam
.704 332	South Vietnam

*Add as instructed under 930–990
‡Add as instructed under 940–990

.704 332 2		National Liberation Front
		Class here Vietcong
.704 332 5		Government forces
.704 334–.704 339		Participation of specific countries and localities

Number built according to instructions under 940–990

Add to base number 959.70433 notation 4–9 from Table 2, e.g., United States participation 959.7043373; however, for North Vietnam, see 959.704331; for South Vietnam, see 959.704332

.704 4	1975–	
.71–.79	Localities of Vietnam	

Add to base number 959.7 the numbers following —597 in notation 5971–5979 from Table 2, e.g., mountain region of northern Vietnam 959.71; then add further as follows:

001–009 Standard subdivisions

Add to 00 the numbers following 00 in notation 001–009 from table under 930–990, e.g., ethnic and national groups 004, ethnic and national groups in mountain region of northern Vietnam 959.71004

01–04 Historical periods

Add to 0 the numbers following 959.70 in 959.701–959.704, e.g., mountain region of northern Vietnam during 1945 to present 959.7104

.8	*Indonesia and East Timor

Subdivisions are added for Indonesia and East Timor together, for Indonesia alone

---

> 959.801–959.804 Historical periods for Indonesia and East Timor together, for Indonesia alone

Class comprehensive works in 959.8

.801	Early history to 1602
.801 1	Early history to 358
.801 2	Period of Hindu kingdoms, 358–1478
.801 5	Period of Muslim rule, 1478–1602
.802	1602–1945
.802 1	Period of Dutch East India Company, 1602–1800
.802 2	Periods under control of British and Netherlands governments, 1800–1945
.802 21	1800–1808
.802 22	Administration of Herman Willem Daendels, 1808–1811

*Add as instructed under 930–990

.802 23	1811–1942
	Including Java War, 1825–1830
.802 24	Period of Japanese occupation, 1942–1945
.803	1945–1998

Class here 20th century; period of Republic, 1950 to present

For 1900–1942, see 959.80223; for 1942–1945, see 959.80224; for 1998 to present, see 959.804

.803 5	Administration of Soekarno, 1945–1967

Including period as United States of Indonesia, 1949–1950

.803 7	Administration of Soeharto, 1967–1998
.804	1998–
.804 1	1998–2004

Including administration of B. J. Habibie, 1998–1999; administration of Abdurrahman Wahid, 1999–2001

Class here administration of Megawati Soekarnoputri, 2001–2004

.804 2	Administration of Susilo Bambang Yudhoyono, 2004–2014
.804 3	Administration of Joko Widodo, 2014–
.81–.86	Localities of Indonesia

Add to base number 959.8 the numbers following —598 in notation 5981–5986 from Table 2, e.g., Sumatra and neighboring islands 959.81; then add further as follows:
001–009   Standard subdivisions
        Add to 00 the numbers following 00 in notation 001–009 from table under 930–990, e.g., ethnic and national groups 004, ethnic and national groups in Sumatra and neighboring islands 959.81004
01–04   Historical periods
        Add to 0 the numbers following 959.80 in 959.801–959.804, e.g., Sumatra and neighboring islands during 1998 to present 959.8104

.86	*Lesser Sunda Islands (Nusa Tenggara)
.87	*East Timor
.870 1	Early history to 1520
.870 2	1520–1945
.870 3	1945–1999

Class here 20th century

For 1900–1945, see 959.8702

.870 31	1945–1975

*Add as instructed under 930–990

.870 32	1975–1999
.870 4	1999–
	Class here period as Democratic Republic of East Timor, 2002–

.9   *Philippines

.901	Early history to 1564
	Including 16th century
	For 1564–1599, see 959.902
.902	Spanish period, 1564–1898
.902 7	Period of insurrection against Spanish, 1896–1898
.903	United States period, 1898–1946
	Class here 20th century
	For 1946–1999, see 959.904
.903 1	Philippine-American War, 1898–1901
.903 2	Period of United States rule, 1901–1935
.903 5	Period of Commonwealth, 1935–1946
.904	Period of Republic, 1946–
	For 2001 to present, see 959.905
.904 1	Administration of Manuel Roxas, 1946–1948
.904 2	Administration of Elpidio Quirino, 1948–1954
.904 3	Administration of Ramon Magsaysay, 1954–1957
.904 4	Administration of Carlos Garcia, 1957–1961
.904 5	Administration of Diosdado Macapagal, 1961–1965
.904 6	Administration of Ferdinand Marcos, 1965–1986
.904 7	Administration of Corazon Cojuangco Aquino, 1986–1992
.904 8	Administration of Fidel V. Ramos, 1992–1998
.904 9	Administration of Joseph Ejercito Estrada, 1998–2001
.905	2001–
.905 1	Administration of Gloria Macapagal-Arroyo, 2001–2010
.905 2	Administration of Benigno S. Aquino III, 2010–2016
.905 3	Administration of Rodrigo Duterte, 2016–

*Add as instructed under 930–990

.91–.99   Localities of Philippines

> Add to base number 959.9 the numbers following —599 in notation
> 5991–5999 from Table 2, e.g., Luzon island and adjacent islands 959.91;
> then add further as follows:
>> 001–009   Standard subdivisions
>>> Add to 00 the numbers following 00 in notation 001–009
>>> from table under 930–990, e.g., ethnic and national groups
>>> 004, ethnic and national groups in Luzon island and
>>> adjacent islands 959.91004
>> 01–05   Historical periods
>>> Add to 0 the numbers following 959.90 in 959.901–959.905,
>>> e.g., Luzon island and adjacent islands during 2001 to
>>> present 959.9105

960   History of Africa

.01–.09   Standard subdivisions

> As modified in notation 001–009 from table under 930–990

.1   **Early history to 640**

.2   **640–1885**

.21   640–1450

> Including 7th century, 15th century

> *For 600–640, see 960.1; for 1450–1499, see 960.22*

> *See Manual at 930–990: Add table: Centuries*

.22   1450–1799

.23   1800–1885

.3   **1885–**

.31   1885–1945

> Class here 20th century

> *For 1945–1999, see 960.32*

.312   1885–1914

.314   1914–1918

.316   1918–1945

.32   1945–1999

.324   1945–1949

.325   1950–1959

.326   1960–1969

.327   1970–1979

.328   1980–1989

.329   1990–1999

.33	2000–
.331	2000–2019
.331 1	2000–2009
.331 2	2010–2019
.332	2020–2029

961   *Tunisia and Libya

Class here North Africa

For early history to ca. 640, see 939.7

(.01)   Early history to ca. 640

(Optional number; prefer 939.7)

Add to base number 961.01 the numbers following 939.70 in 939.701–939.705, e.g., Carthaginian period 961.012

.02   Periods of Arab rule and Ottoman Empire, ca. 640–1830

.022   Period of Arab rule, ca. 640–ca. 1520

Including 7th century

For 600–ca. 640, see 939.705

.023   Period of Ottoman Empire, ca. 1520–1830

(Option: Class here Tripolitan War with the United States; prefer 973.47. Class here United States War with Algiers; prefer 973.53)

.03   Period of European conquest and hegemony, 1830–1950

Including 19th century, 20th century

For 1800–1830, see 961.023; for 1950–1999, see 961.04

.04	1950–1999
.045	1950–1959
.046	1960–1969
.047	1970–1979
.048	1980–1989
.049	1990–1999
.05	2000–
.051	2000–2019
.051 1	2000–2009
.051 2	2010–2019
.052	2020–2029

*Add as instructed under 930–990

.1	*Tunisia

For early history to 647, see 939.73

(.101)	Early history to 647

(Optional number; prefer 939.73)

Add to base number 961.101 the numbers following 939.730 in 939.7301–939.7305, e.g., Carthaginian period 961.1012

.102	Period of Arab rule, 647–1516

Including 7th century

For 600–647, see 939.7305

.103	Period of Ottoman Empire, 1516–1881
.104	1881–1956

Class here 20th century

For 1956–1999, see 961.105

.105	1956–
.105 1	Administration of Habib Bourguiba, 1956–1987
.105 2	Administration of Zayn al-'Ābidīn Bin 'Alī, 1987–2011
.105 3	2011–

Class here administration of Beji Caid Essebsi, 2014–2019

.2	*Libya

For early history to 644, see 939.74; for Cyrenaica to 642, see 939.75; for Marmarica to 642, see 939.76

(.201)	Early history to 644

(Optional number; prefer 939.74)

Add to base number 961.201 the numbers following 939.740 in 939.7401–939.7405, e.g., Carthaginian period 961.2012; however, for Cyrenaica, Marmarica to 642, see 961.2

.202	644–1911
.202 2	Period of Arab rule, 644–1551

Including 7th century, 16th century

For 600–644, see 939.7405; for 1551–1599, see 961.2024

See Manual at 930–990: Add table: Centuries

.202 4	Period of Ottoman Empire, 1551–1911
.203	Period of Italian rule, 1911–1952

*Add as instructed under 930–990

.204	1952–2011

                    Class here 20th century

                       For 1900–1911, see 961.2024; for 1911–1952, see 961.203

.204 1	Reign of Idris I, 1952–1969
.204 2	Period of Muammar Qaddafi, 1969–2011
.205	2011–

962   Egypt, Sudan, South Sudan

.000 1–.000 8	Standard subdivisions of Egypt, Sudan, South Sudan

                    As modified in notation 001–008 from table under 930–990

.000 9	Archaeology; historical periods; areas, regions, places in general; collected biography of Egypt, Sudan, South Sudan
.000 900 9	Archaeology

                            Notation 09009 from Table 1 as modified below

.000 900 902–.000 900 909	Specific subdivisions of archaeology

                                  Add to base number 962.00090090 the numbers following 009090 in notation 0090902–0090909 from table under 930–990, e.g., serials treating archaeology of Egypt, Sudan, South Sudan 962.000900905

.000 901–.000 905	Historical periods

                              Add to base number 962.00090 the numbers following —090 in notation 0901–0905 from Table 1, e.g., Egypt, Sudan, South Sudan during 20th century 962.000904

.000 91–.000 99	Areas, regions, places in general; collected biography

                      As modified in notation 0091–0099 from table under 930–990

.001–.009	Standard subdivisions of Egypt

                    As modified in notation 001–009 from table under 930–990

(.01)	Early history to 640

                  (Optional number; prefer 932)

                  Add to base number 962.01 the numbers following 932.0 in 932.01–932.02, e.g., period of New Kingdom 962.0114

>   962.02–962.05   Historical periods of Egypt

        Class comprehensive works in 962

        For early history to 640, see 932

        (Option: Class early history to 640 in 962.01; prefer 932)

.02	Period of Arab rule, 640–1517

Including 7th century

For 600–640, see 932.023

.024	Mameluke period, 1250–1517
.03	Period of Ottoman Empire, 1517–1882
.04	Period of British occupation and protectorate, 1882–1922
.05	1922–
.051	Reign of Fu'ād I, 1922–1936
.052	1936–1953

Class here reign of Faruk I, 1936–1952

Class Israel-Arab War, 1948–1949, in 956.042

.053	1953–1970

Including administration of Mohammed Naguib, 1953–1954; period of United Arab Republic, 1958–1961

Class here administration of Gamal Abdel Nasser, 1954–1970

Class Sinai Campaign, 1956, in 956.044; class Israel-Arab War, 1967, in 956.046

For Syrian part of United Arab Republic, see 956.910421

.054	Administration of Anwar Sadat, 1970–1981

Class Israel-Arab War, 1973, in 956.048

.055	Administration of Muḥammad Ḥusnī Mubārak, 1981–2011
.056	2011–

Including administration of Muḥammad Mursī, 2012–2013; of 'Abd al-Fattāḥ Sīsī, 2014 to present

.1–.3   Localities of Egypt

Add to base number 962 the numbers following —62 in notation 621–623 from Table 2, e.g., Lower Egypt 962.1; then add further as follows:
001–009   Standard subdivisions
            Add to 00 the numbers following 00 in notation 001–009
            from table under 930–990, e.g., ethnic and national groups
            004, ethnic and national groups in Lower Egypt 962.1004
(01)   Early history to 640
            (Optional number; prefer 932.1–932.3)
            Add to 01 the numbers following 932.0 in 932.01–932.02, e.g.,
            Lower Egypt during period of New Kingdom 962.10114
02–05   640 to present
            Add to 0 the numbers following 962.0 in 962.02–962.05, e.g.,
            Lower Egypt during 1922 to present 962.105

.4   ***Sudan and South Sudan**

        Subdivisions are added for Sudan and South Sudan together, for Sudan alone

        For Sudan, see 962.5–962.8; for South Sudan, see 962.9

>   962.401–962.404 Historical periods for Sudan and South Sudan together, for Sudan alone

        Class comprehensive works in 962.4

.401   Early history to 500

.402   500–1820

.402 2   Period of Christian kingdoms, 500–1504

.402 3   Period of Funj Sultanate, 1504–1820

.403   Period as Anglo-Egyptian Sudan, 1820–1956

        Including 20th century

        Class here period of Egyptian and British rule

        For 1956–1999, see 962.404

.404   1956–

.404 1   1956–1969

        Class here Sudanese civil war, 1955–1972

.404 2   Administration of Ja'far Muḥammad Numayrī, 1969–1985

.404 3   1985–

        Class here administration of Omar Hassan Ahmad al-Bashir, 1996 to present; Sudanese civil war, 1983–2005

        For Sudanese civil war during 1983–1985, see 962.4042

>   **962.5–962.8 Sudan**

        Class comprehensive works in 962.4

.5   ***Northern states of Sudan**

        For early history to 500, see 939.78

(.501)   Early history to 500

        (Optional number; prefer 939.78)

        Class here ancient Ethiopia (a part of what is now modern Sudan, not modern Ethiopia), Nubia, Kush

        See also 963.01 for ancient history of modern Ethiopia

---

*Add as instructed under 930–990

.502–.504   500–

>   Add to base number 962.50 the numbers following 962.40 in
>   962.402–962.404, e.g., period of Christian kingdoms 962.5022

.6   *Khartoum state and east central states of Sudan

.601–.604   Historical periods

>   Add to base number 962.60 the numbers following 962.40 in
>   962.401–962.404, e.g., period as a part of Anglo-Egyptian Sudan
>   962.603

.62–.64   Localities of Khartoum state and east central states of Sudan

>   Add to base number 962.6 the numbers following —626 in notation
>   6262–6264 from Table 2, e.g., Khartoum state (Kharṭūm wilāyat) 962.62;
>   then add further as follows:
>   001–009   Standard subdivisions
>   Add to 00 the numbers following 00 in notation 001–009
>   from table under 930–990, e.g., ethnic and national
>   groups 004, ethnic and national groups in Khartoum state
>   (Kharṭūm wilāyat) 962.62004
>   01–04   Historical periods
>   Add to 0 the numbers following 962.40 in 962.401–962.404,
>   e.g., Khartoum state (Kharṭūm wilāyat) during period as a
>   part of Anglo-Egyptian Sudan 962.6203

.7   *Darfur region of Sudan

.701–.704   Historical periods

>   Add to base number 962.70 the numbers following 962.40 in
>   962.401–962.404, e.g., period as a part of Anglo-Egyptian Sudan
>   962.703

.8   *Kordofan region of Sudan

.801–.804   Historical periods

>   Add to base number 962.80 the numbers following 962.40 in
>   962.401–962.404, e.g., period as a part of Anglo-Egyptian Sudan
>   962.803

.9   *South Sudan

>   Class comprehensive works on Sudan and South Sudan in 962.4

.901–.903   Early history to 1956

>   Add to base number 962.90 the numbers following 962.40 in
>   962.401–962.403, e.g., period as a part of Anglo-Egyptian Sudan
>   962.903

.904   Period as part of Republic of the Sudan, 1956–2011

.904 1   1956–1969

>   Class Sudanese civil war, 1955–1972 in 962.4041

---

*Add as instructed under 930–990

.904 2   Administration of Ja'far Muḥammad Numayrī, 1969–1985

                Class here period of Southern Sudan Autonomous Region, 1972–1983

.904 3   1985–2011

                Class here administration of Omar Hassan Ahmad al-Bashir, 1996–2011

                Class Sudanese civil war, 1983–2005 in 962.4043

.905   2011–

.905 1   2011–

.93–.95   Localities of South Sudan

                Add to base number 962.9 the numbers following —629 in notation 6293–6295 from Table 2, e.g., Upper Nile states 962.93; then add further as follows:
                001–009   Standard subdivisions
                                Add to 00 the numbers following 00 in notation 001–009 from table under 930–990, e.g., ethnic and national groups 004, ethnic and national groups in Upper Nile states 962.93004
                04–05   Historical periods
                                Add to 0 the numbers following 962.90 in 962.904–962.905, e.g., Upper Nile states during 2011 to present 962.9305

963   *Ethiopia and Eritrea

                Subdivisions are added for Ethiopia and Eritrea together, for Ethiopia alone

---

>   963.01–963.07 Historical periods for Ethiopia and Eritrea together, for Ethiopia alone

                Class comprehensive works in 963

.01   Early history to 640

                See also 939.78 for ancient Ethiopia (a part of what is now modern Sudan, not modern Ethiopia)

.02   640–1543

                Including 7th century

                For 600–640, see 963.01

.03   1543–1855

                Including 16th century, 19th century

                For 1500–1543, see 963.02; for 1855–1899, see 963.04

                See Manual at 930–990: Add table: Centuries

.04   1855–1913

.041   Reign of Theodore II, 1855–1868

*Add as instructed under 930–990

.042	1868–1889
	Class here reign of John IV, 1872–1889
.043	Reign of Menelik II, 1889–1913
	Including Ethiopian War, 1895–1896
.05	1913–1941
	Class here 20th century
	For 1900–1913, see 963.043; for 1941–1974, see 963.06; for 1974–1999, see 963.07
.053	Reign of Lij Yasu, 1913–1916
.054	Period of Jah Rastafari (Haile Selassie) as regent and king, 1917–1930
.055	Reign of Haile Selassie (Jah Rastafari) as emperor, 1930–1974
	For reign during 1935–1936, see 963.056; for reign during 1936–1941, see 963.057; for reign during 1941–1974, see 963.06
.056	Italo-Ethiopian War, 1935–1936
.057	Period of Italian rule, 1936–1941
.06	1941–1974
	Including deposition of Haile Selassie, 1974
.07	1974–
.071	1974–1991
	Including Ogaden War, 1977–1978
	Class here chairmanship of Mengistu Haile-Mariam, 1977–1991; Somali-Ethiopian conflicts, 1978–1991
.072	1991–
.072 1	1991–2012
	Class here prime ministership of Malas Zénāwi, 1995–2012
	Class Somalia Civil War during 1991–2009 in 967.73053
.072 2	Prime ministership of H#āylamāryām Dasālañ, 2012–2018
.072 3	Prime ministership of 'Abey 'Ahmed 'Ali, 2018–

.2–.4　**Localities of Ethiopia**

> Add to base number 963 the numbers following —63 in notation 632–634 from Table 2, e.g., central Ethiopia and eastern Ethiopia 963.2; then add further as follows:
>
> 001–009　Standard subdivisions
> > Add to 00 the numbers following 00 in notation 001–009 from table under 930–990, e.g., ethnic and national groups 004, ethnic and national groups in central Ethiopia and eastern Ethiopia 963.2004
>
> 01–07　Historical periods
> > Add to 0 the numbers following 963.0 in 963.01–963.07, e.g., central Ethiopia and eastern Ethiopia during 1974 to present 963.207

.4　***Northern Ethiopia**

> Number built according to instructions under 930–990
>
> Including period of kingdom of Aksum
>
> *For period of kingdom of Aksum in Eritrea, see 963.501*

.5　***Eritrea**

.501　　Early history to 640

.502　　640–1543

> Including 7th century
>
> *For 600–640, see 963.501*

.503　　1543–1855

> Including 16th century, 19th century
>
> *For 1500–1543, see 963.502; for 1855–1889, see 963.504; for 1889–1899, see 963.505*
>
> *See Manual at 930–990: Add table: Centuries*

.504　　1855–1889

.504 1　　Reign of Theodore II, 1855–1868

.504 2　　1868–1889

> Including reign of John IV, 1872–1889

.505　　Period of Italian control, 1889–1941

> Class here 20th century
>
> *For 1941–1952, see 963.506; for 1952–1999, see 963.507*

.506　　Period of British control, 1941–1952

.507　　1952–

.507 1　　Period of union with Ethiopia, 1952–1993

*Add as instructed under 930–990

.507 2   1993–

964   *Morocco, Ceuta, Melilla, Western Sahara, Canary Islands

Subdivisions are added for Morocco, Ceuta, Melilla, Western Sahara, Canary Islands together; for Morocco alone

(.01)   Ancient history to 647

(Optional number; prefer 939.712)

Add to base number 964.01 the numbers following 939.7120 in 939.71201–939.71206, e.g., Roman period 964.014

>   964.02–964.05 Historical periods of Morocco

Class comprehensive works in 964

For early history to 647, see 939.712

(Option: Class early history to 647 in 964.01; prefer 939.712)

.02   Periods of Arab and Berber rule, 647–1830

.021   647–ca. 1050

Including 7th century, 11th century

For 600–647, see 939.71206; for ca. 1050–1099, see 964.023

See Manual at 930–990: Add table: Centuries

.023   Ca. 1050–ca. 1550

Including 16th century

For ca. 1550–1599, see 964.025

.025   Ca. 1550–1830

.03   1830–1899

Including Spanish-Moroccan War, 1859–1860 (Option: Class Spanish-Moroccan War in 946.072)

Class here 19th century

For 1800–1830, see 964.02

.04   1900–1956

Class here 20th century; period of French and Spanish protectorates, 1912–1956; reign of Muḥammad V, 1927–1961

For 1956–1999, see 964.05; for reign of Muḥammad V during 1956–1961, see 964.051

.05   1956–

.051   Later portion of reign of Muḥammad V, 1956–1961

---

*Add as instructed under 930–990

.052   Reign of Hassan II, 1961–1999

.053   Reign of Mohammed VI, 1999–

.1   Ceuta and Melilla

.100 1–.100 9   Standard subdivisions

> Add to 964.100 the numbers following 00 in notation 001–009 from table under 930–990, e.g., ethnic and national groups 004, ethnic and national groups in Ceuta and Melilla 964.1004

.101–.108   Historical periods

> Add to 964.10 the numbers following 946.0 in 946.01–946.08, e.g., Ceuta and Melilla during reign of Juan Carlos I, 1975–2014 964.1083

.2–.6   Localities of Morocco

> Add to base number 964 the numbers following —64 in notation 642–646 from Table 2, e.g., Tangier-Tétouan region 964.2; then add further as follows:
>
> 001–009   Standard subdivisions
>> Add to 00 the numbers following 00 in notation 001–009 from table under 930–990, e.g., ethnic and national groups 004, ethnic and national groups in Tangier-Tétouan region 964.2004
>
> (01)   Ancient history to 647
>> (Optional number; prefer 939.7122–939.7126)
>> Add to 01 the numbers following 939.7120 in 939.71201–939.71206, e.g., Tangier-Tétouan region during Roman period 964.2014
>
> 02–05   647 to present
>> Add to 0 the numbers following 964.0 in 964.02–964.05, e.g., Tangier-Tétouan region during reign of Mohammed VI, 1999 to present 964.2053

.8   *Western Sahara

.801   Early history to 1888

.802   Spanish period, 1888–1976

.803   Moroccan period, 1976–

> Including Moroccan and Mauritanian period, 1976–1979

.9   *Canary Islands

.906   Early history to 1402

.907   Periods of French, Portuguese, Spanish rule, 1402–1927

.908   Period as Provinces of Spain, 1927–

> Class here 20th century
>
> *For 1900–1927, see 964.907*

.908 1   1927–1939

---

*Add as instructed under 930–990

.908 2	Period of Francisco Franco, 1939–1975
	Add to base number 964.9082 the numbers following 946.082 in 946.0824–946.0827, e.g., 1960–1969 964.90826
.908 3	Reign of Juan Carlos I, 1975–2014
.908 4	Reign of Felipe VI, 2014–

965   *Algeria

For early history to 647, see 939.714

(.01)	Early history to 647
	(Optional number; prefer 939.714)
	Add to base number 965.01 the numbers following 939.710 in 939.7101–939.7105, e.g., Roman period 965.014
.02	647–1830
.022	Periods of Arab and Berber rule, 647–1516
	Including 7th century
	For 600–647, see 939.7106
.024	Period of Ottoman Empire, 1516–1830
.03	Period of French rule, 1830–1962
	Class here 19th century
	For 1800–1830, see 965.024; for 1900–1962, see 965.04
.04	1900–1962
	Class here 20th century
	For 1962–1999, see 965.05
.046	‡Period of Revolution, 1954–1962
.05	1962–
.051	1962–1965
.052	1965–1979
.053	Administration of Chadli Bendjedid, 1979–1992
.054	1992–
	Class here administration of Abdelaziz Bouteflika, 1999 to present

*Add as instructed under 930–990
‡Add as instructed under 940–990

.1–.7   Localities of Algeria

> Add to base number 965 the numbers following —65 in notation 651–657
> from Table 2, e.g., northwestern provinces of Algeria 965.1; then add further as
> follows:
>
> 001–009   Standard subdivisions
> > Add to 00 the numbers following 00 in notation 001–009
> > from table under 930–990, e.g., ethnic and national groups
> > 004, ethnic and national groups in northwestern provinces of
> > Algeria 965.1004
>
> (01)   Early history to 647
> > (Optional number; prefer 939.7141–939.7143)
> > Add to 01 the numbers following 939.710 in
> > 939.7101–939.7105, e.g., northwestern provinces of Algeria
> > during Roman period 965.1014
>
> 02–05   647 to present
> > Add to 0 the numbers following 965.0 in 965.02–965.05, e.g.,
> > northwestern provinces of Algeria during 1962 to present
> > 965.105

.5   *Northeastern provinces of Algeria

> *For early history to 647, see 939.72*

(.501)   Early history to 647

> Class here Numidia
>
> (Optional number; prefer 939.72)
>
> Add to base number 965.501 the numbers following 939.720 in
> 939.7201–939.7206, e.g., Roman period 965.5014

.7   *Sahara provinces of Algeria

> *For early history to 647, see 939.77*

(.701)   Early history to 647

> Class here Gaetulia
>
> (Optional number; prefer 939.77)

966   *West Africa and offshore islands

.01–.03   Historical periods

> Add to base number 966.0 the numbers following 960 in 960.1–960.3, e.g.,
> early history to 640 966.01

.1   *Mauritania

.101   Early history to 1903

.101 6   300–1200

> Class here comprehensive works on period of Ghana Empire
>
> *For period of Ghana Empire in Mali history, see 966.2301*

*Add as instructed under 930–990

.101 7	1200–1500
	Class here period of Mali Empire
.103	French period, 1903–1960
	Class here 20th century
	For 1900–1903, see 966.101; for 1960–1999, see 966.105
.105	1960–2005
.105 1	1960–1978
	Class here administration of Mokhtar Ould Daddah, 1961–1978
.105 2	1978–1984
	Class here administration of Khouna Ould Haidallah, 1980–1984
.105 3	1984–2005
	Class here administration of Maawiya Ould Sid'Ahmed Taya, 1992–2005
.106	2005–
.106 1	2005–2009
.106 2	Administration of Mohamed Ould Abdel Aziz, 2009–
.2	***Mali, Burkina Faso, Niger**
.201	Early history to ca. 1900
.201 7	1200–1400
	Class here period of Mali Empire
	For period of Mali Empire in Mauritanian history, see 966.1017
.201 8	1400–1500
	Class here period of Songhai Empire
.202	French period, ca. 1900–1960
	Class here 20th century
	For 1960–1999, see 966.203
.203	1960–
.23	*Mali
.230 1	Early history to 1902
	Class comprehensive works on Mali Empire in 966.2017
.230 3	Period as French Sudan, 1902–1960
	Class here 20th century, French period
	For 1900–1902, see 966.2301; for 1960–1999, see 966.2305

*Add as instructed under 930–990

.230 5	1960–
.230 51	1960–1991
	Class here administration of Moussa Traoré, 1968–1991
.230 52	1991–2002
	Class here administration of Alpha Oumar Konaré, 1992–2002
.230 53	Administration of Amadou Toumani Touré, 2002–2012
.230 54	2012–
	Class here administration of Ibrahim Boubacar Keïta, 2013–
.25	*Burkina Faso
.250 1	Early history to 1897
	Including kingdom of Mossi
.250 3	French period, 1897–1960
	Class here 20th century; period as Upper Volta, 1919–1932 and 1947–1984
	For 1960–1999, see 966.2505
.250 5	1960–
.250 51	1960–1983
.250 52	Administration of Thomas Sankara, 1983–1987
.250 53	Administration of Blaise Compaoré, 1987–2014
.250 54	2014–
	Class here administration of Roch Marc Christian Kaboré, 2015 to present
.26	*Niger
.260 1	Early history to 1900
.260 3	French period, 1900–1960
	Class here 20th century
	For 1960–1999, see 966.2605
.260 5	1960–
.260 51	Administration of Hamani Diori, 1960–1974
.260 52	1974–1999
	Including administration of Seyni Kountché, 1974–1987
.260 53	Administration of Mamadou Tandja, 1999–2010
.260 54	2010–

*Add as instructed under 930–990

.3   ***Senegal**

.301   Early history to 1895

> Including kingdom of Tekrur

.303   French period, 1895–1960

> Class here 20th century

> *For 1960–1999, see 966.305*

.305   1960–

.305 1   1960–2000

> Including administration of Abdou Diouf, 1981–2000; Confederation of Senegambia, 1982–1989

> *For Gambian part of Senegambia, see 966.51031*

.305 2   Administration of Abdoulaye Wade, 2000–2012

.305 3   Administration of Macky Sall, 2012–

.4   ***Sierra Leone**

.401   Early history to 1787

.402   Period as a British colony, 1787–1896

.403   Period as both colony and protectorate, 1896–1961

> Class here 20th century

> *For 1961–1999, see 966.404*

.404   1961–2007

.404 1   1961–1971

.404 2   Administration of Siaka Probyn Stevens, 1971–1985

.404 3   Administration of Joseph Saidu Momoh, 1985–1992

.404 4   ‡1992–1998

> Class here chairmanship of Valentine E. M. Strasser, 1992–1996; Sierra Leone civil war, 1991–2002

> *For Sierra Leone civil war during 1991–1992, see 966.4043*

.404 5   Administration of Ahmad Tejan Kabbah, 1998–2007

.405   2007–

.405 1   Administration of Ernest Bai Koroma, 2007–2018

.405 2   Administration of Julius Maada Bio, 2018–

.5   ***Gambia, Guinea, Guinea-Bissau, Cape Verde**

---

*Add as instructed under 930–990
‡ Add as instructed under 940–990

.51	*Gambia
.510 1	Early history to 1807
.510 2	Period as a British colony, 1807–1965
	Class here 20th century
	For 1965–1999, see 966.5103
.510 3	1965–
.510 31	Administration of Dawda Kairaba Jawara, 1965–1994
	Including period as a part of Senegambia, 1982–1989
	Class comprehensive works on Senegambia in 966.305
.510 32	Administration of A. J. J. Jammeh, 1994–2017
.510 33	2017–
	Including administration of Adama Barrow, 2017–
.52	*Guinea
.520 1	Early history to 1882
.520 3	Period as French Guinea, 1882–1958
	Class here 20th century
	For 1958–1999, see 966.5205
.520 5	1958–
.520 51	Administration of Ahmed Sékou Touré, 1958–1984
.520 52	Administration of Lansana Conte, 1984–2008
.520 53	2008–
.520 532	Administration of Alpha Condé, 2010–
.57	*Guinea-Bissau
.570 1	Early history to 1879
.570 2	Period as Portuguese Guinea, 1879–1974
.570 3	1974–
.570 31	1974–1980
.570 32	First administration of João Bernardo Vieira, 1980–1999
.570 33	1999–2005
.570 34	Second administration of João Bernardo Vieira, 2005–2009
.570 35	2009–
.58	*Cape Verde

*Add as instructed under 930–990

.580 1		Early history to 1900
.580 2		1900–1975
.580 3		1975–
.580 31		Administration of Aristides Pereira, 1975–1991
.580 32		Administration of António Mascarenhas Monteiro, 1991–2001
.580 33		Administration of Pedro Verona Rodrigues Pires, 2001–2011
.580 34		Administration of Jorge Carlos de Almeida Fonseca, 2011–

.6   **Liberia and Côte d'Ivoire**

.62   *Liberia

.620 1   Early history to 1847

.620 2   1847–1945

         Class here 19th century

         For 1800–1847, see 966.6201

.620 3   1945–2003

         Class here 20th century

         For 1900–1945, see 966.6202

.620 31   1945–1980

.620 32   Administration of Samuel K. Doe, 1980–1990

.620 33   1990–2003

         Class here administration of Charles Ghankay Taylor, 1997–2003

.620 4   2003–

.620 41   2003–2018

         Class here administration of Ellen Johnson-Sirleaf, 2006–2018

.620 42   Administration of George Weah, 2018–

.68   *Côte d'Ivoire (Ivory Coast)

.680 1   Early history to 1904

.680 3   French period, 1904–1960

         Class here 20th century

         For 1900–1904, see 966.6801; for 1960–1999, see 966.6805

.680 5   1960–

.680 51   Administration of Félix Houphouët-Boigny, 1960–1993

.680 52   Administration of Henri Konan Bédié, 1993–1999

*Add as instructed under 930–990

.680 53	1999–2011
	Class here administration of Laurent Gbagbo, 2000–2011
.680 54	Administration of Alassane D. Ouattara, 2011–

.7   *Ghana

See also 966.1016 for Ghana Empire

.701	Early history to 1874
.701 6	Period of Akan states, 1295–1740
	Including Akwamu, Bono kingdoms
.701 8	Period of Asante (Ashanti) empire, 1740–1874
	Including 18th century
	For 1700–1740, see 966.7016
.703	Period as Gold Coast, 1874–1957
	Including British Togoland, 1914–1957
	Class here 20th century, British period
	For 1957–1999, see 966.705
.705	1957–
.705 1	1957–1979
	Including administration of Kwame Nkrumah, 1957–1966
.705 2	1979–2001
	Class here administration of Jerry J. Rawlings, 1981–2001
.705 3	Administration of John Agyekum Kufuor, 2001–2009
.705 4	2009–

.8   Togo and Benin

.81	*Togo
.810 1	Early history to 1894
.810 2	Period as Togoland, 1894–1914
.810 3	Period as French Togoland, 1914–1960
	Class here 20th century
	For 1900–1914, see 966.8102; for 1960–1999, see 966.8104
.810 4	1960–
.810 41	1960–1967
.810 42	Administration of Gnassingbé Eyadéma, 1967–2005

*Add as instructed under 930–990

.810 43		Administration of Faure Gnassingbé, 2005–
.83	*Benin	

See also 966.9301 for kingdom of Benin

.830 1	Early history to 1904
.830 18	Period of kingdom of Dahomey, 1600–1904
.830 3	French period, 1904–1960

Class here 20th century

For 1900–1904, see 966.83018; for 1960–1999, see 966.8305

.830 5	1960–
.830 51	1960–1991

Class here first administration of Mathieu Kérékou, 1972–1991

.830 52	Administration of Nicéphore Dieudonné Soglo, 1991–1996
.830 53	Second administration of Mathieu Kérékou, 1996–2006
.830 54	Administration of Boni Yayi, 2006–2016
.830 55	Administration of Patrice Talon, 2016–
.9	***Nigeria**
.901	Early history to 1886
.903	Period as a British colony, 1886–1960

Class here 20th century

For 1960–1999, see 966.905

.905	1960–
.905 1	1960–1967
.905 2	Period of Nigerian Civil War, 1967–1970
.905 3	1970–1999

Including administration of Ibrahim Badamosi Babangida, 1985–1993

.905 4	Administration of Olusegun Obasanjo, 1999–2007
.905 5	Administration of Umaru Musa Yar'adua, 2007–2010
.905 6	Administration of Goodluck Ebele Jonathan, 2010–2015
.905 7	Administration of Muhammadu Buhari, 2015–

*Add as instructed under 930–990

.91–.98   Localities of Nigeria

> Add to base number 966.9 the numbers following —669 in notation 6691–6698 from Table 2, e.g., Lagos State 966.91; then add further as follows:
>
> 001–009   Standard subdivisions
>> Add to 00 the numbers following 00 in notation 001–009 from table under 930–990, e.g., ethnic and national groups 004, ethnic and national groups in Lagos State 966.91004
>
> 01–05   Historical periods
>> Add to 0 the numbers following 966.90 in 966.901–966.905, e.g., Lagos State during 1960 to present 966.9105

967   *Central Africa and offshore islands

> Class here Sub-Saharan Africa (Africa south of the Sahara)
>
> *For each specific part of Sub-Saharan Africa not provided for here, see the part, e.g., Nigeria 966.9*

.01–.03   Historical periods

> Add to base number 967.0 the numbers following 960 in 960.1–960.3, e.g., early history to 640 967.01

.1   *Cameroon, Sao Tome and Principe, Equatorial Guinea

> Class here Islands of Gulf of Guinea, Lower Guinea area

.11   *Cameroon

.110 1   Early history to 1884

.110 2   Period as Kamerun, 1884–1916

> Class here German period

.110 3   Anglo-French period, 1916–1959

> Class here 20th century
>
> *For 1900–1916, see 967.1102; for 1960–1999, see 967.1104*

.110 4   1960–

.110 41   Administration of Ahmadou Ahidjo, 1960–1982

.110 42   Administration of Paul Biya, 1982–

.15   *Sao Tome and Principe

.150 1   Early history to 1975

.150 2   Period of Republic, 1975–

.150 21   First administration of Manuel Pinto da Costa, 1975–1991

.150 22   Administration of Miguel Trovoada, 1991–2001

.150 23   Administration of Fradique Bandeira Melo de Menezes, 2001–2011

.150 24   Second administration of Manuel Pinto da Costa, 2011–2016

*Add as instructed under 930–990

.150 25	Administration of Evaristo Carvalho, 2016–
.18	*Equatorial Guinea
.180 1	Early history to 1469
.180 2	Portuguese, British, Spanish periods, 1469–1968

         Including 20th century

         For 1968–1999, see 967.1803

.180 3	1968–
.180 31	Administration of Francisco Macías Nguema, 1968–1979
.180 32	Administration of Teodoro Obiang Nguema Mbasogo, 1979–
.183–.186	Localities of Equatorial Guinea

         Add to base number 967.18 the numbers following —6718 in notation
67183–67186 from Table 2, e.g., Malabo 967.186; then add further as
follows:
        001–009   Standard subdivisions
                        Add to 00 the numbers following 00 in notation
                        001–009 from table under 930–990, e.g., ethnic and
                        national groups 004, ethnic and national groups in
                        Malabo 967.186004
        01–03   Historical periods
                        Add to 0 the numbers following 967.180 in
                        967.1801–967.1803, e.g., Malabo during 1968 to present
                        967.18603

.2	***Gabon and Republic of the Congo**
.201	Early history to 1910
.203	Period as French Equatorial Africa, 1910–1959

         Class here 20th century; comprehensive works on French Equatorial
Africa

         *For 1900–1910, see 967.201; for 1959–1999, see 967.205; for
Ubangi-Shari as part of French Equatorial Africa, see 967.4103; for
Chad as part of French Equatorial Africa, see 967.4302*

.205	1959–
.21	*Gabon
.210 1	Early history to 1839
.210 2	French period, 1839–1960

         Including period as a part of French Equatorial Africa; 19th century,
20th century

         Class comprehensive works on French Equatorial Africa in 967.203

         For 1800–1839, see 967.2101; for 1960–1999, see 967.2104

.210 4	1960–

*Add as instructed under 930–990

.210 41	1960–1967
.210 42	Administration of Omar Bongo, 1967–2009
.210 43	2009–
	Class here administration of Ali Ben Bongo, 2009–
.24	***Republic of the Congo**
.240 1	Early history to 1885
.240 3	Period as Middle Congo, 1885–1960
	Class here 20th century, French period
	Class comprehensive works on French Equatorial Africa in 967.203
	For 1960–1999, see 967.2405
.240 5	1960–
.240 51	1960–1979
.240 52	First administration of Denis Sassou Nguesso, 1979–1992
.240 53	1992–1997
.240 54	Second administration of Denis Sassou Nguesso, 1997–
.3	***Angola**
.301	Early history to 1648
.302	1648–1899
	Including 17th century
	For 1600–1648, see 967.301
.303	1900–1975
.304	1975–
.304 1	Administration of António Agostinho Neto, 1975–1979
.304 2	‡Administration of José Eduardo dos Santos, 1979–2017
	Class here Angolan Civil War, 1975–2002
	For Angolan Civil War during 1975–1979, see 967.3041
.304 3	Administration of João Lourenço, 2017–

*Add as instructed under 930–990
‡Add as instructed under 940–990

.31–.35   Localities of Angola

> Add to base number 967.3 the numbers following —673 in notation
> 6731–6735 from Table 2, e.g., Luanda 967.32; then add further as follows:
>
> 001–009   Standard subdivisions
>> Add to 00 the numbers following 00 in notation 001–009
>> from table under 930–990, e.g., ethnic and national groups
>> 004, ethnic and national groups in Luanda 967.32004
>
> 01–04   Historical periods
>> Add to 0 the numbers following 967.30 in 967.301–967.304,
>> e.g., Luanda during 1975 to present 967.3204

.4   *Central African Republic and Chad

.41   *Central African Republic

.410 1   Early history to 1890

.410 3   Period as Ubangi-Shari, 1890–1960

> Class here 20th century, French period, period as part of French
> Equatorial Africa
>
> Class comprehensive works on French Equatorial Africa in 967.203
>
> *For 1960–1999, see 967.4105*

.410 5   1960–

.410 51   1960–1979

.410 52   1979–1993

> Class here administration of André Kolingba, 1981–1993

.410 53   Administration of Ange-Félix Patasse, 1993–2003

.410 54   Administration of François Bozizé, 2003–2013

.410 55   2013–

> Including administration of Michel Am-Nondokro Djotodia,
> 2013–2014; of Faustin-Archange Touadéra, 2016 to present

.43   *Chad

.430 1   Early history to 1850

> Including 19th century, kingdom of Kanem
>
> Class Kanem-Bornu in 966.9801
>
> *For 1850–1899, see 967.4302*

.430 2   Colonial period, 1850–1960

> Including period as part of French Equatorial Africa; 20th century
>
> Class comprehensive works on French Equatorial Africa in 967.203
>
> *For 1960–1999, see 967.4304*

---

*Add as instructed under 930–990

.430 4	1960–
.430 41	1960–1975
.430 42	1975–1982
.430 43	Administration of Hissein Habré, 1982–1990
.430 44	Administration of Idriss Déby Itno, 1990–

.5   ***Democratic Republic of the Congo, Rwanda, Burundi**

.51   *Democratic Republic of the Congo

.510 1	Early history to 1885
.510 2	Belgian period, 1885–1960
.510 22	Period as Congo Free State, 1885–1908
.510 24	Period as Belgian Congo, 1908–1960

Class here 20th century

For 1900–1908, see 967.51022; for 1960–1999, see 967.5103

.510 3	1960–
.510 31	1960–1965
.510 33	Administration of Mobutu Sese Seko, 1965–1997

Class here period as Zaire, 1971–1997

.510 34	1997–

Including administration of Laurent-Désiré Kabila, 1997–2001

Class here administration of Joseph Kabila, 2001 to present

.511–.518   Localities of Democratic Republic of the Congo

Add to base number 967.51 the numbers following —6751 in notation 67511–67518 from Table 2, e.g., Kinshasa 967.5112; then add further as follows:

    001–009   Standard subdivisions
                 Add to 00 the numbers following 00 in notation 001–009 from table under 930–990, e.g., ethnic and national groups 004, ethnic and national groups in Kinshasa 967.5112004

    01–03   Historical periods
                 Add to 0 the numbers following 967.510 in 967.5101–967.5103, e.g., Kinshasa during 1960 to present 967.511203

.57   *Rwanda and Burundi

.570 1	Early history to 1899
.570 2	German period, 1899–1917

*Add as instructed under 930–990

.570 3	Belgian period, 1917–1962

Class here 20th century

For 1900–1917, see 967.5702; for 1962–1999, see 967.5704

.570 4	1962–
.571	*Rwanda
.571 01	Early history to 1899
.571 02	German period, 1899–1917
.571 03	Belgian period, 1917–1962

Class here 20th century

For 1900–1917, see 967.57102; for 1962–1999, see 967.57104

.571 04	1962–
.571 041	1962–1973
.571 042	Administration of Juvénal Habyarimana, 1973–1994
.571 043	1994–
.571 043 1	Civil War of 1994
.572	*Burundi
.572 01	Early history to 1899
.572 02	German period, 1899–1917
.572 03	Belgian period, 1917–1962

Class here 20th century

For 1900–1917, see 967.57202; for 1962–1999, see 967.57204

.572 04	1962–
.572 041	1962–1993
.572 041 5	Administration of Jean-Baptiste Bagaza, 1976–1987
.572 042	1993–2005
.572 043	2005–

.6	***Uganda and Kenya**

Class here East Africa

.601	Early history to 1894
.603	1894–1961

Class here 20th century

For 1961–1999, see 967.604

*Add as instructed under 930–990

.604	1961–1999
.605	2000–
.605 1	2000–2019
.605 11	2000–2009
.605 12	2010–2019
.605 2	2020–2029
.61	*Uganda
.610 1	Early history to 1894
	Including kingdoms of Ankole, Buganda, Bunyoro, Busoga, Karagwe
.610 3	British period, 1894–1962
	Class here 20th century
	For 1962–1999, see 967.6104
.610 4	1962–
.610 41	First administration of A. Milton Obote, 1962–1971
.610 42	Administration of Idi Amin, 1971–1979
.610 43	Second administration of A. Milton Obote, 1980–1985
.610 44	Administration of Yoweri Museveni, 1986–
.62	*Kenya
.620 1	Early history to 1895
.620 3	British period, 1895–1963
	Class here 20th century
	For 1963–1999, see 967.6204
.620 4	1963–
.620 41	Administration of Jomo Kenyatta, 1963–1978
.620 42	Administration of Daniel Arap Moi, 1978–2002
.620 43	Administration of Mwai Kibaki, 2002–2013
.620 44	Administration of Uhuru Kenyatta, 2013–

*Add as instructed under 930–990

.622–.629   Localities of Kenya

> Add to base number 967.62 the numbers following —6762 in notation 67622–67629 from Table 2, e.g., Mombasa 967.6236; then add further as follows:
>
> 001–009   Standard subdivisions
>> Add to 00 the numbers following 00 in notation 001–009 from table under 930–990, e.g., ethnic and national groups 004, ethnic and national groups in Mombasa 967.6236004
>
> 01–04   Historical periods
>> Add to 0 the numbers following 967.620 in 967.6201–967.6204, e.g., Mombasa during 1963 to present 967.623604

.7   *Djibouti and Somalia

> Class here Somaliland

.71   *Djibouti

.710 1   Early history to 1881

.710 3   French period, 1881–1977

.710 32   Period as French Somaliland, 1881–1967

> Class here 20th century

> *For 1967–1977, see 967.71034; for 1977–1999, see 967.7104*

.710 34   Period as French Territory of the Afars and Issas, 1967–1977

.710 4   1977–

.710 41   Administration of Hassan Gouled Aptidon, 1977–1999

.710 42   Administration of Ismail Omar Guelleh, 1999–

.73   *Somalia

.730 1   Early history to 1884

> Including kingdom of Mogadishu

.730 3   Period of British and Italian control, 1884–1960

> Class here 20th century

> *For 1960–1999, see 967.7305*

.730 5   1960–

.730 51   1960–1969

.730 52   Administration of Maxamed Siyaad Barre, 1969–1991

> Class Somali-Ethiopian conflicts, 1978–1991, in 963.071

---

*Add as instructed under 930–990

.730 53	1991–2000
	Class here Civil War, 1991 to present
	For Civil War, 2000 to present, see 967.73054
.730 54	2000–
.8	***Tanzania**
.801	Early history to 1884
.802	German period, 1884–1916
.803	1916–1964
	Class here British period, 1916–1961; 20th century
	For 1900–1916, see 967.802; for 1964–1999, see 967.804
.804	Period as United Republic, 1964–
.804 1	Administration of Julius K. Nyerere, 1964–1985
.804 2	Administration of Ali Hassan Mwinyi, 1985–1995
.804 3	Administration of Benjamin W. Mkapa, 1995–2005
.804 4	Administration of Jakaya Khalfan Mrisho Kikwete, 2005–2015
.804 5	Administration of John Pombe Joseph Magufuli, 2015–
.81	*Zanzibar Region and Pemba Region
.810 1	Early history to 1700
.810 2	Period of Arab rule, 1700–1890
.810 3	Period as a British protectorate, 1890–1963
	Class here 20th century
	For 1963–1999, see 967.8104
.810 4	1963–
.810 41	1963–1985
.810 42	1985–1995
.810 43	1995–2005
.810 44	2005–
.82	*Mainland regions of Tanzania
.820 1	Early history to 1884
.820 2	German period, 1884–1916

*Add as instructed under 930–990

.820 3	Period as Tanganyika, 1916–1961

Class here 20th century, British period

For 1900–1916, see 967.8202; for 1961–1999, see 967.8204

.820 4	1961–
.820 41	1961–1985
.820 42	1985–1995
.820 43	1995–2005
.820 44	2005–
.822–.828	Localities of mainland regions of Tanzania

Add to base number 967.82 the numbers following —6782 in notation
67822–67828 from Table 2, e.g., Dar es Salaam 967.8232; then add
further as follows:
001–009   Standard subdivisions
                Add to 00 the numbers following 00 in notation
                001–009 from table under 930–990, e.g., ethnic and
                national groups 004, ethnic and national groups in Dar
                es Salaam 967.8232004
01–04   Historical periods
                Add to 0 the numbers following 967.820 in
                967.8201–967.8204, e.g., Dar es Salaam during 1961 to
                present 967.823204

.9	***Mozambique**
.901	Early history to 1648
.902	1648–1900

Including 17th century

Class here Portuguese period, 1648–1975

For 1600–1648, see 967.901; for 1900–1975, see 967.903

.903	1900–1975
.905	1975–
.905 1	Administration of Samora Machel, 1975–1986
.905 2	Administration of Joaquim Alberto Chissano, 1986–2005
.905 3	Administration of Armando Emílio Guebuza, 2005–2015
.905 4	Administration of Filipe Jacinto Nyusi, 2015–

*Add as instructed under 930–990

.91–.99   Localities of Mozambique

      Add to base number 967.9 the numbers following —679 in notation
      6791–6799 from Table 2, e.g., Maputo 967.91; then add further as follows:
       001–009 Standard subdivisions
            Add to 00 the numbers following 00 in notation 001–009
            from table under 930–990, e.g., ethnic and national groups
            004, ethnic and national groups in Maputo 967.91004
       01–05 Historical periods
            Add to 0 the numbers following 967.90 in 967.901–967.905,
            e.g., Maputo during 1975 to present 967.9105

968 Republic of South Africa and neighboring southern African countries

     Class here southern Africa

.000 1–.000 8   Standard subdivisions of southern Africa

      As modified in notation 001–008 from table under 930–990

.000 9   Archaeology; historical periods; areas, regions, places in general;
      collected biography of southern Africa

.000 900 9   Archaeology

      Notation 09009 from Table 1 as modified below

.000 900 902–.000 900 909   Specific subdivisions of archaeology

      Add to base number 968.00090090 the numbers
      following 009090 in notation 0090902–0090909
      from table under 930–990, e.g., serials treating
      archaeology of southern Africa 968.000900905

.000 901–.000 905   Historical periods

      Add to base number 968.00090 the numbers following —090
      in notation 0901–0905 from Table 1, e.g., southern Africa
      during 20th century 968.000904

.000 91–.000 99   Areas, regions, places in general; collected biography

      As modified in notation 0091–0099 from table under 930–990

.001–.009   Standard subdivisions of Republic of South Africa

      As modified in notation 001–009 from table under 930–990

\>   968.02–968.07 Historical periods of Republic of South Africa

     Class comprehensive works in 968

.02   Early history to 1488

.03   Period of European exploration and settlement, 1488–1814

.04   1814–1910

.041   1814–1835

     Class here Mfecane (Difaqane)

.042	Great Trek, 1835–1838
.044	1838–1854
.045	1854–1899

See also 968.2046 for First Anglo-Boer War

.048	‡South African War (Second Anglo-Boer War), 1899–1902

(Option: Class South African War [Second Anglo-Boer War] in 941.081)

.048 3	Participation of specific groups of countries, of specific countries, localities, groups

Number built according to instructions under 940–990

Class military participation of specific countries, localities, groups in 968.0484. Class a specific activity with the activity, e.g., efforts to preserve or restore peace 968.0481

.048 31	Great Britain
.048 32	Orange Free State and South African Republic

Standard subdivisions are added for either or both topics in
. heading

[.048 34–.048 39]	Participation of specific countries and localities

Do not use; class in 968.0483

[.048 42]	Land operations

Do not use; class in 968.0484

.049	1902–1910
.05	Period of Union, 1910–1961

Class here 20th century

For 1900–1902, see 968.048; for 1902–1910, see 968.049; for 1961–1999, see 968.06

.052	Prime ministership of Louis Botha, 1910–1919
.053	First prime ministership of Jan Christiaan Smuts, 1919–1924
.054	Prime ministership of James Barry Munnik Hertzog, 1924–1939
.055	Second prime ministership of Jan Christiaan Smuts, 1939–1948
.056	Prime ministership of Daniel François Malan, 1948–1954
.057	Prime ministership of Johannes Gerhardus Strijdom, 1954–1958
.058	Prime ministership of Hendrik Frensch Verwoerd, 1958–1966

Including Sharpeville Massacre, 1960

For 1961–1966, see 968.061

‡Add as instructed under 940–990

.06	Period as Republic, 1961–

> For 1994 to present, see 968.07

.061	Period of prime ministership of Hendrik Frensch Verwoerd under republic, 1961–1966
.062	Prime ministership of B. J. Vorster, 1966–1978
.062 7	1976–1977

Class here Soweto and related riots

.063	Administration of P. W. Botha, 1978–1989
.064	Administration of F. W. de Klerk, 1989–1994
.07	1994–

Class here post-apartheid period of Republic of South Africa

.071	Administration of Nelson Mandela, 1994–1999
.072	Administration of Thabo Mbeki, 1999–2008
.073	Administration of Kgalema Motlanthe, 2008–2009
.074	Administration of Jacob Zuma, 2009–2018
.075	Administration of Cyril Ramaphosa, 2018–
.2	***Gauteng, North West, Limpopo, Mpumalanga, former homelands (national states) of Republic of South Africa**
.203	Early history to 1835
.204	1835–1910

Class here 19th century

> For 1800–1835, see 968.203

.204 2	Period of Great Trek and Boer settlement, 1835–1852
.204 5	Period as South African Republic, 1852–1877
.204 6	Period of British control, 1877–1881

Including First Anglo-Boer War, 1880–1881

.204 7	1881–1899
.204 75	Jameson raid, 1895–1896
.204 8	Period of South African (Second Anglo-Boer) War, 1899–1902
.204 9	Period as Transvaal Colony, 1902–1910

*Add as instructed under 930–990

.205   Period of Union, 1910–1961

              Class here 20th century; period as province of Transvaal, 1910–1996

              Add to base number 968.205 the numbers following 968.05 in
              968.052–968.058, e.g., period of World War II 968.2055

              *For 1900–1902, see 968.2048; for 1902–1910, see 968.2049; for
              1961–1999, see 968.206*

.206–.207   Period of Republic, 1961–

              Add to base number 968.20 the numbers following 968.0 in
              968.06–968.07, e.g., period of administration of Nelson Mandela
              968.2071

.22–.29   Localities of Gauteng, North-West, Limpopo, Mpumalanga, former
              homelands (national states) of Republic of South Africa

              Add to base number 968.2 the numbers following —682 in notation
              6822–6829 from Table 2, e.g., Gauteng 968.22; then add further as follows:
              001–009   Standard subdivisions
                         Add to 00 the numbers following 00 in notation 001–009
                         from table under 930–990, e.g., ethnic and national groups
                         004, ethnic and national groups in Gauteng 968.22004
              03–07   Historical periods
                         Add to 0 the numbers following 968.20 in 968.203–968.207,
                         e.g., Gauteng during 1994 to present 968.2207

.29   Former homelands (Former national states)

              Limited to pre-1997 periods

              *For a specific homeland or part of a homeland, see the homeland or the
              part, e.g., Ciskei 968.755*

.4   *KwaZulu-Natal

              Province of Republic of South Africa

.403   Early history to 1824

.403 8   Period of early Nguni kingdoms, ca. 1500–1816

              Including kingdoms of Mthethwa, Ndwandwe, Qwabe

.403 9   Reign of Shaka, 1816–1828

              For reign of Shaka during 1824–1828, see 968.4041

.404   1824–1910

              Class here period of Zululand, 1816–1879

              For reign of Shaka, see 968.4039

.404 1   Period of early British settlement, 1824–1835

              Class here reign of Dingaan, 1828–1840

              For reign of Dingaan during 1835–1840, see 968.4042

---

*Add as instructed under 930–990

.404 2	Period of Great Trek and Boer settlement, 1835–1843
	Including Battle of Blood River, 1838; republic of Natalia
.404 5	Period as a British colony, 1843–1899
	Including reign of Cetewayo, 1872–1879; Zulu War, 1879; annexation of Zululand, 1897
.404 8	Period of South African (Second Anglo-Boer) War, 1899–1902
.404 9	1902–1910

.405   **Period of Union, 1910–1961**

Class here 20th century; period as province of Natal, 1910–1996

Add to base number 968.405 the numbers following 968.05 in 968.052–968.058, e.g., period of World War II 968.4055

For 1900–1902, see 968.4048; for 1902–1910, see 968.4049; for 1961–1999, see 968.406

.406–.407   **Period of Republic, 1961–**

Add to base number 968.40 the numbers following 968.0 in 968.06–968.07, e.g., period of administration of Nelson Mandela 968.4071

.41–.49   **Localities of KwaZulu-Natal**

Add to base number 968.4 the numbers following —684 in notation 6841–6849 from Table 2, e.g., Amajuba District Municipality 968.41; then add further as follows:

    001–009   Standard subdivisions

           Add to 00 the numbers following 00 in notation 001–009 from table under 930–990, e.g., ethnic and national groups 004, ethnic and national groups in Amajuba District Municipality 968.41004

    03–07   Historical periods

           Add to 0 the numbers following 968.40 in 968.403–968.407, e.g., Amajuba District Municipality during 1994 to present 968.4107

.5   *Free State

Province of Republic of South Africa

.503	Early history to 1828
.504	1828–1910

Class here 19th century

For 1800–1828, see 968.503

.504 2	Periods of Great Trek and as Orange River Sovereignty, 1835–1854
.504 5	Period as Orange Free State, 1854–1899
.504 8	Period of South African (Second Anglo-Boer) War, 1899–1902

*Add as instructed under 930–990

.504 9	Period as Orange River Colony, 1902–1910
.505	Period of Union, 1910–1961

Class here 20th century; period as province of Orange Free State, 1910–1996

Add to base number 968.505 the numbers following 968.05 in 968.052–968.058, e.g., period of World War II 968.5055

> *For 1900–1902, see 968.5048; for 1902–1910, see 968.5049; for 1961–1999, see 968.506*

.506–.507	Period of Republic, 1961–

Add to base number 968.50 the numbers following 968.0 in 968.06–968.07, e.g., period of administration of Nelson Mandela 968.5071

.51–.57	Localities of Free State

Add to base number 968.5 the numbers following —685 in notation 6851–6857 from Table 2, e.g., Thabo Mofutsanyana District Municipality 968.51; then add further as follows:

    001–009   Standard subdivisions

                Add to 00 the numbers following 00 in notation 001–009 from table under 930–990, e.g., ethnic and national groups 004, ethnic and national groups in Thabo Mofutsanyana District Municipality 968.51004

    03–07   Historical periods

                Add to 0 the numbers following 968.50 in 968.503–968.507, e.g., Thabo Mofutsanyana District Municipality during 1994 to present 968.5107

.7	***Northern Cape, Western Cape, Eastern Cape**

Provinces of Republic of South Africa

.702	Early history to 1488
.703	Period of exploration and settlement, 1488–1814
.703 1	1488–1652

Including 17th century

> *For 1652–1699, see 968.7032*

.703 2	Period of Dutch control, 1652–1795

Class period of control by Batavian Republic in 968.7033

.703 3	1795–1806

Including periods of British occupation, 1795–1803, control by Batavian Republic, 1803–1806

.704	1806–1910

*Add as instructed under 930–990

.704 2	Period of British control, 1806–1854
	Including period of Great Trek
	Class period of British occupation, 1795–1803, in 968.7033
.704 5	Period of self-government, 1854–1899
.704 8	Period of South African (Second Anglo-Boer) War, 1899–1902
.704 9	1902–1910

.705   **Period of Union, 1910–1961**

Class here 20th century; period as province of Cape of Good Hope, 1910–1996

Add to base number 968.705 the numbers following 968.05 in 968.052–968.058, e.g., period of World War II 968.7055

> *For 1900–1902, see 968.7048; for 1902–1910, see 968.7049; for 1961–1999, see 968.706*

.706–.707   **Period of Republic, 1961–**

Add to base number 968.70 the numbers following 968.0 in 968.06–968.07, e.g., period of administration of Nelson Mandela 968.7071

.71–.75   **Localities of Northern Cape, Western Cape, Eastern Cape**

Add to base number 968.7 the numbers following —687 in notation 6871–6875 from Table 2, e.g., Northern Cape 968.71; then add further as follows:

001–009	Standard subdivisions
	Add to 00 the numbers following 00 in notation 001–009 from table under 930–990, e.g., ethnic and national groups 004, ethnic and national groups in Northern Cape 968.71004
02–07	Historical periods
	Add to 0 the numbers following 968.70 in 968.702–968.707, e.g., Northern Cape during 1994 to present 968.7107

.8   *Namibia, Botswana, Lesotho, Eswatini

.801–.803   **Historical periods**

Add to base number 968.80 the numbers following 960 in 960.1–960.3, e.g., 20th century 968.8031

.81   *Namibia

.810 1	Early history to 1884
.810 2	German period, 1884–1915
.810 3	South African period, 1915–1990
.810 4	1990–
.810 41	Administration of Sam Nujoma, 1990–2005

*Add as instructed under 930–990

.810 42		Administration of Hifikepunye Lucas Pohamba, 2005–2015
.810 43		Administration of Hage Gottfried Geingob, 2015–
.83	*Botswana	
.830 1		Early history to 1885
.830 2		Period as Bechuanaland, 1885–1966

Class here 20th century, British period

For 1966–1999, see 968.8303

.830 3		1966–
.830 31		Administration of Seretse Khama, 1966–1980
.830 32		Administration of Sir Ketumile Masire, 1980–1998
.830 33		Administration of Festus Gontebanye Mogae, 1998–2008
.830 34		Administration of Seretse Khama Ian Khama, 2008–2018
.830 35		Administration of Mokgweetsi Eric Keabetswe Masisi, 2018–
.85	*Lesotho	
.850 1		Early history to 1868
.850 2		Period as Basutoland, 1868–1966

Including 20th century

Class here British period

For 1966–1999, see 968.8503

.850 3		1966–
.850 31		First reign of Moshoeshoe II, 1966–1990

Class here prime ministership of Leabua Jonathan, 1966–1986

.850 32		1990–

Including second reign of Moshoeshoe II, 1995–1996; prime ministerships of Pakalitha Bethuel Mosisili, 1998–2012 and 2015–2017; prime ministerships of Thomas Motsoahae Thabane, 2012–2015 and 2017 to present

Class here reigns of Letsie III, 1990–1995 and 1996 to present

.87	*Eswatini	
.870 1		Early history to 1840
.870 2		British period, 1840–1968

Including 19th century, 20th century

For 1800–1840, see 968.8701; for 1968–1999, see 968.8703

---

*Add as instructed under 930–990

.870 3	1968–
	Including reigns of Sobhuza II, 1968–1982; Mswati III, 1986 to present

.9   ***Zimbabwe, Zambia, Malawi**

.901   Early history to 1888

.902   Period of British control, 1888–1953

          Class here 20th century

          For 1953–1963, see 968.903; for 1964–1999, see 968.904

.903   Period as Federation of Rhodesia and Nyasaland (Central African Federation), 1953–1963

          Class here prime ministership of Roy Welensky, 1956–1963

.904   1964–

.91   *Zimbabwe

.910 1   Early history to 1889

          Including Karanga kingdoms of Changamire, the Monomotapas

.910 2   Period as Southern Rhodesia, 1889–1953

          Class here 20th century, British period

          For 1953–1963, see 968.9103; for 1964–1980, see 968.9104; for 1980–1999, see 968.9105

.910 3   Period of federation, 1953–1963

.910 4   Period as Rhodesia, 1964–1980

          Class here prime ministership of Ian Douglas Smith, 1965–1979

.910 5   Period as Republic of Zimbabwe, 1980–

.910 51   Administration of Robert Gabriel Mugabe, 1980–2017

.910 52   2017–

.94   *Zambia

.940 1   Early history to 1890

          Including kingdoms of the Barotse, of the Bemba

.940 2   Period of British control, 1890–1953

          Including periods as North-eastern Rhodesia and North-western Rhodesia provinces, 1890–1911; as Northern Rhodesia, 1911–1953

          Class here 20th century

          For 1953–1963, see 968.9403; for 1964–1999, see 968.9404

.940 3   Period of federation, 1953–1963

*Add as instructed under 930–990

.940 4	Period as Republic of Zambia, 1964–
.940 41	Administration of Kenneth D. Kaunda, 1964–1991
.940 42	Administration of Frederick Chiluba, 1991–2002
.940 43	Administration of Levy P. Mwanawasa, 2002–2008
.940 44	2008–
.97	*Malawi
.970 1	Early history to 1891
	Including kingdom of Malawi
.970 2	Period as Nyasaland, 1891–1953
	Class here 20th century, British period
	For 1953–1963, see 968.9703; for 1964–1999, see 968.9704
.970 3	Period of federation, 1953–1963
.970 4	1964–
.970 41	Administration of H. Kamuzu Banda, 1964–1994
.970 42	Administration of Bakili Muluzi, 1994–2004
.970 43	2004–2014
	Including administration of Joyce Hilda Banda, 2012–2014
	Class here administration of B. W. T. Mutharika, 2004–2012
.970 44	Administration of A. Peter Mutharika, 2014–2020
.970 45	Administration of Lazarus McCarthy Chakwera, 2020–

969   †South Indian Ocean islands

.1	*Madagascar
.101	Early history to 1895
	Including kingdoms of Betsimisaraka, Boina, Menabe, Merina
.103	French period, 1895–1960
	Class here 20th century
	For 1960–1999, see 969.105
.105	1960–
.105 1	1960–1975
	Class here administration of Philibert Tsiranana, 1960–1972
.105 2	First administration of Didier Ratsiraka, 1975–1993

*Add as instructed under 930–990
†Add as instructed under 930–990; however, do not add historical periods

.105 3	1993–1997
.105 4	Second administration Didier Ratsiraka, 1997–2002
.105 5	Administration of Marc Ravalomanana, 2002–2009
.105 6	Administration of Andry Rajoelina, 2009–2014
.105 7	Administration of Hery Rajaonarimampianina, 2014–

.4 **†Comoro Islands**

.41 †Comoros (Federal and Islamic Republic of the Comoros)

.45 †Mayotte

.6 **†Seychelles**

.7 **†Chagos Islands**

.8 **†Réunion and Mauritius**

.81 *Réunion

.810 2 Early history to 1946

.810 4 Period as a Department of France, 1946–

Class here 20th century

For 1900–1946, see 969.8102

.82 *Mauritius

.820 1 Early history to 1810

.820 2 Period of British rule, 1810–1968

Including 20th century

For 1968–1999, see 969.8203

.820 3 1968–1992

.820 4 Period as republic, 1992–

.820 41 Administration of Cassam Uteem, 1992–2002

.820 42 2002–2012

Class here administration of Aneerood Jugnauth, 2003–2012

.820 43 Administration of Kailash (Rajkeswur) Purryag, 2012–2015

.820 44 2015–

Including administration of Ameenah Gurib-Fakim, 2015–2018

.9 **†Isolated islands**

Including Amsterdam, Cocos (Keeling), Crozet, Kerguelen, Prince Edward, Saint Paul

*Add as instructed under 930–990
†Add as instructed under 930–990; however, do not add historical periods

970   **History of North America**

.001–.003   Standard subdivisions

.004   Ethnic and national groups

.004 001–.004 009   Standard subdivisions

.004 05–.004 09   Specific ethnic and national groups with ethnic origins from more than one continent, of European descent

Add to base number 970.0040 the numbers following —0 in notation 05–09 from Table 5, e.g., general history and civilization of people of European descent in North America 970.00409

.004 1–.004 9   Specific ethnic and national groups

Add to base number 970.004 notation 1–9 from Table 5, e.g., general history and civilization of North American native peoples in North America 970.00497
(Option: Class North American native peoples in North America in 970.1; class specific native peoples in 970.3)

Class history and civilization of North American native peoples in a specific place before European discovery and conquest with the place, without using notation 00497 from table under 930–990, e.g., Aztecs before 1519 972.018

.005–.009   Standard subdivisions

As modified in notation 005–009 from table under 930–990

>   970.01–970.05 Historical periods

Class comprehensive works in 970

.01   Early history to 1599

.011   Early history to 1492

Including pre-Columbian claims

For Chinese claims, see 970.012; for Norse claims, see 970.013; for Welsh claims, see 970.014

.012   Chinese claims

.013   Norse claims

.014   Welsh claims

>   970.015–970.019 Period of European discovery and exploration

Class comprehensive works in 970.01

.015   Discoveries by Columbus

.016   Spanish and Portuguese explorations

Standard subdivisions are added for either or both topics in heading

.017	English explorations
.018	French explorations
.019	Explorations by other nations
.02	1600–1699
.03	1700–1799
.04	1800–1899
.05	1900–
.051	1900–1918

> Class here period of World War I, 1914–1918

.052	1918–1945

> Class here period of World War II, 1939–1945

.053	1945–1999

> Class here 20th century

> *For 1900–1918, see 970.051; for 1918–1945, see 970.052*

.053 4	1945–1949
.053 5	1950–1959
.053 6	1960–1969
.053 7	1970–1979
.053 8	1980–1989
.053 9	1990–1999
.054	2000–
.054 1	2000–2019
.054 11	2000–2009
.054 12	2010–2019
.054 2	2020–2029

(.1) **North American native peoples**

> (Optional number; prefer 970.00497)

> Class special topics in 970.3–970.5

(.3) **Specific native peoples**

> (Optional number; prefer 971–979 with use of subdivision 00497 from table under 930–990, e.g., the Hopi in Arizona 979.100497458)

> (Option: Arrange alphabetically by name of people)

> Class government relations with specific native peoples in 970.5

(.4) **Native peoples in specific places in North America**

(Optional number; prefer 971–979 with use of subdivision 00497 from table under 930–990, e.g., native peoples in United States 973.0497, in Arizona 979.100497)

Add to base number 970.4 the numbers following —7 in notation 71–79 from Table 2, e.g., Indians in Arizona 970.491

Class specific native peoples in specific places in 970.3; class government relations in specific places in 970.5

(.5) **Government relations with North American native peoples**

(Optional number; prefer 323.1197 for comprehensive works; a specific subject with the subject, e.g., Black Hawk War 973.56, relation to the state in Canada 323.1197071)

History and policy

> ## 971–979 Countries and localities

Class comprehensive works in 970. Class specific native peoples in a specific place with the place in 971–979, plus notation 00497 from table under 930–990, e.g., the Hopi in Arizona 979.100497458
(Option: Class native peoples in specific places in North America in 970.4)

971 *Canada

.01	Early history to 1763
.011	Early history to 1632
.011 1	Period before European discovery and exploration
.011 2	Norse explorations
.011 3	French explorations
.011 4	English explorations
.016	Period of French and English expansion, 1632–1689

Class here 17th century

For 1600–1632, see 971.011; for 1689–1699, see 971.018

.016 2	Period of Company of New France, 1632–1663
.016 3	1663–1689

*Add as instructed under 930–990

.018   Period of struggle of France and England for supremacy, 1689–1763

Including periods of War of the League of Augsburg, 1688–1697; War of the Spanish Succession, 1701–1714; War of the Austrian Succession, 1740–1748
> (Option: Class here North American aspects of War of the League of Augsburg, War of the Spanish Succession; prefer 973.25. Class here North American aspects of War of the Austrian Succession; prefer 973.26)

Class here comprehensive works on period as a French royal province, 1663–1763; 18th century

Class North American aspects of War of the League of Augsburg, War of the Spanish Succession in 973.25; class North American aspects of War of the Austrian Succession in 973.26; class comprehensive works on War of the League of Augsburg in 940.2525; class comprehensive works on War of the Spanish Succession in 940.2526; class comprehensive works on War of the Austrian Succession in 940.2532

> *For 1663–1689, see 971.0163; for 1763–1791, see 971.02; for 1791–1799, see 971.032*

.018 8   Period of Seven Years' War, 1756–1763

Class expulsion of Acadians in 971.5017; class North American aspects of Seven Years' War in 973.26; class comprehensive works on Seven Years' War in 940.2534

(Option: Class here North American aspects of Seven Years' War; prefer 973.26)

.02   Period of early British rule, 1763–1791

.022   1763–1774

Including Quebec Act, 1774

(Option: Class here Pontiac's conspiracy, 1763–1764; prefer 973.27)

.024   Period of American Revolution, 1774–1783

Including settlement of Loyalists from United States, 1774–1789

> *For settlement of Loyalists during 1783–1789, see 971.028*

.028   1783–1791

Class here Constitutional Act, 1791

.03   Period of Upper and Lower Canada, 1791–1841

Class here 19th century

> *For 1841–1867, see 971.04; for 1867–1899, see 971.05*

.032   1791–1812

.034   Period of War of 1812, 1812–1814

(Option: Class here War of 1812; prefer 973.52)

.036   1814–1837

.063 3	Prime ministership of Louis Stephen Saint-Laurent, 1948–1957
.064	1957–1999
.064 2	Prime ministership of John G. Diefenbaker, 1957–1963
.064 3	Prime ministership of Lester B. Pearson, 1963–1968
.064 4	First prime ministership of Pierre Elliott Trudeau, 1968–1979
.064 5	Prime ministership of Joe (Charles Joseph) Clark, 1979–1980
.064 6	Second prime ministership of Pierre Elliott Trudeau, 1980–1984

Including prime ministership of John Turner, 1984

.064 7	Prime ministership of Brian Mulroney, 1984–1993

Including prime ministership of Kim Campbell, 1993

.064 8	1993–1999

Class here prime ministership of Jean Chrétien, 1993–2003

For prime ministership of Jean Chrétien during 2000–2003, see 971.071

.07	2000–
.071	Later portion of prime ministership of Jean Chrétien, 2000–2003
.072	Prime ministership of Paul Martin, 2003–2006
.073	Prime ministership of Stephen Harper, 2006–2015
.074	Prime ministership of Justin Trudeau, 2015–
.1	***British Columbia**
.101	Early history to 1790
.102	Period of settlement and colony, 1790–1871

Including colony of New Caledonia

Class here 19th century

For 1871–1899, see 971.103

.103	Period as a Province of Canada, 1871–

For 1945–1999, see 971.104; for 2000 to present, see 971.105

.104	1945–1999

Class here 20th century

For 1900–1945, see 971.103

.105	2000–

*Add as instructed under 930–990

.11–.18	Localities of British Columbia

Add to base number 971.1 the numbers following —711 in notation 7111–7118 from Table 2, e.g., northern coastal region of British Columbia 971.11; then add further as follows:
    001–009   Standard subdivisions
            Add to 00 the numbers following 00 in notation 001–009 from table under 930–990, e.g., ethnic and national groups 004, ethnic and national groups in northern coastal region of British Columbia 971.11004
    01–05   Historical periods
            Add to 0 the numbers following 971.10 in 971.101–971.105, e.g., northern coastal region of British Columbia during 2000 to present 971.1105

.2 *Prairie Provinces

.201	Early history to 1869

    Including Rupert's Land

.202	1869–1945
.203	1945–1999

    Class here 20th century

    For 1900–1945, see 971.202

.204	2000–
.23–.27	Localities of Prairie Provinces

Add to base number 971.2 the numbers following —712 in notation 7123–7127 from Table 2, e.g., Alberta 971.23; then add further as follows:
    001–009   Standard subdivisions
            Add to 00 the numbers following 00 in notation 001–009 from table under 930–990, e.g., ethnic and national groups 004, ethnic and national groups in Alberta 971.23004
    01–04   Historical periods
            Add to 0 the numbers following 971.20 in 971.201–971.204, e.g., Alberta during 2000 to present 971.2304

.3 *Ontario

.301	Early history to 1791
.302	Period of Upper Canada and Act of Union, 1791–1867

    Class here 19th century

    For 1867–1899, see 971.303

.303	Period as a Province of Canada, 1867–

    For 1945–1999, see 971.304; for 2000 to present, see 971.305

*Add as instructed under 930–990

.304   1945–1999

                Class here 20th century

                For 1900–1945, see 971.303

.305   2000–

.31–.38   Localities of Ontario

                Add to base number 971.3 the numbers following —713 in notation
                7131–7138 from Table 2, e.g., northern Ontario region and Georgian Bay
                region 971.31; then add further as follows:

                001–009   Standard subdivisions
                             Add to 00 the numbers following 00 in notation 001–009
                             from table under 930–990, e.g., ethnic and national groups
                             004, ethnic and national groups in northern Ontario region
                             and Georgian Bay region 971.31004
                01–05   Historical periods
                             Add to 0 the numbers following 971.30 in 971.301–971.305,
                             e.g., northern Ontario region and Georgian Bay region during
                             2000 to present 971.3105

.4   ***Quebec**

.401   Early history to 1763

.401 2   Early history to 1608

                Including period of explorations by Jacques Cartier, 1534–1535

.401 4   French period, 1608–1763

                Including 18th century

                For 1763–1799, see 971.402

.402   British period, 1763–1867

                Including period of Lower Canada, 1791–1841; 19th century

                For 1867–1899, see 971.403

.403   Period as a Province of Canada, 1867–

                For 1945–1999, see 971.404; for 2000 to present, see 971.405

.403 1   Beginning of confederation, 1867–1897

.403 2   1897–1936

.403 3   1936–1945

.404   1945–1999

                Class here 20th century

                For 1900–1945, see 971.403

---

*Add as instructed under 930–990

.404 1	1945–1960

Class here comprehensive works on second administration of Maurice Duplessis, 1944–1959

For second administration of Maurice Duplessis during 1944–1945, see 971.4033

.404 2	1960–1976
.404 3	1976–1985
.404 4	1985–1994
.404 5	1994–1999
.405	2000–
.41–.47	Localities of Quebec

Add to base number 971.4 the numbers following —714 in notation 7141–7147 from Table 2, e.g., northern region of Quebec 971.41; then add further as follows:

001–009   Standard subdivisions

Add to 00 the numbers following 00 in notation 001–009 from table under 930–990, e.g., ethnic and national groups 004, ethnic and national groups in northern region of Quebec 971.41004

01–05   Historical periods

Add to 0 the numbers following 971.40 in 971.401–971.405, e.g., northern region of Quebec during 2000 to present 971.4105

.5	***Atlantic Provinces**

Class here Maritime Provinces

For Nova Scotia, see 971.6; for Prince Edward Island, see 971.7; for Newfoundland and Labrador, see 971.8

.501	Early history to 1763

Including 18th century

For 1763–1799, see 971.502

.501 7	1604–1763

Class here expulsion of Acadians, 1755 and 1758; comprehensive works on Acadia

For a specific part of Acadia not provided for here, see the part, e.g., Acadia in Nova Scotia 971.601

.502	Period as British colonies, 1763–1867

Including 19th century

For 1867–1899, see 971.503

---

*Add as instructed under 930–990

.503	Period as provinces of Canada, 1867–
	For 1945–1999, see 971.504; for 2000 to present, see 971.505
.504	1945–1999
	Class here 20th century
	For 1900–1945, see 971.503
.505	2000–
.51	*New Brunswick
.510 1	Early history to 1784
	For expulsion of Acadians, see 971.5017
.510 2	Period as separate province, 1784–1867
	Including 19th century
	For 1867–1899, see 971.5103
.510 3	Period as a Province of Canada, 1867–
	For 1945–1999, see 971.5104; for 2000 to present, see 971.5105
.510 4	1945–1999
	Class here 20th century
	For 1900–1945, see 971.5103
.510 5	2000–
.511–.554	Localities of New Brunswick

                  Add to base number 971.5 the numbers following —715 in notation 71511–71554 from Table 2, e.g., Restigouche County 971.511; then add further as follows:

           001–009   Standard subdivisions

                        Add to 00 the numbers following 00 in notation 001–009 from table under 930–990, e.g., ethnic and national groups 004, ethnic and national groups in Restigouche County 971.511004

           01–05   Historical periods

                        Add to 0 the numbers following 971.510 in 971.5101–971.5105, e.g., Restigouche County during 2000 to present 971.51105

.6	***Nova Scotia**
.601	Early history to 1763
	Including 18th century
	For expulsion of Acadians, see 971.5017; for 1763–1799, see 971.602

*Add as instructed under 930–990

.602   Period as a British colony, 1763–1867

         Including 19th century

         For 1867–1899, see 971.603

.603   Period as a Province of Canada, 1867–

         For 1945–1999, see 971.604; for 2000 to present, see 971.605

.604   1945–1999

         Class here 20th century

         For 1900–1945, see 971.603

.605   2000–

.61–.69   Localities of Nova Scotia

         Add to base number 971.6 the numbers following —716 in notation 7161–7169 from Table 2, e.g., northern counties of Nova Scotia 971.61; then add further as follows:

         001–009   Standard subdivisions

                Add to 00 the numbers following 00 in notation 001–009 from table under 930–990, e.g., ethnic and national groups 004, ethnic and national groups in northern counties of Nova Scotia 971.61004

         01–05   Historical periods

                Add to 0 the numbers following 971.60 in 971.601–971.605, e.g., northern counties of Nova Scotia during 2000 to present 971.6105

.7   *Prince Edward Island

.701   Early history to 1769

         Including 18th century

         For expulsion of Acadians, see 971.5017; for 1769–1799, see 971.702

.702   Period as separate province, 1769–1873

         Including 19th century

         For 1873–1899, see 971.703

.703   Period as a Province of Canada, 1873–

         For 1945–1999, see 971.704; for 2000 to present, see 971.705

.704   1945–1999

         Class here 20th century

         For 1900–1945, see 971.703

.705   2000–

*Add as instructed under 930–990

.71–.77   Localities of Prince Edward Island

> Add to base number 971.7 the numbers following —717 in notation 7171–7177 from Table 2, e.g., Prince County 971.71; then add further as follows:
>
> 001–009   Standard subdivisions
>
> > Add to 00 the numbers following 00 in notation 001–009 from table under 930–990, e.g., ethnic and national groups 004, ethnic and national groups in Prince County 971.71004
>
> 01–05   Historical periods
>
> > Add to 0 the numbers following 971.70 in 971.701–971.705, e.g., Prince County during 2000 to present 971.7105

.8   ***Newfoundland and Labrador, Saint Pierre and Miquelon**

> Class here Newfoundland

>   971.801–971.805   Historical periods for Newfoundland and Labrador

> Class comprehensive works in 971.8

.801   Early history to 1855

> Including 19th century
>
> *For 1855–1899, see 971.802*

.802   1855–1934

.803   Period of suspension of parliamentary government, 1934–1949

.804   Period as a Province of Canada, 1949–

> Class here 20th century
>
> *For 1900–1934, see 971.802; for 1934–1949, see 971.803; for 2001 to present, see 971.805*

.805   2001–

.81   St. John's

.810 01–.810 09   Standard subdivisions

> Add to 971.8100 the numbers following 00 in notation 001–009 from table under 930–990, e.g., ethnic and national groups in St. John's 971.81004

.810 1–.810 5   Historical periods

> Add to base number 971.810 the numbers following 971.80 in 971.801–971.805, e.g., St. John's during period of suspension of parliamentary government, 1934–1949 971.8103

.82   *Labrador

---

*Add as instructed under 930–990

.820 1	Early history to 1763
	Including 18th century
	For 1763–1799, see 971.8202
.820 2	Period when claimed by Lower Canada (Quebec) and Newfoundland, 1763–1927
.820 3	Period as dependency of Newfoundland, 1927–1949
.820 4	Period as part of Province of Newfoundland and Labrador, 1949–
	Class here 20th century
	For 1900–1927, see 971.8202; for 1927–1949, see 971.8203; for 2001 to present, see 971.8205
.820 5	2001–
.88	†Saint Pierre and Miquelon
.9	***Northern territories**
.901	Early history to 1870
	Including 19th century
	For 1870–1899, see 971.902
.902	1870–1945
.903	1945–1999
	Class here 20th century
	For 1900–1945, see 971.902
.904	1999–
.91	*Yukon
.910 1	Early history to 1898
.910 2	1898–1945
.910 3	1945–1999
	Class here 20th century
	For 1900–1945, see 971.9102
.910 4	1999–
.92	*Northwest Territories (1870–1999)
	See also 971.93 for Northwest Territories (1999–); also 971.95 for Nunavut

*Add as instructed under 930–990
†Add as instructed under 930–990; however, do not add historical periods

.920 1–.920 4	Historical periods
	Add to base number 971.920 the numbers following 971.90 in 971.901–971.904, e.g., 1945–1999 971.9203
.93	*Northwest Territories (1999–)
	See also 971.92 for Northwest Territories (1870–1999)
.930 1–.930 4	Historical periods
	Add to base number 971.930 the numbers following 971.90 in 971.901–971.904, e.g., 1945–1999 971.9303
.95	*Nunavut
.950 1–.950 4	Historical periods
	Add to base number 971.950 the numbers following 971.90 in 971.901–971.904, e.g., 1945–1999 971.9503
.952–.958	Localities of Nunavut

Add to base number 971.95 the numbers following —7195 in notation 71952–71958 from Table 2, e.g., Kitikmeot Region 971.955; then add further as follows:

001–009	Standard subdivisions
	Add to 00 the numbers following 00 in notation 001–009 from table under 930–990, e.g., ethnic and national groups 004, ethnic and national groups in Kitikmeot Region 971.955004
01–04	Historical periods
	Add to 0 the numbers following 971.950 in 971.9501–971.9504, e.g., Kitikmeot Region during 1999 to present 971.95504

972   Mexico, Central America, West Indies, Bermuda

Class here Middle America

.000 1–.000 8	Standard subdivisions of Mexico, Central America, West Indies, Bermuda together
	As modified in notation 001–008 from table under 930–990
.000 9	Archaeology; historical periods; areas, regions, places in general; collected biography of Mexico, Central America, West Indies, Bermuda together
.000 900 9	Archaeology
	Notation 09009 from Table 1 as modified below
.000 900 902–.000 900 909	Specific subdivisions of archaeology
	Add to base number 972.00090090 the numbers following 009090 in notation 0090902–0090909 from table under 930–990, e.g., serials treating archaeology of Mexico, Central America, West Indies, Bermuda together 972.000900905

*Add as instructed under 930–990

.000 901–.000 905		Historical periods

> Add to base number 972.00090 the numbers following —090 in notation 0901–0905 from Table 1, e.g., Mexico, Central America, West Indies, Bermuda together during 20th century 972.000904

.000 91–.000 99   Areas, regions, places in general; collected biography

> As modified in notation 0091–0099 from table under 930–990

.001–.009   Standard subdivisions of Mexico

> As modified in notation 001–009 from table under 930–990

> 972.01–972.08   Historical periods of Mexico

> Class comprehensive works in 972

.01   Early history to 1519

.016   Classical period, ca. 100–ca. 900

.017   Ca. 900–1325

> Class here period of Toltec empire, ca. 900–ca. 1200

.018   Aztec period, 1325–1519

> Including 14th century

> *For 1300–1325, see 972.017*

.02   Conquest and colonial period, 1519–1810

.03   Revolutionary period and period of independence, 1810–1822

.04   Periods of first empire and republic, 1822–1845

> Class here 19th century

> *For a part of 19th century not provided for here, see the part, e.g., period of second empire 972.07*

.05   Period of war with United States, 1845–1848

> (Option: Class here Mexican War; prefer 973.62)

.06   Period of reaction and reform, 1848–1861

.07   Period of European intervention, 1861–1867

> Class here period of second empire, 1864–1867; comprehensive works on administration of Benito Juárez, 1858–1872

> *For administration of Benito Juárez during 1858–1861, see 972.06; for administration of Benito Juárez during 1867–1872, see 972.0812*

.08   Period of Republic, 1867–

.081   1867–1917

.081 2   1867–1876

.081 4	Porfiriato, 1876–1910
	Class here administrations of Porfirio Díaz, 1876–1880, 1884–1910
.081 6	Period of Mexican Revolution, 1910–1917
.082	1917–1964
	Class here 20th century
	For 1900–1910, see 972.0814; for 1910–1917, see 972.0816; for 1964–1999, see 972.083
.082 1	Administrations of Venustiano Carranza and Adolfo de la Huerta, 1917–1920
.082 2	Administration of Alvaro Obregón, 1920–1924
.082 3	Administration of Plutarco Elías Calles, 1924–1928
.082 4	Administrations of Emilio Portes Gil, Pascual Ortiz Rubio, Abelardo L. Rodríguez, 1928–1934
.082 42	Administration of Emilio Portes Gil, 1928–1930
.082 43	Administration of Pascual Ortiz Rubio, 1930–1932
.082 44	Administration of Abelardo L. Rodríguez, 1932–1934
.082 5	Administration of Lázaro Cárdenas, 1934–1940
.082 6	Administration of Manuel Avila Camacho, 1940–1946
.082 7	Administration of Miguel Alemán, 1946–1952
.082 8	Administration of Adolfo Ruiz Cortines, 1952–1958
.082 9	Administration of Adolfo López Mateos, 1958–1964
.083	1964–2000
.083 1	Administration of Gustavo Díaz Ordaz, 1964–1970
.083 2	Administration of Luis Echeverría, 1970–1976
.083 3	Administration of José López Portillo, 1976–1982
.083 4	Administration of Miguel de la Madrid Hurtado, 1982–1988
.083 5	Administration of Carlos Salinas de Gortari, 1988–1994
.083 6	Administration of Ernesto Zedillo Ponce de León, 1994–2000
.084	2000–
.084 1	Administration of Vicente Fox Quesada, 2000–2006
.084 2	Administration of Felipe Calderón Hinojosa, 2006–2012
.084 3	Administration of Enrique Peña Nieto, 2012–2018
.084 4	Administration of Andrés Manuel López Obrador, 2018–

.1–.7   Localities of Mexico

Add to base number 972 the numbers following —72 in notation 721–727 from Table 2, e.g., northern states of Mexico 972.1; then add further as follows:

     001–009   Standard subdivisions

                  Add to 00 the numbers following 00 in notation 001–009 from table under 930–990, e.g., ethnic and national groups 004, ethnic and national groups in northern states of Mexico 972.1004

     01–08   Historical periods

                  Add to 0 the numbers following 972.0 in 972.01–972.08, e.g., northern states of Mexico during period of Republic, 1867 to present 972.108

> **972.8–972.9   Other parts of Middle America**

Class comprehensive works in 972

.8   *Central America

.801   Early history to 1502

.802   Period of European discovery, exploration, conquest, 1502–1535

.803   Colonial period, 1535–1821

         Including 16th century

           For 1500–1502, see 978.801; for 1502–1535, see 978.802

.804   1821–1899

         Including period of United Provinces of Central America, 1823–1840

.805   1900–

.805 1   1900–1944

         Class here 20th century

           For 1944–1979, see 972.8052; for 1979–1999, see 972.8053

.805 2   1944–1979

.805 3   1979–1999

.805 4   2000–

.81   *Guatemala

.810 1   Early history to 1502

.810 16   Mayan period, ca. 300–ca. 900

         Class here comprehensive works on Mayan period in Middle America

           For a specific aspect of the Mayan period not provided for here, see the aspect, e.g., Mayan period from ca. 900 to 1325 in Mexico 972.6017

*Add as instructed under 930–990

.810 2	Period of European discovery, exploration, conquest, 1502–1524
.810 3	Colonial period, 1524–1821

Including 16th century

For 1500–1502, see 972.8101; for 1502–1524, see 972.8102

.810 4	1821–1871

Class here 19th century

For 1800–1821, see 972.8103; for 1871–1899, see 972.81051

.810 42	1821–1839

Class here period as a part of United Provinces of Central America, 1823–1839

.810 44	1839–1871

Class here administration of Rafael Carrera, 1839–1865

.810 5	1871–
.810 51	1871–1931
.810 52	1931–1986

Including Civil War, 1960–1996

Class here 20th century

For 1900–1931, see 972.81051; for 1986–1999, see 972.810531

.810 53	1986–
.810 531	1986–2000
.810 532	Administration of Alfonso Portillo, 2000–2004
.810 533	Administration of Oscar Berger Perdomo, 2004–2008
.810 534	Administration of Álvaro Colom Caballeros, 2008–2012
.810 535	Administration of Otto Pérez Molina, 2012–2015
.810 536	2015–

Class here administration of Jimmy Morales, 2016 to present

.811–.818		Localities of Guatemala

Add to base number 972.81 the numbers following —7281 in notation 72811–72818 from Table 2, e.g., Guatemala department 972.811; then add further as follows:
001–009   Standard subdivisions
    Add to 00 the numbers following 00 in notation 001–009 from table under 930–990, e.g., ethnic and national groups 004, ethnic and national groups in Guatemala department 972.811004
01–05   Historical periods
    Add to 0 the numbers following 972.810 in 972.8101–972.8105, e.g., Guatemala department during 1871 to present 972.81105

.82	*Belize	

.820 1	Early history to 1502

.820 2	Period of Spanish discovery and colonization, 1502–1638

.820 3	1638–1862

Including 17th century, 19th century

Class here period of British involvement, 1638–1963; 18th century

For 1600–1638, see 972.8202; for 1862–1963, see 972.8204

.820 4	Period as a British colony, 1862–1981

Including period as self-governing colony, 1964–1981

Class here 20th century

For 1981–1999, see 972.8205

.820 5	1981–

.821–.826	Localities of Belize

Add to base number 972.82 the numbers following —7282 in notation 72821–72826 from Table 2, e.g., Corozal District 972.821; then add further as follows:
001–009   Standard subdivisions
    Add to 00 the numbers following 00 in notation 001–009 from table under 930–990, e.g., ethnic and national groups 004, ethnic and national groups in Corozal District 972.821004
01–05   Historical periods
    Add to 0 the numbers following 972.820 in 972.8201–972.8205, e.g., Corozal District during 1981 to present 972.82105

.83	*Honduras	

.830 1	Early history to 1502

.830 2	Period of Spanish discovery, exploration, conquest, 1502–1542

*Add as instructed under 930–990

.830 3	Colonial period, 1542–1821
	Including 16th century
	For 1500–1502, see 972.8301; for 1502–1542, see 972.8302
.830 4	1821–1838
	Class here period as a part of United Provinces of Central America, 1823–1838
.830 5	1838–
.830 51	1838–1924
	Class here 19th century
	For 1800–1821, see 972.8303; for 1821–1838, see 972.8304
.830 52	1924–1978
	Class here 20th century
	For 1900–1924, see 972.83051; for 1978–1999, see 972.83053
.830 53	1978–
.830 531	1978–1982
.830 532	Administration of Roberto Suazo Córdova, 1982–1986
.830 533	Administration of José Azcona H., 1986–1990
.830 534	Administration of Rafael Leonardo Callejas Romero, 1990–1994
.830 535	Administration of Carlos Roberto Reina, 1994–1998
.830 536	Administration of Carlos Flores Facussé, 1998–2002
.830 537	Administration of Ricardo Maduro, 2002–2006
.830 538	Administration of Manuel Zelaya, 2006–2009
.830 54	2009–
.830 541	2009–2014
	Class here administration of Porfirio Lobo Sosa, 2010–2014
.830 542	Administration of Juan Orlando Hernández, 2014–
.831–.838	Localities of Honduras

Add to base number 972.83 the numbers following —7283 in notation 72831–72838 from Table 2, e.g., northern departments of Honduras 972.831; then add further as follows:

001–009   Standard subdivisions

           Add to 00 the numbers following 00 in notation 001–009 from table under 930–990, e.g., ethnic and national groups 004, ethnic and national groups in northern departments of Honduras 972.831004

01–05   Historical periods

           Add to 0 the numbers following 972.830 in 972.8301–972.8305, e.g., northern departments of Honduras during 1838 to present 972.83105

.84	*El Salvador
.840 1	Early history to 1524
.840 2	Period of Spanish discovery, exploration, conquest, 1524–1542
.840 3	Colonial period, 1542–1821

        Including 16th century

            For 1500–1524, see 972.8401; for 1524–1542, see 972.8402

.840 4	1821–1859

        Class here 19th century

            For 1800–1821, see 972.8403; for 1859–1899, see 972.8451

.840 42	1821–1839

        Class here period as a part of United Provinces of Central America, 1823–1839

.840 44	1839–1859
.840 5	1859–
.840 51	1859–1931
.840 52	1931–1979

        Class here 20th century

            For 1900–1931, see 972.84051; for 1979–1994, see 972.84053; for 1994–1999, see 972.84054

.840 53	1979–1994
.840 54	1994–
.840 541	Administration of Armando Calderón Sol, 1994–1999
.840 542	Administration of Francisco Flores Pérez, 1999–2004
.840 543	Administration of Elías Antonio Saca, 2004–2009
.840 544	Administration of Carlos Mauricio Funes, 2009–2014
.840 545	Administration of Salvador Sánchez Cerén, 2014–

*Add as instructed under 930–990

.841–.843   Localities of El Salvador

> Add to base number 972.84 the numbers following —7284 in notation 72841–72843 from Table 2, e.g., western departments of El Salvador 972.841; then add further as follows:
>
> 001–009   Standard subdivisions
>> Add to 00 the numbers following 00 in notation 001–009 from table under 930–990, e.g., ethnic and national groups 004, ethnic and national groups in western departments of El Salvador 972.841004
>
> 01–05   Historical periods
>> Add to 0 the numbers following 972.840 in 972.8401–972.8405, e.g., western departments of El Salvador during 1859 to present 972.84105

.85   *Nicaragua

.850 1   Early history to 1502

.850 2   Period of Spanish discovery, exploration, conquest, 1502–1527

.850 3   Colonial period, 1527–1821

> Including 16th century
>
> *For 1500–1502, see 972.8501; for 1502–1527, see 972.8502*

.850 4   1821–1893

> Class here 19th century
>
> *For 1800–1821, see 972.8503; for 1893–1899, see 972.85051*

.850 42   1821–1838

> Class here period as a part of United Provinces of Central America, 1823–1838

.850 44   1838–1893

.850 5   1893–

.850 51   1893–1934

> Class here period of interventions by United States, 1909–1933

.850 52   1934–1979

> Class here 20th century
>
> *For 1900–1934, see 972.85051; for 1979–1990, see 972.85053; for 1990–1999, see 972.85054*

.850 53   1979–1990

> Including first administration of Daniel Ortega, 1985–1990

.850 54   1990–

.850 541   Administration of Violeta Barrios de Chamorro, 1990–1997

.850 542   Administration of Arnoldo Alemán, 1997–2002

*Add as instructed under 930–990

.850 543		Administration of Enrique Bolaños Geyer, 2002–2007
.850 544		Second administration of Daniel Ortega, 2007–
.851–.853	Localities of Nicaragua	

> Add to base number 972.85 the numbers following —7285 in notation 72851–72853 from Table 2, e.g., Pacific departments of Nicaragua 972.851; then add further as follows:
> 001–009   Standard subdivisions
> > Add to 00 the numbers following 00 in notation 001–009 from table under 930–990, e.g., ethnic and national groups 004, ethnic and national groups in Pacific departments of Nicaragua 972.851004
> 01–05   Historical periods
> > Add to 0 the numbers following 972.850 in 972.8501–972.8505, e.g., Pacific departments of Nicaragua during 1893 to present 972.85105

.86	*Costa Rica	
.860 1	Early history to 1502	
.860 2	Period of Spanish discovery, exploration, conquest, 1502–1560	
.860 3	Colonial period, 1560–1821	

> Including 16th century

> *For 1500–1502, see 972.8601; for 1502–1560, see 972.8602*

.860 4	1821–1948
.860 42	1821–1838

> Class here period as a part of United Provinces of Central America, 1823–1838

.860 44	1838–1948
.860 5	1948–

> Class here 20th century

> *For 1900–1948, see 972.86044*

.860 51	1948–1986	
.860 52	1986–2014	
.860 521		First administration of Óscar Arias Sánchez, 1986–1990
.860 522		Administration of Rafael Angel Calderón Fournier, 1990–1994
.860 523		Administration of José María Figueres, 1994–1998
.860 524		Administration of Miguel Angel Rodríguez, 1998–2002
.860 525		Administration of Abel Pacheco, 2002–2006
.860 526		Second administration of Óscar Arias Sánchez, 2006–2010

*Add as instructed under 930–990